# Texas Plays

★ ★ ★ ★ ★ ★ ★ ★ ★ ★ ★ ★ ★ ★ ★ ★

SOUTHWEST LIFE & LETTERS

*A series designed to publish outstanding new fiction*

*and nonfiction about Texas and the American Southwest*

*and to present classic works of the region in handsome*

*new editions.*

General Editors:

Suzanne Comer, Southern Methodist University Press

Tom Pilkington, Tarleton State University

# Texas Plays

★ ★ ★ ★ ★ ★ ★ ★ ★ ★ ★ ★ ★ ★ ★ ★ ★

EDITED BY

WILLIAM B. MARTIN

SOUTHERN METHODIST

UNIVERSITY PRESS

DALLAS

Library of Congress Cataloging-in-Publication Data
Texas plays / edited by William B. Martin.
    p.   cm.
  Includes bibliographical references.
  Contents: A cloud of witnesses / Ramsey
Yelvington — The trip to Bountiful / Horton Foote
— Who's happy now? / Oliver Hailey — Patio/Porch
/ Jack Heifner — The regions of noon / R.G. Vliet
— El jardín / Carlos Morton — Lu Ann Hampton
Laverty Oberlander / Preston Jones — Ladybug,
ladybug, fly away home / Mary Rohde — Lone star/
Laundry and bourbon / James McLure.
  ISBN 0-87074-300-7 — ISBN 0-87074-301-5
(pbk.)
  I. Texas—Drama.   2. American drama—
Texas.   3. American drama—20th
century.   I. Martin, William B. (William Bizzell),
1926–
PS558.T4T38   1990
812'.54099764—dc20   89-42893
                 CIP

The editor gratefully acknowledges receipt of a grant
from the Organized Research Committee of Tarleton
State University in 1982, which funded preliminary
investigations important to the development of this
book.

# CONTENTS

Preface, ix

★   Ramsey Yelvington, 1
*A Cloud of Witnesses*, 9

★   Horton Foote, 67
*The Trip to Bountiful*, 75

★   Oliver Hailey, 125
*Who's Happy Now?*, 131

★   Jack Heifner, 177
*Patio*, 185
*Porch*, 201

★   R. G. Vliet, 221
*The Regions of Noon*, 229

★   Carlos Morton, 267
*El Jardín*, 275

★   Preston Jones, 299
*Lu Ann Hampton Laverty Oberlander*, 307

★   Mary Rohde, 351
*Ladybug, Ladybug, Fly Away Home*, 357

★   James McLure, 407
*Lone Star*, 415
*Laundry and Bourbon*, 441

★   Sources, 468

# PREFACE

A solid body of respectable Texas plays does exist, but they have received such scant attention from the familiar guides that even careful readers are often unaware of them. There has been a tendency for the heralds of Texas literature—from J. Frank Dobie and Mabel Majors to A. C. Greene, Tom Pilkington, Jim Lee, and Don Graham—to pan quickly over dramatic literature, or stage plays. Most commentators make obligatory remarks about the existence of Texas playwrights, mention a familiar name or two, and then seem glad to get on to more congenial territory. Cultural journalists in the state, when pressed to comment on drama in Texas, prefer to focus on revered theater directors or on motion pictures, which have broad-based popularity and commercial appeal.

Plays pose recognition and study problems that discourage all but the most determined. Unlike novels, poems, and essays, plays are not readily available to readers. If they are published at all, it is most commonly in the form of acting scripts, which are not reviewed, distributed widely, or acquired regularly by libraries, even distinguished ones. It is difficult for those outside the theatrical community to borrow reading scripts of unpublished plays. And it is even harder to learn about works that have been performed outside of one's own area of the state. Texas theaters are clustered in four metropolitan areas: Houston, Dallas–Fort Worth, Austin, and San Antonio. Newspaper critics in one city seldom cover performances outside their immediate vicinity. Ramsey Yelvington once wrote bitterly that it was easier to get a critic from New York to attend a performance of a Texas play and write a notice than it was to get critics from several representative Texas cities to do the same.

My obvious intention in this anthology is to make good Texas plays accessible to a wide range of students and general readers, those who live in rural areas and small towns as well as those residing in cities where professional dramatic performances are frequent. It is hoped that if readers experience representative examples from among the best of Texas drama on the printed page—a mode of perception that offers advantages as well as disadvantages—they will have a better understanding of the range of literary expression provided by the state's writers. Another desired benefit is an increased demand for performances of these and similar plays that deal searchingly and seriously with characters and subjects of immediate concern to Texans.

It would have been impossible to compile this anthology thirty years ago. The works simply were not there. The urbanization, wealth, and cultural sophistication necessary for the development of Texas theater were lacking. As an urban form, drama is a late arrival on any cultural scene: it demands populations large enough to provide sufficient audiences. These audiences, in turn, need leisure time, a sense of community, a certain level of discretionary income, and a sophisticated sensibility. Playwrights can stretch the receptivity of their audiences—and they must respond somewhat to audience demands—but they cannot produce a body of quality drama for those who desire only titillation, reassurance, or, in the words of the scholar-critic John Gassner, "facile, farcical, and melodramatic entertainment."

The beginnings of such an environment in Texas can be traced to the post-WWII years of the forties and fifties, when a handful of creative pioneers stimulated the theater climate. Some of these innovators were academics; others were theater directors and founders. All gave their audiences a sense of participating in the creation of something different and exciting. Margo Jones, of Theatres '47 through '55 in Dallas, once said: "I want our age to be a golden age. . . . I like living in the age of the airplane and television, and I want to live in an age when there is great theatre everywhere." An official publication of the Alley Theatre in Houston noted of the theater's founding, "Let us, from the start, be quite clear that this was a revolt."

Working separately or cooperatively, these pioneers convinced Texas audiences that they did not need to travel to established cultural centers to experience vital theater, nor did they need to rely on warmed-over Broadway productions interpreted by road-show companies. Instead, regional theaters, without the support of New York leadership or values, could offer their own productions of a high artistic standard. Today theaters across the state carry on the tradition: the Alley and Stages theaters in Houston, the Theater Center and Theatre Three in Dallas, the Zachary Scott Theatre and the Capitol City Playhouse in Austin, and the Guadalupe Theater and ACT in San Antonio.

The years since the 1940s and 1950s have seen dramatic achievements and the fulfillment of promise in Texas theater—only to be followed by stagnation. Civic pride and federal funding in the sixties and seventies transformed basic playing spaces into elaborate stage complexes. Heightened political consciousness and sharp social division led to the development of issue-oriented and minority theater. Growing internationalism, declining provincialism, and expanding higher education created an environment more receptive to dramatic experiment. In the late seventies and early eighties, Texas political clout, Texas oil wealth, and that phenomenon dubbed "Texas chic" combined to create a boom-town atmosphere in which no dream seemed impractical and expansion appeared unlimited. The late eighties, however, brought a fall in oil prices and changes in the political climate. As the costs of art facilities became more burdensome, cutbacks and closures became more frequent. The tide of immigration into the state reversed, and some of the theater's shining figures retired or moved to areas with better economic potential. In 1987, Jerome Weeks, a critic with the *Dallas Morning News*, pointed out that there was not "a single Dallas theater in good [financial] shape" and that several were being kept alive by the families of the artistic directors. In the nineties, theater in Texas faces a time of retrenchment.

Yet Texas has gone too far to turn back. The state is no longer provincial and no longer remote from cultural activity. It has educational institutions and performance centers to guarantee that future generations will be exposed to high artistic standards and opportunities for career development. Perhaps most important, Texas now has a generous supply of examples to demonstrate that being born and educated within the state's borders is not inconsistent with the highest achievement in theater and in other arts.

In compiling this anthology, I have made no attempt to rigorously define *Texas play* or to balance choices of writers or works to fit a plan. Not all of the nine authors represented are native Texans, and a majority make their homes in either New York or California. Those who are not natives, however, have studied and lived in Texas long enough for it to constitute a significant influence. Although not without practical experience, none of these playwrights came to the stage directly from the saddle; all but one have university degrees and most have more than one. All have given serious attention to the distinctive characteristics of life in Texas and are represented by works that contribute to its greater appreciation and understanding. Also, of course, they have dealt with the "problems of the human heart in conflict with itself" and with the universal struggles for knowledge, ease, and love that transcend boundaries.

All but one of the plays are set completely within the state, and the remaining one is set both in Texas and in the Garden of Eden, either nearby neighborhoods or a far cry from each other, depending on one's orientation. Specific locations suggest the regional diversity that is so characteristic of the state and that mitigates against the definitiveness of any single work or scene.

The nine plays illustrate a variety of forms and styles. Comedy, both broad and thoughtful, predominates, but the anthology also includes a heroic play in verse, a melancholy lyric play, an allegory, and a straightforward realistic drama. Two playwrights are represented by pairs of related one-act plays. Some of the works are widely known through motion picture and television adaptations, but others have had only infrequent production and are relatively unfamiliar.

I would like to think that this collection will be the forerunner of many to be compiled by a variety of editors. Certainly this one is not definitive. It is, however, the first collection of Texas plays to appear since *Three Southwest Plays* in 1942 and has an obvious gap to fill. Some of the selections will no doubt provoke controversy, but I am confident that there will be broad concurrence in the majority of my choices. In closing, I can only hope that this volume will direct more attention to a distinguished body of playwrights who have served their region and their art well.

# Ramsey Yelvington

★ ★ ★ ★ ★ ★ ★ ★ ★ ★ ★ ★ ★ ★ ★

## ★ THE PERSON

Ramsey Yelvington was born in West Point, Texas, between Smithville and La Grange, in 1913. The son of a Baptist minister and a fourth-generation Texan, he took pride in his heritage. He attended public schools in San Antonio and later Howard Payne University and Baylor University without taking a degree. After working as a radio writer and announcer in Austin, Houston, Corpus Christi, and San Antonio, he served three years in the United States Army Corps of Engineers. Then, at the age of thirty-five, he wrote his first play, *Home to Galveston.* Produced by Paul Baker at his Southwest Summer Theater in Waco, this play marked the first of many happy collaborations between the two.

In the ensuing years, Yelvington completed B.A. (1962) and M.A. (1963) degrees from Baylor University, wrote eighteen long plays and five short ones, served as Playwright-in-Residence at Baylor under a Rockefeller Foundation Fellowship, and taught playwriting at Southwest Texas State University in San Marcos until he died in 1973—on the opening night of his play *The Folklorist.*

In addition to his playwriting and teaching, Yelvington acted in his plays; wrote a book of Hill Country sketches; edited *Dramatic Images,* a volume of plays for the church; spoke widely; and wrote a series of columns for the *Fort Worth Star-Telegram* called "Theater Southwest"—all while tending land and cattle in Boerne and Wimberley. Throughout his career he championed regional drama, insisting that the level of production in Texas was outstanding and that the greatest need was for active, intelligent critical attention to guide the development of both audiences and playwrights.

Considered Texas's foremost playwright during most of his career, Yelvington was fortunate in his professional associates. Paul Baker, at Baylor University and later at the Dallas Theater Center, and Dr. James Barton, at Southwest Texas State University, gave him personal support and his plays quality productions. The best-known performances of a Yelvington work were those given *A Cloud of Witnesses* (also called *The Drama of the Alamo*) at San José Mission in San Antonio beginning in 1955 and continuing, with some interruption, until 1962.

Characteristically, Ramsey Yelvington's epitaph reads simply, "Texas Playwright and Baptist."

## ★ THE PLAY

*A Cloud of Witnesses,* although written first, occupies the historical middle position in Yelvington's Texian Trilogy. Preceding it, *Women and Oxen* describes emigration from the United States into the Mexican state of Texas and portrays events in Gonzales leading to the Texas Revolution in 1835. Concluding the trilogy, *Shadow of an Eagle* focuses on Sam Houston, "The Runaway Scrape," and the Texans' final victory at San Jacinto in 1836.

The legendary hold that the Battle of the Alamo has on Texans' imaginations foredooms a modern stage version to one or another kind of failure. If the playwright treats the subject with awe, the work is likely to be dismissed as one-dimensional pageantry and hero worship. If the playwright deviates from the familiar version, the work can be labeled as revisionist and considered damaging to Texans' respect for their heroic past. *A Cloud of Witnesses* errs more in the first direction than the second, but Yelvington uses his historical knowledge and skillful dramaturgy to make the familiar fresh and to counter charges of excessive hero worship and jingoism.

By setting his play in the present and making the stage action a self-conscious re-creation intended to rekindle the concept of freedom in modern minds—a morality-tale struggle between Satan's view of history as cyclical force and the Romantic view of history as determined by courage and sacrifice—Yelvington diverts attention from the historical event to its contemporary meaning. By bringing up personal weaknesses of Crockett, Bowie, and Travis and challenging such staples of legend as Colonel Travis's drawing a line with his sword for volunteers to cross, the author makes his work more acceptable to modern viewers conditioned to doubt. And by calling attention to the participation of Mexicans on the Texan side and including an official report of postbattle activity by the alcalde of San Antonio de Bexar, he gives his play a refreshing breadth of view.

A chorus made up of widows of the men from Gonzales introduces a classical element that heightens the dignity and universality of the work. Their suffering, made palpable, gives balance and depth to the heroic accolades accorded the Alamo's defenders. Perhaps the play's most moving lines are spoken by these Widows of Gonzales when their husbands, answering Colonel Travis's plea for re-inforcements, enter the besieged fortress, and its gates close behind them.

> Did anyone hear the Gate open?
> The double Gates swing out,
> Open, like *Jaws?*
> No, but we heard it CLOSE.
> In our sleep,
>
> .  .  .
>
> Warm yet with the warmth of memory of a man gone;
>
> .  .  .
>
> We heard the Gate creaking,
> We heard it groan in place
> And a LOCK drop.
> A *great—Lock—drop.*

The play deserves attention and respect in spite of its weaknesses, which include didacticism, inflated language, and intrusive stage techniques. Through 134 performances under widely different playing conditions, *A Cloud of Witnesses* has continued to move audiences and win critical acclaim. It tackles headlong, with originality and courage, the emotional center of Texas myth. It is a creation not of a cautious or prudent playwright but of a heroic one unwilling to doubt either the necessity of dealing with the largest of subjects or the capacity of his art to do them justice.

A recent significant production, in commemoration of the Texas Sesquicentennial, took place in February and March 1986 at Southwest Texas State University under the direction of Jay Jennings.


★ THE WORKS

Ramsey Yelvington carried with him a strong sense of Victorian earnestness that had its roots in his father's Protestant ministry and his long association with education. Although it would be wrong to say that he used the stage as either pulpit or lectern, it is clear that Yelvington took the calling of playwright seriously. His extensive body of work, consisting of twenty-three plays, correctly suggests dedication and industry. With few exceptions, his plays express a conviction that heroes exist and that morality and ideas matter. Some of his notable works depict major actions in Texas history; others have contemporary settings and deal with the philosophical facing of death, ethical issues related to college football, and racial and generational conflict.

Yelvington's best-known plays, those making up his Texian Trilogy—*Women and Oxen, A Cloud of Witnesses,* and *Shadow of an Eagle*—are historical and are realized on a grand scale. They differ, however, from most of the familiar "outdoor genre" by a more complex use of language and by a consciousness of stagecraft derived from the playwright's long association with Paul Baker. Yelvington wrote all his plays with Baker's famous enveloping stage with its side extensions in mind, and the expansiveness of his plays reflected some of the scale of his subject while straining the theater's ability to contain them. In an interview Yelvington said: "I try to put the texture of a novel on stage through multiple sets. Looking for the thickness of a novel, I want to show the ins and outs and suggestions through many characters." This "thickness" that he sought and that constitutes one of the strengths of his works also leads to a recognizable weakness—a lack of focus. His plays have large casts, often mixed styles, and are undeniably wordy. They stand significantly above the level of their predecessors largely for two reasons. Unlike plays of ephemeral entertainment concerned with offering audiences ingenuity and titillation, these plays seriously expound local and universal truths, and unlike heroic one-dimensional portrayals of history, they deal with unpleasant and contradictory truths instead of avoiding or denying them. Yelvington wanted his audiences to share his perceptions of the grandeur and strength of Texas's heroes, but he refused to oversimplify beyond a responsible point.

Although Yelvington possessed an optimism he associated with his region and its history—what he called "the land and its progenitors"—his was not the optimism of the uninformed or the sentimental. His honesty and his experience of living close to nature in hard country precluded that. It was an optimism based on his convictions, both of human potential and of divine guidance.

## LIST OF WORKS

### THE TEXIAN TRILOGY

*A Cloud of Witnesses,* 1955
*Shadow of an Eagle,* 1961
*Women and Oxen,* 1965

### OTHER FULL-LENGTH PLAYS

*Home to Galveston,* 1949
*Cocklebur,* 1950
*Choir Boy,* 1951
*Inland Sailor,* 1952
*Widow's Walk,* or *The Sail,* 1952
*The Long Gallery,* 1953
*The Seeker,* or *The Conversion of Roger Williams,* 1956
*The World by the Tail,* 1957
*The Will to Win,* 1958
*The Marble Horseman,* 1965
*One,* 1965
*Montezuma Alley,* 1969
*Pastor Blake at the Mercy Seat,* 1970
*The Folklorist,* 1971
*The Governors,* 1971

### ONE-ACT PLAYS

*The Choir,* 1958
*Could Statues Speak,* 1958
*Korea,* or *The Golden Stair,* 1958
*Sunshine Sisters,* 1959
*Go! Fly a Kite,* 1960

### PAGEANTS

*There Was a Woman,* 1954
*Challenge and Response,* 1957

### NARRATIVES

*The Roaring Kleinschmids.* Boerne: Texas Highland Press, 1950.

### RECOMMENDED READINGS

Baker, Paul. "Introduction." In *A Cloud of Witnesses,* by Ramsey Yelvington.
Austin: University of Texas Press, 1959.

Cooke, Nan. *Ramsey Yelvington: Texan Playwright.* Master's thesis, Southwest Texas State University, 1975.

Rosenfield, Paul. "Bard of the Southwest." *Dallas Times Herald Magazine,* July 16, 1961, p. 25.

"Stage-Struck Texas." *Life,* December 22, 1958, pp. 122–32.

Yelvington, Ramsey. "The Regional Playwright." *Texas Libraries* 29 (Summer 1967): 137–45.

# A Cloud of Witnesses

★ ★ ★ ★ ★ ★ ★ ★ ★ ★ ★ ★ ★ ★ ★ ★ ★ ★

# CAST OF CHARACTERS

WITNESSES: Those who died at the Alamo, both Texans and Mexicans, and some who died later, including the widows of Gonzales

COLONEL WILLIAM BARRET TRAVIS: Leader

SATAN

WIDOWS OF GONZALES

PRIVATE PURDY REYNOLDS

SERGEANT MAJOR HIRAM WILLIAMSON

COLONEL DAVY CROCKETT

LIEUTENANT WILLIAM BONHAM

DR. AMOS POLLARD

GUERRERO, ABAMILLO, ESPARZA, FUENTES, LOSOYA, NAVA: Mexicans who fought beside the Texans

COLONEL JAMES BOWIE: Commander of the Volunteers

DON REFUGIO DE LA GARZA: Curate

TEXAN SOLDIERS: Regulars and Irregulars

SOLDIER ONE

SOLDIER TWO

SOLDIER THREE

CAPTAIN ALMERON DICKINSON: Captain of the Artillery

MRS. DICKINSON

JOHNNY KELLOGG: Sixteen-year-old boy from Gonzales

MEXICAN DANCER

JOHN SMITH: Scout

DR. JOHN SUTHERLAND: Scout

TAPLEY HOLLAND

GREEN B. JAMESON: Alamo engineer

JOSÉ BATRES: Aide-de-Camp of the President of the Republic

ISAAC MILLSAPS: Volunteer

GEORGE TAYLOR, EDWARD TAYLOR, and JAMES TAYLOR: Brothers, volunteers

SENTRY ONE

SENTRY TWO

SERGEANT JOHN MacGREGOR

MRS. ALSBURY, MRS. ESPARZA, MRS. LOSOYA, MISS NAVARRO: Mexican women whose men fought beside the Texans

MEXICANS

MAJOR ROBERT EVANS

JACOB WALKER: Cannoneer

SANTA ANNA

FRANCISCO RUÍZ: Alcalde of San Antonio de Bexar

DON RAMÓN MUSQUIZ: Political chief

VICENTE FILISOLA: Mercenary general in the Mexican army, Italian national

MOSES ROSE: Satan

# ★ PROLOGUE

*(Spoken before the play by* DR. POLLARD.*)*

No, it hasn't begun.

But I am in the play—as you'll see later—if you look carefully.

Then what am I doing here? I am here to make an explanation which might or-dinarily be written in the program. But since we have reasonable doubts as to whether such explanations are ever read, I am become—you might say—both you and part of the program too.

Now the theme of this play needs no explanation. It's quite clear. It concerns the cost of freedom. But the method, or technique, of the presentation—well, we thought it just might bear a little introduction. Because it isn't what you're accus-tomed to seeing.

You see, the author didn't wish merely to demonstrate what you already know: how a band of brave men died in the cause of freedom at an old church turned into a fortress, called the Alamo. He wished also to point you an application, a meaning, as well: to show the event, then go beyond it and say what it means—or can mean—to us today.

Therefore, he chose an older way of saying it. This is meant deliberately to startle you into a keener, sharper sort of recognition—to make an old story fresh and vital, which is the purpose of all serious literature.

In technique the play derives from the morality play of the Middle Ages, from the Greek theater, and also from the Japanese. And it borrows something from the bal-lad singer, too.

There is in this play a figure representing Satan. This is the tie with the old mo-rality plays. Satan is the Alamo's critic. He questions the actions of these men.

There is also in the play a chorus of women. The Greeks used choruses in their plays centuries ago, as did the Japanese. The chorus of women in this play are the widows of Gonzales. They represent the thirty-three women in the area of that town whose husbands died in the fall. They, as did the Greek choruses, sometimes act as narrators, telling the story; sometimes they are themselves, telling how it was to remain at home; again, they enter into the play as collective or individual partici-pants—as you'll see.

The style of the play is frequently in the rhyme of the ballad. This, of course, you'll hear.

And finally, the title of this drama of the fall of the Alamo is *A Cloud of Wit-nesses*—taken from the Apostle Paul's statement in the Bible, which says: "Where-fore, seeing we also are compassed about with so great a cloud of witnesses, let us lay aside every weight, and the sin which doth so easily beset us, and let us run with patience the race that is set before us, looking unto Jesus the author and finisher of our faith; who for the joy that was set before him endured the cross, despising the shame, and is set down at the right hand of the throne of God."

*A Cloud of Witnesses* has been called "a contemporary morality play."

And so it is.

*Darkness. The sound of wings in the darkness overhead, descending. Voices calling.*

   *The* WITNESSES, *those who died at the Alamo, both Texans and Mexicans, and some who died later, including the widows of the volunteers from Gonzales, have entered.*

WOMAN. *(High voice.)* Here?
MAN *(*REYNOLDS*).* Here?
WOMAN. *(Medium voice.)* Here?
MAN *(*BOWIE*).* Here.
WOMAN. *(High voice.)* Is this the place?
MAN (CROCKETT). Yes, this is the place.
WOMAN. *(High voice.)* A sort of box . . .
WOMAN. *(Medium voice.)* Roof and walls . . .
WOMAN. *(Low voice.)* Strange. It's—
MAN *(*BOWIE*).* Dark.
WOMAN. *(Low voice.)* No light.
WOMAN. *(Medium voice.)* I had forgotten. No light.
MAN *(*BONHAM*).* There will be light.
WOMAN. *(Low voice.)* I know. I know.
WOMEN. *(All voices.)* We know all.
WOMAN. *(Low voice.)* What is this place called?
MAN *(*BOWIE*).* The place is called *theater.*
WOMAN. *(Low voice.)* Oh, yes. Theater.
LEADER (TRAVIS). The question is irregular, but is everyone all right? It was a
   long descent.
WOMEN. *(All voices.)* We are fine.
TEXANS. *(All voices.)* So are we.
LEADER *(*TRAVIS*).* And our erstwhile enemies, how are they?
MEXICANS. *(Four or five men, distantly.)* Muy bueno.
LEADER *(*TRAVIS*).*
   Splendid.

   We know our mission here.
   It is not new.
   We must once again attempt to get through;
   We must try again to reach the Ear of Man.

   This is not new.

   The particular occasion, however,
   Is in response to a Universe Call;
   You heard it—
   I heard it—

An urgent Call
To witness an enactment
Of the siege and fall of the Alamo.

We know how in this we are implicated:
We died there.

ALL VOICES. Yes.

TEXANS. *(All voices.)*
How by our deaths in the Alamo,
How from our dust
The mammoth Thing, Freedom,
Received a forward thrust
That has continually reverberated.

LEADER *(TRAVIS).*
You are likewise aware: the continuance of these reverberations is our special care.

ALL VOICES. Yes!

LEADER *(TRAVIS).*
But you also know: we are strictly limited.
Our interest may assume no more than a general pressure,
Something primitive;
Something to which Man may respond, or not respond, at pleasure.
As rain.
Or pain.
Or any variable weather.

So, again, let us attempt to get through.
All. Together.

ALL VOICES. Man.

LEADER *(TRAVIS).* Again.

ALL VOICES. Man!

LEADER *(TRAVIS).* Again!
> *(Some distance away, and at a different level, there is now a diffused red-and-green light. In its midst, at first indistinct, there appears a single tall figure, and they all audibly draw in their breath. The figure, when clear, is* SATAN.*)*

SATAN. Did someone call?

ALL VOICES. You!

SATAN. Yes. Whom did you expect?

LEADER *(TRAVIS).* Well . . . Mankind. At the very least a man!

SATAN. Won't I do?

ALL VOICES. Emphatically—No!

LEADER *(TRAVIS).* You are not acceptable.

SATAN. Not even as an antagonist? Is chivalry dead everywhere? I am the loyal opposition! *(There is no reply.)* Forgive me this intrusion then, but—I'm speaking to Colonel William Barret Travis—correct?

DAVY CROCKETT. *(After a silence.)* You might as well give Old Nick his devil's due.

SATAN. Thank you, Sir! Colonel Crockett. Am I right?

CROCKETT. I be.

SATAN. Be sure you're right, then push ahead!

CROCKETT. You remember those words of mine?

SATAN. I remember all the words of all mankind.

CROCKETT. Then what a full slop jar your head must be!

WILLIAM BARRET TRAVIS *(for he is the* LEADER*).* Why are you here?

SATAN. It's simple enough. Aside from my being in a degree everywhere, I came because you called. Just now I heard your wistful voices poking about space in a dispirited and apprehensive search for the Ear of Man; lamenting, I believe, you couldn't get his attention. True?

TRAVIS. We do not lament.

SATAN. Well . . . whatever your intent, you didn't get through.

TRAVIS. No. We could, if only we were better understood.

SATAN. Alas, the complaint that outlasts the worm.

WOMEN. *(All voices.)* The Call was urgent.

MEN. *(All voices.)*

We seem to be under special duress
On this particular occasion
To make a particular impress.

WOMEN. *(All voices.)* If we longed, we would long for success.

SATAN. I see.

WOMEN. *(All voices.)*

Yes.
Although utterly aloof,
Washed of either approval or reproof,
Knowing all truth—
We,
Who own the total discernment of eternity,
With our thousand-thousand compassing eyes must nevertheless
Put on the dark glass;
Be almost blind.
Why?

SATAN. You don't know? *You* ask *me? (Their silence is shamed assent.)* This is preposterous. Well, if I must, I must.

This much you know: You were directed here to witness a play, an enactment of the siege and fall of the Alamo—because you either died there or were in some way involved. What you apparently do not know is that the condition for which most of you died—the condition in which my Enemy puts such unaccountable store—freedom, I believe you call it, is currently in a rather—shall we say—vulnerable position. It seems that today the term is become confused. The meaning is now everywhere debated. It is not clear-cut, as in your time. And your deed, your deaths, though generally revered, are . . . oh, something in a niche; something cloudy in a baroque picture frame. *Great*, of course; but so . . . remote.

People and times were so *different* then! *(SATAN enjoys this a moment.)*

Oh, you have done a fair job of keeping your memory alive, with your general pressures. Politicians wouldn't miss speaking there. Various individuals and organizations regularly place wreaths there. Why, that interesting addition they made to the front of the Alamo chapel is one of the most readily identified façades in the world! *(Pauses, then ironically.)* Though of course it wasn't there in your day.

Don't you see? The place takes precedence over the ideal! The place is hallowed! The place is a thousand times more photographed than the lesson learned! And you!—I will prove to you ere this evening is out that you are no more valid to this audience than jittering words of a theater marquee or a lurid sign by the highway or a sales pitch on television! Modern man knows how to take heroes. He cuts them down to size—his own size. And this audience will diminish you! *(A pause.)*

You are quiet.

ALL VOICES.

You have made it clear

Why you, and we, are here.

SATAN. I am good at that.

TRAVIS. Yes, you are, and also the other way around! What we wish to know is why you are being so free with us. We suspect a trap!

SATAN. Not a trap! Can't you see? A challenge! During the performance, in whose thrall will this audience be? Yours, or mine?

MAN. *(This sequence is spoken very rapidly.)* Is this audience so exceptional?

MAN. The potential is there.

MAN. All audiences are exceptional.

MAN. The potential is always there.

WOMAN. Still . . . we must exercise care.

TRAVIS. *(To SATAN.)* But . . . how may we be sure this audience will assist us to come through?

SATAN. Neither I nor the Power I defy can assure you that. Man is, of all weather vanes, the most unpredictable cock, turning betimes with the wind, then sometimes not.

TRAVIS. What do you suggest?

SATAN. Only this: Concentrate. Center your powers. For a time withdraw your gentle, misty goodwill from the man on the hill, on the plain, in the cave, in the air, the country town, in the city, on and under the sea. Draw your forces together and, in a black-centered lightning-forked storm, force alarm down here! And I meanwhile will not even hold to their lassitude. I will let fall . . . all. *(And with the opening of his clenched fist, the dropping of his hand, he begins to fade.)*

ALL VOICES. And we shall concentrate . . . all.

SATAN. Do. Invoke their wills.

ALL VOICES. Audience. *(At the first summoning of the audience the WITNESSES begin to take on added form and color, gradually lighting into brilliant clarity. If seen*

*through a scrim to this point, the scrim should rise at the peak of their exhortation.*
SATAN, *meanwhile, disappears.)*

SATAN. Invoke their better selves.

ALL VOICES. Audience!

SATAN. Plead with them!

ALL VOICES. *Audience!*

SATAN. *Plead!*

ALL VOICES.

> *For the love of good and right—*
> *To keep out darkness—*
> *To bring the light—*

SATAN. *Intercede! Plead!*

ALL VOICES.

> *Do not let the good act die!*
> *Audience! Audience,* TRY!

> *(The scrim has risen. The* WITNESSES *are now brilliantly visible, the light gold, the sky blue.* SATAN *is out of sight.)*

CROCKETT. *(After they have all adjusted themselves a bit to the light and other— mortal—strictures.)*

Golden light.

Golden silence.

SATAN. *(Out of sight, but near the* WITNESSES.*)* Are you a lover of silence, Colonel Crockett? In your earth-time it seems to me you were as garrulous as the next.

CROCKETT. Garrulous? I know the word and I sometimes was. *(Suddenly looking around.)* Where did the fellow go?

ALL VOICES. We have the unpleasant feeling we don't know!

MAN. I feel . . . constricted.

MAN. I feel . . . shrunken.

MAN. I feel . . . bound!

MAN. I feel . . . dwarfed!

WOMAN. I . . . ohhhh—I *feel!*

SATAN. *(In yet another location, possibly higher up.)* Why, Colonel, you do your talent an injustice. Were you not lionized as a speaker in sedate Boston? Were you not applauded as an orator in both the broadclothed East and the buckskinned West? In the Halls of Congress was there a man more appreciatively listened to than Colonel Davy Crockett?

ALL VOICES. True!

CROCKETT. In those times I admit to a bellows lung and a trip-hammer tongue and a powder-keg pride to set it off.

SATAN. And now you are changed?

CROCKETT. I be.

SATAN. How?

CROCKETT. You are leading me on, but I will speak this once and have done.

ALL VOICES. Hear! Hear!

CROCKETT. There was another word I learned in those times, in my time in the velvety-padded congressional high roost-chamber, where the enduring marble rang to the hammerings and chiselings of the founding words from the blistered tongues of the artisans of the new-quarried marble-block nation. And the word I learned was *resolved.*

ALL VOICES. Resolved.

CROCKETT. Resolved!

ALL VOICES. A thing *resolved* is a thing done; finished; settled; agreed upon; proved; held forever!

CROCKETT. Aye! To illustrate:

We will say you have walked a great while, as I have, in the visioning silence of the wilderness; the Great American Wilderness. And we will say you have come, as I have, onto the bank of a breakneck hopping and skipping brook. And there you suddenly stand in a shower of gold, a yellow waterfall of light pouring down where the tall soldiery of trees push back the forest throng and leave a silver path; you stand stock-still as green statuary in raining awe at the sight of water and light, the pulsing cold sliver that tugs at turtle-back stones and finning forests of stringing weed that weaves like some queer viscera in the agate body of the snaking river. It is some little time before you recollect how long you have waited for water.

Then, humble-crouched down in the living and breathing fathering and mothering mud, down on your creaking-sawhorse praying-mantis bones, you the said-to-be master bow, and wait. See the little millions? See the soot-sized little whing-ding devils rise like so many blinded maddened flies? Oh what a black crusty nest you've kicked into! If they could they'd sting you swell you black and blue, suck your blood and needle you through! But the little buggers can't get to you. For whilst you wait outside their glassy cage they too wait outside your blue and cloud palisade; you prisoned in shifting shade, they prisoned in their sliding, jellied glades; manacled pair, dragging alike your iron water and clanking air!

So the little living things have their dwarfling madding fling; played and playing their drip-drop part, rivered along from heart to heart, now they're spent. Now spinning in the looking sun, belly and back, turning, turning, in funeral driftings to the same old drum, down they come.

And I, watching the millions and missing the trillions, down on caney crooked pious knees in the green-grained mud listening for the primeval thud of the Universe; I, David Crockett, drank and drank.

ALL VOICES. Hear! Hear!

CROCKETT. *Was man ever freer than that?* I think not! And to that way of life, that God-given blood-bought Freedom, sweet as wandering in the wilderness, sweet as stumbled-on spring water, I shall through the aeons doff my old coonskin hat!

But now my life and times on earth are like to that ever-living sediment: *resolved.* What I did lives on and on. What I am become drinks now of the Silence and Freedom of God.

GROUP ONE *(Men)*.
>Oh, the cobbled streets of Dublin
>Are yet a-hivin' and a-bubblin'
>On the tongues of Ireland's sons
>Wherever the Race yet runs!

GROUP TWO *(Women)*.
>In rude wilderness homestead
>Or ivoried parliaments of the dead
>Our Davy's tongue is slick as ever
>A verra, verra clever feller!

CROCKETT. I thank you.

GROUP ONE *(Men)*.
>When into one gourd there's poured
>Blood of Celtic and Norman lord
>There's mixed a draught as bucking-colt frisky
>As blended Scotch and Irish peat-bog whiskey!

CROCKETT. Aye! I was but a watery limb of a mighty oak! Crocketts and Hawkinses go away way back, but I was never one to dillydally over a long-cold track. My own father fought in the Revolution at the Battle of King's Mountain, and I had it from himself direct his blood turned the leaves early and a redder red, for he said he bled like a stuck hog all up and down the side of old King's Mountain. But he never felt his blood so rare a compliment as to light there and wait for his monument!

WOMEN. No. He didn't. John Crockett moved—

CROCKETT. On! On into the golden Carolinas.

WOMEN. And then?

CROCKETT. On! On again, into smoky-blue Tennessee.

WOMEN. Why?

CROCKETT. Why? Why, because—why because, as he often said to me, he said: "John Crockett be twenty-one, white, and free!"

WOMEN. Fiddle-footed and fancy-free, that's what John Crockett be; and his son Davy followed right in his steps!

CROCKETT.
>I learned early it don't pay to answer
>The complaint of a woman
>Or the cry of a panther.

WOMEN. Or the cry of a baby, maybe?

CROCKETT. I was a good provider.

WOMEN.
>A good provider.
>Of stringy bear-meat and neighbor's borried cider!
>Of a dirt-floored cabin made of logs
>And a passel of mangy drawed hound-dogs!
>A good provider.

Of silver and dishes?
A rain-bar'l of wiggle-tail wishes!
And china? Not even pewter!
A *great* provider.
All you could ever afford
Was a filed-down hunting knife
And a hollowed-out gourd!
And as for social life, what fun!
Davy off on a ring-tail tooter
While Polly stays home to get the chores done!

CROCKETT. *Some*body had to look after the place!

WOMEN.

But for the *male* of the species, that would be a disgrace!
And when she'd got the hundred chores done—
*Then,* we suppose, Polly could look forward to an evening's fun?

CROCKETT. Well . . . some, I reckon.

WOMAN. Some of what?

CROCKETT. Some of whatever she'd got!

WOMEN. Rot! All she'd got was *your* children.

CROCKETT. Polly never seemed to mind!

WOMEN.

Then you—like most males—were merely blind!
Oh, we know what the men in the armies say,
We've heard the laughing manly regiments:
"To keep your woman happy while you're away
Just—keep—her—pregnant!"
We've heard women say it and say it so often:
"Better I were dead and in my coffin."
Then turn right around and soften.

CROCKETT. Her death was a terrible blow.

WOMEN.

Oh! . . . what you men don't know!
There are things in a home—any home—
That working together will gradually hone
A conscientious woman to the very bone.
Let alone
The empty, hopeless, dreary mess
Of starting from scratch in a wilderness.

CROCKETT.

I allow it maybe was the drip of day to day
Caused my little Polly to be carried away.
And yet I think I grieved her fair,
Fell on her coffin and kissed her hair;
Carried next my heart in my breast pocket

A snippet of hair in her little gold locket—
Though I afterwards in some campaign lost it.

WOMEN. In the Widow *Patton* campaign?

SOLDIER *(from Tennessee)*.

Now you Gonzales women, looka here—
You're treating our Colonel a shade severe.
Ain't you kind of overlooking
He was a widower, with two children to rear?

WOMEN.

Posh! We're not overlooking anything!
As soon as he'd wore little Polly Finley out
He turned himself right square about,
Put his courting cap on
And went after the widow Elizabeth Patton!

CROCKETT. And may I respectfully inquire the harm?

WOMEN.

You may and there wasn't any, you might say.
Elizabeth owned a snug little farm.
And more than that
It gave you a place to hang your coonskin hat;
A sort of axle-hub for the Crockett round
Of running for Congress or running after hounds;
A place to cache your gunpowder and cap
And then skedaddle all over the map.

CROCKETT. As a congressman and elected representative of the people it was my duty and privilege to move about, to listen to my constituents' grievances, to mend and keep on mending my political rail fences.

WOMEN. Until they threw you out.

CROCKETT. The people are sovereign!

WOMEN. A generous attitude; meaning, we suppose, you bowed out gracefully, you took defeat well? *(A pause.)* Did you?

CROCKETT. I . . . told my constituents I would go to Texas, and they could go to hell.

PURDY REYNOLDS.

At this juncture—bearing, of course, the utmost respect—
There's a question I'd like to interject.
Among you ladies,
The so-called Widows of Gonzales—

WOMEN. So-called!

REYNOLDS.

Yes. Were there none who, later, like Colonel Crockett,
Sought, shall we say, other solace?
  *(They are silent.)*
Then I ask you bluntly:

Did each of you stubbornly retain
The dear and hallowed name,
A name written in a husband's own gore
On the Alamo's blood-slick sacrificial floor?
Did you enduringly march primly to bed
With a widow's pillow for a widow's lone head?
  (*Again, they are silent.*)

CROCKETT.

They mostly married again, that's what they did,
Some of 'em several,
And some, I'm told, went to the very devil!

WOMEN.

We confess.
There were those of us who succumbed to the second wilderness.
To the bitter blank wall
And the nightfall
And the unanswered call.
We were not hunters, but hearth-keepers;
We were not soldiers, but sweepers and weepers.
With scissors and thread for rifles and lead
We fought.
And marched a thousand miles on a twelve-by-twelve floor.

Be gentle therefore with the Widows of Gonzales
Who, in their extremity, sought other . . . solace.

REYNOLDS. Then see you deal as generously with Colonel Crockett.

WOMEN. We will.

HIRAM WILLIAMSON.

Still,
Colonel Crockett at his popularity peak
Was generally regarded as little more than a freak.
As an example of his statesmanship
There is the record of his attempt
To put through a bill to abolish West Point Military Academy.
At the Alamo we could have used some of that spit and polish about which he
  complained.

TRAVIS.

Sergeant Major Williamson on that point is correct.
Prior to and during the Battle of the Alamo
Both men and certain officers
Were lax in decorum and respect.

REYNOLDS.

But were they not, Colonel Travis, eminently qualified in the decorum of facing
  shot,

With respect to the manner in which they died?

TRAVIS.

Private Reynolds, the men died well.
On the whole they fought and fell
In a manner entirely creditable.
But I should like to point out:
As there is more to living than breath,
There is also more to dying than death;
And lifelong conduct presages beyond a doubt
Whether we're to die with a bleat or a shout!
All die! . . . man, dog, and swatted housefly!
But in the long balladry of Man's valorous deeds
There gapes an ocean 'twixt mere dying and one who heeds
Freedom's clear but hard-to-hear single repeated note,
Mounting higher and higher,
Lost,
Except to the attuned ear;
Lost,
Amid the billion-voiced self-pitying bog-drone of Death's common choir.

REYNOLDS.

But tell me, Sir:
Had they died—as we assume you did—
According to some archaic chivalric letter—
Could they have fought and died any better?

TRAVIS.

Not at the last.
Didn't I make myself clear?
The men *sold* their lives dear.
But the difference . . .
And the preeminence . . .
Is not in sold, but *gave!*
I was no slave caught up a tree,
No Johnny-come-lately for Liberty.
I was not there in an accidental fight,
With some vague notion of redress
To more or less protect a lagniappe headright.
No!
In the midst of a piecemeal war,
From the divining distance of a star
I from the first detected how we are
All of a flock and of freedmen's feather,
But lacking a lead-wether to keep us together;
All of us running and running pell-mell,
Each bleating separately but finding no bell.

It was thus in Freedom's blessed name
I, William Barret Travis, willfully became that castrated ram.
When I fell
I rang that bell.

REYNOLDS.

We remember your words.
Interesting. Revealing. A bit absurd, however,
When held up to the light of psychological investigation by Dr. Pollard and me
    in several midnight conversations.
The repetitive use of the words *death* and *liberty*
Suggested to us a certain schoolboy immaturity;
A very clear-cut indication
Of what medical science terms a death preoccupation.
In fact, we noted in several others this inclination.
Notably, your friend Bonham.

WILLIAM BONHAM.

I never yet read a medical report of a splendid act
That didn't somehow in the end detract;
That didn't leave you feeling a piece of sheerest valor
Was somehow tainted,
Painted white and bloodless with a crazy-house pallor.
To the very end
I was Travis' friend.
And I tell you he had a vision of interaction
That will bear no worded-down detraction;
His clipped and heart-homing words
Were all arrow, tipped with living birds;
He carried waist-stripped leadership
As a cocked and ready pistol at his hip,
And when he blooded Freedom's sword
It bore the unmistakable unction of the Lord.

AMOS POLLARD.

Lieutenant Bonham,
In most respects I agree.
And it certainly isn't for me
To imply Colonel Travis in any willful degree lied.
But you will recollect: I also died.
And young Reynolds and I were at that time
Interested—as a game, to keep from falling asleep—
In tracing out influences that shaped our commander's words and acts.
Colonel Travis was brought up in a fanatical sect.
And the urgently inflammatory words he used so well
Were probably derived
From hearing Baptist preaching

On the urgency of avoiding a Baptist hell.

At any rate, most of his statements were exclamations.

BONHAM.

What else could they have been, in our situation?

REYNOLDS.

Neither can you overlook the manner in which he died,

For—shed of its aura of honor and glory—the best data

Indicates it was probably suicide.

    *(When* BONHAM *would retort.)*

One thing more:

Since here our main occupational task

Appears to be a judgeless reviewing of things past,

And since of our past we are wholly absolved,

And nothing further can really evolve—

I say, why shouldn't we take equally laconic note

Of the official wording of the official report?

BONHAM.

Official report?

Of the Alamo's fall there was no report.

Of this immortal action the thing most cherished

Is that none lived to describe it,

To the last man we everyone perished.

REYNOLDS.

Thermopylae had its messenger of defeat,

The Alamo had none?

BONHAM.

Well . . . very nearly.

REYNOLDS.

What of the women?

BONHAM.

Well, yes, there was afterward a gossipy spinning

Of an unreliable report by the Negroes and women.

REYNOLDS.

If you do not accept the word of Mrs. Dickinson—

BONHAM.

I said I do not accept her word as official!

REYNOLDS.

Then what of the official report of the Mexicans?

TRAVIS.

Now, as then, I offer the most strenuous objections

To accepting the shifty word of any and all Mexicans!

REYNOLDS.

Not even those Mexicans on our side?

TRAVIS.

Not even those who *died* at my side.

REYNOLDS.

Surely by now!—

Surely here!—

Oh, the execrable cloying vestige of Man!

Having been one, still I am at a loss to understand.

GUERRERO.

Ho! Comrades! Amigos! Listen to me:

I was a Mexican.

By my comrades in the Alamo

I was ribbed and called "Old One-Eye Guerrero,"

Because in life I had but one eye.

So I ask it of you:

Caballeros, does your horse pay much attention to the spur

That only ruffles up the fur?

What does the burro with the little load think

When he is now and then jabbed with the stick?

I tell you:

Comrades, he laughs!

Brother, he kicks!

JAMES BOWIE.

You were a strong man, Guerrero,

But you were a little too easily bent

Into the intricate fence of subservience.

Abamillo,

Esparza,

Fuentes,

Losoya,

Nava. Stand!

*(They do so.)*

Do you recognize these men?

TRAVIS.

Certainly. Your men. Bowie's men.

BOWIE.

Bowie's men and Bowie's friends,

Therefore, Bowie's to defend!

TRAVIS.

There is nothing to defend.

BOWIE.

Again we do not see eye to eye.

Where you see nothing I see everything.

When my friend Juan Seguin sent his nephew, Blas Herrera, to Laredo

On February 18 and Blas whipped two horses back

To warn us of Santa Anna's imminent attack—
Who was the commander in his stiff-necked pride
Looked disdain and with his heel replied?

TRAVIS.

It was my mistake.
During a time of poor communication and wild rumor,
When I could not even depend on my own Regular Army men to fill a sentry post,
My mistake, at most,
Was one any careful commander might make.
Does my word for it ease your splenetic humor?

BOWIE.

No. It seems to me you had a word for everything.
No, you made a charge these men were born corrupt.
Now back it up.

TRAVIS.

I made no charge!
I but spoke of birth, irrefutable birth!
They were born Mexican.

BOWIE.

Hold you then, Sir,
Mere accidental birth
May predestine a man's everlasting worth?

TRAVIS.

For certain capacities, yes.
That there were exceptions I with pleasure hasten to attest—but—
Let me ask you:
Will an eagle's shadow over a hen
Get her chick with knowledge of the high winds?
Or some great stallion's drop of seed
Endow the plow mare's foal with racing speed?
No!
In the God-seed
We were freed!
He is the Sire
Of our blood's ancient desire!
In the blood, Sir, is Freedom's mystery,
And in the blood is its transmitted history!

BOWIE.

You men be seated.
    *(They do so.)*

TRAVIS.

Man, don't you see?
These were not born on edge to be free!
The centuries that shaped the bended knee

Withered also the glands that beget Liberty.
When the times turn dire,
When the flesh and the will tire
And the heart is gutted by fire—
What may we expect of those
Drilled to genuflect?
Will they then stand erect?
Should we have thrust our foundling hope
Into hands who know only to hand it to a pope?
No!
These could not have stood alone
Who have no inherited home save guilty, bloody Rome.
And to these born in closed-eyed obedience
I add those genuflecting from wide-eyed expedience!

REFUGIO DE LA GARZA.

Predestinarian Calvinist and Separatist Anabaptist . . .
Intermingled with Southern United States white-skinned prejudice—
Thus, the by-some-esteemed Colonel Travis.
As a member of the neutral band, I stand.
I present the view of the unintoxicated few.

TRAVIS.

De La Garza.
Well I remember you . . . and your neutral view.
Representative of the sneaking culture;
Shepherd of the devious way;
First to reach our burning pyre;
Freedom's first vulture.

DE LA GARZA.

As was my custom
I went to each charted place,
Moving always at the Church's authorized pace.
Colonel Bowie at my hands was baptized;
By me his marriage to Ursula de Veramendi solemnized.
Who are you and what know you of his or my eternal hope?

TRAVIS.

Only this:
Whatever the hope
It is not bound up in Roman rope!

DE LA GARZA.

How fine the line between freedom and rebellion,
Between the misguided zealot and the unredeemed hellion.
Colonel Travis,
What was there in our time on earth
In minutest degree comparable to the freedom of this our later birth?

What, or how,
Comparable to the incomparable Now?
It appears therefore a small and dubious thing you should have found
It necessary to base religious perception on whether man is bound, or unbound;
    rabbit, or hound.
Better, better far!
Spend the snuff-pinch of time on earth in enduring servitude
If it serve to bring man to somewhat understand God's magnitude!
Better bar the doors of the earthly house
To the lion, and leave off chasing the mouse.

TRAVIS.

So have intoned the priest-vested despots through time.
So have they lifted the sorcerer's hood from the misunderstood
And slowly uncurled their string of black-wisdomed pearls,
All the while chanting the selfsame noxious paralyzing rhyme:
Man born of earth fear God.
Fear God and reason not why
He has ordained you in lockjawed misery to breathe a little, then die.
It's a lie!
God does not mock the mortal flock.
It is the earthly shepherd leads them
Into endless pastures of endless rock!
Who showers God with devotions of the empty belly
Showers God with devotions of carnival confetti.
God desires man enter his presence in full stride,
To stand before him, a god-chip, in godly pride;
And, full of the knowledge of a son's place
Stare boldly into the Father's face—
Then—*then,* out of his own will and accord
Bow,
And say: My Lord.

DE LA GARZA. *(Turning away.)*

It is very apparent
God is lenient with the arrogant.

WILLIAMSON.

There is an arrogance exceeds Travis' a country mile:
The arrogance of false solicitude
Backed by the disappearing smile.
As for Colonel Bowie,
When he and his men should have been drilling
They were instead as drunk as lords,
Whooping and hollering and chasing the peons with drawn swords.
The week they should have been preparing
They were instead on a gargantuan spree

That ranged from the barracks at the Alamo
To the palace of the Veramendi.

BOWIE.

Gentlemen, gentlemen. Friends.
You have no way of knowing
How two years before the battle most of my life was over;
How two years before the battle most of me died . . .
With my wife and children in the plague at Monclova.

Much of my life I could wish to amend.

My early years were laid on a keel of wormwood days,
With poverty-warped ambition for rib staves,
And a will of swamp cypress for a hull,
And lean longing for the long oar-pull.
And for my pilot and mate:
Against the caste of Society, a seasoned hate.
So I didn't give a whoop in hell whether sweet or unsavory.
Life was a laugh! With money. I needed quick money!
I looked around and saw it was to be found in slavery.
So it was out of the backs of thousands of blacks
And afterward in faro-wheel deals in timbers and fields,
Hand over hand I yanked myself up, station by station
I parlayed my various deeds into a legended reputation.
Until in the Delta Queen City I was almost accounted reputable;
Until in New Orleans society I was almost—which is not—acceptable!

So with a saddlebag of tinderbox pride
I hit the freedom tide;
The tide you couldn't hold—
The tide that wouldn't be told—
The tide that rolled old '76 Liberty
Westward from the Mississippi.
Came out to Texas to breathe some of that crazy new air,
Where a man with ambition could better practice what the Creole calls *laissez-
    faire*—
Came out to Texas where
There was said to be freedom to spare
And set myself up, a gentleman land speculator,
In the old sun-baked town of San Antonio de Bexar!

And it was there
God sent me
Ursula de Veramendi.

Oh, I too liked the shake a clicking heel makes,
The shutters and sipped wine, guitars and maracás;

And I quickened to the silken laughter
That promises much,
But allows scarce a touch,
Until long, long after!
Yes, I vastly admired the chessmen grace
Of the high-gaited tight-reined Spanish race.
For they were rich and knew how to wear it;
Governors, in demeanor, to warrant the velvet.
Living so the daily round conspired to make one feel
He is engaged in moving through an endless, elegant, Virginia reel;
From birth to the grave a road of finest brocade,
Wine-velvet, blood-red, onyx, black, jade—
Life lived as an imperial parade!

Yet our love was a simple, elemental thing:
Two found water at a mountain spring.
Our coming together: as feather to feather.
Our days all one blue-and-gold weather.

    I cannot liken her laughter.
    I cannot compare her grace,
      Nor the remembered qualities of her face.

But oh, were I to dive to the caves of the sea,
Or climb to the outermost reaches of infinity,
In the remotest float of placeless space
I would see her lover and mother face.
Or were I to enter matter's elemental womb
And tunnel my way back through every tomb
And swim the dim blood-channels of every man—
Back and back and back, till there is nothing to understand—
There, where we were first sown;
There, where God as God is not known;
There in the spume-wrapped bombproof soul-seed home—
If,
Aeons above,
One word fell from your lips, my beloved—
In my deep I would wake from that sleep.
*Such was our love's pollenizing power*
*In that shattering hour*
*My soul would a second time burst, and flower!*
WOMEN. *(Softly.)*
Sweet was the love of Jim Bowie,
Slave-trader, gambler, fighter, speculator, roué;
Sweet and pure.

We respect your love.

Your accusers are silent.

*(Far across the plain, in the tower of San Fernando Cathedral, a bell begins to toll.)*
Listen!

That bell!

That tolling bell!

Oh, well, well do we remember what it foretells!

*(The light comes up slowly, as the morning sun on a cold and grey February day, revealing the auditorium as the shadowy, dank interior of the Alamo chapel of that time: a chapel without roof, the remains of which, with rock from the crumbling walls, litter the floor. Stage front, across the apron, is the entrance to the Alamo, looking out toward San Fernando. If the façade of the present-day Alamo is used, it should be constructed in two tiers, the heroes standing as in niches, like statues; and it should be an open construction, so that the audience may see out. It is effective to presume the audience as having been seated outside the Alamo chapel to this point in the play, and as inside the chapel, the defenders all around, during the remainder of the play.*

*On the stage to the left are two dim rooms.*

*On the stage to the right are bundles of hay and a scaffolding of poles held together with leather thongs.*

*The time is a little before midmorning.*

*Onstage, seen through the façade of the Alamo, the last of the Mexican populace are hurrying away, the final stages of an exodus which had begun about February 18. The Texan soldiers, Regulars and Irregulars, are seen coming into the enclosure of the fort. Some are driving cattle, and we hear their lazy, careless drivers' calls as they herd them inside the three-acre compound. A soldier steps inside the chapel, listens intently to the tolling bells, then drops his scant belongings and disappears outside, calling.)*

SOLDIER ONE. Hey! Y'hear that?

SOLDIER TWO. *(Unseen, with a soft laugh.)* Yeah.

*(Enter CAPTAIN ALMERON DICKINSON and his wife, she with their infant daughter in her arms. They walk hurriedly, she leading the way, as though they had been arguing. At his words, a little past stage center, she turns on him defiantly.)*

DICKINSON. For the last time I'm asking you—*begging* you to—

MRS. DICKINSON. No. No, I will not go.

DICKINSON. But—it's—Do you hear that? Do you know what it means?

MRS. DICKINSON. Of course I hear it. And I know what it means. It means—there's going to be a fight, and if there's a fight my husband will be in it, and if he's in it, I'm in it, and—that's all there is to it.

DICKINSON. You're some woman.

MRS. DICKINSON. I'm your wife.

DICKINSON. Well, I'm glad enough of that, you know—but I'd still like you to make for the settlements; we've still got horses over on Cibolo Creek, and you could be snug in Gonzales before morning, if you was to leave—

MRS. DICKINSON. Almeron!

DICKINSON. All right. I quit. *(He looks around, goes to the door of a side room, peers in.)* I'm right sorry about you having to put up in a place like this, so run-down and . . . all. But the place don't afford nothing extra for nobody, not even Colonel Travis.

MRS. DICKINSON. You won't hear me complainin'.

DICKINSON. They say there's to be some Mexican women stayin' on with us. They'll be company. *(He moves a few steps away.)* I got my work to do.

MRS. DICKINSON. Then do it. *(She is already busily engaged in making a comfortable place for her daughter.)* Be there any water? . . . enough to spare for washing didies and the like, I mean?

DICKINSON. There's water. A well. And they've digged a couple of aqueducts—little creeks, like—into here, if'n the Mexicans don't find 'em and shut 'em off. I'm going. *(He moves a step or two.)* I got my work to do. *(He goes for a final look at the baby.)* She's asleep. You wouldn't think she could sleep with all that goin' on, would you?

MRS. DICKINSON. Almeron! We'll be here. Now you'd best go and see about placing them cannons.

DICKINSON. *(Suddenly mock-soldierly).* Right you are, Ma'am! *(Going, after kissing her lightly.)* It won't take long. We only got eighteen pieces, at last count, and Jameson's mostly got 'em mounted in place already. *(He passes two of his soldiers just entering the chapel; one salutes in a languid manner, the other not at all.)* You men mind these cannon in here, will you? I got to check on the angle of that eighteen-pounder at the southwest corner.

> *(*CAPTAIN DICKINSON *exits, and one of the soldiers slowly climbs up. The second remains at the foot of the scaffold.* MRS. DICKINSON *disappears into one of the side rooms. The bell in San Fernando continues to ring. A third soldier enters and stands listening. He is the boy from Gonzales, sixteen-year-old* JOHNNY KELLOGG.)*

SOLDIER ONE. *(On scaffold, after a moment.)* Hell, I remember that bell.

SOLDIER TWO. Sure. It was the sentry in San Fernando.

KELLOGG. The signal he'd sighted the Meskin army.

SOLDIER ONE. Old Santy Anna.

SOLDIER TWO. At the time it didn't mean nothing to me.

SOLDIER ONE. Me neither.

KELLOGG.
They claimed he seen their lances in the sun,
All lined up horseback, with bugles and banners.

SOLDIER ONE. It was Sesma's cavalry he seen.

SOLDIER TWO. For sure it warn't old Santy Anna!

KELLOGG. He never come that close to the line!

SOLDIER ONE.
One thing I *do* remember:
It was cold as a well-digger's behind!

SOLDIER TWO. That ain't what I was rememberin'.

KELLOGG. Me neither.

> *(Now, at a distance, in a hazy spot of light up high and to the rear, a memory sequence begins. It fades in and out during the following dialogue. First, there is the laughter of women and men, and music; then silence, then the spot of light. Quickly, a Mexican dancer enters the light and begins to dance, accompanied only by her clicking castanets.)*

SOLDIER ONE. What you're rememberin' I bet I know!

SOLDIER TWO. Yeah. *(He licks his lips.)*

SOLDIER ONE. Yeah. The night before.

SOLDIER TWO. Man, did we have the fun!

SOLDIER ONE. Son of a gun!

> *(He slaps his leg, and on the signal there is a burst of laughter from the men and women in the memory picture as a Texan soldier steps into the light and does a quick turn with the dancer. Immediately he releases her and disappears, and the scene fades, but not completely.)*

SOLDIER TWO. You remember that there fandango?

SOLDIER ONE. Sure. On one of them little muddy side streets . . .

KELLOGG. Calle Durango.

SOLDIER TWO. Yeah, that was it. Calle Durango.

SOLDIER ONE. And cold as a well-digger's behind.

SOLDIER TWO. But we was so drunk we didn't none of us mind!

KELLOGG. It was someplace down close to the Square.

SOLDIER ONE. Plaza, Johnny, not Square.

SOLDIER TWO. How do you know, Johnny? Was you there?

KELLOGG. No . . . but one of the fellows that was, said—well—

SOLDIER TWO. What?

KELLOGG. Afterwards he'd wished he'd not. 'Count of—

SOLDIER TWO. What?

KELLOGG. He said, "'Count o' what he got."

SOLDIER ONE. Like as not! *(A moment.)* That was one more fandango.

> *(Now, in a last, magnificent whirl, the dancer appears in brilliant light, and again the Texan soldier, right at the last, takes her about the waist and flings her around . . . and at the same time SOLDIER TWO, on the ground in the Alamo chapel, suddenly does an impromptu version of the same tango, his rather comic. They end at approximately the same moment, with a shout—except that, in the memory scene, the Texan soldier suddenly lifts the dancer in his arms and carries her off, while SOLDIER TWO merely ends with his arms out, empty, remembering. At that instant the memory scene abruptly vanishes.)*

Yeah, that was what I call a real "in-fair."

KELLOGG. Wish I'd a-been there.

SOLDIER TWO. It would of curled your belly hair.

KELLOGG. I don't git what you mean!

SOLDIER ONE. How old was you, Johnny?

KELLOGG. Sixteen.

SOLDIER TWO.

    Sixteen. Bet you could give a fit

    To an old-fashion sugar-teat!

SOLDIER ONE.

    I remember yet

    The one with the big combs and the castanets.

KELLOGG.

    Golly, when I think what all I missed!

    All them wimmin'!

    All that sinnin'!

SOLDIER ONE.

    Oh, I don't know, Johnny, about them women.

    Mostly I found 'em to be all eyes and hair;

    Once you plucked the feathers, there wasn't too much there.

SOLDIER TWO.

    They didn't always smell just quite right,

    Not like a woman ought;

    Too much chili pepper and garlic, I figure—

SOLDIER ONE.

    But oh, my soul, how they clawed and fought.

KELLOGG.

    *All I ever done was to die!*

WOMEN.

    Shame! Shame!

    Shame on you men for the example you set,

    The vows you broke,

    The lusts you whet;

    Shame in the name of this boy's good mother!

BONHAM.

    Ladies.

    Concerning the orgies you've heard the men relate,

    My apologies.

    Rest assured,

    There were those of us who did not participate.

WOMEN.

    Let us hope so.

WILLIAMSON.

    There were men there

    Who wouldn't have turned a hair

    If Cleopatra'd come walking naked across the Square.

WOMEN.

    At any rate

    We're glad our Gonzales men got there late!

BONHAM.

    Late? Yes, but in time
    To insure their names would be forever enshrined!

WOMEN.

    In time . . . to have . . . their names . . . enshrined—
    Another way of saying, in time to die.
    But oh, sometimes! . . .
    Sometimes
    When the wind blew;
    When the winds talked in the flue;
    When in their icy passing
    You could hear them asking, *laughing!*
    When the asking winds blew
    And a door's cold breath
    Whispered death, death,
    And you knew.
    You *knew!*
    Knew before the wind tattled
    Why the latch doors creaked,
    Why the far-off silent battle
    Killed in silence the local cattle,
    Why the empty barns shrieked!

    And oh, sometimes . . .
    When the children cried . . .
    When the new lambs died . . .

    Then

    In our pacing sorrow,
    In our oxen sorrow,
    Today yoked to tomorrow,
    Tomorrow yoked to tomorrow,
    Sorrow to sorrow,
    Tomorrow to tomorrow,
    All yoked,
    Yesterday,
    Today,
    Tomorrow,
    All yoked—
    Dragging sorrow.

    Walking.

    Stopping.

    Stopping in the middle of a beardy old field,
    Picking one-handed what a little war yields.

Digging a hole,
Digging in sorrow,
Burying today,
And burying tomorrow.
Then!—
*Listening to the wind in the dry cornhusks,*
*We groaned aloud: they didn't get there late enough!*
> *(Onstage,* COLONEL WILLIAM BARRET TRAVIS *enters the chapel, followed*
> *by an aide,* COLONEL DAVID CROCKETT, *and the scouts,* JOHN SMITH *and*
> DR. JOHN SUTHERLAND. SUTHERLAND *is being supported by* CROCKETT
> *and* SMITH, *his horse having fallen on him as they were scouting the Mexican*
> *Army on the Laredo Road.)*

TRAVIS. Come in here a moment.

WOMEN. Look! There's Colonel Travis!

BONHAM. So it is. And Crockett and John Smith and Dr. Sutherland.

WOMEN.
The play,
The piece of Time we left Heaven for,
Has begun.

TRAVIS. This report you've made on Sesma's cavalry: is it accurate? Fifteen hundred men. Are you sure?

JOHN SMITH. Well, we didn't check their muster roll with their commanding officer, Colonel, but we did the best we could. Under the circumstances.

DR. JOHN SUTHERLAND. We got a good look at them, Colonel. Calvary. They were drawn up on horseback in a battle line and an officer was riding up and down in front. I judged from twelve to fifteen hundred strong.

TRAVIS. And you agree with that estimate, Smith?

SMITH. Yessir, I do. I've guessed at cattle in a herd as big as that, and them milling, and never come out a hundred wrong, and I'd say Doctor John come pretty close.

TRAVIS. In that case . . . what's the condition of your leg?

SUTHERLAND. Bad. That little rain we had turned to ice and when we spurred to make our getaway my horse slipped and went down. Just for a second, but the damage was done. It's already swollen to where I had to split the top of my boot.

TRAVIS. Then there isn't much chance of your being fit for battle duty, is there?

SUTHERLAND. Not for a few days, no. I can't stand on it at all.

TRAVIS. Can you ride?

SUTHERLAND. Oh yes, I can ride. It isn't pleasant, but I can do it.

TRAVIS. Will you take a message to Gonzales?

SUTHERLAND. I'll make a start.

TRAVIS. Good. We're going to need every able man here, but it's imperative we get word out to the settlements. Our plight, as you can see, will very soon be desperate unless we get reinforcements. We must have help from Gonzales and Goliad.

CROCKETT. Here am I, Colonel. All you've got to do is assign me to someplace and I and my Tennessee boys will defend it or know why.

TRAVIS. That's the kind of talk I like to hear. Colonel Crockett, I want you and your men to man the picket fence just outside, from the corner of the church to the barracks on the south. It's a long stretch, but I know you can do it. We've got a big area to defend here, what appears to be better than two acres, so we're forced to spread ourselves thin. And you'll mostly have to rely on your muskets, though Ensign Jameson has located four four-pounders on the entrenchment to the front.

CROCKETT. We'll defend it, all right. *(He departs, shouting as he passes the stockade.)* All you Tennessee mule-skinners and b'ar-fighters gather here! Tennessee, this-a-way! Over here, at the picket fence!

TRAVIS. *(He sits to write, a sawed-off stump serving as a desk.)* I want you to take this dispatch to Judge Andrew Ponton and the citizens of Gonzales. I'll send another to Fannin at Goliad . . . *(He writes.)* by either Bonham or Johnson, one . . .

WOMEN.
Gonzales.
That was us.
We got the letter. It was read to the whole town by Judge Ponton.
Those who didn't hear it got it from mouth to mouth.
We got it. We understood.
Our men responded.
They answered in their blood.
But we were so upset we never did know exactly what the letter said, except:
   Come.

BONHAM. It said: "The enemy in large force is in sight. We want men and provisions. Send them to us. We have 150 men and are determined to defend the Alamo to the last. Give us assistance. Send an express to San Felipe with news day and night."

   *(Onstage, a soldier reports to Travis, excitedly.)*

SOLDIER. Sir! Sir, they've went and done it!

TRAVIS. Done it? Who?

SOLDIER. The Mexicans!

TRAVIS. They've done what?

KELLOGG. The Mexicans have run up a red flag on San Fernando! They've run up the red flag that means no quarter!

TRAVIS. *(Rising, going outside to see.)* Then we'll give them as good as they give! We'll answer them with a cannon shot!

SOLDIER ONE. Which one, Sir?

TRAVIS. The one at the southwest corner, the eighteen-pounder, the biggest one we've got!

SOLDIER THREE *(Two soldiers have been frantically loading the cannon.)* We're loaded, Sir!

TRAVIS. Then ready—

KELLOGG. Ready!—

SOLDIER THREE. Ready!—

TRAVIS. *Fire! (The big cannon booms out, and almost as it sounds, a man bearing a small white flag marches out from the farthest end of the fort, straight toward the Mexican lines. The soldier is* GREEN B. JAMESON, *Alamo engineer, being sent to parley by command of* JAMES BOWIE. TRAVIS, *watching, and understanding his intent, storms.)* Who is that man? Where is he going?

AIDE. It looks like . . . it walks like—Jameson. It is, Sir! It's Benito Jameson!

TRAVIS. Jameson? A white flag? By whose command?

SOLDIER. They say it's a parley, Sir. He was sent out by Colonel Bowie.

TRAVIS. Bowie? Then Bowie assumes more than his share of the command. What does the man mean? I heard no call to parley. He has bugles in his ears! Tell Colonel Bowie I wish to see him. Here.

SOLDIER. Colonel Bowie is sick, Sir. He's lying down. Yesterday he fell off a scaffold while he was helping to mount a cannon. Some say he was sick then. Today he's in a fever and can barely get up.

TRAVIS. Then I'll go to him. *(Striding off.)* I'll learn what this is all about. For the good of the Command we've got to have this thing threshed out! Either he gives me good reason, or else I have no alternative to call his action other than— treason!

> *(Exit* TRAVIS, *followed by the aide. The light fades to a stormy green. It thunders, distantly. It could be either thunder, or cannon. It is almost dark.)*

WOMEN.

What did Jim Bowie's note say?

Did he have a valid reason?

Or was it—as Travis thought—*treason?*

JAMESON. *(Rising among the* WITNESSES.*)* It was I who carried the flag of truce and the note from Colonel Bowie, and there was no trace of treason in it. As Commander of Volunteers, Colonel Bowie had a perfect right to send it. There were more Volunteers than Regular Army soldiers in the Alamo. The note said: "I wish to ascertain if it be true that a parley was called during the firing of our cannon. For this reason I send my second aide, Benito Jameson, under guarantee of a white flag which I believe will be respected by you and your forces. God and Texas! Fortress of the Alamo, February 23rd, 1836."

WOMEN. We *know* how the Mexicans replied.

JOSÉ BATRES. *(Rising from among the* WITNESSES.*)* But do others? I myself penned the reply, and I should like to read it. If you please. To keep the record clear.

BONHAM. Go ahead. I never did hear it.

BATRES. Thank you, Lieutenant Bonham. As the Aide-de-Camp of his Excellency, the President of the Republic, I reply to you according to the order of his Excellency, that the Mexican Army cannot come to terms under any conditions with rebellious foreigners to whom there is no other recourse left, if they wish to save their lives, than to place themselves immediately at the disposal of the Supreme Government from whom alone they may expect clemency after some considerations are taken up. God and Liberty! José Batres. *(He sits, immediately, after clicking his heels and bowing.)*

WOMEN.
>God and Texas.
>God and Liberty.
>So many people pulling at God's coattails.
>So many causes trying to get His attention.
>All claiming, pulling, tugging;
>A few, perhaps, praying for His intervention;
>Fewer still for absolute arbitration,
>The weeding out of every motive,
>Tracing out for Time's good, Man's good,
>Then choosing.
>Yet His Steady Finger did.
>
>But oh, sometimes, many times, it seemed to us
>Ours was such a little war, a little fuss
>In which nothing much was coming to pass.
>That somehow our men's going was like summer dust,
>And must
>In a little while,
>Where the horses passed,
>Fall back to the grass.
>Fall back to us.
>Had we but *known*
>How Man stumbles on joy but runs toward sorrow;
>Had we but *known*
>How hard death is, how featureless is the face of tomorrow;
>Then we should have adjusted life's hideous asides,
>>In the dark room,
>>The padded mind's room . . .
>And there, if we must—since we must—
>>To peek.
>Then shriek on silent shriek
>Give release to our silent horror!

BONHAM.
>Women, God did well
>When He made you our softer selves.
>Cut off from you men grow hard.
>And William Travis and I were pulled from Woman's breast
>As the harvester pulls certain fruit before the rest;
>We were pulled early,
>Pulled while yet hard,
>Broken off by the harvesting hand of the Lord that others might better grow.

It was during that wet and cold night of February 23 and early the following day William Barret Travis wrote lines that had no woman softness in them; lines that didn't rouse Fannin in time or Houston in time or enough of anybody in time . . . but have since roused the World for All Time:

"To the People of Texas and All Americans in the World—Fellow Citizens and Compatriots: I am besieged with a thousand or more of the Mexicans under Santa Anna. I have sustained a continual bombardment and cannonade for twenty-four hours and have not lost a man. The enemy has demanded a surrender at discretion, otherwise, the garrison are to be put to the sword, if the fort is taken. I have answered the demand with a cannon shot, and our flag still waves proudly from the walls. *I shall never surrender or retreat.* Then, I call upon you in the name of Liberty, of patriotism, and everything dear to the American character, to come to our aid with all dispatch. The enemy is receiving reinforcements daily and will no doubt increase to three or four thousand in four or five days. If this call is neglected, I am determined to sustain myself as long as possible and die like a soldier who never forgets what is due his own honor and that of his country. VICTORY OR DEATH."

WOMEN. *(Softly.)* Rosanna Cato wrote every line.

BONHAM. *(Startled.)* What?

WOMEN. *(Louder.)* Rosanna Cato wrote every line.

BONHAM. Who?

WOMEN.
Rosanna, the child-wife Travis refused again to see;
The wife from whom he imagined himself forever free.

BONHAM.
Oh yes. His wife.
I never knew if the report of her unfaithfulness was true;
But I do know, of course, in such a case, what a man's honor commands
  him to do.
Or . . . could the Hand of God been picking there, too?
I don't know.
It does seem strange, though—now I think of it:
I never heard him mention her, not one time—

WOMEN. Nonetheless, she wrote every line!

*(Lights up immediately onstage, the following afternoon. All the defenders of the Alamo have been called together. They are just inside the chapel, in a loose semicircle, and as the lights come up they cheer.* COLONEL TRAVIS, *across the chapel, is haranguing them. In the group may be seen* JAMES BOWIE, *resting on a cot toward the front, his face pale with illness. The day is cold and grey.)*

BOWIE. *(After a fit of coughing, rising on one elbow.)* Men, I want it understood that from this time onward Colonel Travis is your commanding officer. I'm sick, boys . . . sick. But I'm with you. Sick or well, heaven or hell, I'm with you! *(He breaks off in another attack of coughing.)* I want to give you something. My sword. *(Pushes it toward* TRAVIS.*)* Take it! *(*TRAVIS *does so.)* Use it. Keep it for my word and my pledge to die for freedom. Hold it and wield it as long as you can; until the grip goes out of your white-knuckled hand; until your hand drops open to receive the Keys to the City of God. *(He coughs, briefly.)* But this—*(He lifts his "Bowie knife" aloft.)*—this I keep. Made at my brother's plantation by his black-smith, Jesse Cliffe, and given me by my brother Rezin Bowie. This I keep. And the enemy who takes it for a trophy will first have to wash it clean of enemies' blood.

TRAVIS. *(Contemplating the sword.)*
The sword.
Symbol of authority.
Of valor.
Symbol of chivalry.
Sign of battle.
A drawn sword, the eager blade.
Look at it. Look at it long! . . .
Who made it? Whose, do you suppose, the hand that tempered and shaped it?
Were his thoughts of foreboding?
Did he in his mind's forward eye
Look to the time when men would die,
Die by the stroke of the thing he was moulding?
When in the bellows'd forge he heated it white
Did he dream of the heat of a distant fight?
When out of his head he pulled a hair
And with a stroke cut it, floating in air—
What was the smithy thinking there?
Of a throat cut easily as thread?
Of a blood-bathed, falling head?
No, he felt no sense of guilt
As he plunged it in water to the hilt;
No sweat of conscience over the blade
His great rough hands had made.
Holding it to the light,
Brandishing it in every direction,
He had but one thing in mind: perfection.
Of the sword's grim potential he was but dimly aware,
But the sword's *making* was his special care.
And I say to you men:
As this sword is, your soul is!
Of our soul's potential we are but dimly aware,
But our soul's *making* is God's special care!
And in the forge with our souls I put our nation,
The nation we're making,
And everything we hold dear as—Texans.
What a young thing it is to be called Texan!
Yet already it fires the blood, calls the blood—Texan!
ALL. Texan!

TRAVIS. Texan!

ALL. Texan!

TRAVIS.

How the name gallops!
How the call beckons!
God I verily believe has put us on this anvil,
And God is not one to idly gamble
On the temper of the product of His forge.
He has tested us with His hands and knows we will not yield;
He has weighed us and balanced us and knows by the feel
We are His steel.
We are the point of His sword.
And if the point be blunted
The blade, Freedom's life, is daunted;
But if the *point* enters in—
Even though it break as it enters—
The wound in which Freedom's steel was left
Was never yet known to mend!
Men! The Mexicans have handed us a coward's choice
Of living under a despot without a governing voice,
Or running away.
Everything dear to our conscience they've sought to gag,
And now they taunt us with a blood-red flag.
*Will we run away?*

TEXANS. NO! NO!

TRAVIS. *Will we stay?*

TEXANS. YES! YES!

WOMEN. *(Softly under as Travis continues to exhort.)*

Like a camp meeting
In a brush arbor
The men are swayed
By Travis' ardor.

Cling! Clang!
Clong! Clong!
Beated steel
On an anvil gong.

Beating you
On His anvil gong!

Do they know
What he's doing?
Do they know
Death they're wooing?

Now they sway
To and fro . . .
 *(Louder.)*
*Tapley Holland's*
*The first to go!*
 *(Swiftly).*
Some step quickly
And some step slow,
Some take a dare
Some say a prayer
Some smirk
And some just don't care!
 *(A pause, then slower, softer.)*
Isaac. Isaac Millsaps,
You with seven children and a blind
 wife—
What did you think when pledging
 your life?

ISAAC MILLSAPS.
 Why, it happened quick as a wink.
 Fact is—I guess a man didn't have
 *time* to think!

WOMEN.
 And the Taylor boys,
 George, Edward, James,
 Eighteen, twenty, twenty-two—
 Boys, what prompted you?

TAYLOR BROTHERS.
 We don't know.
 We don't know.
 We can't seem to remember.
 All we know is
 We looked at George, our older brother,
 And then we looked at one another,
 And George said:
 "Let's go."
 *(Disguised as one of the colonists onstage* SATAN *now steps forward. The actors stop and stare at him in wonder, sensing his identity.)*

SATAN. And now may I have just a moment to explain why I didn't cross over the line? Because, like all myths and legends that spring up without corroboration from the most unlikely situations, this scene never happened. It's rank fiction. It's pure myth. There was never any line to cross over!

WOMEN. *(They are outraged.)*
 Oh is that so?

TRAVIS.
See this sword?
A drawn sword!

Unsheathed, naked,
To be clothed in blood!
Look at it!
Look at it long!
*You* are this blade
And God made you strong!

Who will follow me?
Follow the sword?
Follow the sword
Of our precious Lord!
Here I draw a blood-red line
For you to cross
Or stay behind.
Who will be first
To follow me,
To throw down his life
For Liberty?

Well, we know you,
And even if what you said were true,
We know our men
And we say, true or untrue,
*It would have been just like them!*
    *(Lights go up immediately.)*

           *Curtain*

# ★ ACT II

*It is the eighth day, March 1, 1836, about ten o'clock in the evening. A sentry walks slowly back and forth.*

WOMEN.
It is the eighth day.
It is the eighth day of waiting.
There has been fighting. Some.
Mostly there has been waiting.
Not a man has been lost.
There has been ample time now to think it over:
What they have pledged themselves to do:
To die, if necessary.
That necessity is not yet fully apparent.
The *step,*
The dreaded *step,*
The *one* step forward,
The *last*—
Has not been taken.
The one requiring final reconciliation has not been taken.
That time has not yet arrived.
    *(Brighter.)*
It is the first day of March.
At home little spots of green in the protected places,
In the pastures, in the bottoms, are beginning to show.
Next to the warmth of houses, trees prematurely bud and leaf.
Though slowly, some things begin to grow.
We are hopeful, impatient with *winter,*
*Impatient* to be in our gardens,
To make things *green,* to make things grow!
But it's . . . slow.
And off there a hundred miles in the Alamo, it's . . .
SENTRY. Slow.
    *(Very, very softly, somewhere in the enclosure, a young soldier is heard singing and playing a guitar. The song is "Come to the Bower," and he sings it over and over.)*
SOLDIER ONE. *(After listening awhile.)* Wish he'd git off that same song all the time.
SOLDIER TWO. Why?
SOLDIER ONE. It reminds me of somethin'.
SOLDIER TWO. Oh.
SENTRY. Slow.

*(ALMERON DICKINSON and his wife come from one of the side rooms and stand a moment. Quietly, they embrace.)*

SOLDIER ONE. *(After a moment.)* That's what I mean.

SOLDIER TWO. Yeah.

SOLDIER ONE. *(After watching DICKINSON exit, and MRS. DICKINSON stand a moment looking after him, then reenter the room.)* Ain't no place for a woman.

SOLDIER TWO. No, it ain't. *(The soldier singing "Come to the Bower" breaks off.)* Do you ever catch yourself wonderin' where you're at? I ain't asleep. My eyes are open. But things turn hazy. Like that song, there. Did he stop? *(A moment.)* I feel myself driftin' off. Like I'm drowning with my eyes open, and I can't figure out where I'm at or what I'm doing. Then I come to with a jerk and shiver like a wet dog. I shiver and shiver till I think I can't quit; until I finally just wear out and start drifting off again. *(Pause.)* You ever git like that?

SOLDIER ONE. Yeah. Sort of like. The way I feel I'm so tired I'm divided up: I'm divided into my feet, my belly, my eyes, and where this damn gun's rubbed my shoulder raw. If'n there's any more to me I can't tell it.

SENTRY. *(Stopping.)* My feet feel as big as tubs, and the tubs full of half-froze water; my belly like it'd been stretched and tacked on the wall of a crib; and you could light a cigar at one of my eyes if'n you was to hold it a foot away!

SOLDIER ONE. *(After a moment.)* Wish you hadn't mentioned tobacco. I got a craving that would pull a stump.

SOLDIER TWO. Yeah. And coffee. I keep thinkin' little wisps of coffee-smell come floating by, and then I think I see whole platoons of steaming cups crossing and recrossing right before my eyes. Man, I'd dance with old Santy Anna for a cup right now!

SOLDIER ONE. *(After a moment.)* Tobacco. What I wouldn't give for a chew of tobacco . . .

SOLDIER TWO. Coffee. Just the smell of boilin' coffee . . .

*(Soldier begins singing and playing "Come to the Bower.")*

SENTRY. *(Suddenly picking up his gun and marching off, fiercely.)* And there he goes with that damn song again! *(But the SENTRY has scarcely taken six steps when the sound of voices approaching drowns the music, and all stop, listening and peering out.)*

SOLDIER ONE. Here somebody comes!

*(Enter CROCKETT, REYNOLDS, POLLARD, and JOHN MACGREGOR.)*

CROCKETT. Evenin', boys.

SOLDIERS. Evenin', Colonel, evenin'.

CROCKETT. Any sign of reinforcements coming?

SENTRY. No sir. Ain't a sign anywheres, ain't much stirring.

REYNOLDS. It seems to me they've had plenty of time . . . if they're coming.

POLLARD. You'd think so. Bonham's been to Goliad and Gonzales twice. Smith's at Gonzales now. But people are slow to take alarm.

CROCKETT. Maybe they're holding a farewell ball before the soldiers take off. MacGregor, speaking of balls, where's that instrument o' yours, if instrument it be!

JOHN MACGREGOR. Instrument it is and a noble one, too, Colonel. Besides the hunting horn, the bugle, and perhaps the ram's horn o' Joshua, there be none so manly as the bagpipe.

CROCKETT. And none so hard to coax a tune from?

MACGREGOR. The tunes are there. They but require a Scot's ear to detect 'em.

CROCKETT. The sounds you get on it, it seems to me, would better suit the fiends o' hell.

MACGREGOR. If the pipes do better seem to suit the fiends o' hell, sir, then 'tis all to my instrument's credit, and to me. That is that for which it was constructed: to summon the clans to war. And what, might I ask, would the playin' o' your fiddle bring, the scrapin' o' the gut? A host o' howlin' tomcats, like as not!

CROCKETT. I like the sauce of your remarks, MacGregor, if not the wail o' your pipes. And I'm thinking it might stir our boys' faltering blood if we was to fight— the fiddle, that is, against the pipes. What do you say we try it? A contest. Right now. Tonight.

MACGREGOR. I accept the challenge. The contest will be unequal, o' course, but . . . don't you worry. I'll not play me best.

CROCKETT. Then get your weapon, mon, and if it's dreadful noise we're judgin' on, then I'm agreed—you've already won!

MACGREGOR. *(As he goes for the bagpipe.)* If you fiddle like you talk, Crockett, then I'm already lost!

CROCKETT. It could be a musical duel would stir up the coals in our boys and add a mite o' warmth for another long night's watch.

POLLARD. Our fires could use some stirring.

REYNOLDS. They're low tonight.

CROCKETT. Aye. But not burnt out!

REYNOLDS. No. Not out.

CROCKETT. All they need is to be poked about.

POLLARD. Men can go just so long without sleep.

CROCKETT. How long?

POLLARD. And be effective? Three days—four—in rare men, five.

CROCKETT. In rare men—five.

REYNOLDS. And we're already into the seventh!

POLLARD. But you couldn't say we were altogether effective.

CROCKETT. No. But dead from the neck up and walking in their sleep I'll take our boys one against any ten of Santa Anna's Mexicans.

POLLARD. Ten? One against ten? They'll have to do better than that. Santa Anna may have as many as five thousand men out there. No, one to ten won't do, Colonel. It'll have to be nearer one to thirty-three. Unless we get reinforcements.

REYNOLDS. That's pretty long odds on men dead for sleep, with no coffee, not enough ammunition, and not much to eat.

POLLARD. Mighty long.

CROCKETT. But not too long!

POLLARD. I hope you're right. But I'd feel a lot better if Fannin came.

REYNOLDS. Yes. And a hundred or so from Gonzales.

POLLARD. I was wondering if we hadn't maybe better bring Jim Bowie in here. The men have got their hands full. He's running a high fever and a lot of the time he's out of his head. I thought maybe the women here might look after him. He'd be a lot better off.

CROCKETT. Yes, he would. I'd plum forgot about there being any women here. *(He sees them, huddled with the children and two Negroes, at the far side of the stage.)*

POLLARD. I hesitated bringing him in here because what he's got could be contagious. It has the look of typhoid, with other complications.

CROCKETT. At any rate we can feel out their attitude. *(They walk toward the women, about halfway.)* Ladies, are all of you well?

MRS. DICKINSON. We're making out. About as well as the men.

POLLARD. Mrs. Dickinson, Colonel, wife of the Captain of Artillery.

CROCKETT. Yes, I know Mrs. Dickinson . . . and the other ladies, who are they?

POLLARD. Mrs. Alsbury I know. The others . . . I'm sorry, I don't.

MRS. DICKINSON. Mrs. Esparza, Mrs. Losoya, and Miss Navarro. And the children. They do not all speak English.

CROCKETT. I see. Ladies, although I regret it, we have need of your services. Colonel Bowie, as you may know, is very sick. Dr. Pollard is of the opinion his disease may even be highly contagious. However, the soldiers have as much as they can do, and we were wondering if you could possibly relieve them of looking after the Colonel. You would, of course, be running some risk.

MRS. DICKINSON. We are running a bigger risk just being here. Bring him to us. We'll put him in a room to himself and keep the children away.

*(The playing of the bagpipe is heard at a distance.)*

POLLARD. *(To REYNOLDS.)* Purdy, get some of the men to help you bring Bowie into the chapel.

*(REYNOLDS goes; CROCKETT is already striding away, calling.)*

CROCKETT. All right, boys! Get ready for the battle of the century: John MacGregor versus me! A fight to the finish between the fiddle and the pipes! Concert tonight! Everybody gather round except them that's walking post or on the lookout! Gather here! *(Growing fainter.)* Gather here for the fight between the fiddle and the pipes! First, my honored opponent, Sergeant John MacGregor! *(In the distance may be heard the skirl of the bagpipe, followed by a weak response, a few halfhearted yells and laughter; then Crockett plays, and again the response is weak. As he fiddles a hoedown, the dialogue below continues, over.)*

SOLDIER ONE. *(At a cannon on the wall.)* Did you hear what Doctor Pollard said just now?

SENTRY ONE. How could I? I was walking my post. Or I reckon I was. I could have been asleep.

SOLDIER ONE. He said the odds was one to thirty-three.

SENTRY ONE. He did?

SOLDIER ONE. Yeah. He said there was one of us to maybe every thirty-three of them. About a hundred and fifty to five thousand. If'n we don't pretty soon git some more men.

SENTRY ONE. I don't look for none. Not now. *(Pause.)* Do you?

SOLDIER ONE. I don't know. But I do wish they'd come on if'n they're coming. Either them or the Mexicans, one. I just wish *something* would git done!

SENTRY TWO. *(After a moment of listening.)* Listen to that!

SOLDIER TWO. *(After another pause.)* It'll take a devil of a lot better'n that to light a fire under me.

SENTRY TWO. I figure our fire's about out.

SOLDIER TWO. You know what? I was just thinking.

SENTRY TWO. What?

SOLDIER TWO. If'n these fellers can come through the Mexican lines *this*-a-way, it's a cinch we could go out through them Mexicans *that*-a-way! Ain't it?

SENTRY TWO. *(Considering.)* Yeah. Them scouts come in and go out all the time.

SOLDIER TWO. You know, we could just take off and leave this place. Walk right off. Couldn't we? Run away.

SENTRY TWO. *(A pause, uncertainly.)* We could.

SOLDIER TWO. A mile from here a man could lie down in some brush, or maybe a barn even, and sleep a week with nobody the wiser. *(They are silent, thinking of it.)* Only, we ain't the runnin' kind.

SENTRY TWO. *(Rising a little, but still under the spell.)* A cup o' coffee and a warm featherbed.

SOLDIER TWO. We fired a couple o' times at old Santy Anna's headquarters to-day, and hit it, too—but he wasn't to home, they say.

SENTRY TWO. I heard 'em cheer. *(A pause.)* Well, reckon I best make me another round. *(He is on the point of departure when, from the southeast side of the fort, there comes a distant shout. Then others, coming closer and closer.)*

SOLDIER TWO. What you reckon it is?

SENTRY TWO. I don't know but I'm going to see!

    *(He goes at a trot. The women in the chapel wake and whisper excitedly. The women* WITNESSES *also begin to stir.)*

MRS. DICKINSON. Is it the Mexicans coming?

SOLDIER. I don't know. I don't hear no guns. But I can't see!

SENTRY. *(Bursting inside the chapel.)* Hurrah! Hurrah!

SOLDIER. What is it, man? Who is it?

SENTRY. The men from Gonzales! They got here! They got here!

    *(He rushes back outside.)*

SOLDIER. Thank God. Thank God.

    *(Now the women* WITNESSES *sit up in alarm. They speak.)*

WOMEN. Our men. Our men.

    *(Now* CROCKETT *and* MACGREGOR *lead a joyous march about the enclosure, playing the bagpipe and the fiddle, the men shouting wildly, happily. In the course of their marching they do a turn through the chapel, and* CROCKETT *shouts.)*

CROCKETT. Dr. Pollard! Dr. Pollard! These are your rare men! We are your rare men!

(*Dancing in single file, they wave their rifles and exit whooping.*)

SOLDIER. (*At the cannon, after a pause.*) I wonder how many there are. They don't look like very many to me . . .

(*The lights fade on stage center as the music continues briefly, then out.*)

WOMEN. (*Leaping up as though rousing hurriedly from beds.*)

*Our* men!
Who could lie in a featherbed
A cherry-wood bed,
Who could lie passively asleep
When our men have entered the Fort?
Did anyone hear the Gate open?
The double Gates swing out,
Open, like *Jaws?*
No, but we heard it CLOSE.
In our sleep,
In our goose-down featherbeds.
Our hearts heard it first
And raised the solid shout,
Beat as fist on stolid bone,
Breastbone,
Beat, beat, beat
Till we wakened in our featherbeds,
Our cherry-wood beds
Warm yet with the warmth of memory of a man gone;
Beat, beat, beat
Till face downward
In the musty ticking
We heard the Gate grating
We heard the Gate creaking,
We heard it groan in place
And a LOCK drop.
A *great—Lock—drop.* (*A moment, one woman pulls free, as it were, from the hold of the group, and with a muffled scream runs across to the place where two men have just dropped the great bar in place across the double gates. Then she is brought back.*)
O God!—that *Silence!*
OPEN!
OPEN THE GATE!
OPEN!
THAT GATE IS THE LID OF A COFFIN!

(*The* WOMEN *sink to their knees, speak softly.*)

O let us pray.
Let us pray.

*(The lights fade quickly from the* WOMEN. *Now the scene is the same, except that the mood is drearier, the area in greater disarray, the defenders haggard beyond belief. They move as in a trance. The ensuing is meant to suggest the continuous time from the evening of March 3 to the evening of March 5. The lighting should suggest various stages of day and night, turning at an accelerated rate but always revealing contrastingly harsh, bright realities against hidden, murky unreality. It is eight o'clock in the evening as the scene begins, and we hear the voices of the* MEXICAN WITNESSES, *either one or a group.)*

MEXICANS.
> Now they took us seriously,
> The arrogant whites;
> Now they knew.
> From the tenth day onward
> They must have known.
> They could smell it:
> Contaminating the ground,
> Fouling the air,
> In their clothing,
> In themselves:
> The sickly odor
> Presaging death.
> They knew.
> They knew.
> Our cannon hounded them by day and by night.
> Wolves of "no sleep" ripped at the flanks of the penned sheep;
> While we laughed and played cards the fanged battalion called "no sleep"
>     fought our fight!

TEXAN WITNESSES.
> No sleep,
> No sleep,
> For the Alamo's keepers
> No sleep.

TRAVIS.
> By day
> By night,
> Alike,
> All alike.
> Day, or night.
> Alike.
> Day-shaded
> Night-shaded
> Mutated
> Slated
> Day,

And night,
Alike;
Translated
Into something
Grey.
Decay grey.

SOLDIER'S VOICE. *(A cry of pain.) We can't keep it up, we can't keep on this-a-way!*

TEXANS.
No sleep.
No sleep.

TRAVIS.
Feet,
Feet,
Walking,
Walking,
Tired,
Tired feet.
A bite to eat.
*A bite to eat!*
Feet . . .
Keep . . .
*Going!*

SOLDIER'S VOICE. I just got to have some sleep!

TRAVIS. Will!

TEXANS. Will!

TRAVIS. Steeling . . . the *will!*

TEXANS. WILL!

TRAVIS.
In the thigh,
In the groin,
Keep going. *(More rapidly.)*
Back of the eye,
Base of the neck,
Ball of the foot,
Pit of the back,
Wherever the flesh weakens,
Attack!

TEXANS. Attack!

TRAVIS. Shove it back!

TEXANS. Back!

TRAVIS. *(Slower, softer.)*
Back.
Back.

SENTRY. *(Slumping down.)* Bonham just come in.

TRAVIS and TEXANS. *(Softly.)* Back.

SOLDIER. Where from?

TRAVIS and TEXANS. *(Very softly.)* Back. (TRAVIS *has disappeared.)*

SENTRY. I don't know.

SOLDIER. Seems to me he's always just coming back or just going.

SENTRY. He looked whipped this time.

SOLDIER. Thinks he's playing cadet at that Carolina college where he went to.

SENTRY. I hear Smith's leaving out again.

SOLDIER. With another note?

SENTRY. Yeah. I reckon.

SOLDIER. That's a joke.

SENTRY. Yeah. Colonel must've sent out a dozen. All he catched was thirty-two men.

SOLDIER. That Fannin. They'd ought to hang him.

SENTRY. All them notes Travis writes. Reckon what they say.

SOLDIER. Ain't much telling. But if'n they're like him they'll jump right out at you. Feller's got a spring coiled in him. Steel spring.

SENTRY. Got something that keeps him going all right. Bet he laid old Fannin out proper.

SOLDIER. He'd ought to. And them others at the Convention, too.

SENTRY. How's Jim Bowie doing?

SOLDIER. He's about done for.

SENTRY. Some say he had TB all along.

SOLDIER. For minutes on end he don't seem to breathe; then he takes a new lease and starts all over again. Sometimes the women have to hold him to the bed.

SENTRY. That can't last long.

SOLDIER. You don't know. Can't tell. Sometimes they hold on and on.

SENTRY. *(After pause.)* You been thinkin' about—dyin'?

SOLDIER. *(After pause.)* Yeah. *(Pause.)* Some.

SENTRY. These last two days and nights I've come close. I catch myself drawing away from myself. I catch myself grinning at my old carcass walking post beside me. Then again I'm higher up and I look down, down into me like I was leaning over and looking down a well; I feel lost; woods-and-world lost and torn between something, something like staying, or going. I feel like if'n just one little cobwebby thread was to give, I'd be at peace. But I can't let go.

SOLDIER. Yeah. We got to hold on.

*(Slowly and deliberately the Mexicans begin a distant cannonade.)*

SOLDIER. There them Mexicans go again.

SENTRY. I don't know if I can git up or not.

SOLDIER. They're keeping them cannons hot.

SENTRY. *(Rising very slowly).* One more time around.

*(TRAVIS enters. He salutes the departing sentry.)*

SOLDIER. *(Cannoneer.)* Had I ought to answer 'em with a shot, Sir?

TRAVIS. No. No, save your shot. Save it as long as you can. (TRAVIS *stands looking*

*toward the room where* BOWIE *lies.* MRS. DICKINSON *comes out.)* Is Bowie still
alive?

MRS. DICKINSON. I don't know how, but he is.

*(She rejoins the other women. Enter* MAJOR ROBERT EVANS.*)*

ROBERT EVANS. Did you send for me, Sir?

TRAVIS. *(Turning away from* BOWIE'*s room.)* Yes. Evans, I don't know, of course,
how or when, but I think . . . this may be the beginning of the end. I have no way
of knowing *how* it will end. But as soldiers we know our duty. We will not avoid it.

EVANS. No, Sir.

TRAVIS. If, when the assault comes, the enemy should gain entrance, as a last measure I want you to light a torch and explode the old powder in the magazine here.

EVANS. Yes, Sir.

TRAVIS. Evans.

EVANS. Sir?

TRAVIS. Do you pray?

EVANS. I . . . sometimes try, Sir.

TRAVIS. Then Evans, pray now. *(On his words,* TRAVIS *strides away.)*

EVANS. Sir, where can I find you if you're needed?

TRAVIS. *(Calling back as he goes.)* At the breach where the wall is down. You'll find
me there, standing my ground!

> *(*EVANS *examines the magazine, then goes out. The cannonade builds to a terrifying
> climax. Pieces of the wall crumble and fall. The women cower and the children cry.
> The cannoneer is heard to pray, just a word now and then of the Twenty-third
> Psalm. Then, with amazing abruptness, the cannonade stops. And the ensuing quiet
> is all the more oppressive. For at least twenty seconds not a word is spoken.)*

TEXAN WITNESSES. There were plenty of things about that night that didn't
seem real. I know that.

KELLOGG. *(After a slight pause.)*

> That night I looked up in the sky
> And I couldn't imagine what it was like to die.
> That night I kept thinking, now let me try:
> What—what is it like—to die?
> And all I could think was:
> Same old sky.
> And here I am.
> Me! Johnny Kellogg!
> Sixteen years old!
> From Gonzales.
> Little wart on my little finger on my left hand.
> Five feet seven and one-half inches tall, marked on the wall in our own front
>     room at home.
> Hair that won't hardly ever stay down account of I got a cowlick.
> Toes wiggle, fingers wiggle . . . and ears too, when I try . . . a little.
> That's funny, ain't it? . . . when you think about it:

Cowlick!

Didn't no cow ever lick me. *(A moment.)*

I was so *sleepy.*

SOLDIER.

When they stopped firing

Everybody dropped where he was at,

Right in his tracks . . .

KELLOGG. I slept on the wall . . .

ALL SOLDIERS.

Flat on our faces,

Flat on our backs.

KELLOGG.

I slept snuggled up to a cannonball.

And the last thing I thought was:

Same old sky . . .

But I wonder—what it's like—*what it's going to be like, to die!*

*(And now there is another period of silence as the defenders of the Alamo sleep. Only* TRAVIS *and a stolid sentry are up. The sentry stands upright and still as a statue on the wall some distance away.* TRAVIS *moves restlessly among the sleeping men. He comes inside the chapel. He mounts the upper tier. He hears a distant, indistinct shout.)*

MEXICANS. *Viva la Republica Mexicana! Viva Santa Anna!*

*(The shout is followed almost immediately by a single urgent, harsh bugle call. Then silence again, during which the sleepy* TEXANS *begin to sit up and rub their eyes, unwilling to believe they have heard anything. The rush and tramp of soldiers' running feet is heard, coming closer and closer.* TRAVIS, *vibrantly alert, peers into the night.)*

TRAVIS. To your posts, men, to your posts! *(*TRAVIS *leaps down from the wall.)* Everybody up! Everybody up! The Mexicans are here!

SENTRY. *(Echoing him.)* The Mexicans are here! The Mexicans are here! Everybody up!

TRAVIS. *(Frantically.)* Come on, men, the Mexicans are upon us! They're here! They're here *now!*

*(*TRAVIS *rushes out and is seen no more.)*

CROCKETT. *(Sticking his head in the door.)* Tennessee! Tennessee! You men from Tennessee, follow me! Follow old Davy Crockett! *(As he goes.)* Follow . . . old . . . Davy . . . Crockett! . . .

SOLDIER. It's them all right! *Thousands* of 'em!

CANNONEER. Cannon One ready to fire, Sir!

WILLIAMSON. *(On ground, center.)* Not yet! Not yet, man! Hold your fire! *(Outside the walls the Mexicans are now yelling.)*

CROCKETT. *(His voice not far away.)* That's right! Hold your fire! Let 'em git closer! Make every shot count! Git—set—Git—*(The Mexican band at the southeast corner strikes up "Degüello.")* Now! Let 'em have it! FIRE! *(The rifles of the*

TEXANS *crackle, the cannons roar, the enemy shrieks, the* TEXANS *yell. The clash is brief. The* MEXICANS *fall back.)*

SOLDIER. *(On the wall.)* They're falling back!

SOLDIER. *(Outside.)* We held 'em!

SOLDIER. *(Jubilant.)* Man, they took to their scrapers, what I mean!

CROCKETT. Yeah. But they ain't had enough. They're coming back for more! Git ready. Git ready, boys . . . because *here they come!*

WILLIAMSON. Load your guns! Fast! Fast!

SOLDIER. *Here they come!*

WILLIAMSON. *(Shrilly.)* Faster! Faster! You've got to load faster!

SOLDIER. *(Ramming shot into a rifle.)* Fast as I can, Sir! I can't do it no faster!

WILLIAMSON.

I know it, but—

All right. Get ready—

Hold your fire—

Aim—aim for the chest and belly—

Aim—

Ready—

Steady—

Steady—

FIRE!

*(Again the yells of the* TEXANS *and the shrieks of the* MEXICANS, *the roar of the cannon and the splatter of the muskets. This time, however, a few* MEXICANS *reach the top of the walls, some of the* TEXANS *are killed, some are wounded. The cannoneer in the chapel,* JACOB WALKER, *is wounded, though not critically. He is out of ammunition for his cannon. The* MEXICANS *have a second time fallen back, but there is little jubilation among the Alamo's defenders.)*

SOLDIER. We held 'em off again.

SOLDIER. One more time leastways.

SOLDIER. I wonder can we do it again.

SOLDIER. Yeah.

WILLIAMSON. Load your guns!

SOLDIER. We're loaded, Sir.

WILLIAMSON. *(Oblivious.)* Then faster! Fast! Faster! Fast! Faster! . . .

SOLDIER. *(As* WILLIAMSON *continues, under.)* Reckon he ain't never heared o' takin' your time and shinin' your glasses.

SOLDIER. Reckon not.

WILLIAMSON. Fast! Faster!

WOMEN WITNESSES. We couldn't sleep.

WILLIAMSON. Fast! Faster! *Faster!*

WOMEN. The wind shrieked.

WILLIAMSON. *Faster* man, *faster!*

SOLDIER. Can't, Sir! We're clean out of cap and powder!

WOMEN. Couldn't eat.

WILLIAMSON. Oh my God!

WOMEN. Couldn't sleep!

SOLDIER. *(In a rising hysteria.)* What'll we do now? What'll we do now, Sir? What'll we do now?

WOMEN. *(On top of, above, and below.)*
Somewhere something
Shook the air . . .

WILLIAMSON. Oh my God, I don't know! I don't *know!*

WOMEN.
And we felt the tremor
Everywhere! . . .

SOLDIER. What, Sir? What? I can't *hear!* . . .

SOLDIER. *Here they come!*

WOMEN. *Everywhere!*

WILLIAMSON. *Load the guns!*

WOMEN. In the top of the pine . . .

SOLDIER. *There ain't no time!*

WOMEN. In the bowed-down oak . . .

SOLDIER. *(Despairing.)* Oh, there ain't any more time . . .

WOMEN.
Everywhere
Everywhere

SOLDIER. *Lord God save us now!*

WOMEN. Something awoke . . .

SOLDIER. *(Softly.)* Save us now . . .

WOMEN. Something spoke . . .

CROCKETT. Don't give in! Give 'em the knife, give 'em the knife! . . .

WOMEN. The whining pine . . .

CROCKETT. *Give 'em the knife and the butt o' your gun!*

WOMEN. And the bull-voiced oak!

CANNONEER. I'm hit! I'm hit! I'm hit!

CROCKETT. *Bust their skulls! Club 'em down!* (The MEXICANS *are now coming over the walls into the enclosure; fighting is hand to hand.)*

CANNONEER. Oh my God. I'm . . . hit.

WOMEN.
Owls called
And we heard the panther
(KELLOGG *comes rushing onstage.)*

KELLOGG. Come on! Come on! I'll show you how I did it! I'll show you how I died! Look! Look! Everybody look! Over here! See me? See? *This is the way I died!* (*A Mexican dragoon runs him through with a bayonet, then can't get the bayonet out in time and is brained from behind by* DAVY CROCKETT.)

WOMEN.
We were there!
At home we were there!

*(As the* WOMEN *continue,* MAJOR ROBERT EVANS *runs toward the magazine with a lighted torch and is shot down before he reaches it.)*

Because everywhere
The wind came calling
Howling the news
Everywhere, everywhere
Running the road before us
Wild of look and streaming hair
Everywhere
News blown to us
News bitterly known to us
The dry-wind news
The hollow-howl news
Tongue-falling-out news
Drought news
Blue-norther news
News borne on buzzard wings!
Felt with our gaping minds
Blind.
Blind as bats.

Then on our bowed heads
Down came the news;
An axe; and a world.
Down. Down. Down.

*(MRS. DICKINSON leaves the group and goes searching among the dead for her husband. She finds him and kneels beside him. Then JACOB WALKER, the wounded gunner who has been hiding undetected, comes running from his hiding place and clings to her as the MEXICANS who have flushed him advance, bayonets fixed. MRS. DICKINSON stands and attempts to shield him. The MEXICANS bayonet WALKER and lift him high.)*

WOMEN. *(Quietly narrating, as MRS. DICKINSON slowly rejoins the group.)*
With their bayonets they thrust and lifted him high—
    As Mrs. Dickinson afterward used to say,
    like pitchforks stuck in a bale of hay—
Jacob Walker, gunner from Nacogdoches, the last to die—
Save five,
Hungry for life,
Who were later brought from the long barracks
    where they had been hiding beneath some mattresses.
Five who shall go nameless.
True, they were sick; true, some were wounded. Yes.
But go look in Jim Bowie's room.
Jim Bowie was sick.
He was almost dead.

He had only his big hunting knife.
*But go look in his room!*
> (SANTA ANNA, *the Mexican dictator, enters the chapel. While his aides stand at attention, he disdainfully inspects the carnage. Finding the body of* CROCKETT, *he snorts derisively and touches the body with the toe of his boot. During his inspection, the five sick and wounded* TEXANS *are brought from the long barracks and lined up just outside the chapel. An aide calls* SANTA ANNA's *attention to them. He pauses a moment, then turns his back on them as a signal.)*

SANTA ANNA. *Pues no es cosa. Escade!*
> (*And his soldiers run the prisoners through with their bayonets. After another brief look around, he exits. A pause. Then the* WOMEN *resume in a quiet, matter-of-fact, sad tone.*)

WOMEN.
Now there is surprisingly little to be done or said.
The Mexicans have had their fill.
For there is after all
No quiet to match the quiet following the kill.
When the quick nimble prey is forever still—still forever;
When the slender stamen of throat has been cut
And the soft covering of gut rent open
Revealing—what? All there is. Nothing.
O then with the grey shutter that draws over the staring eyes
Draws also a shutter over your own suddenly naked eyes.
Beneath the dropped wing of the crook of your arms
Hide your dull eyes.
Hide your white face.
Embrace! Embrace!

How *cold* your skin.

Win? Did someone say, *Win?*

There is no quiet like the quiet after the kill.
> (*Enter* FRANCISCO RUÍZ, *Alcalde of San Antonio,* DON RAMÓN MUSQUIZ, *and the curate,* DON REFUGIO DE LA GARZA. *Slowly the bodies are being carried to the area beyond the chapel. In the interim of dialogue, below, the* WITNESSES *slowly resume their positions in the niches of the Alamo façade.*)

RUÍZ.
I should like to make my report.
As you can see, we have our work.

WOMAN.
The politician has his mission.
Don Pancho—Francisco Ruíz, Alcalde of San Antonio de Bexar.
With our permission.

RUÍZ. Thank you. When the Mexican Army entered the walls, I with the political chief, Don Ramón Musquiz, and other members of the corporation, accompanied by the curate, Don Refugio de la Garza, who by Santa Anna's orders had assembled during the night at a temporary fortification on Protero Street, with the object of attending the wounded, et cetera. As soon as the storming commenced, we crossed the bridge on Commerce Street, with this object in view, and about one hundred yards from the same, a party of Mexican Dragoons fired upon us and compelled us to fall back on the river to the place we had occupied before. Half an hour had elapsed when Santa Anna sent one of his aides-de-camp with an order for us to come before him.

On the north battery of the fortress convent lay the lifeless body of Colonel Travis on the gun carriage, shot only through the forehead. Toward the west and in a small fort opposite the city, we found the body of Colonel Crockett. Colonel Bowie was found dead in his bed in one of the rooms on the south side.

Santa Anna ordered wood to be brought to burn the bodies of the Texans. About three o'clock in the afternoon of March 6, we laid the wood and dry branches, upon which a pile of bodies was placed, more wood was piled on them, then another pile of bodies was brought, and in this manner all were arranged in layers. Kindling wood was distributed through the pile, and above five o'clock in the evening it was lighted. The dead Mexicans of Santa Anna—*(It has now turned dusk, and in the courtyard beyond the Alamo façade the soldiers may be seen bringing the bodies and stacking them. Then the fires are lit—there are three stacks in various locations—and for a while they burn brightly, then gradually die away as the play ends.)—* were taken to the graveyard, but not having sufficient room for them, I ordered some to be thrown into the river, which was done on the same day.

    *(*RUÍZ *and his companions move briskly away to get on with their work.)*

WOMEN.

And this was the news which, reaching us,
Sent us mad.
This was the sharp bit-in-the-bloody-mouth news,
The news that wouldn't spit out;
This was the news we swallowed and couldn't keep down,
This the news that *erupted into San Jacinto!*

    *(From among the* MEXICAN WITNESSES *now steps* VICENTE FILISOLA, *mercenary general in the Mexican Army, an Italian national.)*

VICENTE FILISOLA. Before we go, I should like to add a word not found in my already well-thumbed report on the siege and fall of the Alamo.

WOMAN.

Vicente Filisola, general, mercenary, Italian national,
In the pay of the Mexican Army.

FILISOLA.

Yes. I should like to say that,
By these men's deaths,
I was at the time, and later, impressed;
As my memoirs attest.

TEXANS. So you were impressed!

FILISOLA.

Yes. Taking all things into consideration, however,

Though impressive,

I could not but conclude you men blundered.

TEXANS.

Yet you—

FILISOLA.

Yet I—true. Sometimes wondered.

But really now, what had you to gain by dying? What lose by—withdrawing?

You could have fought another and more propitious day—did not Houston do
    that very thing?

To the mercenary soldier such fruitless dying was—frankly—mystifying.

TEXANS.

At the foot of the cross of the crucified Christ

There were those who were impressed.

No more, no less.

Impressed.

O be more! *Be more!*

To this audience we turn in compassion,

Making as we do our honest confession:

Of Man and his mortal lot

Some important things we had forgot:

The loneliness.

The half-light.

The confusion.

And the barrier, Time.

Wherefore on Man's behalf we call attention to our Father.

O our Father,

Man is so awfully, terribly alone.

O our Father,

He has traveled so many generations

And in sand digged his miserable, impermanent home.

Heads grow heavy with fact on fact;

Eyes become bleary, then blind;

Everywhere he scratches and scratches,

Digs and digs, shreds and shreds,

Adds stack on stack on stack;

Born with a scabrous itch that no scratching relieves—

Born to this awful searching—

Born to bear this mountain humpback, incomplete learning—

Isn't it about time you turned him back?

Isn't it time you lifted him out of what never can be?

We wait for your answer.

What shall Man do?

What shall we do?

*(Enter* SATAN, *disguised as a bedraggled colonist, the mythical* MOSES ROSE, *who is said to have been the only man to leave the Alamo in order to escape the fighting.)*

SATAN. *(He speaks humbly.)* Am I intruding? Interrupting? I saw the play was closing and I came as fast as I could. I was not in the play. I am not, strictly speaking, a Witness. My position—even my existence—is questioned.

I am Moses Rose. Legend says I fled the Alamo. Legend says I was a coward.

Yes, I did leave the Alamo. But I was no coward. I had fought in two wars before I came to this country and I had simply learned my lesson. A lesson this audience might well learn. My verdict is that these men of the Alamo were caught up in a false emotion, for a cause that would have lived whether they died or not. Listen: Live out your life and champion no cause that cannot be defined "bread," and "bread" alone. *(Abruptly he flings off his hat and lifts his head, revealing his identity.)*

All nations, all civilizations, rise and fall, are cyclical. Their going is inevitable. So why throw yourselves under an avalanche? This Law, this Avalanche, is Nature! Today the very term for which you men died is argued. No definition is totally accepted, totally agreed upon. You've been looking at Man at short range. Answer me—answer truthfully: *Hasn't Freedom changed?*

*(He goes.)*

TEXANS.

Who was that?

Moses Rose?

We don't remember any Moses Rose.

Do we?

*(They mumble among themselves.)*

Who was Moses Rose?

WOMEN.

There is always a Moses Rose.

Really—didn't you recognize him?

TEXANS.

We thought we felt the evil presence. Satan!

WOMEN.

Of course!

Isn't he said to be myth? Isn't he legend?

Yet you are free and he tempted you—

TEXANS.

With a question!

WOMEN.

Yes!

Can he by one simple question so easily confuse you?

Do you not remember the place, the time?
Do you forget so soon?

TEXANS.

We remember.
We remember the cold, the hunger, the hurt;
We remember the crying for sleep, the pain.

WOMEN.

But do you remember the condition?
Do you remember the cause, the reason why?

TEXANS.

We remember. We recall:
The siege. The fall.
And the reason why.
It was for Freedom that we died.
And the condition *is* the same—Freedom has not changed!
Our dying kept it living, kept it safe,
And from our dust, the mammoth thing, Freedom,
Received a forward thrust
That has continually reverberated.

O our Father!
Again we make our prayer!
Help us! Help us to go anywhere!
Make us as a boundless mother;
Make us as a spirited lover;
Make us as a warning cloud to hover, and hover.
And wherever Man is
Let Him remember us—
Us discover—
Until He rips open the final discovery
There before Him is Freedom Forever—
Until then,
Let us be his reminding and remembering cover!

WOMEN. *(After a pause.)* Is the play over?

MEN. The play is over.

WOMEN. And the audience. What of it? Do you think—

MEN.

We do not know.
For them we cannot decide.

WOMEN. But the freedom you won for them—

MEN.

By them must be claimed.
They must try.
It must be for them the reason, the why.

Only this we know:
We died there.
And from our dust
The mammoth Thing, Freedom,
Received a forward thrust.
The reverberations we continued
Are something to which Man may respond,
Or not respond,
At pleasure.

WOMEN.
O Thou Man.
Fortunate, fortunate Man!
To WILL and CAN!

MEN. *(Growing faint.)*
O Thou Man.
Fortunate, fortunate Man.
To Will, and . . . Can.
*(The sound of wings ascending, ascending—Wind, then wind dying.)*

*Curtain*

# Horton Foote

★ ★ ★ ★ ★ ★ ★ ★ ★ ★ ★ ★ ★ ★ ★ ★

## ★ THE PERSON

Born in Wharton, Texas, in 1916, Horton Foote visits there often and emotionally has never left it. He draws strength and inspiration from the past and present of Wharton and has set almost all of his plays in Harrison, Texas, which is his fictional equivalent for Wharton. Harrison has served Foote somewhat as Bradleyville did Preston Jones or Jefferson did William Faulkner. In spite of the fact that Foote's career has required him to live in or near major cities, his view of life remains attuned to that part of Texas that drew its culture from the American South.

At the age of sixteen Foote left home to pursue an acting career. His training took him first to Dallas and to Pasadena, California, and then to New York, where he began writing plays, originally with the intention of providing roles for himself and actor friends. *Texas Town*, his first full-length play, was presented in 1941, but his early acclaim came as a writer of television scripts during the much-heralded "Golden Age of Television Drama" in the 1950s. In addition to such original dramas as *A Young Lady of Property*, *The Midnight Caller*, and *The Trip to Bountiful*, Foote the television writer has to his credit two distinguished adaptations of works by William Faulkner, *Old Man* and *Tomorrow*.

In recent years, Foote has become widely known and respected as a writer of film scripts, which he now finds as artistically satisfying as stage plays. He followed his Oscar-winning script for Harper Lee's *To Kill a Mockingbird* (1962) with original scripts for *Baby, the Rain Must Fall* (1964) and *Tender Mercies* (1983), the latter earning him his second Academy Award. He began what he hoped would become a series of personal films, based on events in his family history, with *1918* (1985) and *On Valentine's Day* (1986). Both of these featured his actress-daughter, Hallie.

Foote's outstanding personal characteristics are his self-effacing, gentle nature and his persistence. The first has resulted in, among other things, a circle of loyal colleagues and family members who want to work with him. Actors and actresses as well as directors and producers repeatedly choose to associate themselves with Foote. Robert Duvall, Geraldine Page, Kim Stanley, Fred Coe, Alan J. Pakula, and Ken Harrison are notable examples. The second quality, persistence, accounts for Foote's unswerving commitment to writing one kind of play in spite of the fact that it became unfashionable and was for a decade or more unwanted. As he said to Samir Hachem in an interview for *Horizon:* "You have to trust the sun and the rain and the summer. . . . You can't force things, you have to trust."

With his wife's encouragement and with a determination akin to that of his rural forebears, Foote has remained true to his vision and is now enjoying a second wave of success. Thirty-six years ago he was featured in a *Life* magazine article entitled "Bright Galaxy of Playwrights" and was heralded along with Paddy Chayefsky, Tad Mosel, and three others as America's best hope for raising television drama to a significant cultural level. The year 1986 ended with two of his plays running concurrently in New York and with Foote being described as "Dramatist of the Hour" by Don Hulbert, the *Dallas Times-Herald*'s drama critic. The playwright was then seventy years old. The following year Grove Press announced plans to publish his nine-play series *The Orphans' Home Cycle* and then brought out the first volume. Late in 1988 Foote supervised the production of his play *The Habitation of Dragons* in Pittsburgh. In 1989 he filmed *Convicts* in Louisiana and wrote a television script of Flaubert's *Madame Bovary.*

It is paradoxical and delightful that such a traditional gentleman who respects and typifies old-fashioned virtues and social forms now commutes so easily between Wharton and Waxahachie in Texas and Greenwich Village in New York; Foote has been more successful than any other American dramatist in producing works for the technically demanding large and small screens as well as for the stage.

★   THE PLAY

*The Trip to Bountiful* began as a television play on NBC's "Goodyear Playhouse" in 1953. It was then adapted for the stage in 1954 and played for thirty-nine performances on Broadway. Interestingly, it was produced by Stella Holt, who was responsible for giving Ramsey Yelvington's work its only New York exposure with a production of *The Long Gallery*. After Horton Foote's movie career blossomed in the 1980s, *The Trip to Bountiful* was filmed; recently that film version was released on videocassette, the work thus completing a journey that began and ended on the television screen.

Throughout its transformations, *The Trip to Bountiful* has been treasured for outstanding interpretations of its larger-than-life central character, Mrs. Carrie Watts, acted first by Lillian Gish and more recently by Geraldine Page, who capped her motion picture career with an Academy Award–winning performance of Mrs. Watts in 1985. Foote's understanding of the importance of the performer to the success of his works, and his uncompromising determination, are both illustrated by his refusal for over twenty years to allow *The Trip to Bountiful* to be filmed with any of a number of popular but inappropriate stars whom Hollywood producers proposed. If he could not have Lillian Gish or Geraldine Page cast in the lead, he was content to postpone filming indefinitely.

In common with most of Foote's other plays, this one has as its setting Wharton and the surrounding area in Southeast Texas. Wharton is of course fictionalized as Harrison. Readers unfamiliar with Texas who are inclined to think of the state in terms of ranching or oil wells will have to make adjustments, for Foote's country is neither barren nor sparsely settled; it is more southern than western, is less than fifty miles from the coast of the Gulf of Mexico, and was associated in its heyday with the river-bottom farming of cotton, corn, and sugarcane. Families in this area have histories that feature endurance rather than migration as a response to cyclic vicissitudes.

Houston, sixty miles away and the nearest city, represents the new urban Texas; Bountiful, the abandoned past. Mrs. Watts's desperate journey back to Bountiful constitutes the play's central action, and the beneficent effect that the return to the ruined family home has on her and her son, Ludie, powerfully expresses the strength to be gained from contact with the dignified rhythms of rural life.

Foote has said that his plays tend to feature either young characters coming to accept life or old characters coming to terms with death. In this play Mrs. Watts expresses the latter and her son, Ludie, the former. Having completed her journey and accepted the necessity of returning to Houston to die, Mrs. Watts responds to the healing quality of the rural setting. Now she is better able to face the humiliations of life with her trivial daughter-in-law, Jessie Mae, who wants to visit Hollywood as badly as Mrs. Watts wants to visit Bountiful and who structures her life around visits to the drugstore, the beauty parlor, and the movie theater. Ludie, after reexperiencing Bountiful and facing memories he had thought too painful to bear, is better prepared to reenter the urban struggle for a decent life.

The play is deceptively simple. Its conservative preference for elements of the rural scene—birds, woods, warm breezes from the Gulf—over those of the city—noisy radios, irate neighbors, colliding automobiles—is certainly unremarkable. The three primary characters represent clear-cut, near stereotypical positions. So apparently simple a play could easily be dismissed. Its charm and power lie in its detail of observation and speech and in the moral strength of its appealing major characters, Mrs. Watts and her son, who prevail amid trying circumstances with dignity and without complaint.

The 1985 motion picture of *The Trip to Bountiful*, coproduced by Foote himself and featuring such outstanding players as Geraldine Page, John Heard, Carlin Glynn, and Rebecca de Mornay, is the version of the play that will probably linger longest in collective memory and exert the strongest influence on future interpretations. But there continue to be numerous regional-theater productions of this popular play, including two well-received Texas productions in 1989, at Austin's Zachary Scott Theatre and at Houston's Grace Theater.

## ★ THE WORKS

Horton Foote's plays can be placed in two primary groups: the eight plays published in the 1956 volume titled *Harrison, Texas,* including *The Midnight Caller* and *The Trip to Bountiful,* and the nine that make up the series *The Orphans' Home Cycle.* This latter group is based on characters and events in Foote's own parents' history and covers the time between 1902, the date of Horace Robedaux's father's death, and 1928, the date of the death of his wife's father. Although major events such as World War I, an influenza epidemic, and bank failures contribute to the subject matter of the plays, the immediate focus is always on the personal. Outside events become important largely as forces to challenge the will of individuals and families. Overall, the dominant mood is one of restrained optimism slowly surfacing through pain and struggle.

*Chekhovian* is an adjective admirers of Foote's plays often use to describe them. *Sleepy* and *uneventful* are harsh judgments sometimes uttered by those impatient with the plays. Unquestionably, restraint is a major characteristic of Foote's plays. They do not feature large effects or move toward dramatic climaxes. Even when violent events do take place, often offstage, the characters' responses are underplayed and the tranquility of the prevailing mood is not ruptured.

The subtle movements that take place within a calm frame offer good actors fine opportunities. Without excellent acting, however, any of the plays can come across as flat. Maybe Foote's own training and experience as an actor give him special confidence in the contribution that excellent acting can make. Perhaps the television medium itself, for which so many of the early plays were written, is also an explanation, since it magnifies detail and is uncongenial to large effects.

In contrast to Ramsey Yelvington's plays, which have a consciously dramatic surface and which suffer when their demand for response becomes exaggerated, Foote's encourage the audience to explore beneath the matter-of-fact surface and are unsatisfying only when the effort is disproportionate to the insight revealed.

Foote's plays reward rereading and are best appreciated in a group. Extensive exposure to his characters and settings through a number of plays helps a reader or spectator to recognize the significance of actions that, in a single play, might seem minor. The power of Foote's unobtrusive technique is cumulative.

## LIST OF WORKS

### MAJOR PLAYS

*Only the Heart,* 1944
*The Chase,* 1952
*The Traveling Lady,* 1954
*The Habitation of Dragons,* 1988
*Dividing the Estate,* 1989

Published in *Harrison, Texas: Eight Television Plays by Horton Foote* (New York: Harcourt, Brace and Company, 1956):
*The Death of the Old Man* *, 1953
*Expectant Relations,* 1953
*John Turner Davis* *, 1953
*The Midnight Caller* *, 1953
*The Tears of My Sister* *, 1953
*The Trip to Bountiful,* 1953
*A Young Lady of Property* *, 1953
*The Dancers* *, 1954
*Also included in *Selected One-Act Plays of Horton Foote,* ed. Gerald C. Wood.
Dallas: Southern Methodist University Press, 1989.

*The Orphans' Home Cycle,* written 1974–77, consisting of the following nine plays:

Published in *Courtship, Valentine's Day, 1918: Three Plays from "The Orphans' Home Cycle"* (New York: Grove Press, 1987):
*Courtship*
*Valentine's Day*
*1918*

Published in *Roots in a Parched Ground, Convicts, Lily Dale, The Widow Claire: The First Four Plays of "The Orphans' Home Cycle"* (New York: Grove Press, 1988):
*Roots in a Parched Ground*
*Convicts*
*Lily Dale*
*The Widow Claire*

Published in *Cousins and The Death of Papa: The Final Two Plays of "The Orphans' Home Cycle"* (New York: Grove Press, 1989):
*Cousins*
*The Death of Papa*

Published in *Selected One-Act Plays of Horton Foote,* ed. Gerald C. Wood (Dallas: Southern Methodist University Press, 1989):
*The Old Beginning,* 1952
*The Oil Well,* 1953
*Blind Date,* 1982
*The Man Who Climbed the Pecan Trees,* 1982
*The Roads to Home (The Dearest of Friends, A Nightingale, Spring Dance),* 1982
*The One-Armed Man,* 1985
*The Prisoner's Song,* 1985
*The Road to the Graveyard,* 1985
*The Land of the Astronauts,* 1988

FILM SCRIPTS

*Storm Fear,* 1956
*To Kill a Mockingbird,* 1962
*Baby, the Rain Must Fall,* 1964
*Tender Mercies,* 1983
*The Trip to Bountiful,* 1985
*1918,* 1985
*On Valentine's Day,* 1986
*Courtship,* 1987
*Convicts,* 1989

NOVELS

*The Chase.* New York: Rinehart and Co., 1956.

RECOMMENDED READING

Barr, Terry, and Gerald C. Wood. "'A Certain Kind of Writer': An Interview with Horton Foote." *Literature/Film Quarterly* 14 (1986): 226–37.

"Bright Galaxy of Playwrights." *Life,* October 25, 1954, pp. 77–78, 81–82.

Davis, Ronald L. "Roots in Parched Ground: An Interview with Horton Foote." *Southwest Review* 73 (Summer 1988): 298–318.

Edgerton, Gary. "A Visit to the Imaginary Landscape of Harrison, Texas: Sketching the Film Career of Horton Foote." *Literature/Film Quarterly* 17 (1989): 2–12.

Freedman, Samuel G. "From the Heart of Texas." *New York Times Magazine,* February 9, 1986, pp. 31–50, 61–63, 73.

Hachem, Samir. "Foote-Work." *Horizon* 29 (April 1986): 39–41.

Weales, Gerald. "The Video Boys." In *American Drama Since World War II.* New York: Harcourt, Brace, and World, 1962.

Wood, Gerald C. Introduction to *Selected One-Act Plays of Horton Foote,* edited by Gerald C. Wood. Dallas: Southern Methodist University Press, 1989.

# The Trip to Bountiful

★ ★ ★ ★ ★ ★ ★ ★ ★ ★ ★ ★ ★ ★ ★ ★ ★

# CAST OF CHARACTERS

MRS. CARRIE WATTS

LUDIE WATTS

JESSIE MAE WATTS

THELMA

HOUSTON TICKET MAN

A TRAVELER

SECOND HOUSTON TICKET MAN

HARRISON TICKET MAN

SHERIFF

TRAVELERS

# SCENES

ACT I: A Houston Apartment

ACT II: The Trip

ACT III: A Country Place

# PRODUCTION NOTES

ACT I

> The bedroom and living room of a Houston apartment. The walls of these two rooms can be defined by the placement of furniture and by the use of certain necessary fragments of flats needed to contain a door or a window frame.

ACT II

> The Houston bus station, a seat on a bus, the Harrison bus station. The Houston and Harrison bus stations require no more than a bench each and cutouts to represent ticket windows. Two chairs are all that are required for the bus seats.

ACT III

> The house at Bountiful. Since this house is seen through the eyes and heart of Mrs. Watts, the actual house can be as symbolic or as realistic as the individual designer chooses. An atmospheric description of this set is included in the text for groups wanting to make use of it.

*The curtain rises. The stage is dark. The lights are slowly brought up and we see the living room and bedroom of a small three-room apartment. The two rooms have been furnished on very little money. The living room is downstage right. In the living room is a sofa that at night has to serve as a bed. It has been made up for the night. Upstage left of the room is a door leading out to the hallway, kitchen, and bathroom. At the opposite end of this hallway is a door leading to the bedroom. To get back and forth, then, between these two rooms it is necessary to go out into the hallway. Center right, in the living room, is a window looking out on the street. Above the window is a wardrobe in which* MRS. WATTS' *clothes and other belongings are kept. On top of the wardrobe are a suitcase and* MRS. WATTS' *purse. A rocking chair is beside the window, and about the room are an easy chair and another straight chair. Center, in the living room, is a drop-leaf table with two straight chairs at either end. On the table are a small radio and a book. Upstage center is a door leading to the outside stairs. Against the rear wall, stage right, is a desk and on the desk are a phone, a newspaper, and a movie magazine.*

*A full moon shines in the window. The two rooms are kept immaculately.*

*The bedroom is smaller than the living room. There is a bed with its headboard against the upstage center wall. A small table with a bed light stands by the bed. Right center is a vanity with its back against the imaginary wall separating the living room from the bedroom. There are two straight chairs in the room, one in front of the vanity. Upstage left is a closet with dresses hanging in it.*

*In the living room a woman of sixty is sitting in the rocking chair, rocking back and forth. She is small and thin and fragile. The woman is* MRS. WATTS. *She lives in the apartment with her son,* LUDIE, *and her daughter-in-law,* JESSIE MAE.

*The lights are out in the bedroom and we can't see much.* LUDIE *and* JESSIE MAE *are both in bed.* JESSIE MAE *is asleep and* LUDIE *isn't.*

LUDIE *slips out of his bed, in the bedroom. He starts tiptoeing out the door that leads to the hallway.*

MRS. WATTS *continues to rock back and forth in the chair. She doesn't hear* LUDIE. *She hums a hymn to herself, "There's not a friend like the lowly Jesus."*

*Then she hears* LUDIE.

LUDIE *is in his early forties. He has on pajamas and a robe.* LUDIE *has had a difficult life. He had been employed as an accountant until his health broke down. He was unable to work for two years. His mother and his wife are both dependent on him, and their small savings were depleted during his illness. Now he has started working again, but at a very small salary.*

MRS. WATTS. Don't be afraid of makin' noise, Sonny. I'm awake.

LUDIE. Yes, Ma'm.

*(He comes into the living room. He comes over to the window.* MRS. WATTS *is looking back out the window, rocking and singing her hymn. He stands behind his mother's chair looking out the window at moonlight. We can clearly see his face now. It is a sensitive face. After a moment* MRS. WATTS *looks up at* LUDIE. *The rocking ceases for a second.)*

MRS. WATTS. Pretty night.

LUDIE. Sure is.

MRS. WATTS. Couldn't you sleep?

LUDIE. No, Ma'm.

MRS. WATTS. Why couldn't you sleep?

LUDIE. I just couldn't. *(*MRS. WATTS *turns away from* LUDIE *to look out the window again. She starts her rocking once more, and hums her hymn to herself. She is opening and closing her hands nervously.)* Couldn't you sleep?

MRS. WATTS. No. I haven't been to bed at all. *(Outside the window in the street we hear a car's brakes grind to a sudden stop.)*

LUDIE. There's going to be a bad accident at that corner one of these days.

MRS. WATTS. I wouldn't be surprised. I think the whole state of Texas is going to meet its death on the highways. *(Pause.)* I don't see what pleasure they get drivin' these cars as fast as they do. Do you?

LUDIE. No, Ma'm. *(A pause.* MRS. WATTS *goes back to her humming and her rocking.)* But there's a lot of things I don't understand. Never did and never will, I guess. *(A pause.)*

MRS. WATTS. Is Jessie Mae asleep?

LUDIE. Yes, Ma'm. That's why I thought I'd better come out here. I got to tossin' an' turnin' so I was afraid I was gonna wake up Jessie Mae. *(A pause.)*

MRS. WATTS. You're not worryin' about your job, are you, Sonny?

LUDIE. No, Ma'm. I don't think so. Everybody seems to like me there. I'm thinking about askin' for a raise.

MRS. WATTS. You should, hard as you work.

LUDIE. Why couldn't you sleep, Mama?

MRS. WATTS. Because there's a full moon. *(She rocks back and forth opening and closing her hands.)* I never could sleep when there was a full moon. Even back in Bountiful when I'd been working out in the fields all day, and I'd be so tired I'd think my legs would give out on me, let there be a full moon and I'd just toss the night through. I've given up trying to sleep on nights like this. I just sit and watch out the window and think my thoughts. *(She looks out the window smiling to herself.)* I used to love to look out the window back at Bountiful. Once when you were little and there was a full moon, I woke you up and dressed you and took you for a walk with me. Do you remember?

LUDIE. No, Ma'm.

MRS. WATTS. You don't?

LUDIE. No, Ma'm.

MRS. WATTS. I do. I remember just like it was yesterday. I dressed you and took you outside and there was an old dog howlin' away off somewhere and you got scared an' started cryin' an' I said, "Son, why are you cryin'?" You said someone had told you that when a dog howled a person was dyin' some place. I held you close to me, because you were tremblin' with fear. An' then you asked me to explain to you about dyin', an' I said you were too young to worry about things like that for a long time to come. *(A pause.)* I was just sittin' here thinkin', Sonny. *(She looks up at* LUDIE. *She sees he is lost in his own thoughts.)* A penny for your thoughts.

LUDIE. Ma'm?

MRS. WATTS. A penny for your thoughts.

LUDIE. I didn't have any, Mama. *(She goes back to her rocking.)* I wish we had a yard here. Part of my trouble is that I get no exercise. *(A pause.)* Funny the things you think about when you can't sleep. I was trying to think of the song I used to like to hear you sing back home. I'd always laugh when you'd sing it.

MRS. WATTS. Which song was that, Son?

LUDIE. I don't remember the name. I just remember I'd always laugh when you'd sing it. *(A pause.* MRS. WATTS *thinks a moment.)*

MRS. WATTS. Oh, yes. That old song. *(She thinks for another moment.)* What was the name of it?

LUDIE. I don't know. *(A pause.)*

MRS. WATTS. Let's see. Oh, I hate not to be able to think of something. It's on the tip of my tongue. *(A pause. She thinks. She recites the words.)*
"Hush little baby, don't say a word.
Mama's gonna buy you a mockin' bird.
And if that mockin' bird don't sing,
Mama's gonna buy you a diamond ring."
I used to think I was gonna buy you the world back in those days. I remember remarking that to my Papa. He said the world can't be bought. I didn't rightly understand what he meant then. *(She suddenly turns to him, taking his hand.)* Ludie. *(He looks down at her, almost afraid of the question she intends to ask. She sees his fear and decides not to ask it. She lets go of his hand.)* Nothin'. Nothin'. *(A pause.)* Would you like me to get you some hot milk?

LUDIE. Yes, Ma'm. If you don't mind.

MRS. WATTS. I don't mind at all. *(She gets up out of her chair and exits to the kitchen.* LUDIE *repeats the lines of the song to himself quietly.)*

LUDIE.
"Hush little baby, don't say a word.
Mama's gonna buy you a mockin' bird.
And if that mockin' bird don't sing,
Mama's gonna buy you a diamond ring."
*(Another car comes to a sudden stop out in the street, screeching its brakes. He peers out the window, his face close against the screen, trying to see the car.* JESSIE MAE *is awakened by the screech. She gets out of bed and puts on a dressing gown.)*

JESSIE MAE. *(From the bedroom.)* Ludie! Ludie!

MRS. WATTS. *(Reenters from hallway.)* You want butter and pepper and salt in it?

LUDIE. Yes, Ma'm, if it's not too much trouble.

MRS. WATTS. No trouble at all. *(Exits to hallway.)*

JESSIE MAE. *(From the bedroom.)* Ludie.

LUDIE. Come in, Jessie Mae. Mama isn't asleep.

> *(JESSIE MAE goes out the bedroom into the living room. She immediately turns on the lights, flooding the room with an ugly glare. JESSIE MAE was probably called very cute when she was young. Now she is hard, driven, nervous, and hysterical.)*

JESSIE MAE. Why don't you turn on the lights? What's the sense of sitting around in the dark? I don't know what woke me up. I was sleeping as sound as a log. All of a sudden I woke up and looked over in bed and you weren't there. Where is your mama?

LUDIE. In the kitchen.

JESSIE MAE. What's she doing out there?

LUDIE. Fixing some hot milk for me.

JESSIE MAE. *(She glances out the hallway.)* Putter, putter, putter. Honestly! Do you want a cigarette?

LUDIE. No, thanks. *(JESSIE MAE takes cigarettes and a lighter from her dressing gown pocket. She struggles with the cigarette lighter.)*

JESSIE MAE. Do you have a match? My lighter is out of fluid. I have to remember to get some tomorrow. *(LUDIE lights her cigarette. A pause. She takes a drag off her cigarette. LUDIE gives her a package of matches.)* Thanks. Couldn't you sleep?

LUDIE. Uh-uh.

JESSIE MAE. How do you expect to work tomorrow if you don't get your sleep, Ludie?

LUDIE. I'm hopin' the hot milk will make me sleepy. I slept last night. I don't know what got into me tonight.

JESSIE MAE. You didn't sleep the night before last.

LUDIE. I know. But I slept the night before that.

JESSIE MAE. I don't think your mama has even been to bed. *(MRS. WATTS comes in from the hallway with the milk.)* What's the matter with you that you can't sleep, Mother Watts?

MRS. WATTS. It's a full moon, Jessie Mae.

JESSIE MAE. What's that got to do with it?

MRS. WATTS. I never could sleep when there's a full moon.

JESSIE MAE. That's just your imagination. *(MRS. WATTS doesn't answer. She hands LUDIE the hot milk. He takes it and blows it to cool it off before drinking. JESSIE MAE goes over to a small radio on the drop-leaf table and turns it on.)* I don't know what's the matter with you all. I never had trouble sleepin' in my life. I guess I have a clear conscience. The only time that I remember having had any trouble sleeping was the night I spent out at Bountiful. The mosquitoes like to have chewed me up. I never saw such mosquitoes. Regular gallow nippers. *(The radio plays a blues. JESSIE MAE picks up a movie magazine from the desk and sits in the chair by the radio.)* Mother Watts, where did you put that recipe that Rosella gave me on the phone today?

MRS. WATTS. What recipe was that, Jessie Mae?

JESSIE MAE. What recipe was that? She only gave me one. The one I wrote down while I was talkin' to Rosella this mornin'. You remember, I asked you to find me a pencil.

MRS. WATTS. Yes, I remember something about it.

JESSIE MAE. Then I handed it to you and asked you to put it away on the top of my dresser.

MRS. WATTS. Jessie Mae, I don't remember you havin' given me any recipe.

JESSIE MAE. Well, I did.

MRS. WATTS. I certainly have no recollection of it.

JESSIE MAE. You don't?

MRS. WATTS. No, Ma'm.

JESSIE MAE. I swear, Mother Watts, you just don't have any memory at all anymore.

MRS. WATTS. Jessie Mae, I think I . . .

JESSIE MAE. I gave it to you this mornin' in this very room and I said to please put it on my dresser and you said I will and went out holding it in your hand.

MRS. WATTS. I did?

JESSIE MAE. Yes, you did.

MRS. WATTS. Did you look on your dresser?

JESSIE MAE. Yes, Ma'm.

MRS. WATTS. And it wasn't there?

JESSIE MAE. No, Ma'm. I looked just before I went to bed.

MRS. WATTS. Oh. Well, let me look around. *(She gets up and goes out the door into the hallway.* JESSIE MAE *paces around the room.)*

JESSIE MAE. I swear. Have you noticed how forgetful she's getting? I think her memory is definitely going. Honestly, it just gets on my nerves. We're just gonna have to get out a little more, Ludie. No wonder you can't sleep. You get up in the morning, you go to work, you come home, you have your supper, read the paper, and then go right off to bed. Every couple I know goes out three or four times a week. I know we couldn't afford it before, so I kept quiet about it. But now you're working again I don't think a picture show once or twice a week would break us. We don't have a car. We don't go to nightclubs. We have to do something.

LUDIE. OK. Why don't we go out one night this week?

JESSIE MAE. I mean, I think we have to. I was talkin' to Rosella about it this morning on the phone and she said she just didn't see how we stood it. Well, I said, Rosella, we have Mother Watts and it's hard for us to leave her alone.

LUDIE. When did you and Rosella get friendly again?

JESSIE MAE. This morning. She just all of a sudden called me up on the telephone. She said she would quit being mad if I would. I said shucks, I wasn't mad in the first place. She was the one that was mad. I told her I was plain-spoken and said exactly what I felt and people will just have to take me as I am or leave me alone. I said furthermore, I had told her the truth when I remarked that the beauty parlor must have seen her coming a long way down the road when they charged her good money for that last permanent they gave her. She said she agreed with me now entirely and had stopped patronizing that beauty shop. *(A pause. She goes back to her movie magazine.)* Rosella found out definitely that she can't have any children . . . (MRS. WATTS *comes into the living room. To* MRS. WATTS.*)* Walk, don't run. (MRS. WATTS *looks around the room for the recipe. A pause.)* You know your mother's pension check didn't come today. It's the eighteenth. I swear it was due. I just can't understand the government. Always late. *(Looking up from her reading—then to* MRS. WATTS.*)* Did you find it?

MRS. WATTS. Not yet.

JESSIE MAE. Well, then forget about it. Look for it in the morning.

MRS. WATTS. No, I'm going to look for it until I find it. (MRS. WATTS *goes out of the room.)*

JESSIE MAE. Honestly, Ludie, she's so stubborn. *(She goes back to her movie magazine. Turns the radio dial—the radio plays a popular tune.)* I just love this song and this singer: I could just listen to him all day. (JESSIE MAE *begins to sing with the singer. There is an immediate knocking upstairs. She continues singing louder than ever. The knocking continues. Finally she jumps up out of her chair. She is very angry.)* Now what are they knocking about? Do you consider this on too loud?

LUDIE. No sense in arguing with them, Jessie Mae.

JESSIE MAE. They'd like it if we didn't breathe.

LUDIE. Well, it is kinda late. (LUDIE *turns the radio down.* JESSIE MAE *yawns. She goes over to the sofa with the movie magazine.)*

JESSIE MAE. Who played the captain in *Mutiny on the Bounty?*

LUDIE. Search me.

JESSIE MAE. They're running a contest in here but I never saw such hard questions. *(A pause. She looks up at* LUDIE.*)* Rosella said Jim used to have trouble sleepin'. She said a man told him to lie in bed and count backwards and that would cure him. He tried it and she said it did. She said you start with a hundred and instead of going forward you go backwards. One hundred, ninety-nine, ninety-eight, ninety-seven, ninety-six, ninety-five . . . She said it would just knock him out.

LUDIE. Jessie Mae, maybe we can take in a baseball game one night this week. The series is getting exciting. I think Houston has the best team they've had in a long time. I'd sure like to be there when they play Shreveport. *(Pause.)* I used to play baseball back at Bountiful. I used to rather play baseball than eat, when I was a kid.

JESSIE MAE. Come on, let's go to bed. *(She gets up. There is another screech of brakes.)* There goes another car smashed up. *(She runs to the window and stands looking out.)* Nope, they missed each other. Six cars smashed up on the freeway to Galveston I read yesterday in the Chronicle. One right on top of another. One car was trying to pass another car and ran right smack into a third car. Then the ones behind both cars started pilin' up. A lot of them were killed. I bet they were all drunk. Been down to Galveston, gamblin', likely. I think the whole of Houston goes into Galveston gambling and drinking. Everybody but us. I don't see how some people hold down a job the way they drink and gamble. Do you?

LUDIE. No . . . I don't.

JESSIE MAE. That's why I told Rosella I could hardly keep from callin' up your boss and givin' him a piece of my mind for payin' you the salary he pays you. Like I said to Rosella, you're so steady and so conscientious and they just take advantage of your good nature. Maybe you're too steady, Ludie. *(*LUDIE *has taken a book off the drop-leaf table. He goes to the chair, reading it. A pause.* MRS. WATTS *goes into the bedroom. She turns on the lights in the bedroom and begins a systematic search for the recipe. To* LUDIE.*)* Rosella was glad to hear you're workin' again. She said she was cleanin' out some drawers night before last and had come across some pictures of you and me she'd taken when we started goin' together. I said I don't care to see them. No, thank you. *(*MRS. WATTS *is looking, now, in* JESSIE MAE'*s vanity drawer. She finds the recipe.)* The passin's of time makes me sad. That's why I never want a house with the room to keep a lot of junk in to remind you of things you're better off forgetting. If we ever get any money you wouldn't catch me buying a house. I'd move into a hotel and have me room service. *(*MRS. WATTS *comes into the living room, holding the recipe.)*

MRS. WATTS. Here's your recipe, Jessie Mae.

JESSIE MAE. Thank you but I told you not to bother. Where did you find it? *(She takes the recipe.)*

MRS. WATTS. In your room.

JESSIE MAE. In my room?

MRS. WATTS. Yes, Ma'm.

JESSIE MAE. Where in my room?

MRS. WATTS. In your dresser drawer. Right-hand side.

JESSIE MAE. In my dresser drawer?

MRS. WATTS. Yes, Ma'm. I looked on top of the dresser and it wasn't there an' something said to me . . . *(*JESSIE MAE *rises and angrily throws her package of matches down on the table.)*

JESSIE MAE. Mother Watts.

MRS. WATTS. Ma'm.

JESSIE MAE. Ludie, how many times have I asked her never to go into my dresser drawer?

MRS. WATTS. I thought you wanted me to find your recipe?

JESSIE MAE. Well, I don't want you to go into my dresser drawers. I'd like a little privacy if you don't mind.

MRS. WATTS. Yes, Ma'm. *(She turns away. She is trying to avoid a fight.)*

JESSIE MAE. *(She is very angry now. She takes* MRS. WATTS *by the shoulder and shakes her.)* And just let me never catch you looking in them again. For anything. I can't stand people snoopin' in my dresser drawers. *(*MRS. WATTS *grabs the paper from* JESSIE MAE *and throws it on the floor. She is hurt and angry.)*

MRS. WATTS. All right. Then the next time you find it yourself.

JESSIE MAE. Pick that recipe up, if you please.

MRS. WATTS. Pick it up yourself. I have no intention of picking it up.

JESSIE MAE. *(Shouting.)* You pick that up!

MRS. WATTS. *(Shouting back.)* I won't!

LUDIE. Mama.

JESSIE MAE. *(Shouting even louder.)* You will!

LUDIE. Jessie Mae. For God sakes! You're both acting like children. It's one-thirty in the morning.

JESSIE MAE. You tell her to pick that up.

MRS. WATTS. I won't. (MRS. WATTS *stubbornly goes to her rocking chair and sits.)*

JESSIE MAE. *(Screaming.)* You will! This is my house and you'll do as you're told. *(*LUDIE *walks out of the room. He goes into his bedroom.* JESSIE MAE *crosses to* MRS. WATTS.*)* Now. I hope you're satisfied. You've got Ludie good and upset. He won't sleep for the rest of the night. What do you want to do? Get him sick again? *(There is a knocking upstairs.* JESSIE MAE *screams up at them.)* Shut up. *(To* MRS. WATTS.*)* You're going too far with me one of these days, old lady.

*(*JESSIE MAE *walks out of the room.* MRS. WATTS *is ready to scream back at her, but she controls the impulse. She takes her anger out in rocking violently back and forth.* JESSIE MAE *throws open the door to the bedroom and comes in.* LUDIE *is sitting on the edge of the bed. She marches over to the vanity and sits. She starts to throw things around on top of the vanity. After a moment,* LUDIE *gets up and starts toward her.)*

LUDIE. Jessie Mae.

JESSIE MAE. I just can't stand this, Ludie. I'm at the end of my rope. I won't take being insulted by your mother or anyone else. You hear that?

*(*LUDIE *rises and stands uncomfortably for a moment. He turns and goes out the bedroom door and into the living room. He stands by the living room door looking at his mother. She stops her rocking. She goes and picks up the recipe.* LUDIE *sees what she is doing and tries to get there first. He is not able to. She hands the recipe to him. He stands there for a moment looking at it. He turns to his mother and speaks with great gentleness.)*

LUDIE. Mama. Will you give this recipe to Jessie Mae?

MRS. WATTS. All right, Ludie. *(She takes the recipe. She starts out of the living room and* LUDIE *stops her. He obviously hates asking the next question.)*

LUDIE. Mama, will you please tell Jessie Mae you're sorry?

MRS. WATTS. Ludie . . .

LUDIE. Please, Mama.

MRS. WATTS. All right, Ludie.

LUDIE. Jessie Mae.

*(*MRS. WATTS *goes out of the room to the bedroom.)*

JESSIE MAE. What do you want, Ludie?

LUDIE. Mama has something to say to you.

JESSIE MAE. What is it? *(*MRS. WATTS *hands her the recipe.)*

MRS. WATTS. I'm sorry, Jessie Mae, for throwing the recipe on the floor.

JESSIE MAE. I accept your apology.

> (MRS. WATTS *goes out, reappears in living room.*)

JESSIE MAE. *(Calling.)* Come on, Ludie. Let's all go to bed.

LUDIE. All right. *(He starts for the living room door.)*

JESSIE MAE. *(Calling.)* And you'd better go to bed too, Mother Watts. A woman your age ought to have better sense than to sit up half the night.

MRS. WATTS. Yes, Ma'm. Good night, Ludie.

LUDIE. Good night, Mama.

> (*He waits until his mother sits in the rocking chair and then he turns the lights off in the living room and goes into the bedroom, taking his book with him.* MRS. WATTS *buries her face in her hands. She is crying.*)

LUDIE. *(Now in bedroom.)* Jessie Mae. I know it's hard and all, but for your own sake, I just think sometimes if you'd try to ignore certain things.

JESSIE MAE. Ignore? How can you ignore something when it's done right under your very nose?

LUDIE. Look, Jessie Mae.

JESSIE MAE. I know her, Ludie. She does things just to aggravate me. Well, I hope she's happy now. She aggravated me. Now you take her hymn singin'. She never starts until I come into a room. And her poutin'! Why sometimes she goes a whole day just sittin' and starin' out that window. How would you like to spend twenty-four hours a day shut up with a woman that either sang hymns or looked out the window and pouted? You couldn't ignore it and don't tell me you could. No. There's only one thing to do and that's to say quit it, every time she does something like that until she stops for good and all.

LUDIE. I'm not sayin' it's easy, Jessie Mae. I'm only sayin' . . .

JESSIE MAE. Well, let's change the subject. I don't want to get mad all over again. She keeps me so nervous never knowing when I leave whether she is going to try to run off to that old town or not.

LUDIE. Well, she's not going to run off again, Jessie Mae. She promised me she wouldn't.

JESSIE MAE. What she promised and . . .

LUDIE. Now, she can't run off. Her pension check hasn't come. You said yourself . . .

> (MRS. WATTS *hears them. She goes to the edge of the rug, lifts it up, and takes the pension check. She stands there for a moment, looking at it, trying to decide whether to take this in to* JESSIE MAE.)

JESSIE MAE. Well, I am not too sure that that check hasn't come. Sometimes I think she hides that check and I tell you right now if it is not here tomorrow I am going to search this house from top to bottom.

LUDIE. Well, I know the check will come tomorrow.

JESSIE MAE. I hope so. Rosella says she thinks it's terrible how close I have to stay here. Well, I told Rosella ever since your mother started that running-off business I don't feel easy going. I used to love it when I could get up from the breakfast table with an easy mind and go downtown and shop all morning, then get a sandwich and a coke, or a salad at the cafeteria, see a picture show in the afternoon and then come home. That was fun. Shhh. I think I hear your mother still up.

*(MRS. WATTS has decided not to give them the check. She is now sitting in her rocking chair, rocking and looking out the window. LUDIE comes into the living room. She puts the check inside her nightgown.)*

LUDIE. Mama. Are you still up?

MRS. WATTS. Yes. I don't feel like sleeping, Ludie. You go on back to bed and don't worry about me.

LUDIE. All right, Mama.

*(He goes back to bedroom.)*

JESSIE MAE. Was she still up?

LUDIE. Yes.

JESSIE MAE. I knew it. I never get to go out of the house except for the beauty parlor. I'm not giving that up for anyone. I told Rosella that. I said no one was more faithful to a husband than I was to Ludie, when he was sick, but even then I went out to the beauty parlor once a week. I mean, I had to.

LUDIE. I wanted you to.

JESSIE MAE. I know you did. *(JESSIE MAE sings absentmindedly. She is sitting at the vanity, brushing her hair, putting on face lotion, etc. A pause.)* Next time I see one of those little portable radios on sale, I'm going to get one. It would be nice to have by our bed. It would be so much company for us. *(A pause.)* That was a good supper we had tonight, wasn't it?

LUDIE. Uh-huh. Mama is a good cook.

JESSIE MAE. Yes. She is. I'll have to hand that to her. And an economical one. Well, she enjoys cooking. I guess you're born to enjoy it. I could never see how anyone could get any pleasure standing over a hot stove, but she seems to. *(A pause.)* Rosella asked me if I realized that it would be fifteen years this August since we were married. I hadn't realized it. Had you? *(LUDIE thinks for a moment. He counts back over the years.)*

LUDIE. That's right, Jessie Mae. It'll be fifteen years this August.

JESSIE MAE. I hate to think of time going that fast. *(A pause.)* I never will forget the night I came home and told Rosella you had proposed. I thought you were the handsomest man alive.

LUDIE. And I thought you were the prettiest girl.

JESSIE MAE. Did you, Ludie? I guess I did have my good features. People used to tell me I looked like a cross between Joan Crawford and Clara Bow. And I thought you were the smartest man in the world. I still do. The thing that burns me up is that you don't let other people know it. Do you remember Sue Carol in the movies?

LUDIE. Sure.

JESSIE MAE. I loved her. She was my ideal when I was growing up. She was always so cute in whatever she did. I always tried to act like her, be good company and a sport. *(A pause.)* Sue Carol's married to Alan Ladd now. They've got a bunch of kids. Well, she can afford them. They've got servants and I don't know what all. *(LUDIE has his book in his hand. He is walking around the room.)*

LUDIE. Jessie Mae, I've just got to start makin' some more money. I'm thinkin' about askin' for a raise. I'm entitled to it. I've been there six months now. I haven't been late or sick once. I've got to do it. I've got to ask for a raise tomorrow. *(He continues to walk around the room.)* I'm gonna walk into Mr. Douglas' office the first thing in the mornin' and I'm just gonna take the bull by the horns and I'm gonna say, Mr. Douglas, I've got to have a raise starting as of now. We can't live on what you pay us. We have my mother's pension check to help us out and if we didn't have that I don't know what we'd do.

JESSIE MAE. Well, I would.

LUDIE. I don't understand it, Jessie Mae. I try not to be bitter. I try not to . . . Oh, I don't know. All I know is that a man works eight years with a company. He saves a little money. He gets sick and has to spend two years in bed watching his savings all go. Then start all over again with a new company. *(A pause. He sits on the bed, placing his book on it.)* Of course, the doctor says I shouldn't worry about it. He says I've got to take things like they come. Every day, and that's what I try to do. But how can you help worryin' when you end up every month holding your breath to see if you're gonna make ends meet. *(JESSIE MAE gets up from the vanity. She crosses to the bed.)*

JESSIE MAE. You can't help being nervous. A lot of people get nervous. *(She sits on the bed and picks up the book.)* What's this book?

LUDIE. It's mine. I bought it at the drugstore coming home from the office.

JESSIE MAE. *How to Become an Executive.* What's that about?

LUDIE. It tells you how to prepare yourself for an executive position. It looks like there might be some helpful things in it. *(LUDIE takes the book and leans back against the headboard of the bed, reading. JESSIE MAE restlessly looks around the room.)*

JESSIE MAE. You sleepy, Ludie?

LUDIE. No, not yet.

JESSIE MAE. I'm not either. I wish I had something good to eat. I wish the drugstore was open. We could get us some ice cream. I wish I had my movie magazine.

LUDIE. Where is it?

JESSIE MAE. In the living room. *(LUDIE starts off the bed.)*

LUDIE. I'll get it.

JESSIE MAE. No, honey. I don't want to get your mother awake. *(JESSIE MAE lies across the foot of the bed. She hums and gets off the bed.)* I think I'll get me a cigarette. Want me to get you one?

LUDIE. Thanks. I think I will have one. I can get them.

JESSIE MAE. No. You rest. *(She goes to the vanity and gets a package of cigarettes.)* Rosella cried like her heart would break when she told me she couldn't have children. *(She lights a cigarette and gives one to LUDIE.)*

LUDIE. Thanks.

JESSIE MAE. She wanted to know how I stood it not havin' children. I said I don't know about Ludie 'cause you can't always tell what he feels, but I stand it by never thinking about it. *(She walks back to the foot of the bed and sits.)* I have my own philosophy about those things, anyway. I feel things like that are in the hands of the Lord. Don't you, Ludie?

LUDIE. I guess so.

JESSIE MAE. I've been as good a wife to you as I know how. But if the Lord doesn't want to give us children, all the worryin' in the world won't help. Do you think?

LUDIE. No. It won't.

JESSIE MAE. Anyway, like I told Rosella, I don't have the money to be runnin' around the doctors about it, even if I wanted to. *(A pause.)* Do you have an ashtray?

LUDIE. Right here. *(LUDIE gets an ashtray from the vanity and brings it to her.)* Jessie Mae, if I get a raise the first thing I want you to do is buy yourself a new dress.

JESSIE MAE. Well, thank you, Ludie. *(She goes back to the vanity and puts pin curlers in her hair. She puts a hairnet on and is finished by the end of speech.)* Besides, when you were sick what would I have done if I'd had a bunch of kids to worry me? Your mother said to me the other day, Jessie Mae, I don't know how you and Ludie stand livin' in the city. What are you talkin' about, I said. I didn't start livin' until I moved to the city. Who but a fool would want to live in the country? She wouldn't even listen to my arguments. Honestly, she's so stubborn. I declare, I believe your mother's about the stubbornest woman in forty-eight states. *(She looks at herself in the vanity mirror and then gets up laughing.)* Well, I don't look like Joan Crawford now. But who cares? I don't. What are you thinking about?

LUDIE. Oh, I was just thinking about this book. *(A pause. LUDIE gets into bed.)*

JESSIE MAE. Ludie, do you ever think back over the past?

LUDIE. No.

JESSIE MAE. I don't either. I started today a little when Rosella brought up that fifteen year business. But I think it's morbid. Your mother does that all the time.

LUDIE. I know.

JESSIE MAE. Turn your head the other way. *(He does so. She takes her dressing gown off and slips into bed.)*

LUDIE. My boss likes me. Billie Davison told me today he was positive he did. Billie has been there ten years now, you know. He said he thought he liked my work a lot. *(A pause.)* Feelin' sleepy now?

JESSIE MAE. Uh-huh. Are you?

LUDIE. Yes, I am. Good night.

JESSIE MAE. Good night.

*(LUDIE turns off the bed light by the side of the bed. MRS. WATTS is rocking back and forth in her rocker now, working her hands nervously, humming quietly to herself. LUDIE hears her and sits up in bed. He gets out of bed and goes into the living room.)*

LUDIE. Mama.

MRS. WATTS. I'm all right, Ludie. I'm just still not sleepy.

LUDIE. You're sure you're feelin' all right?

MRS. WATTS. Yes, I am.

LUDIE. Good night. *(He starts out of the room. She turns to him.)*

MRS. WATTS. Ludie, please, I want to go home.

LUDIE. Mama, you know I can't make a living there. We have to live in Houston.

MRS. WATTS. Ludie, son, I can't stay here any longer. I want to go home.

LUDIE. I beg you not to ask me that again. There's nothing I can do about it.

   *(LUDIE goes back to the bedroom. He gets into bed.)*

JESSIE MAE. Was she still up?

LUDIE. Uh-huh. Good night.

JESSIE MAE. Good night.

   *(MRS. WATTS is standing at the back of the rocking chair. She paces around the room thinking what to do. She listens for a moment to see if they are asleep. She decides they are and quietly takes a suitcase down from the top of the wardrobe. She waits a moment then takes some clothing from the drawer of the cupboard and puts them in the suitcase, then she quietly closes it and hides the suitcase under the sofa. She then goes back to her chair, sits, and is rocking back and forth violently as the lights fade.)*

*Curtain*

# ★ ACT I

## SCENE II

*At rise of curtain,* MRS. WATTS *is discovered sleeping in the rocker.* JESSIE MAE *is in bed.* LUDIE *is offstage in the bathroom, washing.* MRS. WATTS *awakens, looks for the check, finds it inside her nightgown, and hides it under the mattress. She looks out the window to see the time, runs over to* LUDIE's *bedroom to see if he's awake, and runs into the kitchen to put some water on for coffee, calling as she goes.*

MRS. WATTS. Ludie, it's eight-fifteen by the drugstore clock . . .

LUDIE. *(Calling back, offstage.)* Yes'm. *(*MRS. WATTS *is back in the living room with a breakfast tray and dishes.* JESSIE MAE *has gotten out of bed and is at the vanity.* LUDIE *sticks his head in the living room door.)* Good morning, Mama.

MRS. WATTS. Good morning, son.

LUDIE. Did you get any sleep at all last night?

MRS. WATTS. Yes. Don't worry about me. *(*MRS. WATTS *goes back into the kitchen, takes the tray out with her.* MRS. WATTS *comes back with the tray and finishes setting the table, humming to herself, absentmindedly.* JESSIE MAE *hollers from the next room.)*

JESSIE MAE. It's too early for hymn singing. *(*JESSIE MAE *comes into the living room.)*

MRS. WATTS. Good morning, Jessie Mae.

JESSIE MAE. Good morning, Mother Watts.

    *(*MRS. WATTS *goes out to the kitchen.* JESSIE MAE *turns on the radio and we hear a popular song. She goes out to the bathroom.* LUDIE *enters the living room from the hallway, puts his jacket on the chair.)*

JESSIE MAE. *(Calling.)* Ludie, turn that radio down, please, before they start knocking again. *(*MRS. WATTS *enters from the kitchen with coffee, which she sets on the table.)*

LUDIE. *(At the radio.)* Would you like me to turn it off?

JESSIE MAE. *(Calling.)* Oh, you might as well.

MRS. WATTS. I'll have your toast ready for you in a minute. *(Crosses into the kitchen.* JESSIE MAE *enters the living room from the hallway as* MRS. WATTS *is rushing out.)*

JESSIE MAE. Walk, don't run. I've just got to get me out of this house today, if no more than to ride downtown and back on the bus.

LUDIE. *(Sits at table, drinking coffee.)* Why don't you?

JESSIE MAE. If Mother Watts' pension check comes I'll go to the beauty parlor. I'm just as tense. I think I've got a trip to the beauty parlor comin' to me.

LUDIE. You ought to go if the check comes or not. It doesn't cost that much. *(*MRS. WATTS *comes in with toast.)*

JESSIE MAE. Mother Watts, will you skip down and see if the mail has come yet? Your pension check ought to be here and I want to get me to that beauty parlor.

MRS. WATTS. Yes, Ma'm. *(MRS. WATTS goes out for the mail at outside door. JESSIE MAE looks after her suspiciously.)*

JESSIE MAE. Ludie, she's actin' silent again. Don't you think she's actin' silent again?

LUDIE. I hadn't noticed. *(He takes a last swig out of his coffee.)*

JESSIE MAE. Well, she definitely is. You can say what you please, but to me it's always a sure sign she's gonna try and run off when she starts actin' silent.

LUDIE. She's not going to run off again, Jessie Mae. She promised me last time she wouldn't. *(He starts up from the table.)*

JESSIE MAE. She just better not. What do you want, Ludie?

LUDIE. I want more coffee.

JESSIE MAE. Well, keep your seat. I'll get it.

LUDIE. No, I'll get it.

JESSIE MAE. No. I want to get it. You'll have a tiring day ahead of you. Now rest while you can. *(She goes out to the hallway for coffee. MRS. WATTS enters.)*

MRS. WATTS. Where's Jessie Mae?

LUDIE. In the kitchen.

MRS. WATTS. There was no mail, Jessie Mae. *(JESSIE MAE comes in with coffee.)*

JESSIE MAE. Had it been delivered yet?

MRS. WATTS. I don't know.

JESSIE MAE. Did you look in the other boxes to see if there was mail?

MRS. WATTS. No, Ma'm. I didn't think to. *(MRS. WATTS goes to the bedroom.)*

LUDIE. I'll look on my way out. Why don't we have an early supper tonight? Six-thirty if that's all right with you and Mama. After supper I'll take you both to the picture show.

JESSIE MAE. That's fine. What would you like to see, Ludie?

LUDIE. Whatever you want to see, Jessie Mae. You know best about picture shows.

JESSIE MAE. Do you want to go downtown or to one of the neighborhood movies? *(She picks up a paper from the desk.)*

LUDIE. Whatever you want to do, Jessie Mae.

JESSIE MAE. Maybe it would do us good to go downtown. There's something about walkin' into the Majestic or the Metropolitan, or the Loew's State that just picks me up. People dress so much nicer when they're going to see a movie downtown. Of course, on the other hand, I could stand a good double bill myself.

LUDIE. *(Half to himself.)* I want to get to the office a little early this morning. Mr. Douglas is usually in by nine. I'd like a chance to talk to him before the others get there. I think I'm doin' the right thing, askin' for a raise. Don't you?

JESSIE MAE. Sure. I think I'll phone the beauty parlor for an appointment. I hope I can still get one. *(She goes to the phone on the desk. MRS. WATTS has been making up the bed. She stops when she hears JESSIE MAE dial the phone and goes to the bedroom door to listen.)* Hello, Rita. This is Jessie Mae Watts. Can I have an appointment for my hair? The usual. Uh-huh. *(She laughs.)* Four o'clock. Nothin' earlier. All right. See you then. *(She hangs up the phone.)* Well, I can't get an appointment until four o'clock.

LUDIE. I'm ready to go. Wish me luck on my raise.

JESSIE MAE. Good luck, Ludie. *(He kisses her on the cheek. He calls into the bedroom.)*

LUDIE. Goodbye, Mama.

MRS. WATTS. Goodbye, son. *(*MRS. WATTS *goes back to making up the bed.)*

LUDIE. Goodbye, Jessie Mae.

JESSIE MAE. So long. Holler if there's any mail down there so we won't be runnin' up and down lookin' for mail that won't be there.

LUDIE. *(Calling back.)* All right. *(Exits outside door.)*

JESSIE MAE. *(Calling into the bedroom.)* That pension check should have been here yesterday, shouldn't it, Mother Watts?

MRS. WATTS. *(Calling back and trying to seem unconcerned.)* I reckon so.

LUDIE. *(Calling from offstage downstairs.)* No mail for us.

JESSIE MAE. All right! I can't understand about that pension check, can you?

MRS. WATTS. No, Ma'm. *(*JESSIE MAE *casually takes* MRS. WATTS' *purse off the wardrobe and looks inside. Finding nothing, she closes it and puts it back.)*

JESSIE MAE. I sure hope it isn't lost. You know you're so absentminded, you don't think you put it around the room someplace by mistake and forgot all about it. *(*MRS. WATTS *comes into the living room.)*

MRS. WATTS. I don't believe so. *(*JESSIE MAE *looks around the room.* MRS. WATTS *watches anxiously everything she does.)*

JESSIE MAE. You know you said you lost that check once before and it took us five days to find it. I came across it under this radio.

MRS. WATTS. I don't think I did that again, Jessie Mae.

> *(*JESSIE MAE *begins a halfhearted search of the room, looking under a vase, a pillow on the sofa, and when she gets to the corner of the rug where the check is hidden, she stoops as if to look under it, but it is only a strand of thread that has caught her attention. She picks it up and goes over to the radio, looking under that.* JESSIE MAE *gives up the search and* MRS. WATTS *goes back to the bedroom.* JESSIE MAE *calls after her.)*

JESSIE MAE. What could I do 'til four o'clock? What are you gonna do today?

> *(*JESSIE MAE *goes into the bedroom.)*

MRS. WATTS. Well, I'm going to give the kitchen a good cleaning and put fresh paper on the shelves and clean the icebox.

JESSIE MAE. Well, I have a lot of things I have to do. I got some drawers I can straighten up. Or maybe I'll put some flowers on that red dress of mine. If I wear the red dress tonight. I really don't know yet which dress I'm going to wear. Well, if I wear my red dress tonight, I'll wear this print one to the beauty parlor. *(She has taken a dress out of her closet and goes out the hallway to the bathroom to try it on.* MRS. WATTS *decides to use this opportunity to run into the living room to get the check.* JESSIE MAE *hears her running and calls to her from the bathroom before she can reach the rug.)* Mother Watts! *(*MRS. WATTS *quickly finds something to do in the living room.)*

MRS. WATTS. Yes, Ma'm.

> *(*JESSIE MAE *comes into the living room.)*

JESSIE MAE. There you go again. You never walk when you can run. *(*JESSIE

MAE *goes back into the bathroom.* MRS. WATTS *quickly reaches under the rug and gets the check. She puts it inside her dress. Then she takes the dishes out to the kitchen.* JESSIE MAE *continues to lecture her from the bathroom.)* You know it's none of my business, and I know you don't like me to suggest anything, but I don't think a woman your age should go running around a three-room apartment like a cyclone. It's really not necessary, Mother Watts. You never walk when you can run. *(JESSIE MAE comes out to the living room with the dress on. She watches MRS. WATTS.)* I wish for once you'd listen to me.

MRS. WATTS. I'm listening, Jessie Mae.

JESSIE MAE. You're not listening to a word. Mother Watts, are you feeling all right? You look a little pale.

MRS. WATTS. I'm feeling fine, Jessie Mae. *(JESSIE MAE zips up her dress, straightens out the skirt etc. during following speech.)*

JESSIE MAE. That movie magazine Ludie brought me last night is running a contest. First prize is a free trip to Hollywood. I'd like to enter it if I thought I could win. I wouldn't win. I don't have that kind of luck. I want you to look at the hem of this dress for me, to see if it's straight.

MRS. WATTS. Yes, Ma'm. *(MRS. WATTS gets a tape measure from her wardrobe and measures the dress.)*

JESSIE MAE. I'm gonna make Ludie take me to Hollywood one of these days. I want to visit Hollywood as bad as you want to visit Bountiful.

MRS. WATTS. It measures straight, Jessie Mae. *(She returns the tape measure to the wardrobe and starts to make her own bed.* JESSIE MAE *walks restlessly around the living room.)*

JESSIE MAE. Do you need anything from the drugstore?

MRS. WATTS. Just let me think a moment, Jessie Mae.

JESSIE MAE. Because if you do, I'd walk over to the drugstore and have me a fountain Coke with lots of chipped ice. We don't need toothpaste. We don't need toothbrushes. I got a bottle of Listerine yesterday. Can you think of anything we need from the drugstore?

MRS. WATTS. Did you get that nail polish you mentioned?

JESSIE MAE. Oh, yes I have that. I hate to wait around here until four o'clock. I think I'm gonna call Rosella and tell her to meet me at the drugstore for a Coke. *(She goes to the phone and dials.* MRS. WATTS *is humming to herself as she finishes making up her bed.)* Will you stop that hymn singing? Do you want me to jump right out of my skin? You know what hymns do to my nerves. *(MRS. WATTS stops her humming.)* And don't pout. You know I can't stand pouting.

MRS. WATTS. I didn't mean to pout, Jessie Mae. I only meant to be silent.

JESSIE MAE. *(Hangs up the phone.)* Wouldn't you know it. She's not home. I bet she's at the drugstore right now. I think I'll go on over to the drugstore and just take a chance on Rosella's being there. *(JESSIE MAE begins to put her hat on.* MRS. WATTS *has gotten a hand sweeper from the kitchen and is sweeping around the room.)* I can't make up my mind what movie I want to see tonight. Well, I'll ask Rosella. Will you stop that noise for a minute. I'm nervous. *(MRS. WATTS stops sweeping and gets a dustrag from the kitchen. She begins to dust the room.* JESSIE MAE *continues putting on her hat and arranging her dress in front of the mirror.)* You know when I first came to Houston, I went to see three picture shows in one day. I went to the Kirby in the morning, and the Metropolitan in the afternoon, and the Majestic that night. People don't go to see picture shows the way they used to. Well, I'm ready. *(She turns to* MRS. WATTS.*)* I just want you to promise me one thing. That you won't put a foot out of this house and start that Bountiful business again. You'll kill Ludie if he has to chase all over Houston looking for you. And I'm warning you. The next time you run off I'm calling the police. I don't care what Ludie says. *(*JESSIE MAE *starts out of the room.)* If Rosella calls just tell her I'm at the drugstore. *(*MRS. WATTS *has done her best to continue dusting the furniture during the latter speech, but she has been getting physically weaker and weaker. Finally in a last desperate attempt to keep* JESSIE MAE *from noticing her weakness she grabs hold again of the sweeper, trying to support herself. She sways, drops the sweeper, and reaches for the sofa to keep from falling, just as* JESSIE MAE *is ready to leave the room.)* Mother Watts . . . *(*JESSIE MAE *runs to her. She is very frightened.)*

MRS. WATTS. *(Trying desperately to control herself.)* I'm all right, Jessie Mae.

JESSIE MAE. Is it your heart?

MRS. WATTS. No. Just a sinkin' spell. Just let me lie down on the sofa for a minute and I'll be all right.

JESSIE MAE. Can I get you some water?

MRS. WATTS. Thank you. *(*JESSIE MAE *runs into the kitchen for water.)*

JESSIE MAE. (Offstage, from the kitchen.) Do you want me to call a doctor?

MRS. WATTS. No, Ma'm.

JESSIE MAE. Do you want me to call Ludie?

MRS. WATTS. No, Ma'm. *(*JESSIE MAE *reenters the living room with a glass of water.* MRS. WATTS *drinks it.)*

JESSIE MAE. Are you feelin' better?

MRS. WATTS. Yes, I am, Jessie Mae. *(*MRS. WATTS *gets up off the sofa.)*

JESSIE MAE. Do you think you ought to get up so soon?

MRS. WATTS. Yes, Ma'm. I'm feeling much better already. I'll just sit here in the chair.

JESSIE MAE. All right. I'll sit here for a while and keep you company. *(*MRS. WATTS *sits in her rocking chair.* JESSIE MAE *sits in her chair, restless as a cat.)* How do you feel now?

MRS. WATTS. Better.

JESSIE MAE. That's good. It always scares the daylights out of me when you get one of those sinkin' spells. Of course, like I told you this morning, you wouldn't be having these sinkin' spells if you'd stop this running around. Well, it's your heart. If you don't want to take care of it no one can make you. But I tell you right now all I need is to have an invalid on my hands. I wish you'd think of Ludie. He's got enough to worry him without your gettin' down flat on your back. *(Phone rings. She goes to it.)* Oh, hello, Rosella. I tried to call you earlier. Oh. You're at the drugstore. That's what I just figured. Well, I'd like to, Rosella, but Mother Watts has had a sinking spell again and . . .

MRS. WATTS. You go on, Jessie Mae. I'm gonna be all right. I'll just rest here. There's nothing you can do for me.

JESSIE MAE. Are you sure?

MRS. WATTS. Yes, Jessie Mae. I'm sure.

JESSIE MAE. Well, all right then. Rosella, Mother Watts says she won't need me here. So I think I will come over for a little while. All right. I'll see you in a few minutes. Goodbye. *(She hangs up the phone.)* Now you're sure you'll be all right?

MRS. WATTS. Yes, Jessie Mae.

JESSIE MAE. Well, then I'll go on over. Now you call me at the drugstore if you need me. You hear?

MRS. WATTS. Yes, Ma'm.

> *(JESSIE MAE goes out the entrance to stairs. MRS. WATTS sits for a moment, rocking and using all her will to get her strength back. After a moment she slowly and weakly gets up and goes to the door, listening. She is sure JESSIE MAE has gone. She gets her suitcase from under the bed. Then she remembers the check, which she takes out, and goes to the desk to endorse it. She takes writing paper and an envelope from the desk at the same time. While MRS. WATTS is endorsing the check, JESSIE MAE comes running back in. MRS. WATTS doesn't see her until she has opened the door.)*

JESSIE MAE. I forgot to take any money along with me. *(JESSIE MAE is in such a hurry she doesn't see MRS. WATTS. She goes into the bedroom to get her money, which she takes from the vanity. MRS. WATTS has just time to get the suitcase and get it back in the wardrobe, stuff the check inside her dress, and get back to the writing desk when JESSIE MAE comes in again.)* Who are you writing to?

MRS. WATTS. I thought I'd drop a line to Callie Davis, Jessie Mae. Let her know I'm still alive.

JESSIE MAE. Why did you decide to do that all of a sudden?

MRS. WATTS. No reason. The notion just struck me.

JESSIE MAE. All right. *(She starts out.)* But just in case you're trying to put something over on me with that pension check, I've told Mr. Reynolds at the grocery store never to cash anything for you.

> *(She goes out the door. MRS. WATTS again stands quietly waiting. Then she goes to the door, listening. She decides JESSIE MAE has really gone. She gets her hat and coat from the wardrobe. She gets her suitcase and goes quietly out the door.)*

*Curtain*

*The lights are brought up on part of a bus terminal in Houston, Texas. It is placed stage right. Upstage center right of this area is a door to the street. Downstage right is an exit to washrooms, etc.*

*There is a man sitting on one of the benches eating a sandwich. A pretty blond girl, carrying a suitcase and a magazine, is standing at the ticket window right center waiting to buy a ticket. A man is standing behind her. The girl's name is* THELMA.

*The* TICKET MAN *is busy on the telephone. He puts the phone down and comes to the front of the window.*

TICKET MAN. Yes?

THELMA. I want a ticket to Old Gulf, please.

TICKET MAN. Yes, Ma'm. *(He reaches for a ticket.)* Here you are. You change busses at Harrison.

THELMA. I know. How much, please?

TICKET MAN. Four eighty.

THELMA. Yessir. *(She gives him the money and steps out of line. Goes to bench and sits, reading a magazine. The man steps up to the window.)*

MAN. Ticket to Leighton.

TICKET MAN. Leighton. Yes, indeed. *(*MRS. WATTS, *carrying a suitcase and purse, comes into the terminal from the street entrance. She is looking all around her to see if* JESSIE MAE *or* LUDIE *has put in an appearance. Satisfied that they haven't, she hurries to the ticket window. She gets in line behind the man. She is humming the hymn to herself and keeps an eye on the doors all the time.* TICKET MAN *hands the man his ticket.)* Be seven sixty, please.

MAN. Yessir. *(He gets the money for the* TICKET MAN. *Two people have come up behind* MRS. WATTS. *The man gives the* TICKET MAN *the money for the tickets, the* TICKET MAN *reaches for change.)*

TICKET MAN. Seven sixty out of ten dollars.

MAN. Thank you. *(He takes his change and exits.* MRS. WATTS *is so busy watching the doors that she doesn't notice it's her turn.)*

TICKET MAN. *(Calling.)* Lady. *(She is still so absorbed in watching, she doesn't hear him.)* Lady. It's your turn. *(*MRS. WATTS *turns and see she is next in line. She moves up to the counter.)*

MRS. WATTS. Oh, yes. Excuse me. I'd like a ticket to Bountiful, please.

TICKET MAN. Where?

MRS. WATTS. Bountiful.

TICKET MAN. What's it near?

MRS. WATTS. It's between Harrison and Cotton.

TICKET MAN. Just a minute. *(He takes a book from behind the window on a shelf. He looks inside it.* MRS. WATTS *is again watching the doors. He looks up.)* Lady.

MRS. WATTS. Oh. Yessir.

TICKET MAN. I can sell you a ticket to Harrison or to Cotton. But there's no Bountiful.

MRS. WATTS. Oh, yes there is, it's between . . .

TICKET MAN. I'm sorry, lady. You say there is, but the book says there isn't. And the book don't lie.

MRS. WATTS. But . . . I . . .

TICKET MAN. *(Impatiently.)* Make up your mind, lady. Cotton or Harrison. There are other people waiting.

MRS. WATTS. Well . . . let me see . . . How much is a ticket to Harrison?

TICKET MAN. Three fifty . . .

MRS. WATTS. Cotton?

TICKET MAN. Four twenty.

MRS. WATTS. Oh, yes. Well, I'll have the one to Harrison, please.

TICKET MAN. All right. That'll be three fifty, please.

MRS. WATTS. Yessir. *(She reaches for her pocketbook and is about to open it. She turns to the* TICKET MAN.) Can you cash a pension check? You see I decided to come at the last minute and I didn't have time to stop by the grocery store.

TICKET MAN. I'm sorry, lady. I can't cash any checks.

MRS. WATTS. It's perfectly good. It's a government check.

TICKET MAN. I'm sorry. It's against the rules to cash checks.

MRS. WATTS. Oh, is that so? I understand. A rule's a rule. How much was that again?

TICKET MAN. Three fifty.

MRS. WATTS. Oh, yes. Three fifty. Just a minute, sir. I've got it all here in nickels and dimes and quarters. *(She opens her purse and takes a handkerchief out. The money is tied in the handkerchief. She unties it, places it on the counter, and begins to count out the amount for the ticket. She counts half aloud as she does it. She shoves a pile of silver toward the* TICKET MAN.) Here. I think this is three fifty.

TICKET MAN. Thank you. *(He rakes the money into his hand. She ties her hand-kerchief back up.)*

MRS. WATTS. That's quite all right. I'm sorry to have taken up so much of your time. *(She picks up her suitcase and starts off.)*

TICKET MAN. Here, lady. Don't forget your ticket. *(She comes running back.)*

MRS. WATTS. Oh, my heavens. Yes. I'd forget my head if it wasn't on my neck. *(She takes the ticket and goes away. The man next in line steps up to the window.* MRS. WATTS *goes back to the entrance. She peers out and then comes back into the bus station. She comes down to the bench.* THELMA *is seated there, reading. Looks up from her magazine. There is an empty space next to her.* MRS. WATTS *comes up to it.)* Good evening.

THELMA. Good evening.

MRS. WATTS. Is this seat taken?

THELMA. No, Ma'm.

MRS. WATTS. Are you expectin' anyone?

THELMA. No, Ma'm.

MRS. WATTS. May I sit here then?

THELMA. Yes, Ma'm. (MRS. WATTS *puts the suitcase down along the side of the bench. She looks nervously around the station. All of a sudden she jumps up.*)

MRS. WATTS. Would you watch my suitcase, honey?

THELMA. Yes, Ma'm.

MRS. WATTS. I'll be right back.

THELMA. Yes'm.

(MRS. WATTS *goes running back toward the door to the street.* THELMA *watches her go for a minute and then goes back to reading her magazine. The* TICKET MAN *is joined by the man who is to relieve him for the night. They greet each other and the first* TICKET MAN *leaves the bus station.* MRS. WATTS *comes back to the bench. She sits down and takes a handkerchief out of her purse. She wipes her forehead.*)

MRS. WATTS. Thank you so much.

THELMA. That's all right. (MRS. WATTS *wipes her brow again.*)

MRS. WATTS. Little warm isn't it when you're rushing around?

THELMA. Yes'm.

MRS. WATTS. I had to get myself ready in the biggest kind of hurry.

THELMA. Are you going on a trip?

MRS. WATTS. Yes, I am. I'm trying to get to a town nobody ever heard of around here.

THELMA. What town is that?

MRS. WATTS. Bountiful.

THELMA. Oh.

MRS. WATTS. Did you ever hear of it?

THELMA. No.

MRS. WATTS. You see. Nobody has. Well, it's not much of a town now, I guess. I haven't seen it myself in thirty years. But it used to be quite prosperous. All they have left is a post office and a filling station and a general store. At least they did when I left.

THELMA. Do your people live there?

MRS. WATTS. No. My people are all dead except my son and his wife, Jessie Mae. They live here in the city. I'm hurrying to see Bountiful before I die. I had a sinking spell this morning. I had to climb up on the bed and rest. It was my heart.

THELMA. Do you have a bad heart?

MRS. WATTS. Well, its not what you call a good one. Doctor says it would last as long as I needed it if I could just cut out worrying. But seems I can't do that lately. (*She looks around the bus station again. She gets up out of her seat.*) Excuse me. Would you keep your eye on that suitcase again?

THELMA. Yes, Ma'm. (MRS. WATTS *hurries back to the entrance of the bus station.* THELMA *picks up her magazine and goes back to reading.* MRS. WATTS *comes hurrying back to the seat. She doesn't sit down, but stands over by the side.*) Lady. Is there anything wrong?

MRS. WATTS. No, honey. I'm just a little nervous. That's all. (*She hurries back toward the door. This time she opens it and goes outside.* THELMA *goes back to her reading.* MRS. WATTS *comes running back in. She hurries over to the seat and picks up the suitcase. In her confusion, she drops her handkerchief on the floor. Neither she nor* THELMA *sees it fall.)* Say a prayer for me, honey. Good luck.

THELMA. Good luck to you.

(MRS. WATTS *goes running out toward the rest room.* LUDIE *comes in the outside door to the bus station. He stands a moment at the entrance, looking all around. He wanders slowly down until he gets to the bench where* THELMA *is sitting. He pauses here, looking out in front of him and to each side.* JESSIE MAE *comes in. She is in a rage. She walks over to* LUDIE.)

LUDIE. You want to sit down, Jessie Mae?

JESSIE MAE. Yes, I do. If you want to look around, go ahead. I'll wait here.

LUDIE. You looked carefully in the coffee shop?

JESSIE MAE. Yes.

LUDIE. Want me to bring you a Coke?

JESSIE MAE. No.

LUDIE. Want me to buy you a movie magazine?

JESSIE MAE. Yes.

LUDIE. All right. I'll be right back. *(He goes back out the outside door he came in, looking around as he goes.* JESSIE MAE *sits down next to* THELMA. *She takes out a package of cigarettes. She gets her lighter. It doesn't work. She opens her purse and starts looking for a match. She can't find one. She turns to* THELMA.)

JESSIE MAE. Excuse me. Do you have a match? My lighter's out of fluid. *(*THELMA *reaches in the pocket of her jacket. She finds matches and gives them to her.)* Thank you. *(She lights her cigarette and hands the matches back to* THELMA. JESSIE MAE *takes a deep drag off her cigarette.)* I hope you're lucky enough not to have to fool with any in-laws. I've got a mother-in-law about to drive me crazy. At least twice a year we have to try and keep her from getting on a train to go back to her hometown. *(She takes another drag off her cigarette.)* I swear, she always has to spoil everything. My husband was goin' to take us to a double bill tonight at the picture show for the first time in I don't know when. I had called the beauty parlor for an appointment and I couldn't get one till 4 o'clock, see, and I was nervous sitting around the house, and so I went to the drugstore for a fountain Coke and I come home and what did I find . . . no Mother Watts. So I had to call my husband at the office and say the picture show was off. We've got to go looking for Mother Watts. Oh, she's so stubborn. I could just wring her neck. Her son spoils her that's the whole trouble. She's just rotten spoiled. Do you live with your in-laws?

THELMA. No.

JESSIE MAE. Well, you're lucky. They're all stubborn. My husband is as stubborn as she is. We should be over at the depot right now instead of sitting here. She always tries to go by train, but no. We wait at one railroad station five minutes and the other railroad station for five minutes and because she isn't there, right then, he drags me over here. And don't ask me why she always tries to go by train. That's just how she is. *(She takes another drag off her cigarette. It has gone out.)*

Could I trouble you for another match, please? My cigarette has gone out. *(THELMA gets the match for her. JESSIE MAE takes it and lights her cigarette.)* Of course, there hasn't been a train to that town in I don't know when. But if you try to tell her that she just looks at you like you're making it up. Always before we've been there waitin' for her when she walks into the railroad station, but today I was too trustin'. I gave her all the time in the world to get away. Well, we're payin' for it now. I told Ludie at breakfast she had that silent look, and I bet she tries to run away. But no, he said she wouldn't, because she had promised she wouldn't, and Ludie believes anything she says. I'm just worn out. I've had my fourth Coca-Cola today, just to keep my spirits up. People ask me why I don't have any children. Why? I say I've got Ludie and Mother Watts. That's all the children I need. *(LUDIE comes in with a movie magazine. He comes up to JESSIE MAE.)* What did you bring me? *(He shows her the magazine.)* Oh, I've seen that one.

LUDIE. *(He puts it absentmindedly under his arm. He looks around the station.)* Have you seen Mama?

JESSIE MAE. No, you goose. Do you think I'd be sittin' here so calm if I had! Personally, I think we're wastin' our time sittin' here. She always tries to go by train.

LUDIE. But she can't go by train, Jessie Mae.

JESSIE MAE. She doesn't know that.

LUDIE. She's bound to by now. What time did she leave again?

JESSIE MAE. I don't know what time she left. I told you I called from the drugstore at 11:30 and she was gone, the sneaky thing.

LUDIE. Well, you see she's had the time to find out a lot of things she hasn't known before. *(JESSIE MAE gets up and goes to him.)*

JESSIE MAE. I don't care what you say, Ludie. My hunch is that she's at one of those train stations. We've always found her there. You know how she is. Stubborn. Why, she won't believe them at the depot if they tell her there's not a train to Bountiful. She says there is and you watch, as far as she's concerned that's how it'll have to be. Ludie, I know she's there. I'm never wrong about these things.

LUDIE. All right. Have it your way. Let's go.

JESSIE MAE. Well, now we're here we might as well inquire from someone if they've seen her wanderin' around.

LUDIE. I thought you said she wouldn't come here.

JESSIE MAE. I said I didn't think she would come here. I don't know what the crazy thing will do. I could wring her neck. I can tell you that. I ought to be sitting at the beauty parlor right this very minute.

LUDIE. All right, Jessie Mae. Let's go on back to the depot.

JESSIE MAE. Will you stop rushing me around. I'm so mad I could chew nails. I tell you again I think we ought to just turn this whole thing over to the police. That would scare her once and for all.

LUDIE. Well, we're not going to call any police. We've been through that once and we're . . .

JESSIE MAE. It's for her own good. She's crazy.

LUDIE. *(He is very angry with her.)* Now why do you talk like that? You know Mama isn't crazy. *(A pause.)* I just wish you wouldn't say things like that.

JESSIE MAE. (JESSIE MAE *has taken off her hat, and hands it to* LUDIE. *She is combing her hair and freshening her makeup during the following speech.)* Then why does she keep runnin' off from a perfectly good home like this? To try and get to some old swamp. Don't you call that crazy? I mean, she doesn't have to turn her hand. Hardly. We only have a bedroom and a living room and a kitchen. We're all certainly very light eaters, so cooking three meals a day isn't killing her. And like I told her this morning. She wouldn't be havin' her sinkin' spells if she'd start walkin' like a normal human bein' and not go trottin' all over the place. I said, Mother Watts, please tell me why with a bad heart you insist on running . . . (LUDIE *is getting more and more embarrassed. He sees people looking at them.)*

LUDIE. Well, let's don't stand here arguing. People are looking at us. Do you want to go to the depot or not? (JESSIE MAE *turns and sees they're being watched. She lowers her voice but not her intensity.)*

JESSIE MAE. It's your mother. I don't care what you do. Only you better do something. Let me tell you that, or she's gonna clonk out some place. She'll get to Bountiful and die from the excitement and then we'll have all kinds of expenses bringing her body back here. Do you know what a thing like that could cost? Do you realize she had a sinkin' spell this mornin'?

LUDIE. I know. You've told me a hundred times. What can I do about it, Jessie Mae?

JESSIE MAE. I'm trying to tell you what you can do about it. Call the police.

LUDIE. I'm not going to call the police.

JESSIE MAE. Oh, you won't.

LUDIE. No.

JESSIE MAE. Then I think I will. That'll settle it once and for all. *(She goes outside.* LUDIE *looks around for a minute, then sits down dejectedly in the seat next to* THELMA. THELMA *has been watching the preceding scene. She has tried not to be seen by them, but the audience should know that she has taken in every single word.* LUDIE *reaches in his back pocket and takes out a handkerchief. He mops his forehead. He notices the magazine under his arm. He takes it in his hand and turns to* THELMA.*)*

LUDIE. Would you like this? I never read them, and my wife has seen it.

THELMA. Thank you. *(She takes the magazine and puts it in her lap. She goes back to her reading.* LUDIE *looks on the floor and sees the handkerchief that was dropped by* MRS. WATTS. *He reaches down and picks it up. He recognizes it. He gets up and goes running over to the ticket window.)*

LUDIE. Excuse me. Did an old lady come here and buy a ticket to a town named Bountiful?

TICKET MAN. Where?

LUDIE. Bountiful!

TICKET MAN. Not since I've been on duty.

LUDIE. How long have you been on duty?

TICKET MAN. About fifteen minutes.

LUDIE. Where is the man that was on before?

TICKET MAN. He's gone home.

LUDIE. Oh. *(He walks away thinking what to do next. He sees* THELMA *and goes to her.)* Excuse me, Miss.

THELMA. Yes?

LUDIE. I found this handkerchief here that belongs, I think, to my mother. She's run off from home. She has a heart condition and it might be serious for her to be all alone. I don't think she has much money, and I'd like to find her. Do you remember having seen her?

THELMA. Well . . . I . . .

LUDIE. She'd be on her way to a town called Bountiful.

THELMA. Yes, I did see her. She was here talkin' to me. She left all of a sudden.

LUDIE. Thank you so much. *(*JESSIE MAE *has come back in.* LUDIE *goes up to her.)*

JESSIE MAE. Ludie.

LUDIE. I was right. She was here. The lady there said so.

JESSIE MAE. Well, it's too late now.

LUDIE. But this lady was talking to her.

JESSIE MAE. We're not going to wait. The police and I talked it over.

*(*THELMA *takes advantage of their argument to slip out of the station.)*

LUDIE. *(Turning on* JESSIE MAE.*)* You didn't really call them!

JESSIE MAE. I did, and they said in their opinion she was just trying to get our attention this way and we should just go home and pay her no mind at all.

LUDIE. How can I go home with Mama . . .

JESSIE MAE. The police tell me they have hundreds of cases like this every day. They say such things are very common among young people and old people, and they're positive that if we just go home and show her that we don't care if she goes or stays, she'll come home of her own free will.

LUDIE. Jessie Mae . . .

JESSIE MAE. Now, we're going to do what the police tell us to. They say she will come home when she's tired and hungry enough and that makes a lot of sense to me. Now, Ludie, I wish you'd think of me for a change . . . I'm not going to spend the rest of my life running after your mother.

LUDIE. All right, Jessie Mae. *(He stands there, thinking.)*

JESSIE MAE. Now, come on, let's go. Come on. *(She starts out.* LUDIE *pauses for a moment, thinking. He goes after her.)*

LUDIE. All right. But if Mama is not home in an hour I'm going after her . . .

JESSIE MAE. Honestly, Ludie, you're so stubborn.

*(They go out as the lights are brought down. Over the loudspeaker we hear the stations being called: Bus leaving for Newton, Sugarland, Gerard, Harrison, Cotton, Old Gulf, Don Tarle . . . In the darkness we hear the sound of a bus starting, then the noise of the traffic of a downtown city. Brakes grinding, horns honking. This is brought down to almost a whisper. The lights are brought up on the center section and we see a seat in the bus.* MRS. WATTS *and* THELMA *are sitting there.* MRS. WATTS *is gazing out into the night.* THELMA *is casually glancing at the movie magazine. After a moment* MRS. WATTS *turns to her.)*

MRS. WATTS. Isn't it a small world? I didn't know we'd be on the same bus. Where do you go, honey?

THELMA. Harrison.

MRS. WATTS. Harrison!

THELMA. Yes. I change busses there.

MRS. WATTS. So do I go there. Isn't that nice? It that a moving picture magazine?

THELMA. Yes, Ma'm. Would you like to look at it?

MRS. WATTS. No, thank you. *(She leans her head back on the seat and turns her head away.)* The bus is nice to ride, isn't it?

THELMA. Yes. It is.

MRS. WATTS. I'm sorry I couldn't take a train, though.

THELMA. I tried to go by train, but you couldn't get connections tonight.

MRS. WATTS. I know. When I was a girl I used to take excursions from Bountiful to Houston to Galveston. For the day, you know. Leave at five in the morning and return at ten that night. The whole town would be down to see you get off the train. I have such fond memories of those trips. *(A pause. She looks over at* THELMA.*)* Excuse me for getting personal, but what's a pretty girl like you doing travelling alone?

THELMA. My husband has just been sent overseas. I'm going to stay with my family.

MRS. WATTS. Oh, I'm sorry to hear that. Just say the Ninety-first Psalm over and over to yourself. It will be a bower of strength and protection for him. *(She begins to recite with closed eyes.)* "He that dwelleth in the secret place of the most high, shall abide under the shadow of the Almighty. I will say of the Lord, He is my refuge and my fortress: My God; in Him will I trust. Surely He shall deliver thee from the fowler and the noisome pestilence. He shall cover thee with His feathers and under his wing shalt thou trust: His truth shall be thy shield and buckler." *(*THELMA *covers her face with her hands—she is crying.* MRS. WATTS *looks up and sees her.)* Oh, I'm sorry. I'm sorry, honey.

THELMA. That's all right. I'm just lonesome for him.

MRS. WATTS. Keep him under the Lord's wing, honey, and he'll be safe.

THELMA. Yes, Ma'm. *(She dries her eyes.)* I'm sorry. I don't know what gets into me.

MRS. WATTS. Nobody needs be ashamed of crying. I guess we've all dampened our pillows sometime or other. I have, goodness knows.

THELMA. If I could only learn not to worry.

MRS. WATTS. I know. I guess we all ask that. Jessie Mae, my daughter-in-law, don't worry. What for? she says. Well, like I tell her, that's a fine attitude if you can cultivate it. Trouble is I can't any longer.

THELMA. It is hard.

MRS. WATTS. I didn't use to worry. I was so carefree as a girl. Had lots to worry me, too. Everybody was so poor back in Bountiful. But we got along. I said to Papa once after our third crop failure in a row, whoever gave this place the name of Bountiful? His Papa did, he said, because in those days it was a land of plenty. You just had to drop seeds in the ground and the crops would spring up. Cotton and corn and sugar cane. I still think it's the prettiest place I know of. Jessie Mae says it's the ugliest. But she just says that I know to make me mad. She only saw it once, and then on a rainy day, at that. She says it's nothing but a swamp. That may be, I said, but it's a might pretty swamp to me. And then Sonny, that's my boy, Ludie, I call him Sonny, he said not to answer her back. He said it only caused arguments. And nobody ever won an argument with Jessie Mae, and I guess that's right. *(A pause. She looks out into space.)*

THELMA. Mrs. Watts . . .

MRS. WATTS. Yes?

THELMA. I think I ought to tell you this . . . I . . . I don't want you to think I'm interfering in your business . . . but . . . well . . . you see your son and your daughter-in-law came in just after you left . . .

MRS. WATTS. I know. I saw them coming. That's why I left so fast.

THELMA. Your son seemed very concerned.

MRS. WATTS. Bless his heart.

THELMA. He found a handkerchief that you had dropped.

MRS. WATTS. Oh, mercy. That's right, I did.

THELMA. He asked me if I had seen you. I felt I had to say yes. I wouldn't have said anything if he hadn't asked me.

MRS. WATTS. Oh, that's all right. I would have done the same thing in your place. Did you talk to Jessie Mae?

THELMA. Yes.

MRS. WATTS. Isn't she a sight? I bet she told you I was crazy . . .

THELMA. Well . . .

MRS. WATTS. Oh, don't be afraid of hurting my feelings. Poor Jessie Mae, she thinks everybody's crazy that don't want to sit in the beauty parlor all day and drink Coca-Colas. She tells me a million times a day I'm crazy. That's the only time Ludie will talk back to her. He gets real mad when she calls me crazy. I think Ludie knows how I feel about getting back to Bountiful. Once when I was talkin' about somethin' we did back there in the old days, he just broke out cryin'. He was so overcome he had to leave the room. *(A pause.* MRS. WATTS *starts to hum "There's Not a Friend Like the Lowly Jesus.")*

THELMA. That's a pretty hymn. What's the name of it?

MRS. WATTS. "There's Not a Friend Like the Lowly Jesus." Do you like hymns?

THELMA. Yes, I do.

MRS. WATTS. So do I. Jessie Mae says they've gone out of style . . . but I don't agree. I always sing one walking down the street or riding in the streetcar. Keeps my spirits up. What's your favorite hymn?

THELMA. Oh, I don't know.

MRS. WATTS. The one I was singin' is mine. I bet I sing it a hundred times a day. When Jessie Mae isn't home. Hymns make Jessie Mae nervous. *(A pause.)* Did Ludie mention my heart condition?

THELMA. Yes, he did.

MRS. WATTS. Poor Ludie. He worries about it so. I hated to leave him. Well, I hope he'll forgive me in time. So many people are nervous today. He wasn't nervous back in Bountiful. Neither was I. The breeze from the Gulf would always quiet your nerves. You could sit on your front gallery and smell the ocean blowing in around you. *(A pause.)* I regret the day I left. But I thought it was the best thing at the time. There were only three families left there then. Farming was so hard to make a living by, and I had to see to our farm myself; our house was old and there was no money to fix it with, nor send Ludie to school. So I sold off the land and gave him an education. Callie said I could always come back and visit her. She meant it, too. That's who I'm going to stay with now. Callie Davis. I get a card from her every Christmas. I wrote her last week and told her to expect me. Told her not to answer though on account of Jessie Mae opens all my mail. I didn't want her to know I was going. She'd try to stop me. Jessie Mae hates me. I don't know why, but she hates me. *(A pause.)* Hate me or not. I gotta get back and smell that salt air and work that dirt. I'm gonna spend the whole first month of my visit workin' in Callie's garden. I haven't had my hands in dirt in twenty years. My hands feel the need of dirt. *(A pause.)* Do you like to work the ground?

THELMA. I never have.

MRS. WATTS. Try it sometimes. It'll do wonders for you. I bet I'll live to be a hundred once I can get outside again. It was being cooped up in those two rooms that was killing me. I used to work the land like a man. Had to when Papa died . . . I got two little babies buried there. Renee Sue and Douglas. Diphtheria got Renee Sue. I never knew what carried Douglas away. He was just weak from the start. I know Callie's kept their graves weeded. Oh, if my heart just holds out until I get there. *(A pause.)* Where do you go from Harrison?

THELMA. Old Gulf. My family have just moved there from Louisiana. I'll stay there with them until my husband comes home again.

MRS. WATTS. That's nice.

THELMA. It'll be funny living at home again.

MRS. WATTS. How long have you been married?

THELMA. A year. My husband was anxious for me to go. He said he'd worry about my being alone. I'm the only child and my parents and I are very close.

MRS. WATTS. That's nice.

THELMA. My father being in the oil business we've always moved around a lot. I guess I went to school in fifteen different towns along the Coast. I guess moving around like that made me and my mother and father even closer. I hoped so my mother and daddy would like my husband and he'd like them. I needn't have worried. They hit it off from the very first. Mother and Daddy say they feel like they have two children now. A son and a daughter.

MRS. WATTS. Isn't that nice? I've heard people say that when your son marries you lose a son, but when your daughter marries you get a son. *(A pause.)* What's your husband's name?

THELMA. Robert.

MRS. WATTS. That's a nice name.

THELMA. I think so. But I guess any name he had I would think was nice. I love my husband very much. Lots of girls I know think I'm silly about him, but I can't help it. *(A pause.)*

MRS. WATTS. I wasn't in love with my husband. *(A pause.)* Do you believe we are punished for what we do wrong? I sometimes think that's why I've had all my trouble. I've talked to many a preacher about it, all but one said they didn't think so. But I can't see any other reason. Of course, I didn't lie to my husband. I told him I didn't love him, that I admired him, which I did, but I didn't love him. That I'd never love anybody but Ray John Murray as long as I lived and I didn't, and I couldn't help it. Even after my husband died and I had to move back with Mama and Papa I used to sit on the front gallery every morning and every evening just to nod hello to Ray John Murray as he went by the house to work at the store. He went a block out of his way to pass the house. He never loved nobody but me.

THELMA. Why didn't you marry him?

MRS. WATTS. His papa and my papa didn't speak. My papa forced me to write a letter saying I never wanted to see him again and he got drunk and married out of spite. I felt sorry for his wife. She knew he never loved her. *(A pause.)* I don't think about those things anymore. But they're all part of Bountiful and I guess that's why I'm starting to think of them again. You're lucky to be married to the man you love, honey.

THELMA. I know I am.

MRS. WATTS. Awfully lucky. *(A pause. She looks out the window.)* Did you see that star fall over there?

THELMA. No.

MRS. WATTS. It was the prettiest thing I ever saw. You can make a wish on a falling star, honey.

THELMA. I know. It's too bad I didn't see it.

MRS. WATTS. You take my wish.

THELMA. Oh, no.

MRS. WATTS. Go on. I've gotten mine already. I'm on my way to Bountiful.

THELMA. Thank you. *(A pause.* THELMA *closes her eyes.* MRS. WATTS *watches her for a moment.)*

MRS. WATTS. Did you make your wish?

THELMA. Yes, I did.

(MRS. WATTS *leans her head back on the seat. She hums to herself.* THELMA *leans her head back, too. They close their eyes. The lights fade. The lights on the area stage left are brought up. It is the Harrison bus station. An old man is inside the ticket window, with his head on the ledge, asleep. He wakes up. He comes out of the cage into the room, yawning and stretching. We hear a bus pull up in the distance and stop. He starts for the entrance of the bus station, as* THELMA *comes in carrying her suitcase and* MRS. WATTS' *suitcase.)*

TICKET MAN. Want any help with those bags?

THELMA. No, thank you. *(The* TICKET MAN *turns a light on in the station.* THELMA *takes the bags and puts them down beside a bench. She goes over to the* TICKET MAN.*)* Excuse me.

TICKET MAN. Yes?

THELMA. Is the bus to Old Gulf going to be on time?

TICKET MAN. Always is.

THELMA. Thank you. (THELMA *goes back to her seat near the suitcases.* MRS. WATTS *comes in. She sees the* TICKET MAN. *She speaks to him.*)

MRS. WATTS. Good evening. (*To* THELMA.) What time is it, honey?

THELMA. Twelve o'clock.

MRS. WATTS. Twelve o'clock. I bet Callie will be surprised to see me walk in at twelve o'clock.

THELMA. Did you tell her you were coming today?

MRS. WATTS. No. I couldn't. Because I didn't know. I had to wait until Jessie Mae went to the drugstore.

THELMA. My bus is leaving in half an hour.

MRS. WATTS. Oh, I see. I guess I'd better be finding out how I'm going to get on out to Bountiful.

THELMA. You sit down. I'll find the man.

MRS. WATTS. Thank you. (*She sits on the bench.* THELMA *goes over to the* TICKET MAN *at the door. He is busy bringing in morning papers left by the bus.*)

THELMA. Excuse me again.

TICKET MAN. Yes?

THELMA. My friend here wants to know how she can get to Bountiful.

TICKET MAN. Bountiful?

THELMA. Yes.

TICKET MAN. What's she going there for? (MRS. WATTS *comes up to the* TICKET MAN.)

MRS. WATTS. I'm going to visit my girlhood friend.

TICKET MAN. I don't know who that's gonna be. The last person in Bountiful was Mrs. Callie Davis. She died day before yesterday. That is they found her day before yesterday. She lived all alone so they don't know exactly when she died.

MRS. WATTS. Callie Davis!

TICKET MAN. Yes, Ma'm. They had the funeral this morning. Was she the one you were going to visit?

MRS. WATTS. Yessir. She was the one. She was my friend. My girlhood friend. (MRS. WATTS *stands for a moment. Then she goes to the bench. She seems very old and tired and defeated.* THELMA *crosses to the* TICKET MAN.)

THELMA. Is there a hotel here?

TICKET MAN. Yes'm. The Riverview.

THELMA. How far is it?

TICKET MAN. About five blocks.

THELMA. Is there a taxi around?

TICKET MAN. No, Ma'm. Not this time of night.

THELMA. Thank you. (*The* TICKET MAN *goes back into the ticket window.* THELMA *goes over to* MRS. WATTS *at the bench. She speaks to her with great sympathy.*) What'll you do now, Mrs. Watts?

MRS. WATTS. I'm thinking, honey. I'm thinking. It's come as quite a blow.

THELMA. I'm sorry. I'm so sorry.

MRS. WATTS. I know. I know. (*A pause. Her strength and her will reviving.*) It's come to me what to do. I'll go on. That much has come to me. To go on. I feel my strength and my purpose strong within me. I'll go on to Bountiful. I'll walk those twelve miles if I have to. *(She is standing now.)*

THELMA. But if there's no one out there what'll you do this time of night? *(THELMA gets her to sit back down.)*

MRS. WATTS. Oh, yes. I guess that's right.

THELMA. I think you should wait until morning.

MRS. WATTS. Yes. I guess I should. Then I can hire someone to drive me out. You know what I'll do. I'll stay at my own house, or what's left of it. Put me in a garden. I'll get along fine with the help of my government checks.

THELMA. Mrs. Watts, the man says there's a hotel not too far away. I think you'd better let me take you there.

MRS. WATTS. Oh, no thank you. I wouldn't want to waste my money on a hotel. They're high as cats' backs you know. I'll just sleep right here on this bench. Put my coat under my head, hold my purse under my arm. *(She puts the coat down on the bench like a pillow. She begins to look around for her purse. She has lost it.)* My purse! *(She begins to search frantically.)* Have you seen my purse, honey?

THELMA. Why, no. *(They begin to look around for it.)*

MRS. WATTS. Oh, good heavens. I remember now. I left my purse on the bus. *(THELMA runs to the entrance and looks out.)*

THELMA. You're sure you left it there?

MRS. WATTS. *(Joining her.)* Yes. I am. I remember now. I didn't have it when I got off that bus. I kept thinking something was missing, but then I decided it was my suitcase that you had brought in for me. What am I gonna do, honey? All I have in the world is in that purse. *(THELMA and MRS. WATTS go back to the ticket window. The TICKET MAN is drowsing.)*

THELMA. Excuse me again.

TICKET MAN. Yeah?

THELMA. This lady left her purse on the bus.

TICKET MAN. All right. I'll call ahead. How can you identify it?

MRS. WATTS. It's a plain brown purse.

TICKET MAN. How much money?

MRS. WATTS. Thirty-five cents and a pension check.

TICKET MAN. Who was the check made out to?

MRS. WATTS. To me. Mrs. Carrie Watts.

TICKET MAN. All right. I'll call up about it.

MRS. WATTS. Oh, thank you. You're most kind.

THELMA. How long will it take to get it back?

TICKET MAN. Depends. If I can get ahead of the bus at Don Tarle, I can get them to send it back on the Victoria bus and it should be here in a couple of hours.

MRS. WATTS. That's awful kind of you. *(He goes.* THELMA *and* MRS. WATTS *go back to the bench.)* I don't know what I would have done without you.

THELMA. Try not to worry about the purse.

MRS. WATTS. I won't. *(They sit on the bench.)* I'm too tired to worry. Be time enough to start worrying when I wake up in the morning.

THELMA. Why don't you go on to sleep now if you can?

MRS. WATTS. Oh, I thought I'd stay up and see you off.

THELMA. No. You go on to sleep.

MRS. WATTS. I couldn't go right off to sleep now. I'm too wound up. You know I don't go on a trip every day of my life. *(The* TICKET MAN *comes over to them on the bench.)*

TICKET MAN. You're lucky. Bus hadn't gotten to Don Tarle yet. If they can find the purse it'll be here around five.

MRS. WATTS. Thank you. Thank you so much.

THELMA. Make you feel better?

MRS. WATTS. Yes. It does. Of course, everything has seemed to work out today. Why is it some days everything works out, and some days nothing works out. What I mean is, I've been trying to get on that bus for Bountiful for over five years. Usually Jessie Mae and Ludie find me before I ever get inside the railroad station good. Today, I got inside both the railroad station and the bus station. Bought a ticket, seen Ludie and Jessie Mae before they saw me. Hid out. Met a pretty friend like you. Lost my purse, and now I'm having it found for me. I guess the good Lord is just with me today. *(A pause.)* I wonder why the Lord isn't with us every day? It would be so nice if He was. Well, maybe then we wouldn't appreciate so much the days when He's on our side. Or maybe He's always on our side and we don't know it. Maybe I had to wait twenty years cooped up in a city before I could appreciate getting back here. *(A pause.* THELMA *rests her head back on the bench.* MRS. WATTS *rests her head. She hums her hymn.)* It's so nice being able to sing a hymn when you want to. I'm a happy woman, young lady. A very happy woman.

THELMA. I still have a sandwich left. Will you have one?

MRS. WATTS. Sure you don't want it?

THELMA. No. I'm full.

MRS. WATTS. Then I'll have a half, thank you. *(*THELMA *gets the sandwich from her suitcase and unwraps it.)*

THELMA. Take the whole sandwich. I'm not hungry.

MRS. WATTS. No, thank you. Just half. You know I don't eat much. Particularly if I'm excited. *(She rises and stands nibbling on the sandwich and walking around the room.)* You know, I came to my first dance in this town.

THELMA. Did you?

MRS. WATTS. Yes, Ma'm. It was the summertime. My father couldn't decide if he thought dancin' was right or not. But my mother said she had danced when she was a girl and I was gonna dance. And so I went. The girls from all over the county came for this dance. It was at the Opera House. I forget what the occasion was. Somethin' special though. *(A pause. She looks at* THELMA. *She goes over to her.)* Do you know something, young lady? If my daughter had lived I would have wanted her to be just like you.

THELMA. Oh, thank you.

MRS. WATTS. *(With great tenderness.)* Just like you. Sweet and considerate and thoughtful.

THELMA. Oh, no . . . I'm . . .

MRS. WATTS. Oh, yes. Sweet and considerate and thoughtful. And pretty.

THELMA. Well, thank you. *(A pause.)* Mrs. Watts . . . I hope you don't mind my askin' this, but I worry about your son. Are you going to let him know where you are?

MRS. WATTS. Oh, yes, Ma'm. As soon as I get that check cashed I'm going to send him a telegram. *(The* TICKET MAN *comes by checking his watch as he passes.* MRS. WATTS *follows after him.)* I was tellin' my little friend here that I came to my first dance in this town.

TICKET MAN. Is that so?

MRS. WATTS. Yes. And I've been to Harrison quite a few times in my life, shopping.

TICKET MAN. *(To* THELMA.*)* You'd better get outside, Miss. Bus will be up the road. It won't wait this time of night unless it sees we have a passenger.

THELMA. All right. *(She gets her suitcase.)* Goodbye, Mrs. Watts.

MRS. WATTS. *(Following her to the door.)* Goodbye, honey. Good luck to you. And thank you for everything.

THELMA. That's all right. Good luck to you.

MRS. WATTS. Thank you.

> *(*THELMA *kisses her.* THELMA *goes out into the night, followed by the* TICKET MAN. MRS. WATTS *stands at the door watching* THELMA. *We hear a bus pulling up.* MRS. WATTS *waves. We hear the bus leave. The* TICKET MAN *comes back inside the bus station.)*

TICKET MAN. Are you gonna stay here all night?

MRS. WATTS. I have to. Everything I have is in that purse and we can't go anyplace without money.

TICKET MAN. I guess that's right. *(He starts away.)*

MRS. WATTS. Do they still have dances in Borden's Opera House?

TICKET MAN. No, Ma'm. It's torn down. They condemned it, you know. *(He starts on. He pauses.)* Did you ever know anybody in Harrison?

MRS. WATTS. I knew a few people when I was a girl. Priscilla Nytelle. Did you know her?

TICKET MAN. No, Ma'm.

MRS. WATTS. Nancy Lee Goodhue?

TICKET MAN. No, Ma'm.

MRS. WATTS. The Fay girls?

TICKET MAN. No, Ma'm.

MRS. WATTS. I used to trade in Mr. Ewing's store. I knew him to speak to.

TICKET MAN. Which Ewing was that?

MRS. WATTS. George White Ewing.

TICKET MAN. He's dead.

MRS. WATTS. Is that so?

TICKET MAN. Been dead for twelve years.

MRS. WATTS. Is that so?

TICKET MAN. He left quite a bit of money, but his son took over his store and lost it all. Drank.

MRS. WATTS. Is that so? One thing I can say about my boy is that he never gave me any worry that way.

TICKET MAN. Well, that's good. I've got one boy that drinks and one boy that doesn't. I can't understand it. I raised them the same way.

MRS. WATTS. I know. I've known of other cases like that. One drinks. The other doesn't.

TICKET MAN. A friend of mine has a girl that drinks. I think that's the saddest thing in the world.

MRS. WATTS. Isn't it? *(A pause.)*

TICKET MAN. Well. Good night.

MRS. WATTS. Good night. *(The* TICKET MAN *stands waiting to switch off the light while* MRS. WATTS *takes her suitcase and coat and makes a bed for herself on the bench. She lies down. He goes inside the ticket booth. He sticks his head out the cage.)*

TICKET MAN. Good night.

MRS. WATTS. Good night.

> *(He turns the light inside the ticket window out.* MRS. WATTS *is humming quietly to herself. Her humming fades away as the lights are faded out. The lights are brought up. The* TICKET MAN *is in his office sound asleep and snoring slightly. The door opens and a man comes in. He is the* SHERIFF. *He stands by the door for a moment looking around the bus station. He sees* MRS. WATTS *lying on the bench asleep. He goes over to her and looks down. He stands for a moment watching her sleep. He looks over at the ticket window and sees the man is asleep. The* SHERIFF *goes over to the* TICKET MAN. *He shakes him.)*

SHERIFF. Come on, Roy, wake up.

TICKET MAN. Yeah? *(He opens his eyes. He sees the* SHERIFF. *He comes out to the* SHERIFF.*)* Oh, hello, Sheriff.

SHERIFF. How long has that old woman been here?

TICKET MAN. About four hours.

SHERIFF. Did she get off the bus from Houston?

TICKET MAN. Yessir. I know her name. It's Watts. She left her purse on the bus and I had to call up to Don Tarle about it.

SHERIFF. Have you got her purse?

TICKET MAN. Yes. It just came.

SHERIFF. She's the one, all right. I've had a call from the Houston police to hold her until her son can come for her.

TICKET MAN. She said she used to live in Bountiful.

SHERIFF. Yeah. I believe I remember some Wattses a long time ago over that way. I think that old ramshackly house about to fall into the Brazos River belonged to them.

TICKET MAN. That right? They must have been before my time. She asked me about a lot of people I never heard of. She claimed she was going to visit Miss Callie Davis. I told her she was dead. What do the police want her for?

SHERIFF. Police don't. It's her son. He wants to take her back home. Claims she's not responsible. Did she act crazy to you?

TICKET MAN. Not that I noticed. Is she crazy?

SHERIFF. They say so. Harmless, but hipped on running away from Houston to get back here. *(He starts over to her to wake her up. He stands looking at her for a moment. He comes back to the* TICKET MAN.*)* Poor old thing. She's sleeping so sound. I don't have the heart to wake her up. I'll tell you what, I'll go down and call Houston . . . tell them she's here. Her son is coming in his car. He should be here around seven-thirty. I'll be back in ten minutes. If she gives you any trouble just call me. Keep your eye on her.

TICKET MAN. All right. *(The* SHERIFF *goes out and the* TICKET MAN *follows him. He comes back in carrying a crate and bumps it accidentally against the door. This makes* MRS. WATTS *up. She opens her eyes. She looks around trying to remember where she is. Then she sees the* TICKET MAN.*)*

MRS. WATTS. Good morning.

TICKET MAN. Good morning.

MRS. WATTS. Could you tell me the time?

TICKET MAN. It's around four-thirty.

MRS. WATTS. Thank you. Did my purse arrive?

TICKET MAN. Yes, Ma'm. *(He reaches under the ticket window to a ledge and gets the purse for her. He hands the purse to her.)*

MRS. WATTS. Thank you so much. I wonder if you could cash a check for me?

TICKET MAN. I'm sorry. I can't.

MRS. WATTS. It's a government check and I have identification.

TICKET MAN. I'm sorry. I can't.

MRS. WATTS. Do you know where I could get a check cashed?

TICKET MAN. Why? *(She starts to gather up her coat and suitcase.)*

MRS. WATTS. I need money to get me started in Bountiful. I want to hire someone to drive me out there and look at my house and get a few groceries. Try to find a cot to sleep on. *(She has the coat and suitcase.)*

TICKET MAN. I'm sorry, lady. You're not going to Bountiful.

MRS. WATTS. Oh, yes, I am. You see . . .

TICKET MAN. I'm sorry, lady. You're not going anyplace right now. I have to hold you here for the sheriff.

MRS. WATTS. The sheriff?

TICKET MAN. Yes, Ma'm. *(A pause.)*

MRS. WATTS. You're joking with me!? Don't joke with me. I've come too far.

TICKET MAN. I'm sorry. That's how it is.

MRS. WATTS. What has the sheriff got to do with me?

TICKET MAN. He came a few minutes ago while you were asleep and said I was to keep you here until your son arrived in his car this morning.

MRS. WATTS. My son hasn't got a car, so I don't believe you. I don't believe you.

TICKET MAN. It's the truth. He'll be here in a little while, and you can ask him yourself. *(A pause.)*

MRS. WATTS. Then you're not joking?

TICKET MAN. No. *(She takes her coat and suitcase and runs for the entrance. He senses what she is going to do and gets there first—blocking her way.)*

MRS. WATTS. All right. But I'm going, do you understand? You'll see. This is a free country. And I'll tell him that. No sheriff or king or president will keep me from going back to Bountiful.

TICKET MAN. All right. You tell him that. *(She comes back into the room. She is desperate.)*

MRS. WATTS. What time is my son expected?

TICKET MAN. Sheriff says around seven-thirty.

MRS. WATTS. What time is it now?

TICKET MAN. I told you around four-thirty.

MRS. WATTS. Where can I get me a driver?

TICKET MAN. Ma'm?

MRS. WATTS. If you can get me a driver, I can make it to Bountiful and back way before seven-thirty . . .

TICKET MAN. Look, lady . . .

MRS. WATTS. That's all I want. That's all I ask. Just to see it. To stand on the porch of my own house, once more. Walk under the trees. I swear, I would come back then meek as a lamb . . .

TICKET MAN. Lady . . .

MRS. WATTS. Last night, I thought I had to stay. I thought I'd die if I couldn't stay. But I'll settle for less now. Much, much less. An hour. A half hour. Fifteen minutes.

TICKET MAN. Lady, it ain't up to me. I told you the sheriff.

MRS. WATTS. *(Screaming.)* Then get me the sheriff.

TICKET MAN. Look, lady . . .

MRS. WATTS. Get me the sheriff. The time is going. They'll have me locked in those two rooms again soon. The time is going . . . the time is . . .

*(The SHERIFF comes in. The SHERIFF goes over to MRS. WATTS.)*

SHERIFF. Mrs. Watts?

MRS. WATTS. Yessir. *(She looks up at him. She puts the coat and suitcase down.)* Are you the sheriff?

SHERIFF. Yes, Ma'm.

MRS. WATTS. I understand my son will be here at seven-thirty to take me back to Houston.

SHERIFF. Yes, Ma'm.

MRS. WATTS. Then listen to me, sir. I've waited a long time. Just to get to Bountiful. Twenty years I've been walkin' the streets of the city, lost and grieving. And as I've grown older and my time approaches, I've made one promise to myself, to see my home again . . . before I die . . .

SHERIFF. Lady . . . I . . .

MRS. WATTS. I'm not asking that I not go back. I'm willing to go back. Only let me travel these twelve miles first. I have money. I can pay . . .

SHERIFF. I think that's between you and your son.

MRS. WATTS. Ludie? Why, he's got to do whatever Jessie Mae tells him to. I know why she wants me back. It's for my government check.

SHERIFF. I don't know anything about that. That's between you and your son.

MRS. WATTS. Won't you let me go?

SHERIFF. No. Not unless your son takes you.

MRS. WATTS. All right. Then I've lost. I've come all this way only to lose. *(A pause. She stands behind the bench supporting herself. She seems very tired and defeated. She speaks very quietly and almost to herself.)* I've kept thinking back there day and night in those two rooms, I kept thinkin' . . . and it may mean nothin' at all to you, but I kept thinkin' . . . that if I could just set foot there for a minute . . . even . . . a second . . . I might get some understanding of why . . . Why my life has grown so empty and meaningless. Why I've turned into a hateful, quarrelsome old woman. And before I leave this earth, I'd like to recover some of the dignity . . . the peace I used to know. For I'm going to die . . . and Jessie Mae knows that . . . and she's willful and it's her will I die in those two rooms. Well, she won't have her way. It's my will to die in Bountiful. *(She sobs and starts to run out of the bus station. The SHERIFF stops her. She suddenly seems very weak, and is about to fall. He has her arm, supporting her.)*

SHERIFF. Mrs. Watts.

MRS. WATTS. Let me go those twelve miles . . . before it's too late. *(A pause. For a moment her strength seems to come back.)* Understand me. Suffering I don't mind. Suffering I understand. I never protested once. Though my heart was broken when those babies died. I could stand seeing the man I love walk through life with another woman. But this fifteen years of bickering. Endless, petty bickering . . . It's made me like Jessie Mae sees me. It's ugly. I won't be that way. *(An anguished cry.)* I want to go home. I want to go home. I want to go . . . *(She is unable to speak any more. She is on the verge of collapse. The SHERIFF helps her over to the bench and settles her there. The SHERIFF calls to the TICKET MAN.)*

SHERIFF. Roy, hurry. Call a doctor. *(She summons up her last bit of strength to get free.)*

MRS. WATTS. No. No doctor. Bountiful . . . Bountiful . . . Bountiful. *(The SHERIFF holds her. There is a very fast CURTAIN.)*

# ★ ACT III

*It is early morning. The lights are slowly brought up and we can see the house and the
yard of* MRS. WATTS' *old house in Bountiful. The house, with a sagging porch
before it, is stage right. The entrance to the yard is upstage center.*

*The house is an old, ramshackle two-story country place that hasn't been painted
for years. Vines are growing wild over it, coralvine and Virginia creeper and fig vine.
The roof of the front porch is sagging and one of the supporting posts is completely
gone. The floorboards of the front porch are rotting away and the steps leading to the
porch are loose. The yard has gone to weeds, and wildflowers are everywhere: butter-
cups, dandelions, and wild iris. In the early morning light there is a peace and tranquility and a wild kind of beauty about the place that is moving and heartwarming
and in its own way lovely.*

*The* SHERIFF *and* MRS. WATTS *come in upstage center walking very slowly.
They stop every few minutes while she looks at the house and the yard.* MRS.
WATTS *is carrying her purse.*

MRS. WATTS. I'm home. I'm home. I'm home. Thank you. I thank you. I thank
you. I thank you. *(They pause for a moment in the yard.* MRS. WATTS *is obviously
still quite weak.)*

SHERIFF. You'd better sit down and rest for a while. You don't want to overdo it.

MRS. WATTS. Yessir. *(She sits on a tree stump in the yard.)*

SHERIFF. Feeling all right?

MRS. WATTS. Yes, I am. I feel ever so much better.

SHERIFF. You look better. I hope I've done the right thing in bringing you here.
Well, I don't see what harm it can do. As long as you mind the doctor and don't
get overexcited.

MRS. WATTS. Yessir. *(A pause. She looks around the yard again.)*

SHERIFF. Soon as you've rested for a little I'll go on back to my car and leave you
alone. You can call me if you need anything. I'll stay out here until your son
arrives.

MRS. WATTS. Thank you. You've been very kind. *(A bird calls. She and the*
SHERIFF *sit listening to it. It whistles once again.)* What kind of a bird was that?

SHERIFF. Redbird.

MRS. WATTS. I thought that was a redbird, but I hadn't heard one in so long, I
couldn't be sure. *(A pause.)* Do they still have scissortails around here?

SHERIFF. Yes, Ma'm. I still see one every once in a while when I'm driving around
the country.

MRS. WATTS. I don't know of anything prettier than a scissortail flying around in
the sky. *(A pause.)* My father was a good man in many ways, a peculiar man, but a
good one. One of the things he couldn't stand was to see a bird shot on his land.
If men came here hunting, he'd take a gun and chase them away. I think the birds

knew they couldn't be touched here. Our land was always a home to them. Ducks and geese and finches and blue jays. Bluebirds and redbirds. Wild canaries and blackbirds and mockers and doves and ricebirds . . . *(During the latter speech she gets up and begins to pick weeds out of the yard. At the end of the speech the* SHERIFF *gently stops her and leads her to the porch of the house. She sits on a step.)*

SHERIFF. Ricebirds are gettin' thicker every year. They seem to thrive out here on the coast.

MRS. WATTS. I guess a mockin'bird is my favorite of them all.

SHERIFF. I guess it's mine, too.

MRS. WATTS. I don't know, though. I'm mighty partial to a scissortail. I hope I get to see one soon.

SHERIFF. I hope you can.

MRS. WATTS. My father was born on this land and in this house. Did you know my father?

SHERIFF. No, Ma'm. Not that I can remember.

MRS. WATTS. I guess there are not many around here that remember my father. I do, of course, and my son. Maybe some old-timers around Harrison. *(A pause.)* It's funny, ever since I've been here I've been half expectin' my father and my mother to walk out of the house and greet me and welcome me home. *(A pause.)* When you've lived longer than your house or your family, maybe you've lived too long. *(A pause.)* Or maybe it's just me. Maybe the need to belong to a house and a family and a town has gone from the rest of the world.

SHERIFF. How big was your farm, Mrs. Watts?

MRS. WATTS. Three hundred and seventy-five acres were left when my papa died and I sold off all but the house and the yard. *(A pause.)* You say the store burned fifteen years ago?

SHERIFF. Yes, Ma'm. What was left of it. You see with the good roads we have now in the county, the little towns and their country stores are all disappearing. The farmers ride into Cotton or Harrison to trade . . .

MRS. WATTS. But what's happened to the farms? For the last five miles I've seen nothing but woods . . .

SHERIFF. I know. The land around Bountiful just played out. People like you got discouraged and moved away, sold off the land for what they could get. H. T. Mavis bought most of it up. He let it go back into timber. He keeps a few head of cattle out here. That's about all . . .

MRS. WATTS. Callie Davis kept her farm going.

SHERIFF. Yes. She did. She learned how to treat her land right and it began paying off for her toward the end. I've heard she was out riding her tractor the day before she died. Lonely death she had. All by herself in that big house.

MRS. WATTS. There are worse things. *(The sun is up full now, filling the stage with light.)*

SHERIFF. Looks to me like you're going to have a pretty day.

MRS. WATTS. I hope so. My daughter-in-law has never seen our place in the sunshine. I expect my son will bring her along with him. I'd hate for her to have to see it again in the rain. *(A pause. The* SHERIFF *looks at her.)*

SHERIFF. Feeling more rested now?

MRS. WATTS. Oh, yes, I am.

SHERIFF. Good. Then I'll be getting on back to my car. You just call me if you need anything.

MRS. WATTS. Thank you.

*(He gets up and walks to the corner of the yard. Just before he goes out he turns and waves.* MRS. WATTS *waves back to him. She sits on the steps for a moment watching him go out. When he is out of sight, she rises slowly from the steps and goes along the porch. When she comes to the front door she stops and stands for a moment. She slowly opens the door and goes inside the house as the lights fade. The lights are slowly brought up. The* SHERIFF *comes into the yard. He goes up to the steps of the porch.)*

SHERIFF. *(Calling.)* Mrs. Watts. Mrs. Watts. Mrs. Watts. *(He runs up on the porch as he calls her.* MRS. WATTS *comes out of the house. She has left her purse inside the house.)*

MRS. WATTS. Yessir.

SHERIFF. It's seven-thirty. Your son and his wife are here.

MRS. WATTS. Yessir.

SHERIFF. They're out on the road in their car. They said they had to hurry on back. I told them I'd come get you.

MRS. WATTS. Yessir. Won't you ask them to please come in for a minute?

SHERIFF. Well, all right. I'll have to be gettin' on back to town now myself, Mrs. Watts. *(He holds his hand out. She takes it.)* Good-bye, and good luck to you.

MRS. WATTS. Thank you. You'll never know what this has meant to me.

SHERIFF. Glad I could oblige. *(He starts away as* LUDIE *comes into the yard.)* Oh, Mr. Watts. I was just coming to tell you your mother wanted you to come in for a few minutes.

LUDIE. Thank you. *(The* SHERIFF *goes up to him.)*

SHERIFF. I've got to be getting back on into town.

LUDIE. All right, Sheriff. Thank you for everything you've done.

SHERIFF. Don't mention it. I was glad I could oblige. You folks have a nice trip home.

LUDIE. Thank you.

SHERIFF. Good-bye, Mrs. Watts.

MRS. WATTS. Good-bye, Sheriff.

SHERIFF. So long, Mr. Watts.

LUDIE. Good-bye, Sheriff. *(He goes out.* MRS. WATTS *and* LUDIE *watch him go.* LUDIE *walks up on the porch to his mother. They both seem embarrassed and ill at ease.)* Hello, Mama.

MRS. WATTS. Hello, son.

LUDIE. How do you feel?

MRS. WATTS. I'm feelin' better, Ludie.

LUDIE. That's good. They told me at the bus station you had another attack.

MRS. WATTS. Yes, I did. All the excitement, I guess. But I feel fine now.

LUDIE. Yes'm.

MRS. WATTS. I got my wish.

LUDIE. Yes'm. *(LUDIE walks away from the porch down to the corner of the yard.* MRS. WATTS *follows him.)*

MRS. WATTS. I hope I didn't worry you too much, Ludie. But I just felt I had to . . .

LUDIE. I know, Mama.

MRS. WATTS. You see, son, I know it's hard for you to understand and Jessie Mae . . . understand—But . . .

LUDIE. Yes, Ma'm. I understand, Mama. It's done now. So let's forget about it.

MRS. WATTS. All right, Sonny. *(A pause.)* You did bring Jessie Mae, didn't you?

LUDIE. Yes, Ma'm.

MRS. WATTS. Well, now she's here isn't she going to get out of the car and look around a little?

LUDIE. She didn't seem to want to, Mama.

MRS. WATTS. You asked her?

LUDIE. Yes, Ma'm. *(A pause.)*

MRS. WATTS. Did you ask about your raise, son?

LUDIE. Yes, Ma'm, and Mr. Douglas told me he liked my work and he'd be glad to recommend a raise for me.

MRS. WATTS. Oh. *(A pause.)* The sky's so blue, Ludie. Did you ever see the sky so blue?

LUDIE. No, Ma'm. *(A pause.)*

MRS. WATTS. Callie Davis died.

LUDIE. Is that so? When did that happen?

MRS. WATTS. They don't rightly know. They found her dead. She'd been ridin' a tractor the day before they found her. Buried her yesterday. *(A pause.)*

LUDIE. Mama, I should have made myself bring you here before. I'm sorry but I thought it would be easier for both of us not to see the house again.

MRS. WATTS. I know, Ludie. *(A pause.)* Now you're here, wouldn't you like to come inside, son, and look around?

LUDIE. I don't think I'd better, Mama. I don't see any use in it. It would just make me feel bad. I'd rather remember it like it was. *(A pause.* MRS. WATTS *looks at the house. She smiles.)*

MRS. WATTS. The old house has gotten kind of run down, hasn't it?

LUDIE. Yes, it has. *(She starts back toward the house slowly.)*

MRS. WATTS. I don't think it'll last out the next Gulf storm.

LUDIE. It doesn't look like it would. *(She turns and looks at him standing in the yard.)*

MRS. WATTS. You know who you look like standing there, Ludie?

LUDIE. Who?

MRS. WATTS. My papa.

LUDIE. Do I?

MRS. WATTS. Just like him. Of course, I've been noticing as you grow older you look more and more like him. My papa was a good-looking man.

LUDIE. Was he?

MRS. WATTS. You've seen his pictures. Didn't you think so?

LUDIE. I don't remember. It's been so long since I looked at his picture.

MRS. WATTS. Well, he was always considered a very nice-looking man. *(A pause.)* Do you remember my papa at all, son? *(*MRS. WATTS *sits on the steps of the porch.)*

LUDIE. No, Ma'm. Not too well. I was only ten when he died, Mama. I remember the day he died. I heard about it as I was coming home from school. Lee Weems told me. I thought he was joking and I called him a liar. I remember you takin' me into the front room there the day of the funeral to say good-bye to him. I remember the coffin and the people sitting in the room. Old man Joe Weems took me up on his knee and told me that Grandpapa was his best friend and that his life was a real example for me to follow. I remember Grandmama sitting by the coffin crying and she made me promise that when I had a son of my own I'd name it after Grandpapa. I would have, too. I've never forgotten that promise. *(A pause.)* Well, I didn't have a son. Or a daughter. *(A pause.)* Billy Davidson told me his wife is expecting her fourth child. They have two girls and a boy, now. Billy Davidson doesn't make much more than I do and they certainly seem to get along. Own their own home and have a car. It does your heart good to hear them tell about how they all get along. Everybody has their job, even the youngest child. She's only three. She puts the napkins around the table at mealtimes. That's her job. Billy said to me, Ludie, I don't know how I'd keep going without my kids. He said, I don't understand what keeps you going, Ludie. What you work for. I said, Well, Billy . . . Oh, Mama, I haven't made any kind of life for you, either one of you and I try so hard. I try so hard. *(He crosses to her.)* Oh, Mama. I lied to you. I do remember. I remember so much. This house. The life here. The night you woke me up and dressed me and took me for a walk when there was a full moon and I cried because I was afraid and you comforted me. *(He turns abruptly away from his mother and walks to the downstage corner of the porch.)* Mama, I want to stop remembering . . . It doesn't do any good to remember. *(A car horn is heard in the distance—loud and impatient. He looks in the direction of the horn.)* That's Jessie Mae.

MRS. WATTS. Whose car did you come in? *(He crosses to her.)*

LUDIE. I borrowed Billy Davidson's car. He didn't want me to have it at first. You know people are funny about lending their car, but then I explained what happened and he was nice about it. *(The car horn is heard again.)* We have to start back now, Mama. Jessie Mae is nervous that I might lose my job.

MRS. WATTS. *(Frantically trying to find an excuse not to leave.)* Didn't you ask for the day off?

LUDIE. No, Ma'm. I only asked for the morning off.

MRS. WATTS. What time is it now?

LUDIE. Must be after eight. We were a little late getting here.

MRS. WATTS. We can drive it in three hours, can't we, Ludie?

LUDIE. Yes, Ma'm, but we might have a flat or run into traffic or something. Besides, I promised Billy I'd get his car back to him by twelve.

MRS. WATTS. Son, why am I going back at all? Why can't I stay?

LUDIE. Mama, you can't stay. You know that. Now come on. *(He takes her by the arm. She starts to get up from the steps. When she is about halfway up she collapses, crying. She cries passionately, openly, bitterly.)*

MRS. WATTS. Ludie. Ludie. What's happened to us? Why have we come to this?

LUDIE. I don't know, Mama.

MRS. WATTS. To have stayed and fought the land would have been better than this.

LUDIE. Yes'm. *(She gets up.)*

MRS. WATTS. Pretty soon it'll all be gone. Ten years . . . twenty . . . this house . . . me . . . you . . .

LUDIE. I know, Mama. *(A pause. She looks into his suffering face. She looks around. She speaks with great tenderness.)*

MRS. WATTS. But the river will be here. The fields. The woods. The smell of the Gulf. That's what I always took my strength from, Ludie. Not from houses, not from people. *(A pause.)* It's so quiet. It's so eternally quiet. I had forgotten the peace. The quiet. And it's given me strength once more, Ludie. To go on and do what I have to do. I've found my dignity and my strength.

LUDIE. I'm glad, Mama.

MRS. WATTS. And I'll never fight with Jessie Mae again or complain. *(She points out into the distance.)* Do you remember how my papa always had that field over there planted in cotton?

LUDIE. Yes, Ma'm.

MRS. WATTS. See, it's all woods now. But I expect someday people will come again and cut down the trees and plant the cotton and maybe even wear out the land again and then their children will sell it and go to the cities and then the trees will come up again.

LUDIE. I expect so, Mama.

MRS. WATTS. We're part of all this. We left it, but we can never lose what it has given us.

LUDIE. I expect so, Mama.

> *(He takes her by the arm and they start walking out.* JESSIE MAE *comes into the yard.)*

JESSIE MAE. Ludie. Are you coming or not?

LUDIE. We were just startin', Jessie Mae.

MRS. WATTS. Hello, Jessie Mae.

JESSIE MAE. I'm not speakin' to you. I guess you're proud of the time you gave us. Dragging us all the way out here this time of the mornin'. If Ludie loses his job over this, I hope you're satisfied.

LUDIE. I'm not goin' to lose my job, Jessie Mae.

JESSIE MAE. Well, you could.

LUDIE. All right, Jessie Mae.

JESSIE MAE. And she should realize that. She's selfish. That's her trouble. Always has been. Just puredee selfish. Did you tell your Mama what we were discussing in the car?

LUDIE. No. We can talk it all over driving back to Houston.

JESSIE MAE. I think we should have it all out right here. I'd like everything understood right now. *(JESSIE MAE opens her purse and takes out a piece of paper.)* I've gotten everything written down. Do you want to read it or do you want me to read it to you, Mother Watts?

MRS. WATTS. What is it, Jessie Mae?

JESSIE MAE. It's a few rules and regulations that are necessary to my peace of mind. And I think to Ludie's. Ludie says you may have a few of your own to add and that may be and I'm perfectly willin' to listen if you do . . . First of all, I'd like to ask you a question.

MRS. WATTS. Yes, Ma'm. *(MRS. WATTS sits on the steps.)*

JESSIE MAE. Just what possessed you to run away? Didn't you know you'd be caught and have to come back?

MRS. WATTS. I had to come, Jessie Mae. Twenty years is a long time.

JESSIE MAE. But what if you had died from the excitement! Didn't you know you could have died?

MRS. WATTS. I knew.

JESSIE MAE. And you didn't care?

MRS. WATTS. *(With great dignity.)* I had to come, Jessie Mae.

JESSIE MAE. Well, I hope it's out of your system now.

MRS. WATTS. It is. I've had my trip. That's more than enough to keep me happy the rest of my life.

JESSIE MAE. Well, I'm glad to hear it. That's the first thing on my list. *(She reads from list.)* Number one. There'll be no more running away.

MRS. WATTS. There'll be no more running away.

JESSIE MAE. Good. *(She takes the list up again.)* Number two. No more hymn singing, when I'm in the apartment. When I'm gone you can sing your lungs out. Agreed?

MRS. WATTS. Agreed.

JESSIE MAE. Number three.

LUDIE. *(Interrupting.)* Jessie Mae, can't this wait till we get home?

JESSIE MAE. Now, honey, we agreed that I'm going to handle this! *(She goes back to the list.)* No more pouting. When I ask a question, I'd like an answer. Otherwise I'll consider it's pouting.

MRS. WATTS. All right.

JESSIE MAE. Fourth. With the condition that your heart is in I feel you should not run around the apartment when you can walk.

MRS. WATTS. All right, Jessie Mae.

JESSIE MAE. That's all. Is there anything you want to say to me?

MRS. WATTS. No, Jessie Mae.

JESSIE MAE. I might as well tell you now I'm not staying in the house and watching over you anymore. I am joinin' a bridge club and going to town at least twice a week. If you go now, it'll just be your funeral. You understand?

MRS. WATTS. I understand.

JESSIE MAE. All right. *(She puts the list away.)*

LUDIE. And, Mama, we also agreed that we're all gonna try our best to get along together. Jessie Mae also realizes that she gets upset sometimes when she shouldn't. Don't you, Jessie Mae?

JESSIE MAE. Uh-huh.

LUDIE. So let's start by trying to have a pleasant ride home.

JESSIE MAE. Allrightie. *(She takes a cigarette and the lighter from her purse. The lighter works and she lights her cigarette. She crosses down to the far edge of the house.)* Is there any water around here? I'm thirsty.

LUDIE. I don't think so, Jessie Mae. Mama, is there any water around here?

MRS. WATTS. No. The cistern is gone. *(JESSIE MAE notices a scratch on her shoes. She is furious.)*

JESSIE MAE. Look at my shoes! I've got scratches on them. They're my good pair. I ought to have my head examined for wearing my only good pair of shoes out here in this old swamp.

LUDIE. *(Looking out in the distance.)* When I was a boy I used to drink in the creek over there, Jessie Mae. We had a cistern, but I always preferred to drink out of the creek. It seemed to me the water always tasted so much better. *(JESSIE MAE crosses over to the far end of the stage looking out at the creek in the distance.)*

JESSIE MAE. Well, you wouldn't catch me drinking out of any creek. I knew a man once that went on a huntin' trip and drank out of a creek and caught something and died.

MRS. WATTS. There's nothin' like cistern water for washin' your hair with. It is the softest water in the world. *(A bird calls in the distance.)* That's a redbird.

JESSIE MAE. A what?

MRS. WATTS. A redbird.

JESSIE MAE. Oh. I thought you said that. They all sound alike to me. Well, come on. Let's get going. Do we go back by the way of Harrison?

LUDIE. Yes.

JESSIE MAE. Good. Then we can stop at the drugstore. I'm so thirsty I could drink ten Coca-Colas. Are you all ready?

MRS. WATTS. Yes'm. *(They start out. JESSIE MAE looks at her.)*

JESSIE MAE. Where's your purse?

MRS. WATTS. Are you talkin' to me, Jessie Mae?

JESSIE MAE. Who else would I be talkin' to? Since when did Ludie start walkin' around with a pocketbook under his arm? *(MRS. WATTS looks around.)*

MRS. WATTS. Oh, I guess I left it inside.

JESSIE MAE. Where? *(She starts toward the door of the house.)*

MRS. WATTS. I'll get it. *(She turns to go into the house.)*

JESSIE MAE. No. I want to go. You'll take all day. Where did you leave it?

MRS. WATTS. In the parlour. Right off the front hall.

JESSIE MAE. All right. I'll get it. You wait here. *(She starts into the house. She turns and sees them walking off.)* I said wait here now. I don't want to be left alone in this ramshackly old house. No telling what's running around in there.

MRS. WATTS. There's nothing in there.

JESSIE MAE. There might be rats or snakes or something.

LUDIE. I'll go.

JESSIE MAE. No. I'll go. Just stay here so if I holler you can come. *(She goes inside the house.* LUDIE *turns to his mother.)*

LUDIE. Mama.

MRS. WATTS. It's all right, Ludie, son. *(JESSIE MAE comes back out with the purse.)*

JESSIE MAE. Here's your purse. Now where's the money for that government check?

MRS. WATTS. I haven't cashed it.

JESSIE MAE. Where is it?

MRS. WATTS. It's right inside the purse. *(JESSIE MAE opens the purse and begins to search again.)*

JESSIE MAE. No. It isn't.

MRS. WATTS. Here. Let me look. *(JESSIE MAE hands her the purse and MRS. WATTS, too, begins to rummage around. All of a sudden she bursts out laughing.)*

JESSIE MAE. What's the matter with you?

MRS. WATTS. That's a good joke on me.

JESSIE MAE. Well, what's so funny?

MRS. WATTS. I just remembered. I left this purse on the bus last night and caused a man a lot of trouble because I thought the check was in there. *(She is overcome by laughter again.)* And do you know that check wasn't in that purse all that time?

JESSIE MAE. Where was it?

MRS. WATTS. Right here. *(She reaches inside her dress and takes it out.)* Been here since yesterday afternoon. *(JESSIE MAE reaches for the check.)*

JESSIE MAE. Give it to me before you go and lose it again.

MRS. WATTS. I won't lose it.

JESSIE MAE. Now don't start that business again. Just give it to me.

LUDIE. *(Interrupting angrily.)* Jessie Mae.

JESSIE MAE. Well, I'm not going to—

LUDIE. *(With great positiveness).* We're going to stop this wrangling once and for all. You've given me your word and I expect you to keep your word. We have to live together and we're going to live together in peace.

MRS. WATTS. It's all right, Ludie. *(She gives the check to JESSIE MAE.)* Let Jessie Mae take care of the check. *(JESSIE MAE accepts the check. She looks at it for a moment and then grabs MRS. WATTS' purse. She opens it and puts the check inside.)*

JESSIE MAE. Oh, here. You keep the check. But don't go and lose it before you get home. *(She puts the purse back in MRS. WATTS' hand. She starts offstage.)* Well, come on. Let's go. *(She leaves. LUDIE goes to his mother.)*

LUDIE. Mama, if I get the raise you won't—

MRS. WATTS. It's all right, Ludie. I've had my trip. You go ahead. I'll be right there. *(LUDIE starts out. MRS. WATTS points up in the sky.)* Look, isn't that a scissortail?

LUDIE. I don't know. I didn't get to see it if it was. They fly so fast. *(LUDIE takes one last look at the house.)* The house used to look so big.

*(He goes out. MRS. WATTS stands for a moment looking into the sky. Then she*

*drops gently onto her knees, puts her hands in the dirt. She kneels for a moment holding the dirt, then slowly lets it drift through her fingers back to the ground. She begins to walk slowly out until she gets to the corner of the yard. She pauses for a moment, taking one last look at the house, speaks quietly.)*

MRS. WATTS. Good-bye, Bountiful, good-bye. *(Then she turns and walks off the stage.)*

*Curtain*

# Oliver Hailey

★ ★ ★ ★ ★ ★ ★ ★ ★ ★ ★ ★ ★ ★ ★ ★

★   THE PERSON

Born in Pampa, Texas, in 1932, Oliver Hailey grew up in both West Texas and East Texas, childhoods that he has drawn upon for dramatic subject matter. He attended the University of Texas, where he took his B.F.A., and the Yale School of Drama, where he took his M.F.A. In between, he worked as a reporter for the *Dallas Morning News* and while there met and married his wife and fellow author, Elizabeth Forsythe Hailey (*A Woman of Independent Means* and *Joanna's Husband and David's Wife*). Recently his teen-aged daughter, Kendall, brought out her own book, *The Day I Became an Autodidact and the Advice, Adventures, and Acrimonies That Befell Me Thereafter.*

Although Hailey has family and professional ties in Texas, he is not primarily a Texas playwright by residence or subject. He currently lives in Los Angeles, where he, Michael Cristofer, and Ted Tally have been said to make up the Mark Taper Forum's family of playwrights. The settings of Hailey's plays are diverse: *Father's Day, Hey You, Light Man!* and *Continental Divide,* for example, take place in New York, while *I Won't Dance* occurs in Los Angeles. His reputation is as wide-ranging as the locales of his plays and their productions. He has won both New York and Los Angeles drama awards, and his plays have been produced from Ashland, Oregon, to Edinburgh, Scotland.

In addition to writing original work for the stage, Hailey has done an adaptation of August Strindberg's *The Father,* has taught playwriting for UCLA, and has had an active career in motion pictures and television. He served as the program consultant for the *Mary Hartman, Mary Hartman* television series and as the story editor for *McMillan and Wife.* In 1975 two of his stage plays—*For the Use of the Hall* and *Who's Happy Now?*—were performed on PBS Television. The latter was repeated several times on KERA-TV in Dallas.

Like Horton Foote, Hailey benefits from being a part of a close, mutually supportive family. Both men have talented wives and children who actively encourage and assist them with their work. Their dramatic uses of family as subject matter, however, are quite different. While Foote's attention is directed toward the relationship between family and circumstance, toward the family as impacted by outside events, Hailey's is concentrated on the family's internal dynamics, on the excruciating difficulty of communication and the discovery of shareable satisfactions.

★   THE PLAY

*Who's Happy Now?* is a courageous play that mixes genres and gets away with it. On the surface it is a wildly funny farce peopled with stock western characters. The action takes place in a cliché of a bar in an utterly stylized West Texas town complete with sagebrush and a bartender called Pop. Even on that level it succeeds. Familiar character types—such as Faye Precious, the waitress and "other-woman"; Horse, the unrepentant, philandering butcher-father; and Mary Hallen, the long-suffering wife-mother—are exaggerated to fresh levels of manic behavior. However, Hailey keeps audiences from dismissing his main characters as predictable stereotypes by giving each at least one distinctive trait.

When Horse's family hold his birthday party in the bar because he usually does not go home, when they decorate the bar with crossed strings of weiners and sawdust from the floor of the butcher shop, when they present Horse with a birthday cake made of meat because he can't stand regular cake and can drink beer with this kind, and when they then try to honor him with a hilariously awful song, the audience recognizes that it is in the territory of the comically bizarre. Yet in the same scene and in the earlier act when Mary Hallen feeds her six-year-old son, Richard, a cereal-and-milk supper in the bar so he can have some time with his father, albeit time shared with his father's mistress as well, it is clear that the emotion and intent are sincere and painfully worthy of respect. Only the form of expression is ridiculous.

This play depicts a family, each member of which wants to play his or her role responsibly yet hurts others because of received notions of what this role should be. Horse, with his hard work, heavy drinking, manly aggressiveness, sentimentalization and desexualization of his mother and his wife, lusty enjoyment of extramarital sex, and distrust of learning, has much in common with the West Texas image of manhood. Mary Hallen, with her complementary concept of proper wifeliness, is willing to subdue her sexuality, to channel it into fantasy, and to accept humiliation and brutality at her husband's hands in order to nurture and educate her son and to be the respectable wife to whom her husband returns, eventually, every night. In this society, with its disharmonious expectations of gender roles, family life is necessarily a field of pain and compromise. In Act II, Horse and Mary's son, Richard, says movingly, "Oh, Mama—when you do something like this, I know you and Dad could be happy." But his mother answers knowingly, "You worry too much about people being happy."

The character of the mother is split and played by two actresses, one onstage and usually referred to as Mary Hallen and another seated in the audience and referred to as Mama by the character playing both the young Richard onstage and also the playwright. The function of this double role becomes clear when the onstage play ends. The playwright then explains to "Mama" in the audience that the play, which left Mary Hallen with Horse, is false both because of his promise to soften the degree of her humiliation in the dramatized version of their story and because the "true" resolution, her escape to live with him, could not be made to work onstage. The last line of the play—"Oh God, Mama, I'm sorry. I should never have made you quit him"—is spoken by Richard as the playwright and ironically indicates that the playwright, bound by his social role as son, has brought his mother pain through his well-intentioned, sentimental love instead of rescuing her from violence and embarrassment. It further suggests that the artistic demands of the drama reveal that which had been obscured by good intentions in the real world.

A notable production of *Who's Happy Now?* (directed by Stanley Prager) opened at the Village South Theatre, New York City, on November 17, 1969, with the following cast:

| | |
|---|---|
| *Richard Hallen* | Ken Kercheval |
| *Pop* | Stuart Germain |
| *Mary Hallen* | Teresa Wright |
| *Horse Hallen* | Robert Darnell |
| *Faye Precious* | Rue McClanahan |
| *Mother in Audience* | Janet Sarno |

## ★ THE WORKS

Two of Oliver Hailey's plays have Texas settings. *Who's Happy Now?* takes place in a fictional West Texas town called Sunray. *Kith and Kin* is set in deep East Texas. Both of these plays have strong autobiographical elements and both deal with family relationships in a broadly comic manner. Hailey has said that he consciously seeks a perspective that will let him approach sensitive material comically; such a perspective, he feels, not only makes the play fresher but also allows relationships to be probed more deeply.

All of his plays feature highly inventive scenes characterized by comic exaggeration, yet they are never far from the painfully serious. Hailey accepts the playwright's responsibility to entertain, and he considers his plays to be failures if they do not give audiences immediate pleasure, regardless of the important insights they may convey. The surfaces of his plays, as well as the depths, attract attention. Running through his works is an evident and sometimes insistent theatricality that clearly draws on a background of solid scholarship. Hailey's frequent juxtapositions of diverse emotional material and thwarting of conventional expectations make his works a far cry from the straightforward realism commonly associated with Texas. An example is his use of the title *Father's Day*, which in the context of the drama refers to the day of the month when three fathers exercise their visitation rights with their children.

Hailey's plays are sophisticated. They are complex, they are serious, and they are stagy. Their focus of attention is the family and its importance, but instead of the pathos that American dramatists usually draw from this subject, the prevailing mood of Hailey's plays is comic irony.

Unfortunately, Hailey and his works have not received extended critical commentary. Journalistic reviews are, at their best, inadequate instruments to deal with the range and complexity of his plays, and Hailey has experienced more than a reasonable share of shallow and scathing notices.

## LIST OF WORKS

### PLAYS

*Hey You, Light Man!*, 1961
*Child's Play: A Comedy for Orphans*, 1962

*Home by Hollywood,* 1964
*Animal,* 1965
*Picture,* 1965
*First One Asleep, Whistle,* 1966
*Who's Happy Now?,* 1967
*Continental Divide,* 1970
*Criss Cross,* 1970
*Father's Day,* 1970
*Orphan,* 1970
*For the Use of the Hall,* 1976
*And Where She Stops Nobody Knows,* 1977
*Triptych* (earlier version of *Kith and Kin*), 1978
*I Can't Find It Anywhere,* 1979
*Red Rover, Red Rover,* 1979
*I Won't Dance,* 1982
"About Time" (part of *24 Hours—A.M. and P.M.),* 1983
*Round Trip* (freely adapted from August Strindberg's *The Father*), 1984
*Kith and Kin,* 1986
"Starkers" (part of *The Bar Off Melrose*), 1987

## RECOMMENDED READING

Dinsdale, Katherine. "Elizabeth and Oliver." *D Magazine* 10 (July 1984): 155–57, 166.

Hailey, Elizabeth Forsyth. *Joanna's Husband and David's Wife.* New York: Delacorte, 1986.*

Hailey, Kendall. *The Day I Became an Autodidact and the Advice, Adventures, and Acrimonies That Befell Me Thereafter.* New York: Delacorte, 1988.*

Lahr, John. "Oliver Hailey." In *Showcase I: Plays from the Eugene O'Neill Foundation,* edited by John Lahr, 13–16. New York: Grove Press, 1970.

Schwartz, Maryln. "Interview." *Dallas Morning News,* June 11, 1978.

* These two works, a novel by Hailey's wife, Elizabeth, and a personal chronicle by his teen-aged daughter, are very informative about the playwright's career and his remarkable family. Both describe relatives and associates from whom dramatic characters have been developed.

# Who's Happy Now?

★ ★ ★ ★ ★ ★ ★ ★ ★ ★ ★ ★ ★ ★ ★ ★ ★ ★

## CAST OF CHARACTERS

RICHARD HALLEN

POP

MARY HALLEN

HORSE HALLEN

FAYE PRECIOUS

## SCENES

The action of the play takes place in a barroom in the small Texas town of Sunray.

ACT ONE: 1941

ACT TWO: 1951

ACT THREE: 1955

*The set is a barroom. The bar runs along the stage right wall. Downstage are two tables for two. Upstage center is a gaudy jukebox. Upstage left is the front door. Upstage center behind the juke is a large window. Upstage left a door leads to the toilet. Downstage left is an upright piano. A small door behind the bar, stage right, leads to* POP's *storeroom. A large picture of F.D.R. hangs on the upstage right wall, flanked by an American flag and a Texas flag. "Welcome" in rope letters hangs above the bar.* RICHARD, *a lean, good-looking fellow about thirty, enters from the rear of the audience with a woman on his arm. He escorts her to a seat in the second row of the theatre, then climbs onto the stage. He turns directly to the audience, smiles.*

RICHARD. My mother's here tonight. Stand up, Mama. *(He begins to clap for her as she stands briefly.)* It's the first night she's seen the show. I tried to get her to come sooner—a rehearsal maybe—when things were a little more relaxed—but she chose tonight. Guess why. *(He sings.)*
HAPPY BIRTHDAY TO YOU,
HAPPY BIRTHDAY TO YOU,
HAPPY BIRTHDAY, DEAR MAMA,
HAPPY BIRTHDAY TO YOU.
*(And then again to the full audience.)* So the show may be a little different tonight. Because it's the story of her life. And mine. And his. And . . . our family in Sunray, Texas. She warned me a long time ago she'd kill me if I ever told it the way it really was. Look at her down there right now—frowning. My mother means business. When I first admitted I was going to do this play, "Don't," she begged me. "None of the neighbors ever knew a thing, Richard. I never told anybody anything. They would've loved to know—but they never did. Promise me they never will." Well, I've tried to . . . by disguise. Like Richard. Richard's not my real name. *(He winks at his mother.)* And the play's full of that kind of thing. So no matter who might drop in from our neighborhood, they'd have a pretty hard time figuring it out. Like the set . . . *(He shouts offstage.)* Will you bring up the lights now, please? *(The stage lights come up to full.)* A bar. The whole play takes place in this bar. Mama—have you ever been in a bar in your life? Okay—the lady who's playing you is going to be in this bar all night tonight. *(He laughs.)* How's that for disguise? Everybody who knows you knows you'd never go in a bar—right? Okay! Okay—let's begin. *(And then as an afterthought to his mother.)* I'll be playing the boy—all three ages. Remember me at six, Mama? Act One.
*(He exits into the wings as the sound of wind begins, increases, howls. After a moment the front door opens and* POP, *a wiry man in his sixties, struggles in. With him comes a tumbleweed.* POP *hurls the tumbleweed outside again.* POP *is the bartender, wears an apron. The wind howls even louder while* POP *has the door open. He must struggle to shut it.)*
POP. I'm blind. That dust blinded me!

*(He goes behind the bar, fills a glass with what looks like a shot of whiskey, splashes it in his eyes. After a beat he drinks what is left. The front door opens and* MARY HALLEN *enters with her son,* SONNY. RICHARD *plays the part of* SONNY, *with only suggestions that he is six years old. They, too, must fight the outside wind as they push the door shut. The boy looks up at his mother, crying.)*

SONNY. I can't see, Mama.

MARY. Did you see us waving?

POP. I did not!

SONNY. And my mouth is full of stuff.

MARY. *(To* POP.*)* Can we at least have a wet rag—to wipe our faces clean?

POP. I don't see why any teetotaler comes out on a night like this.

MARY. You close and we won't come out.

POP. I can't close just to keep you home. I got my business here.

MARY. And I got my business here! *(To* SONNY.*)* How's your throat?

SONNY. I still got stuff in my mouth. Look. *(He extends his tongue fully, then coughs.)*

MARY. Clear your throat and keep it clear. *(Wiping his mouth.)* I want your voice ready when I give the signal—remember?

SONNY. When will you give the signal?

MARY. We have to look for the right time.

POP. What are you up to, Mary Hallen?

MARY. A little surprise for Horse. Nothing to worry you.

POP. Horse get home last night?

MARY. Horse gets home every night!

POP. When?

MARY. Finally! Don't try to make trouble, Pop.

POP. You're the troublemaker—in here every night!

SONNY. I want a drink, Mama.

POP. Glad to hear it! That's what this place is for—drinks! Step right up!

MARY. *(Suddenly enraged.)* I swear to God, any man in this place ever give my boy another beer and I'll kill him! And that includes you and him and her!

POP. That's the chance you take when you bring a kid in a place like this!

MARY. Handing a child of six a bottle of beer and telling him it's orange soda pop. To this day Sonny won't go anywhere near orange soda pop! You've ruined orange soda pop for my boy.

SONNY. I want a drink, Mama.

MARY. Sonny, don't say drink. In here. Say water.

SONNY. I was hoping for soda pop. *(In a whisper.)* Any color but orange.

POP. *(Leaning over the counter.)* We don't sell soda pop—no color! This ain't a soda pop place! You don't make money off soda pop!

MARY. You keep Coca-Colas and you give him one right now. And you give me one, too! I know you keep them. I've seen a certain somebody drinking them!

POP. Where's your dime? *(*MARY *hesitates, then opens her purse, proudly pulls forth a bill, hands it to* POP.*)* Twenty dollars! I never knew you to get *any* money. Horse says butchers don't make enough money to give their wives any.

MARY. Just get our Cokes, please. That's your business! And make sure they're cold.

SONNY. *(A stage whisper.)* Don't tell him about the musical encyclopedias.

MARY. I'm not. Shut up. *(As POP goes for the Cokes, MARY begins to unwind her hair, which is extremely long and which she usually wears in a large bun at the back.)*

POP. *(Noticing as she unwinds it.)* You should let your hair down more often, Mary.

MARY. It came undone in the wind.

POP. You look good that way.

MARY. *(Removing a brush from her purse, combing her hair somewhat vainly.)* I know I do.

POP. You used to wear it that way all the time. I know why you stopped.

MARY. I chose to stop.

POP. Horse caught that salesman fooling with it, didn't he?

MARY. *(Suddenly pulling her hair to her, as if it had been bothered.)* Sonny—did you understand any of that?

SONNY. No, Mama.

MARY. Go play with the jukebox. *(SONNY moves to the jukebox.)* I chose to stop. I came to realize some men have no control when it comes to long, beautiful hair. *(She combs proudly.)*

POP. What was that salesman doing—when Horse caught him?

MARY. That salesman had no control.

POP. What was he doing?

MARY. Pop, some things are so personal between a man and his wife a bartender has no right knowing them—but I'll tell you, anyway. Because I'm sick of your innuendoes!

POP. My what? Is that Mexican? A Mexican word? Watch out! I know Mexican!

MARY. I let Horse catch that salesman! Deliberately let Horse catch him running fingers through my hair.

POP. That all he was doing? Running his fingers through it?

MARY. Every week. It was like an obsession. Every week. He'd come in the store to sell Horse an order of meat, and he'd sneak those fingers into my hair. When Horse wasn't looking, of course. I kept asking him to stop—to use control— Horse would kill him if he caught him. Well, he said he was running his hand through hair up and down the state, and most of the wives seemed to appreciate it.

POP. Did you appreciate it?

MARY. I said I appreciated it, but I didn't like it. And my husband wouldn't like it either. He said not to be so sure about that, oftentimes it was surprising how the husbands seemed to appreciate it too.

POP. Not Horse.

MARY. I said Horse wouldn't, he said I might be surprised, I said why don't you do it in front of him and see, he said he just might, I said do! About that time Horse came out of the icebox, I turned my back to the salesman, my hair just flowing down before him, and he being a man of no little temptation, he began to run those fingers up and down my hair, up and down my hair. *(She makes a running gesture with her finger.)* Then we both turned to Horse, all the time those fingers going in and out of my hair.

POP. Yeh?

MARY. Well, a big smile crossed Horse's face. And then he said to the salesman, Let me take your hand. And the man turned to me, and he said, See, I told you you might be surprised. And so he let go of me and gave the hand to Horse, and Horse grabbed hold of it, slammed it on the block, and chopped off two fingers!

POP. Horse is a fine man with a cleaver. I just wish I could've seen it.

MARY. I remember one finger landed in Mrs. Worsham's grocery basket. She about died. But Horse was within his rights. The insurance company said so. They didn't have to pay that salesman a penny. Not even for the one they couldn't sew back on.

POP. *(Turning to* SONNY.*)* You got yourself a papa, boy!

SONNY. When's Papa coming?

MARY. *(Quietly.)* Shut up, Sonny.

POP. I hear Faye Precious is having to run the café by herself this week. Mrs. Moot is on vacation.

MARY. Where'd she go?

POP. She said she was going home to bed. That's what Mr. Moot wanted. "I just want you to come home and get in bed with me, Mrs. Moot." When people can get that happy in bed, it's sad they have to get out of it—ain't it?

MARY. I've thought that.

POP. *You've* thought that?

MARY. Yes. I have.

POP. I guess anybody who's ever been in bed's thought it.

MARY. You know what I dream sometimes? In fact, I dream it often. It is what you would call a . . . recurring dream.

POP. What?

MARY. I am standing at the end of Main Street—and I slowly take off all my clothes—and then I walk to the other end of Main Street.

POP. In what kind of light?

MARY. Broad daylight. And nobody stops me.

POP. Boy—when you dream, you dream.

MARY. I thought you'd think so. *(She crosses to the window, stares out proudly.)*

POP. You know what Mrs. Moot said last week? You and Faye Precious look alike. A little. She said.

MARY. I don't look like any WAITRESS! My mother would kill you saying I looked like a waitress. If there was one thing she didn't want Jane and me to be—well, it was two things—a waitress and a nurse. I can remember Jane lying down on the bed and crying, begging so hard for Mama to let her go to nursing school. But Mama stood over that bed and said bed is right—and bed is where you'll be if you become a nurse—or a waitress. Those are the other two words for whore, she said. Don't you ever call me a waitress again, Pop. I'm a married woman. And prouder of it than any waitress or nurse has to be of her calling.

*(Suddenly the front door is pushed open and* HORSE *enters, followed by* FAYE PRECIOUS. *She is slightly younger than* MARY *and* HORSE, *vividly made up.* HORSE *is a large, boisterous man in his mid-thirties.)*

SONNY. Hi, Papa.

HORSE. Hi, Hamburger!

SONNY. Don't call me Hamburger!

HORSE. *(To* MARY.*)* No weather too bad to bring him out?

MARY. He has the right to spend the evening with his father . . . doesn't he?

FAYE. Of course he does. *(She crosses to* SONNY, *pats his chin.)* Every little boy does.

SONNY. Mama, she touched me.

MARY. Don't touch him, Faye Precious.

FAYE. Sorry, Mrs. Hallen.

MARY. *(She takes her handkerchief, quickly wipes clean the spot where* FAYE *has touched* SONNY.*)* All right, Sonny—it's time for your supper. *(She reaches into her purse, pulls out a bottle of milk, a large box of Post Toasties and a bowl.)*

HORSE. Now ain't that a supper? No wonder he's such a runt.

FAYE. Mrs. Hallen, you know you could bring him by the café just any night and I'd fix him a good hot supper. You too.

HORSE. *(Slaps* FAYE*'s behind.)* The best!

MARY. *(As she serves* SONNY.*)* This is perfectly fine—he has a hot lunch and a cold supper. Nobody needs a hot both.

HORSE. That woman never would fix me a hot supper.

MARY. There's always somebody to do it, isn't there?

FAYE. *(Anxious to change the topic, taking off her hat and beginning to examine it.)* Oh— my feather! I shouldn't of worn it! But I do like to dress up a little in the evenings! Poor feather.

HORSE. I'll buy you another feather, Faye Precious. *(He yanks the feather from her hat, throws it away.)*

FAYE. Don't talk like that, Horse. *(Turning quickly to* MARY.*)* He's never bought me a thing, Mrs. Hallen. Don't let him get your goat. I wouldn't let him buy me anything. You know I wouldn't. Waitresses make enough.

HORSE. Two beers, Pop!

FAYE. Oh, can't I have a Coke, Horse? Please!

HORSE. Beer!

POP. Horse—you're in a mean mood tonight.

HORSE. Why wouldn't I be? I was short twenty dollars tonight—checking up at the register—first time it's ever happened to me! Two beers—and hurry!

POP. Well, Faye Precious didn't steal it. You don't have to take it out on her—force her to drink beer!

HORSE. I ain't gonna be the only person in this bar drinking! Two is gonna drink! Me and Faye Precious!

FAYE. How come it's gotta be us two all the time?

HORSE. Get those beers up here, Pop!

POP. No! I won't serve beer to them what don't want it!

MARY. Yeh? What about my boy? You served him, didn't you? And he didn't want it! If you'll serve children don't want it, you should serve grown women don't want it either.

HORSE. Yeh—you sure should! Damn good point, Mary! We got you there, Pop!

POP. *(Serving two beers.)* Yeh—you got me! *(FAYE PRECIOUS gives MARY a hurt glance as she accepts her beer.)* I'm sorry, Faye Precious. I'd put some flavoring in it if it was anything else. But there's nothing you can do to beer.

FAYE. Oh, I know. Why God came up with beer—after he'd invented chocolate and Coca-Cola, I don't know!

HORSE. Just take big swallows, Faye Precious. And don't whine.

FAYE. *(Groaning in the face of her beer.)* That's not whining—that's gagging. *(But finally taking as big a swallow as she can manage.)* Oh, my—oh, my, my! *(She turns to MARY.)* You're a lucky woman, Mrs. Hallen.

MARY. *(Nodding.)* I do enjoy a Coke in the evening.

HORSE. Where did you get money, Mary?

POP. *(With a smile at MARY.)* I was wonderin' when.

MARY. *(Avoiding POP's stare.)* I found a fifty-cent piece.

HORSE. A fifty-cent piece.

MARY. This afternoon. On the sidewalk.

HORSE. And you're already blowing it to Coke? *(He turns to POP.)* I always wondered how she'd handle herself with money, Pop. *(And then to MARY.)* Well, you're handling yourself pretty poorly, Mary!

MARY. Want to play the jukebox, Sonny?

HORSE. That lousy noisemaker—no! I won't have that thing going! *(And then to FAYE PRECIOUS, who is struggling with her beer.)* And stop spitting beer, Faye Precious!

SONNY. I love that box, Mama.

MARY. I know you do, honey. Here. *(She hands him a nickel and he runs to the jukebox.)*

HORSE. So help me, you put that nickel in there, Hamburger, and I'll dance with Faye Precious!

FAYE. Oh, please, no—no! I'm feeling a littly woozy, Horse.

POP. No dancing in here, Horse! Law doesn't allow it.

HORSE. You turn it into a music dance hall with that no-good machine and I'll dance! I'm warning you, Mary, I'll dance with Faye Precious and I'll hold her tight! I will!

FAYE. Oh, my goodness.

MARY. You think I care?

HORSE. I know you care! You always have and you always will! Because you're my wife! Face that, Mary. Face it! *(MARY stares at him for another moment. As she hesitates, a smug smile crosses his face. Seeing this, she turns abruptly to* SONNY, *nods her permission to put the nickel in the jukebox.* SONNY *does. A Western tune blares forth.* HORSE *quickly grabs* FAYE PRECIOUS *by the arm, yanks her from her chair.)* Okay, Faye Precious—you asked for it!

FAYE. I didn't do a thing, Horse! *(As* HORSE *swings her past* MARY.*)* Oh, Mrs. Hallen, you've really got it in for me, haven't you? *(*HORSE *dances* FAYE PRECIOUS *wildly about the room. He is as inept as he is vigorous.)*

POP. *(Following them—almost as if the three of them were dancing.)* Stop it, Horse! You can't do that! It's against the law! Dancing's against the law in here!

MARY. Come on, Pop—who'd call what he's doing dancing?

HORSE. I'm dancing!

MARY. You're jumping and hugging!

POP. Okay, Horse—you asked for it! *(*POP *moves to the jukebox, unplugs it. The music stops abruptly.)*

FAYE. Thank goodness! *(But then she grabs her stomach.)* Oh, I'm sick! I'm sick!

HORSE. Is that beer you're spittin'?

FAYE. *(Running toward the toilet door.)* Among other things!

HORSE. Faye Precious, will you never learn!

FAYE. Will *you* never learn! Did it ever occur to you maybe you expect too much from women!

HORSE. No! *(*FAYE PRECIOUS *bangs shut the rest room door.* HORSE *begins to pound on it. She throws it open, roars.)*

FAYE. Well, you do! *(She slams the door again.* HORSE *pounds again. A beat later this sound is duplicated by* MARY *pounding on the jukebox for her nickel to return. But it does not, so she crosses to* POP.*)*

MARY. Give me back my nickel, Pop.

POP. What nickel?

MARY. *(She points to the jukebox.)* The song wasn't over when you stopped it.

POP. I had to. The law.

MARY. I didn't break it. And I didn't get my nickel's worth.

POP. *(Grudgingly giving her the nickel.)* You're a hard woman with money, Mary Hallen.

MARY. I'm a good woman with money. What do you think, Horse?

HORSE. I like what I just seen, yeh.

MARY. Sit at our table a little. While she's in there.

HORSE. Why?

MARY. I'll buy you a beer.

HORSE. Out of your fifty-cent piece?

MARY. Yes.

HORSE. *(He stares at her—hesitates for the briefest moment.)* Hell, yes, I'd like a beer out of your money, Mary.

SONNY. Hi, Papa.

HORSE. Hi, Hamb—boy. *(*SONNY *beams.)*

MARY. Pop—two beers and another Coke!

HORSE. Two beers?

MARY. I'll try. As a little present to you.

HORSE. Beer's twenty cents a bottle, Mary. Two bottles is forty—the Cokes you already had is a dime—fifty. And another Coke makes it fifty-five. *(MARY is already reaching in her purse for the money—now she suddenly stops.)*

MARY. I didn't realize beer was so much—twenty cents.

HORSE. *(Staring at her.)* And you just got fifty?

MARY. *(Returning his stare.)* That's right. *(There is a long moment before he speaks—with no indication of what is in his mind. But then he smiles.)*

HORSE. I'll stand you the nickel.

MARY. Thank you, Horse.

HORSE. You're all right, Mary. *(He slaps her on the back, gets a handful of her long, flowing hair.)* Aren't you wearing your hair a little different?

MARY. *(She fluffs the hair toward him.)* It came undone in the wind. I thought maybe you'd enjoy it this way tonight.

HORSE. Maybe I will and maybe I won't. Don't push me, Mary. *(There is a pause as SONNY makes a whistling sound by blowing into his Coke bottle.)*

MARY. I don't push. Sonny, why don't you take off your papa's boots? . . . Make him more comfortable. *(She points toward HORSE's feet. SONNY misunderstands.)*

SONNY. *(A loud stage whisper.)* Is that the signal? Ready for me to do it?

MARY. Not yet. Just take off his boots now. *(SONNY straddles HORSE's leg, removes a boot—then the other boot. HORSE cannot resist giving SONNY a kick with the removal of the second boot. But SONNY happily cradles HORSE's feet in his lap. POP brings the beers and Coke. MARY and HORSE lift their beers.)*

HORSE. *(Offering his beer as a toast to her.)* Damn you, Mary!

MARY. Thank you, Horse. *(HORSE and MARY sip their beers, SONNY drinks his Coke. Slowly HORSE reaches over as if to kiss MARY. But before they can kiss, SONNY, as RICHARD, rises and stops them.)*

RICHARD. No—I don't want the kiss in the play. Remember that time, Mama? It was at the Walkers' picnic. You did try to drink beer. You were ashamed afterwards. But I was proud of you. And it was the only time I ever saw you kiss him. The kiss isn't in the play tonight. We've tried it, but it doesn't look real. But it was real—that time you kissed him. Admit it. *(He sits again, assumes his role as SONNY.)*

HORSE. I'll say one thing for you, Mary—you're not spitting your beer.

SONNY. She's drinking beer! You're drinking beer, Mama—did you know that?

MARY. Yes—I know.

SONNY. Does it taste good, Mama?

MARY. *(Again with her eye on HORSE.)* It's tasty.

HORSE. *(Slaps MARY on the back again.)* You're all right, Mary! I just may buy *you* one. *(She gives a smile that betrays that one is quite enough.)*

SONNY. I'll be glad when I can drink beer.

MARY. Don't say that! Horse, don't let him say that.

HORSE. Don't ruin the party, you little brat!

SONNY. I did taste it once—didn't I, Mama? Once. *(*MARY *puts her beer down, stares hard at* HORSE. HORSE *looks at her, then turns to* SONNY.*)*

HORSE. You're really out to ruin the party, aren't you, Hamburger? Get lost, you little bastard! Leave my wife and me alone.

MARY. Don't talk to him like that, Horse!

HORSE. He's ruining out party!

MARY. It's not a party.

HORSE. It could be. Sometimes. If we could ever shake him.

MARY. We don't have parties.

HORSE. I have parties! *(He suddenly runs his fingers through* MARY's *hair—roughly. She rises abruptly, turns away, ties her hair up again.* HORSE *shouts.)* Faye Precious, get back in here! *(*SONNY *turns around in his chair, away from* HORSE, *sobs.)*

MARY. Don't cry, Sonny.

HORSE. You cry and I'll whack you, Hamburger!

MARY. You won't.

SONNY. He will.

MARY. Why can't you ever treat him nice?

HORSE. Because I don't like him. I just don't like him. I've never liked the kid. That's why.

SONNY. *(As* RICHARD.*)* I know it sounds too mean, Mama. I know *he* had a *special* way of saying it. *(And then to the audience.)* It was almost like a carnival barker does—when he's got the best attraction on the midway. "I don't like him! I just don't like him! I've never liked the kid! Right this way!" The way we're doing it, I feel like an orphan. *(He pats the actor playing* HORSE *consolingly on the arm, then resumes his position.)*

HORSE. *(Attempting to duplicate the way* RICHARD *has delivered the line.)* I don't like him. I just don't like him. I've never liked the kid. *(*RICHARD *nods approvingly to his mother in the audience.)*

MARY. Okay, Sonny. Now. Now.

SONNY. What?

MARY. You know. It.

SONNY. Oh—the song! Now? Hot dog!

MARY. Don't say it—just do it.

HORSE. I don't like songs!

MARY. You're not going to believe this, Horse—he did it all by himself. Practically.

HORSE. Did what?

MARY. The little tune, the rhymes—he rhymed it—he did it all. Go on, Sonny— sing it.

HORSE. I don't like songs, Mary.

MARY. Shut up and listen, Horse! Okay, Sonny—sing it! *(*MARY *sits at the piano, begins to play.)*

SONNY.

> MY NAME IS SONNY.
> AND I'M FROM SUNRAY,
> BORN ON A SUNDAY AFTERNOON.
> SUNRAY'S A SUN TOWN,
> SUNUP TO SUNDOWN
> WHEN THERE'S A SUNRAY, TEXAS MOON.
>
> MY NAME IS SONNY.
> I'M MAMA'S SUNBEAM,
> I'M MAMA'S SUNBEAM EV'RY DAY,
> AND VERY SUN-GLAD
> TO HAVE A SUN-DAD
> IN SUNRAY, TEXAS, U.S.A.
>> *(At the song's conclusion applause is heard from* FAYE PRECIOUS—*standing at the toilet door.)*

FAYE. That's wonderful! Just wonderful, Sonny!

MARY. And he did the rhymes by himself practically.

HORSE. What are rhymes?

MARY. Sun-glad and sun-dad—that's what rhymes are. Glad and dad happen to rhyme. And Sonny thought them up.

HORSE. *(To* SONNY.) You did that?

SONNY. Yes, sir. *(There is a moment as* HORSE *stares at* SONNY, *evaluating him. Then* HORSE *turns away in disgust.)*

HORSE. Shit!

FAYE. It's just wonderful! Let me sing it—can I?

> MY NAME IS SONNY
> AND I'M FROM SUNRAY—

SONNY. No, you can't sing it! Stop her, Mama!

FAYE. Why can't I?

SONNY Your name's not Sonny, that's why.

MARY. Sonny—you should be proud someone wants to sing your song.

SONNY. Do we like her, Mama?

MARY. You should be glad anyone wants to sing your song. Sing it, Faye Precious.

FAYE. Thank you, Mrs. Hallen.

> MY NAME IS SONNY
> AND I'M—

SONNY. Your name's still not Sonny! *(*HORSE *gives the boy an angry glare—points a finger for the boy to behave himself.)*

FAYE. *(She glares at* SONNY *for a moment, then begins again—* MARY *at the piano.)*

> HIS NAME IS SONNY
> AND HE'S FROM SUNRAY,
> BORN ON A SUNDAY AFTERNOON.

SUNRAY'S A SUN TOWN,

SUNUP AND SUNDOWN,

WHEN THERE'S A SUNRAY, TEXAS MOON.

Come on, join me, Sonny. We'll make a little harmony. *(He hesitates, glances at his mother.* MARY *hits a couple of notes of harmony to encourage him.)*

FAYE AND SONNY.

MY NAME IS SONNY.

I'M MAMA'S SUNBEAM,

I'M MAMA'S SUNBEAM EV'RY DAY,

AND VERY SUN-GLAD

TO HAVE A SUN-DAD

IN SUNRAY, TEXAS, U.S.A.

FAYE. *(She hugs* SONNY.*)* You're a genius, Sonny! You are!

SONNY. *(Wrapped in* FAYE PRECIOUS' *embrace—struggling to speak to his mother.)* Mama—she's touching—

MARY. It's all right, Sonny. She appreciates your talent.

HORSE. *(Watching* FAYE *hug* SONNY, *rises.)* Beer and steer!

FAYE. What?

MARY. Horse just made a rhyme. Sit down, Horse.

SONNY. It's a good rhyme, Papa.

HORSE. I didn't ask you! You shut up!

MARY. Anybody can rhyme words. The trick is to put them into songs.

HORSE. Well, it's a dumb trick and it ain't my trick maybe.

MARY. Certainly isn't.

HORSE. Thank God! My trick happens to be breaking down a beef! *(To* SONNY.*)* Can you do that? Can anybody here do that? Speak up! Anybody?

FAYE. My, no, Horse—I can't even bear to watch you do it.

HORSE. Why can't you watch? Something wrong with breaking down a beef? You think something's wrong with it?

FAYE. 'Course I don't.

HORSE. Juries do. They won't put a butcher on a jury. They think he's too cruel to be on a jury. Did you know that? *(This is not spoken to* POP.*)*

POP. Yeh—I knew it.

HORSE. Oh, boy, it hurt me when I found that out!

FAYE. I didn't mean nothing like that, Horse. It just makes me a little woozy to watch you do it.

HORSE. Lots of things make you woozy, Faye Precious. *(*FAYE PRECIOUS *looks at him for a moment, then suddenly turns away, begins to sob.)* Oh hell! You crying, Faye Precious?

FAYE. I was thinking of my late husband, and what used to make him woozy. So woozy he'd lose his stomach. Every time. *(She sobs loudly.)*

POP. What?

FAYE. He said he'd die if I ever told. Of course . . . now he's dead. *(Another sob.)*

HORSE. Tell it! What was it?

FAYE. *(A pause.)* Love. Love is what made him woozy.

MARY. Love?

FAYE. Making it.

MARY. Sonny, go to the bathroom.

SONNY. I don't need to!

HORSE. Get in there and *try!* *(SONNY obeys.)*

FAYE. I was careful as I could be about the way I said it, Mrs. Hallen.

HORSE. She hasn't even said it. You get it, Pop?

POP. *(Snickering.)* I think I do.

HORSE. I think I do too. You telling us, Faye Precious, every time this old fellow took you to bed, then he'd have to get right back up, go to the—

FAYE. That's enough, Horse!

POP. Every time, Faye Precious?

FAYE. *(Crying.)* From the wedding night on. I was so innocent, for the first few weeks I just thought that was part of it. And I felt so sorry for men. But then he came to me, poor worn-out thing, and he said, "Faye Precious, I just can't keep this up."

HORSE. Should of said he just couldn't keep it down!

FAYE. Horse—please!

POP. So what happened?

MARY. No details, Faye Precious.

FAYE. It's okay, Mrs. Hallen. It's not a bad answer. We just vowed to give it up, my husband and me.

MARY. Give it up?

HORSE. Hell!

FAYE. *(Crying.)* He told me he was sorry as he could be, he'd looked forward to it all his life . . . but now it was here . . . well, it just wasn't what he'd hoped it'd be. And we'd have to stop, or he might die from it. And you could see he was already beginning to waste away.

POP. So you gave it up?

HORSE. Nobody can give it up.

MARY. Could you, Faye Precious?

FAYE. Well, we were doing real fine. For three weeks. Only then—three weeks to the day after we made the vow—my husband . . . passed away.

POP. Died?

MARY. How?

FAYE. Well, the Amarillo doctor said it was a liver ailment, but the Dumas doctor said it was pneumonia—but I always said he just . . . lost the will to live.

HORSE. That's an awful story, Faye Precious. Damn, I'm depressed! Give me a beer, Pop.

FAYE. *(Still crying.)* I didn't mean to depress you, Horse. But . . . well . . . life happens to be a little depressing.

HORSE. You think I don't already know that? I know life is depressing! Why do you think I bring you here every night?

FAYE. I'm sorry, Horse. Maybe if I sang for you?

HORSE. I hate songs!

FAYE. It's the best thing I do.

HORSE. *(Laughs.)* It is not!

FAYE. See—you're cheering up already. *(She laughs.)*

POP. You could've been a singer, Faye Precious, 'stead of a waitress if you'd wanted. *(He has aimed this remark at* MARY.*)*

FAYE. I know it. Several of my regular customers will not eat until I have sung.

HORSE. Singing is not the thing Faye Precious does best!

FAYE. I wish you would please not talk that way in front of Mrs. Hallen, Horse.

MARY. I'm used to it, Faye Precious.

FAYE. I don't see how you *got* used to it, Mrs. Hallen. It still embarrasses me to death—everything Horse says about him and me in front of you. Why, every night I come through that door and see you and the boy sitting here again, I just want to die!

MARY. You'd feel better if the boy and I stayed home?

FAYE. Oh—a lot better! Why don't you try that some night, Mrs. Hallen? Huh?

HORSE. You think I haven't told her to stay home? You tell her—see where it gets you!

MARY. We've stayed home, Faye Precious.

FAYE. When? I can't remember you missing a night.

MARY. At first. We tried staying home. But it's no life for the boy—at home. He falls asleep before Horse gets there. Now me—I don't. I always wait up.

FAYE. You wait up for Horse every night? I don't think I knew that.

MARY. I'm married to him. I'm the last one to see him—every night.

FAYE. Well, that's nice.

MARY. But I bring the boy here so he can know his father too.

SONNY. *(Entering from the toilet.)* Yeh—and this place has the jukebox. *(He runs to the jukebox, begins to punch the selection buttons.)*

POP. You bet it does! This is a first-class place!

MARY. This is the only place the boy gets a chance to know Horse. And it's impor-tant for a boy to know his father. *(And then turning directly to* HORSE.*)* Even Horse knows what a father can mean to a boy. How a *father* can—

HORSE. Shut up, Mary—damn you! *(A beat.)* Oh, hell, I'm thinking about him already! You did that to me, Mary Hallen! I'm thinking about my papa again! *(He begins to cry—heaving with sobs.)* Help me stop it! Help me, Mary! *(His head falls on the table as he sobs violently.* MARY *crosses quickly to him.* FAYE *moves away—not knowing how to help.* MARY *stands behind him, consoling.)*

MARY. Think about him a little. It's okay. It'll go away in a minute. *(*HORSE *reaches for* MARY's *hand—squeezes it tightly.)*

FAYE. *(Softly—to* MARY.*)* What kind of a man was his father—just wonderful?

(MARY *nods affirmatively. But* HORSE *speaks from deep within his sobs, beating a fist on the table.*)

HORSE. Wonderful! Wonderful! Oh, Goddamn, how I loved that man! How I loved him! And it ain't easy for me to say something like that, is it, Mary?

MARY. *(Wistfully.)* No.

HORSE. *(He suddenly pulls himself together, lifts his head, wipes an eye.)* I'm going to tell her what he was, Mary—okay? Just tell her what he was. *(But then he breaks into sobs again.)* You tell her!

MARY. He was a lawyer, Faye Precious.

HORSE. That's all I'm telling you. A lawyer. I'm a meatcutter and he was a lawyer. That's enough to say, ain't it, Faye Precious?

FAYE. Oh—it's fascinating. (HORSE's *head falls on the table again as he struggles to gain control.* SONNY *rises and moves to him.*)

SONNY. Don't cry, Papa—please.

HORSE. *(His head still lowered.)* You get away! Get away! *(Again he is crying.)* Mary, keep him away from me. (MARY *signals to* SONNY *to move away, but* SONNY *stands firm.*)

SONNY. *(As if by rote.)* When you break down the beef, you break it into halves and then into the front quarter and the hindquarter. In the front quarter you get the shoulder roasts and the club steaks. And in the hindquarter you get the T-bones, and then the sirloins, and then the round steaks and the rump roast. Right, Papa?

HORSE. *(Slowly looking up.)* How'd you learn that? (SONNY *remains silent.*) How'd he learn it, Mary? How?

MARY. He's a bright boy, I've been telling you. He sees the charts on your back wall and . . .

HORSE. I know grown meatcutters never learned them. Damn you, boy! There are full-grown meatcutters don't know that stuff! *(He suddenly pulls* SONNY *to him.)* I'm glad I remembered my papa, Mary. I'm glad you made me remember him. I always will remember him. Just like I hope my boy will always remember me.

SONNY. Oh—I won't forget you.

MARY. *(Her hand on* HORSE's *shoulder as he holds* SONNY.) Let me buy you another beer, Horse.

HORSE. *(Warmly—his mind still on his father.)* Out of your money, Mary?

MARY. Yes.

HORSE. *(Suddenly cold and hard.)* Mary Hallen—you should be out of your money by now!

MARY. Oh, my God yes—I am.

HORSE. Unless you are who I think you are!

MARY. Who?

HORSE. The person that lifted twenty dollars from my cash register this afternoon!

MARY. Horse—I would never take money from you.

HORSE. Except for him! (HORSE *suddenly shoves* SONNY *aside.)* You think I don't remember the price of them musical encyclopedias? Eighteen seventy-five! I told you two weeks ago today, no, I would not pay for musical books inside my house! It is two weeks to the day, I bet they are already at the post office C.O.D. waiting for your eighteen seventy-five! Which leaves one dollar and one quarter for you to be blowing in this bar, like the fool that you are! Okay, hand it over!

MARY. No, Horse—I don't . . .

HORSE. Hand it over! *(He grabs her purse, begins to slam objects onto the table—the box of Post Toasties, the bottle of milk, several toys. Finally he holds the purse upside down—but it is empty, no money falls out. He turns again to* MARY.) Okay, Mary Hallen, I'll strip you if I have to!

MARY. Strip me?

HORSE. Strip you! I know you got it and I'm gonna find it.

MARY. Strip me. *(She unbuttons her blouse, removes it, throws it at* HORSE. *He stands staring in disbelief.)* I'll help you.

HORSE. Not in front of the kid, for God's sake, Mary!

MARY. In front of the town. *(She takes off a shoe, flings it at him, and then moves to the front door. She opens the door, dashes out.)*

POP. *(Running to a window, peering out.)* Look at that—she's slinging clothes every which way.

HORSE. *(Also at the window—for a moment afraid to go out.)* Holy hell—it's just like her dream.

POP. You know about her dream?

HORSE. *You* know about her dream? My God, what kind of woman am I married to?!

POP. *(He glances out the window again.)* I don't know—but from the looks of it, you better get out there and start claiming her.

HORSE. *(Glances out the window again—shudders.)* Hell, I can't just go out in the middle of Main Street and start chasing a naked woman. What will people think of me?

POP. It's your wife!

HORSE. Yeh—but suppose they don't spot her face—and think I'm just out chasing a naked woman. Then again, suppose they *do* spot her face? What kind of marriage will folks think I got—wife out there running naked?

POP. Then you better get going and get her back in here! I'll help you catch her.

HORSE. The hell if you will.

*(HORSE exits, slams the door sharply after himself.)*

POP. *(After waiting only a beat.)* The hell if I won't!

*(And out the door he goes, leaving FAYE PRECIOUS and SONNY alone. There is a pause as FAYE PRECIOUS stares at SONNY. Finally she speaks.)*

FAYE. Sonny . . . your mama's mind has snapped!

*(And then she runs out the door. SONNY, unaffected by any of it, crosses to the Post Toasties, gets his bowl, begins to pour—and a wad of dollar bills and coins falls from the Post Toasties box. He quickly stuffs the money in his pocket. Then he turns, as RICHARD, and speaks directly to his mother in the audience.)*

RICHARD. I guess I got that idea for the naked run, Mama, remembering those encyclopedias—and how mad he was about you buying them—and how he came home that night and sliced up all your dresses—and even your underwear—and left you with nothing to wear. Which is where I've left you. End of Act One.

    (RICHARD *moves off into the wings as the houselights come up.*)

*Curtain*

# ★ ACT II

*It is now 1951, and the bar's decor has been changed somewhat. The large photograph of F.D.R. has been replaced by one of Harry Truman. "Welcome" has faded considerably, indicating that the word has hung for several years. These permanent decor touches, however, are secondary to the bar's current disarray, which consists of assorted party supplies scattered about the counter and on the tables—ribbons, meat hooks, a basket of wieners, a box of white aprons and butcher hats, a box of sawdust, a rake.*

*POP stands at the bar surveying the room with disgust. RICHARD stands over the basket of wieners. He pulls strings of wieners from the basket, begins to hang them.*

POP. What are you doing with *them?*

RICHARD. Going to hang wieners from the ceiling. Two rows maybe—crisscross. You scatter the sawdust. I sneaked out his rake. *(He points toward the rake in the corner.)*

POP. *(Moving to scatter sawdust.)* You think this'll put Horse in a party mood? Work all day, come over here, and find his bar's been turned into another meat market?

RICHARD. I wish we had meat blocks—instead of tables. Fancy cafés do that sometimes.

POP. Meat blocks? You're lying to me, boy.

RICHARD. I read it in a book!

POP. No wonder he hates you—you sure are a smart ass.

RICHARD. I can't help reading.

POP. 'Course you can! Why can't you?

RICHARD. Once you learn how, it's a habit. If you'd learn how, you'd know what I mean.

POP. I can read! *(He points to the large rope word.)* Welcome!

RICHARD. I mean sentences.

POP. Oh. *(A pause as he stares at RICHARD.)* You want you and Horse to be pals, you know what'd I'd do? Give up reading!

RICHARD. I couldn't give up reading.

POP. Try! You ain't tried! Do it like Alcoholics Anonymous—they just promise not to drink today, that's all. You promise not to read today. And from day to day. You can make it—I know you can!

RICHARD. It doesn't bother you you can't read?

POP. I can read words and I don't miss sentences.

RICHARD. That's the way Horse is, he knows lots of words.

POP. Sure, and you hang onto the ones you already got. Most of 'em. Might dump a few of the fancy ones. Like *bane of our existence.*

RICHARD. You remember that?

POP. You hurt Horse awful calling him that. When he found out what *bane* meant, he was hurt.

RICHARD. I went through a smart-aleck period, didn't I?

POP. You sure did. Smart-ass period.

RICHARD. I'm over it. I'm gonna be different.

POP. What changed you?

RICHARD. You just change, don't you?

POP. Yeh—you do. And you're changing at a high rate of speed right now, too, ain't you, boy? Horse and me was wondering the other night if it wasn't about time for it. Got hair under your arms yet?

RICHARD. *(A beat.)* Got it everywhere! Had it everywhere for a couple of years now. I'm sixteen, Pop!

POP. You're gonna be all right, boy!

RICHARD. I want to be like you and Horse, Pop.

POP. *(Slams a fist on the bar.)* Men!

RICHARD. *(Awkwardly slams a fist on the bar.)* Men.

POP. You're off to a good start! And after what you just told me—now you got a little more going for you—you're not going to miss reading nearly as much as you think you will.

RICHARD. But I won't end up like Horse—with two women. Not me.

POP. Probably not. Not many that lucky.

RICHARD. I wouldn't do that to two women. To either of them. You know what that does to a woman? Even to Faye Precious. To be one of many?

POP. She's one of two.

RICHARD. After a while she can't help but feel betrayed, let down, whipped, defeated, destroyed . . .

> *(FAYE gaily opens the front door, popping her head in. She wears her waitress costume. She sees that RICHARD has finished stringing wieners across the ceiling.)*

FAYE. Oh—it's so festive! Fes—tive! When you give a party, Sonny, you give a party!

RICHARD. I got your song ready, Faye Precious. *(He pulls sheet music from his hip pocket.)*

FAYE. I can't wait! I told Horse just to meet me here tonight—so I'll have time to run home and change—maybe put on something to match the wienies. *(She glances at the wieners hanging overhead.)* If I can come up with something.

RICHARD. *(Watching FAYE as she begins to read the sheet music.)* I hope you like it.

FAYE. I'll love it—if it just doesn't have too much of the meat market in it. You know what I mean, that last little song of yours—how did it go?

RICHARD. "Please Be Frank"?

FAYE. I forgot about that one. I was thinking of "My Love Is on the Block." I sometimes worry about you. *(A beat as she smiles at him sadly—then explains.)* Having to spend so much time in the meat market. It could hinder your career.

RICHARD. But this is a happy birthday song.

FAYE. *(Reading the sheet music.)* Yes. And what an interesting idea making a happy birthday song so sad.

RICHARD. I didn't mean it to be sad. Is it?

FAYE. Well . . . I'm a little depressed. Sadness just has a way of creeping into your work, Sonny.

RICHARD. Don't sing it sad, Faye Precious.

FAYE. Oh, I won't. If I sung your stuff sad, on top of all the sadness in it—"my love is on the block, my heart is at stake"—why, people just couldn't bear it. *(She again looks at the sheet music.)*

RICHARD. You don't like it.

FAYE. It's a sweet little song—I just hope it don't set Horse to crying.

RICHARD. He won't cry. It's his forty-first birthday. He didn't die at forty. He'll be happy.

FAYE. He sure don't look forty-one, that dad of yours. Pop, give me and Sonny a couple of Cokes, and then I'll hurry on home. Let me buy, okay?

RICHARD. Thank you. *(She sits at a table,* RICHARD *joining her. She hums the tune from the sheet music.)*

FAYE. I got this already.

RICHARD. How old do you think I look, Faye Precious?

FAYE. I don't know . . . what are you, thirteen?

RICHARD. Sixteen!

POP. *(Serving the Cokes, winking at* FAYE.*)* And all man, if you know what we mean, Faye Precious.

RICHARD. *(Turning away.)* Why did you have to say that?

FAYE. Kindly turn back around here, Sonny Hallen! My goodness, you think I didn't already know that little secret about you? Why, a woman can spot that the minute it happens.

RICHARD. She can? How?

FAYE. *(With a wink.)* By looking.

RICHARD. Wow—you sure talk frank, Faye Precious.

FAYE. I know it. And I know I shouldn't. But everybody seems to enjoy it so much I hate to cut it out.

RICHARD. I enjoy it, too . . . I like you, Faye . . . *Precious.*

FAYE. My goodness, what you'll say for a free Coke, Sonny Hallen!

RICHARD. Did you know I used to hate you?

FAYE. You didn't!

RICHARD. I did.

FAYE. Sonny, does your mother still hate me?

RICHARD. Does that matter?

FAYE. Yes! I just hate to be hated!

RICHARD. Me too, Faye Precious. I'm the same. And Horse hates me.

FAYE. Oh, he doesn't.

RICHARD. I could've said Mama doesn't hate you—but I didn't.

FAYE. Okay—he hates you a little.

RICHARD. I wish we all liked each other.

FAYE. Well, I like you and I like your mother and I like Horse. And you like me and you like your mother and you like Horse. And your mother likes you . . . and she likes Horse, too . . . And Horse . . . well, he likes me. See—that's a lot of liking.

POP. Crap—I'm going to the toilet! *(He exits.)*

RICHARD. You like Horse a lot, don't you?

FAYE. He's the sweetest man I ever knew.

RICHARD. I wish . . .

FAYE. What?

RICHARD. No.

FAYE. Come on, say it. If it's hard to say it'll just be that much more interesting to hear.

RICHARD. I wish when I grew up . . . I'd seem as sweet to you as Horse does.

FAYE. Why, Sonny . . . you've got my whole body in goose bumps.

RICHARD. I do?

FAYE. Want to feel them?

RICHARD. Sure.

FAYE. Here. Touch. *(She extends an arm.* RICHARD *runs three fingers slowly, gently across her arm. And then again.)* Oh, my, they're getting bigger. *(She retrieves her arm, cradles it.)* Don't you worry about your future. You're gonna be sweetness itself. *(She rises—a little desperate.)* I better be going!

RICHARD. No. Let me buy *you* a Coke now.

FAYE. Oh, no—I know when I've had enough. *(She hurries to the door.)* Bye-bye, sweetness. *(She waves at the door, exits.)*

RICHARD. *(Crossing to the piano, playing as he sings.)*

MY LOVE IS ON THE BLOCK
AND MY HEART IS AT STAKE.
DON'T CHUCK MY HEART AWAY.
IT'S TOO TENDER TO BREAK.

MY LOVE IS ON THE SCALE
AND IT'S RIGHT IN ITS PRIME.
THE CHOICE IS YOURS TO WEIGH.
WRAP MY LOVE WHILE THERE'S TIME.

YOU MAKE EACH ENCOUNTER SO RICH AND SO RARE.
JUST LEAN ON MY SHOULDER AND TELL ME YOU CARE.
MY LIFE IS GROUNDLESS AND GRISLY AND YOUR
LOVE IS THE ONLY CURE.

MY LOVE IS ON THE RACK
AND IT'S TIME TO TAKE STOCK.
MY HEART IS ON THE LAM.

TAKE MY LOVE OFF THE BLOCK.

TAKE MY LOVE OFF THE BLOCK!

*(As he finishes the song, he picks up the two Coke bottles he and* FAYE *drank from, holds one in each hand, stares at them for a moment, and then brings them slowly together until they touch. He then turns downstage to speak with his mother in the audience.)* I did fall a little in love with her, Mama. I know I wasn't seeing her the way you did. This is the way I saw her. Can you understand now, Mama? *(He gets only silence from his mother.)* Oh.

> *(He returns upstage as* HORSE *staggers through the doorway.* HORSE *carries several half-empty liquor bottles and a bloody apron over his shoulder. He drops the apron on the bar.)*

HORSE. I'm dying! Where is everybody? I went home for help but your mama wasn't there.

RICHARD. You don't usually go home.

HORSE. I'm not usually dying! When I'm dying I go home! She's gotta remember that!

RICHARD. You've already started celebrating?

HORSE. *(Putting the liquor bottles on a table.)* Every salesman remembered me with a bottle—only nobody remembered what I drink! From whiskey to gin to rum—and one no-good brought tequila. I hate Mexicans! *(He has staggered to the toilet door, begins to pound on it.)* This is locked!

POP. *(Shouting through the door.)* I'm in here!

HORSE. Well, open up!

POP. *(Again shouting through the door.)* Those who don't drink it here got no right to lose it here!

HORSE. Okay—sell me a beer. I'll lose that for you, too. *(Now* POP *opens the toilet door.)*

POP. One beer—coming up!

HORSE. *(Exiting hurriedly into the toilet.)* Everything coming up! *(*MARY *enters with a bundle, which she proudly unwraps, revealing a cake box.)*

MARY. Here's the cake.

RICHARD. You made a cake? For him?

MARY. I did. And then dropped it when I heard him coming in the front door. I barely got out the back door. Why did he come home?

HORSE. *(From the toilet.)* Pop—you're out of towels!

POP. He went home to die—only he couldn't find you and he refused to do it alone—now he's doing it in my clean toilet! Coming, Horse! *(*POP *exits into the toilet.)*

RICHARD. *(Lifting the cake box lid.)* Let me see it.

MARY. It's ruined. The legs flattened out when I dropped it.

RICHARD. *(Looking into the cake box but not removing the cake—the audience doesn't see it.)* Legs? Oh, Mama—a cake like a meat block! How'd you ever think of that?

MARY. I don't know—it just came to me.

RICHARD. The first one you ever baked him?

MARY. I used to offer. But you don't offer to bake a birthday cake, do you? You just bake it.

RICHARD. I hope he won't drink so much he can't eat it—be too sweet for him.

MARY. *(Removing a bottle from her purse.)* I took care of that.

RICHARD. *(Seeing the bottle.)* Ketchup?

MARY. It's all made of meat.

RICHARD. Oh! Mama—when you do something like this, I know you and Dad could be happy. *(A glance at the mother in the audience.)*

MARY. You worry too much about people being happy.

RICHARD. I don't just worry. I do something. You wait—before this party is over, I'm going to make you and Dad happy. Forever.

MARY. Now that'd be quite a trick.

HORSE. *(Stomping from the toilet, followed by* POP.*)* Okay, Pop, set me up a beer and we'll get it all going again! *(And then to* MARY.*)* Where the hell were you? I went home first—figured you'd want to watch if I died!

MARY. I was helping Sonny with the party.

HORSE. What party?

RICHARD. Look around, Dad. You haven't even noticed.

HORSE. I been too close to death to—*(But he has looked up at the wieners—is now squinting at them.)* Hey, what are those? Hanging up there? You know what they look like to me? Know what?

POP. I bet I do, Horse! I bet I know what you're thinking! *(Laughing.)* 'Cause that's always been what wieners made me think of. Are you the same way, Horse?

HORSE. Hell, everybody's that way. Wieners are the best-selling little item I have. *(He laughs.)*

MARY. That's enough, Horse. Richard did this for you—a surprise.

HORSE. Hung up all them for his papa, did he? Boy, what does that mean? Mary, I bet he really did it for you. You always was a big one for wieners!

MARY. Stop it in front of the boy.

HORSE. *(Crossing to* MARY.*)* What's the trouble—gone already, Mary? Whisper two dirty words in her ear, Pop, and she's hotter than hell. Always has been.

POP. Which two?

HORSE. *(Whispering into* MARY's *ear.)* Any two! But she has a leaning toward little ones—like—

MARY. *(Quietly, enjoying it—but embarrassed in front of the boy.)* Shut up, Horse. Damn you.

RICHARD. Don't worry about me—I know as much as anybody in this room.

HORSE. Since when? You don't know nothing about nothing!

RICHARD. I know about sex.

HORSE. *(He takes a long pause before speaking.)* Don't you use that word in front of your mother, boy! And you better not know anything! I'm your father and I haven't told you a word. Not a word has passed my mouth! And it's the father tells the son. Right, Pop?

POP. That's the way, Horse. If you want the boy to grow up straight.

HORSE. Straight or dead—them's the choices!

RICHARD. I've already been told. You waited too long to tell me.

HORSE. I waited till I was good and ready! And found the right words! I feel them coming on now. Sit down, boy.

RICHARD. I already know them.

HORSE. Right when I'm ready? You better not! Did you tell him, Mary? Any boy will talk with his mother is just plain dirty. And so's she!

RICHARD. I didn't learn from her. She never told me a word.

HORSE. *(Glaring at* MARY.*)* She'll talk about anything. She thinks that's part of being educated!

MARY. I was waiting for you, Horse. Since he had the chance to learn from a master.

HORSE. You're mean, Mary Hallen. *(Pause.)* But you are right! *(And then turning to* RICHARD.*)* Who?! Who told you?

RICHARD. I can't say who he is. He swears you to secrecy. He says he holds the world's record. He's told a hundred and twenty-seven kids.

HORSE. What?!

POP. How do you know how many he's told? How do you keep up?

RICHARD. You just pass him on the street and ask him—any day. "Dutch, how many so far?" And he'll shout out the number.

HORSE. Dutch Vogel. *(*RICHARD *remains silent.* HORSE *suddenly lifts him by the arm, holds him.)* Dutch Vogel?!

MARY. There's only one Dutch in town.

HORSE. *(Returning* RICHARD *to the stool.)* Yeh—Dutch Vogel!

POP. He's a married man.

HORSE. Damn Germans, they stick their noses into everything! How many you say he's told?

RICHARD. He'll kill me if he finds out I told you.

HORSE. How many?!

RICHARD. A hundred and twenty-seven.

HORSE. There hadn't been a hundred twenty-seven kids in this town! Has there, Pop?

POP. No.

RICHARD. I know that. Sometimes he drives over to Dalhart and Dumas—tells kids over there. ·

HORSE. Hell—I got a feeling there's something wrong with that man!

POP. My feelings exactly!

HORSE. *(Staring at* RICHARD.*)* And I also got a feeling any boy picks it up that way—there's something wrong with him, too.

MARY. Well, that just about wrecks the future of Sunray, Dumas, and Dalhart, doesn't it?

HORSE. What future? Damn dead towns! A hundred and twenty-seven boomtown bastards, that's what they are! Born of poor fools didn't have the sense to move on

when the towns moved on. Towns move on, you know. Why, Sunray is somewhere out in California by now. On the ocean. But dumb fools listen to their
dumb wives and sit in these God-forgotten places, trying to pretend they're still
towns—that Sunray never moved on up to Oklahoma, then over to Colorado.
Why, Dalhart's in Alaska now. A salesman told me he saw it up there on his vacation. Gave it my regards, he said. Pop, give me a beer. Damn, I'm depressed!

RICHARD. This should be the happiest night of your life.

HORSE. HAPPY?!

RICHARD. You lived to be forty-one. You didn't die when you were forty—like
your father.

HORSE. You think that makes me happy? I'm so ashamed I didn't die at the same
age he died I could die! Oh, how I loved that man!

RICHARD. But that's why I planned the party! No telling how many more years
you're gonna live now!

HORSE. *(Roaring.)* Well, it just so happens I was only living to be forty—I made no
plans for forty-one! I couldn't believe it when today came and I was still here!
You look forward to something all your life and then it doesn't happen, and you
have to go on . . . you want me to celebrate that?

MARY. You didn't want to die. You wouldn't even take a road trip this year, so afraid
a car wreck might get you.

HORSE. I was scared to die, yes! Always have been—I admit it! You butcher as
many animals as I have, look 'em in their dead faces, you'd be scared to die, too.
But I still *wanted* to die! In memory of him! *(He bursts into sobs.)*

POP. Here's your beer.

HORSE. *(Hoisting the beer.)* In memory of him! Betrayed by all but me! Married to
the sorriest woman ever lived!

RICHARD. Was my grandmother sorry?

HORSE. A tramp of the first water! Tell him, Mary—I don't care—tell him what
kind of blood he's got in him.

RICHARD. What was wrong with her?

POP. Yeh. I never knew she was a tramp.

MARY. She wasn't.

HORSE. Don't try to defend my mother—just because it's my birthday!

RICHARD. What did she do?

HORSE. She quit him—that's what she did! She quit my papa and married another
man. Damn, I do not believe in people quitting people. *(He strikes the table with
his fist.)*

MARY. She didn't quit him—he died.

HORSE. It's the same thing—you leave one man and you go to another one! Besides, you're forgettin' the important part, Mary—she married that other bastard
on the day of my papa's funeral. *(He is crying loudly now.)*

MARY. You know, I believed that for years. Until we went to visit her just before she
died. And she got out the marriage license to Mr. Nunn, her second husband,
and showed us the date—cried showing it—one year after Horse's daddy died.

HORSE. *(Sobbing.)* Well, I thought it was the same day! I was still crying about my papa when it happened!

RICHARD. How old were you?

HORSE. *(A sob.)* Sixteen!

RICHARD. Just like I am now.

HORSE. Nothing like you are! I loved my papa! I left that whore the night she married the new bastard!

MARY. They had no money. She married again so Horse could stay in school.

HORSE. That's a lie. I knew why she married again! Don't forget, I was sixteen! And if I hadn't been old enough to figure it out, my buddy would of told me anyway. He said it to me, "She wants it again"—that's what he said. "She likes it." You think that didn't just about kill me? My own mother? She liked it? She wanted it again? She couldn't go on living without it? You see, that's the kind of mama I had, boy. And the kind of grandmama you had. What do you think of that?

RICHARD. Is it wrong for women to like it?

HORSE. I'm not talking about women—I'm talking about *mothers!* How would you feel if you found out *your* mother liked it? *(RICHARD gives MARY a quick, inquiring look—she turns slowly away, but we spot a slight smile. HORSE notices none of this. The front door opens and FAYE PRECIOUS enters, dressed gaily. The others sit dejected.)*

FAYE. Oh, heck—the party's already started!

RICHARD. No, it hasn't—you're right on time. Here—everybody put on hats and aprons. *(From a box he has removed white butcher hats and aprons.)*

HORSE. Where'd you get clean aprons?

RICHARD. *(Distributing them.)* I hid them at the first of the week.

HORSE. *(During this speech HORSE goes for his bloody apron on the bar—shows it to RICHARD.)* That's why we ran out—I been wearing a bloody apron for two days! You know what it does to customers, you wait on them in bloody aprons? They lose respect for you. Plus their appetites!

RICHARD. I only took five.

HORSE. You got no feeling for the meat business—you got to keep their minds off blood as much as possible!

FAYE. He's right, Sonny. A butcher come at me with blood on his apron, I'm finished. *(Everyone now stands holding a paper hat and apron.)*

RICHARD. Well, since I have them, won't you put them on? Please?

FAYE. Sure we will. It's like a costume party, isn't it? What a cute idea, Sonny. How'd you ever think of it? *(She begins to put on her apron and hat.)*

HORSE. Don't mess up one of my aprons, Faye Precious!

FAYE. I'm not going to butcher anything! I told you—the very idea makes me woozy. Don't be so mean, Horse. Put yours on.

HORSE. No!

FAYE. Yes, come on. *(She puts the butcher hat on him.)* Nobody in the world ever looked cuter under a butcher hat than you—forgive me, Mrs. Hallen, but it's true, you know it is. Now stand up, Horse. *(She puts the apron around him.)* Why, you get that white apron on you—well, there never was such a man, was there, Mrs. Hallen? *(*MARY *stands silent, holding her apron and hat, staring at* HORSE.*)*

RICHARD. Please, Mama, put yours on. *(He begins to help* MARY; *she permits this.)* Come on, Pop, you too!

POP. Will I get a piece of the cake? I seen it over there.

RICHARD. Sure—but first we're going to have the song. Sing it now, Faye Precious.

HORSE. I hate songs! No songs on my birthday!

FAYE. I practiced this song almost one hour and I'm gonna sing it!

MARY. What song, Richard?

RICHARD. I wrote it for Dad's birthday. A surprise.

HORSE. If you got something to say to me, say it—don't sing it!

MARY. And taught it to her—she's going to sing it?

RICHARD. *(An awareness of his mother in the audience.)* You know how she is, Mama—she loves to sing my songs. If I didn't teach it to her, she'd pick it up first time she heard it anyway.

FAYE. That's true, Mrs. Hallen. That's the way I am. I just pick them up. Did you want to sing it to him?

MARY. You know better.

FAYE. I thought I did—unless things changed overnight. But sometimes they do, Mrs. Hallen. I always hope for the best for you—you know that.

RICHARD. *(At the piano.)* Ready, Faye Precious?

FAYE. And on key—always! *(But* HORSE *rises with irritation.)* Sit down, Horse— I'm about to sing it.

HORSE. I'm going to the toilet.

FAYE. Not till I've sung, you're not. *(At the toilet door, her arms outstretched.)*

HORSE. I got to go!

FAYE. Sit down, cross your legs, and shut up! *(She pushes him back into a chair.)* You'd take the happy out of happy anything, Horse! *(She composes herself, smiles, nods to* RICHARD. HORSE *very subtly crosses his legs.* RICHARD *plays as* FAYE *sings.)*

THERE'S ONE DAY IN EACH YEAR
THAT IS YOURS WHEN IT'S HERE,
IT'S THE DAY THAT BELONGS TO YOU.
AND EACH TIME IT APPEARS
THROUGH A LIFETIME OF YEARS
IT'S THE DAY THAT BELONGS TO YOU.

THE PEOPLE WHO LOVE YOU
WILL ALWAYS THINK OF YOU,
WANTING TO KEEP YOU CLOSE BY THEIR SIDE.
SO TO WHOM IT CONCERNS
MANY HAPPY RETURNS
OF THE DAY THAT BELONGS TO YOU—

*(They all turn to* HORSE *for his reaction, but he remains silent, disgusted.)*

RICHARD. You did it beautiful, Faye.

FAYE. I just love it, Sonny. I do.

RICHARD. You like it, Mama?

MARY. Very nice. *(But spoken with considerable coolness.)*

HORSE. Hell if it is. It's supposed to be a happy birthday song, ain't it? It don't say happy or birthday. I like the real one better. Sing that one, Faye Precious. *(*FAYE *glances at* RICHARD.*)* Go on—sing it!

FAYE. You mind, Richard? It's not as depressing as this one, you keep saying *happy* over and over, you know. I think that's what Horse is missing.

HORSE. That's the one. Sing it!

FAYE.

HAPPY BIRTHDAY TO YOU,

HAPPY BIRTHDAY TO YOU—

HORSE. Wait a minute! When somebody starts singing that song, everybody else joins in—if they're honest-to-God celebrating somebody's birthday. That's the way that song is sung! Start over and join in!

FAYE. *(A desperate glance at the others for support.)*

HAPPY BIRTHDAY TO YOU . . .

*(Gesturing with her hands to pull them into the song.)*

RICHARD, MARY, POP, AND FAYE. *(As the others join in, they do it with no spirit, no joy. The song ends with a painful flatness.)*

HAPPY BIRTHDAY TO YOU,

HAPPY BIRTHDAY, DEAR HORSE,

HAPPY BIRTHDAY TO YOU.

HORSE. *(Sniffling.)* Now that kind of got me—all of you singing it to me.

MARY. You're cruel—Sonny wrote his song as a birthday present for you.

HORSE. That little song was his birthday present to me? Well, isn't this a lousy party!

RICHARD. Give him your cake, Mama.

POP. Yeh—let's have the cake.

HORSE. I hate cake! You'd like to see me sick all night, wouldn't you, Mary Hallen? That'd be a party for you!

RICHARD. It's not that kind of cake. *(He lifts the cake from its box, holds it before* HORSE. *This is the first time the audience has seen the cake. There are four legs, now somewhat squashed, under it.)*

HORSE. Hell—it's not even a cake. What is it?

FAYE. I get it—a meat block! See the legs, Horse. A cake like a meat block. Why, Mrs. Hallen, you're as clever as Sonny.

HORSE. Yeh—they're both out to get me. Cake'd poison me faster than anything.

RICHARD. Taste it, Dad—it's a different cake. *(*RICHARD *begins to cut slices.)*

HORSE. Cake's cake. I won't touch it! Another beer, Pop.

FAYE. *(Taking a piece.)* I'll taste it.

POP. *(Coming from the bar for his piece.)* Me too!

FAYE. Why, that's real unusual—what is that?

MARY. *(Gives* FAYE *the ketchup.)* Have some ketchup, Faye Precious.

HORSE. Ketchup on cake? You trying to kill her, too? Oh, you are mean, Mary Hallen.

FAYE. It's good, Horse, and I bet with ketchup it'll just be wonderful.

POP. It does need ketchup. Strangest cake I ever tasted.

HORSE. You're all crazy—give me a piece! *(He takes a piece, takes a bite.)* Why, what is this? Wait a minute—I know! I'd know this anywhere! It's meat! This is meat! If that ain't the damnedest, stupidest—pass the ketchup, it ain't bad.

RICHARD. *(Proudly handing him the ketchup.)* Here, Dad.

HORSE. Tasty! Damn tasty! This is the first cake I ever been able to eat. First cake anybody could ever eat with beer! *(He sips the beer.)* That's kind of a invention, ain't it? Did you invent this for me, Mary?

RICHARD. Yes—she did.

HORSE. It's good. Damn good. I can eat all of it. *(POP is reaching for another piece.)* Stay out of there, Pop—it's my cake and I'm eating it! *(HORSE takes another piece.)* This is one good idea—a meat cake. I like you people when you come up with good ideas!

RICHARD. I'm full of them—open this, Dad. *(From the top of the piano RICHARD removes a large black case.)*

HORSE. Why, what's that?

MARY. What is it, Richard?

FAYE. A birthday present, I bet.

HORSE. From you, boy?

RICHARD. From me and Mama.

MARY. Not from me. I didn't know about it.

RICHARD. *(A whisper to MARY.)* I couldn't tell you, but it's from you.

MARY. Whose money?

RICHARD. I saved it.

MARY. Then it's from you.

POP. Open it, will you, Horse?

HORSE. Shut up, old man. This is my party and I'll open it soon as I know who it's from. Have you two decided?

MARY. From Richard.

HORSE. Thank you, boy. *(Slowly he opens the case.)* Well, holy hell! Look at this!

POP. Ain't they fancy!

FAYE. They're beautiful, Horse! A whole new set of meat tools. I get a little woozy looking at them, but they're beautiful.

HORSE. Look at that cleaver. *(Examining it proudly.)* That's better than the one I own. Where'd you get the money, boy?

RICHARD. I been saving two years.

MARY. Why, Richard?

HORSE. Why? Because I'm his father and it's my birthday! Right, boy?

RICHARD. Right, Dad!

HORSE. Hell, I'm about to cry.

RICHARD. You haven't even heard it all yet, Dad.

MARY. All what?

RICHARD. I want your old set of tools. I want them for mine. I've decided to be a meatcutter. Like you. I'm telling you tonight I'm becoming a meatcutter—like my dad. Forever.

FAYE. Isn't that sweet, Horse?

HORSE. You mean that, boy?

RICHARD. I do.

MARY. That's quite a decision.

RICHARD. It's the one I've made.

HORSE. Who says you'll make a good meatcutter?

RICHARD. You said I got talent for it.

HORSE. What about your talent for other things?

MARY. Yes!

HORSE. Shut up, Mary. You keep out! *(And then again to* RICHARD.) What about it?

RICHARD. What?

HORSE. You write little songs, don't you?

RICHARD. You don't think they're any good, do you?

HORSE. Well, adding it all up, I'd say you got more talent for meat cutting than you got for songs—yeh.

RICHARD. Then let me be one.

HORSE. *(Extending a hand to shake with* RICHARD.) You make me proud, boy!

RICHARD. *(Shaking hands.)* That's what I want to do—always. *(*MARY *turns sharply away.* RICHARD *starts to move to her, but* HORSE *stops him.)*

HORSE. I tell you what, boy—let's give that song of mine—my birthday song—another listen. It might grow on me. You remember that song, "I'm Dreaming of a White Christmas"?

RICHARD. Sure.

HORSE. I didn't give a damn for that song first time I heard it. But they just kept playing the bastard on the radio so much, kind of wore you down. Faye Precious, sing it again—wear us down! *(*FAYE *crosses to* RICHARD, *whispers in his ear that they should speed up the song. They do—considerably.)*

FAYE.

THERE'S ONE DAY IN EACH YEAR
THAT IS YOURS WHEN IT'S HERE,
IT'S THE DAY THAT BELONGS TO YOU.
AND EACH TIME IT APPEARS
THROUGH A LIFETIME OF YEARS
IT'S THE DAY THAT BELONGS TO YOU.

THE PEOPLE WHO LOVE YOU
WILL ALWAYS THINK OF YOU,

WANTING TO KEEP YOU CLOSE BY THEIR SIDE.
SO TO WHOM IT CONCERNS
MANY HAPPY RETURNS
OF THE DAY THAT BELONGS TO YOU—
*(A long silence when the song is finished.)*

RICHARD. It's no "White Christmas," Dad.

FAYE. I sung it the best I could.

MARY. He's just a boy. A boy wrote that!

HORSE. Shut up, Mary—he knows bad stuff when he hears it! He ain't the world's greatest meatcutter but he's not much of a songwriter either. Are you, boy?

RICHARD. *(He turns again to the piano, quietly crumples his sheet music, and drops it on the floor. He then rises, moves toward his father.)* No, sir. But it's okay—you won't have to hire me. I didn't mean that. That's not the plan. I plan to work somewhere else. Some other town. *(He turns sharply to* FAYE.*)* If Faye Precious will go with me?

MARY. Who?

HORSE. Faye Precious?

FAYE. Me?

POP. Well, I'll be damned—like father like son.

RICHARD. No! I want to *marry* Faye Precious.

FAYE. Oh, my God!

MARY. *(Stunned.)* Richard—Richard.

HORSE. What is this, Faye Precious?

FAYE. I don't know, Horse. I do remember touching his hand a little this afternoon—God, I didn't mean to—and I guess he just must have gone to pieces.

RICHARD. I've been planning this for a long time. Will you marry me?

HORSE. Hell, no, she won't marry you! Are you crazy, boy? You're a child—she could be arrested.

FAYE. Could I? Oh, my God—I just touched his hand!

RICHARD. I'm going to marry Faye Precious and take her away with me, and be a meatcutter and support her, and we'll live in another town, and you can come visit us sometimes and we'll come visit you and Mama sometimes! And that's it!

HORSE. So that's it! Why, you dirty little bastard—you are crazy. Your son's crazy, Mary!

MARY. Of course he is—and you drove him there. He grew up watching you and that . . . that—

HORSE. Watch what you call her!

FAYE. Yeh—watch what you call me!

MARY. WAITRESS! *(And then a nod to* POP, *to confirm what she equates with waitress.)*

HORSE. Oh, I been too good to you, Mary Hallen—that's my whole trouble! Me and Faye Precious coming in here every night—associating with you and the boy. We didn't have to do that, you know. We could've just gone off and—

FAYE. *(Clapping her hands to drown out* HORSE*'s speech.)* Horse, for God's sake, shut your filthy mouth! You already heard what she thinks of me.

HORSE. I don't care. I want her to know the truth about me! I could've been a lot more wicked than I am, Mary! And I should've! Oh, I wanted to be a lot more! I just ached to be more wicked! Lots more than I am!

MARY. *(Striking* HORSE *hard across the face.)* Impossible!

HORSE. Why, you devil! Why did you do that? You never hit me before in your life!

MARY. You've destroyed my son!

HORSE. I haven't touched him—but if he causes a wife to lay hands on her own husband, then it's time to touch him. *(He turns to* RICHARD.*)* You've ruined my life for . . . *(And then quickly turning to* MARY.*)* How old is he?

MARY. Sixteen.

HORSE. Sixteen years! And I'm going to put an end to it. Now! *(He suddenly picks up the cleaver.)*

MARY. Horse—for pity's sake!

FAYE. Oh, my—I'm getting woozy. Don't swing that thing, Horse!

HORSE. *(Throwing out his arms for help.)* Then somebody hold me down—you know how I am with a cleaver!

FAYE. Pop, hold him down!

POP. Not me! I know how he is with a cleaver! *(*POP *ducks behind the bar.* HORSE *swings the cleaver again, moving toward* RICHARD.*)*

FAYE. Do something, Mrs. Hallen!

MARY. He wouldn't touch Richard! Wouldn't dare.

FAYE. The hell he wouldn't! I'm woozy as hell, but I'll have to stop him. Stop, Horse! Stop, stop! *(She throws herself between* HORSE *and* RICHARD, *but* HORSE *continues advancing, slowly swinging the cleaver.* FAYE PRECIOUS *sticks a hand into the path of the cleaver, then jerks it back quickly.)* Oh, son of a bitch, Horse, I could just kill you, you damn meatcutter! Look what you've done to me! *(She holds up an injured finger, but* HORSE *ignores it, continues advancing on* RICHARD. FAYE PRECIOUS *runs to the table, takes the ketchup bottle, pours ketchup up and down her white apron, arms, face, hair, then turns screaming to* HORSE.*)* Look! Look, Horse! What you've done to me! Turn and look, you damn meatcutter!

HORSE. *(Turning, seeing* FAYE.*)* Holy hell—I told you I'm a devil with a cleaver! Faye Precious—what have I done to you? *(He drops to his knees, wraps his arms about* FAYE*'s legs, dropping the cleaver.)*

MARY. I will say this for you, Faye Precious—you do have a way with him.

FAYE. Yeh—got him to his knees, don't I, Mrs. Hallen? *(She winks at* MARY, *but then looks down.)* But looking down at all this "blood." Oh, my God, I shouldn't have looked . . . I'm feeling so woozy . . .

HORSE. *(Holding* FAYE *by the legs, sobbing.)* Faye! What have I done?!

FAYE. I'm fainting, Mrs. Hallen—oh, God, I'm fainting. Catch me, Mrs. Hallen—catch me! *(And* FAYE PRECIOUS *does collapse—into* MARY*'s arms,* HORSE *still holding tightly to her legs.* RICHARD *moves toward the audience.* FAYE, HORSE, *and*

MARY *freeze in position, but they remain lighted and visible.)*

RICHARD. *(On the forestage, illuminated by a spotlight.)* My plan had been to save your marriage. To get you and him closer together. And that's how close I got you. About as close as I'd ever be able to get you. And so I left. Struck out on my own. To make my fortune—and formulate another plan. Because what do you do if you can't join them? Why you split them asunder, don't you, Mama?

*(The spotlight goes out, the stage goes to dark. The houselights come up.)*

*Curtain*

*The stage is dark, but as* RICHARD *enters, there is a soft light on him. He is wear-*
*ing a light coat, carrying a suitcase, spinning a 45-rpm record on his finger. He*
*speaks directly to his mother.*

RICHARD. How do you like the idea of me as a songwriter, Mama? How's that for
  disguise? Wait till you see me in this act. I become successful. I've been away
  from home for a few years now—with just occasional trips back. Not that I wasn't
  old enough to be on my own. But were the three of you old enough to be left
  alone? I never thought so—and that's why I was always anxious to get back.
  *(Hammering begins.)* But before I could this time . . .
    *(The hammering grows louder. He laughs, shrugs, watches as* POP *enters from the*
    *toilet, then exits. The lights on the stage come up full. It is now 1955, and the bar's*
    *large photograph of Truman has been replaced by one of Dwight Eisenhower. The*
    *faded "Welcome" sign still hangs.* POP *stands at the toilet door staring in. More loud*
    *hammering is heard from within. And then* HORSE's *shout.)*
HORSE. Finished! Hand me in my toothbrush, Pop! *(*POP *hands him the toothbrush.*
  HORSE *disappears in the toilet again.* POP *again stares inside.)*
POP. I didn't see your razor before. You going to do your shaving in there, too?
HORSE. I'm going to do my everything in here. That woman has humiliated me for
  the last go-round!
POP. I don't like you taking over my toilet! That's a public place, you know.
HORSE. *(Standing in the door—admiring his work.)* Who's going to notice a little
  toothbrush hanging there?
POP. Suppose they use it?
HORSE. Who?
POP. The public.
HORSE. They better damn not!
POP. You better put your name over it—a little sign.
HORSE. And let it get out all over town this is where I brush my teeth now?
POP. You care who knows?
HORSE. Of course I care! I'm ashamed to death of it! What respectable husband
  wouldn't be?
POP. I told you there'd come a night you'd get home too late.
HORSE. The point is I get home every night. And then to get there and come upon
  what I did. To see my toothbrush holder nailed outside on the front porch—my
  razor hanging there by it. Why, that broke my heart! *(*POP *laughs.)* You think it's
  funny?
POP. I do.
HORSE. So did Mary. That's when I let her have it.
POP. You hit her?

HORSE. She was doubled over with laughter—I straightened her back up.

POP. You shouldn't of hit her.

HORSE. What about what she done? Nailing my personals to the front porch. Like she expected me to use them out there.

POP. Maybe she did.

HORSE. Sure she did. That was the funny part to her. Well, I showed her! I yanked those devils right from the wall. And told her I was taking them elsewhere—I was taking my personals elsewhere—going to use them elsewhere for the rest of my life. I tell you, Pop, that bothered her a lot more than slugging her did.

> *(Suddenly the front door flies open and* FAYE PRECIOUS *races in, wearing her waitress costume. She is carrying a bowl of salad. She is followed by* MARY, *who wears a black scarf to conceal her right eye.)*

FAYE. I don't have nothing! I don't even know what you're talking about!

MARY. You do! You've got it! And I want it back! I'm gonna get it back if I have to search you!

FAYE. I don't have it! Horse, thank God you're here! She came running into the café right at the busy dinner hour. *(She slams the bowl of salad on the bar.)*

MARY. I'll strip you if I have to, Faye Precious.

FAYE. She yelled that right in front of the customers. I could've died. *(A pause— softly.)* Horse, for God's sake, where's your toothbrush?

HORSE. That what you want, Mary? You think she's got it?

MARY. I know she's got it!

FAYE. I ain't got it!

HORSE. *(With a snap of the fingers.)* Oh, I wish I'd thought to give it to her!

FAYE. But you didn't! Tell her you didn't!

POP. Of course he didn't, Mary.

MARY. Then who? Who's got it?

POP. I got it! I ended up with the whole damn mess. Look in there! *(*MARY *crosses rather haughtily to the rest room door, looks inside, stands staring for a moment, then enters the toilet, returns carrying the toothbrush. She crosses to her table, sits quietly, holding the toothbrush in her hand. They all stare at her. Finally* HORSE *crosses to her.)*

HORSE. Happy now? *(For an answer,* MARY *lifts her scarf, reveals her bruised eye, then quickly pulls down the scarf again. But there is time for* FAYE *to see the eye, too.)*

FAYE. My goodness, Horse—look at that eye. That was a terrible thing to do to her.

HORSE. *(Smiling at* MARY.) That wasn't the terrible thing I did to her. I've hit her before—but I never moved my personals before. I hope I don't have to do that again. But I tell you what I am doing, Mary Hallen—I'm leaving that toothbrush *holder* nailed up in there . . .

POP. Damn.

HORSE. I can use it anytime I get the urge. So watch yourself, Mary Hallen. *(He leans over, speaks directly into her face.)* Watch yourself! *(*MARY *remains silent.)*

POP. I wouldn't push my luck, Horse.

HORSE. *(He gestures with an arm in the direction of each woman.)* I've been pushing it all my life. Haven't you noticed? *(And he sails from the bar, out the front door.* FAYE *moves to* MARY, *but* MARY *continues to sit staring forward. Finally* FAYE *speaks with a touch of envy.)*

FAYE. Remember the time Horse hit me?

MARY. He never hit you!

POP. 'Course he didn't.

FAYE. He did too! I got stitches at the back of my head. Want to see the scar? *(She lifts her hair, tries to get* MARY *to look, but* MARY *will not.)*

POP. How come nobody ever heard about it before?

FAYE. We hushed it up. Didn't want anybody to worry about us having troubles, or anything. *(A beat as she turns to* MARY *again.)* We've got lots of things in common, Mary.

MARY. I realize we have a great deal in common, Faye Precious. In fact, I would say there is only one thing we don't have in common.

FAYE. *(Innocent.)* What don't we have in common? Tell me. *(But* MARY *remains silent, facing forward, daring* FAYE *to figure out what it is.)*

POP. She's holding it in her hand! *(*MARY *still holds tightly to* HORSE*'s toothbrush.)* His toothbrush. *She's* got it—and it looks like she's gonna keep it.

FAYE. Oh. *(She stares at* MARY, *and then at the toothbrush.)* Well . . . I sure hope you'll be happy with it. *(*MARY *rises proudly, turns, and exits out the front door.* FAYE *shrugs at* POP.*)* I do. *(Moving to the window, peering after* MARY.*)* The way she took on, you'd think the toothbrush was close to being the key to marriage.

POP. Don't worry, Faye Precious—you got the key.

FAYE. *(Not registering* POP*'s comment, staring out the window.)* Uh-oh! Look who's coming up the street. *(*FAYE *races to the door, opens it, shouts.)* Hurry, Mary—you can hide in the toilet!

MARY. *(Dashing in.)* Did you see who that was? He's coming back! I don't want him to see me looking like this.

FAYE. *(A consoling arm about* MARY.*)* 'Course you don't. Duck in the toilet and I'll think fast and come up with something! *(Pushing* MARY *into the toilet.)* Got it already! *(She shuts the toilet door, turns to* POP.*)* Quick, Pop—take this dollar, go to the drugstore, get a pair of sunglasses.

POP. Sunglasses?

*(The front door opens and* RICHARD *enters wearing a light coat and carrying a suitcase—he is obviously older now.)*

FAYE. Well, look who's back! Richard Hallen, my sweetheart! Got a kiss for Faye?

RICHARD. Hi, Faye Precious. Sure. *(He puts down his suitcase, crosses to her.)*

FAYE. *(Whispering to* POP.*)* Go on, Pop—get 'em!

POP. I'm gonna buy them got little stars on the edges.

FAYE. Just hurry!

RICHARD. What you up to, Pop? *(*POP *pats* RICHARD *on the back as he hurries toward the front door.)*

POP. Glad you're back, boy! We sure missed you a lot—and you sure missed a lot! *(And he is gone.)*

FAYE. My kiss, please. *(RICHARD reaches to kiss her, touches the back of her head with his hand.)* Oh—careful of my scar.

RICHARD. Scar?

FAYE. It acts up sometimes.

RICHARD. What scar?

FAYE. Didn't you know about my scar—would you like to see it? *(She bends her neck, parts her hair so that he can see it.)* Twelve stitches.

RICHARD. *(Staring at the scar.)* How did that happen?

FAYE. Horse. Knocked me against the coffee urn at the café. You never knew about that?

RICHARD. No. Why?

FAYE. Oh, it was my fault. I was telling a customer about that spring night that . . . that . . . *(And then panic—remembering that it was RICHARD's mother.)*

RICHARD. That what?

FAYE. *(So gently.)* That a lady in this town kind of went crazy—and ran naked. Were you old enough to remember that?

RICHARD. No.

FAYE. *(Enormous relief.)* Oh, good! *(And then relish at being allowed to continue her story.)* Well, she did—and she was such a fast runner, finally the sheriff had to form a posse to catch her. Every man in the county volunteered. Out all night, up and down the hills looking for her. And reports over the radio—men pouring in from Dalhart, Dumas—even Amarillo to help out. Mainly degenerates. And Horse leading the pack. About dawn they found her, brought her home—but then they couldn't find Horse. Didn't find him until almost noon. He'd fallen in a ditch and couldn't get out. I'd remembered him saying he was the first man down—and hundreds of men ran right over him looking for her. But when I was telling it to this customer, well, I didn't know Horse was in the café. And suddenly he just roared, "It never happened—none of it—no woman ever ran naked in this town"—and he knocked me against the coffee urn. *(She shows RICHARD the scar again.)*

RICHARD. He did that?

FAYE. You know how Horse is—always banging away at people he loves. Might get you in the back of the head—might be . . . *(A weak laugh.)* right in the eye.

RICHARD. Where's Mama, Faye? I called her soon as I got off the bus.

FAYE. Stay gone long as you have, can't expect people to still be standing where you left them. *(RICHARD turns toward the door.)*

RICHARD. Look, Faye, I want to find Mama. I'll be back later. *(He heads for the door.)*

FAYE. No—wait.

RICHARD. Why? *(A beat.)* Something's happened.

FAYE. You know how Horse is—always banging away at people he—

RICHARD. He hit her?

FAYE. *(Spoken rapidly on top of his line.)* Just a light one. *(She gestures with her fist—as if slugging someone lightly.)*

RICHARD. Where is she?

FAYE. First there's something you got to understand, Richard.

RICHARD. What?

FAYE. This morning—for the first time in their married lives—he took away his toothbrush—only she came over here and got it right back. You know why? Because she wanted it back! Because she intends to keep it. Forever. I don't know why you are back here, but I hope you can understand that, Richard.

RICHARD. Can you understand it, Faye?

FAYE. I'm explaining it to you, ain't I? *(But then she begins to cry.)* You remember that time you asked me to marry you?

RICHARD. Yes.

FAYE. That wasn't the worst idea anybody ever had. If I'd just known enough to take quick advantage of a good offer. It might of just been nice and wonderful. What do you think, honey?

RICHARD. *(An awareness of the mother in the audience.)* I'm older now, Faye. Maybe it seems a little silly to me now.

FAYE. I guess I'm not any older. It just sounds sweet and beautiful to me.

RICHARD. Did you ever think you'd get to marry him?

FAYE. Horse? I knew her from the beginning too, didn't I? Besides, the way he feels about people quitting people, it never entered my mind. I thought he was Catholic for the longest time. Didn't realize he was just moral.

RICHARD. You *never* thought you and Horse would be together?

FAYE. You asking me if I ever made a plan? The answer's no—never. And the same can be said of Horse. *And* of her. She sat over there with you—and no plan. And me over here with him—and no plan. And him not even wanting a plan. Not a plan among us.

RICHARD. Well, I have. I've got one.

FAYE. I'd love to hear a good plan.

POP. *(Entering with a small sack.)* Got 'em! She'll look like a movie star.

FAYE. *(Rising)* I'll take them to her.

RICHARD. *(Also rising.)* She's in there? I want to see her.

FAYE. *(Taking the package from POP.)* Just a minute! She wants to look right when you see her. *(FAYE exits into the toilet. RICHARD turns to POP.)*

RICHARD. How bad did Horse hit her?

POP. She's kept it hid with a little black handerchief.

RICHARD. *(Slamming a fist on the bar.)* I could just kill him when he does something like that!

> *(POP slams his fist on the bar, too—smiles consolingly at RICHARD. They silently acknowledge a moment similar to this that happened once before. Suddenly the front door opens and HORSE stands—proudly holding a beefsteak between his hands.)*

HORSE. Finest piece of beefsteak in West Tex—*(But he sees* RICHARD.*)* Oh . . . my boy's back.

RICHARD. Just in time, I'd say.

HORSE. Better not say much. Better keep that mouth out of my business.

RICHARD. When you start slugging her, it's not just your business anymore.

HORSE. What happened between her and me was a little home accident—my business! You come on home and I'll see if I can't fix up a little home accident for you!

POP. More people kill each other in homes than ever do in bars.

RICHARD. I won't be coming into your home anymore.

HORSE. Oh, you won't? What's that supposed to do—break your pappy's heart?

POP. Horse, don't talk to the boy that way—he may be serious.

HORSE. Hell, he better be—better not be lying to his papa! I'm all excited about this news. So long, Sonny! You set that one to music and *I'll* sing it!

FAYE. *(Racing in from the toilet.)* Horse, stop it! Think we can't hear you in there? Wall's paper-thin and now she's crying again. You get out of—*(She spies the beefsteak.)* Oh—a piece of beefsteak. Now wasn't that thoughtful! You do have a tender side, Horse. *(Taking the steak.)* Ooh—and so does this. But you get back to the meat market now—so Mary can get herself composured and come out—it's stuffy in there!

HORSE. I was just bidding my boy good-bye—but I can make it quick. GOOD-BYE, BOY! *(And then at the door—as an afterthought.)* For God's sake at least *try* to do a few of the things I done.

> *(He waves a farewell hand, turns, and exits proudly. There is a moment's silence, then* FAYE *turns to* RICHARD *as* POP *exits through the small door behind the bar.)*

FAYE. What did you mean—you'd never go in his house again?

> *(*MARY *suddenly appears from the toilet, wearing the sunglasses.)*

MARY. I know what he meant.

RICHARD. Mama!

MARY. It's all in the song.

RICHARD. Song? *(But she moves directly to the piano, begins to play and sing.)*

MARY. *(Singing.)*

> FREE,
> EV'RYONE WANTS TO BE FREE,
> FREE FROM A LOCK AND A KEY.
> EV'RYONE—

FAYE AND MARY. *(*FAYE *smiles, joins* MARY *in singing.)*

> INCLUDING ME.
> FLIGHT,
> EV'RYONE WANTS TO TAKE FLIGHT,
> FLIGHT FROM THEIR FEARS IN THE NIGHT.
> EV'RYONE

INCLUDING ME.

BEYOND THE ROCKS

OUT WHERE IT'S CALM AND SERENE,

OUT WHERE NO BREAKERS ARE SEEN,

THAT'S WHERE I LONG TO ROAM—

RICHARD. How did you learn that? You've never seen that song.

MARY. Let us finish. Don't you like the way we're doing it?

RICHARD. How did you get it?

FAYE. *(She points to the jukebox.)* By listening and listening.

RICHARD. They got a record here already? How? I was bringing one home in my suitcase.

FAYE. The man owns the juke brought it in day before yesterday. He was excited as us. First time it's ever happened in his territory.

RICHARD. I didn't figure they'd send them out before I got back. I have one in my suitcase just for you, Mama. To put on our player.

MARY. I've already heard it several times.

RICHARD. Damn, I wanted to be here when you heard it!

MARY. If you'd told me what you were up to, I'd of waited.

RICHARD. I wasn't ready—I wasn't sure it'd come true. But it has! And now I got a plan! Wait till you hear it!

MARY. I already know it. Let's finish the song, Faye. I like the way we sing it.

FAYE AND MARY.

JUST DRIFTING ON AND ON

BENEATH A SAPPHIRE CROWN

AND OH, SO HAPPY TO BE WHERE

THE SUN DOESN'T EVER GO DOWN.

*(During the song,* RICHARD *crosses downstage, stares out at the mother in the audience.)*

BEYOND THE ROCKS,

OUT WHERE A HEARTACHE CAN CEASE,

OUT WHERE THERE'S NOTHING BUT PEACE,

*(MARY silences FAYE with a touch of her hand, finishes the song alone.)*

MARY.

THAT'S WHERE *HE* LONGS TO ROAM

AND HE'D NEVER,

NO NEVER

COME HOME.

*(A beat—and then she speaks.)* Your plan.

FAYE. Is that it? You really never coming back again?

RICHARD. That's just part of it. I want you to come with me.

FAYE. Who?

RICHARD. My mother.

FAYE. Oh.

RICHARD. That's the whole plan. You're not going to believe the money I'll have—they like several of my songs and all my ideas. I'll take you anywhere you want to go.

FAYE. Go? Where in the world does she want to go? You don't like to travel, do you, Mary?

MARY. When did you start calling me Mary?

FAYE. Oh—sometime this afternoon, I guess.

RICHARD. This is between her and me, Faye Precious. You're leaving Horse and Faye Precious—let them have what they want!

FAYE. And what in the world do we want? Would you tell me that one?

RICHARD. Each other.

FAYE. You got a way of putting things that's disgusting! You're not about to leave here, are you . . . Mrs. Hallen?

MARY. You don't want to be left with him?

FAYE. Why, you got a streak in you like your boy's, don't you? *(She begins to cry.)* What have I ever done to you people?

RICHARD. You don't want him?

FAYE. Want him? I don't understand any of this! I love him like all the rest of you, that's all. What's happening to everybody all of a sudden?

RICHARD. Maybe we don't love him so much.

FAYE. You do too! Don't you, Mrs. Hallen?

MARY. I'm not so sure, Faye Precious.

FAYE. Oh, don't say that! Don't you see what this is? Don't you? Your boy's in love with me! Yes! Has been for years. Will we ever forget that night he tried to get me to marry him? Well, he can't have me! *(She stands proudly.)* I've made that so clear. And now, to get revenge on his daddy—who does have me—he wants to take you away. It's revenge, Mrs. Hallen. Revenge over his lust for *me!* But I'm not going to let it happen. Because I know who to tell! And if you don't think he'll come right back over here—and he won't be carrying a steak this time! And you know what I mean! And another thing! This is one time Faye Precious will not raise her already sliced finger to save you! *(She raises her already sliced finger, then turns and runs from the bar.* RICHARD *stares silently at* MARY.*)*

RICHARD. Mama, I want you to come with me. To Nashville, Tennessee. That's where they made my record. It's a good place to live. We're going to pack your suitcase right now. There's a bus that way in twenty minutes. *(*MARY *turns silently away.)* Mama, you don't know how it's hurt me all these years—watching all this.

MARY. You think it hasn't hurt me? It killed me to have you see. *(A beat.)* I left him once—took you and left him.

RICHARD. You never left him.

MARY. Once. You weren't three. We took the bus out. But it hadn't got ten miles when I spotted his old pickup out the rear window—following. Another mile and he'd caught up with us and run that bus right off the road into a ditch. Three passengers were injured. I said I could've been injured. But he said, "Hell, I knew which side to run it off the road on—I knew which side you were sitting on, Mary."

RICHARD. You wanted him to run it off the road.

MARY. I was headed back home to my mama and papa. Back to *East* Texas. Where there is nobody in the world who'd run a bus off the road for you. Much less have the good sense to run it off on the proper side. *(A beat.)* And allow me to come climbing out safely. And back to him.

RICHARD. For how long?

MARY. A night. Which can be enough.

RICHARD. I want better than that for you, Mama. A lot better. I want to show you what it's like when somebody really cares about you. You've never known that. Let me show you. I love you, Mama. *(He drops to his knees beside her, glances at his mother in the audience.)*

HORSE. *(Pushing the front door open.)* I heard that! I heard it! Right outside this door! It came through the door! *(Pointing to* RICHARD, *still on his knees.)* Look at him there—on his knees! Oh, I had my eyes on the two of you for years! I want the truth, and I want it fast! You and her going away together? Is that your plan?

RICHARD. That's it.

HORSE. Well, if that don't beat any plan of man or beast! That's the filthiest, dirtiest thing I ever heard of! My own wife and my own boy running off together! Son of a bitch!

FAYE. I told you, Horse.

HORSE. I know you did. Son of a bitch! *(And then turning to* MARY.) Mary—what have you got to say for yourself?

MARY. The boy wants me to live with him, Horse.

HORSE. Shut your dirty mouth, Mary! Don't speak it no plainer than I already spoke it.

RICHARD. *(Suddenly moving to his suitcase.)* Come on, Mama. I'll help you pack. We can have the rest of your things shipped.

FAYE. Don't count on me to help ship anything, Mrs. Hallen. I won't do it.

RICHARD. Then she can do without them. She'll have new things. And nice ones. *(*HORSE *grabs* RICHARD *violently by the throat, slams him against the bar.)*

HORSE. Look, you—I've had it with you!

MARY. Leave the boy alone.

HORSE. *(Continuing to hold* RICHARD *by the neck, turning sharply to* MARY.) Then you tell him good-bye forever. Say good-bye to your boy! *(Tightening his grip on* RICHARD's *neck.)* Tell him! So long, Sonny!

MARY. You won't hurt him!

HORSE. I'll kill him! *(*RICHARD *makes a groaning sound as* HORSE *continues to hold him tightly.)*

MARY. Let him go, Horse!

HORSE. If he'll go by himself! That's the only way! *(He loosens his hands from* RICHARD's *throat for a moment.)* Will you?

RICHARD. *(Winded but loud.)* No!!

HORSE. *(Tightening his hands about* RICHARD *again.)* Okay—goodbye to my only son!

FAYE. My God, Mrs. Hallen—do something! I don't want to watch the boy die right here!

POP. Hell, I never thought I'd have to invent a rule about killing in here. No dancing or killing, Horse! *(*HORSE *continues his grip on* RICHARD's *throat. There are desperate groans from* RICHARD *now.)*

MARY. *(Finally a shout.)* I won't go, Horse!

HORSE. *(Still strangling* RICHARD.*)* Never? Say never, Mary! You'll never go! *(There is a pause—*MARY *hesitates.)* You better say it fast—the boy's dying right here in my hands!

MARY. *(From deep within herself.)* I'll never go, Horse! Never! Never!

HORSE. *(Still strangling* RICHARD.*)* Thank you, Mary. Thank you. My marriage is saved.

FAYE. Let go of the boy, Horse.

HORSE. *(Releasing* RICHARD.*)* Sure. Sure. *(*RICHARD *is gagging.* HORSE *slaps him on the back.)* You'll be all right in a minute, boy. Just get your breath. Your papa's got a grip like a bear, you got to remember that.

RICHARD. *(Still gasping for breath, looking at* HORSE.*)* Why do you want her to stay?

FAYE. Sonny, *when* is your bus due to leave?

RICHARD. Why do you want her?

HORSE. Don't make your last words to me smart-ass, boy. Don't do it!

RICHARD. *(A plea.)* Why?

HORSE. *(*HORSE *stares at* RICHARD *in disbelief—then shakes his head, explains as simply as he can.)* Because she's my wife—that's why. I was the first man ever took that little innocent virgin to bed and I'm going to be the last man takes her to bed. Because that's marriage. *(He points at* MARY.*)* That woman there has stayed within the bounds of marriage and she's going to continue staying there, difficult as it is. She is no whore. She's better than my own mama. She's the only thing in my life that's . . . that's so good I could . . . I could show her to God, if I wanted to. And you're not taking that away from me—nor anybody else. She's my fine thing, damn you. My fine thing. *(He sits at the table, puts his head in his hands, begins to cry.)*

FAYE. I always said he thought awful highly of you, Mrs. Hallen. Don't cry, Horse—please. That was so sweet. Wasn't it, Mrs. Hallen? *(But* MARY *only stares at* HORSE. RICHARD *crosses silently to his suitcase, picks it up.)*

MARY. You really going?

RICHARD. What can I do here?

FAYE. *(Nervous—urging him to leave.)* Nothing. It's all been done—a long time ago.

MARY. You can kiss me good-bye. *(*HORSE *lifts his head from the table, watching as* RICHARD *moves to* MARY. *She opens her arms to embrace him.)*

HORSE. Just good-bye! *(*MARY *and* RICHARD *kiss briefly and then he again turns to exit.)*

MARY. Say something to him, Horse—please.

HORSE. What?

MARY. Something!

HORSE. Boy!

RICHARD. *(Pausing—turning to* HORSE.*)* Yes.

HORSE. How the hell you going to make a living? You're no first-class meatcutter, you know that?

RICHARD. On my songs.

HORSE. I heard that one in there. *(He points to the jukebox.)* You going to make a living from them?

RICHARD. Yes.

HORSE. How? You trying to tell me every time I pop a nickel in there it goes to you?

RICHARD. Part of it. Something like that.

HORSE. You gonna have to live on my nickels?

RICHARD. Yes, sir.

HORSE. Well, don't say your papa never gave you a helping hand. *(He crosses to the jukebox, reaches for a nickel, slams it into the machine. They stand staring at each other as the song begins. It is "Beyond The Rocks," the song* FAYE PRECIOUS *and* MARY *sang earlier in the act, but it has been recorded by a rock-and-roll group.)* It's got a nice little beat to it, boy!

RICHARD. Yes, sir.

HORSE. *(*HORSE*'s foot begins keeping time to the music.)* Look at that—it's got my foot going. I feel like dancing. *(He moves toward* FAYE PRECIOUS.*)*

RICHARD. *(Quickly setting down his suitcase, reaching* FAYE PRECIOUS *first.)* So do I. Faye Precious—a farewell dance?

FAYE. Sure, honey, but don't you miss that bus.

HORSE. *(A flash of anger.)* Pop—I thought you always said there was no dancing in this place!

POP. I'm an old man. I can't enforce all the rules. I'm going to concentrate on no killing. *(*HORSE *glares angrily at* FAYE PRECIOUS *and* RICHARD *for another moment as they dance. Then suddenly he turns to* MARY.*)*

HORSE. Can you dance, Mary?

MARY. As well as you can, Horse.

HORSE. I hope that's true! *(He grabs her by the waist, begins to dance, swinging her about the floor.* HORSE *shouts at* RICHARD.*)* How's this for dancing, boy?

RICHARD. It's fine, Papa. It's wonderful.

HORSE. You bet it is! Mary's almost as good a dancer as me, by God!

> *(*HORSE *continues to swing* MARY *about the floor.* RICHARD *and* FAYE *cease to dance. He seats her at the table, kisses her lightly on the cheek, picks up the suitcase, and moves to the front door. From there he waves to her and to* POP. MARY *and* HORSE *are unaware as they continue dancing.* RICHARD *turns, now watching as the playwright.* FAYE *leans back in her chair, watches* HORSE *and* MARY, *beams with genuine happiness, patting her foot, clapping her hands.* MARY *lets down her long hair, continuing to dance with* HORSE. *The hair flows freely. So does* MARY.*)*

*RICHARD puts down his suitcase. The music from the jukebox becomes softer, HORSE's dancing less wild. RICHARD crosses downstage, speaks directly to his mother in the audience.)*

RICHARD. Well, I said at the beginning I wouldn't show it the way it really happened. And I didn't, did I, Mama? That stuff about you still doing his laundry—even after he moved in with her. Why, you would have stayed there all your life, sending over clean laundry and birthday cakes—I know you would have. I thought it was so wrong at the time—but it was the only ending I could make work on the stage. Oh God, Mama, I'm sorry. I should never have made you quit him.

*(The woman seated in the audience suddenly rises, steps toward the stage, pauses to stare up at RICHARD, then turns and moves to the rear exit. RICHARD stares after her, speaks the word* Mama *softly, then turns, stares at HORSE and MARY. They continue to dance. HORSE runs his fingers through MARY's long hair. After another moment of this the lights fade to dark.)*

*Curtain*


NOTE: The mother in the audience should be played as realistically as possible. The actress playing the part should not be listed in the program. She should be as unrecognizable to members of the audience as possible. If spoken to by members of the audience, she should answer them briefly but realistically—continuing to "play" the role of the playwright's mother. It is also suggested that she not mingle with the audience during intermissions, but slip discreetly into the dressing rooms if that is possible. Her reactions to the play itself should be subdued and controlled—never with any excessive display of emotion.

# Jack Heifner

★ ★ ★ ★ ★ ★ ★ ★ ★ ★ ★ ★ ★ ★ ★ ★ ★

★ THE PERSON

Born in 1946 in Corsicana—the small, blackland, cotton and oil town famous for its Collin Street Bakery fruitcakes—Jack Heifner moved first to Dallas, fifty miles away, to attend Southern Methodist University and then, after receiving his B.F.A. in theater in 1968, to New York, where he now lives. Like Horton Foote, he visits his hometown often and keeps his ties to his earlier way of life close. In spite of having dramatized many of the community's limitations and foibles, he is a popular native son who is celebrated on his returns. Corsicana's resident theater has produced Heifner's most widely known play, *Vanities*, which features portraits of three vacuous cheerleaders loosely based on locally recognizable originals, and has also produced *Patio/Porch*, which comically uses local lore. Jack Heifner Day was declared on December 22, 1977, and the playwright was honored with a reception by the mayor in the public library.

By growing up in a small community within easy driving distance of a city, Heifner enjoyed benefits of both. As a public school student, he was frequently bussed to theatrical performances in Dallas, and as a precocious child performer in Corsicana, he was assured of frequent opportunities to sing and recite before indulgent audiences. He admits to having been an avid seeker of popularity until well into his college years. Since then, in his works, he has dealt frequently with the American "popularity trap" as a theme.

Heifner's attendance at SMU coincided with the university's new emphasis on theater arts, and he had the fortunate experience of acting with visiting professionals. Although he soon became convinced that his future lay in the theater, he did not make an early commitment to writing. Educated as a complete theater professional, he was confident that he could always find a job, behind the scenes if not onstage. In Texas he worked at the Scott Theatre in Fort Worth and at Theatre Three in Dallas before graduating and taking a job in New York with Joseph Papp's Shakespeare Festival in 1968. Unquestionably, the practical stage knowledge Heifner gained through his experiences as actor, technician, stage manager, director, and even producer has contributed to his success as a playwright. Performers and technicians trust his judgment and consult him during rehearsals about much more than lines.

As a cofounder of the Lion Theatre Company and a member of the New Dramatists, both in New York, Heifner has stayed close to experimental productions and has gained from his associations with the playwrights Christopher Durang, James McLure, and David Mamet. He has also maintained old associations: the original director of *Vanities* in both New York and Los Angeles was his college roommate, Garland Wright, now the artistic director of the Guthrie Theater in Minneapolis. In 1987 Heifner returned to SMU, where he spent a week closely involved with a student production of his play *Bargains*. Set in a small-town Texas dry-goods store, the play communicates the emotional center the store occupies in the life of an aging spinster clerk.

★ THE PLAYS

*Patio/Porch* is a pairing of two one-act plays written to work as a unit for a theatrical evening. Usually they are presented together, but occasionally *Porch*, the major and first written of the two, is combined with a different one-act. In the 1986 Edinburgh Fringe Festival, for example, *Porch* was paired with Heifner's *Twister*.

Like most of Heifner's plays, *Patio/Porch* deals with the ways that small-town society limits and shapes the lives of its inhabitants, usually women. Also, this pair of plays expresses the author's acute theatrical sensibility, here in response to the implications of emotionally charged domestic spaces. As Heifner writes in the epigraph to the Dramatists Play Service edition of the plays: "The patio is an escape from a world that is empty. The porch is a spot from which one can watch the emptiness pass by."

Through the lives of its two characters, the sisters Jewel and Pearl, *Patio* demonstrates the two options that the small Texas town offers its unencumbered inhabitants—to go or to stay. The dreams of both Jewel and Pearl, however, are so limited and media-defined that neither choice seems likely to offer advantages over the other for personal fulfillment. Jewel's movie-magazine dream is structured around such possessions as a waterbed, Fonz posters, a red Thunderbird, and the ultimate—a trailer house parked in the middle of the "O" of "HOLLYWOOD" spelled out on the hillside overlooking America's dream capital. Pearl's *Better Homes and Gardens* dream is centered on her perfect living room with its pink velvet sofa, end tables, and swag lamps, and on her showplace bathroom with every sparking tile demonstrating the result of joyous hours of scrubbing.

*Porch*, originally commissioned by PBS, is a much darker and more thoughtful comedy, which powerfully expresses the mutual dependency of aging mother and fading daughter. Delegated by gender and tradition to secondary roles, the women sit immobile on their porch and watch what passes for the world go by while remaining locked in their dance of death. Inherited money is the weapon used by the widowed Dot to keep her daughter in thrall: "How would you get your own home? Huh? How'd you pay for it? What money you have belongs to me. I won't give you the money."

Health and a pathetic sexuality are the weapons Lucille uses to assert her potential for escape. She maliciously reads her mother the obituaries from her newspaper and threatens to "walk across the street and marry Old Man Ferguson. . . . I could do that! Unless it's God's will that I should stay here for forty-five more years letting you make me miserable."

Running beneath the comic surface constructed of the exaggerations and posturing of the two characters and a string of grotesque small-town anecdotes is a serious explication of interrelated middle-class responsibilities: the parent must support the feckless child, and the daughter must care for the aging parent. *Porch* brings out the bitterness and antagonism implicit in such imposed obligations—and does so without violating the play's comic mode.

In May 1986, there were consecutive productions of *Patio/Porch* at the Warehouse Theater in Corsicana and at Theatre Three in Dallas. Both were directed by Tom Troup and starred Ronnie Claire Edwards in the roles of Jewel and Lucille, which she had played in New York and Los Angeles, and Carole Cook in the roles of Pearl and Dot. Cook's performance in the latter role brought accolades from the *Dallas Observer*'s critic Mitch Owens, who said that she was "in glorious form—bringing to life one of the South's most frightening creatures—the bulldozing matriarch with a Bible at her side and a black belt in dishing guilt."

★   THE WORKS

Like other Texas plays, Jack Heifner's have attracted favorable attention because of their comic use of Texas idiom and their portrayal of regional eccentrics. The Texas-born critic Rex Reed has lauded the playwright for his "recording of the wavy rhythms and colorful colloquialisms of Texas jargon," but of course Heifner has done much more than merely record that jargon. He has created his own effective stage diction that is true to the way Texans really talk. In many cases he has drawn his characters from life and readily admits that natives of Corsicana can recognize the sources. An actor himself, he has written richly rewarding roles and has benefited from having them interpreted by such talented comic actresses as Fannie Flagg, Carole Cook, Ronnie Claire Edwards, and Sandy Duncan.

Heifner's dramas, though, are distinguished from those of other Texas playwrights in several ways. Most noticeable of these is the visual impact of his plays. It is characteristic that the staging concept of *Vanities*—having the three principals costume themselves and make themselves up before each act in full view of the audience—was developed a year before the play itself was written. That device, and patterning the action around periods in the lives of three central characters rather than two or only one, account more than anything else for the play's astonishing success—a run of 1,785 performances Off-Broadway and thousands of productions across the country and abroad. A single cheerleader would have required a characterization complex enough to justify extended analysis. Two would have set up a conflict or a choice, whose resolution would have had to show one or the other as preferable. But three cheerleaders serve as samples of a type whose similarities are revealing and whose differences are merely diverting. In fact it was the inauthentic staging of HBO's television version that most upset the author and, in his opinion, led to the production's failure. Another example of a theatrically striking device, which partially redeems one of Heifner's weakest plays, is the opening scene of *Running on Empty*, in which a glamorous jet-setter burns her designer dresses for warmth in a penthouse fireplace. The fantasy play is set in a futuristic world that has depleted its supply of fossil fuels, and high-fashion synthetics, it seems, are made of flammable petroleum derivatives.

Unlike many dramatic evocations of small-town life, Heifner's have an edge and a dark side that is not overwhelmed by nostalgia or even by the broad comedy that is often in generous supply in such plays. Heifner is seriously concerned about the choices available for his characters and the results of those choices. Mary, Kathy, and Joanne of *Vanities*, Jewel of *Patio*, and Jackie Lee of *Casserole* leave their small towns and discover that they are inadequately prepared for what they encounter, or settle cynically for small, mean dreams, or find that they are cut off forever from significant involvement with the families they left behind. Other characters—such as Pearl of *Patio*, Lucille and Dot of *Porch*, and Sally of *Bargains*—make the decision to stay and are diminished by the demands of dependents or by the barrenness of small-town life.

Heifner's imagination is rich and seething, but when it is not successfully channeled, it can produce excess and disorder as well as wit and novelty. Consequently, his plays fall into two categories: the restrained and the diffuse. The first, not surprisingly, includes his successes, all of which are sharply restricted by such factors as acting space, number of characters, or situation. The second, exemplified by *Casserole* and *Running on Empty*, may represent more fully the fertility of Heifner's imagination. Each of these plays contains delightful moments that, unfortunately, are sandwiched between scenes characterized by self-indulgence and disorder. *Casserole* mixes a plot about a precocious actor returning home for his father's funeral with grotesque caricatures of relatives so determined to keep the flow of donated food uninterrupted that they resort to intrigue and violence to postpone the funeral. *Running on Empty* carries the specter of cities devoid of petroleum to extremes: a starving character scuffles with birds for berries, and a stylish host serves purely imaginary delicacies. Both plays, but especially *Casserole*, contain several potentially noteworthy plays in embryo. A comparison of the two groups of Heifner's plays, the restrained and the diffuse, leads to an increased appreciation for the playwright's ability to edit himself in his best works and to constrain his creative abundance.

## LIST OF WORKS

### PLAYS

*Casserole*, 1975
*Vanities*, 1976
*Porch*, 1977
*Patio*, 1978
*Music Hall Sidelights* (adapted from Colette), 1978
*Star Treatment* (with songs by Janis Ian), 1980
*Running on Empty*, 1982
*Tornado*, 1983
*Smile* (a musical based on the film by the same name), 1983
*Twister*, 1984
*Tropical Depression*, 1984
*Natural Disasters* (a combination of *Twister* and *Tropical Depression*), 1985

*Bargains,* 1987
*Pageant* (contributing author), 1988
*Boy's Play,* 1989

RECOMMENDED READING

"Heifner, Jack, 1946–." In *Contemporary Authors,* edited by Frances C. Lochner, 105:213–14. Detroit: Gale, 1982.

# Patio

★ ★ ★ ★ ★ ★ ★ ★ ★ ★ ★ ★ ★ ★ ★ ★ ★

CAST OF CHARACTERS

JEWEL: A woman in her mid-thirties. She wears slacks, a blouse, and plenty of jewelry. Her hair is ratted high on her head.

PEARL: A woman in her mid-thirties. She wears a sundress and sensible shoes.

Both characters speak with Texas accents.


SETTING

*The concrete patio of a prefabricated, modern brick house. There is a patio table, a barbecue pit, a cyclone fence, and a few tiny trees. The backyard is decorated for a party. Paper garlands, Oriental lanterns, paper party items are scattered about. Despite the decorations, the setting looks very dry and hot. A sliding-glass door leads from the patio into the house.*

PEARL. Would you look? *(She is inside the house.)*

JEWEL. At what? *(She is up on a ladder on the patio.)*

PEARL. Come here and look.

JEWEL. Honey, I can't. I'm trying to put up these lanterns of yours.

PEARL. You should see this.

JEWEL. Sweetheart, I'm halfway up this ladder with an armload of Oriental shades. Where am I supposed to put them? On the roof?

PEARL. In my fruit trees.

JEWEL. Oh, for Pete's sake . . . *(To herself.)* I didn't need a ladder to put these in her fruit trees. *(She comes down and starts putting them in the two tiny trees by the patio.)* I'll have to bend over to put them in her fruit trees.

PEARL. *(Finally entering from the sliding door.)* Oh, I could just scream.

JEWEL. What is it? What's wrong?

PEARL. Do you know there's not a cube of ice in my freezing compartment? Not a cube? Come look!

JEWEL. I can't come look. You've got me doing this.

PEARL. Is it too much to ask for a few cubes of ice when I want to make limeade? Huh?

JEWEL. I don't think so.

PEARL. I tell you, one of these days I'm gonna get a new icebox . . . a big one . . . with one of those automatic ice machines. It's gonna turn out cubes faster than I can use them. I'm gonna have to throw away ice! In the future, when I decide to make limeade, I'm not going to have to go through all this worry. *(PEARL exits back into the house.)*

JEWEL. Well, I hope not. *(To herself.)* Lord, there ain't enough places for all these. *(Shouting to PEARL.)* Pearl, you bought too many lanterns!

PEARL. There should be just enough.

JEWEL. Just enough for what? *(She throws the lanterns over the fence.)*

PEARL. *(Entering again with more party things.)* You know, I may have goofed. May have put the hot dogs on too early. Jumped the gun on them. *(She crosses to the barbecue.)*

JEWEL. So?

PEARL. So, I've got to get them off before they burn. Oh . . . by the time we want to eat, they'll be like ice. We're going to have hot limeade and cold wienies. It's all backwards and isn't that always the way things turn out when you try and plan something pretty?

JEWEL. Well, it does look pretty. It all looks real nice.

PEARL. And . . . I must apologize for the table setting.

JEWEL. Apologize? What for?

PEARL. For the napkins.

JEWEL. You got napkins.

PEARL. Not the right ones . . . not the ones that match. You'd think if they were gonna carry the centerpiece and the paper cups and plates they'd have the good sense to know a person would want the napkins. I mean, it's all part of a set and I like things to be finished. Don't you?

JEWEL. Well, I don't miss those napkins. I took one look at your decorations and the fact that your napkins don't go with your plates did not enter my mind.

PEARL. You wouldn't kid me, would you?

JEWEL. Girl, I don't care one way or the other whether you have those Snoopy napkins.

PEARL. Are you sure? Don't just humor me.

JEWEL. Sure, I'm sure.

PEARL. I'm just doing this for you, you know?

JEWEL. Sure, I know. Now you just sit down and relax. You've been running around like a chicken with her head cut off. Sit down, Pearl. *(She does.)* It all looks finished. See, I finally got all the lanterns in place. Don't they look nice? I tell you, Pearl, when it comes to decorations you wrote the book.

PEARL. I'll rearrange those lanterns in a minute. *(She is up and moving around again.)* First, I'd better put this centerpiece over the hole in the table. Cover up the hole.

JEWEL. What's wrong with the way I did the lanterns?

PEARL. I wish I had gotten the umbrella for this. That's what the hole is for and somehow it looks sort of silly without it. It's an umbrella table!

JEWEL. I want you to know I've hung a lantern on every twig in this yard.

PEARL. I could have used a little shade out here all these years.

JEWEL. You could have used some bigger trees.

PEARL. You know, I always thought I'd get back down there and get that umbrella. I always thought that.

JEWEL. Well you thought wrong.

PEARL. Well I didn't get enough stamps.

JEWEL. How many books?

PEARL. Sixteen.

JEWEL. That seems like a lot of books to waste on an umbrella.

PEARL. Not if you need the shade.

JEWEL. Besides, I thought you were saving up for a concrete bird bath.

PEARL. I was, but I changed my mind.

JEWEL. Was it too many books?

PEARL. No . . . no, it was only eight. But I just decided I didn't care to have all those little birds bathing in my backyard. Nasty pooh.

JEWEL. Well, that makes some sense.

PEARL. For a long time I thought getting that umbrella was the most important thing. They say people aren't supposed to sit in the sun too much.

JEWEL. Well, you know, rich people do . . . sunbathe, suntan.

PEARL. And you know, they are just asking for trouble . . . sunburn, sunstroke. I don't know why some people want to burn themselves up? Do you?

JEWEL. No, you've got me stumped.

PEARL. However, I never had much choice except to sit in the sun, because I never got the stamps together to get that umbrella.

JEWEL. Get your mind off the umbrella. You'll drive yourself crazy.

PEARL. What if they discontinue it? What if, by the time I buy enough groceries and gas to get my sixteen books together . . . what if, I go down there and they tell me there's no way to get it? Do I have to live the rest of my life with a table with a hole in the middle and nothing to put in it?

JEWEL. Well, there are other things you could put in that hole.

PEARL. Other things? Like what?

JEWEL. Well . . . well . . . you could run yourself up a flagpole.

PEARL. Oh, don't be silly. What would I want with a flagpole? Then I'd have to get a flag.

JEWEL. I guess one thing leads to another doesn't it?

PEARL. Sure it does. Besides, I think a flagpole would just look silly in the middle of a picnic table. It's not proper.

JEWEL. I guess you're right.

PEARL. Can you see me running out here day and night running a flag up and down a pole? I'd go crazy.

JEWEL. Let's just drop it.

PEARL. Not to mention rain. You couldn't leave an American flag out in the rain. I'd have to worry about that. What if I was downtown and it started to rain and my flag was up?

JEWEL. Well, I guess it would just get wet.

PEARL. Well, sure it would and I'm not about to have a wet American flag on my conscience. I've got enough to worry about.

JEWEL. You sure do. Now you just forget about that silly hole and sit. Who knows, you just might decide you want to get rid of this table completely. Just begin again with all new patio things.

PEARL. I just might cover up this entire patio with astroturf.

JEWEL. That sounds great. Up-to-date. Just sit down, Pearl.

PEARL. I will, I will . . . but I just have to redo those lanterns and I've gotta put the candles in these holders. Now what has happened to the tapers?

JEWEL. What do we need candles for? It's broad daylight out here.

PEARL. *Better Homes and Gardens* says, "Any hostess knows a properly appointed party table includes tapers."

JEWEL. If it's dark.

PEARL. No, not "if it's dark." One *must* have tapers to offset . . . to balance the centerpiece on a fancy table. Haven't you ever been to a party?

JEWEL. You know I've been to parties . . . plenty. I just never knew of anyone who burned candles in the daytime. (PEARL *is looking all over the yard for the tapers.*)

PEARL. You don't burn them dumbo. They're for looks. Oh, don't you remember when you went to Esther's wedding and she had candles on her reception table?

JEWEL. I didn't notice.

PEARL. Well, that's always been the difference between you and me. I see every-thing. Old eagle-eyes. And, I tell you, Esther had two tapers on each side of her centerpiece. Yes sir, she had blue candles on each side of that arrangement of blue carnations in the white swan.

JEWEL. She used a swan?

PEARL. She sure did. And, confidentially, I didn't think it was all that clever. I didn't see what a swan had to do with getting married.

JEWEL. Maybe it meant marriage is for the birds! Ha, ha, ha! *(JEWEL has broken herself up,* PEARL *is not laughing.)*

PEARL. I think, if I had been Esther, I would have put those carnations inside a wedding bell or coming out of the top of a church steeple. That makes more sense than using a bird.

JEWEL. HA! HA! HA!

PEARL. I can't figure out for what occasion I would use a swan.

JEWEL. HA! HA! HA!

PEARL. What's wrong with you?

JEWEL. Nothing . . . nothing. I just got the giggles.

PEARL. I'm glad you're having a good time . . . "a successful party means people had a good time."

JEWEL. Well, I am . . . ha, ha, ha.

PEARL. Are any of your friends gonna come see you off or have I just worked my-self silly for nothing?

JEWEL. Now don't get mad, but I had to invite Mary Louise and Minnie Beth.

PEARL. I'm not mad.

JEWEL. You know I've worked alongside them every day for years.

PEARL. I'm not mad.

JEWEL. It seemed rude not to let them come!

PEARL. *I'm not mad!* Even though I suppose it slipped your mind that Minnie Beth drinks?

JEWEL. So what?

PEARL. And I hope she knows that I have not included any alcohol in my party plans.

JEWEL. Now don't you worry about that. Minnie Beth always travels with her own six-pack.

PEARL. And did I tell you that the last time I saw Mary Louise, she didn't even bother to say "hello"?

JEWEL. Maybe she didn't see you.

PEARL. She saw me. I was standing right in front of her in the checkout line and all I said was, "Mary Louise, you look thirty years younger." And she just turned up her nose and rolled her cart into another lane.

JEWEL. Well, I think that was the wrong thing to say, Pearl. She's very touchy. Be-sides . . . she just turned twenty-seven.

PEARL. I like Mary Louise. She's done wonders after her tragedy.

JEWEL. You said it. I couldn't lose my mind and pop back that fast.

PEARL. They say for three days in that sanitarium she didn't remember a thing. Not even her name. Then on the fourth day, she woke up, remembered who she was . . . and broke down and cried like a baby.

JEWEL. I'd cry too if I woke up and found out I was Mary Louise.

PEARL. Isn't that the truth? But I like Mary Louise. So . . . with Wanita, Katherine . . .

JEWEL. And Sylvia and Faith.

PEARL. And us . . . are we talking about eight?

JEWEL. Ten's about right.

PEARL. Well, two of them may not get to eat. At this point, I figure I've got about eight wienies that haven't been reduced to ashes.

JEWEL. Don't you worry. Sylvia said she'd bring a pie of some sort. My bet would be apple. And you know Wanita always brings that congealed salad you love.

PEARL. And I guess Katherine will bring her usual "surprise" dish.

JEWEL. The surprise always remains even after you've eaten it. Everyone wondering . . . "what was that?"

PEARL and JEWEL. *(Together.)* Surprise!

PEARL. Now . . . let me get the picture. Come here. *(She gets a magazine.)* So what do you think? *(Showing* JEWEL *the picture).*

JEWEL. It's perfect, Pearl. The very thing. You've lifted that party right out of *Better Homes and Gardens* and into your backyard. Good for you, girl!

PEARL. Oh, I don't know. I mean, I got all they called for . . . the Snoopy decor, with the exception of those napkins . . . and the tapers. Same menu. The same . . . all the same. But it doesn't look the same. Maybe what's off is the way you did those lanterns.

JEWEL. Actually, Pearl, what's out of whack is your backyard. See here in the photo? All those shade trees and leafy bushes? If you'll notice what you've got back here, honey, it's tiny twigs and scrawny shrubs.

PEARL. Well, that's not my fault.

JEWEL. I didn't say it was.

PEARL. I can't help it if the soil is so poor nothing will grow. I tried for years to get Buddy to put some more fertilizer out, but he was too gol-darned lazy. Finally I bought a bag of store-bought manure and spread it around, but it didn't help. I've done my best to get things to grow, so don't blame me if the backyard's bare.

JEWEL. I'm casting no blame, honey. All I'm saying is that you created the same lovely decorations they have right in this magazine, but you just don't have nature on your side. It still looks pretty. Childish, but pretty.

PEARL. Childish? How can you say that? This article is about, "How To Throw A Summer Garden Party." It's about that and that's just what I've done.

JEWEL. But down here at the bottom it says, "Suitable for children ages three to ten."

PEARL. Where?

JEWEL. Down here. *(Pointing to the magazine.)*

PEARL. Well, I didn't see that.

JEWEL. And I thought you saw everything.

PEARL. The print's too fine. They should have made it bigger if they intended me to read it.

JEWEL. Now see, here . . . here on the next page? Here we have your adult garden party. See? It's got a South Sea Island theme.

PEARL. *(Getting angry.)* I don't happen to like the South Seas.

JEWEL. See? You got your fishnet and flamingoes . . . a luau decor. It's Hawaiian. And it's appropriate for ages fifteen and up. That's our group. The one we're in. Snoopy's for children.

PEARL. Well, I happen to love Snoopy. Just look how cute he is.

JEWEL. I didn't say he wasn't cute.

PEARL. I only read *Peanuts* for Snoopy. Don't you?

JEWEL. I have nothing against the dog.

PEARL. So, I'm sorry to say, when it comes to figuring out who likes what at which age, *Better Homes and Gardens* is dead wrong. Right?

JEWEL. All right. Okay. You win, Pearl. I'm sorry that I even brought it up. I guess that's why they call it *Better Homes and Gardens*, not GREAT *Homes and Gardens*.

PEARL. *(She picks up the centerpiece and screams.)* Oh heck! I could just have a hissy fit! Look!

JEWEL. What is it? What's wrong?

PEARL. LOOK! *(She is indicating the centerpiece.)* The candles were under the centerpiece and they've done melted all over Snoopy. He's got this red mess all over his tail.

JEWEL. It looks okay . . . just pull them off.

PEARL. It does not look "okay." It looks awful!

JEWEL. It looks okay, I tell you.

PEARL. *(Furious.)* And I tell you it does not look okay for Snoopy to have two candles stuck to his little butt.

JEWEL. Just pull them off.

PEARL. Oh! How could you think of messing him up? How dare you attack my decorations!

JEWEL. Just listen to me! *(She grabs the Snoopy, pulls the candles off, and the tail too . . .* PEARL *goes hysterical and* JEWEL *is equally shocked.)*

PEARL. Oh! Oh! You've ruined him! You . . . you murderer!

JEWEL. *(She grabs* PEARL *by the shoulder and shakes her.)* Now you just pull yourself together! Pull yourself together, baby sister, and listen to me! No one cares if you have candles, no one cares if you have paper lanterns, no one gives a damn if Snoopy loses his tail! Do you hear me? No one cares!

PEARL. I try so hard to do things right. I care!

JEWEL. I know you do.

PEARL. And you tell me no one gives a damn?

JEWEL. That's right, Pearl. Nobody does. That's what's the matter with people, but that sure is the way it is. No one gives a damn, darling.

PEARL. But I do.

JEWEL. Well it won't get you anywhere.

PEARL. I don't understand you, Jewel. You used to care. Care as much as I do. How can you be so hard? What's happened to you?

JEWEL. Oh, yes, honey . . . I used to care. I spent my time working and working trying to make people happy, worrying about how they were going to like my work, worrying about "doing it right" . . . and they didn't care. When I enrolled in the Lady Linda School of Beauty, I wanted to be the best damn hairdresser on the face of this earth. Curling, coloring, stripping, frosting, dyeing, waving . . . I did it all. I learned every aspect of the scalp. When you pour a bottle of peroxide on a woman's head you gotta know what you're doing. Leave a bleach job on one second too long and do you know what you've got? Huh?

PEARL. No!

JEWEL. A handful of blonde hairs that ain't attached to nothing!

PEARL. Oh, my God!

JEWEL. It's tricky, Pearl . . . doin' hair is a dangerous business.

PEARL. Are you scared?

JEWEL. Oh, I used to be . . . used to be when some woman would come in, I'd practically faint. I'd always be scared. What if I push an orange stick too far into the cuticle when I'm giving a manicure? It would be like having bamboo shoots under the fingernail. What if I put a black rinse on someone's hair and the next day the woman calls me and says she's got a black pillowcase . . . that the rinse didn't take, that her husband reached over and touched her hair and ended up with a handful of soot!

PEARL. Oh, no!

JEWEL. Oh, yes! Those, Pearl, are the hazards of hairdressing.

PEARL. So what do you do? How do you face it?

JEWEL. Confidence, Pearl, confidence. First, I learned that hairdressing is no art. It is a science. When you put bleach on someone's hair . . . you set a timer. When the timer goes off . . . you wash her off. No guessing. When someone calls up and says her rinse rubbed off, you blame it on her. Tell her she's had so many dye jobs that she abused her hair . . . make her feel guilty . . . make another five dollars by giving her a hot oil treatment. And you know what a hot oil treatment does to her hair?

PEARL. No.

JEWEL. It fries it. Then you recommend a "conditioning treatment" and charge her another two-fifty. Then you throw an eyelash and eyebrow dye into the bargain and you've got her hooked. Ruin a woman's hair and you've got a customer for life. She's dependent on you . . . I mean, what does a woman want when it comes to her hair?

PEARL. I don't know.

JEWEL. No . . . and she don't know . . . she just wants it to be there . . . no trouble . . . no worry. She wants it to sit on her head like a monument. She doesn't know the first thing about making it look the way I can make it look. All she cares is that it sits there . . . shining . . . colorful . . . and immovable like a giant cow patty. She doesn't want it to be easy to take care of, because she wants me to take care of it. She doesn't care what I have to do, as long as she has to do nothing. And you know what? I don't care if she don't care. I could put my life's work, all the knowledge I know onto a woman's head . . . work myself silly . . . and she'll go out, jump into the lake, get it all wet, come back, and want me to fix it.

PEARL. Doesn't that break your heart?

JEWEL. It used to . . . I used to sit down and cry when somebody would come in ruined after I'd spent three hours on the most perfect sausage curls you ever laid eyes on. Broke my heart. How could she ruin my masterpiece? But then, I got hard . . . bitter about it. Now . . . I don't give a damn . . . I look at her . . . she's hysterical . . . needs it all fixed up before the husband comes home and sees her at her worst . . . she's at my mercy . . . I control her hair . . . and I look at her and say, "I don't have time . . . I'm booked up." She goes into a fit . . . pleads for my help . . . and I eventually work her in and charge her double. I take five minutes . . . sweep her whole messed-up head into a hairstyle . . . rat it, spray it . . . laugh to myself about how silly she looks, and she pays me, tips me, and goes out thanking me for her life. She doesn't care about her hair . . . not how healthy it is, not if it's dying from all the dye, not if her scalp is rotted . . . she just wants to look nice when she faces her man. Caring, Pearl, is a thing of the past . . . just like my customers don't care about the life of their hair, nobody cares whether your centerpiece has its tail. *(She has been on a sermon and doesn't realize it.)*

PEARL. No matter what you say, Jewel . . . I care . . . I care about doing things right . . . and if my napkins don't match, and the food is a mess, and Snoopy's missing his tail . . . there's no way I'm going to say, "To hell with it!" That has always been the difference between you and me, me and Buddy, me and every-body else. I care. For instance, Buddy used to complain all the time . . . he couldn't understand why I could spend five hours cleaning the bathroom, why I would scrub every tile until it sparkled . . . he couldn't understand that.

JEWEL. I'm with him.

PEARL. He used to say he felt guilty about using the bathroom . . . that I had taken away its function and turned it into a showplace.

JEWEL. You'll have to admit, Pearl, that you are a fanatic when it comes to the bathroom.

PEARL. I am not . . . I don't care if someone messes it up as long as they under-stand that I will always feel the urge to clean it after they finish. It's no reflection on them. It applies to everyone.

JEWEL. It is, however, a bit offputting that you stand outside the door with your sponge and Ajax in hand waiting for people to finish. Always asking, "When will you be through?"

PEARL. I can't live in a dirty house.

JEWEL. Nobody's ever been in your house. When people ring the front doorbell, you always holler for them to come around here to the back.

PEARL. I don't want people tracking dirt into the living room.

JEWEL. Has anyone ever been in the living room? I can't remember a time when guests haven't been "off limits" in there.

PEARL. Do you know how many years I've worked to get that room just right . . . how long it's taken to reach perfection?

JEWEL. No . . . I don't know . . . all I do know is that you might as well put some velvet ropes across the doorways . . . you've turned it into a museum. Why have a living room, if not to live in it?

PEARL. Doing that living room was the high point of my life . . . you don't understand that, Buddy never could. I always wanted a pink velvet sofa, so I saved and saved and finally I got it. It took all my married years to get that and the end tables and the swag lamps. Buddy used to say, "Why don't you just get something else for that room?" And I would always say, "I'd rather do without than have crap." It applies to everything. It's my philosophy of life. Finally, Buddy said, "Would you rather do without me?" And I said, "I guess so, Buddy, because you are crap." I didn't want a bad marriage anymore than I want bad furniture.

JEWEL. You know, I think he built this patio as some sort of oasis. Someplace where he could relax, get his hands dirty, drink his can of beer in peace. I think Buddy understood you very well.

PEARL. I can't look at this patio without thinking of him. I've tried to make it my own. I've put plastic flowers in the beds . . . they're easy to wash off . . . and nothing will grow. I've hosed it down several times a day . . . but this patio remains slightly dirty and therefore will always be just like Buddy.

JEWEL. You know I've always liked Buddy.

PEARL. Well, you should have married him then . . . or marry him now if you like him so much.

JEWEL. And I think Buddy always liked me.

PEARL. Maybe more than he liked me.

JEWEL. Lord, he was a good-looking man. Football hero. He'd drive that convertible of his up and down the street and the two of us would just die . . . collapse in ecstasy. He had that sort of attraction a man has when he comes from a broken home . . . from the wrong side of the tracks. Like a Marlon Brando or a James Dean. Sort of tough and trashy. You'll have to admit that Buddy was one damn good-looking punk.

PEARL. Yeah, well, I certainly *did* marry him for his looks. I picked out my crystal, my silver, and my husband all at the same time. But, you know, tastes change. What's attractive to a seventeen-year-old girl . . . torn T-shirts and dirty jeans . . . begins to turn off a thirty-five-year-old woman.

JEWEL. But you've got to admit Buddy had a great sense of humor. Lordy, that man could make me laugh . . . one joke after another.

PEARL. He had a filthy mouth.

JEWEL. His jokes weren't dirty.

PEARL. Filthy.

JEWEL. *(Remembering.)* Yes . . . filthy.

PEARL. Buddy had me to clean and cook, and you to joke with. I used to be in the house and hear the two of you out here just hooting. I always wondered what was so funny? Every time I came out here the two of you would stop laughing. What would our lives have been like if you hadn't dropped by all the time?

JEWEL. Not as much fun, I expect.

PEARL. Maybe I would have tried harder. I never had to be entertaining. You always provided the floor show. You and Buddy would laugh and laugh, have some beers, run off to the bowling alley. I'd stay here and clean the oven or do something constructive. Then he'd come home after being out all night with you and climb in the bed with me. It didn't make much sense. Why did you hang around so much?

JEWEL. I thought you liked having me here.

PEARL. I never said that.

JEWEL. Well, you never said you didn't.

PEARL. There were a lot of things I never said. I think after Buddy and I got married, I never said I loved him. Isn't it funny how when you're going together or engaged, how many times you say, "I love you." All the time . . . "*I love you.*" Then I got married and I got busy with the house; and he got busy with his job . . . and I think I forgot to tell him I loved him anymore. I guess it slipped my mind. Or else I took it for granted. Then one morning I woke up and realized I was no longer a wife. I didn't have a husband, so I was no longer a wife. So . . . all I was left with, then and now, at the end of a bad marriage is the perfect furniture I always wanted and a house and this patio, which I've always hated. I should have said more . . . done more.

JEWEL. There's all the time in the world, Pearl, to get over it.

PEARL. All the time in the world? What does that mean?

JEWEL. You've got your whole life ahead of you.

PEARL. I'll have my whole life ahead of me when I'm eighty.

JEWEL. I guess you're right.

PEARL. Maybe I've got my whole life behind me. I never wanted a career. You did. I never wanted to run around with a new guy each night. You did. I only wanted Buddy. So did you. I got him. You didn't. Or did you? I lost him. Where am I now?

JEWEL. I guess Buddy was the only man either one of us ever loved. But I'm glad you got him.

PEARL. Oh, I wish you had. Things might be different today. Or it might have been different with Buddy if I'd taken time off from cleaning and decorating to have a child or something. But childbearing just seemed sort of messy. And now, you're moving off and I'm just sort of stuck here in my museum. It'll be a lonely old life and I'll miss you. Miss you dropping by for coffee on your way to work . . . miss showing you my new recipe or dress pattern. Who will I show things to?

JEWEL. Pearl, honey, why don't you get out now and then? Have some fun? Go on a date?

PEARL. A what?

JEWEL. A date . . . you know, dates? With men? Girl, you've got a good setup here. Any man would consider you a prime target for marriage.

PEARL. Oh, Lord, I sure don't want another man. It's not so nice to have a man around my house.

JEWEL. Oh, but I'll bet you get you one. Someday soon some good-looking son of a gun is going to come along, fall head over heels for you . . .

PEARL. And mess up my living room. I don't want it messed up.

JEWEL. Are you scared to take a second chance?

PEARL. Do I have to remind you that I have been married? That you're the one who never tied the knot? Talk about afraid. What are you scared of?

JEWEL. Well, it's certainly not of getting my living room dirty. I don't care what people do on my sofa.

PEARL. You're the next one in line to be a bride.

JEWEL. Listen, honey, I may be a Miss; but I'm sure not missing anything. I'm footloose and fancy-free. And that's why I'm going away. I've spent my whole life in this hick town. Gone as far as I can go here. You know, there's a great calling for hairdressers in this world. I can pretty well name my price anywhere. I'll bet you as soon as I get moved and walk into Neiman-Marcus or Vidal Sassoon's shop . . . with my experience, my expertise . . . he'll offer me a job on the spot. Vidal'll fall all over me. If I was hooked up with some man, I couldn't do that . . . I'd be tied down. And I don't want to spend the rest of my life in this dead place. I want to live.

PEARL. And you think I don't?

JEWEL. So I'm taking off. I got too much to do. I worry all the time that I'm not going to get it all done before I die or before something worse happens.

PEARL. Something worse?

JEWEL. And you know what I hate most? When you think of something you want to do . . . like something real fun and with-it and today; and people say: "Oh, you're too old for that. You should have done that when you were young." The problem is, when I was young, I didn't know what was fun or with-it or today.

PEARL. Oh, Jewel, face it . . . you were always wild. Always, as they call it, "doing your thing."

JEWEL. Well, I'm doing it better now. When I get my new apartment set up with my waterbed and the posters of the Fonz all over the walls . . .

PEARL. That's just awful.

JEWEL. When I get my pad set up and get on my work schedule at Neiman's or Vidal's . . . I'm going back to school . . . be a coed.

PEARL. A coed? To school? What for?

JEWEL. To study the one thing that's going to put me over the top in this world.

PEARL. What's that?

JEWEL. Facials.

PEARL. What?

JEWEL. A woman's face is her fortune and there's a fortune to be made on facials. Then, with all the money I'm making, I'll buy me a big red Thunderbird and drive up and down dressed up real pretty. I'll take trips . . . to New York and Hollywood. I might even move to Hollywood and go to work for Max Factor. Do up the stars' hair and faces. You've seen pictures of that big sign on the side of a mountain that spells out "HOLLYWOOD"? Well, I just might live there! Buy me a trailer house and park it smack dab in the middle of the "O"! The sky's the limit! The world's my oyster! Now how do you like them apples?

PEARL. We are so different.

JEWEL. Isn't that the truth.

PEARL. Were we ever alike?

JEWEL. Well, you copied me. When I went out for Baton Twirler in high school, so did you. We both had those felt skirts with poodles on them. Of course mine was blue and yours was pink.

PEARL. Yeah, well, I've always been stuck on pink.

JEWEL. With me left-handed and you right . . . me tall and you short . . . I guess we never really were alike, but we like each other and Lord knows we've had plenty of good times together.

PEARL. Especially when we were young. You were always getting me into trouble and Mama was always threatening to send us both off to an orphanage.

JEWEL. We weren't at all what Mama intended . . . two gems, a Jewel and a Pearl.

PEARL. If Mama could see us now . . . two big, old, grown-up girls.

JEWEL. She still wouldn't like us much. She used to say: "I see more of their daddy in those two every day. It makes me sick." *(They both laugh . . . the following is a shared recall.)*

PEARL. Remember when Mama hung that sign in front of the house: "Beware! There's one word that will make this dog attack." And she never would tell anybody what the word was.

JEWEL. Strangers wouldn't open their mouths for fear they'd be ripped apart.

PEARL. And we didn't even have a dog! *(Laughter.)* Oh, Jewel, I'll never forget when we were about sixteen and you were out parking with Chester Herrod . . . parking down there in the cemetery. Buddy and I climbed up in a tree, shook all the branches, went "woooooo," and scared the two of you to death. Whatever made you two park in the cemetery?

JEWEL. Well, what were you doing there?

PEARL. Parking, too. That was some crazy idea of fun.

JEWEL. And we'd take the bus up to Dallas to the state fair . . . go to the midway, ride the rides, eat ourselves silly on cotton candy and corny dogs. You and me and Cousin Gladys.

PEARL. Poor Gladys . . . to this day they've never found out what made her drive over the side of that bridge. She never drank. Never drove fast. I guess she just lost control and went off. I don't think she meant to. She just, for a second, lost control . . . went off and there was no coming back.

JEWEL. They never found her. I guess she floated out of the car, down the river, and out into the Gulf of Mexico.

PEARL. Broke her daddy's heart. After Gladys left him he just went out into the garage, turned on the table saw, ran it across his neck . . . chopped his head off.

JEWEL. Nothing like that ever happened in this town before or since.

PEARL. Nope. That was the most excitement we ever had growing up.

JEWEL. Yep. Those sure were the good old days. *(A moment of silence as the recall ends . . .* PEARL *looks over and studies* JEWEL *for a moment.)*

PEARL. Well, it's almost four o'clock. I guess the girls will be here soon. About time for us to get this over with so you can get on your way . . . leave the past behind you . . . leave me behind you. First, Buddy . . . now, you.

JEWEL. I'll be back soon.

PEARL. No you won't. Not soon. Take it from me . . . people don't come rushing back to something they were dying to leave. I know.

JEWEL. Pearl, I wish you'd at least think about starting over.

PEARL. Start over and do what?

JEWEL. Well, whatever you want.

PEARL. I did what I wanted. I've had what I want.

JEWEL. All you want?

PEARL. Everything but a patio umbrella.

JEWEL. You talk like life is about complete.

PEARL. Well, about.

JEWEL. Don't you dream of anything beyond getting your house in order?

PEARL. I don't think so. No.

JEWEL. Well, then what?

PEARL. Well, maybe I'll never get that umbrella. Never really go down and trade those stamps. Then I'll still have a dream . . . something to look forward to. Don't you worry about me.

JEWEL. Oh, but I will. And just for the record . . . just so you'll know . . . *(She grabs* PEARL *in an embrace.)* Oh, hell, honey . . . I'm gonna be lost without my Pearl.

PEARL. So promise you'll take care.

JEWEL. I will.

PEARL. And write me.

JEWEL. I will.

PEARL. And you won't end up marrying Buddy.

JEWEL. I won't. Like I said, darling, you always copied me. I have never copied you. *(They both laugh.)* I'd better run inside and freshen my face. This may be the last time any of you are going to see it for awhile. I'm going to the little girls' room. Don't you follow me with that Ajax!

*(They both laugh and* JEWEL *exits.)*

PEARL. *(Yelling.)* And, Jewel, on your way back see if that old refrigerator's made any ice.

JEWEL. *(From inside the house.)* Okey-doke.

PEARL. *(She wanders around the patio, finishing up the party decorations.)* Oh, heavens, I hate this patio. Even all decorated . . . I still hate it. Just dirt and dust and pitiful little fruit trees. Probably never will bear fruit. Can barely bear the weight of a paper lantern. *(Pause and she continues to wander about.)* Hot. Could use some shade. Yeah, I sure could use that umbrella. *(Pause.)* No, I will do without. I've got to learn to do without. *(She goes to the table and picks up the centerpiece.)* Poor little Snoopy. Little tail all off. Poor little thing. Don't you look behind, cause if you do you'll just look back and find there's nothing there. *(Pause . . . she puts the centerpiece down . . . then looks down at it and straight at the audience with a shock of recognition.)*

*Curtain*

# Porch

★ ★ ★ ★ ★ ★ ★ ★ ★ ★ ★ ★ ★ ★ ★ ★ ★

# CAST OF CHARACTERS

DOT: A woman about seventy. She sits in a wheelchair and fans herself with a paper fan (the type one used to get from funeral parlors). She wears an old housedress and bedroom slippers.

LUCILLE: A woman about forty-five. She wears a two-piece swimsuit (the kind that Esther Williams would have worn). She also has on plastic jewelry and rubber thong sandals. Lucille has red hair. She reads the newspaper continuously.

Both characters speak with Texas accents.

# SETTING

*The porch of an old Victorian house. The steps are broken and the house is in need of a paint job. The porch has a rocking chair surrounded by magazines and newspapers. There is a wheelchair and lots of junk is scattered about. The yard around the porch is dry and hot looking, with a few weeds and flowers growing. A screen door leads from the porch into the house. A sound track or live sound effects of an ice-cream truck and hot rods are required (as indicated in the script).*

*(The sound of the ice-cream truck is heard playing "Pop Goes the Weasel.")*

DOT. *(In her wheelchair.)* Lucille! Lucille! Get back out here! It's the Good Humor!

LUCILLE. *(From inside the house.)* What'd you want?

DOT. Ice cream.

LUCILLE. What?

DOT. Hurry! Throw something on and run get me an ice cream! Oh, Lucille, you're so slow. He's done gone. Turned the corner. You made me miss it.

LUCILLE. *(Coming out onto the porch.)* Miss what? What's to miss?

DOT. Forget it! You're too late.

LUCILLE. I had to go in the house for a minute.

DOT. What for? To admire your figure?

LUCILLE. *(Sitting.)* I forgot my newspaper.

DOT. Your newspaper. So you're just gonna rock in your rocker and read?

LUCILLE. Yes. *(LUCILLE begins to read the paper.)*

DOT. Well, I sure don't want to read. I'm burning up. *(LUCILLE pays no attention to DOT.)* Oh, Lord, it's hot. Do you ever remember it being so hot? *(Short pause.)* Hot as a firecracker! Aren't you just burning up? *(Short pause.)* I'm just dripping wet. Every part of me. Aren't you wet? *(Short pause.)* I don't know how you can read when it's so hot. I can't do a thing, I tell you. My energy is sapped.

LUCILLE. Don't think about it.

DOT. I'm not thinking about it . . . I'm just about to die, that's all.

LUCILLE. You want to go in and wash your face or have a Coca-Cola or something?

DOT. I wanted an ice cream. That would have cooled me off. *(Short pause.)* You've been reading that all afternoon while I sit here suffering. It must be good.

LUCILLE. What?

DOT. I said, it must be good! You've had your head buried in that paper half the day.

LUCILLE. What?

DOT. I take it the news is good? God, good God . . . it's hot as Hades.

LUCILLE. You want some ice? All chipped up, like a snowcone?

DOT. Like a snowcone?

LUCILLE. *(Irritated.)* Like a cone.

DOT. Oh . . . ooh . . . remember when Old Man Hayes used to come by selling those cones? Every day? I'd be out on the porch, cause Daddy wouldn't let me go outside in the sun. He'd say: "Stay up on the porch, Dottie. You've got fair skin. If you go out you'll get burned." He'd say that. Wouldn't even let me go out to the curb and buy a snowcone from Old Man Hayes. He was afraid I'd turn red. That's because I used to be a redhead, like you. So let that be a lesson to you, Lucy.

LUCILLE. Who's Old Man Hayes?

DOT. Oh, you knew Old Man Hayes. Think, Lucy! You knew him.

LUCILLE. I did?

DOT. Marion's daddy. Marion Hayes . . . that gal I went to school with. Marion Hayes . . . everybody called her "mayonnaise." Whatever happened to her?

LUCILLE. She's probably dead.

DOT. I wonder. I really do.

LUCILLE. I don't remember her either.

DOT. Oh, you do.

LUCILLE. Marion Hayes?

DOT. God, she was skinny. Marion Hayes. Her daddy sold snowcones in the summer and hot tamales in the winter. He had that tamale cart. Used to push it up to the corner by the Continental bus station. It was red and he rolled those tamales in newspapers. Well, not the tamales themselves . . . they were in corn shucks. But your order of tamales came to you in a newspaper. Like the one you're reading. Whatever happened to him?

LUCILLE. How should I know?

DOT. Whatever happened to her?

LUCILLE. *(Very irritated.)* I said, I don't know her. *(LUCILLE goes back to reading.)*

DOT. Poor Marion . . . skinny little thing. But tall. Wore glasses. We used to ride by the tamale stand and hang our heads out the car window and scream at Old Man Hayes. We'd scream, "Where's my cat?" or "dog." "Where's my dog?" We were accusing him of making those tamales out of cat meat. Dog meat. Poor old Marion didn't have a chance with her daddy selling snowcones in the summer and tamales in the winter. Nobody liked her because of it. I guess she just up and moved when she had the chance. Went somewhere where nobody knew her past. I guess she just did. Didn't she?

LUCILLE. Huh?

DOT. Didn't she move?

LUCILLE. I guess.

DOT. Well, I guess she'd just have to . . . wouldn't she? Well?

LUCILLE. Well, what? *(She slams the paper down.)*

DOT. Well . . . it didn't seem to make much difference if your daddy ran the chili factory. That didn't hurt the kids in that family. They are well thought of. Nobody went around screaming, "Where's my dog," to them. But then, they used to drive that truck around . . . it was shaped like a chili can and had two beavers in the back . . . for *Beaver Brand. Beaver Brand Chili.* They used to have two stuffed beavers in the pickup truck in a cage. Nobody questioned whether it was beef or beaver. Did they? *(Short pause.)* Isn't it odd?

LUCILLE. What?

DOT. Odd?

LUCILLE. I guess. *(She goes back to reading.)*

DOT. Well, of course, it's odd. God . . . I could drop dead or melt. Can people melt?

LUCILLE. What?

DOT. Melt? Like *Little Black Sambo* . . . melt? Turn into butter?

LUCILLE. Beats me.

DOT. Why butter?

LUCILLE. What?

DOT. Why did the tigers turn into butter? Why? What for?

LUCILLE. I don't know.

DOT. It doesn't make any sense. They ran round and round until they turned into butter?

LUCILLE. Yes.

DOT. Why? How? Tigers turning into butter. What would Sambo do with it? What would a little colored boy want with all that butter?

LUCILLE. I don't know.

DOT. It makes no sense to me. It's one of the wonders of the world. *(Short pause.)* Hot, hot, hot, hot, hot! *(Short pause.)* About finished?

LUCILLE. What?

DOT. With your paper?

LUCILLE. About.

DOT. About time.

LUCILLE. It gets my mind off the heat.

DOT. Hot. Whew it's hot!

LUCILLE. Wish it would rain.

DOT. Wouldn't help. Would just turn into steam. Humidity. If you got to be hot, dry heat is less hot. Not that I want *any* heat . . . just if we've got to be hot, then it's better not wet. Whew wee! Drip, drip, drip! Sweat's running out like sap out of a maple. Whew ooh! *(Pause.)* And . . . *(Short pause.)* there's not a soul on the street.

LUCILLE. No.

DOT. Yes, I saw one person pass by this morning. Want to know who? Well?

LUCILLE. Well, what?

DOT. Guess who?

LUCILLE. Who?

DOT. Guess! Guess! Oh, Lucille, play a guessing game. Guess who? Guess who?

LUCILLE. I haven't any idea, who?

DOT. Edna Baggett! That's who.

LUCILLE. Oh?

DOT. So Edna came out of her house, crossed the street, got in front of the Christian Church, then just turned around and went back home. I said, "Edna, is it hot enough for you?" And she said, "Girl, you can fry an egg on the sidewalk out here." Could you do that? Fry an egg on the sidewalk?

LUCILLE. I've heard of it.

DOT. Without any grease? How? It would stick and you couldn't eat it, but I guess it would prove how hot it is. Wouldn't it? If you wanted to waste an egg. Would you?

LUCILLE. What?

DOT. Waste an egg to prove a point?

LUCILLE. What?

DOT. Oh, read your paper. Just read on. Me, myself, well . . . I'm getting a wrist ache. Fan, fan, fan, fan, fan. If I was skinny, like you, I wouldn't be so hot. Aren't skinny people cooler? Isn't that what they say? Fat makes you hot?

LUCILLE. So they say.

DOT. I just don't know why it won't melt. Fat melts. I could turn into butter then I'd be as cool as a cucumber. Why are cucumbers cool? *(Short pause.)* Because they're skinny?

LUCILLE. *(She screams.)* I guess.

DOT. Oh, just read your paper! Just loll around and read! I'm trying to figure out what makes people cool.

LUCILLE. I thought you decided it was because of thinness.

DOT. Well, that theory, Lucille, just won't hold water. Because Edna is skinny and she was hot. Marion Hayes was always hot. Always had some sort of perspiration problem. So thinness making people cool isn't always right. Right?

LUCILLE. I guess not.

DOT. You guess? You guess? I know not. That Marion Hayes never gained an ounce in spite of all those tamales. But, then, maybe she didn't eat them? Maybe she knew for sure what they were made of? Edna, however, lost all her weight . . . got thin . . . when she swallowed that pin. I wonder where everyone is? There's nobody down at the corner that way and there's nobody in the cemetery.

LUCILLE. What pin? *(She lowers the newspaper.)*

DOT. Aha! So you *are* listening?

LUCILLE. What pin?

DOT. You really want to know?

LUCILLE. What pin?

DOT. Well . . . oh, you're not really interested. I'll just keep my mouth shut. Read. Read! I'll keep on the lookout for another human being wandering about. Someone to talk to. Read on, Lucy, read on!

LUCILLE. Okay. *(She goes back to reading the newspaper.)*

DOT. *(After a pause.)* Nothing. No one. Not a soul. Whole place is empty. Ah, well . . . *(She pauses, then slaps the newspaper with her fan.* LUCILLE *slams the paper down and listens.)* When Edna was selling dresses, she was trying to fit someone one day, unpinned something, put the pin in her mouth, and next thing she knew it was gone. There! I said it!

LUCILLE. Gone?

DOT. Honey, they looked and looked for that pin. They looked through everything she passed. But she never let it out. To this day that pin is somewhere in Edna's body. Either that or she never swallowed it, but she swears she did. At times she'll sit down and can feel it stick her! But it only happens when she sits and only sometimes. She says that must prove the pin is somewhere in her behind. Shall I go on?

LUCILLE. Go on.

DOT. Well, I saw it happen one day, when I was at her house . . . that was several years ago, of course. I saw her sit, heard her carry on, and I think it's actually that chair she's got in her den. I sat on it, that chair, and I felt the pin, too. Must be a spring sticking up. Naturally, I didn't let on to Edna. It would break her heart to know she's suffered ten years over that pin and the pain is actually caused by her furniture. If she ever had that chair recovered she'd probably feel okay, but how could that make up for ten years of pain?

LUCILLE. I don't know. *(LUCILLE goes back to reading.)*

DOT. Well, I don't either.

LUCILLE. No.

DOT. Oh, well . . . it's one of life's mysteries. *(She sings.)* "Ah, sweet mystery of life at last . . ." *(Pause, she sings again.)* "Ah, sweet mystery of life at last I've found you, Ah, . . ." *(LUCILLE slams the paper down and stares at DOT.)* Well, I won't sing. I'll just fan myself. Fan, a fan, a fan! *(The sound of hot rods are heard as they scream by on the street.)* Oh! Oh! Oh! Lucille, I wish those hot rodders would stay off the street. Shut up! Get lost . . . you beatniks!

LUCILLE. They cut through here on their way to the Dairy Queen. *(LUCILLE goes back to reading.)*

DOT. I know. I know. This used to be a residential neighborhood. Quiet. Relaxed. All-American. Just people and their dogs. Now they've put that old Dairy Queen down at the end of the block. Right down practically in the cemetery. And down the other way they got a "do-it-yourself" car wash and a Taco Bell. They tore down the loveliest homes to build that junk. The whole block is a slum, Lucille. We just live in a shanty in old shanty town. And there ain't nothin' I can do about it. Just sit and watch the whole place go straight to hell. Ain't nothin' I can do, except fan. Fan, fan, fan! *(Pause.)* Is it interesting?

LUCILLE. What?

DOT. The news?

LUCILLE. I can't tell yet.

DOT. When will you know?

LUCILLE. When I finish, I guess.

DOT. Well, you just let me know.

LUCILLE. I will.

DOT. I sure don't want to waste my time reading if it's not interesting. Why be hot and bored at the same time? I'm already hot, so why be bored?

LUCILLE. It's not boring.

DOT. But it's not interesting.

LUCILLE. But it's not boring.

DOT. Wouldn't you hate to get all the way to the end and hate all the news? Every bit of it? Isn't it awful you have to get to the end before you know? I hate for the news to disappoint me. It's almost always bad. I just hate it! You hear me? I hate it!

LUCILLE. I hear you. You're screaming.

DOT. Well, I'm making a point. Bad news is for the birds! For the birds, Lucille! And that's my point! I made it. That's it. *(Short pause.)* Oh, Lord, I've done worked myself into a lather. I'm an excitable person, Lucille, and you've got me all worked up.

LUCILLE. Well, simmer down.

DOT. I'm trying, I'm trying. But you made me lose my temper. I'm too hot now. Hot and bothered. I just might die. I might kick the bucket. What would you do if I did, Lucy? You'd probably just read your newspaper wouldn't you? Huh?

LUCILLE. *(Still reading the paper.)* Hey, remember Old Lady Thigpin?

DOT. Well, sure I do. I've got a good memory. Is she in the paper?

LUCILLE. The old woman with that little shop featuring fried pies?

DOT. Yes . . . that's her. God, those little pies are good. Nobody makes a fried pie like Mrs. Thigpin does.

LUCILLE. Did. She died.

DOT. She did?

LUCILLE. Dead.

DOT. Was she cooking when she croaked? Cooking pies?

LUCILLE. How should I know?

DOT. Well, what does the paper say?

LUCILLE. She died.

DOT. But how? Why? That's incomplete! I want to know it all! The full story. Don't just tell me she's dead!

LUCILLE. And remember Betsy Withrow? That cute little girl that had the Shetland pony?

DOT. Yes. No . . . did she die?

LUCILLE. No. But the pony did. And that woman who took in ironing? Mrs. O'Neal?

DOT. Oh, no.

LUCILLE. *(Looking* DOT *right in the eye.)* Died. Dead. Had a stroke.

DOT. I don't doubt it. With all this heat, it's too hot to iron. Stop reading all that bad news, Lucy. You'll get depressed. I want you to listen to me.

LUCILLE. What? *(*LUCILLE *puts down the paper.)*

DOT. Listen to me. Do you know that my hair's all stuck to the back of my neck? All stuck up in little ringlets? Hot! Whew! Why don't you give me a shampoo? Whew! Why don't you do up my hair real pretty?

LUCILLE. What for?

DOT. It'll get your mind off your troubles. All those deaths. Busy hands are happy hands, Lucille.

LUCILLE. My hands are happy enough. *I* may be miserable, but my hands are happy.

DOT. Ah, ha, ha, ha! Lucy, you are a scream!

LUCILLE. Am I?

DOT. A regular comedian! Ha, ha, ha! Oh, don't make me laugh so hard. Stop cracking jokes, Lucille.

LUCILLE. I didn't say anything funny.

DOT. You did! You did! Lucille, you are a monkey! A baboon!

LUCILLE. Oh, calm down. You'll bust a gut. Just calm down.

DOT. All right! All right! I'm getting myself under control. Okay. Now see? I'm calm.

LUCILLE. Good. Control yourself.

DOT. I will. *(LUCILLE waits for DOT to calm down . . . then goes back to reading her newspaper. DOT is quiet for a moment . . . then screams again. Looking offstage.)* Oh! Lookee! Look! There's that little Vickery boy! Shoo! Shoo! Tom Vickery, you get out of my rosebushes! Lucille, run out there and shoo him out of my rosebushes! Out! Get out! If you don't move, I'll call your mommy, Tom Vickery! *(DOT suddenly stops screaming and rolls her wheelchair close to LUCILLE. She speaks quietly.)* Oh, for God's sake, Lucille, did you hear what I just said? I forgot Mrs. Vickery has passed on. Poor little orphan. What a shame. What an unfortunate thing for me to say. Still . . . *(A short pause.)* It doesn't make any sense that he should be stealing my roses. Does it? Just because he's an orphan? Besides, he takes my roses, goes home, makes corsages out of them, and sells them. My roses!

LUCILLE. Maybe he's putting your flowers on his mamma's grave?

DOT. Don't be silly, he sells them! Sold me one . . . back when I used to go downtown. There he was, in front of the Woolworth's peddling corsages, so I bought one from the boy, came home, and found my bushes stripped bare! I bought my own flowers, Lucille. Twenty-five cents for my own roses! Don't that beat all? Don't that just make you sick? Huh? Poor little orphan probably needs the quarter, but that don't make it right. Does it?

LUCILLE. What?

DOT. Stealing! Swiping my flowers so the child can play like he's a florist?

LUCILLE. No.

DOT. No. Having no mamma don't make it right. *(Yelling.)* "Thou shalt not steal," Tom Vickery! Get out of my rose bed! Shoo! Shoo! *(To LUCILLE.)* That's what children do when they don't have a mamma. Isn't that right, Lucille?

LUCILLE. What?

DOT. Isn't that how children go wrong?

LUCILLE. It's not his fault. He didn't kill his own mamma, did he?

DOT. Well, of course not. She was killed by that elephant. I'll bet she'd be sick to death if she could see how her son's turned out.

LUCILLE. Any way you look at it she's dead. What elephant?

DOT. Poor woman's probably turning over in her grave right now. Every time her son steals my flowers, I'll bet she turns right over. Does a flip. *(LUCILLE puts her paper down and really asks the following question.)*

LUCILLE. What elephant?

DOT. *(Ignoring the question.)* I'll tell you, I learned my lesson about stealing when I was a little girl. Yes, I did. I went into the five-and-dime and lifted a lip rouge. I was only about six and didn't have any sense. My daddy whipped me. When I came home wearing lip rouge, he knew I'd stole it. What's a six-year-old doing owning a lip rouge? I should have known to steal something more in my age range. But me, I never liked toys, I just wanted to be pretty. The only thing you were ever caught stealing was a pair of black panties that had red lettering across the front. They said, "Saturday Night." You were never interested in makeup. You stole undies. *(LUCILLE has gone back to her newspaper . . . bored with DOT's story.)* Lucille, you are a peculiar thing. Ha, ha! Funny, now that I'm old enough to wear lipstick every day there are times I just go without it. Of course, I wouldn't do that if we had company. But just sitting here on the porch, I think it's okay not to wear it. I think on my own porch I can sit with a natural face. Well?

LUCILLE. Well, what?

DOT. I don't have to get all done up, do I?

LUCILLE. Not for me. Not if you don't want to.

DOT. I'm not talking about what I want, I'm referring to what's proper. Would Jackie Onassis sit on her screened-in porch without her face on?

LUCILLE. I don't know. Find out from her.

DOT. How can I? I don't even know her. Never met the gal. I don't know where to turn.

LUCILLE. Pray, I guess.

DOT. Pray? To who? What am I going to do, ask the Lord Jesus for makeup advice? Don't be silly. *(She laughs.)* Lucille, you're a card.

LUCILLE. A what?

DOT. A card! A card! Oh, never mind. Read your paper. Me . . . I'll just fan. Fan, fan, fan. Ha, ha! Hum . . . well, it's dead outside. No one's out and about. Dead as a doornail. What's a doornail? Hum-hum-hum. *(A pause. Suddenly.)* Black Diamond!

LUCILLE. What?

DOT. His name was Black Diamond. *(LUCILLE, confused, again puts the newspaper in her lap.)*

LUCILLE. Who?

DOT. The elephant.

LUCILLE. What?

DOT. The beast that killed that little boy's mommy.

LUCILLE. Yes?

DOT. Yes, what?

LUCILLE. Is that all?

DOT. That's it, honey.

LUCILLE. He killed her?

DOT. Like a doornail.

LUCILLE. Why?

DOT. Because she drove up in her convertible. Drove right up to where that elephant was getting a drink of water. Can you imagine? Getting that close to an elephant? I guess when you're looking for a parking place and need it bad enough, you'll park anywhere.

LUCILLE. So?

DOT. So what?

LUCILLE. How did parking there get her killed?

DOT. Simple. The elephant reached over, picked Mrs. Vickery up out of her convertible, and slammed her against the side of the sidewalk.

LUCILLE. Why?

DOT. How would I know why? Because she had the top down, I guess.

LUCILLE. Why would an elephant pick a woman up out of a car and kill her?

DOT. Don't ask me. Why did the chicken cross the road? I don't know.

LUCILLE. So what happened?

DOT. They buried Mrs. Vickery.

LUCILLE. To the elephant? What was an elephant doing downtown anyway?

DOT. Well, what do you think he was doing, Lucille? Shopping? Ha, ha! He was in a circus. Why else would an elephant hang around Main Street? Use your head, Lucy!

LUCILLE. So what happened?

DOT. The elephant was buried, too.

LUCILLE. Where?

DOT. I don't know, Lucille. Where do you bury an elephant? Who cares? My point is till this very day, you'll never catch me feeding peanuts to them at the zoo.

LUCILLE. What zoo? We don't have a zoo.

DOT. That's not my point. Beware of elephants, Lucille. They can just reach over, and before you know it, you're a goner. If I were you, I'd steer clear of elephants.

LUCILLE. I've never seen an elephant in my life. Not in person.

DOT. Well, if you do, just ease on by him. Don't park. Don't even go near him. Elephants spell trouble. And that's my point. Now . . . isn't that a better story than anything you've read in that paper today? Isn't it?

LUCILLE. Are you sure that story is true? Why have I never heard it?

DOT. Sure it's true. And you've never heard it because you never listen. Open your ears, Lucy, you've got a lot to learn!

LUCILLE. That's why I'll just read my paper. (LUCILLE *goes back to reading.*)

DOT. I mean about life, Lucy, life! You can't always believe what you read, except in the Bible.

LUCILLE. Why's that the exception?

DOT. Because it's the truth. I never read anything but the Bible, that's why I speak nothing but the truth. "Ye shall know the truth," Lucy, "and the truth shall set ye free."

LUCILLE. Well, I think there's some truth to the newspaper.

DOT. Just some, Lucy, some! How are you going to separate the truth from the lies? You're not smart enough. You didn't do too well in school, did you? I would have felt just awful if I'd been the last in my class.

LUCILLE. Someone's got to be last.

DOT. Seems to me . . . if I knew I was going to be last, I would pull myself up by my bootstraps and try harder.

LUCILLE. I didn't know I was last. I knew I was near the end, but not last.

DOT. Did it just kill you when you found out? Did you just want to go jump in the lake? End it all?

LUCILLE. Like I said, someone's got to be last. Being the one hasn't ruined my life.

DOT. It hasn't helped it any. So get your head out of that paper, you might miss something.

LUCILLE. There's nothing to miss. What's there to miss?

DOT. Plenty. You'll miss something good and never know it. Why read that old paper?

LUCILLE. There are things I want to know.

DOT. Well, you won't find what you want in the paper. What do you want to know? Well . . . what? I'll answer all your questions. Ask me anything. I'm better than a newspaper. Ask me! *(DOT grabs the paper away from LUCILLE.)*

LUCILLE. Do I have to?

DOT. Yes! Ask me a question and I'll tell you no lies.

LUCILLE. Oh, I don't know.

DOT. Where's your curiosity? Pop me a question.

LUCILLE. Oh, well . . . why is it so hot?

DOT. I know that! It is hot because it is summer. See? *(DOT and LUCILLE probably play these kinds of question-and-answer games every day. DOT loves the game.)*

LUCILLE. Well, why do you think you can answer my questions?

DOT. That's so simple. Because I wasn't the last in my class. Give me a hard one.

LUCILLE. Well, why live?

DOT. What? *(LUCILLE usually doesn't ask such serious questions. She is out to stump DOT with this one.)*

LUCILLE. Why live?

DOT. Ah-ha! That's a goodie. That's the sixty-four-thousand-dollar one. The best one yet. And the answer is, Lucy, because God put everyone on this earth for a purpose.

LUCILLE. What's yours?

DOT. Well . . . one doesn't always know.

LUCILLE. So you don't know what you're doing?

DOT. I know, I know . . . I haven't lived all these years in the dark. I know what I'm doing. I'm doing what God is doing with me. And I'll know what I've done when he decides to tell me.

LUCILLE. When will that be? What if some elephant picks you up and slams you against the sidewalk before he lets you know? *(LUCILLE is winning at this point and DOT is not so quick with her answers.)*

DOT. Well, you see . . . I am sure he told Mrs. Vickery her purpose the minute before that elephant threw her.

LUCILLE. And it was, "Mrs. Vickery, you have lived to be killed by an elephant"? Was that it?

DOT. How should I know? Don't be silly! Whatever he told her was between her and God. He didn't tell me . . . he told her. God just expects you to keep on doing whatever it is you do do until he gives you the meaning of what you are doing.

LUCILLE. So you're just going to sit and wait here on the porch?

DOT. Sure I am. What else can I do? Besides . . . it's too hot to do anything else. I'd do something else if it was cool, but it's hot. I didn't make it hot. God did. He knows what I do when it's hot. I sit here. If he didn't like that he'd make it cool. Then I'd go inside and do what I do then.

LUCILLE. Which is?

DOT. Sit in the living room.

LUCILLE. I see.

DOT. Do you, Lucille? Sometimes I wonder. You're so slow to catch on.

LUCILLE. Well, if God made you to sit, maybe he made me slow. *(LUCILLE goes and gets her paper from* DOT.*)*

DOT. No. You did that, all by yourself . . . out of meanness. God does not set your pace. He puts us all at the starting gate and how fast you come out is your business.

LUCILLE. You really think it's the entire purpose of your life to sit on this porch?

DOT. Well, I hope that's it, because if it is then I've done it. Did my duty.

LUCILLE. Maybe I'm doing mine then. Maybe I'm doing exactly what God intends. *(LUCILLE goes back to reading the news.)*

DOT. Now, Lucy . . . I know God means for you to do more than just read the newspaper. I don't think God even likes the paper. I'm sure he'd rather have you read his book. The only one he ever wrote.

LUCILLE. The Bible?

DOT. Yes. *(Singing.)*
  "Oh, the B.I.B.L.E.
  That's the book for me."
  How does that song go?

LUCILLE. I don't remember.

DOT. Oh, you sang it in Sunday School. Remember?

LUCILLE. I never sang it.

DOT. Oh, you did. I got the words but I can't remember the tune.
  "Oh, the B.I.B.L.E.
  That's the book for me,
  La, la, la, la, la, la, la . . ."
  Help me! Help me with the tune! *(The buzzing sound of a fly.)* Whew! Whew! Get away! Get! Silly fly! Get! I'm gonna get you mister! Where'd he go? Oh . . . *(Swat, swat, swat—she hits the fly with her fan.)* DIE! DIE! DIE! *(A short pause.)* Lucille, I got him.

LUCILLE. Well, it can't be said about you, "She wouldn't kill a fly."

DOT. I don't know where that expression came from. I really don't. Why not kill a fly?

LUCILLE. Remember . . . "Thou shalt not kill"? Your B.I.B.L.E. says that.

DOT. That doesn't apply to flies. That means men. "Thou shalt not kill thy fellow man."

LUCILLE. What about women?

DOT. It means women, too. Man means woman.

LUCILLE. Why didn't God say, "Thy fellow man and woman"? He said man. He said fellows.

DOT. He means both! Whatever his reason for writing man, he meant woman. God does not discriminate because of gender.

LUCILLE. What?

DOT. Gender!

LUCILLE. Then answer this . . . why are all the books of the Bible named after men? Why were all the Apostles men?

DOT. Well, I don't know, Lucille.

LUCILLE. Because God is partial to men.

DOT. There are many great women in the Bible, Lucille. There's, of course, Eve and Mary. Actually the two Marys. I always refer to them as Mary and Mary M. Now Mary M. wasn't as nice a girl as plain Mary. Then there was Ruth and sister, Naomi. And . . . and Sarah. Who could forget Sheba . . . the one who cut the hair.

LUCILLE. A beautician?

DOT. No! She cut Solomon's hair. Took away his strength. She didn't cut hair for a living. She was a queen! Now I forget, was Sheba the same as Bathsheba? Or was Sheba a country and Bathsheba the one who messed up Solomon? Or was it Samson and Delilah? Well, it's all confused, but it's all in the Bible. They were all women. They just didn't all know each other like the Apostles did. They sort of went their own ways doing deeds. But God, my dear, does not discriminate against women. After all, he gave us the power to have babies.

LUCILLE. The "power" to have babies?

DOT. That's why he made you the way you are. See how little you know? See what you learn from your newspaper and magazines? You ought to pick up the Good Book. That's where you get all the answers. It's not called *good* for nothing.

LUCILLE. What's it good for?

DOT. It's a total delight. Adventure, drama, pathos, a few laughs . . . not many, but a few. *(A short pause.)* It's very well written. *(A short pause.)* Better than a newspaper. *(She sings.)* "Oh, the B.I.B.L.E. . . ."

LUCILLE. If you say so.

DOT. Boy, you can't beat the Bible.

LUCILLE. *(Suddenly putting down her paper.)* Oh, look, Mr. Ferguson. *(Yelling.)* Yoo-hoo! Mr. Ferguson!

DOT. Lucille, what are you doing? Yelling at that old man? Have you lost your mind?

LUCILLE. *(Getting out of her chair.)* Yoo-hoo! Look, it's me! Over here on the porch! *(She strikes a pose.)* Do you like my swimsuit?

DOT. *(Screaming.)* You have lost it, Lucy, gone berserk! Shut up talking to that old man!

LUCILLE. If you're going to the post office, I sure could use a magazine.

DOT. Oh, Lord, you don't need another thing to read!

LUCILLE. Get me a *Modern Screen* or a *Photoplay*. I'll give you some money when you get back.

DOT. You're not getting a nickel from me, Lucille.

LUCILLE. *(Waving.)* Much obliged! Bye-bye, Freddy!

DOT. Freddy! Lucille, are you crazy? Screaming at that old man? What will people think? Standing there exposing yourself! You're as naked as a jaybird! Hide, Lucy, hide!

LUCILLE. I'm not naked.

DOT. It's as close to naked as you can get in this world. That little swimsuit offers no surprises. Someone's liable to come up here, whisk you off, and turn you into a white slave!

LUCILLE. People don't do that.

DOT. What do you know about people? I've been around and let me tell you it's bad out there. From what I've seen, I warn you, the only really safe place to wear that "bikini" is in the bathroom with the door locked. And if I'd known you could buy such things through the mail, I'd never gotten a 1956 Sears catalogue. What's happened to them? Who can you trust?

LUCILLE. I don't know.

DOT. No, you don't know. You'd never have ordered that if you knew. You threw away nine-ninety-five on that swimsuit, as well as your reputation. Lucille, you don't even swim!

LUCILLE. But I'm awfully cool.

DOT. Yeah, well, I'm plain disgusted! Go on! Throw decency to the wind! I wish there was a little breeze . . . I'm about to die. *(A short pause.)* I said, I'm about to die! Pass on!

LUCILLE. *(She screams.)* So? What can I do about that? Don't scream at me. Yell at God. He controls the weather. Tell him to turn the heat down.

DOT. You think you're very smart. Well, talking smart don't make you have more sense. Smart talk is senseless talk, Lucille, and you don't make no sense. Plum cuckoo, that's you.

LUCILLE. *(Angry, going to her newspaper.)* I've got another question for you.

DOT. You do?

LUCILLE. Do you know Christine Clowe?

DOT. Oh . . . yes. Christine works down at the slacks factory. She's a seat seamer. Is she in the paper? Is she dead?

LUCILLE. No. Arrested.

DOT. No?

LUCILLE. Passed some bad checks.

DOT. She, like you, never did have a lick of sense.

LUCILLE. And Beth Ellen Bonner?

DOT. Arrested?

LUCILLE. No. She called the police and said a prowler broke into her house and used bad language.

DOT. Called her filthy things?

LUCILLE. So it seems.

DOT. I'll bet she owns a bikini, too.

LUCILLE. And that woman who used to sell shoes, Miss Pugh?

DOT. Cussed out? Arrested? Robbed?

LUCILLE. Dead.

DOT. I thought you were reading the police news? Now you're back to the obits?

LUCILLE. I skip around. It makes it more fun.

DOT. Does it? Does it? Well, it just sounds silly, Lucille. Straighten up and fly right!

LUCILLE. What's a three-letter word meaning "Happiness"?

DOT. You're not now doing the crossword?

LUCILLE. Did you know rump roast is one-fourteen a pound at the A&P? Or that "Dear Abby" says that you shouldn't feel obliged to write a thank-you note to someone who's killed your mother, no matter how thankful you are that she's gone?

DOT. No! No! I didn't know any of that. I don't want to know any of that! Stupid. And you made that up about Abby . . . I just know you did.

LUCILLE. Do you? (LUCILLE *is winning this game and is confusing* DOT.)

DOT. Don't bother me with your silly news. What's the use of reading if you're going to make things up?

LUCILLE. Sex.

DOT. My God, what a word! Where did that come from?

LUCILLE. I think that's the three-letter word meaning "Happiness."

DOT. Sex? Sex? Happiness? How would you know? You've never had it! *(The bells of an ice-cream truck are heard coming down the street. The bells play "Pop Goes the Weasel.")* Ooh, ooh . . . here comes the Good Humor! Good Humor! If you had on some clothes you could run out and get me a popsicle.

LUCILLE. I'll go anyway. *(She gets up and starts to go.)*

DOT. Not in the street you don't. If you go out like that, you'll be gone with the wind. (LUCILLE *is defiant.* DOT *is angry.*)

LUCILLE. I'm just going to the curb.

DOT. No, you're not! Curb it, Lucille, no! No! No! (LUCILLE *stops . . . she has heard* DOT.) There he goes. *(The sound of the ice-cream bells fades.)* My one chance to enjoy life. There goes the Good Humor. A cone would have cooled me off! If you had some morals, I would be cool!

LUCILLE. Do you want me to bring my buzz fan out here? Blow the hot air around? Huh?

DOT. Well . . . it doesn't make up for me not getting an ice cream, but at least it shows you've got a heart. It's usually in the wrong place . . . like hanging out of your bathing suit.

LUCILLE. I'll go in the house and get the fan. *(She exits into the house.)*

DOT. *(Yelling.)* And get an extension cord. That way you can plug it in in the living room and pull the fan way out here on the porch. Hear?

LUCILLE. *(From inside.)* I hear you.

DOT. I'm gonna be cool. I'm gonna be cool. Ha, ha!

LUCILLE. *(Coming out of the house with an electric fan.)* Here we go.

DOT. Point it at me! Flip it on! Ha, ha! *(The buzzing sound of the fan is heard when* LUCILLE *turns it on.)*

LUCILLE. There we go. *(They now have to talk over the sound of the buzz fan.)*

DOT. Oh, oh . . . ha, ha! I'm cool! I'm cool! Ha, ha! Did I ever tell you that Poco has a buzz fan in all her bedrooms? Even in the winter?

LUCILLE. Yes. *(*LUCILLE *picks up a magazine and reads.)*

DOT. Yes. Once when I went to visit her, she showed me to my room and said, "Here's your buzz fan," and I said, "Poco, why do I need that?" And she said, "Turn it on for privacy. It drowns out the noise so everyone in the house won't hear what you're doing." Can you believe it? What did she think I would be doing? *(A short pause.)* Oh, dear . . .

LUCILLE. Oh, dear, what?

DOT. That thing sure is loud.

LUCILLE. Yes.

DOT. I can hear it running at night. I can hear it running in your room.

LUCILLE. So?

DOT. You have this buzz fan for coolness, don't you?

LUCILLE. Sure.

DOT. I don't suppose you use it to drown out noise?

LUCILLE. What?

DOT. *(Yelling.)* What do you do in your room?

LUCILLE. Nothing.

DOT. Good.

LUCILLE. Why good?

DOT. I'm glad to know nothing's going on that I shouldn't hear. I don't want you sneaking around on me. You don't do sneaky things do you, Lucy?

LUCILLE. No . . . well, no. Well, sometimes Helen comes over. It's not sneaky, she just comes in.

DOT. When? Helen? Helen who?

LUCILLE. Helen . . . from down the block. I went to school with her and sometimes she drops by when she gets off work at the movie.

DOT. At night?

LUCILLE. She works at night.

DOT. She comes over often? Comes in when I'm asleep?

LUCILLE. What difference does it make? It's my room. I can ask over whoever I like.

DOT. Can you? Can you? Well I know what you like! I suppose you have men in?

LUCILLE. What?

DOT. Men! Men! For God's sake, get rid of this buzz fan! Turn it off! Get rid of it!

LUCILLE. Why?

DOT. I want to know what's going on! I won't have a Watergate under my own roof! Turn that evil fan off! Off! *(*LUCILLE *turns the fan off.)*

LUCILLE. Okay, it's off.

DOT. What have you done to me?

LUCILLE. Nothing. I had a friend over.

DOT. Keep that Helen out! And don't bring men in here. I don't want strangers in my house.

LUCILLE. It's mine, too.

DOT. Daddy left it to me.

LUCILLE. He was my daddy!

DOT. He was my husband! *(A pause.)* I earned this house. I deserve it. It's mine. Children aren't supposed to own their own homes.

LUCILLE. I'm not a child. I wish I had my own home.

DOT. How would you get your own home? Huh? How'd you pay for it? What money you have belongs to me. I won't give you the money.

LUCILLE. You won't even give me enough to take a bus ride.

DOT. I've given you money. I gave you nine-ninety-five and look what you bought.

LUCILLE. I get your point!

DOT. Do you? Do you, Lucille? Your own home? Are you crazy? How in the world would you get one?

LUCILLE. *(This is an outcry of white anger and force . . . she makes perfect sense.)* I could walk across the street and marry Old Man Ferguson. I could do that. After all, that's what you did. Marry an old man, sit on his porch, have a kid, got your own home. What you did didn't take any brains or money. I could walk across the street, do what you did, sit on Freddy's porch, and stare at you. I could do that! Unless it's God's will that I should stay here for forty-five more years letting you make me miserable.

DOT. You wouldn't marry that old man!

LUCILLE. Sit on your porch and watch.

DOT. You don't even know Old Man Ferguson that well.

LUCILLE. I do. I talk to him at night, when you're asleep. Other times I wander down the block and see Tommy Vickery's daddy. Another nice widower. Ferguson's old, Vickery's young . . . both are lonely. So am I.

DOT. Well, you have yourself quite a night life. I'll bet you even hang out with the beatniks at the Dairy Queen?

LUCILLE. Oh, Mama, I have the time of my life when it's past your bedtime.

DOT. What makes you think any man would want to marry you?

LUCILLE. Out of pity. Out of loneliness. I don't know.

DOT. No, you don't know. You see, the whole world's lonely, Lucille. That's the state of things. That's no reason to wander up and down the block talking to the menfolk. Shame on you! That's no reason to marry one.

LUCILLE. But you did! Marry one!

DOT. That don't make it right. It was the one mistake I ever made, but I recovered . . . got over it.

LUCILLE. And got a house.

DOT. Oh, for Pete's sake, Lucy . . . hold your horses! I'm an old woman. I'll be dead soon.

LUCILLE. How soon?

DOT. What?

LUCILLE. How soon? If you make it short, I might stay around to see the end.

DOT. That's silly, you make it sound like you want me dead!

LUCILLE. Right now I wish I knew an elephant.

DOT. You've certainly got a smart mouth. I didn't raise you to be a tart!

LUCILLE. No, well, what did you raise me for?

DOT. Because . . . because you were born, you came along, you were there.

LUCILLE. Well, that's why the chicken crosses the road, Mama. Because it's there. Like Freddy Ferguson's.

DOT. Well . . . well . . . I don't know what to say.

LUCILLE. Finally.

DOT. Well . . . this is a fine how-do-you-do. Well, I think it's time for you to go in. You've had too much exposure, Miss.

LUCILLE. I don't want to go in, thank you.

DOT. Well, I won't sit here and talk to a crazy. You ought to get inside, get on some clothes, and get ahold of yourself.

LUCILLE. Freddy's bound to be back soon with my magazines.

DOT. You wouldn't do that, would you? Leave poor old me and marry that poor old man?

LUCILLE. I'm the one who's poor.

DOT. I'll be gone soon. Just wait. Then you can have this house, run all over creation at night in your silly swimsuit, get yourself involved with a hot rodder . . . if you want. I won't know. Right now I need you.

LUCILLE. For years you've said, "Lucy, don't go, I need you." So I didn't go and all you've needed me for has added up to nothing. I need to go. I got a lot to do.

DOT. After the Lord takes me, you'll be on your own.

LUCILLE. Finally.

DOT. And I'll bet you find out there's nothing to do, Lucy. Nothing is what there is to do. There's no need to go looking for anything you can't have right here. This is the best of nothing. Oh, I know you have dreams. Wild ideas put there by your newspapers and magazines about what's going on in the world. But this is the best place to be, Lucy . . . out here on this porch. When I go to my eternal rest, you can rest right here. Swing on the swing. Rock in the rocker. Watch the world go by. The view is so much better here than it is from Old Man Ferguson's. But don't go outside . . . in the world, Baby. You're a little person and you might get lost. (DOT *reaches out and touches* LUCILLE . . . *as a mother would touch a child.*)

LUCILLE. I'm just going to read, Mama. Read the news of people who got robbed, arrested, or shot. People who got out and did something.

DOT. Good for you.

LUCILLE. Good for me?

DOT. After all, you wouldn't want to wander off. I might start to die and you wouldn't be here. I'm ready to go. Been just waiting for ages. I can't wait to get to heaven. Every night, before I go to sleep, I pray, "Dear God, take me." I've seen the world for seventy some-odd years. Seen my neighbors come and go. Watched Tommy Vickery swipe my roses and Old Man Ferguson trot off to the post office. Seen Lucille grow from a little girl into a grown woman. I've had an eyeful. Seen it all. Everything there is to see from this porch. Yes, Lord, I'm ready to come to heaven and see what the angels are up to! *(A short pause.)* Well . . . I've had it with the porch. I'm going inside, Lucille, and wait. *(*DOT *puts down her fan and rolls her wheelchair inside the house. We hear* DOT *yell from inside.)* Don't run off! *(*LU-CILLE *picks up* DOT*'s fan and begins to fan herself.)*

LUCILLE. *(To herself.)* Sit and rock. Sit and rot. *(A short pause.)* God, it's hot. *(A short pause.)* God, I got to be going. *(*LUCILLE *puts down the fan, goes to the steps of the porch, and begins to step off. She does not leave. The sound of the ice-cream truck is heard again playing "Pop Goes the Weasel.")*

DOT. *(Yelling from inside the house.)* Lucy? Is that the ice-cream man again? Lucille? *(A short pause.)* Yoo-hoo? Lucille? Come put me in the bed! *(*LUCILLE *stares out at the world beyond the steps . . . torn between leaving and the calls from* DOT. *A short pause.)* Lucy? I need you. Are you there? *(A short pause. She sings.)* "When I'm calling you . . . ooh . . . ooh . . . ooh . . . ooh . . . ooh." *(She yells.)* Yoo-hoo? *(*LUCILLE *turns and exits into the house. The sound of "Pop Goes the Weasel" gets louder and louder until the final "Pop.")*

*Curtain*

# R. G. Vliet

★ ★ ★ ★ ★ ★ ★ ★ ★ ★ ★ ★ ★ ★ ★ ★ ★ ★

★ THE PERSON

Born in Chicago in 1929, Russell Gordon Vliet as a child lived the rootless life determined by his father's naval career. His family made homes in Virginia, American Samoa, North Carolina, and Washington State before settling long enough in Texas City, Texas, for him to graduate from high school. With the help of a track scholarship, Vliet entered Southwest Texas State College in San Marcos. After completing both his B.A. and M.A. degrees there, he spent 1953–54, the most artistically formative year of his life, in Rocksprings, Texas (pop. 1,182), on the Edwards Plateau. Here he and his wife, Ann, began their married life teaching in the public schools, and here he became obsessed with the harshly beautiful landscape that would furnish settings for his drama and fiction over the next thirty years.

Vliet is well-known as a distinguished poet and novelist whose critical reputation was rising rapidly when he died in 1984, only weeks after completing his third novel, *Scorpio Rising.* During his sadly abbreviated career he won Ford Foundation and Rockefeller Foundation fellowships, as well as two Texas Institute of Letters awards and, in 1983, the Dobie-Paisano Fellowship.

Reprints of Vliet's novels *Solitudes* (as *Soledad*) and *Rocksprings,* as well as published appreciations by Lyman Grant, Robert Gish, and Tom Pilkington, are likely to further enhance Vliet's standing as a fiction writer, but up to now little note has been taken of his efforts and achievements as a playwright, which was his first career choice. Drama was the center of his interest while he was a student at Southwest Texas State, and it was to the Yale School of Drama that Vliet turned, from 1954 to 1956, for the completion of his education. From the mid-fifties to 1966, dramatic works constituted his major literary projects, and he gained recognition through productions and awards. Although *The Regions of Noon* is the only play that he considered finished and that he wanted included among his authentic works, his dramatic writing is more important to the body of his work than the existence of a single play might suggest. In the various drafts of his intended trilogy, which included *The Regions of Noon,* Vliet struggled with the same themes and passions that inform his later work in other genres. Similarly, the language of Vliet's plays expresses his poetic sensibility and his concern for precise scenic description, which are both more fully realized in his later works.

With finality, Vliet announced to his wife in 1968 that he was a novelist rather than a playwright, a judgment that readers today, provided with hindsight, can concur with. Yet though Vliet's plays may be overshadowed, they are important, and whether read as prologues or as displaced parallels to his works in more congenial forms, they enrich our understanding of this author's powerful and original response to universal, as well as uniquely Texan, experience.

★ THE PLAY

*The Regions of Noon* is a "Western" in the sense that it is set on a ranch in West Texas and concerns a drifter, Clare Borah (Clar Boray in an earlier draft), who arrives during a drought and stays on to win the de facto mistress of the ranch. It is far from a conventional Western, however. Within its painstakingly evoked setting, several generations of the McKennon family struggle against the fierce elements and their own flaws to achieve precarious, partial victories—the only kind possible in these harshly beautiful circumstances. Instead of gunfights, cattle drives, and dance-hall floozies with hearts of gold, Vliet's Western depicts the real demands that the ranching way of life imposed on those who chose, or were chosen, to live it and dramatizes as well the alterations that life made in them. The play's action is bracketed between the drink of water Jo begrudgingly gives the arriving Clare in the initial scene and the dipperful of water he receives in the final scene, which signals her gift of forgiveness and love.

Mrs. Beah McKennon, the desiccated widow of the ranch's founder, has been hardened by life into a selfish, bitter heiress concerned only that her property pass into the hands of her granddaughter and be kept from the competent but despised hands of her husband's illegitimate daughter, Jo, whom he had insisted on rearing forthrightly as his own. Jo has been so ground down by years of unappreciated service to Beah and by the cares of ranch management that she has become suspicious of others and afraid to trust her emotions. The drifter, Clare, has the strength and hard-won knowledge necessary to manage the ranch, but hurts himself and those he cares for with his imprudent ardor. Dessie, the fragile and selfish granddaughter, can only trade on her weakness and beauty for the protection she requires in this environment.

In these "regions of noon"—which I take to be regions of extreme contrast, those between shimmering sunlight and deep shadow and between parched earth and clear, spring-fed streams—mere survival is an accomplishment, and characters are tested to their limits. The spindly pecan seedling growing by the ranch house gallery, a tree that would be a pathetic deformity in a gentle climate, is here a precious affirmation of life against death, and Clare and Jo's imperfect middle-aged love is here a triumph of hope and courage.

Significantly, it is to Spanish, the gentler language of Texas's earlier settlers, that Clare turns in accepting Jo's gift of love. "*Gracias. Gracias, Señora.* (He starts out. He stops and looks once again at Jo. Then he bows once more, in gratitude, debt, homage.) *Gracias.*"

Vliet has an appreciation, rare among Anglo-Texan writers, of the displaced Hispanics' courtly manner and dignity in loss and of their contribution to regional culture. Throughout his works, there is a depiction of Texas's earliest European settlers as cultivated, formal people who lost their land to more aggressively pragmatic, but cruder, Anglo-Saxons. In scene 1 of this play, the Mexican servant philosophically endures Beah McKennon's insults of his language, his homeland, and even his standards of cleanliness.

This recognition given to Texas's Hispanic tradition reflects not only a racial sensitivity on Vliet's part but also an awareness of history—an understanding that the roots of ranching as a way of life were originally Spanish and Mexican and that Texas history did not begin with settlers from Tennessee. Vliet's Mexican characters suggest some of the same continuity in the experience of the land as do Faulkner's "Old People," the Indians.

*The Regions of Noon* was only the second play to receive the prestigious Play of the Year Award from the Southeastern Theatre Conference. It premiered at the Barter Theater in Abingdon, Virginia, on June 27, 1960, in a production directed by Robert Porterfield. Starring were Robert Pastene (Clar Borah), Donna Todd (Dessie McKennon), and Susan Walker (Jo McKennon).

★   THE WORKS

R. G. Vliet's full-length plays are all set in the Edwards Plateau area of West Texas, three on ranches and one in Alto Springs, his fictional version of Rocksprings. All deal with the power of the setting to generate passion and to harden and destroy. The action of *The Regions of Noon* takes place in 1900, that of *Estrella Bajar* (Falling Star) in 1917, and that of *Rockspring* in 1918. *A Friend in Sahara* is set in the 1970s. The plays are loosely interrelated in ways that suggest the classic trilogy form into which Vliet tried for more than ten years to satisfactorily shape them.

The first three plays mentioned above made up the parts of the trilogy as originally planned by Vliet. The last play, *A Friend in Sahara,* has little direct connection with the others. It is not clear from currently available materials whether Vliet had finally abandoned his plan to complete his trilogy when he wrote *A Friend in Sahara* and intended for it to stand alone, or whether he planned for it to serve as the last play in a newly structured trilogy that would begin with *The Regions of Noon,* as before, and would include a middle play combining parts of *Estrella Bajar* and *Rockspring.* Once a Vliet archive is established where all his manuscripts and notes can be studied, this question and others about his authorial intentions will no doubt be answered. Although the plays have few common characters and do not constitute logical parts of a larger unified plot, they do share character types, refer repeatedly to a central incident, and deal with aspects of a common myth.

A ranch is owned and operated by a Hispanic family. Through violence or legal chicanery or both, a strong Anglo opportunist seizes control, both of the land and the widow. The harsh life casts its spell and exacts its toll. The patriarch dies, leaving an heir unwilling or unable to develop the characteristics necessary to maintain power in such country.

In *A Friend in Sahara,* the young wife, Farley, from Houston and Beaumont, suggests these necessary characteristics when she says, "I've got to get a little prickly in the soul, like that brush out there; catclaw, cedar: they stick their needles through the air, they make their own shape." The son, Lee, in *Estrella Bajar* calls attention to the influence of the setting on the ranch's former temporary master as he speaks to his father's body awaiting burial: "You've got a lot of the land and the weather in you, Dad, even strung out like you are. A lot of the sun is latched into your face. The scrub oaks look like they've winded clean into your skin and scratched them wrinkles. And the wind and the dust still crackin' your lips." Maybe the best description of the rawhide-tough rancher's essence comes from the revenge-driven daughter of a dispossessed widow in *Estrella Bajar:* "Put on a cup of coffee, and boil it and boil it and boil it and boil it until there's nothing left but a crust of dry. That's how his heart was."

Throughout the plays, there is awe for the strength and will sufficient to match the elements and the terror of the hardness that the struggle produces. Images of gnarled oaks, creeping brush, and blowing dust mingle in the texts with the calls of doves and mockingbirds, the rattle of mesquite beans, and the smell of cedar to evoke both the hazards and the appeal of the setting. Some of the best lines in the plays are attempts by characters to articulate their feelings about the nature around them. Scene directions by Vliet are marvelously evocative. His dialogue moves all the way from the naturalistically flat to the consciously lyric, a range that sometimes comes, however, at the cost of disconcerting transitions and verbal excesses.

His most satisfying play, *The Regions of Noon,* is also his most restrained and least discursive. Its central characters are concerned with achieving personal goals rather than with imposing their will on the land. Larger conflicts are shown through background and secondary figures.

The middle play of Vliet's trilogy, whether called *Estrella Bajar, Sweetly Sings the Mocker, Billie,* or *The Arid Spell,* and the original final play of the set, *Rockspring,* are compelling but confusing plays with their dark passions, violent scenes, and conflicts extending over generations. They combine poetic moments with gothic ones, incorporating these moments into labyrinthine plots. Content, sometimes satisfying, often overblown, overwhelms form. Regardless, both were highly enough regarded to win prizes: *Rockspring,* the Fred Ballard University of Nebraska Award for playwriting; and *The Arid Spell,* the Wisconsin Players Award.

*A Friend in Sahara* rounds out the picture of West Texas culture developed in the earlier plays by showing how small-town individuals and institutions are corrupted and how diversity is stifled by the ranch-based economy's defensive posture. Unfortunately, the play's social criticism comes across as shrill and sentimental, and the plot is too predictable. But there are always memorable bits, even in Vliet's least satisfying works. Here, there is a sensitive variation on Katherine's English lesson in Shakespeare's *Henry V* when Farley, the idealistic young wife, asks Ponce, the teen-aged victim of prejudice, to speak to her in Spanish in spite of her inability to comprehend it, and he lovingly names the parts of her face and hand in Spanish as he touches them. The attractiveness of Houston, toward which Ponce flees in the last scene as an alternative to Alto Springs, is symbolized by images especially appealing to residents of the sun-scorched hills—fog and the singing of frogs.

## LIST OF WORKS

### PLAYS

*The Regions of Noon* (unpublished), first draft, 1957; final, 1982
*Estrella Bajar* (unpublished), n.d.

*Rockspring* (unpublished), 1959
*A Friend in Sahara* (unpublished), 1978
Note: These plays are impossible to date accurately. They underwent frequent
  revision and exist in several drafts. The first two were in existence in some
  form by 1956. Only *The Regions of Noon*, in a draft dated October 1982, was
  authorized by the author for publication.

POETRY

*Events and Celebrations.* New York: Viking, 1966.
*The Man with the Black Mouth.* Santa Cruz: Kayak, 1970.
*Water and Stone.* New York: Random House, 1980.
*Clem Maverick: The Life and Death of a Folksinger.* Fredericksburg, Tex.: Shearer,
  1983.

NOVELS

*Rocksprings.* New York: Viking, 1973.
*Solitudes.* New York: Harcourt, 1977.
*Scorpio Rising.* New York: Random House, 1985.
*Soledad,* or *Solitudes.* Rev. ed. Fort Worth: Texas Christian University Press, 1986.

RECOMMENDED READING

Gish, Robert. "R. G. Vliet's Lonesome Cowboys: Language of Lyricism in the
  Contemporary Western Novel." *Southwestern American Literature* 9 (Fall 1983):
  5–21.
Grant, Lyman. "Vliet's Emotional Landscape." *Texas Observer,* April 19, 1985,
  pp. 25–27.
Pilkington, Tom. Afterword to *Soledad,* or *Solitudes,* by R. G. Vliet. Fort Worth:
  Texas Christian University Press, 1986.
Vliet, R. G. "On a Literature of the Southwest: An Address." *Texas Observer,*
  April 28, 1978, pp. 18–19.

# The Regions of Noon

★ ★ ★ ★ ★ ★ ★ ★ ★ ★ ★ ★ ★ ★ ★ ★

# CAST OF CHARACTERS

OLD MEXICAN

BEAH McKENNON

WILLIE McKENNON

CLARE BORAH

JO McKENNON

DESSIE McKENNON

TWO BOYFRIENDS

TWO BOYS

THEIR GIRLS


# SCENES

The gallery of the McKennon ranch house and a horse pen on the place, on the Edwards Plateau, Texas, 1900.

SCENE I: An evening in early spring.

SCENE II: Two months later.

SCENE III: A few hours later.

SCENE IV: Three weeks later.

SCENE V: Several days later.

SCENE VI: Two weeks later.

SCENE VII: The next morning.

# ★ SCENE I

*The gallery of the McKennon ranch house, on the Edwards Plateau, Texas. An evening in early spring, 1900.*

*The ranch house, which fills most of the stage, is built almost entirely of a dusty yellowish rock. There is a window and a door, both open to a lack of breeze. A narrow gallery with a rail along it runs the length of the ranch house. Wooden steps rise dead center up to the gallery. Next to the door is a stand with a washbasin on it. Down left stage, in what would be the "yard," is a slender pecan sapling. Its few buds are barely broken into pale green leaf. Some rocks are strung protectively around it.*

*The set is designed as if it were a three-dimensional woodcut print.*

*Sunlight is everywhere, although now at evening it is not so bright. There is a subtle wash of it in the shade of the gallery. Later, as the sun goes down, the light will strike the walls into a harsh dry yellow before leading them into darkness.*

*As the curtain goes up,* BEAH *(pronounced "Bee")* McKENNON *sits hunched and smallish on her rocker, to the right of the steps. She is gaunt, almost skeletonic. The skin has gone taut on her brow. Her face is creased with wrinkles, her hair is a stringy gray, and her eyebrows are of the same stringy-gray, long, crinkled bristles. Her fingers are knotted, cramped, bony. Great languorous blue veins snake out above them at the wrist. She is about eighty.*

WILLIE McKENNON, *seven, sits at the top of the steps. She is barefoot and wears a loose, waistless, red-print, flour-sacking dress. A stack of books is beside her. But right now she is playing with a rubber ball and some pebbles she has for jacks, trying to ignore her granny.*

*Standing just inside the doorway, talking to someone inside, is the* OLD MEXICAN.

OLD MEXICAN. *Gracias. Gracias, Señora Bos. El tiempo cambiara. (He bows twice and turns onto the gallery. His brilliant white hair, moustache, and short beard stand out like cold Mexican silver against the soft brown of his face, heightening the classic Spanish features. He walks stiffly, an old dog. The* OLD MEXICAN *looks at* WILLIE *a moment, clicks something in his pockets.)* Willie? You play game, *si?* With stone? *(He draws a handful of pebbles from his pocket. He stoops stiffly down to* WILLIE, *proffers the pebbles scattered on his palm.) Yo tengo* fine stone too, Willie. *Muchos colores.* From creek. Soon—two month, three month—I go back to *Mejico.* I bring fine stone for *mejicanitos* to play, same like Willie.

BEAH. Well, Ignacio, so you're going back to Mexico purty soon, eh?

OLD MEXICAN. *(He rises reluctantly. He does not look at* BEAH.) *Si, Señora. Regresare a mi hogar.*

BEAH. I said, are you going back to Mexico?

OLD MEXICAN. *Si.* When the work is done.

BEAH. That's what I was asking you. *(Pause.)* Now what's in Mexico that'd make a body trouble to cross the Rio Grande, huh, Ignacio?

OLD MEXICAN. *(He turns to her. He speaks deliberately and with dignity.)* Hay mucho de bueno en Mejico, Señora McKennon. En Coahuila donde yo vivo—

BEAH. What're you talking?

OLD MEXICAN. *(He shrugs.)* Es mi patria. *(*BEAH *snorts. The* OLD MEXICAN *disregards her. He turns back to* WILLIE.*)* Willie? *¡Mira!* I give this, this, this *(He selects some pebbles from his palm.)* fine stone to Willie. For to play game, *si? ¡Ay!* es de mucho colores, si. Este es blanco—how you say: white? *(He holds a pebble against the sky.)* Este es como el cielo. Este es rojo. Ah. *Pinto,* same like the horse. You take *uno, dos, tres, cuatro, cinco, seis,* Willie. *(He gently opens one of her hands and puts the pebbles in it. She closes her hand around them. He chuckles.)* Hand soft like *agua,* Willie. Same like putting stone back in creek.

BEAH. Willie, you get up this minute and wash them hands, if they're all sweaty thataway. Go on. *(The* OLD MEXICAN, *hurt but proud, rises. But* WILLIE *stealthily touches his hand. He smiles.)*

OLD MEXICAN. *(He calls into the house.)* Señora bos. Ya me voy a trabajar en el pasto del sur.

JO. *(Offstage.)* Bueno, Ignacio. ¿Te parece que va a llover?

OLD MEXICAN. *(He looks up at the sky.)* Va a llover.

BEAH. Like hell it'll rain. *(A pause.)*

OLD MEXICAN. I go work now. *Adios.*

WILLIE. *Adios.*

  *(The* OLD MEXICAN *exits.)*

BEAH. Willie. You toss out those dirty old rocks. No telling *what's* on them, Ignacio handling them. *(*WILLIE *puts the stones in her pocket. She goes back to playing with her "jacks," which make soft, clicking noises.)* I declare you're bullheaded. Just like your ma. Not listening to a word I say. *(She takes a deep breath and presses a hand to her breast. A pause pregnant with self-pity.)* Sometimes it gets to thumping so *hard.* *(She runs a sleeve under her nose.)* Like when I say to your ma, hire a white hand. A white hand would put in ten times the work Ignacio turns a hand to. *(She sighs.)* Look at my poor pecan. And just last year that spindly thing was green-up with leaves. Willie, run down there like a good gal and pour it a mite from the basin, honey. Go on. *(*WILLIE *gets the washbasin.* BEAH *rambles on and on, dwindling down through reminiscence.* WILLIE *has heard it all before. She carries water to the tree.)* I tell you, it ain't like it used to be, when your grandpa and Uncle Kelcy was alive. Back in them times Texas was real green. Bluestem and sandlove and Injun grass. And a horse come up to its belly in grass like standing in water. *Ever'*thing growed.

  *(We hear the faint "tink" of a spur. Now* CLARE BORAH *stands at the end of the gallery, right stage.* CLARE *is thirty years old. He is a drifter, as his appearance attests. His face under a growth of sandy stubble is brick-red from the sun. He needs a haircut. He wears a sweat-stained Stetson and "about a dollar and a half's worth of*

clothes." *Only his boots are remarkable: they are expensively handmade, with large Mexican spurs attached.* CLARE *stands with one knee crooked forward, his weight on the right foot, a stance habitual with him when at rest.)*

BEAH. *(She keeps right on talking.)* There was even that whopping old pecan tree over the cabin, dropping pecans onto the roof *pop pop* like it was a rain. *(WILLIE sees* CLARE. *She drops the basin and without a word scampers up the steps and into the house.)* What on *earth?* *(BEAH sees* CLARE. *She gasps.)* Mister! You scairt the daylights out of me.

> *(With* WILLIE *clinging to her skirts,* JO MCKENNON *appears at the door. She is a tall woman, solid but graceful in her motions, with firm, handsome features. She is twenty-eight years old. She wears a dark-gray dress, drawn in at the waist. Her hair is bound up behind her head, a sense of the classic. She is holding a rifle.)*

JO. What do you want? *(A pause.)* I said, what do you want?

CLARE. *(He politely removes his Stetson.)* Ma'm, ain't no need to hold that rifle to me thataway. I'm just riding downcountry *solo solo,* looking for work. Like they say: just a lonesome stranger.

JO. There ain't no work here.

BEAH. You ought not to sneak up on a body thataway.

JO. Not if you don't want to get shot, that is.

CLARE. Well now, I'm sorry about that. On account of I sure weren't aiming on swallering a bullet. What I *was* aiming for was a swaller of water. Or something. Preferably something. *(A pause.)* Water would do just fine.

BEAH. *(Indignantly, pressing a hand to her breast.)* Like to give my heart the flips.

CLARE. *(Lightheartedly.)* Left my horse out there chomping along the fence, where there's a few stalks left. Seems like the grass gets scarcer and scarcer the farther downcountry we ride. Oh, but the folks are friendlier, yes sirree. *(A pause.)* Yep. *(A pause.)* And the sun hotter. Boy howdy, I sure miss the cool of the mountains.

BEAH. What mountains are them?

CLARE. Colorado. New Mexico. Up around Cimarron, New Mexico, last. Right near the Sangre de Cristos. Up there they herd stock into the mountains of a summer and the grass in them meadows is as sweet and green.

BEAH. You don't say? Grass like that in the dead of summer?

CLARE. You can stoop down just about anyplace you've a mind to and get a drink from a creek.

BEAH. Landsakes, somebody. Willie. Can't you see the man's near dying of thirst? Give him a dipper-full.

CLARE. *(He looks at* JO.) That's fine drinking water in them mountains, that is.

BEAH. Well, it ain't near so good here, I can tell you. Hot. For all it's only February and should be spring. Had a big rain last year that washed ever'thing out. Then it clouded up and begun not raining.

CLARE. *(He wipes his mouth with the back of his hand.)* Rain's all wind and wind's all sand, ain't it? *(*BEAH *laughs appreciatively.* JO *steps out of the doorway and dips water from the bucket.* WILLIE *remains half-hidden behind the doorframe.)*

JO. *(She goes to the steps and offers* CLARE *the dipper.)* Here.

CLARE. Well now, that's mighty generous of you, ma'm. *(JO does not move, forcing* CLARE *to come to her. He limps, favoring his left foot.)*

BEAH. You wasn't throwed, was you? *(JO holds the dipper at arm's length.* CLARE *takes the bowl and looks at* JO *a moment. She releases the handle and moves brusquely upstage,* CLARE's *eyes following. Then* CLARE *takes a couple of swallows from the dipper and dashes the rest of the water onto his head. He sits on the gallery with a sigh of satisfaction.)*

CLARE. Mighty fine.

BEAH. What ails your foot?

CLARE. That's nothing. Hooked it on a rail onct, when I was a young one first hired out. Jerked the ankle real bad.

JO. You . . . better get, if you're figuring to hit town by dark. That's nine-odd miles through the brush.

BEAH. No you don't. You just set right there and rest your hat and coat.

CLARE. *(To JO.)* Now ma'm, I don't mean to kick up no row between you and your ma.

JO. That ain't my ma. *(A pause.)*

CLARE. I reckon I *am* plumb tuckered. Been riding sinct before sunup.

BEAH. Them there are just about the jim-dandiest boots.

CLARE. I figure sinct that's about all I own, might as well make them fancy.

JO. You've got two hours to sundown if you don't crave to ride by dark.

CLARE. *(He grins.)* Talk about being hospitable: come on a dugout up in West Texas, there weren't no one in it, but there was this note stuck to the wall that said—now let me see, what did that note say? Said:

20 miles to water.

10 miles to wood.

6 inches to Hell.

Gone back to Missouri.

Make yourself at home.

Which I sure did. *(He laughs.* BEAH *cackles.* CLARE *sees it is not going over with* JO, *though. He looks at* JO.) You got a nice spread of land here, ma'm. Of course, in this country you need plenty, if you're going to pasture cattle.

BEAH. Oh, that ain't Jo's land. Jo here, she's just managing things. *(WILLIE has moved gradually downstage.)* My granddaughter Dessie, she's up in Arkansas now. Her Aunt Selma has the raising of her. Bringing her up to be a real lady. And when Dessie gets growed, this will be her land.

CLARE. *(To JO.)* And there I figured this was all yours, ma'm. *(He grins.)* The way you come at me with that .30-30 like you ownt the whole smackdab U.S.A.

BEAH. My man, A. W. McKennon—ever hear of him?

CLARE. Can't say as I have.

BEAH. He ownt all this land, away back. Then my son, Kelcy, come into it. Then it come to me in trust for Dessie. Purty soon it's going to be all Dessie's, on account of—it's my heart here. I keep telling Jo, I keep making her write. I've got to have my Dessie back. *(She undoes a locket at her throat.)* Here. Look here. This here is her picture.

CLARE. *(He goes to* BEAH *and looks at the locket.)* Which one's her?

BEAH. This is her ma. This here's Dessie.

CLARE. They don't look much different. She had her a purty ma.

BEAH. Poor little Dessie. Never knew her ma past the first hour. And her pa went over the canyon edge the night of that storm—horse, buggy, and all. Dessie never got over it. *(*WILLIE *grabs up her "jacks" from where* CLARE *had been sitting. He sees her.)*

CLARE. Why, howdy. *(*WILLIE *runs into the house.* CLARE *whistles with amusement.)* Look at her go. Faster than a jackrabbit. That's sure a cute little tyke. *(To* JO*.)* That yours, ma'm?

JO. *(Pointedly.)* And she's partial who she talks to.

CLARE. Figured her to look like you. All that black hair. Same eyes too. *(He stares at* JO*.)* Yep, that little bugger has mighty purty eyes. How old is she?

BEAH. Going on seven. Seems like all that critter does is tuck her nose in a book. And her ma here—talking out sums, making out to be a schoolteacher, like that was any way to run a ranch.

CLARE. Well. Guess I'd better git. I don't want to keep you two from fixing supper for the menfolks, when they get in.

BEAH. *What* menfolks?

JO. *(She thuds the rifle butt onto the floor.)* That man's got no right to stick his nose into our business, don't you figure, Beah? And you'll have him telling us his own whole travels in a minute.

BEAH. Well, I declare. There can't a man come *near* this place but what you—

JO. *(To* CLARE*.)* Now maybe you'd better git.

CLARE. Aw ma'm, don't look at me thataway, please. *(He stretches his leg out along the top step.)* I've just got to sit and lazy my foot a minute. Besides, it's been a far piece sinct I rested my eyes on a purty lady. Especially one with a .30-30 growed to her fist.

JO. You're mighty pert, ain't you?

CLARE. Oh my. *(Their eyes meet.* CLARE *grins, shakes his head in admiration. But* JO *outstares him angrily. He nervously lowers his eyes, turns out and looks at the land. A pause. The sun is a hard yellow on his face and on the gallery floor behind.)* Look at that range. All that sun wheeling down on it, section on section of scrub brush and mesquite as far away as you can put an eye to. To look at it just aches you inside like you was full-up of mesquite stickers. God! It must be something, to own all that.

BEAH. If it'd just come a rain. This drouth is killing off the stock.

CLARE. You know, it's a wonder that folks hereabouts ain't thought on it: stocking them new Angora goats onto this kind of country.

JO. There's plenty of ranchers around here has got them things.

CLARE. Mohair. Money. Them things gets fat on brush. Better than sheep, even.

BEAH. *(Coldly.)* My man, A. W., come out here to raise steers. And there ain't going to be nothing *but* steers on this place from here on out.

CLARE. Oh, I ain't no sheepman or goater myself, understand. Give me a good spread of cattle any day. And I been working cows for folks sinct I was knee-high to a grasshopper. I got to say it, I'm right smart of a hand too. Just try me. Running stock, working fence line, fixing windmills. Take that windmill I passed on my way in. I seen right off it needed fixing bad. *(He looks narrowly at* JO.*)*

JO. You can hit town by heading straight through thataway.

CLARE. *(He grins. He shakes his head in admiration.)* Ma'm, you're a mighty hard woman. *(They look at one another. Then he turns away.)* Well, like you been hinting at me all along: *adios. (He starts to go, limping slightly.)*

BEAH. *(Indignant, rising from her rocker.)* Jo, I declare—

JO. *(Sharply.)* Mister. *(More gently.)* Is that ankle acting up?

CLARE. I'll make out. *(He starts to walk off.* JO *moves toward him a step.)*

JO. Wait. You hold on a minute. *(She is disconcerted at having stopped him.)* No, go ahead. No. What I mean is, I ain't going to have you haul into town and then spread it around that I ain't hospitable. What with your bunged-up foot and all. *(Hesitantly.)* You can stay the night.

CLARE. I *told* myself when first I seen you, you had a lady's ways. Not really uppity, for all your shaking that .30-30 at me like a broomhandle.

JO. I'll tell you straight off, mister, I don't trust no one that comes up on folks like you done, without even a holler. You can just skedaddle down to the barn and stay there. I'm mighty handy with this rifle.

CLARE. For a wonder I'm up and kicking. If your eyes was bullets I'd of been full-up of lead by now.

JO. You sure are sassy. *(BEAH cackles. A pause.)* I'll fetch you a blanket.

　　　*(JO goes into the house.* BEAH *begins to cough.* CLARE *goes to her.)*

CLARE. Can I help you, ma'm?

BEAH. *(She clutches his sleeve.)* Let me . . . get my . . . breath. Sometimes . . . inside me here . . . it's like a bird . . . of a sudden fluffs its feathers. I tell you, *I got to have my Dessie back. (BEAH begins to breathe more easily. She glances at the door. She speaks vehemently, under her breath.)* Now, mister. Don't you pay no mind to Jo. She's plain mean. I thank the good Lord she ain't no kin of mine.

CLARE. She seems like a fine enough woman. A right *proud* woman, though.

BEAH. My man, A. W., went out and got *her* on a schoolteacher. They run that woman out of the county. But A. W., no, he was too big. And he brung that thing home to raise, like as if there weren't no shame.

CLARE. Them's mean things to say.

BEAH. And I'll tell you another thing—

　　　*(JO reappears at the door.)*

JO. Here's you a blanket. *(JO tosses the blanket to CLARE, who catches it deftly.)*

CLARE. *Gracias. Gracias, señora.*

JO. Just get on down to the barn. There's hay for your horse. There's a tank if you want to wash up and an old bunk in one of the stalls you can sleep in.

CLARE. Sounds fancier than a hotel.

BEAH. And when you're settled, come up and have a bite to eat.

CLARE. Maybe, if—*(He glances at* JO.*)*

JO. There's grub enough to go around. I'll have Ignacio fetch some down to you.

CLARE. I just might take you up on that. *(CLARE tips his hat and turns to leave.* JO *calls after him.)*

JO. Whatever did you say your name was?

CLARE. Didn't say. Name's Borah. *(He pronounces it "Bo-ray.")* Clare Borah. *(He starts to leave.* JO *calls after him again.)*

JO. Hey, you. Clare Borah. What kind of work did you say you was good for, anyways?

CLARE. *(He grins.)* Ma'm, you name it. Like the saying goes, I'm a lover, a fighter, a bucker, and right smart of a windmill fixer.

    *(CLARE roars with laughter. He goes off.* BEAH *cackles.* JO *stares after* CLARE.*)*

*Curtain*

*The gallery, two months later, late morning.*

*The sunlight pours down, pressing waves of heat from the earth and from the roof and stone walls of the ranch house, withering the pecan, which has managed to squeeze from its branches three or four leaves.*

*A school book lies on the steps.*

*JO enters from left stage. She wears an apron over her dress. Her arms are filled with fluffy, yellow, flour-sacking curtains. She crosses to the steps, in a hurry.*

JO. Lordy, I'm never going to get done. I've got these curtains to put up yet and bread in the oven and—Willie? *(A sharp command.)* Willie. *(WILLIE appears at the door.)*

WILLIE. Mama.

JO. Where did you take off to? I thought you was standing right there. I saw Mr. Borah and Dessie coming through the gate a minute ago. You'd better run down and meet them.

WILLIE. Mama, Grandma's up.

JO. What's she doing up?

WILLIE. I gave her a drink of water like you said, and then she said she was getting up to see Dessie.

JO. Well, she can't get up. You know that. She's too weak. She's got to stay in bed. *(She goes up the steps.* WILLIE *goes to her book, at the top of the steps.)* I'll see about that right now. *(JO stops at the door and turns to* WILLIE.*)* Willie, what on earth are you doing? Didn't I tell you to go down and meet Dessie?

WILLIE. Mama, what's sixteen plus seven?

JO. *(Impatiently.)* Use your fingers.

WILLIE. I ain't got sixteen fingers.

JO. *(Exasperated.)* Willie, you get down there and meet them two like I told you. We'll work on them sums later.

WILLIE. Mama, I ain't never *seen* that Dessie before.

JO. Go *on*, I said.

WILLIE. Oh, all right. *(JO goes into the house.* WILLIE *starts to go off, but she turns right around and runs back.)* Mama, they're here!

*(She runs into the house. A pause.* DESSIE McKENNON *enters.* DESSIE *is fragile, evanescently pretty. Her body is slight and in fact boyish, almost without hips. The pink cotton dress she is wearing emphasizes this. Her narrow wrists, fingers, ankles, neck—the bones inside seem almost bird-thin. Her face is thin, freckled, with pale blue eyes. Her hair is blond—so light that it is as if she has no eyebrows or lashes. She is about seventeen. Her motions are tentative, frightened, even: she touches the rail as if it were a piece of memory. She looks out at the land. She presses*

*a hand to her throat in a gesture of oppression and sorrow.* JO *and* WILLIE *reappear at the door.)*

JO. Dessie. Dessie McKennon. *(DESSIE is startled.* JO *goes to her.)*

DESSIE. *(Shyly and tentatively.)* Hi, Aunt Josie. *(JO embraces her.)*

JO. Landsakes, Dessie. Why, we only got the letter from you yesterday saying you was coming. I ain't even got the curtains up in your room yet. My, you sure have growed.

DESSIE. When I heard about Grandma I packed right up.

JO. Mr. Borah meet you in Alto Springs all right?

DESSIE. Yes'm.

JO. Well, I wanted to meet you there too, but we've got to keep a close eye on your grandma. Your grandma—

DESSIE. It sure is hot. I didn't remember it was so hot.

JO. Dessie, I think we'd better tell you right off. Your grandma—

DESSIE. She's going to be all right.

JO. Three days ago she had her worst spell yet. She's been in bed sinct.

DESSIE. *(She claps her hands to her ears.)* She's going to be all right.

  *(The* TWO BOYFRIENDS *enter, lugging a big black trunk.)*

FIRST BOYFRIEND. Hold your horses, Spud. I can't see a damn thing.

SECOND BOYFRIEND. Well, give it a heave, can't you? *(They start up the steps.)*

FIRST BOYFRIEND. Heavier'n a sonofagun. *(He stumbles. His hat falls off.)* Hold on a minute, I said.

SECOND BOYFRIEND. Howdy, Miss Dessie. I reckon this thing is stuffed with ever' purty thing in the state of Arkansas.

JO. Spud? Jim Bob? What are you two doing way out here?

FIRST BOYFRIEND. Howdy, Miz McKennon. We come on Miss Dessie in town and figured to help out some.

SECOND BOYFRIEND. Where you want this thing put?

JO. Stash it in the parlor, beside the door, boys.

FIRST BOYFRIEND. And there's more where this come from.

JO. Shhh. Don't wake her grandma.

  *(The* TWO BOYFRIENDS *go into the house.* JO *follows them.* WILLIE *is standing near the door.* DESSIE *sits on the steps and starts to cry.)*

WILLIE. Dessie? *(She goes hesitantly down to* DESSIE.*)* Dessie, I got me two new—
  *(JO comes out from the house.)*

JO. What's the matter, Willie?

WILLIE. She's crying, Mama.

JO. *(She goes down to them.)* Dessie, I bet you're awful tired. Why don't you come in and wash up? Then you can rest some.

DESSIE. My grandma. Seems like ever'thing dies around here. Sometimes I wish I was a chunk of wood, dumber than these here steps.

JO. Honey, don't you cry. It can't be helped. *(JO offers her apron.)* Here. Wipe your eyes, before somebody sees you. In a minute you can go to your room and change your things and have a good rest. Your grandma's sleeping now.

WILLIE. *(Shyly.)* Looky, Dessie. I got two new eggs.

DESSIE. Are you Willie?

JO. Go on, Willie. Show Dessie your bird eggs.

DESSIE. *(Snuffling.)* They sure are purty, Willie.

WILLIE. I colleck them. I found these two today, down by the barn. This is a gracklebird's egg, Dessie, see? Ain't it all purty and spottedy-brown? And this here's an owl's egg. So round you could might-near shoot it for marbles. No wonder owls has such round eyes.

JO. Wouldn't that be something—to crack that into a frying pan and get a bug-eyed, fuzzy owl blinking at you, saying, "Oh no, ma'm, don't you fry me." *(They laugh.)*

WILLIE. Know how you do to get their insides out, Dessie? *(DESSIE shakes her head.)* You suck them.

DESSIE. Oh, Willie.

> *(The* TWO BOYFRIENDS *reappear at the door.)*

SECOND BOYFRIEND. Miz McKennon, are them biscuits you're baking? We ain't smelled that good a smell sinct breakfast.

FIRST BOYFRIEND. We ain't ate sinct breakfast.

SECOND BOYFRIEND. Jim Bob, here, he's so hungry his ribs is playing Dixie on the south side of his stomach.

JO. Next thing I know, you two will be asking to stay for dinner. Well, there's plenty enough, I reckon.

SECOND BOYFRIEND. *(He slaps the* FIRST BOYFRIEND *on the back.)* What'd I tell you, Jim Bob? *(He goes down to* DESSIE.*)* We get a little time after dinner, Miss Dessie, we'll send Jim Bob here down to the pens to water the stock and you and me'll have some time to talk, how about that?

FIRST BOYFRIEND. Why, you son of a—Hey, Miss Dessie, you're sitting on my hat. *(DESSIE jumps up. The* FIRST BOYFRIEND *scoops his hat from under her.)*

DESSIE. I'm sorry. I never knew—

FIRST BOYFRIEND. *(He knocks the dust from his hat.)* Aw, that's all right. It don't matter.

SECOND BOYFRIEND. Don't you worry about Jim Bob's hat none, Miss Dessie. His head fits crooked anyways. *(He laughs at his own wit. The* FIRST BOYFRIEND *glowers at him.)*

FIRST BOYFRIEND. Yeah? Well, are you going to stand there with your teeth in your mouth? We better get that wagon unloaded.

SECOND BOYFRIEND. Last one to the wagon's a dirty shikepoke. That'll be you, buddy.

> *(They rush off, almost bumping into* CLARE. CLARE *is lugging a sack of flour. He wears new jeans. His hair is trimmed and his face shaven.)*

CLARE. Here's you your flour. *(He drops the sack onto the gallery. It envelopes him in a cloud of dust.* JO *laughs.)*

JO. You look like a ghost. Why don't you come wash up?

CLARE. I need *something*.

JO. Did you bring me those yard goods from Castleberry's store?

CLARE. *(He hands her a package.)* Here they are.

> *(*DESSIE, *who has been staring at the land, entranced and oppressed, suddenly sucks in her breath.)*

DESSIE. That country—

CLARE. *(He takes off his hat and wipes his brow.)* Lordy, it's hot.

DESSIE. It just goes on and on.

CLARE. Clean to Mexico. *(*JO *has opened the package. A piece of light-green cloth tumbles full-length down her body.* CLARE *watches her.)* Oh my, ain't we all fussed up and purty? Greener than fescue grass in spring.

DESSIE. That sure is purty, Josie.

JO. *(Embarrassed.)* Oh, it's nothing.

CLARE. You get that cut and sewed, Miss Jo, it'll be the purtiest thing this side of the Brazos.

JO. It's just an off-piece of cloth from Castleberry's. To take the place of this old thing. *(She grows momentarily ecstatic. She holds the cloth against her body and turns around a bit.)* To be cool and breezy and this purty stuff all around me. To make me feel like new. Make me feel like—*(She notices that everyone is watching her. She stops abruptly. A pause.)*

CLARE. (Quietly.) That'll be the fanciest dress I've seen in a month of Sundays. *(*JO *nervously rebundles the cloth.)* Well, I better unhitch them horses from the wagon. *(He sees* WILLIE.*)* Howdy, Missy. I brung you something from town too.

WILLIE. What for?

CLARE. *(He dredges a small poke-package up out of his pocket.)* Here. This here's for you.

WILLIE. It ain't my birthday.

CLARE. It ain't Christmas neither. But it's for you.

DESSIE. Go on and open it, Willie. *(She goes to* WILLIE.*)* Let's see what you got, honey. Why, it's some jacks. Now weren't that nice of Mr. Borah? *(To* CLARE.*)* That was awful nice of you. *(*WILLIE *runs into the house.)* What's got into *her?*

CLARE. *(He goes to the washstand. Brusquely.)* Well, I'll leave this stuff on the washstand here. Whew, it's hot. *(He rinses his face and neck and dries on the towel.)* Out in the water lot the grass is all browned up. And down in Mercer's Canyon the water's pinched down to a string of mudholes.

> *(He carries the basin to the edge of the gallery.* BEAH *appears at the door. She is wearing a nightdress. She supports herself against the doorframe.)*

BEAH. Oh no you don't, mister. Slosh that water onto my tree.

JO. Oh my god. You're not supposed to be up.

BEAH. I never in my life spent a whole week onto my back. A. W., he never did neither. The one time he did, that was the time he turnt over dead. *(She moves toward her rocker.* JO *tries to help her.)* Don't touch me. *(*BEAH *sits in the rocker, straight and matriarchal. A pause.)* Well? What are you-all waiting for, sundown? Or me to kick the bucket?

JO. *(She grabs hold of the back of the rocker.)* Clare, help me get her back into the house.

BEAH. Even calling him Clare now, ain't you?

DESSIE. Grandma? *(A pause.* DESSIE *is a bit frightened.)* Ain't you glad to see me?

BEAH. Whatever should I want to see you for?

DESSIE. *(Shocked.)* Grandma, what's the matter? I didn't do nothing.

BEAH. You didn't come in to see me.

DESSIE. *(She goes to* BEAH.*)* You were sleeping, Grandma. But I'm here. I got your letter. That's why I come.

BEAH. You been out here, talking to them. Hearing whatever poison's on their tongues.

JO. *Beah.* That's an awful thing to say.

DESSIE. Grandma, I never seen you like this before.

BEAH. *Why didn't you come in to see me?*

DESSIE. I don't know. I was all mixed up. All that travel—things keep swishing past me. *(She kneels and touches* BEAH*'s sleeve.)* Talk to me, Grandma. What's wrong with seeing Josie? She's my kin.

BEAH. Ain't I your kin?

DESSIE. Yes'm. Yes'm. I remember. You helt me when I was little. You used to sing to me. *(*BEAH *suddenly embraces her.)*

BEAH. It don't matter, I tell you. It don't matter. All this time you've been gone from me. And to die. It don't matter.

DESSIE. You're not *gonna* die, Grandma.

BEAH. Touch me, Dessie. Your hands. My hands. It's the same blood through them. That's all that counts.

DESSIE. *(She touches* BEAH*'s face.)* Your face was so brown onct, Grandma.

BEAH. *(Tears blind her eyes.)* That sun's so bright.

JO. You wouldn't never hold me thataway.

BEAH. You're A. W.'s, not mine. This here's mine. *(She hugs* DESSIE *to her.* JO *goes into the house.* BEAH *speaks to* CLARE, *imperiously.)* Now slosh that water onto my tree.

CLARE. Yes *ma'm.* (CLARE *goes down to the tree.)*

DESSIE. Grandma, you're all cold and sweaty. *(She tries to wipe* BEAH*'s face with a handkerchief.)*

BEAH. Get that frilly thing out of my face. I want to look at you. *(She holds* DESSIE *at arm's length.)* Look how you've growed, right straight up. And the way you hold your arms, like. That's how your ma did. *(To* CLARE.*)* Ain't my grandchild the purty one?

DESSIE. Oh Grandma. *(She rises, embarrassed.)* It sure is hot today. (CLARE *pours water onto the roots of the tree. There is the sound of water trickling, liquid-sweet. It holds the scene a moment, a song to their ears. They all look up at the sky.)* I wish that cloud would bank up and rain.

BEAH. Green up my tree.

CLARE. Sweeten up the pasture grass. *(A pause.* BEAH *fans herself.)*

BEAH. Whew. That sun. Dessie, you and Mr. Borah here get a chance to know each other, on the way out?

DESSIE. *(Whispering.)* He don't talk much, Grandma.

BEAH. *(Loudly.)* He *don't?* I'm sure surprised. Sometimes that man's the biggest—

DESSIE. *(She tugs at* BEAH'*s sleeve.)* Stop it, Grandma. *(*BEAH *laughs loudly.)*

BEAH. Clare Borah, where's your manners? Why don't you show my granddaughter where her room is?

DESSIE. Oh Grandma. *(She runs into the house.* BEAH *calls after her.)*

BEAH. Come back after you're changed, you hear? I got lots to say to you. *(To* CLARE.*)* I declare, she hides her light under a bushel.

CLARE. You reckon she'll get a mind to stay on here?

BEAH. She'd better.

CLARE. Maybe for living out here she's too thin-skinned or something.

BEAH. Now that's the damndest thing I ever heard.

CLARE. Well, I don't know. *(Quickly, grinning.)* But now take you. I bet you was a real rancherwoman, weren't you? Spit through a screen door.

BEAH. *(Flattered.)* Well, now.

CLARE. Or that Jo in there—

BEAH. *(Sharply.)* This here is Dessie's land, not Jo's.

CLARE. Why are you all the time jumping on Jo? You're plain mean to her.

BEAH. She sure has got you fooled, ain't she?

CLARE. How's that?

BEAH. You figure what I mean. She ever say anything about Frank? About her husband?

CLARE. Far as I can make out, the durn fool run out on her.

BEAH. *That* man knew when to light out.

>      *(*JO *reappears in the doorway.)*

JO. What's going on out here?

BEAH. That's what I aim to find out. You and this damned, sassy cowboy—the way you two walk around this place like you thought you ownt it.

JO. I'm going to put you back to bed.

BEAH. Get away from me. *(She rises.)* If you ask me, you're more than half the time running this ranch bass-ackwards. *(*CLARE *and* JO *start toward her. She retreats to the doorway.)* Get away from me, I said. *(She goes into the house. A pause.* CLARE *stomps down to the pecan tree.)*

CLARE. Seems like ever'time I open my mouth it rouses her up.

JO. She's awful sick. You got to put up with it.

CLARE. Well, it makes me mad. Her all the time talking against you. *(A pause.)*

JO. She's never in her life said me a good word. She always favored Kelcy over me. And after that come Dessie.

CLARE. Why's she so mean?

JO. She hates me.

CLARE. After all you done for her? Taking care of her, and working this ranch?

JO. Day on day.

CLARE. That Dessie's just a wobbly-kneed, frilly bugger that don't give a damn for this place.

JO. She owns it.

CLARE. Are you going to let them two tromp all over you? It's you the one was bornt for this place.

JO. I don't want to talk about it.

CLARE. *(He goes toward her.)* It's the gods' truth, and you know it.

JO. *(She is suddenly frightened.)* Get away from me. *(A pause.* CLARE *turns away.)*

CLARE. Yep, that's how it is, ain't it? Well, I've made a plumb fool of myself. *(He goes down the steps.)*

JO. *(Angrily.)* Don't you talk to me that way. It's just—*(She closes her eyes, trying to hold it all in.)* Oh, you can't understand. You just don't know. *(*CLARE *starts to walk away.* JO*'s eyes fly open.)* Borah. Don't you walk off like that. I'm boss here. Don't—leave me. I got to have somebody I can *talk* to. Oh. Oh. It's all your fault. You've woke it all new in me.

CLARE. *(Angrily.)* Why should a one that's never breathed the dust nor been stove-in at the fag end of a day just move right in anytime she's a mind to and take it all from you?

JO. Ever' morning I wake up, sunlight hitting my pillow, and outside there's the mourning doves telling morning, and there's a grasshopper buzz and a breeze pressing through the mesquites, and I crave to take it all in. Swaller it. *(With great longing, squeezing her arms against her chest.)* Say: "That's all mine." Open my mouth and say: "It's mine." Say: "Sun, come down and take me, make me forget all but what's true. Like sunlight's true." I look at these blood lines in my wrist here, say: "Them's mesquite branches. That's what's true." Oh, if being growed might-near a part of this place means anything, it *is* true.

CLARE. It's the gods' truth.

JO. I'm McKennon too. A. W. was my pa too, not just Kelcy's. He taught me all I know about this place. How the deer move of a long twilight and the turkeys sneak. He used to heist me up onto his saddle, take us chousing through the brush after strays. And down there in the pens he'd have me scrambling to lasso a skittery colt and laugh to see which was getting the worst of it, telling me, "Josie, you was bornt for this place." That's A. W. telling me that. That's my pa too.

CLARE. *(He goes to her.)* Oh god, from the first time ever I seen you—

JO. *(In grief.)* Pa. Pa. Why did you ever have to leave me?

CLARE. *(He grasps her by the shoulders.)* Jo. *(He kisses her on the mouth. She breaks away and backs to the doorway. They stare at one another.)* Got to—get—that wagon unhitched. That load took down.

> *(*CLARE *turns abruptly on his heel and goes down the steps and away.* JO *stares after him. Her hand shakes as she touches it to her mouth.)*

*Curtain*

A Cloud of Witnesses *at Texas State Historical Theater at Mission San José in San Antonio, 1958. (Photo courtesy of the San Antonio Conservation Society and Dr. James Barton)*

The Trip to Bountiful *by A.D. Players at Grace Theater in Houston, 1989. Larry Balfe as Ludie Watts, Jeannette Clift George as Mrs. Carrie Watts. (Photo courtesy of A.D. Players)*

Who's Happy Now? *at Mark Taper Forum in Los Angeles, 1967. Betty Garrett as Mary Helen, Peggy Pope as Faye Precious, Warren Oates as Horse, and Warren Berlinger as Richard. (Photo courtesy of Mark Taper Forum and Oliver Hailey)*

Patio *at Theatre Three in Dallas, 1986. Ronnie Claire Edwards as Jewel, Carole Cook as Pearl. (Photo by Susan Kandell)*

*Porch* at *Theatre Three in Dallas, 1986. Ronnie Claire Edwards as Lucille, Carole Cook as Dot. (Photo by Susan Kandell)*

*The Regions of Noon* at *the Barter Theater in Abingdon, Virginia, 1960. Robert Pastene as Clar Borah, Donna Todd as Dessie McKennon, and Susan Walker as Jo McKennon. (Photo courtesy of the Barter Theater)*

El Jardín *by the Puerto Rican Traveling Theater in New York, 1988. Irma-Estel LaGuerre as Eva, Jack Landron as Dios, and Tony Mata as Adán. (Photo courtesy of Puerto Rican Traveling Theater Company, Inc.)*

Lu Ann Hampton Laverty Oberlander *at the Down Center Stage of the Dallas Theater Center, 1973. Sallie Laurie as Lu Ann, Ken Latimer as Red Grover. (Photo by Linda Blase)*

Ladybug, Ladybug, Fly Away Home *at the Down Center Stage of the Dallas Theater Center, 1978. Cheryl Denson as Mama Alice Kayro, Synthia Rogers (standing) as Tish Kayro, Alex Winslow and Beverly Renquist as customers of the Lovely Lady Beauty Shop. (Photo by Linda Blase)*

Lone Star *at Richland College Theater in Dallas, 1987. Darrell Muncy as Ray Caulder, Chuck Sheffield as Roy Caulder. (Photo courtesy of Chuck Sheffield and the Richland College Theater Department)*

# ★ SCENE III

*Out near the horse pen, a few hours later.*

*A live oak dominates the scene. It erupts from a rock fence at right stage and extends its snaky branches to the left. Its myriad oval leaves are a dark, shiny green.*

*The rock fence extends up toward left stage to a wooden gate which connects with a corner of the horse shed.*

*Sunlight crowds down, casting a dark pool of shade under the live oak. It is late evening.*

*CLARE is sitting on the rock fence, in the shade. He takes a swallow from a bottle, recorks the bottle, and sets it against the tree trunk.*

*A horse whinnies in the horse shed. It kicks against the side of a stall.*

*JO appears at left stage, carrying an apron-wrapped plate.*

JO. Oh, there you are. *(CLARE sits up straight. He stashes the bottle behind the fence. JO goes to him.)* Wondered where you went. We've ate supper.
CLARE. That's all right.
JO. I've fetched you this.
CLARE. You didn't need to do that.
JO. I'll just put it here. *(She sets the plate on the rock fence. A pause. She stands as if waiting.)* You ain't sick or nothing?
CLARE. No.
JO. You didn't come up to the house to eat. We was wondering what kept you. *(A pause.)* Clare, don't you mind Willie running off like she done.
CLARE. She ever take them jacks?
JO. I got them right here. I want you to give them to her.
CLARE. She don't take to me none.
JO. She ain't used to having a man around, other than Ignacio. She'll get used to you. *(In the stall the horse whinnies and stamps.)*
CLARE. Listen to that critter kick. He's bruised the frog of his foot. I got to keep him in the stall a few days. *(CLARE stands and starts to go to the horse pen, limping slightly.)*
JO. Does that foot hurt?
CLARE. It's nothing. *(He sits again.)* Since him and me has quit traveling, that horse has gone plumb sour.
JO. Clare, what would you say if we was to send you to San Antonio or somewheres, get a doctor to fix that foot?
CLARE. *(Moved.)* Ma'm, nobody ever—
JO. *(She lowers her eyes.)* It's just, it pains me to see you walk thataway.
CLARE. Christ, I love you, Josie.

JO. *(She looks at him a moment.)* You stay over there. *(She laughs. She sits on the fence and picks at the lichen on a rock. A pause.)* You've never stayed on one job long, have you, Clare? What's the longest you ever stayed?

CLARE. I just might get a notion to set a record here.

JO. Oh, I love it here. You can see clear to the Breaks of the Nueces. *(She touches the rock fence.)* Clare, what if we was to look at these stones right, the way a hawk or a lizard does? Maybe then we'd see it's saying things we can't hardly guess at now. *(She looks out at the land.)* That country. It goes on and on. Sometimes I feel like I could put my hand in a mesquite and *feel* the mystery.

CLARE. You ought to put goats on this place. This ain't no country for cattle. I hear them cows of a night, hangdogged in the brush, lowing for green grass.

JO. I wanted to stock this place with goats onct, but Beah wouldn't stand for it.

CLARE. *(He leans toward her eagerly.)* Jo, listen. I seen a buck onct, pure South African Angora, his fleece brung seventy cents a pound at an auction. *Seventy cents a pound.* A body could make money on that.

JO. *(She smiles.)* I think I love you. (CLARE *stands.)*

CLARE. Ma'm, this ain't boss and hired hand no more. Ain't been for a long time now. (JO *stands, inexplicably frightened.* CLARE *goes to her.)* Jo, I've come a long way, through a lonesome country dry for want of a woman. And two months now athirst for you like you was rain or something.

JO. You've been drinking.

CLARE. I'm sober now. *(He starts to touch her, but she backs away.)*

JO. Let loose of me. *(Fiercely.)* I told you not to drink, as long as you're working for me. *(They stare at one another.)*

CLARE. I can't stand no more of this. You come at me, shy away, come at me, shy away. *(He pulls her to him and kisses her. She submits for a moment, then pushes him away.)*

JO. No no no no. It won't never work, you and me. *(She rushes into his arms again.)* Oh my god, what am I going to do? I've been traveling too, through a lonesome country, flat, for miles flat, where there ain't no love. Never knew my ma. Married a fool that strung love up hanging withering in the sun. (CLARE *kisses her again, gently.)* Clare. Clare. Love me. Be good to me.

CLARE. I'd go through hell and high water for you.

JO. That's like a dove come up to my ear, moaning sweetlike from a branch. *(A pause. This next between them is a phase of tenderness.)*

CLARE. The first time I seen you, I said, now that's a one. The way you helt that rifle was a sight to see. Sun popping off that barrel weren't nothing to the fire popping in your eyes.

JO. *(Ruefully.)* I'd of shot you then, if I'd knowed you was thinking all that.

CLARE. And times you'd come riding up to me, so tall-up and proud in the saddle, looking down at me, giving me orders. You sure like to give a man orders, don't you?

JO. I been working this place so long alone I'd near forgot I was a woman. *(She touches his face.)* I love you, Clare Borah.

CLARE. *(Hungrily.)* Them pretty eyes so wet. That mouth so wet.

JO. *(Tenderly.)* You *have* been a long while alone, ain't you?

CLARE. I been traveling—

JO. I been traveling—

CLARE. And so I come to you. *(They kiss.)*

JO. And Willie to have her a father. Someone to give her things. Someone to teach her things. *(They kiss again.)*

CLARE. *(Joyously.)* Oh my god, what've I been doing with my life? Colorado. Oklahoma. New Mexico. So godawful lonesome. But I was thinking on you, though I never knowed it. All my born days I been headed thisaway.

JO. And I've *been* here. *(A pause.)*

CLARE. And trouble. I've seen a peck of trouble. Sometimes from women. *(A pause.)*

JO. I reckon you can tell me.

CLARE. One thing always leads to another. Oh Lordy, Josie, help me. I swear I ain't never loved no other woman but you.

JO. *(Gently, simply.)* I love you.

CLARE. *(He holds her at arm's length and grins.)* Well, I got to say one thing for trouble. It's brung me here. *(They kiss.)*

JO. *(Dark-tongued and possessive.)* And if there was ever another country you've been through, Clare Borah, under another sun, if ever there was another color eyes, some other woman's lips, if ever you was another, different man—you can forget all that. *(She stares at him.)* The one that was my husband is dead to me. I ain't never had a husband, Clare Borah, until you take me to you.

*Curtain*

# ★ SCENE IV

*The ranch house gallery, about noon, three weeks later.*

CLARE *is on the gallery, smoking a cigarette.* DESSIE *and the* TWO BOY-FRIENDS *enter. The two hover continually about her.*

FIRST BOYFRIEND. *(He slaps dust from his britches with a crumpled hat.)* Well, I reckon I *was* throwed, a little.

SECOND BOYFRIEND. Yep, Jim Bob. A little out of the saddle, a little over that roan's ears, and a little onto your little behind. *(He slaps his thigh and laughs.)*

FIRST BOYFRIEND. You ain't got no reason to laugh, Spud. You was too chicken-hearted to try anyways.

SECOND BOYFRIEND. It's just I got brains enough to see that horse was out for blood.

DESSIE. Hello, Mr. Borah. *(CLARE nods moodily. He goes right on smoking.)*

SECOND BOYFRIEND. Hey, Dess, come set here a spell.

FIRST BOYFRIEND. Yep, let's sit. *(Each offers DESSIE a place on the steps. She considers them warily and finally sits reluctantly between them, one step up. They immediately heist themselves up to that step and sit beside her. Feigning nonchalance, they pull out pocketknives and begin whittling. A pause.)*

DESSIE. It sure is hot and dusty.

TWO BOYFRIENDS. Yep. Yep. *(They whittle.)*

DESSIE. It sure is hot today, ain't it, Mr. Borah?

CLARE. About like always.

DESSIE. That sun's like a crackling in grease.

FIRST BOYFRIEND. *(He stops whittling.)* You go to any rodeos up there in Arkansas, Miss Dessie?

DESSIE. I've been to the county fair.

SECOND BOYFRIEND. *(He stops whittling.)* You mean they don't got no rodeos up there?

FIRST BOYFRIEND. Last year we had us a big rodeo, outside Alto Springs. They brung out this old bull. Was he mean. Like he had a hot poker up his—*(CLARE drops his foot to the gallery floor.)* Well, he was real mean, see? But I rid him.

SECOND BOYFRIEND. Yep, Jim Bob. Until you got throwed.

FIRST BOYFRIEND. *(Furiously.)* Of course, Dessie, it was Spud here who done all the *talking* about riding. He *talked* hisself onto all kinds of critters and into a slew of ribbons without coming in shouting distance of neither. *(To the SECOND BOYFRIEND.)* If you had to wear what ribbons you won you'd of been naked.

SECOND BOYFRIEND. Why you little—

*(They almost fight.* JO *comes from the house. She is wearing an apron and carries a bucket. She has been working.* CLARE *looks at her with concern.)*

JO. Dessie, your grandma won't let me feed her. She swears she ain't going to let nobody put a spoon to her mouth but you. *(DESSIE rises, troubled.)*

FIRST BOYFRIEND. Aw, Miss Dessie, your grandma's going to be all right. You can't keep an old rancherwoman down.

(WILLIE *runs onstage, breathless.*)

WILLIE. *Mama.*

JO. Willie, for goodness sakes. Here I am. (JO *sets the bucket on the steps.* WILLIE *runs to her.*)

WILLIE. You know what Ignacio done?

JO. What'd he do, honey?

WILLIE. He put a spell on that horse. After that boy was throwed, he just walked up to it and—and clicked his tongue and—and the horse let hisself be touched.

FIRST BOYFRIEND. It's the Mexican evil eye, that's what it is. Them Mexicans has all got a little horse in them anyways. They can look a horse in the eye, make it act any way they want.

SECOND BOYFRIEND. If that's so, Jim Bob, there must be a-plenty *burros* you can handle.

JO. Willie, go in the house and clean up. You look like a mess.

WILLIE. Oh, all right. (*She goes into the house.* JO *fetches the other bucket from the washstand.* DESSIE *goes to the door.*)

DESSIE. I'd better go feed Grandma.

FIRST BOYFRIEND. Dessie, wait a minute.

SECOND BOYFRIEND. You better ask her, Dess.

JO. What is it, Dessie?

SECOND BOYFRIEND. Dessie was thinking about having a play-party, huh Dess?

JO. A play-party? Where?

FIRST BOYFRIEND. Here. Ain't that so, Dess?

JO. Is that so, Dessie? Your grandma's awful sick.

SECOND BOYFRIEND. Well, she'll get well and—

FIRST BOYFRIEND. Come on, Miz McKennon.

JO. Well, I don't know. Maybe.

TWO BOYFRIENDS. Whoo-ee. We ain't had a party in I don't know how long.

(DESSIE *goes into the house.*)

JO. Now I didn't say no and I didn't say yes. Just maybe. (*Distracted.*) If—if—somebody'd fetch me some water. (*The* TWO BOYFRIENDS *grab the buckets.*)

SECOND BOYFRIEND. *Ah ha.*

FIRST BOYFRIEND. *San Antone.*

(*They run off, whooping and racing.* JO *leans against a gallery post, exhausted.*)

JO. I had to get rid of them. I can't stand their noise no more. They've been wellnigh *camping* here the past three weeks. Oh, Clare, when will I ever get to see you?

CLARE. (*He takes a step toward her.*) Jo.

JO. I can't take much more of it. Been up with Beah three nights running, and all she does is cuss me.

CLARE. Jesus, I can't stand to see you thisaway.

JO. I want to be alone with you, Clare. Just for a little while, just a mite. Help me. Comfort me.

CLARE. Josie.

JO. Shhh.

(DESSIE *reappears at the door.*)

DESSIE. Now if that ain't the durndest thing.

JO. What's that, Dessie?

(*The* TWO BOYFRIENDS *reenter, carrying buckets of water.*)

DESSIE. Grandma feel *asleep* on me.

FIRST BOYFRIEND. I said I was taking her. Hey, Dessie, I'm the one's taking you to the play-party, ain't I?

SECOND BOYFRIEND. It's me the one. Ain't that right, Dess?

FIRST BOYFRIEND. I asked her first.

SECOND BOYFRIEND. (*Sets his bucket down.*) She ain't going to make a fool out of herself and go with *you.*

FIRST BOYFRIEND. (*Sets his bucket down.*) She is too.

SECOND BOYFRIEND. You got about as much chanct as a stump-tail bull in flytime.

FIRST BOYFRIEND. You tight-britched, tick-brained son of a bitch. (*They collide and wrestle at the foot of the steps.*)

DESSIE. Mr. Borah. Make them quit.

TWO BOYFRIENDS. You want up? You give?

DESSIE. (*She rushes down the steps.*) *Quit it,* you two. *Get up.* (*The* TWO BOY-FRIENDS *sheepishly release their holds and rise.*)

FIRST BOYFRIEND. (*Humbly.*) Miss Dessie, ma'm, I sure would like to escort you.

DESSIE. No.

SECOND BOYFRIEND. I'd be proud to.

DESSIE. Not when you act like that. (*The* TWO BOYFRIENDS *look at one another.*)

TWO BOYFRIENDS. We'll *both* take her. O.K. Fine. Jim-dandy. (*They shake hands.*)

SECOND BOYFRIEND. Whoo-ee. See you at the play-party, Dess.

FIRST BOYFRIEND. Come on, buddy. Let's go. Let's get. Whoo-ee.

SECOND BOYFRIEND. Last one to the horses is a you-know-what.

FIRST BOYFRIEND. That'll be you, buddy. (*They run off, whooping and racing.*)

DESSIE. For certain sure *I* didn't have no say about it. Them are the silliest outfits.

CLARE. They've been stuck out in the brush so long, when they light eyes on a purty gal they go hog-wild.

DESSIE. (*She blushes.*) That ain't so.

JO. You were brought up different, Dessie, is all.

DESSIE. How do you mean, Josie?

CLARE. You ain't used to things so rough. This is a mean country, Miss Dessie, what with the northers of a winter and in the spring the twisters and all the time sun and brush and dust.

JO. If your grandma was to die—

DESSIE. Grandma ain't going to die.

JO. This land would be all yours then.

DESSIE. *(She is appalled.)* I couldn't run this place by myself. Josie, you wouldn't leave this place, would you?

JO. I don't know.

DESSIE. *(Frightened.)* You're trying to tease me.

JO. *(She goes to* DESSIE, *suddenly compassionate.)* Oh you. All that blond hair. There shouldn't a worry press through it. You remember that time I put them frogs in your hair?

DESSIE. Them spring peepers? Down near the stock tank? *(She giggles.)* You were awful to do that.

JO. We caught them in the redbuds. *(*DESSIE *laughs.)*

DESSIE. I recollect I tried to catch that big one, remember? And I slipped and skinned my shin and—and Grandma gave you the licking. *(A pause.)*

JO. I ain't heard them frogs in a long while now. *(A pause.)*

CLARE. Jo ought to put it to you plain and simple, Dessie. It's too rough a country for a one like you.

JO. *(She rises, troubled.)* I got to go in.

> *(*JO *goes into the house.* DESSIE *sits at the top of the steps, looking out.)*

DESSIE. Is this drouth going to keep on keeping on?

CLARE. It just might. You see that thunderhead yonder in the northwest, banked up like a wall? That *is* a wall, holding back the rain. It'll let down rain some-wheres—when it gets to the coast, likely. But not here. Here, it's the sun has it all. It ain't no place for a gal like you. You'd do better up in Arkansas. *(A soft, jerking sob breaks from* DESSIE.*)* What's the matter?

DESSIE. Mr. Borah, I ain't *happy* back up there.

CLARE. You got friends there, ain't you? And play-parties and such?

DESSIE. I hate play-parties. It's like as if my life's so empty I got to fill it up with foolishness. And when it's all over, I'm emptier than ever. *(She looks at* CLARE.*)* Ever'body treats me like a baby. I *ain't* a baby. I'm going on eighteen.

CLARE. Seems to me Jim Bob and Spud wasn't acting like you was no baby.

DESSIE. Oh, them silly outfits. *(A pause.)* I'm sorry, Mr. Borah. I didn't mean to say out all that. *(She turns back out to the land.)* It's being here that makes me think. About Ma, and Papa. My pa was one night killed, off that canyon edge. I ain't thought about that night for a long while now. I've been afraid to think on it. I said I wouldn't never come back here.

CLARE. *(Gently.)* You *shouldn't* of never.

DESSIE. I've been thinking lately of *before* Papa was killed. There was days and days of before. And it seems in my mind like then ever'thing was cool and still green. There was many a time I run out, felt a rain, got called in for getting wet in it.

CLARE. It's a drouth now. *(A pause. Up from the pens, a horse's whinny and the distant, singsong voice of the* OLD MEXICAN.*)*

DESSIE. It's a drouth now, all right. Maybe Josie's right, Mr. Borah. Maybe I ought to go back to Arkansas. It's might-near too much for me here. *(A pause.)* I reckon God gave this land to be used a little while by folks and now He's set on taking it back.

CLARE. Well, He's sending his legions. Sun and dust, scorpions, rattlers, blowflies. I've seen blowflies buzzing around like they was preaching doom. Big and hairy as doom.

DESSIE. *(She swats at a fly. She laughs.)* There's a fat one now. Are you preaching doom, mister? Get away from me, preacher. *(Lightning fast,* CLARE *catches the fly in his hand. It startles* DESSIE. *She goes to him.)* You've got it in your hand, Mr. Borah. I couldn't do that in a thousand years. Let me listen to it buzz. *(She grasps* CLARE*'s closed fist and presses it to her ear.)* I can hear it buzz. It's not buzzing so much now. It's buzzing shorter and shorter. Oh, Mr. Borah, you better let it loose. It's sick and craving to be let loose. *(*CLARE *releases the fly.* DESSIE *looks up.)* What are you staring at me for?

CLARE. Sit down.

DESSIE. Yes sir. *(*CLARE *hunkers down beside her.)*

CLARE. *(Brusquely.)* I'm trying to tell you. How mean this land is.

DESSIE. Yes sir.

CLARE. Onct, when I was riding through New Mexico, heat pushing from the ground like a devil breathing, I come on a cabin. No grass there. Just one big cottonwood, naked like a skeleton, beside a dry run. But there was a man there. That man says, he says to me, "Once that there cottonwood was green." He was waiting for it to green-up again. That man was crazy. And that's just what this land here will do, drive you out or drive you crazy, one. Look at it. So smart, sometimes you can hear it think. *(They stare out at the land. It stretches on and on before them under the sun.)* A man comes along, gets the lay of it, fits all his ways to it, prospers. Then the land changes its weather like a fence lizard its stripes, and a man's done for. Whipped.

DESSIE. Maybe a body's got to change his own ways, if he's going to make out. *(She turns to* CLARE.*)* Maybe there's a way to fit this place. Maybe I ought to stay here. I want to stay. *(*CLARE *rises.)* But I'm afraid. *(*DESSIE *rises, desperate.)* Tell me what I ought to do.

CLARE. You poor little gal.

DESSIE. *(In a sudden, childish tantrum,* DESSIE *throws herself against* CLARE *and pounds him with her fists.)* I ain't no little gal. Don't you call me that.

CLARE. *(He grabs her by her wrists.)* Hold on there!

DESSIE. *Don't you call me that!*

CLARE. Shhhh. Shhhh.

DESSIE. *(She presses against him, sobbing and trying to hit him with her fists.)* I— ain't—no—little—gal.

*Curtain*

# ★ SCENE V

*Several days later.*

*A spotlight is on* BEAH*'s rocker, at the center forefront of the gallery. The rest of the set is in darkness.*

BEAH *is sitting in her rocker. She is wearing a loose, pale-blue nightdress. Her face and hands are pale and her eyes sunken and dark.*

*The spotlight gets slowly brighter as the scene progresses.*

JO'S VOICE. Beah? *Beah.* How did you get out here?

BEAH. I walked out.

JO'S VOICE. You're not supposed to be up.

BEAH. I got to have some sun.

JO'S VOICE. I was bringing you a blanket, like you said. You can't stay out here.

BEAH. Damn it to hell, I wasn't built for four walls. *(She winces.)*

JO'S VOICE. I told you. You're hurting.

BEAH. Once a panther come acrost the yard. I chased it with a frying pan. All that running and my ticker—hadn't—a thump to it. Where's Dessie?

*(A second spotlight comes up on* JO, *at left stage. She remains motionless within it.)*

JO. I sent Willie to fetch her. Dessie's out to the water lot, watching Mr. Borah fix that windmill. Let me get you some broth.

BEAH. I don't want nothing.

JO. You've got to eat something.

BEAH. I don't want nothing from you.

JO. *(In an outburst of rage.)* That's the way it's always been, ain't it? You took it out on me. You made me to work. It was Kelcy always had his way, and Dessie was the purty one. But A. W. was my pa too.

BEAH. I told you never to use that name. You married. You've got your own name.

JO. *(In defiance and rage.)* McKennon. McKennon. My name's McKennon.

BEAH. I hate you.

JO. Then hate me. For being bornt. For wearing a name. It could of been so different. I could of loved you. I saw you could be good. You were good to Dessie. And you worked hard like me. Can't you see we're someways so much alike? We know the land. We know the brush. Onct you could ride a horse as good as me. And this ranch, this house, we've lived here all our lives.

BEAH. Look at that—spot—on the rafter. It's been there twenty years.

JO. Say something good to me onct.

BEAH. I wish A. W.'s bones could feel, and pack rats were gnawing on their salt, and whatever beetles. I've never forgiven him.

JO. You don't know what the word means. *(We hear the voices of* DESSIE *and* CLARE.*)* There's Dessie now. I'll get you some broth.

*(The spotlight on* JO *goes out.* CLARE *and* DESSIE *walk into the light at the platform.* DESSIE *is dressed in summer white.)*

DESSIE. *(She sees* BEAH.*)* Grandma oughtn't to be out here, Mr. Borah.

CLARE. Tell Jo her wrench is on the gallery. *(He sets a wrench down on the gallery steps.* BEAH *starts.* CLARE *turns to leave, but* DESSIE *stops him.)*

DESSIE. No, wait. Wait, Mr. Borah. Grandma don't look right.

BEAH. *Dessie?*

DESSIE. I'm right over here, Grandma.

BEAH. Come over here, honey, where I can see you.

DESSIE. *(To* CLARE, *whispering.)* Mr. Borah, I'm scairt.

BEAH. Are you coming?

DESSIE. Yes, Grandma. *(She goes to* BEAH. CLARE *follows her partway.)*

BEAH. Don't be frightened, honey. It's all right. Give me—your hand. *(She takes* DESSIE's *hand.)* Yes. Yes. That hand's so sweet. *(A pause.* BEAH *is momentarily breathless.)* I wish—I had my old room back. In the old house. Cool. And right outside my door that big pecan. *(*DESSIE *tries to remove her hand, but* BEAH's *grasp is fierce.)*

CLARE. I'd better go fetch Jo. *(He starts up the steps.)*

BEAH. Who's that over there?

DESSIE. Mr. Borah, Grandma. We were out to the water lot. I've been learning all about this place.

BEAH. *(She cackles.)* Flies to honey. I knowed it. *(She suddenly lies back, breathing heavily. A pause.)* Ever'thing's so—green today. The way A. W. always liked it. All that range grass. And rain softening up the ground for the plow.

DESSIE. Grandma, are you all right?

BEAH. *(To* CLARE.*)* Come over here, mister. *(A pause.)* Well. Ain't you going to mind a dying woman?

DESSIE. No, Grandma. You're going to be all right.

BEAH. Come over here, I said. *(*CLARE *goes to her.)* There now. That's better. *(*BEAH *laughs, then gags. She presses a hand to her breast and mumbles something unintelligible.)*

DESSIE. What, Grandma?

BEAH. Dessie? I ever tell you how your ma and pa was hitched?

DESSIE. No, Grandma.

BEAH. We built a big brush arbor. It gave lots of shade. Folks come from miles around. From Devil's River, even. Your pa had on new britches and a borrowed coat. Oh, he was all in a sweat. *(She laughs. Her breath catches, and her hand goes again to her breast. For a moment she does not breathe. It is as if she were gone deep into herself. At last she takes a deep breath. She is enraptured.)* Then—here—come— your ma. Small woman. Just like you. Small hands. Like yours. *(She holds* DESSIE's *hand to her face.)* White. She was done up in white. And her hands, her arms, her face—so white. I declare, it made the sun shine rings around her. And her hair so bright. Sometimes I think your ma was too white a woman for these parts. And she said, *Miz McKennon,* I'm *scairt.* And I held her hand. Like—this. Sweet,

sweet Sarah. (DESSIE *tries to pull away, but* BEAH *will not let go.)* And the preacher took their two hands. (BEAH*'s left hand hovers in the air like a bird for a moment. Then she grasps* DESSIE*'s hand with both hands.)* And he said. The word. (BEAH*'s smile slides into a shape of grief.* DESSIE *manages to pull her hand free.)* Oh my poor, lost children. (BEAH*'s eyes are closed. A sly grin cracks her face.)* Is—that— rain?

DESSIE. No, Grandma. That's just a fly buzzing. (BEAH *strains forward from the rocker. Her eyes spring open.)*

BEAH. Who's that blocking my door? A. W., is that you standing between me and the light?

DESSIE. Oh, there ain't nobody there.

BEAH. *Alvin Worthy McKennon.* What are you blocking my sight for? I want to see out. See all that rain. My pecan tree—dropping—pecans. (BEAH *falls back. The spotlight dims.* CLARE *kneels and touches* BEAH*'s wrist.* DESSIE *looks at him. Then she throws herself sobbing across her grandmother's lap.)*

DESSIE. Grandma. Grandma. I won't let you leave me.

CLARE. Dessie, it can't be helped.

DESSIE. That's all I ever knowed. First my ma. Then my pa. And now this. *(She suddenly jumps to her feet.)* I can't stand it. *(She starts to laugh.* CLARE *grasps her and shakes her.)* There ain't nothing real but this.

CLARE. *Quit. (She stops. He releases her and she stares blankly at him.)*

DESSIE. *(After a pause. She speaks as if from a great distance.)* It's like a river come out of the ground, and it drowns ever'thing. It don't matter how much light shines onto it, it takes ever'thing with it, filled with all the dark it come from, all the blind places a hundred miles deep, right under our feet. *(Tears spring to her eyes.)*

CLARE. Don't cry. There ain't no help atall for it.

DESSIE. Oh, Mr. Borah, take me away from here. Take me anywheres, to China or Egypt, where I don't got to be myself no more.

CLARE. What?

DESSIE. I ain't nothin' atall. I might as well be dead.

CLARE. That ain't so. Don't you think like that. *(He takes her by the wrist.)* Christ, there's a hundred thousand men would think you was a fine woman. (DESSIE *stares down at his hand. Suddenly she grasps her clenched fist, forces it upward, kisses the back of* CLARE*'s wrist.)*

DESSIE. Help me! Save me from myself! *(She weeps.* CLARE *stares at her a moment. He takes her to him. He strokes her head.)*

CLARE. I wish I could. *(The spotlight goes out.)*

*Curtain*

# ★ SCENE VI

*The gallery, two weeks later, night.*

*A pair of saddlebags is hanging from one of the rails.*

*A cloud crosses the moon, darkening the scene. The gradual release of the moon is accompanied by one long, intense, rising note from a fiddle. The instant the moon is freed, the note breaks from its peak and evolves into a fast square-dance tune.*

*Moonlight. The gallery posts are like whitened ribs. Down in the yard the sapling, bleached and skeletonic, pokes from the ground. The ranch house door is half open, and dancers pass back and forth behind it. In the ranch house windows, the curtains lift and fall: a night breeze on the plateau.*

*Two couples are courting in the shadows at the edge of the gallery.*

JO. *(Offstage. From behind the house.)* Come and get it. *(The music stops. There is clapping and chatter. Then the sound of the guests diminishes.)*

FIRST BOY. Hey, let's go eat.

HIS GIRL. Let's don't.

FIRST BOY. Come on. *(He pulls her offstage, around the side of the house.)*

HIS GIRL. Well I never.

> *(The* SECOND BOY *and* HIS GIRL *keep right on courting.* CLARE *appears in the doorway.)*

SECOND BOY. Shhh. *(*CLARE *goes down to the steps and glances about. He pulls a bottle out from under the steps, uncaps it, and takes a good, stiff swallow. He pauses, listening. He tucks the bottle into his pocket and goes off. The* SECOND BOY *snickers.)* Going to have hisself a *snort. (The* SECOND BOY *and* HIS GIRL *laugh. They kiss. He whispers in her ear.)*

HIS GIRL. No. *(He whispers again.)* No, I said. *(She laughs. He pulls her toward right stage.)* No, no, no, no.

> *(He leads her off. A pause. The* TWO BOYFRIENDS *rush out of the house. The* FIRST BOYFRIEND *forces the* SECOND BOYFRIEND *against the wall and pins him there.)*

FIRST BOYFRIEND. You damned ornery bastard, you.

SECOND BOYFRIEND. Let go.

FIRST BOYFRIEND. You've been hogging her, that's what. I ain't had one dance with her.

SECOND BOYFRIEND. I ain't danced with her but twict.

FIRST BOYFRIEND. You're a liar.

SECOND BOYFRIEND. Ain't you got eyes? Who's Dessie been staring at all evening? Who's she sit next to ever' chance she gets? It ain't me.

FIRST BOYFRIEND. You mean—?

SECOND BOYFRIEND. How'd you guess?

FIRST BOYFRIEND. We got to get her away from him.

SECOND BOYFRIEND. Come on.

> *(The door opens. It is* DESSIE.*)*

DESSIE. Oh. I thought—

TWO BOYFRIENDS. Hi, Dess. They're dishin' out the barbecue. Let's get us some grub.

DESSIE. I can't even make out what you two are saying.

SECOND BOYFRIEND. Go on, Jim Bob. Take her around back.

FIRST BOYFRIEND. Huh?

SECOND BOYFRIEND. Get her somethin' to *eat,* for crissake. *(He shoves the* FIRST BOYFRIEND *toward* DESSIE.*)*

DESSIE. I don't want to eat yet. Can't I just get some fresh air and quiet for a spell? Purty please?

FIRST BOYFRIEND. Sure. Let's just set and talk.

DESSIE. Well, I just want to sit by myself for a spell.

SECOND BOYFRIEND. *Sssst. (*CLARE *reenters.* DESSIE *rises eagerly.)* Come on, Dessie. Let's go get some grub. *(*CLARE *sees them and turns to go.)*

DESSIE. Mr. Borah. Come on over. *(*CLARE *crosses reluctantly to them.)* We thought we'd set out here and rest ourselves a spell.

SECOND BOYFRIEND. Come *on,* Dess.

DESSIE. If I was a calf they'd have me hog-tied and drug in by now.

FIRST BOYFRIEND. You coming?

DESSIE. Oh, I don't know. I reckon I'll get myself some fresh air.

> *(The* TWO BOYFRIENDS *stalk into the house.)*

CLARE. *(Uneasily.)* Them two whippersnappers've been acting downright persnickety, ain't they?

DESSIE. They been pestering me all evening. *(She leans against a gallery post and looks out.)* That moon's so big.

CLARE. *(He starts up the steps.)* I thought I heard Jo calling chow a minute ago.

DESSIE. Look at them clouds, like twisted-up horses.

CLARE. Giddyap.

DESSIE. *(She laughs.)* You've been so silly tonight.

CLARE. *(Abruptly sober.)* I sure could use some grub in my craw. *(He starts toward the door.)*

DESSIE. Mr. Borah. Clare. *(*CLARE *stops at the door.)* You was so tall-up and purty, standing over there by the fireplace. Especially when you was calling them dances. *(*CLARE *turns to her.)* No, don't you look at me.

CLARE. Miss Dessie—

DESSIE. *(She turns quickly from him.)* That's a fine thing for me to say, ain't it? "Don't you look." When I've been took with looking at you all evening. But I don't want us to look. It'd be more than I could stand. *(*CLARE *fidgets nervously.)* If I was in love I'd tell him ever'thing I ever did and not hold back a single thing.

Onct up in Arkansas when I was fourteen a boy kissed me under a peach tree. I disremember what his name was. Arkansas is such a long ways back. Mudbank rivers and red-dirt hills. Long gone, like in a dream. This here is what's real.

CLARE. Wait a minute, Dess.

DESSIE. This must be what love is. Not hardly able to breathe.

CLARE. Listen, Dessie. It ain't I'm trying to hurt you or nothing—*(A pause.)* What I'm trying to tell you is—Hell's bells. *(He inhales deeply.)* Look, first off I got to feeling sorry for you.

DESSIE. *(She turns to him.)* You don't have to feel sorry for me. I'm alive. I'm breathing. For the first time in my life.

CLARE. Let's just—talk about all this tomorrow. *(Half-drunk he sits on the steps.)* I got too many cobwebs in my head.

DESSIE. I love to hear you talk. To have you teach me things. About this ranch and all.

CLARE. I talk too much.

DESSIE. *(She touches him.)* I remember yesterday, out at the stock tank. Swallows was picking mud at the side of the tank. Waterbugs on top of the water. It was the whole world. And when you helt me I wanted to die and keep it all there. I ain't never been in love before.

CLARE. I ought to butt my brains out on a stooping post oak.

DESSIE. You ain't mad at me or nothing, are you? *(CLARE stands.)*

CLARE. One thing always leads to another.

DESSIE. *(She stands up exultantly.)* It's like the whole world opening. It's like the grass to come green. Like I'd just turnt over in my life and for the first time seen the sun.

CLARE. *Christa'mighty.*
    *(The door opens, and* JO *stands silhouetted there. She is wearing a new dress. Within, the sound of a fiddle being tuned.)*

JO. Oh, there you are.

DESSIE. *(Gaily.)* Hi, Josie.

JO. I seen Clare come out. I didn't know you was out here too, Dessie. *(She closes the door and goes to them. She has a piece of cake on a napkin.)*

DESSIE. We come out to get some fresh air.

JO. It *is* a mite stuffy inside. Here, we just cut the cake. I brung you some white cake, Clare. I'd of brung some for Dessie if I'd knowed she was out here. But it's a big hunk, and you and her can split it. *(She gives the slice of cake to* CLARE.*)*

CLARE. *(Awkwardly.)* Don't you want some?

JO. No. I'm full up.

DESSIE. It's a pretty cake, Josie. You got to tell me the recipe some one of these days.

CLARE. Here's some for you. *(He offers some of the cake to* DESSIE. *Their fingers touch.* DESSIE *giggles.)*

JO. What's so funny?

DESSIE. *(Cramming cake into her mouth.)* Nothing. It's awful good cake.

JO. What have you two been gabbing about out here?

CLARE. *(Quickly.)* Me and Miss Dessie was just now talking about the ranch. *(DESSIE giggles.)*

JO. *(Bewildered.)* What on earth are you laughing about, Dessie?

DESSIE. Oh, nothing. About something that happened at another party onct, I reckon.

JO. Oh. *(She sits.)* My, that's a lot of moon up. Clare, I'll save you some of that cake to put in your saddlebags when you go to ride fenceline tomorrow.

CLARE. That sounds fine.

JO. I got to rest a spell. *(A pause.)* It's nice out here. You'll be heading back to Arkansas purty soon, Dessie. We're going to miss you. *(A crashing noise from within the house.)* Now what on earth's *that?*

DESSIE. You sit. You've been working all day. I'll tend to it.

> *(DESSIE laughs and darts into the house.)*

JO. That's a real good gal. *(She laughs nervously.)* Look at my collar. It's all wrinkled. I can't keep from picking at it with my fingers. I'm still all wound up. All them days of that sick old woman. When those two boys kept pushing for this play-party I couldn't help but say yes. It was like if it didn't come a noise, a twister, music, dancing, *some*thing, I was going to go to pieces. I may go to pieces yet. My tongue keeps right on talking. I don't seem to be able to quit. How do you like my new dress? You ain't said you liked it yet.

CLARE. It's a mighty fine dress.

JO. I've missed you. *(CLARE goes to her and kneels beside her.)*

CLARE. Jo, listen. There ain't never been nobody but you.

JO. Shhh. You don't need to tell me. *(She touches his face tenderly.)*

CLARE. You got such dark eyes. And your forehead so white.

JO. *(Fiercely.)* Soon. Soon. Nobody here but you and me.

CLARE. *(He rises.)* I wish that Dessie was long gone.

JO. She'll be leaving soon. Then it'll just be you and me and Willie. *(Laughter from within.)*

CLARE. I'd like to light out of here right now. Right this minute. Saddle up a horse, ride out, just you and me. Not thinking on nothing but grass and the wind and a live oak tree.

JO. *(She smiles.)* It comes a time when a body has got to quit running, darling.

CLARE. Goddammit. Things always get so *tangled.*

JO. *I love you.*

> *(DESSIE reappears in the doorway.)*

DESSIE. It was them two boys, fighting over the last of the barbecue. I told them to quit. *(Another, louder crash.)*

JO. Clare, maybe you better run inside, keep an eye on them mavericks for me. I been going all day.

CLARE. Ah—all right. I'll do that.

JO. Dessie and me'll be in in a minute.

CLARE. You—sure there ain't nothing you need me out here for?

JO. I just got to rest a mite. *(Inside, someone slides a fresh-rosined bow across a fiddle.)*

CLARE. *(Reluctantly.)* I'll be getting on in then, I reckon.

DESSIE. *(She waves, smiling.)* 'Bye. See you in a minute, Mr. Borah. *(*CLARE *looks at* DESSIE *a moment. Then he goes into the house. Square-dance music in the background frames the following dialogue.)* Borah. That's a purty name, ain't it?

JO. Best thing I did for this ranch was hiring him.

DESSIE. He's smart, ain't he? Like he knows ever'thing.

JO. Well, he gets the work done.

DESSIE. *(She sits beside* JO.*)* I'm tuckered. Didn't know I was so tuckered until now.

JO. Don't get so tired you turn sick, honey.

DESSIE. I wish I was strong like you, Josie. You've been going all day and still fresh as a daisy. I seen you dancing like you hadn't worked a jot.

JO. I love to do the "Little Foot." *(She sings.)* "Put your little foot."

DESSIE. *(She sings.)* "Put your little foot." *(Each moves a foot, in unison, in a delicate, scaled-down version of the dance step.)*

JO and DESSIE. "Put your little foot right out." *(They laugh.)*

DESSIE. You and me like the same dance best.

JO. Oh, all the dances I used to dance when I was younger. "Bird in the Cage" and "Texas Star."

DESSIE. I remember. *(A pause.)*

JO. This here's the first time we've had to really talk together, ain't it? It's nice. That's why I wish you could stay longer. We could talk on all the old things. Remember the time your pa was digging postholes and he gave you a pie plate to scoop out the bottom? You fell in. *(They laugh.)* And those spring peepers in your hair.

DESSIE. Oh, Josie.

JO. Sometimes I think them days was the only good ones there was. It's going to be awful lonesome with you gone, Dessie. *(*DESSIE *laughs again.)* What on earth's making you so silly?

DESSIE. *(She stands.)* I'm *happy.* Like I belonged to ever'thing. Just to suck in air. Did you ever think? How that air comes from ever'wheres, China maybe, and you suck it in and your heart gets like a sparrow about to flip up your gullet and fly out? Or that moon up there. Hey, Moon, I bet you know ever'thing we're thinking.

JO. Only he don't tell. *(A pause.)* You're not *sick* or nothing, are you?

DESSIE. No'm. I'm just *happy.* Josie, am I bad-looking?

JO. You got to fill out some.

DESSIE. I feel puny. Look how puny my arms and neck is. And I feel like I go just straight down. *(*JO *laughs.)*

JO. You never was the strongest. You're thin-boned and easy hurt. I remember when you was little you was always getting sick or hurt or some such thing.

DESSIE. But I ain't bad-looking? And if a body was to look at me they might even think I was good-looking?

JO. I declare. Well, I'll say one thing. If they like freckles they'd say you was good-looking.

DESSIE. Josie, you're awful. *(They laugh. A pause.)* Josie, how can a body tell they're in love?

JO. First you pluck you a daisy.

DESSIE. Oh foo.

JO. Don't tell me some bean pole up in Arkansas has been making eyes at you.

DESSIE. Not up there.

JO. *(Frowning.)* You don't mean here?

DESSIE. Maybe.

JO. Well, that's not love. That's puppy love. Oh, maybe one of them boys—Jim Bob or Spud—has got your fancy for a season, but that's not love. You watch. Pretty soon you'll be back up in Arkansas and forget all about it.

DESSIE. *(She laughs.)* I can't keep it from you. The way you've been talking like I was going to go back to Arkansas in a few days. *(Within, the music stops.)*

JO. You ain't?

DESSIE. *(Gaily.)* No.

JO. You're not going to let a crush on some fool rancherboy turn your head, are you?

DESSIE. Oh, I don't know. Maybe some one of these days I might even get hitched.

JO. Now that's the craziest thing. Don't neither of you know what the word means.

DESSIE. *(Laughs.)* Josie, you don't know what I mean atall.

JO. You wouldn't never be happy in this country.

DESSIE. Him and me might make out just fine. He knows all there is, about ranching and such. We could run this place. He's got good ideas, ways to keep this place going, for all the drouth is so bad. We'll stock the ranch with goats, long-haired Angora ones. I don't know why we ain't done it before, a long ways back. Them things do fine in brush-country like this. *(JO rises slowly, her features frozen in a cold, terrible passion.)* What's the matter, Josie? *(Frightened.)* Josie, what's wrong?

JO. Are you in love?

DESSIE. Yes'm.

JO. Who—are you—in love with, Dessie?

DESSIE. Mr.—Borah.

JO. He wants to—*marry* you?

DESSIE. I don't know.

JO. He—*touched* you?

DESSIE. *(She unconsciously puts a hand to her face. She laughs.)* Oh, Josie! *(A pause.)*

JO. *(Ominously.)* Are you happy, my dear?

DESSIE. I *want* to be.

JO. *(Ominously.)* I'm glad for you.

DESSIE. *(She runs to JO and hugs her. JO doesn't move.)* Oh Josie, you're good. I wish I could do anything on earth for you.

JO. I wish you could.

*(Within the house, the fiddle recommences playing, harshly. The* TWO BOY-
FRIENDS *come out of the house.)*

TWO BOYFRIENDS. Hey Dess, let's dance. They're gonna dance "Ten Pretty
Girls."

DESSIE. I want to stay out here with you, Josie.

TWO BOYFRIENDS. Come on, Dessie. They're about to commence. Come on.
*(They pull* DESSIE *toward the door.)*

DESSIE. Ain't you coming in too, Josie?

TWO BOYFRIENDS. Come *on*, Dess.

*(They pull her into the house. The door remains open.* WILLIE, *in her nightgown,
appears in the doorway. She steps out onto the gallery and closes the door.)*

WILLIE. Mama, I can't sleep. They're making too much noise in there. *(*JO *does not
move or speak.* WILLIE *goes to her.)* I'm tired, Mama. Make them people go home.
*(*JO *grasps* WILLIE *and clutches her to herself.)* What's the matter, Mama? Mama,
you're shaking. You're *squeezing* me!

*Curtain*

# ★ SCENE VII

*The gallery, the next morning.*

*That narrow hush just before sunup. Birds—doves and mockingbirds and such—are making their first, assertive noises.*

*The saddlebags hang from the gallery rail.*

DESSIE *comes out of the house, laughing and pulling* WILLIE. DESSIE *is dressed, but she has not yet put up her hair.* WILLIE *is in her nightgown.*

DESSIE. Come on. You'll miss it.

WILLIE. Miss what?

DESSIE. The sun, silly. I ain't seen the sun come up in I don't know how long. *(*WILLIE *yawns.* DESSIE *claps a hand over* WILLIE's *mouth.)* Look out. You'll swaller it.

WILLIE. Swaller what?

DESSIE. That sun. It's about to come up.

WILLIE. How come you let him kiss you like that?

DESSIE. Who?

WILLIE. You know who. Out to the stock tank.

DESSIE. Willie, you were *follering* us! *(The light grows brighter, changing from amber to white.)*

WILLIE. I'm sleepy.

*(*WILLIE *runs back into the house.* JO *appears at left stage and crosses to the steps. Her dress is torn, her face and arms are scratched, and her hair is disheveled. She carries the rifle.)*

DESSIE. Josie, what are you doing up? I thought you was still asleep. Your new dress is all tore!

JO. He ain't come back for his saddlebags yet?

DESSIE. No'm. But I'm fixing breakfast. Wait a minute, I'll fetch a needle and thread. We'll fix up that dress. Ain't it a purty morning?

*(*DESSIE *goes into the house.* CLARE *appears at right stage. He sees* JO.*)*

CLARE. Jo?

JO. *(She stiffens.)* Good morning, darling. Have you been sleeping, all tight and curly-headed in your bunk?

CLARE. What do you got that .30-30 for?

JO. *(She sinks to the steps, laughing softly.)* To keep me from varmints.

CLARE. *(He goes to her, but his approach is a wide circle of retreat.)* Josie, I been up half the night, hanging around this place, waiting for you to come out.

JO. You kind of missed me.

CLARE. Where in hell have you *been* all night?

JO. I been out walking. Counting fence posts.

*(*JO *laughs strangely.* DESSIE *reappears in the doorway.)*

DESSIE. Good morning, Clare—Mr. Borah. Ain't it a purty morning? There's breakfast almost ready. *(To* JO.*)* Here, let me see that dress. *(She goes to* JO *and sits beside her.)* We'll fix that right quick. *(But* JO *grasps* DESSIE*'s hand.* DESSIE *looks at her, startled.)*

JO. You don't do it that way.

DESSIE. Josie, what's the matter? *(*JO *releases* DESSIE*'s hand.)*

JO. You have fun at that dance, Mr. Borah?

CLARE. *(Uneasily.)* I reckon.

JO. Get a plenty of fresh air? *(She laughs.)* Look at my hair. It's got stickers all through it. I'll wear them stickers like they was jewels, maybe. I'll wear frogs in my hair.

CLARE. *(He reaches for his saddlebags.)* I better get started on that fenceline.

DESSIE. Wait a minute, Clare.

JO. *(Sarcastically.)* Clare. *(*DESSIE *rises.)* The deer were out browsing all night, under that moon. You ever notice how a deer walks? And when they come to a fence, they just sail right on over. High. There ain't nothing sneaky about them.

DESSIE. *(Troubled, glancing from* JO *to* CLARE.*)* I—ain't put your dinner in the saddlebags yet, Mr. Borah. I'll fetch it right now.

*(She goes into the house. A pause.)*

CLARE. Jo? *(*JO *rises.* CLARE *goes toward her. She backs up the steps.)*

JO. Get away from me.

CLARE. For crying out loud. *(A pause.)* What was you and Dessie talking about last night? *(*JO *turns away from him. A long pause.)* Josie, goddammit, *say* something.

JO. *(Sarcastically.)* Josie, Josie, Josie.

CLARE. Hell, Jo, you ain't going to believe ever'thing a little fool like that'll tell you, are you? *(He goes to her and touches her. She cries out and pulls away from him.)* Listen, Jo, we got to straighten this out. Dessie'll be out here any minute. *(Angrily.)* I want to know what nonsense that little ninny was telling you. *(A pause.)* All right, no use shilly-shallying about it. I made a mistake, is what. I got to feeling sorry for Dessie. Next thing I knew, she had it all built up in her head. Are you *listening?* I swear to God, Josie, she don't mean nothing to me. She's just a silly kid. I got to feeling sorry for her, and one thing led to another. For God's sake, *say* something. I was trying not to hurt her, is all. *(*JO *turns slowly back to him.)*

JO. And what about me? What about me?

CLARE. I was going to tell you, going to get this straightened out. When it come the right time.

JO. Why not sooner? Why not come Christmas?

CLARE. *(Choked, bitter and humiliated.)* I reckon I was—afraid.

JO. Of *me?* *(She laughs.)*

CLARE. *(Angrily.)* What are you laughing at?

JO. I been out all night. Walking the brush. Thinking. *Oh God.*

CLARE. I tell you, it ain't all so bad as you think. *(*CLARE *takes a step toward* JO. *She points the rifle at him and he stops.)*

JO. "I'd go through hell and high water for you."

CLARE. We better talk about this later.

JO. "There ain't never been nobody but you, Josie."

CLARE. Point that gun another way.

JO. I'll kill you if I can.

CLARE. Put away that gun, I said.

JO. *Kill you!* (JO *throws herself at* CLARE. *They struggle.* CLARE *wrests the rifle from her and forces her to a step.*)

JO. *(In a fury, weeping.)* I never did you no wrong. You come here a drifter. You would of died in the brush somewheres if it hadn't of been for me. I gave you a job. I gave you the run of this place when you was nothing. (DESSIE *reappears in the doorway.*) I gave you my love. I gave you ever'thing.

DESSIE. *(Shocked.)* Josie!

CLARE. Now listen, Dessie—

DESSIE. *(To* JO.*)* You were—in love with him?

JO. And more. A whole lot more. *(A pause.)*

DESSIE. I—hate—this place. You two have been against me from the start.

CLARE. Hold on a minute.

DESSIE. *I wish I was dead.*

(*She runs back into the house.*)

CLARE. *(He yells after her.)* You wouldn't have it no other way but how it was in your head, Dessie. (JO *rises and backs away from* CLARE.*)*

JO. *(Vehemently.)* Who do you think you are? Did you think you could have your own way, getting the best of us, laughing at us?

CLARE. Ma'm, I ain't laugh—

JO. You think you're the red rooster to ever' woman, don't you? Well, I ain't just any woman.

CLARE. Wait a minute.

JO. *Drifter.* That's what I call you. And I should of remembered it.

CLARE. *(Angrily.)* Sure, tell me off. I'm a shiftless bum. I got a cocklebur under my saddle blanket, does that suit you? Go ahead and say it.

JO. It meant ever'thing on earth to me to of thought well of some one man.

CLARE. All right. I made a mistake. I know it.

JO. I don't hold by mistakes. *(Furiously.)* I wish you'd of never come to this place, do you hear? Your walk, your talk, the everlasting brass of you. It couldn't come down a rain enough to wash all that away.

CLARE. Somewhere there's trees a plenty, and a cool wind, and rain flattening the grass, and I'm gonna *go* there and throw myself onto it and it ain't the steers of hell can drag me back.

JO. Go. Go.

CLARE. It wouldn't *sweat* me none.

JO. *(She laughs hysterically. Abruptly she stops.)* I wish that sun would burn down, set fire to the brush, blacken the deer, turn the rattlers to swirling under rocks, mourning doves to pitching from the limbs, send this house pounding up in smoke against the weather! *(Grievously, wringing her hands.)* How can I live? How can I ever *breathe* again?

CLARE. *(He goes to her and grasps her by the shoulders.)* There ain't never been a one but you, Jo. Not for me, there ain't. There never will be.

JO. Oklahoma, Colorado, New Mexico.

CLARE. *(He shakes her.)* I don't give a damn about them others. Dessie neither. Christ, you're magnificent. From the first time ever I seen you. Aw, Jo. I love you.

JO. Oh. Oh. *(They almost kiss. But* JO *breaks free.)* No. I can't stand it no more. *(*CLARE *stares at her a moment. Then he turns away, dejected, and leans against a gallery post.* JO *moves away from him, wringing her hands.)* Oh god, life's so cruel. The wind. The brush. The stars are nothin' but a pack of stones. We're just alone.

CLARE. I used to say, "Keep drifting, just keep to the brush. Then you won't need nobody."

JO. What's the good of a life if it can't be lived? What's a body doing in this world if he can't make something out of it?

CLARE. *(He looks at her.)* Hell, Jo. *There's you and me.*

JO. *(After a pause.)* One time it was. But I don't hold with rattlers under my front steps.

    *(*WILLIE *appears in the doorway.)*

WILLIE. Mama, Dessie—

JO. *(To* CLARE, *gently.)* Down in the water lot there's your horse. Catch him, throw a saddle on him, and go.

WILLIE. Is he leaving, Mama?

JO. *(She squeezes her eyes shut.)* Shhh. *(*CLARE *strikes the gallery post with his fist.)*

CLARE. Christ, ever'thing I do, it turns to dust. *(He turns back to* JO.*)* I'll be back, I tell you. I'll be back.

JO. That hot sun. I can't even *remember* green.

WILLIE. Where's he going, Mama?

CLARE. I'm going across the Divide. I'm going to catch a panther by the tail and swing him skywide. *(A pause.* CLARE *pushes away from the gallery post.)* I'm going to rope the half of Mexico and haul it behind my saddle. *(He goes to his saddlebags and takes them up. He looks at* JO *a moment. Then he goes down the steps. At the bottom of the steps he stops and turns back to* JO. *A pause.)* Please, ma'm, I got a far piece to go. Let me have a drink of water. *(*JO *goes to the washstand. She dips water from the bucket and returns to the top of the steps. She and* CLARE *look at one another.)*

JO. *(Gently, compassionately.)* Now you know it, Clare Borah. All the ache and the loss, bigger than the sky, crueler than the rain, come to green-up grass, and then leave and let die. *(A pause.)*

CLARE. *(Angrily, almost defiantly.)* I don't care if I ride from here to China. *I'll be back.* *(*JO *holds out the dipper.* CLARE *takes it and drinks from it, looking all the while up at her. A pause.* CLARE *wipes his mouth and hands the dipper back to* JO. *For a moment both their hands are touching the dipper, and they look at one another.)*

JO. Clare Borah, ain't it queer? I love you, for all I know ever'thing you are. *(*JO *takes the dipper. A long pause.)*

CLARE. *(He is overwhelmed with gratefulness and anguish. He removes his hat and bows.)* Gracias. Gracias, señora. *(*CLARE *turns to go. He stops and looks at* JO *again. Then he bows once more, in gratitude, debt, homage.)* Gracias.

    *(*CLARE *goes out. The* CURTAIN *falls.)*

# Carlos Morton

★ ★ ★ ★ ★ ★ ★ ★ ★ ★ ★ ★ ★ ★ ★ ★

★ THE PERSON

Carlos Morton was born Charles Morton in Chicago in 1947 and attended high school in Battle Creek, Michigan. In between, he traveled extensively as his father, a regular army sergeant, was shuttled to various posts in the United States and Latin America. This wandering suited him, and in his adult life he has continued the pattern. He took a B.A. in English at the University of Texas at El Paso in 1975; then he studied drama under Jorge Huerta at the University of California at San Diego, receiving his M.F.A. in 1978. In May 1987 he was awarded a Ph.D. in drama by the University of Texas at Austin.

Morton's work experience has been as scattered as his formal education, and more diverse. Since 1968 he has had jobs as a journalist and an actor in Chicago and as a playwright with the Teatro Campesino of Luis Valdez and the San Francisco Mime Troupe in California. For a time he drove a taxi in New York City. Currently he is a faculty member in the Department of Theatre Arts at the University of Texas at El Paso, having previously taught speech and drama at Laredo Junior College.

Morton is a committed Chicano dramatist whose personal and family life exemplifies many of the complexities and contradictions of American Hispanic culture. One of his immigrant grandfathers, inspired by the sight of a Morton's Salt billboard, changed his name from Perez to Morton to make himself more employable. Later, when Charles embraced the Chicano student movement as an undergraduate, he changed his name to Carlos and worked to relearn the Spanish he had spoken exclusively as a preschool child and to reestablish contact with Hispanic traditions. Although he is the author of a powerful documentary drama about the controversial case of Richard Morales, who died in 1975 while in police custody near Castroville, Texas, Morton derived his information from reports in the *New York Times*.

For many Chicanos, the Rio Grande marks a political abstraction only, not a major separation of peoples. As a border-dweller himself, in Laredo and El Paso, Morton has observed that those living near the border, regardless of the side, feel that they are a part of a larger community and routinely draw on both Mexican and American resources. But he, much more than most, imaginatively transcends barriers of politics, geography, and time. The assassination of Archbishop Romero in San Salvador outrages him as much as the killing of Richard Morales in Texas. Morton's emotional universe, which is identical with his dramatic subject matter, has its historic center in Tenochtitlán, the ancient Aztec capital, and includes oppressed people as far south as Central America and at least as far north as San Antonio, Texas. In 1987 and 1988, plays of his were warmly received by Hispanic audiences in New York when produced under the auspices of Joseph Papp's Festival Latino. In the summer of 1988, Morton's *Johnny Tenorio* was played in Spain, France, and West Germany by a touring theater group from the University of California at San Diego.

No one can question Carlos Morton's credentials as a political activist. His plays are all thesis plays that agitate for social understanding and change, but he is far different from the popular image of the narrow, humorless propagandist. His broad cultural experience, his aesthetic and historical education, and his extensive travel, along with his intelligence and sensitivity, make him a sophisticated spokesman for his race, La Raza.

★   THE PLAY

On its title page, *El Jardín* is designated an *acto*. This is the short dramatic form that Luis Valdez developed for his Teatro Campesino and that he has described as combining the techniques of the German dramatist Bertolt Brecht and the Mexican comic actor Cantinflas. Originally, actos were little more than collectively written agitprop skits played by field workers to dramatize economic conflicts that they and their audiences shared. However, actos came to incorporate sophisticated dramatic techniques from the commedia dell'arte, such as mime, masks, and improvisation, which Valdez brought from his experience with the San Francisco Mime Troupe.

Morton and other Chicano playwrights stretched the limits of the acto form as they strove for artistic achievement in addition to political impact and as they reached for larger audiences. One might use the term of Morton's teacher, Jorge Huerta, and justifiably call *El Jardín* a "super acto" to differentiate it from its more simplistic forebears.

Three elements common to Chicano drama serve to set *El Jardín* apart from the other plays in this volume. First is the immediacy of the mythic dimension. The church and events of Latin American history play vital roles in the daily imagination of many Mexican-Americans. Thus the temptation of Eva (Eve) in El Jardín (The Garden) by Serpiente is neither remote nor abstract. The contemporary imagery and slangy idiom make the characters and their situations not so much modern as timeless or ahistorical. There is an easy blending of Christian and Mechicano myth as the Eva who betrays Adán is told by Serpiente that she worships the god who will one day come with the conquistadores and that she will be Malinche, the Indian who betrayed her race by serving as Cortés's translator and mistress.

Second is the generality of setting. Although the action that is set on the earth in this, the latest, version of the play takes place in El Paso, Texas, in the past Morton has suggested that the name of the producer's own city be used for each production of the play, if that city has a Hispanic community. The printed version of *El Jardín* in *The Many Deaths of Danny Rosales and Other Plays* used Chicago as the setting of the scenes of Adán and Eva's contemporary life. For the Chicano, realities of cultural experience easily transcend political boundaries.

The third element differentiating *El Jardín* is the somewhat bilingual diction. The play's dialogue draws freely on both English and Spanish, just as the Mexican-American community does. An early version had much less English than the text included in this volume and was considerably less accessible to those unfamiliar with colloquial Spanish. Morton rewrote later versions so that the play would appeal to wider audiences. With the aid of the glossary appended here, even the reader totally unfamiliar with Spanish should be able to follow the play's meaning. Morton's remaining Spanish enriches and enlivens the familiar narrative while posing no more difficulty than Robert Burns's or Mark Twain's dialect.

A notable recent production of *El Jardín* was put on throughout the month of August 1988 by the Puerto Rican Traveling Theater in a variety of locations in New York City, ranging from Queens and Far Rockaway to the fountain plaza of Lincoln Center. The director was Jorge Huerta, and the principal players were Jack Landron, Tony Mata, Irma-Estel LaGuerre, and Carlos Carrasco.

★  THE WORKS

Morton's artistic, adult plays vary widely in form and subject, but they lend themselves to grouping. *El Jardín* and *Pancho Diablo* are based on Christian myth. Another group, his largest, derives its subject matter from Mexican-American myth and history. Included in this group are *Los Dorados* and *Rancho Hollywood*, which deal, respectively, with the early Spanish explorers, or the gold seekers, and with California under Mexican rule. Other plays drawing on such sources are *Johnny Tenorio*, which is based both on the legend of Don Juan and on the Mexican Day of the Dead ceremonies, and *Malinche*, which concerns the life of the notorious Mayan mistress and translator of Hernan Cortés.

A final group is made up of two plays based on contemporary events—*The Many Deaths of Danny Rosales* and *The Savior*. The first deals with the violent death of Richard Morales while he was in police custody in Castroville, Texas; the second, with the assassination of Archbishop Romero while he was celebrating Mass in San Salvador.

The recognition that the works of Carlos Morton have already received and the volume and complexity of his body of work are sufficient to assure the playwright national and international attention. Anglo critics and audiences in Texas can little afford to ignore or patronize him and other artists drawing on a different tradition. Although Chicano drama poses challenges for those unaccustomed to it, it rewards those openminded enough to give it an opportunity to speak to them.

It is a truism that Texas is a pluralistic society and that this diversity is one of the state's strengths. The recognition that Texas's population is 20 percent Mexican-American and that 50 percent of all first-graders in the state are Mexican-American has resulted in significant changes in the political arena, but there have not yet been cultural changes that have brought about alteration in the literary canon or in the repertories of mainstream Texas theaters.

Historically, theater in Texas has been a middle-class institution. Productions have been staged in auditoriums financed by conservative business interests or governmental bodies. Performances have been expected to be social events and to entertain or uplift. Controversy, when introduced, has tended to be safely distanced by time or geography.

Chicano drama is proletarian in origin. It has the capacity to enrich mainstream theater, but it does demand adjustments from middle-class WASP audiences. It requires that historical assumptions be examined. It insists that the language and the history of Hispanic America be respected as valuable sources of understanding and delight. It necessitates a toleration of unfamiliar forms and techniques, especially those outside the tradition of realism and those that juxtapose cultural levels and emotional tones.

The strength of Morton's works lies in his fresh blending of wide-ranging and often exotic materials as well as in his sense of commitment. Playfulness can be a benefit, as when Serpiente in *El Jardín* seduces Eva in a language and style common to earthy seductions in *barrio cantinas*. Delightfully, the conventional apple is transformed into *la tuna*, the crimson fruit of the prickly-pear cactus. Less happily, the technique can sometimes come across as arbitrary and superficial. On balance, though, Morton's plays do not resort overmuch to thoughtless laughs or appeals to prejudice. Although stock characters abound and familiar targets of satire recur, the playwright's wit and his eye for the incongruous continue to justify our attention.

## LIST OF WORKS

### PLAYS

*Desolation Car Lot*, 1973
*El Jardín*,* 1974
*The Many Muertes of Danny Rosales* (later version titled *The Many Deaths of Danny
    Rosales*),* 1976
*Los Dorados*,* 1978
*Rancho Hollywood*,* 1979
*Squash* (in collaboration with the San Francisco Mime Troupe), 1979
*Johnny Tenorio*,** 1983
*Malinche*,** 1985
*Lorenzo de Zavala* (children's play), 1986
*The Savior*,** 1986
*Cuentos* (children's play, with Angel Vigil), 1987
*The Foundling*, 1988
*In *The Many Deaths of Danny Rosales and Other Plays*. Houston: Arte Público
    Press, 1983.
**Included in Morton's Ph.D. dissertation, University of Texas at Austin, 1987.

### RECOMMENDED READING

Arrizón, María Alicia. "Estrategias Dramáticas en la Obra de Carlos Morton
    Perez." Master's thesis, Arizona State University, 1986.
Daniel, Lee A. "An Interview with Carlos Morton." *Latin American Theater
    Review* 23 (Fall 1989): 143–50.
Huerta, Jorge. *Chicano Theatre: Themes and Forms*. Ypsilanti, Mich.: Bilingual
    Press, 1982.

Morton, Carlos. *The Many Deaths of Danny Rosales and Other Plays.* Houston: Arte Público Press, 1983.

———. "The Many Masks of Teatro Chicano." *Latin American Theater Review* 12 (Fall 1978): 87–88.

Pross, Edith. "A Chicano Play and Its Audience." *Americas Review* 14 (Spring 1986): 71–79.

Salinas, Judy. "The Image of Woman in Chicano Literature." *Revista Chicano-Riqueño* 4 (Fall 1976): 139–48.

Tatum, Charles. *Chicano Literature.* Boston: Twayne Publishers, 1982.

★ NOTE ON THE LANGUAGE OF *EL JARDÍN*

Much of the charm of *El Jardín* lies in its multicultural reference and partially bilingual diction. Although our "mixed breed of New World people" may eventually blend to form a unified "truly Cosmic Race," as Dios predicts in the last scene, most Anglo readers today will approach the play handicapped at least somewhat by an unfamiliarity with border vernacular of Hispanic origin. Sometimes they will find that recourse to the glossary following the play text will be necessary, but it is hoped that they will attempt at least a first reading without its aid. Even totally strange words will frequently become clear in context, and the playwright often helps by repeating Spanish phrases, parenthetically, in English. The central myth of the play, of course, is familiar to all and provides a framework that facilitates comprehension.

Dios (God) has placed his original human creations, Adán (Adam) and Eva (Eve), in El Jardín (the Garden of Eden). Eva's willful curiosity, combined with the machinations of Serpiente (the serpent), lead to the eating of the forbidden fruit, tuna (fruit of the prickly-pear cactus), and to the fall of the humans into an earthly existence where they must deal with new forms of temptation.

An ignorance of Spanish that might cause a reader to miss some of the play's cross-cultural wit can, on the other hand, prove beneficial by intensifying the play's sense of the exotic and the freshness of its idiom. Pleasure on most journeys into new territory, after all, is piqued by encounters with the unexpected.

# El Jardín

★ ★ ★ ★ ★ ★ ★ ★ ★ ★ ★ ★ ★ ★ ★ ★

## CAST OF CHARACTERS

DIOS (also plays Cristóbal Colón)

EVA

ADÁN (also plays Taíno)

SERPIENTE (also plays Matón, Padre Ladrón, and Muerte)

## SCENES

Paradise, Hell, and Earth

DIOS. Soy la voz de Dios. I am the voice of God. I have been speaking to mis hijos since the first hombre appeared in the universe. His name was Adán and he lived in El Jardín with a woman named Eva who was somewhat of a coquette. Do you remember?

ADÁN. *(In the garden.)* So, you've been talking con ese serpent again, eh?

EVA. Sí pues, so what!

ADÁN. You should be ashamed of yourself!

EVA. Oh, he's not so bad.

ADÁN. What do you mean, tonta, he's evil!

EVA. But he has such a nice slick body. He's soooo ssssslimmmmy!

ADÁN. *(Making the sign of the cross.)* ¡Madre mía! My God, woman, don't you know you should judge a person by his spirit?

EVA. Well, I'm more inclined towards the flesh.

ADÁN. I'm going to tell you something, woman. I catch that snake in the grass around here again, I'm going to wring it around your neck!

EVA. Oh, the way he slides and slithers on the ground . . . he's sooooooooooo evil.

ADÁN. How can you be such a pendeja? Don't you know he'll lead you into temptation?

EVA. He says he wants to teach me about life, about knowledge.

ADÁN. Eva, you're going to get us evicted from El Jardín!

EVA. So what, I'm tired of all that jive the man's been laying down on you. Just look at this place, tame tigers, obnoxious little lambs, I feel like I'm in some kind of zoo. Hey, I want a little action. I want to swing, baby. How come we never go dancing?

ADÁN. Now just a minute! We're not prisoners here. We can leave anytime we want. We have free will. Dios has been very kind to us and under no circumstances do I want to incur His wrath.

EVA. Oh, let Him kick us out . . . see if He can find two other suckers to take our place!

ADÁN.

Are you out of your mind? You want to give up El Jardín?
The rent is free, the air is clean
We got no barrios, got no machines
No one gets rich, no one eats crumbs
We don't need money and we don't drop bombs
We got peace, we got love
We got Dios, we got enough
There's the sun, there's the sea
Here is heaven and here are we
We got the lambs, we got the grass
We are all brothers, there is no class

All creation blends real nice
In the center of Paradise.

EVA. That's just it, we're no better than *worms* to Him!

ADÁN. Or *whales* for that matter! En los ojos de Dios we are all equal!

EVA. Oh, that rap about equality and justice is like a tired old psalm. Listen brother, if we really had freedom in this here cage we'd be able to come and go as we pleased. Why can't we take a trip or a vacation?

ADÁN. Eva, I don't want to go anywhere! I happen to like it here.

EVA. Well I'm bored! I'm stagnating, I'm not satisfied!

ADÁN. Eva, don't be crazy . . .

EVA. All day long I sit around and hear the birds go "tweet, tweet, tweet" and the lambs go "baa, baaa, baaaa"! I want to do something, go shopping, anything. Look at me, I'm naked, I don't have any clothes!

ADÁN. Now I know you're really flipped out! What do you need clothes for? You're beautiful just the way you are.

EVA. Maybe some jewelry, or just a nice hat. Do you really think I am beautiful?

ADÁN. Just look at yourself in this gentle pool . . . come closer. See your reflection in the liquid mirror . . . your bronze skin . . . your long black hair.

EVA. I am beautiful, aren't I?

ADÁN. You are the most beautiful woman in the entire universe.

EVA. Of course I am! I'm the only woman in the universe. Don't try to flatter me!

ADÁN. Eva, querida, just think, you are the only one, you are perfect, you are His creation.

DIOS. *(Voice from above.)* ¡Hola! ¡Hola! What's going on down there?

ADÁN. Nothing, jefe, we were just having a discussion.

DIOS. It sounded like you were shouting. It sounded like disharmony.

ADÁN. Oh no sir, we were only reviewing our theology.

DIOS. Good, any points you want clarified?

ADÁN. No sir, we know it very well.

DIOS. Very good, "In the beginning . . ." *(Voice fades.)*

EVA. "In the beginning, there was nothing . . ." Just what is that supposed to mean?

ADÁN. Exactly what it says. Before Him there was nada, then He came and there was todo.

EVA. But where did He come from?

ADÁN. He has always been here and He will always be here.

EVA. But it doesn't make any *sense.*

ADÁN. It is the word of God!

EVA. Oh brother, that's another thing that bugs the *hell* out of me.

ADÁN. Don't say that word!

EVA. There's no free speech in El Jardín!

ADÁN. Shut up! Don't you say another word!

EVA. Why can't I eat the fruit?

ADÁN. Keep your voice down!

EVA. I'm tired of eating nothing! Why can't I have some carne asada and some hot salsa with frijoles and arroz? I'd even settle for a hamburger with french fries. Or a tequila sunrise!

ADÁN. The serpent promised you all those things!

EVA. He said I could start with dessert.

ADÁN. You keep away from there!

EVA. Such a silly rule about a stupid tree.

ADÁN. Eva, that's the only rule He has laid down. Now, why He doesn't want us eating the Fruit of the Forbidden Tree is none of my concern.

EVA. Don't you see! He's the big ranchero. We're nothing but peons!

ADÁN. For the last time, I'm telling you, I feel great satisfaction living in peace with my fellow creatures. I have no desire to eat them or wear their hides. Why are you so ungrateful? Don't you love me anymore?

EVA. Yes, I love you, te quiero mucho. But it is only a love between brother and sister. I want to love you more, I want to love all of you!

ADÁN. *(Crossing himself.)* Oh my Dios! En el nombre del Padre, el Hijo, el Espíritu Santo . . .

EVA. Why are you blushing?

ADÁN. You make me think sinful thoughts.

EVA. Hmmmmmmmm. Tell me about them. I want to know it all.

ADÁN. No, it's time for my, uh, Bible Study class. See you later!

> *(ADÁN runs out, covering his private parts.)*

EVA. No, don't go, stay here with your Mamasota!

Why can't I have my way
Why do I have to stay
Here in the green Jardín

Sure it's a calm place
Larks sing, gazelles race
It hardly rains at all
Fruit from the trees do fall ·
Creatures both large and small
Love one and they love all
We always sleep late
Angels guard the gate
It never gets cold here
Nothing can be sold here

But I need more than this
More than complacency
Or smug security
I want to dance, I want to shout
I want to leap, I want to fly out
But more than wanting to go
Most important, I want to know

> *(Serpiente enters accompanied by flutes and drums.)*

SERPIENTE. Dig it!

EVA. Ayyyyy, un monster!

SERPIENTE. ¡Qué monster ni que mi abuela! You just don't appreciate style and class. I'm Coco Roco, indigenous down to my alligator-skinned huaraches.

EVA. But you look so feo.

SERPIENTE. Bah! That's the trouble with you hyphenated Mexicans, you can't appreciate other cultures.

EVA. I'm no hyphenated Mexican-American. ¡Yo soy Chicana!

SERPIENTE. ¡Tu madre!

EVA. ¡La tuya que está en vinagre!

SERPIENTE. *(Strutting around, sizing her up.)* Huh, let's check this chick out.

EVA. I'm not a "chick," I'm a mujer. Don't look at me like that, you feathered iguana.

SERPIENTE. Baby, I'm just admiring you in all your perfect innocence.

EVA. Don't touch me, resbaloso.

SERPIENTE. What's the matter, mamacita, don't you dig my movida?

EVA. I guess I have to get used to you. Last time you were just a little snake.

SERPIENTE. I have many faces, you'll see. In this life I am Coco Roco. Fire flames from my mouth and smoke seeps from my ears. The horns at the top of my head are the horns of the bull of fertility and here behind me is the tail of sensuality. My body is made up of the earth which is rich and brown and gives life to all. This girdle of live snakes wound round my middle is further proof of my power of lust . . .

EVA. You're just too much . . .

SERPIENTE. Be careful one of my little snakes doesn't escape and slip into you!

EVA. You beast!

SERPIENTE. You love it!

EVA. Get out of here before I squash you!

SERPIENTE. You don't understand, you don't appreciate me, do you, Eva? That's because you are a white woman living under the European God and your mind is poisoned by their treacherous white ways!

EVA. That's not true. I'm a mestiza, and I'm proud of it.

SERPIENTE. You live in Paradise, worshiping the Lord who will one day come with the conquistadores of España, the bearded ones, and you will be La Malinche, she who will interpret for the white man and betray your own tribe, tu raza. You will even mate with their leader, Hernán Cortés, and the first of a bastard race will be born in Tenochtitlán-México!

EVA. You're lying, I don't believe this will happen.

SERPIENTE. *(Aside.)* She doesn't think I can see into the future. Well, I'll have to show her a little preview of history. Eva, come here . . . do you see that planet way down there?

EVA. What, I don't see anything.

SERPIENTE. The clouds are obscuring your sight—blow them away.

EVA. Oh yes, I see it now, it's blue and green.

SERPIENTE. That's earth. Now focus off the eastern coast of Mexico to a small island in the Caribbean. The year is 1492. Do you see?

*(On the opposite side of the stage enter* TAÍNO *and* CRISTÓBAL COLÓN.*)*

EVA. Who are those men?

SERPIENTE. The man with the flag in his hand is Cristóbal Colón. The other man, scantily dressed, is a native of the island. His name is Borinquén the Taíno. Can you hear what they are saying?

COLÓN. Y nosotros tomamos posesión de estas tierras en el nombre del Rey de España . . .

TAÍNO. *(Circling* COLÓN, *puzzled.)* Caribe? Maya? Seminole?

COLÓN. Y Santo sea el nombre de Dios, Vuestro Rey.

TAÍNO. Aztec? Toltec? Chichimec? Zapotec?

COLÓN. ¿Qué estupideces tratais de decirnos?

TAÍNO. Inca! Inca! No? Illinois! Ohio! Ute! Indiana! *(Laughing at "Indiana.")*

COLÓN. ¡Chingueis tu madreis, imbécileis!

TAÍNO. Ahhhhaaaaa! Polynesia. Malasia. Asia. China? Chop-chop?

COLÓN. ¡No, no, no! España, Europa. Yo Espania. ¡Tu indio, indio!

TAÍNO. ¿Indio? No. Noooooo. Taíno. Taíno. Borinquén. *(Motioning to the land around him.)* Borinquén.

COLÓN. No, indio tonto. Esta es La India. Tu eres indio. Esta isla se llama Puerto Rico. ¿Comprende? *(Speaking very slowly as though he were speaking to a brute.)*

TAÍNO. *(Shrugging his shoulders, he offers* COLÓN *some fruit and tobacco.)* ¡Ummmm, guayaba! ¡Banana! ¡Tobaco!

COLÓN. Hmmmmmmmm. Muy bien. Okay! *(Indicates he is tired after the meal.)* ¿Hotel? ¿Hotel?

TAÍNO. ¿Hotel? ¡No, hotel no! *(*TAÍNO *points across the ocean, indicating* COLÓN *should return from whence he came.)* Caribe, bye bye, adiós!

COLÓN. Espera, amigo. Ahora que ustedes son los sujetos de Su Majestad, será necesario encontrar empleo. *(Breaking into a southern accent.)* I think we going to lay down the Plaza de Armas down there . . .

TAÍNO. ¿Que qué? ¡Espera, acabo de aprender el español!

COLÓN. We'll put the church up here and the embassy over there.

TAÍNO. Ahora, qué estás talking?

COLÓN. Muy bueno, amigo, you learn pronto. Lookee here, you Injuns will provide manual labor, us Europeans boss man.

TAÍNO. Manual labor? Lo conozco. He lives in the same housing project as me.

COLÓN. Amigo, after the conquest . . .

TAÍNO. Which one?

COLÓN. After the colonization, after we put in the freeways, from El Paso to San Francisco, after we put in the Taco Bells with that distinct Spanish architecture, we will have created a great civilization, you and I . . . a monument of cooperation among two culturas, what do you say?

TAÍNO. Sounds great, when do we start?

COLÓN. Right now. The church has to go up first. We'll pay you five coconuts per day.

TAÍNO. Five cocos a day . . . that's not a decent living wage!

COLÓN. Pardner, we ain't even conquered this place yet. We got a high overhead and a low yield for the first few fiscal centuries.

TAÍNO. But my Raza, we will all starve to death.

COLÓN. We'll just have to import two thousand Mau Maus from Africa to finish the job.

TAÍNO. No, we will not do it, for it is slavery! We shall resist.

COLÓN. We got a law says you'll not agitate to form a seditious union.

TAÍNO. You're going to have to build your city over my dead body! *(Taking up arms.)*

COLÓN. That's okay with me, boy. Here, have some whiskey. Here, have some gin. Have some smallpox. Have some tuberculosis! Boy, I really love you all, your spirit, your love of the land, you proud and noble savage you! Why, I'm part Injun myself!

TAÍNO. *(About to strike* COLÓN *down.)* Death to the Europeans!

COLÓN. *(Pulling out a crucifix.)* Behold! Behold! The mighty cross of our Lord, Jesus Christ! Kneel, bow your knees. Feel the power of our Master!

TAÍNO. *(On his knees.)* I am your slave!

    *(Lights out on* TAÍNO *and* COLÓN.*)*

SERPIENTE. So you see, Eva, the Europeans will use God's name to conquer our people and there will be centuries of oppression. And your people, Eva, your brown-skinned Raza, will live their days scratching out a meager existence on earth for the false promise of a glorious place in heaven.

EVA. Dios promised us that the meek would inherit the earth.

SERPIENTE. Only the dirt, Eva, only the miserable dirt of poverty.

EVA. What can I do to prevent this from happening?

SERPIENTE. Eat of the Fruit of the Tree of Knowledge.

EVA. Tell me more!

SERPIENTE.

    Under the light of the skull-white moon
    In the barrios of ancient Aztlán
    A pyramid lies, as tall as the sky
    There on the temple grounds
    Amidst the steaming rites
    There on the sacred stone
    There with my golden knife
    I will slash the holy fruit
    There with my bloody blade
    I will eat your tender heart

EVA. Are you going to do all that to me?! *(Sexually stimulated, enthralled.)*

SERPIENTE. I was only speaking metaphorically, don't take me so literally.

EVA. That's what I like about you: you're so intellectual.

SERPIENTE.

    We have built our temples tall
    Hidden deep in barrio steam
    They will measure most precisely
    What we seek in mescal dreams

In our spacious astral minds
Lies a universe that gleams
Like the cosmos high above
With its stars of crystalline.

EVA. Ay, ay, ay!

SERPIENTE. Shall we go to my altar on the Pyramid of Coco Roco?

EVA. Is it far from here?

SERPIENTE. Only through the Doubting Peaks and into the Valley of the Fascinating Fog!

> *(They exit. Enter* DIOS *and* ADÁN *from the opposite side, walking arm in arm.)*

ADÁN. Dios, I don't know what to do about Eva . . . she's so hardheaded.

DIOS. I know, I made her that way. I fear it will grow to be a trait. You, on the other hand, are much more level-headed. Although I fear you will have a propensity for baldness. Darn it, nothing is perfect! Hey, is it my imagination or are you getting taller?

ADÁN. No sir, My dimensions are from heaven to earth, and from the west to the east as you have decreed.

DIOS. You're so big for your age. It's hard to believe that you are only a few days old. You know, I just started creating this world last Monday. Here it is Saturday. You and Eva were one of my last projects. Maybe I'll take a day off tomorrow.

ADÁN. Dios, what am I going to do with Eva? She's not happy.

DIOS. Unhappy! In Paradise? Impossible! That I can't believe. Huh. See those mountains over there? Don't they look rather crooked? Let me landscape them with a little more finesse. *(He waves his hands and transforms them.)* And look at that river, I think I'll change its color. Maybe Eva needs a change. How about if I make her shorter, fatter, and darker?

ADÁN. No, I like her just the way she is, thank you, in spite of any faults. You see, she's like a different side of me.

DIOS. How strange, I never saw it that way. I, for one, have always been the Father, the Son, and the Holy Ghost. Say, isn't your nose rather large? Would you like a smaller one?

ADÁN. No, no, it's fine the way it is. Let me tell you more about Eva, she keeps talking about the "kid," the "kid."

DIOS. What "kid"? You mean the goat?

ADÁN. No, she speaks of "the kid of our creation."

DIOS. The kid of your creation. That could only mean one thing. She means to bear fruit! But how, if both of you are innocent? Is there something you haven't told me?

ADÁN. She says that if she eats of the Fruit of the Forbidden Tree she will also bear fruit!

DIOS. She's been talking to La Serpiente. I see it all now! That snake has tricked Eva into going down to earth with him. They are on top of a pyramid together!

ADÁN. My God, you've got to stop her! Let's go, where's my angel wings? . . . Shall we take the elevator?

DIOS. No, Adán, I can't help you. This is between Eva and her conscience. Fly quickly!

ADÁN. I'll be back.

*(Depending on the cleverness of the set designer,* ADÁN *can either leap down a trap-door onstage or jump into a pile of trash offstage, creating a loud din.)*

DIOS. ¡Vaya con Dios! *(Sitting down on a cloud, dejectedly.)* Jeeez, maybe I should have posted an archangel or something to guard that damn tree!

*(Down below,* EVA *lies prone atop the pyramid.* SERPIENTE *stands over her with a knife in his hand.)*

SERPIENTE.

Is not this tuna red and ripe
Something to want to make you bite
Into the juices of your brain
Suck out creation, go insane

EVA. ¡Ay, ay, ay! ¡Qué locura!

SERPIENTE.

Would you not like to masticate
Forbidden fruit at this late date
Ingest your mind with this explosion
Blast off from heaven into motion

EVA. ¡Dime más, dime más!

SERPIENTE. Chicana, hembra, woman of the sun, my uh . . . *(Straining for images.)* your skin reflects the beauty of that bronze star! May, uh, my golden knife . . . mate with your brown body!

EVA. What are you going to do, loco?

SERPIENTE. Cut the tuna.

EVA. But it's such a beautiful tuna, so red, so ripe.

SERPIENTE. Stay still, this won't hurt a bit. *(Shrill, strident music is heard.)*

EVA. Noooooooooooooooooo! *(*SERPIENTE *cuts into the tuna.)*

SERPIENTE. Ummmmmmmmmm. This tuna tastes real good. Wanna bite?

EVA. Golly, I don't know.

SERPIENTE. I knew it, you still got religion.

EVA. I better go, Adán is going to be real mad at me.

SERPIENTE. That Jesus-freak! He doesn't have the balls to eat this!

EVA. He does so! *(She grabs the tuna out of his hand.)* Anyway, what's so special about this fruit?

SERPIENTE. Have they kept everything from you, my little torta? This is the Fruit of the Tree of Knowledge. Eat it and you will be injected with all the wisdom of the ages. Not only that, my little enchilada, you will soon learn to deduct and deduce, thereby gaining corporate control of corporal beings.

EVA. I'm not interested in that corporate control stuff, I seek knowledge.

SERPIENTE. My little quesadilla, once you discover the wheel, you'll have the mechanics to build a marvelous civilization.

EVA. Will my people acknowledge this? Will women be appreciated? *(Thunder and lightning build in intensity.)*

SERPIENTE. My little jalapeño, you will be worshiped, idolized, put on pedestals! Take a bite!

EVA. Will I create? *(The sky darkens, wind blows fiercely.)*

SERPIENTE. My little chile pepper, you will create zillions of men and women just as Dios did in his image! Bite it!

EVA. *(Sustained drum roll,* EVA *bites into it.)* Ohhhhhhhhh . . .

SERPIENTE. You did it, my little fajita! You did it! ¡Cuidado, tiene espinas!

EVA. Ouch, it has thorns!

SERPIENTE. That's right, my little taco belle, along with the good comes the bad. And I am the baaaaaaaad. Make no mistake about that!

EVA. ¡Dios mío! I see it all now, you are the devil! *(Thunder, lightning, drenching rain.)*

SERPIENTE. Sí, mujer, I am el mentiroso, el atascado, el borracho, el asesino! ¡SOY EL GRAN CHINGON!

EVA.
What have I done
My mind is reeling
And heaven is wheeling away
I feel suspended in space
And chastity flees from my face
Paradise seems far away
And earth 'neath my feet bids me to stay
For many years and many days
To spend my life in toil and waste
In weeding gardens, cleaning cribs
And needling for Grace

SERPIENTE. *(As* ADÁN *enters.)*
Here comes your man from heaven
To join you here on Earth
Why don't you talk him into
Sharing your worldly berth
As for me, I must flee
See you in a century
        *(Exit* SERPIENTE.*)*

ADÁN. Mi chavalona, why?

EVA.
I ate the apple, I sure did
My heart is thumping, it sure is
My knees are shaking, they sure are
My head is rocking to the stars
But I can see much clearer now
The earth seems much more dearer now

ADÁN.
You don't know what you're saying there
Your eyes are flying everywhere

There's nothing dear about the land
Nothing but work for all us men
Why should we leave the promised land
The home of tigers and of lambs

EVA.

Baby, eat this red ripe fruit
Swear to God, it makes you shoot
Take a bite, it tastes real good
Eat it, honey, wish you would

ADÁN.

You little fool, you've cast us out
of El Jardín where we devout
Had lived an ageless loving life
Without death, without cruel strife

EVA. Adán, eat it . . . if you love me!

ADÁN.

To join her in her cursed state
A life of whim, a life of fate
To leave all that I loved behind
To join the wheel and low and whine
A bigger fool is he than she
To eat from the Forbidden Tree
          *(ADÁN takes a bite, chokes.)*

EVA. Adán, cuidado, it has thorns! *(ADÁN howls in pain.)* Oh, my darling, are they stuck in your throat? I'm afraid you'll never get them out!

ADÁN. ¡Me espiné! I should have never listened to you! Get me a drink of water!
          *(Suddenly, we hear the sounds of civilization, autos, radios, etc.)*

EVA. Oh my God . . . this stream . . . it's polluted! *(Garbage is thrown on the stage.)*

ADÁN. What are you doing running around naked? Go put something on!

EVA. Adán, that never bothered you before!

ADÁN. Well, it upsets me now! Go dress yourself!

EVA. *(EVA puts on a skirt and hands ADÁN some pants.)* Very well. Here, don't you think you ought to practice some modesty?

ADÁN. And cook something, I'm hungry.

EVA. There's nothing to eat, I'm afraid, but the rest of this apple. *(EVA munches on the apple.)* You know, it's rather cold down here.

ADÁN. Look, there's a cave we can sleep in! Go and gather wood for a fire.

EVA. Can't you say "please"!

ADÁN. Vieja, ¡no me agüites! Don't give me a hard time!
          *(As they gather firewood, DIOS appears on a cloud above.)*

DIOS. ¡Hola! Can you hear me?

ADÁN. Of course, Dios, how are you?

DIOS. Fine, it's Sunday, you know, and I was just watching the Northern Lights on my sky screen.

ADÁN. Dios, I know this is supposed to be a day of rest, but I've got to get this work done before dark.

EVA. Adán, who are you talking to?

ADÁN. Shhhh, don't interrupt, can't you hear, I'm talking to Dios.

EVA. I can't hear Him.

ADÁN. Dios, I think Eva and I are going to have a baby!

DIOS. Well, uh, have fun, and, uh, watch out for the dinosaurs.

EVA. Where . . . where is His voice coming from?

DIOS. Adán, tell Eva that from now on she will have to speak to me through you.

ADÁN. Eva, you must speak to Him through me.

EVA. No, don't say that . . . it's not true!

DIOS. "In pain she shall bring forth children, yet her desire shall be for her husband and he shall rule over her."

ADÁN. I will do as you command, my Lord. But will we ever see you again?

DIOS. Perhaps someday I shall send down my son . . .

EVA. Dios, Diosito, por favor, please . . . talk to me!

DIOS. *(As he walks over to a cross.)* To be crucified!

ADÁN. Silence woman! You will be quiet! *(Forcing* EVA *down on her knees.)* Pray, pray for forgiveness!

> *(*SERPIENTE *enters with a whip and rope.)*

SERPIENTE. You see, ever since that day, la mujer no vale madre. Hey don't get mad! This was before the advent of feminism. *(As he lashes* DIOS *to the cross.)* Now then, it's time to celebrate my victory. Come here, Christian, and turn the other cheek.

ADÁN. *(Like a priest before the altar.)*

After millions of years Dios will send His son
A shepherd who leads His flock to safety
But there in Calvary the people will turn against Him
And the father shall sacrifice His only son
So with the shedding of His blood
We will be saved from damnation

EVA.

The spirit is free and ethereal
It hangs suspended between heaven and earth
It is the uplifting of humanity
Giving life the will to rise
It is our life buoy
To which we must cleave after death

> *(Satanic music.* DIOS *is crucified. He screams,* SERPIENTE *laughs. Darkness falls, except for a follow spot on* SERPIENTE.*)*

SERPIENTE. And so, Adán and Eva escaped El Jardín and settled down to a glorious existence on Earth. Besides fratricide, genocide, and infanticide, there have been holy wars, class wars, and gas wars. You mortals have fueled the fires of Hades and entered my domain with bloody smiles on your Aztec faces. And what today? There's Adán and Eva living in middle-class comfort in El Paso, Texas. Isn't that the American Dream?

> *(Lights up on* ADÁN *and* EVA'*s living room, furnished right out of the Sears &*
> *Roebuck catalog. Enter* ADÁN, *dejectedly, dressed in a white shirt and a tie, sport*
> *coat over his shoulder,* Wall Street Journal *in hand. This could be the start of any*
> *sitcom on TV.)*

EVA. *(Voice, offstage.)* Adam, honey, is that you?

ADÁN. Yes, dear.

EVA. *(Entering, dressed in an apron and wearing a blonde wig.)* How was your day at the office? *(*ADÁN *does not answer.)* Would you like a cocktail, dear?

ADÁN. Yes, I could use one.

EVA. *(Picking up a can of ready-made drink.)* Black Russian or tequila sunrise?

ADÁN. Whatever.

EVA. *(Opening the can and handing it to him.)* Now then, what would you like for din-din? Swedish, Chinese, Pakistani, or Polynesian? And then, there's always Mexican.

ADÁN. I had Mexican for lunch. Let's go with . . . oh, whatever you want. *(Mumbling under his breath.)* It all tastes the same anyway.

EVA. No problem. I'll just pop it in the microwave. Thank God for Stouffer's. So, how's the stock market? Did you make some good commissions today?

ADÁN. Let's talk about your day, dear.

EVA. Well, after I tidied up a bit I watched "General Hospital." Holly foiled Oliver's attempt to kill Luke, but Oliver reported back to Basil that Luke and Holly are both in love with that geologist, Mr. Harper.

ADÁN. Luke is in love with Mr. Harper?

EVA. Yes, he's really a transsexual with only one gonad! Isn't that a scream! Oh, but this is so silly. Wait until I tell you the good news. Honey, I am going to be a part-time Mary Kay rep and sell enough cosmetics to help pay for our hot tub! Isn't that wonderful! I could even win a pink Volvo. *(*ADÁN *is very quiet.)* Adam, is something wrong?

ADÁN. Eve, I lost my job. I am no longer an account executive for Ferner, Ferner, Farmer and Fudd. They gave me my two weeks' notice!

EVA. But Adam, weren't you selling more CDs and SLs than any AE? Weren't you bullish on bonds and bearish on . . .

ADÁN. Haven't you been watching the news? We're in the middle of a severe recession. Everybody's cutting back. And the latest hired are the first to be fired.

EVA. Don't worry, Adam, you'll find another job.

ADÁN. Fat chance! The unemployment rate is the highest since the Great Depression. Eve, we could lose this house!

EVA. Oh Adam, we can't let that happen. That's what we worked for all our lives. All those years of schooling, losing our accents, leaving the barrio!

ADÁN. Chin-gow! Why didn't I wait until the interest rates went down before I signed the mortgage note?

EVA. Adam, we'll make it somehow. I'll go to work full-time for Mary Kay.

ADÁN. Who's going to buy cosmetics when they can't even afford groceries?

EVA. I'll sell Amway products. Better yet, I'll sell the Cambridge Diet. Even fat people have to eat!

ADÁN. Jesus, what are we going to do? You work for something all your life and it comes crashing down on you in one day! *(The doorbell rings.)*

EVA. Now, who could that be?

> *(Enter* MATÓN, *dressed in a suit and tie, very professional, with briefcase and calling card. He also wears a pair of dark glasses.)*

MATÓN. You don't know me. My name is Mr. Matón. Mind if I come into your cantón?

ADÁN. *(Exchanging cards with* MATÓN.*)* Adam Martinez, formerly with Ferner, Ferner, Farmer and Fudd. This is my wife, Eve.

MATÓN. Sorry to hear that you lost your position, Mr. Martinez, but I have a product here you might be interested in purchasing. It's called "Sabe."

EVA. "Sabe"? Sounds like an underarm deodorant. Excuse me, haven't we met before?

MATÓN. *(Ignoring her.)* "Sabe" comes from the word *saber*, which means to have knowledge. Are you Chicanos?

ADÁN. Mr. Matón, my wife and I aren't into playing little ethnic games. We are American, Mexican-American. And what do I need "Sabe" for?

MATÓN. You need "Sabe" because the Gringos have taken it away from you. Don't you see? They have not only stolen our land, they have stolen our culture and claimed it as their own. *(Sarcastically, with an Anglo accent.)* Chile con carne, buckaroo, adobe houses, Taco Bells! Take "Sabe" and this will all be given back to you. Now tell me, why do you think you lost your job?

ADÁN. Economic factors; in spite of falling interest rates, the Consumer Price Index has risen. Also, tight money factors by the Fed.

MATÓN. ¡Puro pedo! You know the real reason why you lost your job. *(Pulling a mirror out of his briefcase.)*

ADÁN. No, no.

MATÓN. Yes, yes, it's because of that. *(Showing him the mirror.)*

EVA. What is it? Is that "Sabe"?

MATÓN. You lost your job because you are a Mexican! The only reason they hired you in the first place was because of Affirmative Action. But now, all that has ended!

EVA. Oh, what rubbish!

MATÓN. Do you really think that just because you dress and act and eat and talk like them, they will accept you? Nel, look at your face, it's brown! *(The mirror is having a hypnotic effect on* ADÁN.*)*

ADÁN. How is "Sabe" supposed to help me?

MATÓN. By making you aware of what you are and giving you the huevos to do something about it. With extra-strength "Sabe," we can beat the Gringo.

ADÁN. All right, give it to me, I'll try it. What have I got to lose?

MATÓN. *(He pulls out a bomb from his briefcase;* EVA *shrieks.)* Here it is, vato, how does it feel?

ADÁN. Powerful.

EVA. It's a bomb!

MATÓN. Ahora sí, now you sabe. *(Grabbing* ADÁN *by the hand.)* Come on, we have a lot of catching up to do!

> *(They both exit.)*

EVA. Adam, where are you going? Wait a minute. Wait! *(*EVA *walks over to the crucifix, which is all that is left of God on earth.)* Oh, my God! What are we going to do? We're going to lose all of this and be poor again, just like our parents! It isn't fair, it isn't fair! We worked so hard!

> *(*SERPIENTE *enters, dressed as a priest.)*

SERPIENTE. Poor Eva, she has no one to talk to, tsk, tsk. It's rather difficult to pray to a plastic Jesus, ¿que no? Mejor para mí. Excuse me, won't you? I must minister to the needs of my flock. *(Crossing to* EVA.*)*

EVA. *(Kneeling as though at a confessional.)* Padre, Padre Ladrón?

PADRE LADRÓN. Yes dear, I hear you, loud and clear.

EVA. Padre, I am worried about some of the men Adam is keeping company with. He stays out all night at what they call "rap sessions." During the day he attends rallies and demonstrations in the street.

PADRE LADRÓN. If only men concerned themselves with spiritual matters instead of delving into politics, they would be infinitely happier.

EVA. They speak of wanting to bring down the state by any means necessary.

PADRE LADRÓN. Such militant rhetoric! Eve, has Adam turned into a communist?

EVA. He speaks of the poor overthrowing the rich and creating a just society.

PADRE LADRÓN. I thought so! Communists are the Anti-Christ! And the forces of Lucifer are marshaling like a heinous whirlwind under the red banner of socialism. Adam is associating with the Anti-Christ!

EVA. My God, he even keeps a gun in the house now . . . ever since he took up with Matón!

PADRE LADRÓN. My vow of silence forbids me to speak out, but if I were you I'd call the police. The phone number is 591-2727, ask for Sergeant Taco of the Red Squad.

EVA. He feels frustrated because he lost his job at the brokerage firm where he worked.

PADRE LADRÓN. That's right, and you're also in danger of losing your house. You are six months behind on your payments.

EVA. How did you know that?

PADRE LADRÓN. We hold the note on your house. The Church owns a lot of land. We need monies to carry on God's mission. Now then, anything else bothering you, be it spiritual or physical?

EVA. No. Father, is there anything you can do to help us?

PADRE LADRÓN. Yes, have you and Adam talked about your life in the hereafter?

EVA. What are you talking about?

PADRE LADRÓN. A burial plot. You see, you've got to get your reservations in early! After all, don't you want to be laid to rest in consecrated grounds tended for perpetual care?

EVA. I don't want to talk about no burial plot! I want to talk about how we're going to save our house.

PADRE LADRÓN. Pray, Eve, pray. Meanwhile, I'll have the boys in advertising send you some brochures through the mail. I think the plot is only $130 per month for the rest of your life. Anything else? Any deviant sexual behavior or feelings of abnormal lust?

EVA. Why are you asking me this?

PADRE LADRÓN. *(Moving closer to her.)* Why Eve, you've got to catch these practices in the bud . . . otherwise, your sex organs fall off! *(Trying to fondle* EVA.*)*

EVA. Father!

PADRE LADRÓN. I know about all these things, believe me!

EVA. I don't know why I bother to come to this church! Why are there no women priests?

PADRE LADRÓN. Shhhhh! Calm down, I was only kidding. Now then, that'll be five Hail Marys and ten Our Fathers. Don't forget Bingo on Thursdays and our special Menudo breakfast for those with hangovers on Sunday! Amen!

EVA. That did it! I'm not ever coming back here again. What a fool I've been!
    *(*EVA *exits.)*

PADRE LADRÓN. Well, go somewhere else, join a satanic cult!

DIOS. *(Appearing from up high.)* ¡Diablo miserable!

SERPIENTE. Huh? Did someone say something?

DIOS. You are making a mockery of my church!

SERPIENTE. I thought you had turned into a plastic Jesus.

DIOS. I'm going to show you what a plastic Jesus I am after I wring your neck! You are perverting my flock! *(Goes after* SERPIENTE.*)*

SERPIENTE. ¡Ay! As if the church was so saintly. Remember, in Roma the Papas used to castrate the choirboys so they would always sing in alto.

DIOS. ¡Vicioso! ¡Odioso! *(Chasing* SERPIENTE *around the stage.)*

SERPIENTE. ¡Cuando en Roma, a la Romana! *(As* DIOS *grabs him.)* Ay, ay, beat me, flagellate me, I love it!

DIOS. I thought I locked you up in Hell.

SERPIENTE. *(Rips off his robes and escapes, faces* DIOS *in his underwear.)* And just where do you think you are anyway? Look around you . . . see the greed glowing red in the urban night? Smell the sulphurous air, the running sewers? Don't you see the corruption, can't you feel the hate? This is my Kingdom!

DIOS. Can this be true? Have I been blind all these years? What has happened to my church? What has happened to my people? I must do something. I must show them I am who I am.

*(SERPIENTE has taken this opportunity to slip away. The light fades slowly down on DIOS. On another part of the stage, enter ADÁN dressed as an Aztec prince.)*

EVA. Adam, where have you been? Just look at you, you're practically half naked. What's all this?

ADÁN. Don't you see? I'm re-creating the footsteps of our indigenous forefathers. Deep down inside, this is what we really are: Aztecas!

EVA. Oh, Adam, stop living in the past!

ADÁN. My name is not Adam anymore, it's Mexatexa!

EVA. Mexatexa?

ADÁN. That's right, and take off that silly blonde wig! *(He rips off her wig.)*

EVA. Do you like me better as a brunette?

ADÁN. I like you better as a Chicana!

EVA. Oh Adán, I love you! *(They hug.)* Darling, tell me what's wrong, you look like you haven't slept for days.

ADÁN. I have been at a peyote ceremony with my Native American brothers. I had to release my gabacho/gachupín self and show the real me: ¡Azteca hasta las cachas!

EVA. *(Taking his feathers away.)* Adán, take off those feathers! You're not Aztec, your family is Yaqui from Sonora.

ADÁN. The trouble with you is that *(Slightly hurt.)* you don't take the Movimiento seriously. *(He starts to leave.)*

EVA. Now where are you going?

ADÁN. To a sacrifice!

EVA. Whose sacrifice? Not yours!

ADÁN. No, a gabacho's. The first Gringo we find . . . we're going to sacrifice him to the Gods.

*(Blackout. Lights up at the cantina.)*

ADÁN.
What will I do tonight
Kill a redneck pig
Snuff out his brief life
Like a candle in the dark
With the quick shot through the heart
I'm mad and man enough to do it
And by the devil, I'll go through it.
But what did Eva say
Before I left today

EVA. *(Offstage.)*
If you need help sometime
Call for the Lord Divine
Call out his sweet name, now
Ask him to remain, now
He will never fail you
Once you call he'll save you

ADÁN.

> Yet there is this doubt
> My comrades wait about
> Their fingers pointed at me
> The triggers cocked and ready
> One squeeze and all is bloody
> We murder men tonight

*(*MUERTE *appears to* ADÁN.*)* Who . . . are you?

MUERTE. I am La Muerte. You called for me.

ADÁN. Yes, come with me tonight! I'll kill a redneck pig!

MUERTE. Wonderful! I am at your service. I guarantee my work one thousand percent and I am well-versed in hangings, stabbings, garrotings, dismemberings, poisonings, etc. We also have a special sale on burnings, malnutrition, rat bites, and rapes! *(Taking* ADÁN*'s hand.)*

ADÁN.

> Death will stalk the streets
> A phantom dim with stealth
> When we find our target
> We'll lure them into a trap
> And tie them up with snakes
> And feed them to the rats

MUERTE.

> Death will stalk the streets
> Like a phantom dim with stealth
> It steals into the heart
> And devours it like a fruit
> Soon men will be dead
> They'll rot from desolation
> There is no care in hatred
> Only the revulsion of a soul
> Turning putrid . . .

ADÁN. Ay Muerte, you have sent a cold shiver up my spine!

MUERTE. Don't worry, where you're going, it's plenty warm! Ha! Ha!

ADÁN. Wait a minute . . . I don't want to go through with this!

MUERTE. What? It's too late now. I'm sorry. Once you've signed the contract, there's no turning back. Besides, you're a macho, this is a macho revolution!

ADÁN. No! Nooooooooo!

MUERTE. *(Pulling out a knife.)* Now then, let's get down to business. How do you want it? With a knife? *(Pulls out a gun.)* Or with a gun? Or would you rather bomb them? Or take them down to the cellar, all tied up, and open up their bodies a little at a time to show them how fierce and savage I can be! Anything you want! We can even rip their hearts out and drink their steaming blood!

ADÁN.

> Muerte, leave me be!
> My God, is this really me?

MUERTE. *(Leveling the gun at* ADÁN's *head.)* Are you ready to die for the revolution?

ADÁN. I've everything to lose. Help me, help me choose! *(As* MUERTE *starts to pull the trigger.)*

EVA. *(Entering with* DIOS.*)* No!

DIOS. *(Freezes* MUERTE.*)*
Adán, just think about killing
Killing a man and you're dead yourself
From your own evil hand
Don't think about killing
Killing at all
Death is the victim
Of His own deadly call

MUERTE. *(Breaking free and taking off his mask and cape, revealing himself as* SERPIENTE.*)*
Don't mess with me, He's gotta die
I'm still the king of this Pigsty
    *(*MUERTE *shoots* ADÁN *down,* EVA *screams and goes to him.)*
Adán is a goner, his time has come
To join my company, Hell full of fun

EVA. Diosito mio, please, can't you do something?

DIOS. *(Very dramatically walking over to* ADÁN.*)* Arise Adán! *(Nothing happens.* MUERTE *snickers.)* It worked with Lazarus. *(Clearing his throat.)* Arise Adán!! *(*ADÁN *rises up amidst the sound of heavenly music.)*

EVA. Thank God!

DIOS. You're welcome!

SERPIENTE. Christian! You've thwarted me too much.

EVA. Watch out, Dios! He's turned into a Texas Rinche! *(*SERPIENTE *transforms himself into a Texas Ranger.)*

DIOS. Have no fear children, I declare. For Justice soon will clear the air.

SERPIENTE. I am the only Justice here. That I think is very clear.

EVA. Give way, you fiend, this man is God!

SERPIENTE. If he is God, I slap his face! *(Slapping* DIOS.*)*

DIOS. Ouch!

SERPIENTE. Oh come ye Christian, turn the other cheek. I have another fist for you to meet.

EVA. Dios, don't let him do this to you!

ADÁN. You must strike back and quickly too!

SERPIENTE. You stupid dirty Mexican! Can't you see I'm a Texican?

DIOS. Is this blow in your lexicon? *(Striking down* SERPIENTE.*)*

SERPIENTE. *(Throwing a fit.)* Ahhhhhhhh! No fair! You're supposed to be non-violent!

DIOS. You can turn the cheek once, but twice is too much!
So ends this scene of El Jardín
A Chicano version of the Fall.

This mixed breed of New World people
Indian, Spanish, Negro
Are seeing visions of their own
Which will someday melt with the dreams of others
To form a truly Cosmic Race
  *(Turning to leave with* ADÁN *and* EVA.*)*

SERPIENTE. Hey, not yet, there's still more to talk about.

DIOS. With you? About what?

SERPIENTE. About the dialogue between God and the Devil. Why am I always the fall guy? I have a heart. I cry, sing, bleed, and feel the pangs of love. Look, wouldn't you rather live in peace?

DIOS. But of course.

SERPIENTE. Then, why don't you give me another chance?

DIOS. I don't trust you.

SERPIENTE. I'll try and be more humble. Please? I'm sick to death of my job. It's nothing but torment. The heat is too high!

DIOS. Well, perhaps we can arrange a minor position for you in Purgatory . . .

SERPIENTE. I'd like that. *(As* DIOS *and* SERPIENTE *walk off talking to each other.)*

*Curtain*

## *EL JARDÍN* GLOSSARY

*Ahora que ustedes son los sujetos de Su Majestad, será necesario encontrar empleo.* Now that you are subjects of His Majesty, it will be necessary for you to be put to work.

*Asesino.* Assassin.

*Atascado.* Obstructor.

*¡Azteca hasta las cachas!* Aztec to the hilt!

*Aztlán.* Ancient legendary home of the Aztecs, roughly the southwestern part of the United States.

*Barrios.* Suburbs.

*Borinquén.* Indian name for modern Puerto Rico or its inhabitants.

*Borracho.* Drunkard.

*Cantón.* Area, district.

*Carne asada.* Mexican meat dish.

*¡Chin-Gow!* Oh shit!

*Corazón.* Heart.

*¡Cuando en Roma, a la Romana!* When in Rome, do as the Romans do!

*¡Cuidado, tiene espinas!* Careful, it has thorns!

*¡Diablo miserable!* Miserable Devil!

*¡Dime más, dime más!* Tell me more, tell me more!

*Diosito.* Sweet God.

*Enchilada.* Mexican dish consisting of a tortilla filled with cheese or meat.

*En el nombre del Padre, el Hijo, el Espíritu Santo.* In the name of the Father, the Son, the Holy Ghost.

*¡Espera, acabo de aprender el español!* Stop, I have just learned Spanish.

*Fajita.* Spicy Mexican meat dish.

*Feo.* Ugly, alarming.

*Gabacho.* Anglo, gringo.

*Gachupín.* Spaniard.

*Hembra.* Female.

*Hot salsa with frijoles and arroz.* Hot sauce with beans and rice.

*Huaraches.* Shoes, sandals.

*Huevos.* Literally, eggs; metaphorically, balls.

*Jalapeño.* Hot pepper.

*Jefe.* Chief, boss.

*Ladrón.* Thief.

*La Malinche.* Historical translator and mistress of Cortés; mythically, the ultimate female betrayer.

*La mujer no vale madre.* Women are no damned good.

*¡La tuya que está en vinagre!* Yours [your family] is disagreeable!

*Lo conozco.* I know him.

*Macho.* Overtly masculine, noun or adjective.

*Mamacita.* Little mama, sweet mama.

*Mamasota.* Big mama.

*Matón.* Killer, gangster.

*¡Me espiné!* I am struck, pierced!

*Mejor para mí.* Better for me. It works to my advantage.

*Mentiroso.* Liar.

*Menudo.* Spicy tripe stew that reputedly alleviates hangovers.

*Mescal.* Mexican liquor distilled from the maguey plant.

*Mestiza.* Half-breed, Spanish-Indian.

*Mi chavalona.* My sweetheart.

*Movida.* Moves, actions.

*Muerte.* Death, often represented as a skeletal character in Mexican iconography.

*Mujer.* Woman.

*Nada.* Nothing.

*Pendeja.* Fool.

*Peyote.* Mescal buttons with hallucinatory properties used in Indian religious rituals.

*¡Puro pedo!* Pure flatulence!

*¿Qué estupideces tratáis de decirnos?* What nonsense are you trying to tell us?

*¡Qué locura!* What madness!

*¡Qué monster ni que mi abuela!* Neither a monster or your grandmother!

*¿Qué no?* Right?

*Querida.* Lover, desired one.

*Quesadilla.* Spicy Mexican dish.

*Raza.* Race.

*Resbaloso.* Slippery one.

*Sabe.* Know.

*¡Soy el gran chingón!* I am the big operator, or in black English, I am a bad motha!

*Taíno.* Extinct tribe that belonged to the Arawakan group in the West Indies.

*Tenochtitlán-México.* Aztec capital at the time of the Spanish Conquest; the site of modern Mexico City.

*Te quiero mucho.* I love you very much.

*Todo.* All.

*Tonta.* Foolish woman.

*Torta.* Mexican sandwich on a roll.

*¡Tu madre!* Tell it to your mother or to the marines!

*Tuna.* Fruit of the prickly-pear cactus.

*Tu raza.* Your race.

*Vato.* Fellow, guy.

*¡Vaya con Dios!* Go with God!

*Vieja, no me agüites!* Old lady, don't give me a hard time!

*Y nosotros tomamos posesión de estas tierras en el nombre del Rey de España.* And we take possession of this land in the name of the King of Spain.

*¡Yo soy Chicana!* I am a proud Mexican-American woman!

# Preston Jones

★ ★ ★ ★ ★ ★ ★ ★ ★ ★ ★ ★ ★ ★ ★ ★ ★

★ THE PERSON

Born in Albuquerque, New Mexico, in 1936, Preston Jones died suddenly in Dallas, Texas, in September 1979. His illustrious career as a writer lasted a scant six years; yet he joins Horton Foote as the most widely known of Texas playwrights thanks to a combination of factors, foremost among them being his national exposure. When Jones's Texas Trilogy—made up of *The Knights of the White Magnolia, Lu Ann Hampton Laverty Oberlander,* and *The Oldest Living Graduate*—was given a prestigious, precedent-breaking production at the Kennedy Center in Washington, D.C., in April, May, and June of 1976, it became a major theatrical event. The *Washington Post*'s critic Richard L. Coe compared Jones to Tennessee Williams and said that Jones's plays constituted "far and away the most creative theater yet offered by Kennedy Center." Bruce Cook of *Saturday Review* called him the most promising American playwright to come along in two or three decades. The Trilogy's Broadway opening in September was widely anticipated, but perhaps expectations were too high. The New York critics, whether out of a need to assert their more demanding New York standards or out of an unwillingness to be mere followers of the Washington bandwagon, damned Jones's plays with scarce praise and many reservations. The battle was joined by Jones's supporters in Washington, in Texas, and across the nation. Preston Jones's hopeful march on New York and its disappointing end became part of his legend and one more chapter in the long history of antagonism between regional and New York theater. Maybe Jones's lack of New York appreciation makes Texans even more willing to claim him as their own.

Personally, Jones was a publicist's dream. His western stature and his rugged good looks, his ability to turn a memorable phrase, and his unpretentious sociability all worked to make him a subject of frequent interviews, in which he dramatized himself shamelessly. He was seen by many to be, if not a character from one of his own plays, at least a reassuring image of what a Texas playwright should be—strong, manly, hard-drinking, yet with compassion for the suffering of simple people and an ear for their natural eloquence.

Many of the facts of Preston Jones's life were readily adaptable to the legend, but others resisted conformity to conventional shaping. He was the son of a former lieutenant governor of New Mexico and World War I veteran, J. B. (Jawbone) Jones; his brother was a cattle inspector and rancher in Grants, New Mexico. During university vacations he did manual labor for the Texas Highway Department and played semiprofessional baseball. After joining the Dallas Theater Center, he became a beer drinker and bar conversationalist of heroic stature at such local haunts as The NFL and Joe Miller's.

On the other hand, Jones experienced a traditional Catholic schooling and went on to receive a bachelor's degree from the University of New Mexico and a master's degree in theater from Baylor University through its Dallas Theater Center program. From 1961 until his death he acted a wide variety of modern and classic roles, directed a half-dozen plays, and administered the Theater Center's experimental stage. He was a talented sculptor. His wife since 1964 was Mary Sue (Fridge) Jones, who was one of the Dallas Theater Center's finest actresses and directors and who followed Paul Baker as its managing director in 1982. Jones was the recipient of a Rockefeller Foundation Playwright-in-Residence Fellowship and was represented by one of the nation's best agents, Audrey Wood. When the Trilogy was produced in Washington and New York, its director was the brilliant Alan Schneider.

Although none of Jones's later plays were as successful as the three that made up the Trilogy, the playwright's reputation was still ascendant at the time of his death. A national television production of *The Oldest Living Graduate* starring Henry Fonda was in the works, as was a film script. Before he died Jones had become a frequent spokesman across the state for the arts in general and for theater in particular. Lady Bird Johnson numbered herself among his fans.

Unquestionably the greatest factor contributing to Preston Jones's remarkable development as a playwright was his fortunate association with the Dallas Theater Center, which Paul Baker developed and managed between 1959 and 1982. Its unique environment allowed no separation between performance and education and required that all company members participate in various aspects of theater. The diversity of experience that Jones gained there and the opportunity to work closely with the same congenial, supportive colleagues year after year drew out and nurtured his creativity. He clearly recognized the benefits of his Dallas circumstances and insisted that he would never leave, regardless of the dimensions of his success. As he once said to Bruce Cook, "The advantages of being here as a playwright—my God, they're just enormous."


★   THE PLAY

In three episodes, *Lu Ann Hampton Laverty Oberlander* chronicles twenty years in the life of its title character, from her senior year in high school as bubble-headed cheerleader to her dreary life as single parent with her own teenage daughter and as caretaker to her alcoholic brother and invalid mother. The play's vitality comes from Lu Ann's refusal to admit, or unwillingness to recognize, the barrenness of her existence. Her life in Preston Jones's fictional Bradleyville may well have peaked the week of her high school graduation picnic, but Lu Ann is a Pollyanna who insists on trying to "make lemonade" from the blows that life deals her. Her creator's greatest achievement lies in avoiding clichés of characterization and in blending Lu Ann's audience-pleasing spunk and strength with lines so salty that we are never invited to pity her.

Lu Ann, like the developed characters in *The Knights of the White Magnolia* and *The Oldest Living Graduate,* finds her life as lived in West Texas too desolate to face directly and so constructs bearable comic modifications of it. In her telling, the collapse of her first marriage becomes hilarious farce. "He did it! [Left for good!] Slammed out of the trailer, ground about fourteen gears, knocked over the mailbox, ran over our mangy collie dog, and took off down the road. Never saw him again—he didn't even show up at the divorce trial." Her description of her second husband's death is focused on an anecdote he shared with her about a Kaiser automobile's hood ornament; and her response to the medical opinion that her mother will be a "vegetable" for the remainder of her life is, "Hell, my mama ain't no vegetable, she's a flower, a great old big pretty flower."

As Walter Kerr correctly pointed out in his *New York Times* criticism, characterization in this play is thin and the play makes no statement. On the other hand, it admirably demonstrates Jones's deep affection for his characters, his eye for detail, and his sensitive, actor-storyteller's ear for language. It used to be said that William Saroyan had more good titles than any other American writer. A comparable case could convincingly be made that Jones has more good character names than any other recent dramatist. Lu Ann Hampton Laverty Oberlander stands alongside Col. J. C. Kincaid, Corky Oberlander, Milo Crawford, and Clarence Sickenger as a name that hangs in the memory and delights the ear. And Jones's gift involves more than just characters' names. Whether it is the brands of trucks that Dale Laverty talked so much about—the Kenworths, Macks, Reos, Whites, GMCs, and Internationals; the trailer court he moved his bride to—the Shady Grove Mobile Home Park; or the memorable places his hauling jobs took him to—such as the Top of the World truck stop in Moriarty, New Mexico—they all have a true ring about them. Even Jones's severest critics join his admirers in celebrating the marvelous sound of his lines.

Structurally, *Lu Ann Hampton Laverty Oberlander* is mechanical. Each act follows its predecessor after a ten-year interval. Each of the first two introduces a husband to Lu Ann. Each act presents a phase in the alcoholic decline of her brother, Skip. And each features a comic, narrative set piece. The cyclic closure devices of the last act creak. Lu Ann's daughter, a vulgarized version of her mother twenty years earlier, appears; and Billy Bob Wortman, the rejected suitor of the first act, reappears, to drive home Lu Ann's missed opportunity to escape Bradleyville. Seldom, though, do these flaws diminish the genuine pleasure that audiences receive from the play. Any problems are amply compensated by Jones's celebration of human resilience in response to adversity and by his generous portions of broad comedy.

One of Preston Jones's favorite plays was Thornton Wilder's *Our Town*, and it was unquestionably a strong influence on this play. Both unflinchingly depict the pain and unfairness of life, and both evoke the richness and delight of life as lived by ordinary people in humble surroundings. Jones's West Texas is harsher country than Wilder's New Hampshire, though, and the naive courtship at the Grover's Corners soda fountain is vastly transformed in Grover's bar (Red's) sixty-two years later.

A notable production of *Lu Ann Hampton Laverty Oberlander* opened the record-breaking run of the Texas Trilogy at the Eisenhower Theater of the Kennedy Center, Washington, D.C., on April 29, 1976. Alan Schneider directed. Diane Ladd starred. Graham Beckel and Patrick Hines played supporting roles.

★ THE WORKS

Preston Jones's dramatic works fall naturally into two categories—those that make up the Texas Trilogy and those that do not. The plays of the Trilogy, for better or worse, are the ones on which his reputation largely depends. They are what the playwright Jack Heifner referred to when he said that Jones "certainly is the most representative of Texas culture of any of us." The three plays present views of life in fictional Bradleyville that conform to popular expectations of West Texas; yet each play, in addition, is made memorable through a dimension of dramatic originality. In *The Knights of the White Magnolia*, that extra dimension is furnished by colorful staging of the pathetic, half-forgotten lodge ritual and by the members' desperate attempts to cling to their institution, which had supplied camaraderie and ideals, albeit spurious ones, that had provided relief from harsh nature and unrelenting economics. Also, there is Col. Kincaid's hallucinatory reexperiencing of the horrors of World War I trench warfare, a powerful scene that briefly counterpoints the indolent ineffectuality of the lodge members' present lives. In *The Oldest Living Graduate*, the originality again comes from the character of Col. Jefferson C. Kincaid, whose comic senility, admiration for General "Black Jack" Pershing, nostalgia for a teenage romantic infatuation, and contempt for the vulgarity of contemporary life make him a stage delight and an actor's dream role. *Lu Ann Hampton Laverty Oberlander* could have been merely another detailing of the gritty miseries of a shallow, small-town girl's decline from teenage exuberance and illusion into painful responsibility and boredom. However, the play's virtues prevent this. Each of Lu Ann's unfortunate experiences of marriage is narrated in comic retrospect rather than dramatized on stage. Her sassy profanity gives her at least a rhetorical victory over circumstance. And the focus of the play on the names of the males who have successively determined her fate and on her frivolous delight in selecting the last two on the basis of euphony deflect the audience's attention from pain to poetry, from substance to sound.

Jones's post-Trilogy plays are a diverse lot. With the exception of his minor effort *Juneteenth*, which was commissioned by the Louisville Actor's Theater as one of a series of plays dealing with holidays, none of them utilize a Texas setting or dialect. *A Place on the Magdalena Flats* returns to landscapes of New Mexico familiar to Jones from his youth. It dramatizes a conflict between brothers and is based on Jones's misunderstandings with his older brother, Jim. The play also celebrates the strength required by western ranchers to struggle against drought and other natural hardships and details the personal hardening necessary for survival. Ultimately, though, the play is unsatisfactory because it only presents the different natures of the brothers without resolving their conflict and because interest in the two characters is so equally divided that the play lacks focus.

*Santa Fe Sunshine*, an intended satire of the 1950s Santa Fe art colony, is disappointing. The dialogue lacks wit and lightness of touch, and several targets for ridicule are injudiciously selected. This play was written, as Jones said, in response to the Dallas Theater Center's "desire for a new play by him" and was developed from an old "drawer" manuscript.

*Remember,* his last play, fascinatingly combines a theatrical setting with Jones's deeply held views on the depredations of time and his painful questions about the value of his artistic achievements. The play movingly expresses the self-doubt of the aging central character, Adrian—a Shakespearian actor now reduced to dinner-theater roles—whose lines bitterly lash out at the childhood figures and institutions that he feels have betrayed him by changing with time. Unfortunately, first scheduling demands and later Jones's untimely death prevented this play from undergoing a careful process of revision through experimental performances, as was originally planned. In its present form, *Remember* suffers from special pleading and some improbabilities of plot, but nevertheless contains strong and convincing emotions and humor that match the best of *The Oldest Living Graduate.*

## LIST OF WORKS

### PLAYS

*The Knights of the White Magnolia,* 1973
*Lu Ann Hampton Laverty Oberlander,* 1974
*The Oldest Living Graduate,* 1974
*A Place on the Magdalena Flats,* 1976
*Santa Fe Sunshine,* 1977
*Juneteenth,* 1978
*Remember,* 1979

### RECOMMENDED READING

Bennett, Patrick. "Preston Jones: *In the Jaws of Time.*" *Talking With Texas Writers.*
    College Station: Texas A&M University Press, 1980.
Busby, Mark. *Preston Jones.* Boise, Idaho: Boise State University Press, 1983.
Jones, Preston. "Tales of a Pilgrim's Progress From Bradleyville to Broadway."
    *Dramatists Guild Quarterly* 13 (Winter 1977): 7–18.
McClure, Charlotte S. "Preston Jones." In *American Playwrights Since 1945,*
    edited by Philip G. Kolin, 217–25. New York: Greenwood Press, 1989.
Marek, Annemarie. *Preston Jones: An Interview.* Dallas: New London Press, 1978.
Prideaux, Tom. "The Classic Family Drama is Revived in *A Texas Trilogy.*"
    *Smithsonian* 7 (October 1976): 49–55.
Reynolds, R. C. "Honor, Dreams, and the Human Condition in Preston Jones's
    'A Texas Trilogy.'" *Southern Quarterly* 24, no. 3 (1986): 14–24.
Sewell, Bette Brady. "The Plays of Preston Jones." Ph.D. diss., UCLA, 1984.
Skrabanek, D. W. "The Effect of Time on Character in *A Texas Trilogy.*"
    *Southwestern American Literature* 7 (Fall 1981): 1–8.

# Lu Ann Hampton
# Laverty Oberlander

★ ★ ★ ★ ★ ★ ★ ★ ★ ★ ★ ★ ★ ★ ★ ★ ★

# CAST OF CHARACTERS

LU ANN HAMPTON

SKIP HAMPTON

CLAUDINE HAMPTON

BILLY BOB WORTMAN

DALE LAVERTY

RED GROVER

RUFE PHELPS

OLIN POTTS

CORKY OBERLANDER

MILO CRAWFORD

CHARMAINE

*The time is 1953. The act is set in the living room of* CLAUDINE *and* LU ANN
HAMPTON's *home in Bradleyville. A small frame house in a small frame town.
The room is modestly furnished in Sears-catalogue-type furniture—sofa, table,
chairs, radio, etc. A door upstage left leads to the kitchen. Upstage center door leads to
bedrooms. Stage right is a small front porch section with a functional screen door.*

*As the scene opens,* CLAUDINE *slams through the kitchen door with a bowl of
tangerines and sets it on an end table. She is a heavyset woman in her early forties;
her hair is grayish blond. She is dressed in a housedress and apron—takes the apron
off and puts it on the sofa back. She notes the time and looks out the porch door, then
goes upstairs, picking up sneakers from the landing.* LU ANN *runs on and into the
living room. She is dressed in the blue-and-gold uniform of a Bradleyville cheerleader. She is well built and very blond. She is also very pretty. Small-town pretty,
healthy pretty, clean pretty, Pepsodent-and-Ivory-Soap pretty.*

BILLY BOB. *(Offstage.)* Lu Ann! Lu Ann! Wait up, will ya!
    *(Following* LU ANN *on.* BILLY BOB WORTMAN *is tall and lanky. He wears a
    white shirt, Levi's, boots, and a letter sweater. His crew-cut hair has been dyed
    green.)*
LU ANN. Ma! I'm home!
CLAUDINE. *(Offstage.)* About time!
LU ANN. Well, ah thought ah would die! Ah jest thought ah would curl up and die
    right there on the gym floor. When the coach introduced the basketball team and
    you-all come out there with your hair all dyed green. Well, sir, mah eyes liked to
    jumped plumb outta mah head! Why, Mary Beth Johnson jest hollered. That's
    right, jest hollered right out loud.
BILLY BOB. It was Pete Honeycutt's idea.
LU ANN. Why, ever'one jest laughed and shouted and carried on so. Eveline Blair
    came runnin' over to me shoutin', "Look at the basketball boys, look at the
    basketball boys!"
BILLY BOB. It was Pete Honeycutt's idea.
LU ANN. *(Gestures to the porch—they go out.)* After the assembly we cheerleaders all
    got together and decided we'd do somethin' funny too.
BILLY BOB. Aw, like what?
LU ANN. Now wouldn't you like to know? Mr. Green-headed Billy Bob Wortman.
BILLY BOB. Aw, come on, Lu Ann, what are you-all fixin' to do?
LU ANN. Oh, ah don't know, somethin', somethin' real neat.
BILLY BOB. You cain't dye you-all's hair. Pete Honeycutt already thought that
    one up.
LU ANN. Eveline Blair thought up different shoes.
BILLY BOB. Different shoes?

LU ANN. You know, come to school wearin' one high-heel shoe and one saddle shoe. Somethin' *neato* like that.

BILLY BOB. Yeah.

LU ANN. Ah don't know, though, it might be kinda tricky doin' the Locomotive in a high-heel shoe.

BILLY BOB. Might be at that.

LU ANN. But it might be fun.

BILLY BOB. Shore.

LU ANN. *(Sitting on swing.)* Maybe we can wear them out to the senior picnic.

BILLY BOB. *(Joins her.)* Shore!

LU ANN. We're still goin' in your daddy's Hudson, ain't we?

BILLY BOB. Well, uh, naw, we gotta use the pickup.

LU ANN. The pickup!

BILLY BOB. Yeah, my dad wants the car to go over to Big Spring.

LU ANN. But it's the senior picnic! Mah God, ah don't want to go to mah one-and-only senior picnic in a danged-old pickup.

BILLY BOB. Well, goshalmighty, Lu Ann, ah cain't help it.

LU ANN. What the heck good is it for your dad to have a bran'-new, step-down Hudson Hornet if *we* never get to use the danged old thing.

BILLY BOB. Seems like ever'thin' ah do is wrong.

LU ANN. Boy, that's the truth.

BILLY BOB. Gawlee, Ruthie Lee Lawell and Pete Honeycutt are goin' in his pickup.

LU ANN. So what.

BILLY BOB. Well, nuthin', ah jest mean that it don't seem to bother Ruthie Lee none.

LU ANN. Heck no, it don't bother Ruthie Lee none. Mah Gawd, she almost lives in Pete Honeycutt's pickup seat. I'll bet her bra spends more time on the danged gearshift than it spends on her.

BILLY BOB. *(Shocked.)* Lu Ann Hampton! You know that ain't true.

LU ANN. It is so, too. I seen 'em when they was parked out to the drive-in and she was danged near naked.

BILLY BOB. I never saw nuthin'.

LU ANN. 'Course you never saw nuthin'. You was too busy watchin' the movie. Mah Gawd, you was more worried about old Gary Cooper than Grace Kelly was.

BILLY BOB. Ah liked that movie.

LU ANN. Boy, you shore did.

BILLY BOB. Well, ah did.

LU ANN. No wonder Ruthie Lee has so many chest colds in the wintertime.

BILLY BOB. If Pete and Ruthie Lee was actin' like the way you said, that jest means they don't have any respect for each other.

LU ANN. Or for Gary Cooper.

BILLY BOB. Reverend Stone says that goin' on like that is a sinful sign of no respect.

LU ANN. Oh, brother.

BILLY BOB. People that behave thataway out to drive-ins and such-like is behavin' plumb un-Christian.

LU ANN. Well, at least they were sharin' somethin' more than a danged ol' box of popcorn.

BILLY BOB. A true Christian is pure in mind and body.

LU ANN. I wish you'd stop preachin', Billy Bob. Mah Gawd, ever' time we have somethin' important to discuss, you come up with a danged sermon.

BILLY BOB. What in the world are we discussin' that's important?

LU ANN. Your daddy's step-down Hudson Hornet, that's what!

BILLY BOB. My daddy's . . . For cryin' out loud, Lu Ann, sometimes you drive me absolutely nuts!

LU ANN. Well, you don't have to yell, Billy Bob.

BILLY BOB. Ah told you, an' told you, an' told you that we cain't have the Hudson.

LU ANN. Well, why not?

BILLY BOB. 'Cause my daddy's got to go over to Big Spring!

LU ANN. Well, it seems plumb funny to me that your daddy picked the very day of the senior picnic to go over to Big Spring. Ah mean, doesn't he know that the senior picnic is jest about the most important event in our whole schoolin' career?

BILLY BOB. Ah don't know if he does or not, he jest . . .

LU ANN. Don't hardly seem fair to look forward to somethin' all these years only to have your daddy come along and mess it up.

BILLY BOB. Daddy ain't messed up nothin', he jest . . .

LU ANN. He's only doin' it for spite, Billy Bob.

BILLY BOB. No, he ain't, he's jest . . .

LU ANN. And spite in my book is jest plain sinful and un-Christian. *(She turns to go.)* Good-night, Billy Bob.

BILLY BOB. *(Grabbing her arm.)* Now wait a minute, Lu Ann. *(They are very close now.)* Oh, boy, uh, uh. Ah will talk to Dad tonight and ask for the car again, okay?

LU ANN. Swell, Billy Bob. *(She kisses him.)* Good-night, now.

BILLY BOB. Good-night. By gollies, Lu Ann, ah'm gonna make danged sure we git that car.

LU ANN. Fine.

BILLY BOB. Danged sure!

*(He exits.* LU ANN *watches him for a moment and then enters the house.)*

CLAUDINE. *(Entering down the stairs, singing.)* "Don't let the stars get in your eyes." Well, mah, mah, look who's here. Billy Bob Wortman walk you home?

LU ANN. Yep.

CLAUDINE. Kiss him good-night?

LU ANN. Maybe.

CLAUDINE. Well, ah'm glad your daddy never lived to see the day when his only little girl would be standin' on the front porch smoochin' with one of them worthless Wortman boys.

LU ANN. Oh, Ma.

CLAUDINE. 'Specially one with green hair.

LU ANN. How do you know? You peeked!

CLAUDINE. Didn't done it! It's all over Bradleyville how them ignernt basketball boys poured green dye or somethin' all over their empty heads.

LU ANN. Pete Honeycutt put 'em up to it.

CLAUDINE. That figgers. All them Honeycutts are crazy. God, ah remember once when Pete's *daddy* and me—oh, well, shoot, never mind. See your brother today?

LU ANN. Naw, he said he was goin' to come over to the school but he never.

CLAUDINE. Yeah, well, ah speck he's off runnin' around some place. Lordy, but he worries me, seems like ever since he come home from Korea he's been rollin' around like a tumbleweed. Foolin' around all day long in Sweetwater or Big Spring and drinkin' all night over to Red Grover's bar. All that drinkin' is no good for him, Lu Ann. If he keeps it up he's gonna wind up in the alcohol ward in the state hospital jest like his cousin Wilbur Bentley, you mark mah words. *(She lights up a cigarette.)*

LU ANN. Aw, Ma. Nuthin' like that's gonna happen to Skip.

CLAUDINE. Lord, ah hope not. *(She settles into the armchair.)* Ahh, boy, well now, tell me about the assembly.

LU ANN. Ain't much to tell.

CLAUDINE. Ain't much to tell! Well, if that don't beat all, here you been runnin' around all week talkin' about that-there assembly, and when ah ask you about it, you up and say, "Ain't much to tell."

LU ANN. Oh, gawlee, Ma, it was the same old stuff, dull, dull, dull.

CLAUDINE. Whattayou mean dull, dull, dull?

LU ANN. Oh, you know, first Mr. Palmroy got up and said how the Class of 1953 was one of the best ever at Bradleyville High. Then he had all the teachers stand up and he said how good they were; boy, ah had to laugh at that, but anyway, we gave 'em a big cheer. Then he introduced old Miss Millikan, who's gonna retire this year.

CLAUDINE. Bess Millikan! Retirin'!

LU ANN. Yep, after forty years! Can you imagine?

CLAUDINE. Mah God, Bess Millikan was my English teacher too, twenty-three years ago. Why she musta been a young woman at the time, but even back then we called her "old Miss Millikan."

LU ANN. Well, I cain't imagine her as ever bein' young, gawlee!

CLAUDINE. No, I don't guess anybody ever did. I spoze that's why she was always *Miss* Millikan. I hope you-all had a nice goin'-away for her.

LU ANN. Why, we shore did. Floyd Tatum came out and gave her an orchid.

CLAUDINE. Good.

LU ANN. Then Coach Charlton gave her a letter sweater of her very own to wear to the games.

CLAUDINE. A what?

LU ANN. A letter sweater, with a real Bradleyville letter on the front and a big number 40 on the back. She was gonna give a speech, but she started to cry of course, so we give her a big cheer and she sat down.

CLAUDINE. Why, the poor thing. I feel kinda sorry for her.

LU ANN. Well, I don't see why. Look at all them nice things she got.

CLAUDINE. I know, I know—but even so, it seems—oh, never mind. What happened next?

LU ANN. Then Coach Charlton read off the list of the basketball team and how we almost won district and ever'thing, and then bang, open come the gym doors and here comes the team onto the floor—with green hair! It looked like the Martians had landed or somethin'. Ever'body just hollered and carried on like idiots. We were havin' all kinda fun until stuffy old Mr. Palmroy had us sing the school song and we all went to our classes.

CLAUDINE. Well, it sounds like quite a time.

LU ANN. Uh-huh. But that wasn't the best part. When the noon hour came around, all of us girls that go with the basketball boys pretended that we didn't want to be seen with them.

CLAUDINE. You didn't!

LU ANN. Shore we did. Whenever they'd come around we'd run off. Billy Bob was runnin' after me and fell down into a great old big bunch of tumbleweeds.

CLAUDINE. That figgers.

LU ANN. Pete Honeycutt chased Ruthie Lee Lawell up and down the hall makin' funny noises.

CLAUDINE. Mah, mah, well, you best enjoy yourself while you can, honey, remember that your schoolin' days are the happiest days of your life.

LU ANN. Oh, pooh.

CLAUDINE. Don't "oh, pooh" me, Miss Snippy Face. Ah know what ah'm talkin' about.

LU ANN. Well, if this is the *happiest* time of mah life, ah'm jest not too all fired shore ah want to go on livin'. Gee whiz.

CLAUDINE. You'll eat them words one of these days, believe you me.

LU ANN. What's so doggone happy 'bout dumb old school? I was sittin' there in study hall the other day and I got to lookin' at a picture there on the wall of one of them castles they got over there to Europe and way up in the top part of it was this little tiny door and I got to thinking to myself, boy, what I wouldn't give to git outta here for a spell and go over yonder to where that castle is. Climb up there and open that little door and look out at the trees and gardens and such like and holler out, "Hey, ever'body, look here, look at me. I've just opened the little door that's at the top of the whole wide world!"

CLAUDINE. Well, ah don't know what me and your daddy did wrong in this life to produce such balloon-headed babies. Why weren't you workin' on your lessons 'stead of sittin' there dreamin' up fool notions?

LU ANN. 'Cause ah'm sick and tired of school, that's why! Boy, will I be happy to get out of there. Dumb old Mr. Palmroy grouchin' around and dumb old Mrs.

Willis in dumb old biology class. "Learnin' the ways and means of the life of the plants has importance to learnin' the ways of our fellow human creatures." Boy, ah have to laff at that, I tell you.

CLAUDINE. Well, ah don't know . . .

LU ANN. It's dumb.

CLAUDINE. Well, ah don't know . . .

LU ANN. What's a plant got to do with people? Plants jest sit around doin' nuthin'. Gee whiz.

CLAUDINE. Some plants are mighty pretty.

LU ANN. Do you know that there are plants in this world that eat people?

CLAUDINE. Did Mrs. Willis tell you that?

LU ANN. No, she did not. Ah happen to know *that* for a fact.

CLAUDINE. Well, ah don't believe a word of it.

LU ANN. It's the Gawd's truth. Billy Bob and me jest happened to see a picture out to the drive-in that told us all about it.

CLAUDINE. A movin' picture! That's jest all made-up stuff.

LU ANN. This movie jest happened to be based on actual incidents!

CLAUDINE. Oh pooh.

LU ANN. These fellers went plumb up the Amazon River in a great old big canoe jest to find and film these man-eatin' plants.

CLAUDINE. What'd them man-eatin' plants look like?

LU ANN. They had these big red claw-lookin' outfits that grabbed on to you, you see; then there was this clackity, clackity kind of a noise and *gulp*, that's all she wrote.

CLAUDINE. You're makin' this all up.

LU ANN. Ah am not.

CLAUDINE. You are so, too. You and Billy Bob Wortman ain't never seed a movie out to that drive-in in your life.

LU ANN. What are you talkin' about, we go out there most ever' Sattiday night.

CLAUDINE. Not to watch no movie you don't.

LU ANN. Do too!

CLAUDINE. Don't either! You all go out there to smooch and fool around.

LU ANN. Nasty mind.

CLAUDINE. Nothin' nasty 'bout the truth. Ah don't know why they bother to show a movie at all. They oughter jest line up them pickup trucks and turn the *lights* out for a couple of hours.

LU ANN. Lot you know 'bout it.

CLAUDINE. Ah know a lot more than you think. Hangin' around at the drive-in, dreamin' 'bout castles in the air. Honey, you gotta start some serious thinkin' 'bout after you graduate. Now, are you and Ruthie Lee still wantin' to go to that business college in Big Spring?

LU ANN. Business college? My Gawd, Mama, I'm not goin' through all the trouble of gittin' outta one school jest to turn around and walk right into another one.

CLAUDINE. Well, then how 'bout gittin' you that summer job with me at the hospital? It's the best trainin' in the world if you're goin' to go on and be a nurse.

LU ANN. Oh, ah don't know, Mama. Ah don't want to think about it jest yet.

CLAUDINE. Well, you gotta think about it sometime.

LU ANN. Ah jest wanna *go*, go anywhere. Outta this house, outta this town, plumb outta the state somewhere.

CLAUDINE. Jest wantin' to go ain't gonna git you anyplace. You gotta plan and work and know where you're goin'.

LU ANN. Ah know, ah know!

CLAUDINE. You know, you know! What do you know?

LU ANN. Ah *know* ah don't want to be stuck all mah life in a little old dricd-up West Texas town, emptyin' bedpans at the goddamned hospital, like somebody ah *know!!*

CLAUDINE. *(Looks at her a moment, slightly taken aback by the outburst, then she sighs and slowly shakes her head.)* Ah gotta be gittin' on down to work now. Ah got all the fixin's laid out for you in the kitchen. When your brother gits home, you go ahead and cook the supper, will you?

LU ANN. *(Very low.)* Ah'm sorry, Mama.

CLAUDINE. And if you got schoolwork to do, git it done and don't spend the live-long night playin' that durn radio.

LU ANN. Okay, Mama.

CLAUDINE. *(Going out the door.)* See you later. *(As she exits.)* Confounded kids.

LU ANN. *(Goes straight to the radio and clicks it on. A Western song twangs softly into the room. She starts to dance. The phone rings.)* Comin'. *(She turns down the radio and picks up the receiver.)* Hello . . . Oh, hi, Eveline . . . Nothin', what are you doin'? . . . Chapter 4? Nope, ah haven't read it yet . . . Oh pooh on old Mrs. Willis . . . What? . . . Of course ah'm goin' to the senior picnic . . . You still goin' with Floyd Tatum . . . You-all made up, huh . . . Of course ah'm goin' with Billy Bob, who'd you expect, Milo Crawford? *(She giggles.)* He's got so many blackheads he looks like a pepper shaker . . . *(There is a loud crash outside and we hear* SKIP'*s voice offstage.)*

SKIP. Goddamnit to hell!

LU ANN. Ah gotta go now, Eveline, ah think ah hear mah brother comin' in. See you later, kid, 'bye.

*(She hangs up the phone, turns off the radio, and hurries into the kitchen just as* SKIP *stumbles onto the porch. He is followed by* DALE LAVERTY. *He is dressed in the traditional uniform of West Texas—white shirt, Levi's, cowboy boots, and straw Western hat.* DALE LAVERTY *is a great, honest, shambling sort of fellow. He wears a rumpled, cheap tan suit.)*

SKIP. Come on in this house, Dale. Goddamnit, come on in. Ma! Lu Ann! Where the hell is ever'body? Sit down, Dale. Ma, where the hell are you?

LU ANN. *(Entering from the kitchen.)* Ma's gone down to work.

SKIP. The devil you say. You gittin' the supper?

LU ANN. Yes, ah am.

SKIP. Then to hell with it. *(To* DALE.*)* She couldn't boil a Vyenna sausage.

LU ANN. Well, so much for you then. *(She turns to go back into the kitchen.)*

SKIP. Now hold on a minute, damnit. Ah want you to meet somebody. Dale Laverty, this here is mah little sister, Lu Ann.

DALE. Howdy.

LU ANN. Hello.

SKIP. Dale drove over from San Angelo to visit me today, ain't that somethin'. We was in the same outfit in Korea.

LU ANN. Oh, is that right?

SKIP. Damn right, blastin' them gooks. Old Dale was hell on wheels with a B.A.R., regular John Wayne. Right, Dale?

DALE. Ah never done much really.

SKIP. Never done much! Why, hell's fire, boy, what you talkin' about? Did you know that this-here boy, he, he, uh, he saved mah life over there in Korea?

LU ANN. *(Interested.)* Really?

SKIP. Damn right.

DALE. Aw hell, Skip.

SKIP. Saved your brother's butt, that's what he did. Wanna hear about it?

LU ANN. Lemme turn down the oven and put the salad back in the icebox first.

SKIP. You go ahead and do that little thing, honey.
     *(She exits.)*

DALE. *(Going up to* SKIP.*)* Gawlee, Skip, what are you tryin' to do, ah never saved your life or nuthin'.

SKIP. Shore, shore, I know. So what, we'll jest have some fun with little sister, okay?

DALE. Well, shore, ah guess.

SKIP. Whattayou think of Lu Ann—nice, huh?

DALE. *(Sincerely.)* She's real pretty.

SKIP. Yes, she is. She's mah one-and-only sister and you are mah one-and-only buddy. Only buddy ah got in the whole lousy world.

DALE. Aw hell, Skip.

SKIP. The only one. You saw how them slobs down at Red's acted. Lived in this lousy town all mah life, served mah stinkin' country in Ko-rea, and they wouldn't even buy me a lousy beer.

DALE. Aw come on, Skip, you know that ain't true.

SKIP. The hell it ain't.

DALE. You got lots of friends in this-here town. What about that-there lodge you joined the other day?

SKIP. The Knights of the White Magnolia? Hell, Dale, none of them fellers are friends of mine. Ah joined that-there lodge to get ahead in this town. Damn right, that lodge is jest a steppin'-stone, buddy. I've got ideas that's gonna put this little old town right on its ear.

DALE. By gollies, Skip, if anybody can do it, you can.

SKIP. You're damn right I can. I got plans, buddy, big plans. Remember Corporal Rosenberg?

DALE. Yeah. Old Four-Eyes, the motor-pool clerk.

SKIP. That's the guy. Well, he had two college degrees. That's right, *two*—an A.M. and a F.M., some damn thing like that. Well, one afternoon when we was havin' some beers over to the N.C.O. club, he told me that even with all his education he wished he had my common sense.

DALE. No kiddin'.

SKIP. That's right. You see, Dale, all them college chumps like Rosenberg is good for is like one thing at a time—you know. But commonsense guys like me can move around, ya see. We can be goin' with three or four deals at once. Hell's fire, ah got me a couple of real-estate ideas figgered out over to Sweetwater that are flat gonna make a bundle.

DALE. Gawlee.

SKIP. Damn right. And that ain't all. After ah talk to Old Man Cullers over to the bank, and git me a little capital together, ah'm really gonna put 'er in high gear. You see, Dale, I got all these-here opportunities right out in front of me. And ah got the common sense as how to move out and latch hold of 'em.

DALE. Yeah!

SKIP. But you gotta be careful, you know what ah mean?

DALE. Well, ah . . .

SKIP. You just cain't go rushin' straight into things like a damn fool. No, sir. You gotta move kindly easy-like. Keep your eyes open and slip around. In business you got to know ever' side of things affore you decide to pick up the cards.

DALE. Yeah, ah speck so.

SKIP. Did you know that ah wasn't back in this town of Bradleyville more than five minutes affore old Derwood Herring was over here wantin' me to go in with him in the Western Auto store?

DALE. Them Western Auto stores is damn-good outfits.

SKIP. Hell, yes, they are!

DALE. We got one over to San Angelo.

SKIP. You know what ah told him? I said, "Now look here, Derwood, I appreciate the hell outta you comin' over here." You see, Dale, in business matters you always gotta be polite. "But ah just ain't the kind of feller just to jump on into things this way. No, sir. Ah gotta put my mind to work on it. Look at ever' side of this-here deal. Now, you jest come around again, say, in a month or two, and maybe ah can figger out somethin' for you."

DALE. What did he say to that?

SKIP. What could he say? Hell, Dale, Derwood ain't dumb. He knows the truth of things. He just sorter mumbled somethin' like "Well, all right, Skip, if that's how you feel." Then he got the hell out.

DALE. Did he ever come back?

SKIP. Naw. The backstabbin' s.o.b. went straight over to Earl Parker's place and got him to go partners.

DALE. That was a damn dirty thing to do.

SKIP. Ah was glad, Dale, glad he done it. Who the hell would want to spend the rest of their life runnin' a Western Auto store for Christ's sake?

DALE. Them places ain't much account anyway.

SKIP. Hell, no, they ain't.

DALE. We got one over to San Angelo that ah never liked much.

SKIP. When these real-estate outfits work out, why in ten years or so ah'll not only own that damn Western Auto store but the whole damn block it's sittin' in.

DALE. You'll do 'er too, buddy!

SKIP. You see, Dale, time don't mean a damn thing in the business world. It's what you do with it that counts. How would you like to come over here someday and have old Skip drive you on down to the country club in his new Cadillac, sit around the bar over there with Floyd Kinkaid and all them rich bastards, and talk about oil wells and such like?

DALE. Boy, that would be somethin'.

SKIP. Cain't ever tell, buddy. Why, hell's fire, ah might even buy into that livestock-haulin' outfit you're fixin' to go to work for.

DALE. The Hubbard Brothers?!

SKIP. Hell, yes. Why not? You see, Dale, all ah gotta do is talk to Old Man Cullers over to the bank and then . . .

LU ANN. *(Entering.)* All done.

SKIP. Yeah, that's fine, Lu Ann. You see, Dale, all ah need is a little capital, then . . .

LU ANN. What about the story?

SKIP. What story?

DALE. 'Bout me savin' your life over to Ko-rea.

SKIP. What the hell you talkin' about?

DALE. You know that time when, uh . . . that story you was gonna tell Lu Ann there.

SKIP. Oh yeah, well, let's see now. Remember me writin' to you-all 'bout how I was drivin' them convoy trucks over there?

LU ANN. Shore do.

SKIP. Well, sir. There was that time when the Marines caught hell and was re-treatin' from the Chosan reservoir. Remember readin' that in the newspaper?

LU ANN. Ah think so.

SKIP. Well, we was there! Old Dale and me, a-bringin' them boys down through the hills. Snow on the ground, cold as hell, and by God surrounded by the entire Chinese gook army.

LU ANN. Gawlee.

SKIP. Damn right. The hills was covered by them little slant-eyed bastards like by-God ants! There was five truckloads of us, you see, comin' down this little old dirt road. Cold as hell and dog-assed surrounded. Well, as you can see, we was in somethin' of a fix, but it looked like we was gonna make it out okay. When all of a sudden they come down on us with their heavy artillery. Wham, wham, wham! In nuthin' flat three of our trucks was nuthin' but smokin' ruin.

LU ANN. Smokin' ruin?

SKIP. That's right, smokin' ruin! Then it happened! Bang, they got me! Direct hit, right on my truck! The next thing I know, ah'm lyin' out in the snow with dead bodies of Marines all around me. Well, sir, ah figgered ah'd best git the hell outta there pronto. So ah got up to take off and that's when ah seed 'em comin'.

LU ANN. Who?

SKIP. Who?! The goddamned gooks, that's who! *(To* DALE.*) Who! (Back to* LU ANN.*)* About fifty of 'em comin' like a bat out of hell over this little rise and ever' one of 'em comin' right at me, and ah knew, ah *knew* that ah was standin' there a dead man. Nuthin' ah could do but stand there and watch 'em git closer and closer. Then, then by God it happened!

LU ANN. What?

SKIP. Ah heard a noise behind me and here comes old Dale, drivin' with one hand and shootin' with the other. Cuttin' them gooks down like by-God weeds. He tossed down the B.A.R. and, openin' the door of the truck, reached out and picked me off the ground, threw me into the front seat, and gunned that old truck like Billy Jim hell over the hill and outta there.

LU ANN. Mah gosh.

SKIP. And for doin' that this-here boy was awarded one of the highest medals that this country's got. The Good Conduct Medal with bar.

LU ANN. Wow!

SKIP. Ol' Laverty butt, my best buddy.

DALE. Aw hell, Skip.

SKIP. Yes, sir, that is the man that is sittin' right next to you on the sofa. Old Laverty butt, mah best buddy. *(Suddenly* SKIP *stands up and grasps his stomach.)* Oh God, ah feel it comin' on again.

LU ANN. What's wrong?

SKIP. It's either mah old war wound, or the malaria, or, or—

LU ANN. My God, Skip, what is it?

SKIP. Yes, that's it, ah'm sure that's it.

LU ANN. What?!

SKIP. Oh, gotta go tap this kidney or by God drown.

DALE. Aw hell, Skip. *(*SKIP *laughs and exits. There is a silence as* DALE *and* LU ANN *grope around for a thread of conversation. With great effort.)* So you're a cheerleader, huh?

LU ANN. What?

DALE. Uh—so you're a cheerleader, huh?

LU ANN. Oh, yes.

DALE. That's great.

LU ANN. It's lots of fun.

DALE. Ah'll bet. *(*LU ANN *offers a tangerine—he declines.)*

LU ANN. You—uh—you play any *ball* over in San Angelo?

DALE. Football. Left tackle, that's on the line.

LU ANN. Yes. Ah know.

DALE. We had a good team. You remember Jack Mathis?

LU ANN. Ah don't think so.

DALE. Well, Jack Mathis was our quarterback and he went over to the A and M and made Honorable Mention All Southwestern Conference Second Team Defensive Guard.

LU ANN. That's neat.

DALE. He's the State Farm insurance man in Big Spring now.

LU ANN. No kiddin'?

DALE. That's right. He's doin' real good. Got him one of them ranch-style homes.

LU ANN. Wow. Uh—whatta *you* gonna do now that your army is over and all that?

DALE. Oh, ah got me a job with the Hubbard Brothers.

LU ANN. *(Guessing.)* Truck drivin'?

DALE. Livestock haulers, West Texas and New Mexico. Ah start next week.

LU ANN. Ah see.

DALE. Because of mah army experience ah got me a rig right away. Most guys have to start off as a helper but ah got a rig of mah own right off. Yes, ma'am, big red Mack diesel with air horns and ever'thing. Boy, it's really somethin'.

LU ANN. Ah'll bet.

DALE. Purrs like a kitten. You wouldn't think an engine that big could sound so sweet. Boy, it's really somethin', and they give it to me right off, best old sweetheart in the fleet.

LU ANN. They probably heard about your medal and things.

DALE. *(Taken aback.)* Yeah . . . uh, these your school books?

LU ANN. Biology and history, ugh.

DALE. Boy, ah hated school.

LU ANN. My mama says it's the happiest time of your life. Ever hear anythin' so silly?

DALE. Ah cain't buy that.

LU ANN. Me neither.

DALE. Whattayou gonna do after you graduate?

LU ANN. Gee, ah don't know. Mama wants me to go on to nursin' school.

DALE. That's a good job for a girl.

LU ANN. Ah spoze.

DALE. Mah sister is a dental assistant.

LU ANN. That's a good job.

DALE. Sure is. She makes pretty good money. Her husband works at Hubbard Brothers too.

LU ANN. Really?

DALE. You bet! They got 'em one of those great old big house trailers.

LU ANN. That's neat.

DALE. Shore is. It's got a livin' room, bathroom, kitchen, the works, and the best thing about it is that if you git tired of bein' in one town you can jest hook 'er up and take off, nuthin' to it. Spoze you were livin' in Snyder or Abilene or somewhere and you wanted to move to Amarillo? Well, sir, you jest hook up and take off. Furniture, dishes, clothes, ever'thin', jest take off. Now that is the way to live!

LU ANN. Gosh yes.

DALE. You pull into one of them trailer parks, you see, an' they got ever'thang. Gas, water, washin' machines, swings, septic tanks, some even got swimmin' pools.

LU ANN. Swimmin' pools?

DALE. You bet, and grass and trees and flowers and collie dogs runnin' around.

LU ANN. Gee, it sounds like heaven.

DALE. Yeah.

> *(Their eyes meet for a long moment.* SKIP *reenters.)*

SKIP. Whooee, did ah need that!

DALE. *(Nervously.)* You shore were gone a long time.

SKIP. Well, you know how it is, kid. The longer it is, the longer it takes. You-all gittin' along okay?

DALE. Sure, Skip. Jest fine.

SKIP. Well, now, ain't that real nice. You know, Dale, one of these days old Lu Ann is gonna make some lucky guy one helluva nice wife.

LU ANN. Aw shoot.

SKIP. Whattayou think, old podnah?

DALE. Ah truly believe she will.

SKIP. Damn right. But ah gotta tell you one thing right off. You got competition, boy.

DALE. Ah do?

SKIP. You better believe it. Old Lu Ann's got her a basketball-playin' dude. How many points Billy Bob score agin Snyder, Lu Ann?

LU ANN. Six.

SKIP. You hear that, Dale? Six big ones! God Amighty, what an eye, makes old Bob Cousy look like an amateur.

LU ANN. Billy Bob was doggone good over there to Snyder.

SKIP. Yeah, boy, and a lover too. I hear tell that Lu Ann kissed him so hard the other night that his hair turned as green as alfalfa.

DALE. Sounds like a helluva guy.

SKIP. Damn right! They tell me that when old Billy Bob grows up he's gonna rent his head out to pasture.

LU ANN. *(Playfully hitting at him.)* Oh, you. Now you quit pickin' on Billy Bob, he's a nice boy.

SKIP. Shore he's a nice *boy*, but maybe it's about time you started thinkin' about a nice *man*. An adult, grown-up man, 'stead of some pimply-faced, nose-pickin' kid. Somebody that can shake them bedsprings till your toes curl up and your teeth rattle.

LU ANN. *(Holding her hands over her ears.)* Ah ain't gonna listen no more.

SKIP. Listen to what? Hell, ah never said nuthin'. Hey, Dale, you remember them wooden beds they had in that whorehouse in Tokyo?

DALE. *(Embarrassed and uncomfortable.)* No, Skip, ah, uh, don't, uh, remember.

LU ANN. Ah wish you wouldn't always talk dirty thataway.

SKIP. Who's talkin' dirty? Them wooden beds is a by-God historical fact. We was talkin' about 'em over to mah lodge meetin' the other night, Dale, and old L. D. Alexander said . . .

LU ANN. Boy, that figgers. Bunch of dirty-minded old men.

SKIP. What do you mean "dirty-minded old men"? It jest so happens that some of the most important men in this town are members of the Knights of the White Magnolia.

LU ANN. That ain't the way ah heard it.

SKIP. What ain't the way you heard it? It's the by-God truth. Ain't that right, Dale?

DALE. Well, gawlee, Skip, ah don't know.

SKIP. *(To* LU ANN.*)* You see there?

LU ANN. Sara Beth Phelps was over here the other day and told Mama that she didn't like for Rufe to go to them meetin's 'cause nobody does nuthin' but drink whiskey, play dominoes, and git into big fights.

SKIP. Well, what in the name of Jesus H. Christ does Sara Beth Phelps know anyway!

LU ANN. Rufe Phelps is a member, ain't he?

SKIP. Shore he's a member. That's why Sara Beth don't know a damn thing. 'Cause members ain't spozed to tell nobody, wives or nuthin', what goes on in our meetin's.

LU ANN. How's come?

SKIP. How's come? 'Cause it's secret, that's how's come! We do lots of secret important things.

LU ANN. Shore, shore, like talkin' about wooden beds in Tokyo whorehouses.

SKIP. That was before the meetin', damnit, before the secret stuff. And who the hell ever taught you to say whorehouse! You tryin' to shame the family in front of company?

DALE. Ah, hell, Skip.

LU ANN. You jest said it yourself not two seconds ago.

SKIP. That don't mean you gotta go repeatin' it all over town. How about that, Dale? A little old fatty-legged high-school girl goin' around sayin' dirty words in her own by-God house. Ah don't know what the goddamned world's comin' to.

LU ANN. Pickin' on me ain't gonna change a thing. Ever'body in town knows that that-there lodge ain't worth a hill of beans and you're just puttin' a lot of stock into somethin' that ain't nuthin' at all.

DALE. *(Getting up.)* Well, ah speck ah better . . .

SKIP. That lodge is jest a steppin'-stone, a steppin'-stone, that's all!

LU ANN. Uh-huh. *(She mimes crossing a stream.)* Step, step, kerplunk!

SKIP. Come on, Dale, let's git the hell out of here and go on back to Red's place!

DALE. Well, uh, shore . . .

LU ANN. Mama says, if you keep hangin' out over to Red's place, you're gonna wind up bein' just like Wilbur Bentley.

SKIP. Well, ah don't give a damn if ah do. At least in the alcohol ward ah won't be pestered to death by a big-mouthed little sister. Now come on, Dale, let's go!

DALE. You go ahead, Skip! Ah'll be right with you.

SKIP. *(Exiting.)* Pick on a feller's lodge. Might as well pick on his country or his flag or somethin'. No damn respect, that's the trouble. No by-God respect.

*(He exits. There is a moment of silence.)*

DALE. Old Skip's a lotta fun, ain't he?

LU ANN. Sometimes.

DALE. Lot of that stuff he said earlier he didn't really mean.

LU ANN. Oh, well, ah don't reckin it matters.

DALE. Listen, do you think it would be okay if ah called you some time? Ah mean, uh, you and that feller of yours ain't engaged or nuthin', are you?

LU ANN. Oh, shoot, no, we jest kinda go with each other, you know.

DALE. Shore. Well then, would it be okay?

LU ANN. What?

DALE. If ah maybe could call you or somethin'?

LU ANN. Oh, sure, Dale, that would be real neat.

DALE. Okay, by golly, ah'll jest do that. Real soon.

LU ANN. Swell.

DALE. Well, uh, so long.

LU ANN. So long. See you soon. *(DALE exits. She watches after him for a moment and then crosses into the room. She stands for a moment at the radio.)* Dale Laverty—Dale Laverty, gee, that's a pretty name. *(She switches on the radio; Western music booms forth as the act ends.)*

*Curtain*

# ★ ACT II

*The act takes place in 1963 in Red Grover's bar—a small, dim, beer-smelling West Texas dive. Lots of beer advertisements are on the wall—Coors, Lone Star, Pearl, Miller's, etc. A small wooden bar, a couple of tables and chairs, a beat-up jukebox are onstage. Above the bar is a large sign:* WE RESERVE THE RIGHT TO REFUSE SERVICE TO ANYONE. RED's *place has seen a lot of beer-swilling, head-knocking, gut-rumbling life and looks it.*

*As the scene opens, we find* RED GROVER *standing behind the bar, glumly watching* RUFE PHELPS *and* OLIN POTTS *play checkers.*

RUFE. Watch out there, watch out what you're doin' there!

OLIN. Hell, Rufe, it's mah move.

RUFE. Ah know it's your blamed move. But you cain't move mah checkers. Only yours.

OLIN. Ah ain't movin' yours, only ones ah'm movin' is the black uns.

RUFE. Your finger touched that checker right there and that checker is by God red.

OLIN. Mah finger never touched nuthin'. All ah'm movin' is the black uns.

RUFE. Red seen it. Hey, Red, didn't he touch this-here checker?

RED. Who gives a damn.

OLIN. Ah never touched nuthin'!

RUFE. Did so too!

OLIN. Didn't never either!

RUFE. Done it!

OLIN. Didn't!

RED. For Christ's sake! If you two cain't play that damned game without fightin' about it, then you can by God get the hell outta here.

RUFE. Well, hell, Red, he cheated.

OLIN. Ah never neither.

RED. *(Quietly.)* Ah ain't gonna tell you two again.

RUFE. Ah'm tired of playin' anyway.

OLIN. That's 'cause you're losin'.

RUFE. Shore ah'm losin'. How can anybody win with you a-movin' any damn checker on the board that pleases you?

OLIN. Ah'm only movin' the black uns!

RUFE. Ah never seen nuthin' like you, Olin Potts! Cheat at horseshoes, cheat at checkers, cheat at dominoes, cheat at ever'thang!

OLIN. Ah never cheat at nuthin'! And you know it!

RUFE. Never cheat? How 'bout the last time we went bowlin'. Hey, Red, he knocked down the by-God pinboy and called it a spare.

OLIN. Well, hell, ah figgered he should count for somethin'; 'sides that, a movin' target's harder to hit.

RUFE. *(To* RED.*)* You see there.

RED. Boy, you two are somethin' else. Anybody want another beer?

RUFE. Naw. Ah'm already gittin' the bloats.

RED. How about you, Olin?

OLIN. Two's mah limit, Red.

RED. *(Mimicking.)* "Two's mah limit, Red." Some customers. Sit around here all day long and buy four lousy beers.

RUFE. Ah cain't help it if beer bloats me.

RED. Well, damnit, drink somethin' else!

RUFE. Ah don't like nuthin' else.

RED. Oh, for Christ's sake.

RUFE. What are you-all so all-fired peckish about, Red? Me and Olin never drink more than four beers, ain't that right, Olin?

OLIN. Two's mah limit.

RED. Jesus Christ, some business ah got here. Bloated checker players all day long and by-God drunken maniacs at night.

RUFE. You're talkin' about Skip Hampton, ain't you?

OLIN. What's old Skip done now?

RUFE. Didn't you hear about what he did?

OLIN. Hell no, ah never hear about nuthin'.

RED. Stupid bastard tried to kill himself in here last night.

OLIN. Kill himself!

RED. That's right.

RUFE. Had him a knife, didn't he?

RED. Hell no. The crazy son of a bitch cut his throat with a broken bottle.

OLIN. Cut his throat! Well, whattayou know about that.

RED. Damnedest thing ah ever saw in mah life.

OLIN. What the hell happened?

RED. He came in here about, oh, 2:30 or 3:00 yesterday afternoon, lookin' like hell as usual, and started chuggin' down the old Thunderbird wine. Come about 8:00 he's drunk as billy hell and starts to mouth off again about Ko-rea.

OLIN. Oh, God, not again.

RED. That's right, them same old sad-assed stories. Well, sir, Pete Honeycutt was standin' here at the bar and he turns over to Skip and says, "Why don't you shove it, Hampton—nobody wants to hear that old crap any more—hell, that damned war's been over for *ten years.*"

OLIN. What did he do then?

RED. Well, sir, old Skip looks up and says, "You're a goddamned liar." That's right, jest as cool as you please. "You're a goddamned liar."

OLIN. Skip said that to Pete Honeycutt. My God, what did Pete do?

RED. Hell, you know old Pete Honeycutt, nobody calls him a liar. The next thing I know he's got Skip by the shirt front and slammed up into the corner. "Listen, you sad sack of crap," he says, "this is nineteen and goddamned sixty-three—you ain't no Korean hero no more—you're nuthin' but a stinkin' wino bum, the goddamned town joke!" Then he spins him around and kicks him in the ass. Knocked him right up agin the bar here.

RUFE. God Almighty.

RED. Well, sir, Skip gits up real slow like and ah figger he's gonna tangle with old Pete.

OLIN. Did he?

RED. Hell no. He jest stood there lookin' at Pete for a second and then he started to cry.

RUFE. He did what?

RED. He started bawlin'. Damnedest thing ah ever seen. Stood there like a damned fool and cried like a baby.

OLIN. Whattayou know about that.

RED. Hell, ah liked to died laughin'. The whole place nearly come apart, old Pete jest doubled up and hollered. Jesus, it was funny! Then, by God, while we was laughin' there at him he reached behind him, got this-here beer bottle, broke it on the bar, and pulled the edge across his throat.

RUFE. My God!

RED. Hell, ah thought he was sure-enough dead. Ah mean, the blood jumped clean across the room. It's a damn good thing old Doc Crowley was across the street there to the Dixie Dinette or Skip would be on a slab at Strong's Funeral Home 'stead of the hospital. By God I've seen some pretty wild things in this dump, but last night takes the blue goddamned ribbon. Ah was moppin' up blood and broken glass for an hour.

OLIN. By gollies, ah don't know. It seems to me that ever since our lodge broke up, old Skip's jest sorter gone on downhill.

RED. That's bullshit! Skip Hampton was born goin' downhill, that stinkin' little lush is nuthin' but a washout and a loser.

RUFE. You know the one ah feel sorry for is his mother.

OLIN. Damn right, it's a shame that a fine woman like Claudine Hampton has got a burden like that on her.

RUFE. Two burdens, you're forgittin' about Lu Ann.

RED. Lu Ann, now there's a hot little number for you. *(He chuckles.)* Tough as a damned boot.

RUFE. That girl's plumb wild now, that's a by-God fact.

OLIN. Well, ah don't know.

RUFE. You don't know! Why, hell, Olin, she's been movin' through this town like a tornado ever since she got shed of that husband of hers four or five years ago and moved back from over there to Snyder.

OLIN. Well, ah know all that, but hell, Rufe, she jest blows off a little steam now and again. She ain't *bad* or nuthin' like that.

RUFE. Any woman that would sit around a bar like this-here one drinkin' beer and smokin' cigarettes with a bunch of old hardheaded men is by God down in mah book as *bad!*

RED. Now hold on there, you're talkin' about some of my best customers.

OLIN. By God, Rufe, you got you a plumb narrow mind, ah'll be damned if you don't—

RUFE. Now jest what the hell do you mean by that!

RED. He's tryin' to tell you that you're skinny-brained, Rufe.

RUFE. Who's skinny-brained?

OLIN. You are, that's who, you got a skinny brain in a big fat head!

RED. *(Laughing.)* That's tellin' him, Olin.

RUFE. *(Leaping up.)* By God, Olin, now you've gone too damn far. *(He assumes an old-time fighting stance.)* Git up, git up, so's ah can knock you down.

RED. Attaboy, Rufe!

OLIN. Don't be a damned fool, Rufe, sit down and forgit it.

RUFE. Ah damned well won't forgit it. Now, by God, Olin, git up and fight.

RED. Go ahead, Olin, you can take him.

> *(The door opens and* LU ANN *enters. The years have hardened her prettiness into a tough, smooth gloss. Her figure is still excellent. She is drugstore pretty, cologne-and-lipstick pretty. She wears the white uniform of a beauty operator.)*

LU ANN. What the hell's goin' on in here?

RED. Come on in, Lu Ann, you're jest in time for the fight of the century. We got old Hurricane Skinny-Brain versus Two's-My-Limit Lewis.

LU ANN. My God, what are you and Olin fightin' about now, Rufe?

RUFE. Well, we, ah, er . . .

RED. Go ahead, Rufe, tell her.

OLIN. We was jest arguin' about a bowlin' score, Lu Ann, that's all.

LU ANN. Ah heard about you sports over to the Bradleyville Bowl. Still smackin' down the pinboys there, Olin?

OLIN. Got two last Wednesday.

LU ANN. Damn good goin'.

RUFE. You ought to see 'em jump around when old Olin gits up there—it's plumb comical.

LU ANN. Sounds like it. My gawd, Red, gimme a beer before ah flat dry up and die.

RED. Comin' up, Lu Ann! Whattayou doin' over here today? You and Maud Lowery have another fight?

LU ANN. Aw, that goddamned old bag! What she knows about bein' a beautician wouldn't stuff a horny toad's butt.

RED. Better watch your step, Lu Ann, or Maud's gonna fire you one of these days.

LU ANN. *Fire me!* That'll be the goddamn day. Maud Lowery's Bon-Ton Beauty *Saloon,* for Christ's sake. There ain't a woman in this town comes into that shop wantin' anyone else to do their hair but me. Maud Lowery gits her hands on you and you walk out lookin' like a gunny sack. She couldn't curry a coyote and she's got the sand to call herself a beautician! Hell, ah studied beauty operation, Red, you know that. Probably could have had a shop of my own by now if it weren't for that worthless Dale Laverty.

OLIN. Where is old Dale now?

LU ANN. Who gives a damn. Why, I never hear from him anymore, not since he pulled out on me one fine night with a gut full of hootch and snakes in his boots. Left me to bring up little Charmaine all by mahself.

RUFE. You're livin' with your ma now, ain't you, Lu Ann?

LU ANN. Yep, same old place. Mama helps me take care of Charmaine. She only works part-time over to the hospital now.

RED. Been over to see your brother today?

LU ANN. Sure, sure, ah seen him.

OLIN. How's he gittin' along?

LU ANN. Well, Doc Crowley says he's goin' to be okay but ah don't know, he sure look peekity to me. Boy howdy, what a damn-fool thing to do.

OLIN. Well, he'd had a lot to drink, ah spoze.

LU ANN. Skip always has a lot to drink. Maybe this will slow him down for a little while.

OLIN. *(Getting up.)* Well, ah gotta be gettin' back to the farm. Chores to do. *(To* RUFE.*)* You still wanna set that trotline in the mornin'?

RUFE. Hell, yes, I wanna set that line. I found a place out there on the lake that jest smells catfishy. Pick me up at the house about 4:30, okay?

OLIN. Will do. Well, ah'll see you-all later.

> *(He exits.)*

RUFE. So long, Olin.

LU ANN. You still workin' over to the refinery, Rufe?

RUFE. You bet. Same old job.

LU ANN. How's Sara Beth gittin' along these days?

RUFE. Well, she had the misery in her shoulder again last winter, but other than that she's all right, ah guess.

> *(The door opens and* CORKY OBERLANDER *enters.* CORKY *is an open, friendly-type fellow in his mid-thirties. He wears khaki work clothes and a baseball cap.)*

CORKY. Howdy, Rufe.

RUFE. Hey there, Corky.

RED. Hey, Corky—whattayou say, boy?

CORKY. Don't say it, Red. How 'bout a beer?

RED. Comin' up.

CORKY. *(Spotting* LU ANN.*)* Well, hello there, pretty girl. Hey, Red, who in the world is this pretty little thing?

RED. Lu Ann Laverty, Corky Oberlander.

CORKY. Well, I'm happy to meet you, Lu Ann Laverty.

LU ANN. Well, I'm happy to meet you, Corky Overlander.

RED. Corky here is an inspector with the Highway Department.

CORKY. Yep, got transferred over here from Abilene. Didn't think I was going to like it much till now.

LU ANN. Aw hell.

CORKY. Care to join me at a table?

LU ANN. Suits me.

RUFE. Well, ah gotta be goin'.

RED. Take it easy, Rufe.

RUFE. If I'm late for supper, old Sara Beth will be mad as hell.
    *(He exits.)*

RED. You two want anythin' else?

CORKY. Nuthin' for me, thanks. *(To* LU ANN.*)* How about you?

LU ANN. Naw, ah'm okay.

RED. That figgers. I'm gonna go out back and stack some cases. If anybody comes in, sing out for me, will you?

CORKY. Will do. *(*RED *exits. There is a long pause.)* Well, here we are.

LU ANN. Looks like.

CORKY. Want me to play the jukebox?

LU ANN. Naw, sometimes them damn twangy guitars git into my nose.

CORKY. Yeah, well. How come the white uniform—you a nurse or somethin'?

LU ANN. Nurse? Hell no, ah'm a beauty technician.

CORKY. No kiddin'.

LU ANN. That's right. Ah got me a diploma from the Sanford School of Beauty Culture over there in San Angelo.

CORKY. Well now, that's real fine.

LU ANN. Sure is. Ah went to night school, took me twelve whole months.

CORKY. Twelve months?

LU ANN. That's right. I probably could have finished a whole lot sooner if it weren't for that worthless Dale Laverty.

CORKY. Your husband?

LU ANN. Mah *ex*-husband. Ah'm divorced.

CORKY. Ah see.

LU ANN. You married?

CORKY. Ah was once.

LU ANN. What happened?

CORKY. Oh, ah don't know, Peggy Sue and ah jest never seemed to git along. Seemed like ever'time I was fixin' to move in, she was fixin' to move out. Never could get it together.

LU ANN. Boy, ah know what you mean there, buddy. With me and Dale it was trucks and trailer houses! You ever live in a goddamned trailer house?

CORKY. Nope.

LU ANN. Boy, you ain't missed nuthin'. Cramped, miserable little old tin-boxie outfits—burn up all summer and freeze off all winter. No room to do a damned thing in. Dale would blow a fart and my eyes would water for three days.

CORKY. Sounds like a helluva home life.

LU ANN. Oh, man, it was de-loox. Stay out at them damned trailer parks, might as well live on a tumbleweed farm. Two or three burnt-up little old trees, a couple of splintery teeter-totters, and five hundred rattlesnakes.

CORKY. Rattlesnakes?

LU ANN. You bet your life, *rattlesnakes!* Hell, they used to crawl up under that goddamned trailer house like they owned it.

CORKY. Jesus!

LU ANN. You said it, pal.

CORKY. Why the hell didn't you move into a real house?

LU ANN. Old Dale said he didn't want to be tied down. "Wanna be movin' around," he said, "free as a bird." Boy, there's a laugh for you. We moved from San Angelo to Snyder and that was it. That trailer sat in the Shady Grove Mobile Home Park until the tires rotted off. Hell's fire, that was no way to live. 'Specially after Charmaine come along.

CORKY. Charmaine?

LU ANN. Mah little *girl*. Ah didn't tell you ah had a little girl, did ah?

CORKY. No.

LU ANN. Well, she's just the prettiest little thang around, that's all. Good as gold, never no noise or trouble, no, sir, not even when she was a baby. Didn't even cry at night.

CORKY. Whattayou know.

LU ANN. Well, anyways, here ah was stuck out at the Shady Grove in Snyder with a little baby girl to look after and nuthin' to do all day but hunt rattlesnakes with an O'Cedar mop.

CORKY. What was Dale doin' all this time?

LU ANN. Dale! Hell, he was always off deliverin' cattle for the goddamn Hubbard Brothers. Be gone weeks at a time in that damn truck of his. Then when he was home that's all he could talk about. Trucks. God, ah got sick of it. Kenworth, Mack, Reo, White, GMC, International, hell, you'd think they was presidents of the United States or somethin'. I never went nowhere and he'd come home and gas about all the places he'd been. So one boozy evenin' when he was home lappin' up the Jim Beam and talkin' about the new shower baths at the Top of the World truck stop in Moriarty, New Mexico, ah went right through the roof. "Listen, you flap-mouthed son of a bitch," ah said, "if that cattleshit-smellin' semi you got out in the yard there means more to you than me and li'l Charmaine, why don't you jest haul your butt into the cab and boom on outta here for good."

CORKY. What happened?

LU ANN. He did it! Slammed out of the trailer, ground about fourteen gears, knocked over the mailbox, ran over our mangy collie dog, and took off down the road. Never saw him again—he didn't even show up at the divorce trial.

CORKY. So you come on back here, huh?

LU ANN. Yep. Buried the dog, sold the trailer, picked up Charmaine, and come on home to Bradleyville.

CORKY. That's a damn shame.

LU ANN. What is?

CORKY. Your marriage breakin' up and all that.

LU ANN. Oh, hell, nuthin' to trouble yourself about. Ah think it was probably for the best.

CORKY. Think so?

LU ANN. Sure. Ah'm doin' okay. Got a good job over to the beauty shop, drink a few beers now and then, watch the television, you know.

CORKY. Shore, shore. Ever git the itch to go on any moonlight truck rides?

LU ANN. Long or short haul?

CORKY. Either way you want.

LU ANN. No, thanks. From now on, ah go by automobile or not at all.

CORKY. You're an automobile goer, are you?

LU ANN. Sometimes. What kinda car you got?

CORKY. Chivy.

LU ANN. What year?

CORKY. Bran'-new Impala.

LU ANN. Good model. Hey, remember when they had them step-down Hudson Hornets?

CORKY. Shore do.

LU ANN. There was a helluva car. The fella ah went with in high school had one of them. Boy, we went ever'where in that thang. Step down and saddle up.

CORKY. Lots of leg room, huh?

LU ANN. It was a damn-good car. Went to the senior picnic in that car. Jesus, you shoulda seen ever'body's head turn.

CORKY. Big day, huh?

LU ANN. The best. Gawd, ah'll never forgit it. Me and the captain of the basketball team in a great old big shiny Hudson. Hot damn!

CORKY. Well, ah never owned no Hudson, but ah did have me a Kaiser once.

LU ANN. A Kaiser!

CORKY. A Kaiser. A great old big Kaiser with a silver buffalo-head hood ornament.

LU ANN. God, them was ugly cars.

CORKY. Ugliest cars in the world. They ain't never made anythin' bigger and uglier than my old green Kaiser. Hell, ah bet that damn thing weighed five ton, got about two miles to the gallon, and burned more oil than the *Super Chief.* I had a wreck in that damn thing once—hit an Oldsmobile head on.

LU ANN. What happened?

CORKY. Totaled that damned Olds, tore it to pieces. Put the block right in the backseat, and that Kaiser? One broken headlight. That's right, one broken head-light! That Olds was totaled and the Kaiser only had a broken headlight. That car was by Gawd built. Solid, you know.

LU ANN. They built 'em good back then.

CORKY. Damn right they did. A buddy of mine nearly killed me with that car one time.

LU ANN. How come?

CORKY. Well, we was goin' deer huntin' one year, me and a bunch of guys. Couple of us took a pickup and loaded ever'thin' in the back—the tent, the bedrolls, the rifles, some boxes of chow, all that crap, and took off, with the rest of the guys followin' in my Kaiser. Well, sir, we was movin' on down the road drinkin' six-packs of Pearl and generally jackassin' around when old Len Hanawald, who was drivin' my Kaiser, decided he'd race us. Hell, that car wouldn't do more than sixty goin' straight downhill, but old Len hit the horn and around us he comes.

Well, sir, ah leadfooted that pickup and take him like he's standin' still—about a quarter of a mile down the road ah come to this intersection with a great old big stop sign lookin' right at me. So bein' a good citizen, ah screech to a halt. Ah no sooner get stopped when something makes me look into the rearview mirror and all ah can see is this silver buffalo comin' right at me. Ah mean, the whole rear-view mirror is nuthin' but a big silver buffalo. Next thing ah know, Len has piled into the back of the pickup at sixty fat miles an hour. Hell, we scattered bedrolls, .30-30's, and Campbell's pork and beans all over West Texas. Put mah head smooth through the windshield. Sixteen stitches.

LU ANN. Jeeezus!

CORKY. Knocked out all mah front teeth. These are false. Look real, don't they?

LU ANN. Shore do. Whatever happened to that car?

CORKY. The Kaiser? Oh, ah gave it to mah brother when ah went into the army and he tore it up someway.

LU ANN. That's a damn shame. You got a dime?

CORKY. Yeah. (*He gives her a dime, she plays the jukebox. Song comes on low.*)

LU ANN. Ah got a brother that's pretty good at tearin' up things too.

CORKY. Cars?

LU ANN. *Lives.*

CORKY. Lives!

LU ANN. That's right, pal, lives! His life, mah life, our mama's life. You recollect that king that ever'thin' he touched turned to gold?

CORKY. King Midas?

LU ANN. That's the dude. Well, mah brother, Skip, has a touch too, only ever'thin' he touches goes bad. Cain't hold no job, on the goddamn bum all the time, livin' off my mama like a leech. Now he's flat on his can in the hospital with a cut throat.

CORKY. Was that your brother that did that?

LU ANN. That's the fella. Old playboy Skip. Anythin' for a laugh.

CORKY. Ah've never heard of such a thing. Cuttin' his own throat! Jesus, that makes me goose-pimply jest thinkin' about it. What's wrong with him, is he crazy or somethin'?

LU ANN. No. No, ah don't think Skip's crazy, he jest cain't seem to catch hold of anything, that's all—never seemed to get started. Never married, never held on to a job very long. Jest sorter hung around year after year boozin' it up and dreamin' up big plans.

CORKY. What kind of plans?

LU ANN. Oh, all kinds of plans. Catfish farmin', aluminum siding, uranium pros-pectin', real estate, anythin' that would make a quick buck. Hell's fire, he even went into the chinchilla business.

CORKY. Oh, good God.

LU ANN. Was gonna make a fortune. Built a bunch of cages in the storeroom and bought him some chinchillas. Nuthin' to it, he says. Feed 'em a little alfalfa and let 'em breed away.

CORKY. Sounds easy enough.

LU ANN. Oh, hell yes! He had 'em about a month when the first norther blew in. Course Skip was off drunk somewhere and didn't plug in the 'lectric heater he had in there to keep 'em warm, so they all froze. Poor little old things all humped up in them wire cages froze stiff. Skip came back home and tried to skin 'em, but it was too late then.

CORKY. What kinda work does your brother do now?

LU ANN. Pumps gas over to the Texaco station when he's sober. Aw, to hell with him. Tell me some more about yourself.

CORKY. Well, ah was over to . . .

> (*The door opens and* MILO CRAWFORD *makes a furtive entrance. He glances nervously around.*)

MILO. Hello.

CORKY. Howdy.

LU ANN. Well, ah'll be damned. If it ain't old Milo Crawford.

MILO. Hello. Is, uh, is Red around anyplace?

CORKY. He's out back. *(Calling out.)* Hey, Red, you got a customer.

RED. *(From offstage.)* Tell him to keep his shirt on for a minute, damnit!

MILO. *(Very low.)* No hurry, Red.

LU ANN. Well, how you been there, Milo?

MILO. Oh, fine, jest fine.

LU ANN. Good. *(There is a long pause while* MILO *bumbles around.)*

MILO. Ah beg your pardon, miss, but do ah know you?

LU ANN. Why, of course you do, Milo. My Gawd, we went to high school together.

MILO. Oh, ah see. *(He doesn't.)*

LU ANN. Ah was Lu Ann Hampton.

MILO. You mean you ain't anymore?

LU ANN. Well, no, Milo, ah got married. Mah name is Laverty now.

MILO. Oh, ah see. *(He goes up to* CORKY.*)* Is this Mr. Laverty?

CORKY. Mr. Laverty?!

LU ANN. Good God, Milo, git your head back in the socket! You still don't know me, do you?

MILO. Well, to tell the truth, no, ma'am, ah don't. But Mr. Laverty here looks kindly familiar.

CORKY. Goddamnit, ah ain't Mr. Laverty!

LU ANN. For Christ's sake, Milo, you ain't got the sense God gave a tumblebug.

RED. *(Entering.)* What can ah do for you . . . *(He spots* MILO.*)* What in the name of hell!

MILO. *(Grinning and fawning around.)* Howdy there, Red.

RED. Whattayou doin' in here, Milo, the church burn down or somethin'?

MILO. No, ah, nuthin' like that, Red.

RED. Uh-huh. You know, Milo, if your mama knew that you was in here, she'd flat bust a gusset. She ain't dropped dead or nuthin' like that, has she?

MILO. Oh no, Mama is in real fine health, thank you.

RED. Well, was there anythin' you wanted?

MILO. Oh, ah don't know. Let's see, uh, Miller, Schlitz, Bud, Pearl, uh-huh. All them is kinds of beer, ain't they?

RED. That's right, Milo.

MILO. Ah see. You don't sell Dr Pepper, do you?

RED. No, Milo, we don't.

MILO. Well, then, uh, how about a pack of them potato chips?

RED. Comin' right up, Milo. That'll be fifteen cents.

MILO. They're only a dime over to the drugstore.

RED. Well, this ain't the goddamned drugstore! Now, do you want 'em or not?

MILO. Yes, sir.

RED. Well?

MILO. Well, what?

RED. Milo, don't tell me you have defied God, your mama, and the First Baptist Church to come in here and buy a damned pack of potato chips. Now what the hell else do you want?

MILO. Oh, ah come over here to see if you-all wanted to contribute to the Jaycees' Beautify Bradleyville Campaign.

RED. You're a Jaycee nowadays, are you, Milo?

MILO. Yes, sir, and ah am on the committee to visit the store owners and git them to make a contribution so's we can beautify Bradleyville.

LU ANN. You the same bunch of fellas that put the statue of Colonel Kinkaid in the city park?

MILO. *(With great pride.)* Yes, ma'am, that was us all right.

LU ANN. Ugliest damn thing ah ever saw in mah life.

RED. That damned statue is so ugly even the pigeons won't shit on it. What the hell you monkey nuts got in mind for beautiful this year, Milo?

MILO. The, uh, money goes to repair the cemetery wall.

RED. Oh, it does, does it.

MILO. Yes, the old one is a disgrace to the community. It's full of cracks and splotches and spidery things.

RED. Well, now ain't that a goddamned shame.

MILO. Yes, it is. *(He pulls out a small notebook.)* Now, what can ah put you down for?

RED. Nuthin'.

MILO. Nuthin'?

RED. That's right, pal, nuthin'. N-U-T-H-I-N. As far as ah'm concerned, that splotchy, cracked, old spidery wall is damned fine with me. It's got by God character. Lots more character than this damn town has. Bradleyville. Jesus, how ah ever wound up in this burnt-out collection of cowboys and tumbleweeds is beyond me. For two cents ah'd sell this damn dump and haul ass back to Meridian, Mississippi, where ah by God belong.

MILO. We'd sure hate to see you go, Red.

RED. Oh, hell, yes, you would. You and your mama and the rest of the damn Baptists would hold a regular wake if ah left, wouldn't you? Have a damn parade most likely, with all the goody-goodies on one side of the street and all the booze-soaked, beer-swillin', fat-gutted winos on the other. After ah'm gone, you-all can put up another statue in that patch of dirt you call a city park, make it even uglier than the one of that senile old idiot Colonel Kinkaid. And on the base you can put this-here inscription, *Red Grover, he hated ever' minute of it.* Now, get on outta here, Milo. Ah'm tired of lookin' at you.

MILO. Well, gawlee, Red, ah . . .

RED. Now wait a minute, Milo. Come to think of it, there is somethin' you can do for me.

MILO. Why sure, Red. Ah'd be happy to do anythin' ah can.

RED. Well, sir, you go on back down to that Jaycee meetin' and tell them god-damned deadbeats to git over here and pay their goddamn beer tabs, and ah'll give you enough money to put up a splotchy wall plumb around the whole town of Bradleyville.

MILO. Well, that, uh . . . we, uh . . . they . . .

RED. Now git your ass outta here. Ah got work to do!

MILO. Ah'm goin', ah'm goin'. Ah guess ah better be goin'. It sure was nice to meet you, uh, Mr. and Mrs., uh . . .

CORKY. If you say *Laverty* ah'm gonna belt you!

MILO. Well, uh, no . . . Ah mean . . .

RED. Git outta here!

MILO. Well, it's shore been nice. *(Crosses back for the potato chips.)*

RED. Git!

>    *(MILO exits in a hurry.)*

LU ANN. *(Laughing.)* Old Milo Crawford, by God, he ain't changed in ten years.

RED. *(Muttering.)* Bloated checker players, drunken maniacs, and by-God, bumble-dickin' Jaycees.

>    *(He exits.)*

CORKY. Jest exactly what the hell was that, anyway?

LU ANN. That was a Milo Crawford.

CORKY. You got any more like that around this town?

LU ANN. Naw, old Milo's one of a kind, thank God.

CORKY. Oh, ah don't know. Mah boss over to Abilene would have run him a close second.

LU ANN. Is that a fact?

CORKY. Damn right. God, was ah happy to transfer out of there.

LU ANN. How long you been with the highway?

CORKY. 'Bout eight years.

LU ANN. Red says you're an inspector. What do you inspect?

CORKY. Dirt.

LU ANN. What kinda dirt?

CORKY. The kinda dirt they put on the highway affore they shoot asphalt all over it.

LU ANN. Uh-huh. What else?

CORKY. What else what?

LU ANN. What else do you do?

CORKY. That's it.

LU ANN. Just go around lookin' at dirt?

CORKY. What's wrong with that?

LU ANN. Well, I don't know, it jest seems kindly piddlin'.

CORKY. What do you mean piddlin'? It's a damned important job.

LU ANN. What's so damned important about lookin' at dirt?

CORKY. *(Patiently.)* If the grade of fill underneath the asphalt isn't right, you get holes in the highway, that's what's so damned important about dirt.

LU ANN. Well, you must be doin' a pretty piss-poor job. Ever' goddamned highway in this state is as holey as Billy Graham's mother-in-law.

CORKY. Well, goddamn! What the hell do you know about anythin'. Goddamn beauty operator.

LU ANN. Beauty *technician*, you dumb, dirt-lookin' gourd-head!

CORKY. Dirt-lookin' gourd-head! By God, woman, you can git plumb nasty sometimes.

LU ANN. My mama once told me there was nuthin' nasty about the truth.

CORKY. Oh yeah? Your mama ever say anythin' about sittin' around beer bars and pickin' up strangers!?

LU ANN. Pickin' up strangers! Ah'm not the one that walked in here and said, "Why, looky here, Red, who in the world is this pretty little thing?" Hell, that-there line went out with the by-God *zoot suit.*

CORKY. Yeah, well, ah guess ah jest ain't as up-to-date as the rest of your boy-friends in this dump.

LU ANN. They ain't so bad. Git your nose out of the asphalt someday and maybe you'll learn somethin'.

CORKY. Aw, to hell with it! *(He starts out.)*

LU ANN. Yeah, that's right, go on and go!

CORKY. I'm goin' all right. I'm goin' over to my place, take a shower, change clothes, crank up my old Chivy, and come over to your place and take you out to supper.

LU ANN. You are?

CORKY. Damn right! Where do you live?

LU ANN. 301 North Grand.

CORKY. Seven okay?

LU ANN. Fine with me.

CORKY. Good. Ah'll see you at seven. We'll go over to Big Spring.

LU ANN. Suits me.

CORKY. See you then. *(He starts to exit, then stops and turns.)* Oh, uh, wear somethin' pink, will you?

LU ANN. Pink! What the hell for?

CORKY. Ah like pink, it's a nice color.

LU ANN. Well la-de-da. Lemme tell you somethin', pal, old Peggy Sue mighta been a vision of loveliness in pink, but old Lu Ann in pink looks like somethin' you win at a carnival.

CORKY. Oh, well, hell with it, wear what you want then.

LU ANN. Thanks bunches.

CORKY. Seven, right.

LU ANN. Right. *(He exits. She stands watching the door for a moment, then calls out.)* Hey, Red!

RED. *(Entering.)* Whattayou want?

LU ANN. What kinda name is Oberlander?

RED. Hell, I don't know. German?

LU ANN. Yeah, maybe so. Hum, Oberlander—Corky Oberlander, by gollies, that's a right pretty name, don't you think?

RED. Who gives a damn.

*Curtain*

# ★ ACT III

*The time is 1973 in the Hampton home. There are few changes in the furnishings—new slipcovers, maybe, and a television set in place of the radio. The rabbit ears on top of the set are covered with aluminum foil.*

*As the scene begins,* CHARMAINE *is lying on the sofa reading a magazine. She is the Act I image of* LU ANN. *Small, blond, and pretty. She wears a miniskirt and a sweater. Her transistor radio blares out rock music. The upstage door opens and* SKIP *appears. Time, wear, and booze have taken their toll of* SKIP. *His hair has grayed, he wears thick glasses, and his hands shake. Across his neck is the scar from his suicide attempt, which he makes no effort to conceal. He wears a faded flannel shirt and oversized pants. He crosses to the table and sits down.*

SKIP. For Christ's sake, Charmaine, turn that damn thing off. My head's flat splittin' in two.

CHARMAINE. Aw, go to hell!

SKIP. Aw, please. My head hurts. Ah'm sick.

CHARMAINE. That's tough!

SKIP. I'm gonna tell your ma. Jest see if ah don't.

CHARMAINE. Who gives a damn.

SKIP. Aw, please. That noise is killin' me.

CHARMAINE. Oh, all right. *(Clicks off the radio.)*

SKIP. How you kids can stand that noise is beyond me.

CHARMAINE. Maybe it's because we don't stay up all night messin' up our heads with fortified Thunderbird.

SKIP. I wasn't drinkin'! Ah ain't touched no wine in a long, long time.

CHARMAINE. Shore, shore.

SKIP. It's the God's truth.

CHARMAINE. Then how come you were in the bathroom all mornin' with your head in the commode. Hell, they could hear you gaggin' plumb over to Big Spring.

SKIP. A lot you know, a lot you know. When you drink for a long time and then stop, your stomach shrinks up and you get the mornin' sickness.

CHARMAINE. The mornin' sickness! You're crazy; the only people that gits the mornin' sickness is pregnant women.

SKIP. You're the one that's crazy. Pregnant women git the varicose veins, that's all.

CHARMAINE. The varicose veins?

SKIP. It's caused by lack of iron in the blood cells.

CHARMAINE. Boy, are you dumb—whoever told you that?

SKIP. Ah saw it on the television.

CHARMAINE. That's the dumbest thing ah ever heard.

SKIP. Ah saw it, ah tell you.

CHARMAINE. Oh, you never saw nuthin'. You were probably jest havin' them delirium tremors again.

SKIP. Ah ain't never had them things!

CHARMAINE. Oh no? What about the time you said the bullfrogs was after you?

SKIP. Ah don't remember nuthin' about it.

CHARMAINE. That had to be one of the funniest things ah ever seen in mah life. "Help, help, the whole house is full of bullfrogs."

SKIP. You're makin' this all up.

CHARMAINE. "Git 'em off me, git 'em off me! The whole house is full of bullfrogs!"

SKIP. Keep it up, Miss Smarty Pants, just go on and keep it up and ah'm gonna tell on you.

CHARMAINE. Who gives a hoot what you tell.

SKIP. I know somethin'. Boy, do I know somethin' on you.

CHARMAINE. You don't know nuthin' at all.

SKIP. Oh yes, ah do.

CHARMAINE. Oh—yeah, like what?

SKIP. Like what you and Charles Black was doin' out to Lake Bradleyville last Saturday afternoon.

CHARMAINE. You weren't out there.

SKIP. Ah was so, too.

CHARMAINE. Weren't.

SKIP. Was too. Ah was helpin' old Bowdwin Cassidy out to his bait stand and ah seen you.

CHARMAINE. Boy, what a big fat lie.

SKIP. It ain't either.

CHARMAINE. It just so happens that Charles and me was parked plumb across the lake from Bowdwin's bait stand, so you couldn't have seen a danged thing.

SKIP. Oh no? *(He mimes putting a pair of binoculars to his eyes.)* Peek-a-boo.

CHARMAINE. Do you mean to tell me that you and that damned smelly old Bowdwin Cassidy stood around and spied on Charles and me through binoculars!?

SKIP. Gotcha there, don't I; boy, I really gotcha there.

CHARMAINE. Ah oughta slap your ears off you! You dirty old sneak.

SKIP. You better not try nuthin' like that or ah'll tell. Ah'll tell what me and Bowdwin seen.

CHARMAINE. Well, go ahead. Nobody's gonna believe an old busybody like Bowdwin, and ever'body knows you're crazy.

SKIP. Ah'm not neither.

CHARMAINE. Stupid as a cattle guard. Crazy Skip Hampton.

SKIP. You shouldn't oughta call me names that way.

CHARMAINE. Ever'body in town calls you them names—jest because you're my uncle, ah don't see why ah cain't. *(Shouts out the window.)* Crazy Skip Hampton!

SKIP. Them people in town calls me them names 'cause they're skeered of me.

CHARMAINE. Skeered of you! Boy, that's a hot one. Man, there ain't nuthin' skeered of you.

SKIP. They are skeered of me 'cause ah have killed people.

CHARMAINE. Baloney!

SKIP. In the war, ah killed 'em in the war, lots of people!

CHARMAINE. Run for your lives, ever'body, here comes crazy old Skip.

SKIP. Don't say that! Lu Ann told you not to call me that no more.

CHARMAINE. And the Crazy Man Award of 1973 goes to Skip Hampton!

SKIP. I'm gonna tell your mama on you!

CHARMAINE. Why don't you tell my daddy, you and him was big pals in the Civil War or somethin', why don't you tell him?

SKIP. Ah don't know where he is anymore. He used to come and visit me sometimes, but ah don't know where he is anymore.

CHARMAINE. Well, ah know where he is. Ah went and seen him one time.

SKIP. Aw, you never either.

CHARMAINE. Ah did so, too! Ah heerd that he was workin' for Hubbard Brothers over to San Angelo, so ah got Charles Black to drive me over there and ah seen him.

SKIP. You shouldn't have done that.

CHARMAINE. Why not? Ah got a right to see mah own real daddy, ain't ah? Anyways, ah never talked to him or nuthin'. Ah jest had a feller point him out to me and ah seen him, that's all.

SKIP. How did he look?

CHARMAINE. Fat.

SKIP. Fat?

CHARMAINE. That's right. Old, fat, and kind of dumb-lookin', you know. God, what a letdown. Ah don't know what ah was lookin' for, but it damn sure weren't no dumb fat slob, leanin' up agin a smelly old semi smokin' a cigarette and probably thinkin' about nuthin' at all.

SKIP. Now, listen here, Charmaine. Dale was one damned good old boy and don't you forgit it.

CHARMAINE. Don't forgit it? Aw, cool it, Uncle Bullfrog, ah already have. *(She goes back to her magazine.)*

> *(LU ANN appears on the front porch carrying two large bags of groceries. Now in her late thirties, LU ANN is stouter and mellowed. Her beauty is placid and matronly. She wears a white uniform with her name over the pocket; on the back of the uniform is a blue wagon wheel with "Howdy Wagon" printed around it.)*

LU ANN. Somebody open the door.

CHARMAINE. *(To SKIP.)* You do it.

SKIP. Do it yourself, smarty pants.

CHARMAINE. Go to hell!

SKIP. Same to you!

LU ANN. Somebody open this damn door!

SKIP. Okay, okay, ah'm comin'. *(He opens the screen door.)*

LU ANN. Thanks. *(Crossing to the kitchen.)* Ah heard loud voices comin' outta here. You two ain't been fightin' again, have you? *(She enters the kitchen.)*

SKIP. Ah'm gonna tell on you.

CHARMAINE. Who cares.

SKIP. You got that dress on she don't like.

CHARMAINE. So what!

LU ANN. *(Entering the room.)* Whooee, ah'm bushed! Charmaine, get off your lazy can and put them groceries away.

CHARMAINE. Aw hell.

LU ANN. Git!

CHARMAINE. Oh, all right. *(Getting up.)*

LU ANN. What are you doin' with that damned miniskirt on?

CHARMAINE. Ah'm only wearin' it around the house.

LU ANN. Well, you better. If ah catch you outside in that thing, ah'm gonna paddle somebody's mini butt!

CHARMAINE. Oh, God, Mama, you are absolutely crude. *(She goes into the kitchen.)*

LU ANN. Right on, sister! *(She sits on the sofa and removes her shoes.)* Oh, mah aching feet. Hell, ah bet we said howdy to fifteen new families today.

SKIP. Big Spring is shore gittin' big.

LU ANN. Shore is. You look in on Mama today?

SKIP. Yeah. She's okay.

LU ANN. Give her any dinner?

SKIP. Shore, shore.

LU ANN. Empty her bedpan?

SKIP. Ah don't like to do that.

LU ANN. Ah know, ah know. But it's got to be done.

SKIP. Ah don't like it, Lu Ann, ah really don't. It makes me throw up.

LU ANN. Well, ah'll do it later.

SKIP. Mah stomach jest turns over and over and . . .

LU ANN. Ah'll take care of it after supper. What did you do today?

SKIP. Oh, nuthin'. Watched the television for a while.

LU ANN. Anythin' good on?

SKIP. Henry Fonda was on the afternoon Old West Movie.

LU ANN. That's nice. You, uh, you didn't feel sick again, did you?

SKIP. No.

LU ANN. Well, if you feel up to it tomorrow, that front grass shore needs a good mowin'.

SKIP. Ah'll git on it first thing. Ah was thinkin' too that ah could clear out a little patch over by the shed and put us in some tomaters and okrie.

LU ANN. Fine.

SKIP. We could have 'em fresh off the vine, wouldn't that be nice?

LU ANN. Shore would.

SKIP. Shore. Ah'm gonna git right on that. First thing in the mornin'. Uh, Lu Ann, seein's as how ah'm gonna do all that tomorrow, do you think that maybe tonight you could, uh, maybe?

LU ANN. No! No money, Skip.

SKIP. Well, no, no. Ah was jest thinkin', if ah had maybe a dollar or somethin', ah could have me mah supper over to the Dixie Dinette, then you won't have to go through no trouble a-fixin' me nuthin'.

LU ANN. Now, you know ah keep a tab down there so's you can git you a cheese-burger or a chicken-fried anytime you want. All you gotta do is sign for it.

SKIP. Well, ah know, but maybe if ah go over to Rufe Phelps's place to play a little dominoes, then ah could use a little money, don't you reckin?

LU ANN. Now, Skip honey, you know ah cain't give you no spendin' money.

SKIP. *(Whining with childish logic.)* Why not? Why cain't ah? Ah ain't gonna do nuthin' bad. Why ain't ah even have a dollar in mah pocket? A by-God dollar to buy somethin' with, somethin' ah see in the store—a Coke or a Mars Bar or somethin'. Play a little dominoes or maybe go to the picture show. Jest some pocket change to rattle, buy some cigarettes outta the machine, git me an ice-cream soda or a magazine there at Billberry's Drugstore. Jest stuff like that, Lu Ann, that's all. Ah won't buy me no wine, no, sir, not even a beer. They won't let me in Red's place no more. They won't even let me in the door. How can ah git a drink when ah cain't even git in the door? No, ma'am, there jest ain't no way.

LU ANN. You said all this before, Skip. Said you didn't want a drink and couldn't git one. But you did git it, honey, cain't you remember? You got enough to put you in the state hospital in Terrell. You wanna go back up to Terrell?

SKIP. No! No, ah don't wanna go there no more. It was ugly there and them doc-tors was mean. They put me in a little room and it was cold. They put me in a cage like them chinchillas ah had once. You recollect them chinchillas, Lu Ann, and when it was cold?

LU ANN. Sure, honey. Ah remember, but that's all over now, all gone. We ain't gonna talk about them mean times anymore, are we?

SKIP. No, no more mean times.

LU ANN. Wanna watch the television for a while? The Country Jubilee Show'll be on tonight.

SKIP. No. Ah think maybe ah'll go on over to the dinette for mah supper, but ah'm not gonna have no cheeseburger or chicken-fry, ah'm gonna have me an en-chilada, then ah'll sign the tab. Sign the tab jest like you said. You know, Lu Ann, it's a funny thing how things boil down, ain't it?

LU ANN. Whattayou mean, Skip?

SKIP. When all that stands between a man and the by-God loony bin is his sister's tab down to the Dixie Dinette.

CHARMAINE. *(Entering from the kitchen.)* My Gawd, you know, we got them big red piss ants under the sink again?

LU ANN. Ah'll pick up some bug killer tomorrow.

CHARMAINE. Terrific. Maybe Uncle Skip will chug it down with his mornin' bowl of Cream of Wheat.

LU ANN. Charmaine, that's enough of that. Now, if you got schoolwork to do, why don't you go on up to your room and do it.

CHARMAINE. Can ah take mah radio with me?

LU ANN. Ah don't care. Jest don't play it too loud—you might disturb your grandma.

SKIP. She won't do her homework if she's got that radio.

CHARMAINE. You got to hell!

SKIP. You hear that? Cussin', cussin' at me!

LU ANN. Now that's a by-God 'nuff!

SKIP. She's got that skirt on that you don't like.

CHARMAINE. He's always pickin' on me!

LU ANN. Git on upstairs!

CHARMAINE. Ever'body picks on me! What the hell kinda chance do ah have around here anyway, what with a crazy uncle, a dumb-lookin' daddy, and the god-damned Howdy Wagon for a mama!

*(She turns and exits, slamming the door.)*

SKIP. She went over to San Angelo and saw old Dale.

LU ANN. Yeah, I know. Charlie Black's mama told me about it.

SKIP. She said he was fat and dumb-lookin'.

LU ANN. Yeah, well. What'd she expect me to find here in Bradleyville in 1953, the by-God King of England? *(Pause.)* Ah thought you was goin' on down to the dinette.

SKIP. Ah'm goin', ah'm goin'. You know, Lu Ann, ah was thinkin' it might be nice if ah could maybe leave a little tip.

LU ANN. Oh, for Christ's sake!

SKIP. It would be nice now, and you know it. Leave maybe fifty cents there on the counter.

LU ANN. Git on outta here—ah'm tired of lookin' at you.

SKIP. Ah'm goin'.

*(A figure approaches the porch—*SKIP *sees him and stops.)*

LU ANN. Well, what's keepin' you?

SKIP. Somebody's comin'.

LU ANN. Probably one of Charmaine's skinny boyfriends.

SKIP. Nope, it's a grown man. *(There is a knock at the door.)*

LU ANN. I'll git it. *(She walks to the door.)* What can ah do for you?

BILLY BOB. Mrs. Oberlander?

LU ANN. Yes.

BILLY BOB. Mrs. Lu Ann Hampton Oberlander?

LU ANN. Mrs. Lu Ann Hampton *Laverty* Oberlander, if you want the whole damn handle. Who are you?

BILLY BOB. Ah'm Billy Bob, Billy Bob Wortman.

LU ANN. Billy Bob! Well, Jesus Christ on a crutch. Come on in this house and let me look at you. *(She opens the door and lets* BILLY BOB *in. He wears a black suit and horn-rimmed glasses. His hair is stylishly mod and he now sports a small mustache.)* Lookee here, Skip, it's old Billy Bob—the old preacher-boy himself.

SKIP. *(Shaking hands.)* Howdy, Billy Bob.

BILLY BOB. Hello, Skip, how are you?

SKIP. Fine, fine.

LU ANN. Well, sit down, Billy Bob, or do we call you Reverend nowadays?

BILLY BOB. No, no, just Billy Bob. Plain old Billy Bob. *(He notices* LU ANN'*s bare feet—she sees this and scurries back to her chair to put her shoes on.)*

LU ANN. Well, sit down, plain old Billy Bob. Make yourself at home. God, it's good to see you.

BILLY BOB. Well, it's marvelous to see you, Lu Ann.

LU ANN. *Marvelous?* Listen to that, Skip, listen to mah little old high-school boy-friend usin' them big words.

SKIP. Sounds pretty good.

LU ANN. You wanna cup of coffee or somethin'?

BILLY BOB. No, nothing, thanks.

LU ANN. Sit down, Skip. Quit hangin' around back there.

SKIP. Ah better be gittin' on down to the dinette, Lu Ann. *(To* BILLY BOB.*)* Ah'm havin' me an enchilada tonight.

LU ANN. *(Rising and crossing to him.)* Now, Skip, you're comin' right on home now, hear me?

SKIP. Yeah, ah'll be right on back in.

LU ANN. Well, don't . . . you know.

SKIP. Ah know, ah know. See you all later.
   *(He exits.)*

LU ANN. *(Looking out of the door.)* God, ah hope he don't . . .

BILLY BOB. I know about Brother Hampton's illness, Lu Ann.

LU ANN. Yeah, well, it's nuthin' to trouble yourself about there, Billy Bob.

BILLY BOB. It's my job to trouble myself, Lu Ann.

LU ANN. What? Oh, hell, ah plumb forgot about you bein' a preacher, Billy Bob. My goodness, imagine that. Well, let me look at you. By gollies, that little old mustache is a dandy, ain't it?

BILLY BOB. Yes, well, my congregation rather likes it: it gives me some dignity, don't you think?

LU ANN. Oh, shore. It shore does.

BILLY BOB. I didn't think you'd recognize me with it on.

LU ANN. Oh pshaw, Billy Bob, ah'd know your old hide if ah saw it hangin' on a fence post. Sit down.

BILLY BOB. Yes, thank you.

LU ANN. You know, Billy Bob, ah was real proud to hear you had graduated over there at the Texas Christian University. Ah was livin' in Snyder at the time and my mama wrote me all about it, even sent me the clippings from the *Bradleyville Record.*

BILLY BOB. Well, that's nice.

LU ANN. Oh, shore. Ah even read about you gittin' married. You married a Fort Worth girl, didn't you?

BILLY BOB. Yes, I met Maxine in school. She's a fine woman.

LU ANN. Well, ah jest bet she is. Now, let's see, you have three or is it four children, Billy Bob?

BILLY BOB. Four. Four fine boys.

LU ANN. Well, ain't that nice.

BILLY BOB. You just have the one girl, don't you?

LU ANN. Yes, little Charmaine. Well now, listen to me say *little* Charmaine. She's nearly a growed-up woman now.

BILLY BOB. How old is she?

LU ANN. Seventeen. Can you imagine?

BILLY BOB. My, my.

LU ANN. Yes, she's a chore sometimes, but mostly she's a blessin'. Ah've really got a kick outta watchin' her grow up. Spoiled the devil out of her. But, shoot, what are kids for if it ain't to spoil a little bit?

BILLY BOB. Yes, my boys can be quite the little rascals sometimes too.

LU ANN. Ah wish sometimes that Corky and me coulda give her a little brother or sister—but, well, it jest weren't meant to be.

BILLY BOB. Yes, my mother wrote me about the accident—a real tragedy.

LU ANN. Yes, it was, we wasn't married but a couple of years when it happened. He was out on the job, you see, when his pickup was hit by one of them road machines.

BILLY BOB. Was he killed instantly?

LU ANN. No, he lived for about six or eight hours. Course he was busted up so bad there weren't much hope. They got him over to the county hospital and he passed away there. Ah got to see him once affore he died.

BILLY BOB. That was a blessing.

LU ANN. Yes, it was. They had him in a room with these curtains all around. Poor old Corky, he was all bandaged up with tubes and bottles all over him. When ah got there he opened his eyes and moved his hand a little bit and sorter motioned to me, so ah bent down close to his head and he whispered to me real low like, "Lu Ann, Lu Ann, it hit me again, a buffalo, the biggest goddamn buffalo ah ever seed."

BILLY BOB. What did he mean?

LU ANN. Oh, it was just sort of an old joke we had.

BILLY BOB. You ever think of marrying again?

LU ANN. Oh, Lordy, no. Right after Corky was killed, Mama had her stroke and ah jest sorter settled in to look after her. Ah had already quit my job at the beauty shop so ah got me this-here job drivin' the Howdy Wagon over to Big Spring.

BILLY BOB. You like the work?

LU ANN. Shore. Course ah gotta drive over there of a mornin', but it's not far. And then I like meetin' new people. We git names of new folks movin' into town, you see, and then we drive the Howdy Wagon over to their house and hand out these-here free coupons.

BILLY BOB. What are they good for?

LU ANN. Why, all sorts of thangs. Free bucket of Colonel Sanders' Kentucky Fried Chicken, two free bundles of wash at the washateria, free round of minia-ture golf, five gallons of Fina gasoline, six-pack of Coors beer . . . oops, shouldn't of said that, ah reckin.

BILLY BOB. That's okay.

LU ANN. Well, anyway, all sorts of thangs like that. It's to help the new folks git on to the town, you see.

BILLY BOB. Yes, I understand.

LU ANN. Where do you live now, Billy Bob?

BILLY BOB. Kansas City.

LU ANN. Well, think of that. How do you like the big-city life?

BILLY BOB. We like it very much. I have a fine church there, fine congregation.

LU ANN. Well, ah jest bet you do.

BILLY BOB. Yes, it's nice to be settled down for a while. I'm afraid I've put my family through quite some strain moving around all these years. You knew that I was in missionary work, didn't you?

LU ANN. Ah heard somethin' about it.

BILLY BOB. Oh, yes, indeed. We're here for a little visit. So when I heard you were in town, why, I just had to look you and your mother up. You're about the last of the old high-school gang that's still left around.

LU ANN. Yeah, nobody stays in the little towns anymore.

CHARMAINE. *(Offstage.)* Mama, I cain't work these goddamn algebra problems!

LU ANN. Well, figger it out for yourself. I got company down here.

CHARMAINE. Who?

LU ANN. Billy Bob Wortman.

CHARMAINE. Who the hell's that?

LU ANN. An old friend of mine from high school.

CHARMAINE. Big deal! *(Sound of a door slamming.)*

LU ANN. Confounded kids. Come out on the porch, Billy Bob, ah believe it's a little cooler.

BILLY BOB. Fine. *(They stand for a moment looking out.)* Bradleyville. Do they still put the Christmas lights on the water tower every year?

LU ANN. Shore.

BILLY BOB. I guess nothing much has changed in town, has it?

LU ANN. Oh, we have a few new things.

BILLY BOB. Sure enough?

LU ANN. Uh-huh. The Dairy Queen put in a new parking lot and the drive-in's got *two* screens now.

BILLY BOB. Boy, old Pete Honeycutt would have loved that.

LU ANN. Yeah, ah reckon. Let's see now, the bank's got a whole new front on it, and then of course there's always Mumford County Estates.

BILLY BOB. What's that?

LU ANN. Oh, that's a lake-development outfit we got out to Lake Bradleyville.

BILLY BOB. Really?

LU ANN. Shore. Floyd Kinkaid and Clarence Sickenger got 'em a whole bunch of homes and boathouses and such-like out there.

BILLY BOB. Well, that's progress, I guess.

LU ANN. Shore is. They were gonna put 'em in a golf course but they couldn't get the grass to grow!

BILLY BOB. You know, it's funny, Lu Ann, but I never figured you would stay here in Bradleyville.

LU ANN. Ah did leave once. Got as far as Snyder. Aw, I don't know, Billy Bob, ah spoze ah never did think much further than this-here town—never hankered to. You recollect that time when you and me was spozed to go on the senior picnic and ah run out on you and went to San Angelo with old Dale Laverty?

BILLY BOB. I'll never forget it—my heart was broken for a whole week.

LU ANN. Well, ah think maybe it was then that mah life jest sorter dug itself in. Kindly found its little hollow to stay in. You went on to the college and all them other places, but I jest started a-standin' still. Ah run out on a picnic and ran straight into a rut, you might say—even old Corky couldn't pull me outta it, bless his soul.

BILLY BOB. Oh, I don't know, Lu Ann, there isn't really a lot more in the big cities that isn't right here in Bradleyville.

LU ANN. How's come you never played any basketball while you was there at T.C.U.?

BILLY BOB. My word, you had to be good to play ball there. I was just a little old Bradleyville boy, just wasn't up to snuff.

LU ANN. But you was good, Billy Bob, you was real good.

BILLY BOB. Oh, not really.

LU ANN. But ah recollect you playin' over to Snyder that time—mah, how I used to cheer for you. You recall that, Billy Bob, and the time you-all dyed your hair green?

BILLY BOB. Well, that was a long time ago.

LU ANN. You know, mah mama once told me that them times would be the happiest of mah life, and lookin' back on it all, ah believe she mighta been right. Lordy, but it was fun, wasn't it, Billy Bob? The pep rallies, the bonfires, all them dances . . .

BILLY BOB. Paintin' up them posters when Pete Honeycutt ran for president of the senior class.

LU ANN. Mary Beth Johnson, Eveline Blair, and me leadin' the cheers. Goin' over to the Billberry's Drugstore after the home games with Pete and Ruthie Lee Lawell . . .

BILLY BOB. For chocolate Cokes.

LU ANN. That's right! Pickin' on poor old Milo Crawford. Remember all that, Billy Bob? You know, sometimes when ah'm here alone, ah get out my old Bradleyville High yearbook and just go through it lookin' at them pictures and rememberin'. You ever do that?

BILLY BOB. It's a waste of the Lord's time to dwell on the past, Lu Ann.

LU ANN. Oh, pshaw. The Lord's got lots of time to waste. It's us the clock runs down on! You know, Billy Bob, it's a funny thing, but ah'm about the same age mah mama was when you and me was in high school. My God, ain't that somethin'? It's like ah was her and Charmaine was me and ever'body around us got old and different lookin'.

BILLY BOB. Am I so old and different lookin'?

LU ANN. Oh, no, no, of course not. That's one thing about dwellin' in the past. People you loved back then stay the same. You're still old sweet-smilin', goof-off, green-headed Billy Bob Wortman. That preacher suit and mustache don't fool me none.

BILLY BOB. Yes, well. I haven't really got a lot of time left, Lu Ann. Do you think I could see your mother now?

LU ANN. Why shore. My gosh, here ah am runnin' off at the mouth as usual. Ah'll bring her right on out. We keep her in the downstairs bedroom now because of the wheelchair. *(She goes to the up-center door.)* She don't recognize people much any more, so don't feel bad now if she don't know you.

BILLY BOB. Yes, of course, I understand.

> *(*LU ANN *exits.* BILLY BOB *looks at his watch and fidgets about the room. He glances through* CHARMAINE's *magazine and drops it distastefully.* LU ANN *reenters with* CLAUDINE *in the wheelchair. Her hair is totally white, her waxen hands lie limply on her lap. The stroke has paralyzed one side of her face, and uncontrollable saliva drools from her mouth.* LU ANN *wipes away the saliva from time to time with a clean handkerchief.)*

LU ANN. Here we are. You got a visitor, Mama. Billy Bob Wortman's come all the way from Kansas City for a little visit, ain't that nice? You remember Billy Bob Wortman, don't you, Mama?

BILLY BOB. How are you, Mrs. Hampton?

LU ANN. Why, she's jest as fine as she can be, aren't you, Mama? Be up and outta this old wheelchair just any old day now. Don't you know Billy Bob, Mama? Mah old boyfriend from high school, he's come a long way to see you and say howdy. *(*CLAUDINE *gives no sign of recognition at all; simply stares straight ahead.)*

BILLY BOB. *(Taking* CLAUDINE's *hand.)* Hello there, Mrs. Hampton, how are you? *(Nothing—he drops her hand.)* Can she speak at all, Lu Ann?

LU ANN. No, not a word since her stroke. Ah think that's the biggest shame of the whole business, her not bein' able to talk, 'cause that's one thing Mama loved to do. Couldn't sew, hated to cook, and never read nuthin' but the funny papers, but, oh my, how she loved to talk.

BILLY BOB. Will she be like this from now on—I mean, what do the doctors say?

LU ANN. They say she ain't never goin' to come outta this, not on this earth anyway. So ah jest keep her clean an' fed and ah look after her the best way ah kin.

BILLY BOB. You know, Lu Ann, there are homes for people in her condition. I could look into the church home in Sweetwater if you like.

LU ANN. This is her home, Billy Bob.

BILLY BOB. Well, yes, I know, but it must be a terrible burden.

LU ANN. Aw, it ain't so bad, at least thisaway the burden is mostly on my body—if ah sent her off somewhere, the burden would be on my heart. You know, Billy Bob, them doctors told me that Mama would be a vegetable for the rest of her life—can you imagine that? A vegetable! Hell, my mama ain't no vegetable, she's a flower, a great old big pretty flower.

BILLY BOB. Yes, a creature of God.

LU ANN. You bet.

BILLY BOB. Well, Lu Ann, I really must be going now.

LU ANN. Yep, ah speck them boys will be a-missin' their daddy.

BILLY BOB. It was fine to see you again, Lu Ann.

LU ANN. Well, it was all mah pleasure, Billy Bob. Don't be such a stranger anymore; you come on back anytime and bring the missus and them boys, you hear?

BILLY BOB. Yes, I'll do that. Well, goodbye, Lu Ann, and may the Lord stay by your side.

LU ANN. So long, Billy Bob, and may, uh . . . may you have lots of luck. *(BILLY BOB exits.* LU ANN *stands for a moment watching out the screen door, then she turns and comes back into the room.)* Well now, weren't that somethin', Mama? Who would have guessed that one day old Billy Bob would have him a church way up in Kansas City. Jest cain't ever tell, can you, Mama? Jest cain't ever tell. Oh, hell, look at the time, we done missed most of the Country Jubilee. *(She crosses to the television.)* You know, Mama, if ah'd have played mah cards right ah probably could have been Mrs. Billy Bob Wortman today. That's right, missionary's wife way up there in Kansas City, helpin' to spread the Word. *(She giggles.)* But, you know, Mama, ah jest never could cotton to that boy's name. Billy Bob Wortman. Why, it's jest plain silly-soundin'. *(She flicks on the set. The lights dim as the twang of country music floods into the room.)*

*Curtain*

# Mary Rohde

★ ★ ★ ★ ★ ★ ★ ★ ★ ★ ★ ★ ★ ★ ★ ★ ★ ★ ★

★   THE PERSON

Mary Rohde was born in 1949 in Alamo Heights, Texas, and grew up in that elegant northern suburb of San Antonio. During her early education she was fortunate to come under the influence of Bill and Frances Swinny, he as a teacher and drama director at Alamo Heights High School and she as a professor of speech at Trinity University. From first one and then the other, Rohde received encouragement and sound grounding in theater arts and voice. Graduating from Trinity University in 1971 with a B.A., she spent a year of discovery in New York as a neophyte actress, auditioning, playing small parts, and taking classes—testing her talent and commitment in that most competitive of theatrical environments. She now considers that year invaluable because it gave her growing time and a sense of independence before she returned to Texas to continue her formal education.

In 1972 Rohde began graduate study at the Dallas Theater Center, where she matured as an actress and playwright. In fact, it was the unique organization of the educational program there that was responsible for her beginning to write for the stage. Required on admission to select an alternative concentration to acting, she chose playwriting, almost capriciously, then proceeded to meet the strict standards for entrance set by the playwriting professor, Eugene McKinney. In addition to McKinney's instruction, Rohde benefited from the example of the success of her colleague Preston Jones and from his generous assistance. Like him, she received a Rockefeller Foundation Playwright-in-Residence Fellowship. Just as his works had first attracted national attention at the Theater Center's 1974 Playmarket showcase of new plays, her *Ladybug, Ladybug, Fly Away Home*, in the words of the critic John Lahr, "scooped the pool" at the 1979 Playmarket. His trilogy played Kennedy Center and so also, as the only invited professional offering at the 1980 American College Theater Festival, did her well-received play.

After earning her M.F.A. in 1976 from Trinity University, the Dallas Theater Center's academic affiliation at that time, Mary Rohde became a member of the center's Resident Professional Company. She taught classes in acting and in voice and diction and distinguished herself as an actress in many major roles, including Kathy in *Vanities*, Masha in *The Three Sisters*, Celia in *As You Like It* (in which she very nearly overshadowed the actress playing Rosalind), and Rosealee in *Remember*.

In 1982 Rohde moved to Shreveport, Louisiana, where her husband, Michael Scudday, had accepted a position as the director of a community theater. After several successful years there the family returned to Texas in 1985. Michael now works with a theater supply company based in San Antonio; and Mary, enjoying living in the neighborhood where she grew up, fits her acting and writing careers around the demands of her young daughter and her part-time position with a nearby Montessori school.

★ THE PLAY

One of the most impressive facts about *Ladybug, Ladybug, Fly Away Home* is that it is a first play, a thesis project, by an author less than thirty years old from a sheltered background. Yet it is a tough-minded play that deals uncompromisingly with a major theme of twentieth-century drama. Margie Lynn Bunton, the central character, has deserted her husband and infant child several months before the play's action begins. In act 1, scene 2, she returns to Polly, Texas, and her family to "straighten things out"—without any clear idea of what that will entail but drawn by a pull of the blood. She is a Texas version of Ibsen's Nora Helmer, who so shocked the world of the late nineteenth century by deserting her husband and children at the conclusion of *A Doll's House* in order to discover who she is as a whole person rather than as a supplementary figure to father and husband. But Margie Lynn is different from, and in at least one way is an artistic improvement over, Ibsen's heroine. Actresses playing Nora have always had to struggle to correlate Ibsen's child-wife of the first two acts with his icy rationalist of the last scene, the woman who sets her husband down and explains point by point why her leaving is necessary. Margie Lynn, much more convincingly, can neither understand nor satisfactorily explain her actions. When she tries, her lines echo those of thousands of rebellious teenagers of the American sixties and seventies who compulsively rejected conventional roles and passionately embraced alternative behaviors, often of destructive nature.

The play is feminist in some but not all ways. The male characters are either shadowy off-stage presences, such as Margie Lynn's father, Darrell, and his surrogate, the Major, or clichés, such as Jimmy, the long-suffering husband, and Jack, the boorish uncle. In contrast, the three generations of women in the Kayro family are developed much more fully and sympathetically. The emotional bonds connecting mother, grandmother, and daughter receive major emphasis, and even the sisterhood of whores that Margie Lynn has joined is depicted as mutually supportive. There is, however, no overt politicizing of feminist stances and no strident rhetoric. No doctrinaire solutions are offered for the social problem the play deals with. The play depicts the problem as broadly human rather than gender specific. Mary Rohde has said that she writes plays about women, but not "women's plays," and her practice bears this out.

In addition to the intense struggle of the central character to make an acceptable independent life for herself without rejecting the parts of her heritage that remain valuable to her, the play has other appealing features. Most noticeable is the atmosphere of the small-town beauty parlor, what the *Houston Chronicle*'s drama critic Ann Holmes called "an ammonia-scented little universe" when she nominated *Ladybug* for the American Theater Critics Association 1978–79 Award for Best New Play produced outside New York. Her description, which is included in Otis Guernsey's *The Best Plays of 1978–1979*, continues, "Customers under the dryers at Mama Alice Kayro's shop [The Lovely Lady], cantankerous and overly curious, regale and pry, but set the tone of the town where watching and telling is a preoccupation."

As well as serving as a device for comedy and social comment, the beauty parlor constitutes a convincing link among the play's women characters of various generations and moral persuasions. Margie Lynn is fulfilled by her clandestine return to The Lovely Lady beauty shop at 4 A.M. It is an environment that suggests to her not only scenes of privileged childhood play but also early introductions to female rites and an atmosphere of womanly free expression impossible in mixed company. The whores pamper themselves with shampoos and lotions in the same shop that has given comparable pleasure to the town's respectable matrons during the day.

Many successful comic moments derive from the conflict of manners and styles that result from the incursion of the Major's free-wheeling prostitutes into the precincts of Polly, Texas. Different codes of language and dress provide plentiful opportunities for amusing misunderstandings and embarrassments. Although the girls C. C. and Ginger are stereotypes—one naive and simple, the other tough and savvy—their lines are fresh enough and the pace of the play quick enough to provide a satisfying evening of high-spirited entertainment.

After its initial 1978 production in the Dallas Theater Center's small Down Center Stage, under the direction of Chris Hendrie, *Ladybug, Ladybug, Fly Away Home* was redone, again in cramped quarters, for the 1979 Playmarket. Finally, in January 1980 it was given a full-scale production, again under Hendrie's direction, in the Kalita Humphreys Theater. Featured were Eleanor Lindsay and Cheryl Denson, who had originally created the roles of Margie Lynn and Mama Alice. Also appearing were Mary Sue Jones, who played Eula, and Mary Rohde's husband, Michael Scudday, who played Jack.


★   THE WORKS

Like others who have combined acting and writing careers, Mary Rohde has had to balance the demands of the two for time and creative energy. Since her marriage and the birth of her child about five years ago, both acting and playwriting have played a smaller part in her life, although to keep theatrically active she has seized the opportunities that have presented themselves. In 1981 she wrote and acted in a dramatic introduction to the San Antonio opening of the Texas Women in History exhibit. During the summer of 1987 she and Cheryl Denson, another Dallas Theater Center alumna, played the leads in *A Coupla White Chicks Sitting Around Talking* at the Strand Theater in Galveston, Texas. Rohde currently has an idea for a new play, but at present her dramatic works in addition to *Ladybug* consist only of *Keeper of the Home Fire*, a play set among theater people, and a share of *Pageant*, a collaborative musical about beauty pageants. *Keeper* was performed by the Shreveport Little Theater in June 1986, and *Pageant* was presented by the Arkansas Repertory Theater in Little Rock, Arkansas, in February 1988 and has toured extensively since then.

## LIST OF WORKS

PLAYS

*Ladybug, Ladybug, Fly Away Home,* 1978
*Keeper of the Home Fire,* 1985
*Pageant* (contributing author), 1988

RECOMMENDED READING

Holmes, Ann. "Ladybug, Ladybug, Fly Away Home." In *The Best Plays of 1978–1979,* edited by Otis L. Guernsey, Jr. New York: Dodd Mead and Company, 1980.
Hoyle, Mary Lou. "The Director's Words." In program for production of *Ladybug, Ladybug, Fly Away Home* at Texas Woman's University, October 23–26, 1986.

# Ladybug, Ladybug,
# Fly Away Home

★ ★ ★ ★ ★ ★ ★ ★ ★ ★ ★ ★ ★ ★ ★ ★ ★

# CAST OF CHARACTERS

MAMA ALICE KAYRO, the grandmother, the owner of The Lovely Lady.

TISH KAYRO, the mother, the peacemaker.

MARGIE LYNN KAYRO BUNTON, the daughter, the runaway.

JACK KAYRO, the uncle, a loser, moving from one woman to another like an alcoholic needing one more drink.

JIMMY BUNTON, the husband, unable to understand his own ignorance.

C.C., the friend, after all the things that money can buy.

GINGER, the call girl, not an original thought in her head.

SHORTY, the old friend, the owner of the local beer hall.

EULA SIMMONS, Jimmy's aunt, filled with Baptist self-righteousness.

# ★ PRE-SHOW

*As the audience is entering the theatre,* SHORTY *and* EULA *are already seated under the dryers. The radio in the shop is tuned to a country-western station. The lights in the shop are not up to full. All of the pre-show dialogue is very easy, sometimes lines overlapping each other as though the actors were improvising the scene.* MAMA ALICE *enters from the sink room.*

MAMA ALICE. *(Speaking over the noise.)* Oh my Lord, it's hot! How you doing under there, honey? You think you're dry yet?

SHORTY. *(Shouting.)* Shoot, Mama Alice, my back is already plastered to this chair . . .

MAMA ALICE. Well, let's get you out and have Tish check you. Come on.

SHORTY. My stars, it's warm . . .

MAMA ALICE. I know it. Tish, Tish, honey. Come on out here and check Shorty, she thinks she's dry.

SHORTY. *(Seated in styling chair.)* You think I'm dry?

MAMA ALICE. *(Seated on stool next to* SHORTY.*)* I don't know, honey. (TISH *enters from the sink room.)* Check her, see if she's dry yet, honey.

SHORTY. Ooohwee . . . I'm just wet all over.

TISH. Oh no, Shorty, you're not near ready, still pretty damp. Best get back under.

SHORTY. Oh hell.

MAMA ALICE. Well, why don't you stay out for a little while, cool off a bit. It won't hurt.

TISH. You want something to drink, Shorty?

MAMA ALICE. Oh yeah, that's what I want, one of those pops.

SHORTY. That does sound good.

TISH. What kind you want, Shorty?

SHORTY. Better bring something low-cal.

TISH. O.K. Dr Pepper?

MAMA ALICE. That'd be fine. Sugar-free D.P.
   *(*TISH *exits to the back room.)*

SHORTY. Got to watch my girlish figure, you know.

MAMA ALICE. Oh shoot, who are you kidding? Bet you'd love a beer right now.

SHORTY. Well, hell, yes.

MAMA ALICE. Wouldn't Eula just die if she saw us sitting up here putting away a few? *(They both laugh, glance at* EULA, *who's dozed off under the dryer.)* Would you look at her?

TISH. *(Entering.)* Here you go.

MAMA ALICE. Oh thank you, honey, boy this is just what I needed.

SHORTY. Thank ya, Tish.

TISH. You're welcome, Shorty.

SHORTY. Oh Tish, I was wanting to ask you, you got anything for dry skin? My ole face is so dry, it's about to peel right off.

TISH. You mean like a facial cream or something?

SHORTY. Yeah, something. My skin is just terrible.

TISH. How about some Aloe Vera?

SHORTY. Aloe who?

TISH. Aloe Vera, it's real good for dry skin. Really helps your pores.

MAMA ALICE. Is that that stuff comes from a plant?

TISH. Comes from a cactus, it's a kind of . . .

SHORTY. A cactus?

MAMA ALICE. Yeah, a damn plant.

TISH. What d'you say I give you a trial facial next time you come in?

SHORTY. Well, I don't know.

TISH. Next time you come in. I bet it would really help. O.K.?
    *(She exits to the sink room.)*

SHORTY. Well, O.K., honey. I guess we could give it a try.

MAMA ALICE. I swear she's on a nature kick. That damn beauty supply salesman has been pushing all these "back to nature" things, you know. Gets you to putting cucumber cream on your face, wash your hair with avocado shampoo . . .

SHORTY. My Lord, Mama Alice, I don't want to smell like a salad. *(They both laugh.)*

MAMA ALICE. Oh hell, Shorty. Tish will buy anything from that damn salesman.

SHORTY. I like that shampoo that smells like that fruit though.

MAMA ALICE. Yeah. That strawberry mess, smells pretty good don't it? *(Sniffs* SHORTY's *hair.)* Yeah, smells just like strawberries.

SHORTY. Yeah, I like that.

MAMA ALICE. *(As she gets a cigarette out of her case.)* Hey, I haven't showed you this yet, have I? Guess where I got this?

SHORTY. I don't know, Mama Alice.

MAMA ALICE. Oh come on . . . now guess where this come from.

SHORTY. You sent off to Walter Drake.

MAMA ALICE. No. It was a present. Guess who gimme this.

SHORTY. *(Pause.)* I don't know. Who?

MAMA ALICE. Jack's two little boys.

SHORTY. They did?

MAMA ALICE. Yeah. Those two little towheaded kids. Nancy Joe, you remember Nancy Joe . . . well she sent this and there was a note inside, you know, written by those little boys. It said Grandma, that's what they call me, Grandma. Grandma, light up the world.

SHORTY. *(Laughing.)* You're kidding?

MAMA ALICE. I am not. Now ain't that cute. Light up the world.

SHORTY. You know, Jack was sure cute when he was a little kid.

MAMA ALICE. Oh yeah . . . hard to tell though under all the dirt. I swear he was the dirtiest little boy. Used to set that damn army blanket up outside, over a clothesline. Go out there, stay under that thing, called it his tent. My Lord, one hundred degrees and he'd be under that wool blanket, come inside, sweat and dirt just pouring off of him. Oh but he was having fun, don't you know. *(They laugh.)* Damn army blanket.

SHORTY. *(Laughing.)* Well, he has always been a ringed-tail toot. *(They both take a swig of their soft drink at the same time.)*

MAMA ALICE. You know, I wish I had a TV in this shop. I could hang it up on the wall, you know, like at those motels. We could watch all our programs . . .

SHORTY. You'd have to get some of those, those earplugs, Mama Alice, so's you could hear under the dryers.

MAMA ALICE. Well shoot yeah, wouldn't that be deluxe. Then we could watch Mike Douglas.

SHORTY. You see that program the other day when they had all those child stars on?

MAMA ALICE. Child stars? No, I must a missed that one.

SHORTY. Oh it was real interesting. Talking about how difficult it was growing up in Hollywood, all the problems, you know, being a star . . . drugs and married to all those different people.

MAMA ALICE. D'you see it the other day when they had on that silly-ass little girl . . . oh what was her name, you know . . . every time she talked she shook. *(Demonstrates by shaking.)* Wooooooo . . .

SHORTY. Oh yeah, what was her name? *(They both think.)* Cherry.

MAMA ALICE. No, that's not it. *(Pause.)* Charro.

SHORTY. That's it, Charro.

MAMA ALICE. *(Demonstrating again.)* Wooooo . . . *(They both laugh and drink their soda pop.)*

TISH. *(From the back room.)* Mama Alice, you started mixing that solution yet?

MAMA ALICE. Oh yeah, honey, I'm working on it right now.

SHORTY. Shoot. She works you too hard, Mama Alice.

MAMA ALICE. Oh ain't that the truth.

SHORTY. *(Laughing.)* Shoot.

TISH. You better get Shorty back under that dryer, she'll never get dry . . .

MAMA ALICE. Oh she's already back under, honey . . . yeah, she's fine.

SHORTY. Oh hell's bells . . . don't you go gettin' me in trouble.

MAMA ALICE. Well, I guess you'd better get your head back in the cooker.

SHORTY. Oh Lord. *(MAMA ALICE helps her back under the dryer.)*

MAMA ALICE. There you go. You O.K.?

SHORTY. *(Shouting over the noise of the dryer.)* Yeah . . . I guess.

MAMA ALICE. *(She goes over to the counter and dusts her hands with baby powder before putting on some thin rubber gloves.)* You know, this always reminds me of that doctor, on that TV show, oh what was his name? Used to put on his gloves like this before the big operation.

SHORTY. Oh yeah, I remember him.

MAMA ALICE. You know . . . real handsome fella.

SHORTY. *(Pause.)* Dr. Kildare.

MAMA ALICE. No, not that wimpy little shit, you know . . . the one with all that black hair, used to wear that flap down on his coat . . . show off all that curly black hair . . .

SHORTY. Oh I know the one you're talking about . . .

MAMA ALICE. Oooohwee . . . wuddint he somethin'. Oh damn, what was his name . . . ?

SHORTY. Casey.

MAMA ALICE. Dr. Ben Casey. Dr. Ben Casey.

SHORTY. That's right . . . Dr. Ben Casey.

MAMA ALICE. Oh my Lord . . . he was pretty. What is it the kids are always saying . . . he switched me . . . no . . . he turned me on.

SHORTY. Yeah.

MAMA ALICE. He turned me on. *(She laughs.)* And that ain't as easy as it used to be. *(They both laugh.)*

TISH. *(Still in the back.)* Mama Alice, are you almost through with that solution, you know . . . ?

MAMA ALICE. Oh yeah, honey . . . got it goin' darlin' . . . workin' on it right now.

SHORTY. Oh hell.

MAMA ALICE. You hush and get your head back under that dryer.

*(The members of the audience should all be seated now. The house lights are out, and the stage lights are up to full.)*

# ★ ACT I

*It is mid-August and the temperature has reached well over one hundred degrees for five days straight in this town of Polly, Texas, located just southwest of San Antonio.*

*Onstage is a duplex with a front porch. On one side is the home of* MAMA ALICE KAYRO *and on the other is her beauty shop, The Lovely Lady. It is an old wooden frame house in need of some new paint, and out front are many potted plants. The living room furniture is old, except for a new large color TV. The beauty shop equipment is also old. The hair dryers have the old metal hoods and make a lot of noise when running. There is a back room to the shop where the sinks are and where the supplies are kept.* MAMA ALICE *is pouring smelly permanent wave solution from a larger bottle into smaller ones. She has her hair ratted into a monstrous beehive and the rinse has turned her gray hair rather blue. Her pants are a rainbow of bright colors and she wears fluffy pink bedroom slippers.*

SHORTY. *(Speaking over the noise of the dryer.)* Lord, Mama Alice, what is that stuff?

MAMA ALICE. Permanent wave solution.

SHORTY. It's what?

MAMA ALICE. *(Louder.)* The stuff that curls your hair.

SHORTY. Yeah, I figured that's what it was. Smells like it. That for your $12.50 permanent?

EULA. You give a $12.50 permanent?

MAMA ALICE. *(Calling to the back room.)* Tish . . . Tish, let's order three more gallons of this Golden Curl Wave solution.

TISH. *(Entering and wiping her hands on a towel.)* We order that from the beauty supply in San Antonio, don't we?

MAMA ALICE. Coker's Barber and Beauty Supply on McCullough.

EULA. Tish, this is too hot. *(She tries to adjust the knob on the front of the hood.)* I'm awfully warm under here.

TISH. *(Speaking so she can be heard over the dryer.)* All right, Eula, I've turned it down. If it's still too hot just holler. *(*EULA *smiles and nods in agreement.)*

SHORTY. Tish, mine too, honey, too hot.

MAMA ALICE. Tish, better turn that damn air conditioner on high. I bet it's a hundred degrees outside. *(The phone rings in the shop and also in* MAMA ALICE'S *living room.)* And turn that radio off, honey. I'll get the phone. Lovely Lady . . . hello Mrs. Krausey . . . yes ma'am, for three o'clock this afternoon . . . no, no, she didn't . . . yes, well all right . . . you get to feelin' better and you call me for another appointment . . . all right, I know . . . yes, now you call me . . . O.K. dear, goodbye.

TISH. She break her appointment again?

MAMA ALICE. Says her daughter was supposed to call me yesterday. *(She lights a cigarette.)* She really expect me to believe that?

SHORTY. Who called?

TISH. *(Loudly.)* Mrs. Krausey.

SHORTY. Kathryn Krausey? That poor thing. Her arthritis is something awful. How she gets around at all is amazing. What she want?

TISH. *(As* TISH *takes* EULA *from the dryer.)* She broke her appointment. I think you're dry now, Eula.

SHORTY. Figures.

EULA. Are you sure? I think it's still too damp.

MAMA ALICE. Eula, you hardly have enough hair to wash; it don't take that long to dry.

SHORTY. You think I'm about done?

TISH. Almost, Shorty . . . few more minutes.

EULA. *(To* TISH.*)* That's not her real name, is it?

MAMA ALICE. Shorty, Eula wants to know your real name.

SHORTY. My what?

MAMA ALICE. Your real name, besides Shorty.

SHORTY. *(Laughs.)* Eleanor Marie.

MAMA ALICE. *(Laughing.)* You're kidding?

SHORTY. Now ain't that a kicker? *(To* EULA.*)* I've always been called Shorty. 'Cause I'm so little, petite. My older brother started calling me Shorty before I can even remember and it just sorta stuck.

MAMA ALICE. Tish was scared to death that Margie Lynn would never see five feet.

EULA. Tish is scared of what?

MAMA ALICE. *(Louder.)* I said, Tish thought Margie Lynn was gonna be real short.

SHORTY. *(At the mention of* MARGIE LYNN's *name,* SHORTY *looks a little surprised.)* Yeah, she grew a whole bunch once she got into high school, seems like.

MAMA ALICE. She sure did. Almost two inches in one year, didn't she, Tish? *(*TISH *does not answer.)* I always thought she'd be real tall like her daddy.

SHORTY. How tall is Darrell?

MAMA ALICE. About six feet three inches, I think. He's a good bit taller than Jack.

EULA. I heard that Jack got married again.

MAMA ALICE. Yeah, to some girl in Wichita Falls. Lord, I hope he stays with this one awhile.

SHORTY. Where's Darrell working now, Tish?

TISH. *(Quietly.)* Odessa.

SHORTY. Where?

TISH. In McCamey, out near Odessa.

SHORTY. Working on a rig?

TISH. Yeah.

SHORTY. What?

TISH. Yes, for the McKinley Brothers.

EULA. He sure is out of town a lot. Bet that makes it awful hard on you, don't it, Tish?

TISH. No, I'm used to it. Darrell's been working on oil rigs as long as I've known him.

EULA. Bet he misses that little grandson of his?

MAMA ALICE. He sure does . . . adores that little boy, don't he, Tish?

EULA. How is David Edward? I mean with his mother gone and . . .

TISH. He's fine, just fine.

EULA. You know, Tish, if you ever need some help, I'd be more than happy to keep the baby sometime.

TISH. That's very sweet of you, Aunt Eula, but . . .

EULA. Really, it wouldn't be no trouble for me, and I'd get to see Jimmy again. He used to spend so much time out at the farm. We became very close after my sister passed away. Of course, with all that's happened, I know he's been very busy. *(Pause.)* Did you know Harvey Winder's practically made him a partner at the garage?

MAMA ALICE. I didn't know that. When did all this happen?

EULA. Last week, Jimmy said.

MAMA ALICE. Well what do you know. And I thought Ole Man Winder might close that place down.

EULA. That garage is doing a lot more business now that Jimmy is working there full-time.

MAMA ALICE. Right after his son was killed in that car wreck.

SHORTY. Who was killed?

MAMA ALICE. Harvey Winder's son.

SHORTY. Yeah, car accident. Tragic, real tragic.

EULA. Jimmy was always a good mechanic. His mother swore he could fix anything.

SHORTY. Mama Alice, you need some new magazines around here. I'm getting damn tired of reading about Liz and Dick's first divorce.

TISH. Jimmy's a real hard worker.

EULA. Yes, poor darling, sure hasn't been easy for him. *(Pause.)* I mean his mama dying and then . . . well.

TISH. I know, Eula.

MAMA ALICE. What's Jimmy's dad doing these days? I heard a rumor that he's remarried—that true?

EULA. After Carla died, my brother-in-law insisted on moving to El Paso . . . Jimmy, of course, decided to stay with me.

MAMA ALICE. I knew that. Did he marry some lady out there?

EULA. Yes, I believe he did.

MAMA ALICE. Does Jimmy know this?

TISH. Well, I'm sure he does, Mama Alice, probably just hadn't gotten around to telling us, that's all.

MAMA ALICE. Maybe.

TISH. There, Eula.

EULA. Don't you think the top is a little too full? *(She pats it down.)*

MAMA ALICE. You could use a little fullness, Eula.

EULA. You know, Tish, I really like the way you do Daizel Corey's hair. Do you think you could style mine more like hers? I mean, well, next time maybe?

MAMA ALICE. Daizel Corey has a lot more hair than you do, Eula. She's got more hair and more kids than anyone in Polly.

EULA. *(With great relish.)* And I think she's expectin' again.

SHORTY. Who's expectin'?

MAMA ALICE. Daizel Corey.

SHORTY. Figures. *(She begins to doze off under the dryer.)*

MAMA ALICE. How do you know she is, Eula? She tell you this?

EULA. She didn't have to tell me. I work in the church office every Monday, Tuesday, and Wednesday and so does Daizel . . . but not this week. Called in sick.

TISH. Oh Eula . . . that doesn't necessarily mean she's pregnant.

EULA. Daizel Corey is never sick unless it's morning sickness.

MAMA ALICE. That's right.

TISH. There . . . you like that better, Eula?

EULA. *(Still not really satisfied.)* Yes, well, I guess that will do.

   (JIMMY BUNTON *appears on the front porch, peers in the window, then comes in the shop.)*

TISH. *(Surprised.)* Well hello, Jimmy.

MAMA ALICE. My heavens, Jimmy, we haven't seen you in a month of Sundays.

JIMMY. *(Very uncomfortable, not expecting to see his aunt,* EULA.*)* Hello everybody.

EULA. Hello, honey. Were you looking for me? I'm finished now, all finished. How much do I owe you, Tish?

TISH. I'm not gonna charge you, Aunt Eula, you know that. You're one of the family now.

JIMMY. *(Quietly.)* You don't have to do that, Tish.

TISH. Of course I don't have to . . . but I want to.

MAMA ALICE. Well what can we do for you, Jimmy? I know you didn't come in here for a manicure.

JIMMY. *(Nervously.)* I don't know, Mama Alice . . . can't seem to ever get this grease off my fingers.

MAMA ALICE. *(Laughs.)* Well, you can make an appointment anytime.

EULA. You like my hair this new way, honey?

JIMMY. *(Not noticing anything different.)* You curled it?

EULA. Tish cut it . . .

JIMMY. It looks real nice. *(EULA smiles.)*

MAMA ALICE. Is this a social call, Jimmy, or do you need something?

JIMMY. *(Hesitantly.)* I want to ask a favor.

EULA. What do you need, Jimmy?

JIMMY. Tish, can you keep David Edward tonight? *(*TISH *and* EULA'S *lines overlap.)*

EULA. Oh is that all. I can keep the baby . . .

TISH. Of course I can, Jimmy.

JIMMY. I'm going into San Antonio, pick up some stuff for Mr. Winder. I'll be back late probably.

TISH. Don't you worry about it. I'll pick up little David from Mrs. Ramos's.

EULA. Mrs. Ramos? She takes care of the baby?

TISH. She keeps him during the day sometimes.

EULA. Jimmy, why don't you let me look after David Edward? I'm his great-aunt . . .

JIMMY. Aunt Eula . . . you know it's better that he spends as much time with me as he can. Tish only lives four blocks from me and Mrs. Ramos just lives . . .

EULA. Just who is this Mrs. Ramos?

MAMA ALICE. She's a babysitter, Eula. Very nice lady, speaks two languages.

TISH. Eula, I appreciate your offering; Jimmy and I both do, but we're really doing fine.

MAMA ALICE. You know, Jimmy, you sure look like you could use a haircut.

JIMMY. *(Quickly.)* No I don't. *(*MAMA ALICE *smiles.)* Well, I better get on the road. Thanks again, Tish.

EULA. Jimmy, I need to talk to you. In private.

JIMMY. All right, Aunt Eula. Bye Tish . . . Mama Alice.

MAMA ALICE. Bye Jimmy . . . don't wait so long next time, we never see you anymore.

TISH. Bye Jimmy.

EULA. Wait a minute, honey—I've got to get my bag. *(She starts out the door.)*

SHORTY. *(Waking up.)* Oh bye Eula. You come into town more often . . . *(*EULA *leaves.)* Bye dear. Oh good Lord, I've just got to be dry by now. I'm cooked through and through.

MAMA ALICE. Shorty, Jimmy was just here. You slept right through it.

SHORTY. Jimmy? Well why didn't you wake me? He come to see his Aunt Eula?

TISH. He came to see me.

SHORTY. What'd he want?

TISH. He wanted me to keep the baby tonight since he's got to make a trip into San Antonio.

SHORTY. Oh I bet Eula loved to hear that.

MAMA ALICE. She took Jimmy outside to talk to him, in private.

SHORTY. Oh poor Jimmy.

MAMA ALICE. That woman is the true test of my patience.

SHORTY. Yeah, it's a good thing she lives eighteen miles out of town or she'd be telling all of us how to live our lives in person instead of over the phone.

MAMA ALICE. *(Laughs.)* Ain't that the truth!

SHORTY. Lord, Lord—things have really been rough for him. First his mother dying of cancer. Did you know Carla only weighed eighty-eight pounds when she died? Lingering on for months like she did. Jimmy's daddy used to come into my bar almost every night after he'd been over to the hospital. He came close to a nervous breakdown himself, if you ask me.

MAMA ALICE. Your bar wasn't the only place he was hitting every night.

SHORTY. You're talking about that cocktail waitress at the Rocket, aren't you?

MAMA ALICE. She went to high school with Margie Lynn.

SHORTY. I thought she moved to Waco.

MAMA ALICE. Yeah, after Jimmy caught his daddy with her out at Eula's farmhouse.

SHORTY. After he what?

MAMA ALICE. I thought you knew.

TISH. Mama Alice, please, you have no proof that it ever happened. Jimmy has never said . . .

MAMA ALICE. Jimmy would never say anything to anybody, no matter what he saw. You remember when Jimmy and his dad moved out to the farm with Eula?

SHORTY. Yeah, that was about two months before Carla died. They sold their house to help pay off some of Carla's medical bills.

MAMA ALICE. All right, one night Eula and Jimmy get in Eula's car to go see Carla in the hospital; Eula's gonna spend the night with her. Well, anyway, Jimmy takes Eula's car to one of those big senior parties out at the reservoir . . . he's got a date with Margie Lynn. So, since the party is out at the lake, Jimmy decides to spend the night with his best friend Bobby Nader, instead of driving all the way back to the farm.

SHORTY. Didn't he move to Louisiana or someplace?

MAMA ALICE. Who? Bobby?

SHORTY. Yeah.

MAMA ALICE. *(Pause.)* Yeah, I think he's living in Baton Rouge . . now where was I? Tish, where was I?

TISH. Oh Mama Alice, I really don't remember.

SHORTY. Out at the lake with Jimmy.

MAMA ALICE. Oh yeah, well anyway, to make a long story short . . . Jimmy and Margie have a fight or something and he leaves the party in a huff and drives back to the farm. Well, he finds his daddy and this cocktail waitress in bed together. Now how is that for a sixteen-year-old with his mother dying of cancer and finding his father . . . well, you can imagine.

SHORTY. Oh my Lord. Well, I hope Eula Simmons never hears that story. Poor Jimmy, he has really suffered a lot for such a young man . . . first his mother dying like that, then his daddy running around with that little ole gal, and now with Margie Lynn run off . . . *(*TISH *stops combing* SHORTY's *hair.)* Oh, I'm sorry Tish . . . me and my big mouth. You know my husband used to say I could screw up a dogfight.

TISH. Oh that's O.K., Shorty . . . no need to apologize . . . it's just . . . Mama

Alice, if you don't mind finishing Shorty's comb-out . . . I think I better go get David Edward from Mrs. Ramos.

MAMA ALICE. Sure honey . . . you go on, Tish . . . I'll finish up here on Shorty.

TISH. *(Getting her purse.)* Thank you, Mama Alice. I'll be in tomorrow at eight o'clock to give Mrs. Mitchell her permanent.

MAMA ALICE. That'll be fine, honey. You go on now . . . Bye.

TISH. Bye Mama Alice, bye Shorty . . .

SHORTY. Bye Tish, and honest I'm really sorry . . .

MAMA ALICE. Bye Tish, lean your head back, Shorty. Bye darlin'.

SHORTY. Damn, Mama Alice . . . I'm sorry about that.

MAMA ALICE. Well she did run off, Shorty. What are you apologizing for?

SHORTY. Well, Tish seemed so upset, I thought . . .

MAMA ALICE. Tish is just embarrassed. She's afraid of what other people are thinking and saying about her daughter . . . running off like that, leaving her husband and her baby.

SHORTY. Where d'you think she is?

MAMA ALICE. I don't know, Shorty. I'm surprised I haven't heard from her by now, at least for me to send her some money. Darrell reported her to the highway patrol.

SHORTY. The highway patrol?

MAMA ALICE. Yeah, as a missing person.

SHORTY. Well how is Darrell taking all this?

MAMA ALICE. *(Laughs.)* Oh he's so mad at her it's not even funny.

SHORTY. Darrell's crazy about Margie Lynn.

MAMA ALICE. He's crazy all right. Pampered and spoiled that child and at the same time would snatch her bald-headed if she didn't mind him.

SHORTY. But she's married now.

MAMA ALICE. Yeah, after she talked Jimmy Bunton into saying "I do" then Little Margie didn't have to live in Daddy's house no more.

SHORTY. Now Mama Alice, those two have been sweethearts a long time . . . everybody knew they'd get married. I'm not so sure I didn't talk Pete, rest his soul, into marrying me once upon a time . . . God knows it wasn't his idea.

MAMA ALICE. *(They both laugh.)* My granddaughter is no dummy, no siree. And she's just as stubborn and hardheaded as her father. Oh hell, it hasn't been easy for Tish raising Margie with Darrell out of town more than he's in. Aw, Darrell's crazy about his little girl, but he's not a gentle man; used to tease Jack somethin' awful when they was kids. Jack's always hated his big brother for pickin' on him like that.

SHORTY. Jack's a lot younger than Darrell, ain't he?

MAMA ALICE. Yeah, ten years younger.

SHORTY. You know, I can remember when Margie Lynn and Jimmy used to sneak around in the alley behind my bar. Shoot, they weren't even in high school yet.

MAMA ALICE. I'm sure it was all Margie Lynn's idea.

SHORTY. Lord, I guess. Kids are funny. Bad for business them hanging round my bar . . . reminds some of the customers to go home too early.

MAMA ALICE. Oh hell, there is always someone in your bar.

SHORTY. Well, there better be . . . aw, I like those little curls around the front like that.

MAMA ALICE. You like that . . . well honey, let's nail that thing right on down.

SHORTY. *(MAMA ALICE hands her a plastic face shield with a face painted on the front for her to hold while MAMA ALICE sprays.)* Yeah honey, spray it real good . . . so I won't have to worry with it till I come in again next week. *(Coughs.)* Damn, Mama Alice, what is that stuff? It smells like mosquito repellent.

MAMA ALICE. *(Examines spray can label.)* Well maybe it is . . . somethin' a little extrey.

SHORTY. Oh you go on. *(They both laugh. MAMA ALICE goes and gets the jacket to SHORTY'S pantsuit; SHORTY removes her smock and gets out her money.)*

MAMA ALICE. Oooh I sure do like this. Where'd you get this?

SHORTY. I got that over to Miss Wynant's shop. We'll have to go over there sometime.

MAMA ALICE. You know, I just love bright colors.

SHORTY. Here's $5.50 . . . that right?

MAMA ALICE. Next time what d'you say we put a rinse on your hair?

SHORTY. As long as it don't turn out blue like yours. *(They both laugh.)* And listen, tell Tish to forget what I said . . . I mean about Margie Lynn and all.

MAMA ALICE. Shorty, don't worry about it. See ya next week.

SHORTY. O.K., honey. Bye now.

MAMA ALICE. *(As SHORTY makes her way all the way off.)* Bye darlin' . . . Bye . . . Bye-bye.

SHORTY. *(From off.)* Bye dear . . . bye-bye.

MAMA ALICE. Bye . . . bye . . . bye now. *(She finally closes the door to the shop.)* Oh stars. *(MAMA ALICE goes over and adjusts the window unit and starts to straighten up the shop; she spots SHORTY's letter box and picks it up . . . running for the door.)* Shorty, Shorty. *(Opens the door and calls out.)* Shorty, honey, you forgot your letter box . . .

> *(SHORTY is long gone. MAMA ALICE then closes the door and turns up the radio a little; as she cleans up, she dances to the music, laughing at herself . . . she then gets the idea to call her son JACK. In the meantime, we see JACK KAYRO walk up to the duplex and enter the living room.)*

JACK. Mama. *(He soon spots her through the beauty shop window and observes her on the phone.)*

MAMA ALICE. Hello operator . . . I want to talk to Mr. Jack Kayro, Wichita Falls, the Carousel Motel . . . the number is 442-7878 . . . I don't know the area code, it's Wichita Falls.

JACK. *(Disguising his voice.)* Mama Alice . . . yoo-hoo Mama Alice . . .

MAMA ALICE. *(Yelling.)* I'm next door in the shop.

JACK. Oh Mama Alice, I need my hair fixed.

MAMA ALICE. Who in the hell . . . I'm next door in the Lovely Lady.

JACK. Mama Alice . . .

MAMA ALICE. Well shit . . . what, oh no, operator, I'm not talking to you . . . he checked out . . . well thank you very much.

JACK. Mrs. Kayro, you in there?

MAMA ALICE. *(She goes outside as* JACK *rushes around to the side of the house.)* Who's calling me? *(Not seeing anyone, she looks around, then* JACK *jumps out and grabs her. She screams.)* Good Lord!

JACK. *(Laughing.)* Hello, Mama . . . surprise . . .

MAMA ALICE. Good God damn, Jack Kayro, you scared me to death. Are you trying to give your mother a heart attack?

JACK. Oh, Mama Alice . . . aren't you glad to see your favorite son?

MAMA ALICE. Yeah, I was just trying to reach you at that motel you've been living in. They said you'd checked out.

JACK. That's right. Couldn't stand it a minute longer.

MAMA ALICE. Where's Linda?

JACK. You got a beer, it's too hot to stay out here.

MAMA ALICE. Yeah, I got a beer; there's a six-pack in the icebox. *(They go inside the living room and* JACK *heads for the kitchen while* MAMA ALICE *turns the air conditioner on high.)*

JACK. *(Enters with a can of Pearl beer.)* You got a shop full of wet heads next door?

MAMA ALICE. No, too hot to get your hair fixed today. Business is pretty slow . . . Where's your wife?

JACK. You mean ex-wife, Mama Alice. She is most likely in that asshole of a town, Wichita Falls. After spending some time down at the divorce court.

MAMA ALICE. Good God, Jack! You haven't been married for more than six months.

JACK. Oh no . . . I've been married for more than eleven years . . . just not always to the same woman. *(He laughs.)*

MAMA ALICE. *(Disgusted.)* You are really somethin' else. You know that?

JACK. Yeah, that's what they all say.

MAMA ALICE. Oh they do . . . Linda say that, and Sue Ellen, and what's her name, that kid from Louisiana, what was her name?

JACK. *(He has to think.)* Nayrenne Colby Kayro.

MAMA ALICE. She was hardly seventeen years old.

JACK. *(Smiling.)* Yeah, but she matured early.

MAMA ALICE. Had a phone call the other day from one of your ex-wives.

JACK. Which one?

MAMA ALICE. Who do you think? The only one that ever calls me.

JACK. Nancy Joe.

MAMA ALICE. Yeah.

JACK. And just what in the fuck did she want?

MAMA ALICE. *(Really upset.)* Jack Kayro, don't you ever use that word in my house—do you hear me?

JACK. Oh shit . . . what did Nancy Joe want with you?

MAMA ALICE. She wanted to know where you were.

JACK. You didn't tell anything, did you?

MAMA ALICE. Seems you haven't been sending those child-support checks real regular like.

JACK. *(He empties his beer can.)* Goddamn that woman. What did you tell her?

MAMA ALICE. Nothin'. Said I didn't know where you were. She told me to tell you she's gonna have your ass in jail, even if she has to track you down herself.

JACK. Nancy Joe said that? *(Laughs.)* Well, just let her try . . . she'll never find me and she's gonna wish different if she does. Goddamn that woman. *(He exits to the kitchen for another beer.)* They're all alike, you know, all of 'em . . . all are no good, just after your money.

MAMA ALICE. 'Cept for Cynthia. Bring me a beer, would you, honey? Her daddy was making money hand over fist. Why, he had you working your way up in the business . . . probably gonna leave it to you . . . But oh no, you didn't like workin' for Daddy Ledbetter. You had to start runnin' around with some little teen-age whore, letting the whole town of Pearsall know about it.

JACK. Would you shut up? The only reason I married that pig bitch was for her money . . . so you could take it easy, drive a new car, and act like Miss Got-Rocks here in Polly, Texas. And if you're still so all goddamned interested in her money . . .

MAMA ALICE. Now Jack . . .

JACK. That woman looked like a pig. She had a nose like a goddamn pig. *(He pushes his nose up.)* It was disgusting . . . shit, she was lucky to have a man like me.

MAMA ALICE. Jack, honey, sit down.

JACK. Aw leave me alone. Shit, I come home to see my own mama and she has to start in on me. Don't you ever mention Cynthia or her daddy or two-bit Pearsall again.

MAMA ALICE. Jack, damn it. I'm not just talking about Cynthia. Linda was wife number five. You've been married more times than any man in this town.

JACK. *(Laughs.)* That's for damn sure. This hick town has really gone to hell. Hey where's my sister-in-law? She in the shop?

MAMA ALICE. No, she's gone over to Mrs. Ramos's to pick up David Edward.

JACK. Speaking of little David, anybody heard from my niece?

MAMA ALICE. Nope, not one word.

JACK. You know, when she married Jimmy Bunton I thought . . . shit . . . now that's really stupid and then having that kid . . . but to just run off like that . . . now that's crazy. She could have gotten herself a divorce. She could have come to me for some advice.

MAMA ALICE. You're a fine one to be handin' out marital advice. How long you plannin' on stayin'?

JACK. Few days . . . got all my stuff in my car.

MAMA ALICE. You're just a gypsy . . . a damn gypsy.

JACK. You heard that from Tish. That's what she calls me. My own sister-in-law.

MAMA ALICE. Now don't you start in on Tish. Without her to help in the shop I wouldn't have near as many customers as I do.

JACK. That's the damn truth. You run 'em off faster than you can get their heads under the dryers . . .

MAMA ALICE. What are you goin' to do about Nancy Joe?

JACK. Do? Nothing.

MAMA ALICE. She gonna have you put in jail.

JACK. Aw hell, are we back on that again? Look, can I help it if I'm so irresistible?

MAMA ALICE. Shoot!

JACK. It's all your fault, for raisin' such a handsome boy.

MAMA ALICE. *(Laughs, a smoker's deep hack.)* Handsome, my foot . . . you just talk people into thinking you're good-looking. *(They both laugh.)*

JACK. *(Noticing SHORTY going into the shop.)* Hey—Shorty just went into the shop.

MAMA ALICE. Shorty? Well go tell her I'm over here, honey.

JACK. *(Opens front door and yells.)* Hey Shorty, we're over here.

MAMA ALICE. *(Yelling.)* Goddamn it, Jack, were you raised in a barn? Go over and tell her I'm over here.

JACK. *(He goes over to the shop.)* Hey Shorty . . .

SHORTY. *(Carrying a letter box.)* Oh Lord, Jack Kayro—

JACK. Hiya Shorty. *(Gives her a twirl.)* If you aren't the sweetest sight for sore eyes.

SHORTY. Well when did you get in town—

JACK. Just now.

MAMA ALICE. *(Shouting.)* Jack are you and Shorty comin' back over here or not?

JACK. *(Shouting back.)* We're comin', Mama Alice. Come on, Shorty. *(They both go back over to MAMA ALICE's living room.)*

MAMA ALICE. Hello Shorty. You forgot your letter box!

SHORTY. I bring this box full of stationery every time I get my hair done—and every time I never get one letter written—and it's all your fault, Mama Alice.

MAMA ALICE. Oh shoot! If you didn't like to gossip as much as I do, you might write one of those letters. *(They both laugh.)* Well come on in—sit down—how about a beer?

JACK. Yeah! Come on in, Shorty. Let me get you a beer for a change, on the house.

MAMA ALICE. Oh Jack, now ain't you being charmant.

SHORTY. Charmant?

MAMA ALICE. That means charming—I heard it on the Mike Douglas show. *(They both laugh.)*

SHORTY. What's Jack doing back in town?

MAMA ALICE. Oh Shorty. That damn Jack has gone and gotten himself another divorce.

SHORTY. What? Why he just got married. My word, Mama Alice, how many wives does that . . . *(JACK enters with beers.)* Anyway, she'll probably have that operation next week sometime . . . probably.

MAMA ALICE. Oh thank you, honey.

SHORTY. Thank you, Jack.

JACK. So how's business, Shorty, that bar of yours made you a rich widow yet?

SHORTY. Rich? I doubt that . . .

JACK. You know, what you need to do is expand, open up another bar. *(The phone rings.* MAMA ALICE *gets up to answer it while* JACK *and* SHORTY *continue their conversation.)*

MAMA ALICE. Hello . . . no operator, she's not here right now. Can I take a message? Who's callin' please . . . hello, hello . . . operator . . . *(She hangs up.)*

SHORTY. Oh shoot, Jack . . . it's all I can do to run one bar.

JACK. Well, that's where I could help you out.

SHORTY. You?

JACK. Yeah. You let me manage the new bar and . . .

SHORTY. *(Laughing.)* I may be crazy, honey, but I'm not stupid! *(Noticing* MAMA ALICE.*)* What's the matter, Mama Alice?

MAMA ALICE. Well . . .

JACK. Who was that?

MAMA ALICE. I don't know. They hung up when I asked who was calling. It's damn strange . . . Tish never gets any long-distance calls at the shop. Only one ever calls her long distance anyway is Darrell.

JACK. You think it was Darrell?

MAMA ALICE. No, I don't think it was Darrell.

SHORTY. Well, who was it? *(*MAMA ALICE *doesn't answer.)* It was Margie Lynn!

MAMA ALICE. Oh Shorty, now don't say that.

SHORTY. Oh damn, Mama Alice—I'll bet you dollars to donuts that's who that was.

JACK. Margie Lynn? Well where was she calling from?

MAMA ALICE. I don't know. Shoot, why didn't I ask the operator?

SHORTY. Honey, don't just stand there, call her back, find out where the call came from. *(*MAMA ALICE *dials the operator.)*

JACK. Aw hell, you two are nuts. Operator won't do that.

SHORTY. She will too.

MAMA ALICE. *(On the phone.)* Hello operator. I just received a person-to-person call at this number and I need to know where that call came from . . .

JACK. *(Overlapping the phone conversation.)* I'm telling you she won't do that, I was married to an operator . . .

MAMA ALICE. Could you trace it for me please . . . thank you. *(To* JACK.*)* Would you hush. She's gonna try and trace it now.

SHORTY. You see, I told you.

JACK. Well, they don't like to do it.

MAMA ALICE. *(To phone.)* Yes . . . well thank you very much. Bye.

JACK. Well?

MAMA ALICE. San Antonio. Goddamn, she's only forty-two miles from here.

SHORTY. Oh Mama Alice. Maybe she's on her way home?

MAMA ALICE. You think? Oh Shorty, I don't dare get my hopes up . . . you know I try not to worry but it seems I can't go but a few minutes that I'm not thinking about her . . .

SHORTY. I know, Mama Alice. But don't you fret about this . . . why she's probably on her way home right this minute.

JACK. Aw, you all don't even know it was her that called.

MAMA ALICE. Well, you don't know it wasn't.

JACK. Goddamn it . . . Margie Lynn is nothing but a spoiled brat.

MAMA ALICE. You watch your tongue, Jack Kayro. That's my granddaughter you're talking about.

JACK. Oh yeah . . . well if she were my wife, I'd flatten her so quick, she'd a wished she'd a never run off from me.

MAMA ALICE. Well it's just no wonder that you can't stay married more than five minutes.

JACK. Now Mama Alice, I told you to just lay off me.

SHORTY. Hey Jack, why don't you go and get me another beer, honey?

JACK. I'd be happy to do that for you, Shorty . . . What d'you say you come on back into the kitchen with me. We need to talk about that new bar you're fixin' to open up . . .

SHORTY. *(As she heads out with* JACK.*)* Now just a minute, young Jack, I never said nothing about opening up another bar . . .

JACK. We'll call it the Angel of Lights . . .

SHORTY. The Angel of Lights? *(They exit.)*

MAMA ALICE. Oh dear Lord, I hope she's coming home.

JACK. *(Coming back in.)* Mama? I . . . your little boy is just starvin' to death out here . . . come on back and fix me somethin' to eat.

MAMA ALICE. I'm coming honey. *(She exits as lights fade.)*

*Curtain*

# ★ ACT I

## SCENE II

*Later, about four in the morning. We see* JACK *asleep on the living room couch. Then three women approach The Lovely Lady.* MARGIE LYNN *is dressed in a skimpy T-shirt and a tight pair of designer jeans,* GINGER *is in a dress and high-heeled sandals,* C.C. *is dressed in tight white cotton pants and a T-shirt with "Bitch" written across the front.*

C.C. My God, Margie, where in the shit are you taking us? *(Laughs.)* Talk about Americana. *(She and* GINGER *both laugh.)*

MARGIE. Would you two please shut up? I'm warnin' you, if you wake my grandmother, you'd better run for your life.

GINGER. Run for your life? *(Laughs.)* What she gonna do? Shoot me?

MARGIE. Yeah, she might.

C.C. O.K., where are the cameras? God, I hope somebody's filming this.

MARGIE. Shut up. *(Whispering.)* Now wait here, I've got to find the key. *(*MARGIE *goes to the porch.)*

C.C. *(To* GINGER.*)* Doesn't this remind you of something Lucy and Ethel would do? *(They both giggle.)*

MARGIE. SSSH! *(She finds the key under one of the plants on the front porch and unlocks the door to the shop. Then she motions the others inside. She turns on the little light at the desk and the one over the manicurist's table.)* This is all the light I'm gonna turn on.

C.C. I'm not believing this place.

GINGER. *(Excited.)* Oh this is cute. Can I be first? Who wants to wash my hair?

C.C. Don't you feel like you'd walked back into time . . . say about twenty-five years? Look at this equipment; it's ancient. Hey, Margie, suppose I could get the latest Vidal Sassoon look?

MARGIE. *(Laughs.)* C.C., this is Polly, Texas. Vidaaal who? *(They both laugh.* GINGER *attempts to open a door at the back of the shop.)* Ginger, shit, leave that door alone.

GINGER. I was just looking.

MARGIE. That leads to Mama Alice's house.

GINGER. Ooops. I'm sorry. Well, who's gonna do my hair?

C.C. Do your own damn hair.

GINGER. Oh shut up. Where can I wash my hair, Margie?

MARGIE. That room back there. See the sinks. There's shampoo and towels in the cabinets up above.

GINGER. O.K. Be back in a jiffy.

C.C. So this is the little shop you grew up in?

MARGIE. Yeah. My mama used to bring me here almost every day. Set my playpen up in this very corner.

C.C. How charming.

MARGIE. My favorite toys were plastic rollers, the little purple ones, and empty cans of spray net.

C.C. No dolls?

MARGIE. Oh sure . . . only the kind with hair you could fix.

C.C. God, it's hot in here. Can't we turn that thing on? *(She walks over to the air conditioner.)*

MARGIE. No. It makes too much noise . . .

C.C. And we'll wake dear grandmama what's her name. *(She picks up a stuffed toy.)* This one of your leftover toys?

MARGIE. *(Realizing it's her child's toy.)* No. How about that manicure I promised you? Come on, sit down.

C.C. Well, it's about time. That belongs to your kid, doesn't it?

MARGIE. *(Busying herself setting up the table.)* Yeah, it does, C.C.

C.C. Your mom take care of him? It's a little boy, right?

MARGIE. Yeah. David Edward. Jimmy takes care of him, too.

C.C. Jimmy's your husband?

MARGIE. Yeah.

C.C. You keep in touch with your mother, don't you?

MARGIE. Yeah, I call her. She's the only one who knows where I am.

C.C. And she keeps her mouth shut?

MARGIE. *(Smiles.)* Mama and I have been keeping secrets for years. We had to.

C.C. What happens if your dad finds out?

MARGIE. He won't find out.

C.C. Maybe so. But it sure is going to be hell for your mom if he does.

MARGIE. *(Trying to be very casual.)* I guess I better give her a call . . . I mean as long as I'm here.

C.C. I was wondrin' what took you so long. You didn't bring us down here just to do my nails. *(MARGIE gets up and goes to the phone and calls.)* Maybe you fooled Ginger, but not me, sweetie . . . I figured you had something up your sleeve just as soon as the Major left for Houston.

MARGIE. Hello Mama, it's me, Margie Lynn . . . If Daddy's there, just say it's a wrong number and hang up . . . Well, I'm here, Mama . . . at the shop. I'm fine, I drove down with a couple of my friends; they thought it might be fun to see an old beauty shop like this one . . . No, I'm just visiting, that's all . . . about an hour . . . of course I want to see you . . . how's little David? *(C.C. starts humming Brahms's lullaby and MARGIE glares at her to be quiet.)* What? . . . No, you stay there . . . no Mama, I promise I'll come by the house before we leave. O.K. . . . it won't be long . . . O.K. See you in a little bit . . . Bye.

C.C. Oh brother, aren't you something.

MARGIE. Huh?

C.C. *(As MARGIE returns to the table.)* Why in the holy hell did you drag Ginger and me down here . . . if you just wanted to see your mother, why all this bullshit about playing beauty shop?

MARGIE. I didn't know for sure if I was gonna see her.

c.c. Oh Miss Margie . . . you lie.

MARGIE. I just didn't want to come back by myself . . . O.K.?

c.c. What are you afraid of?

MARGIE. *(Upset.)* Look, I'm sorry if you're having such a lousy time.

c.c. Hey, calm down. What's the matter with you?

MARGIE. Nothing.

c.c. You miss this place.

MARGIE. Are you kidding?

c.c. You want to come back? Come back home again?

MARGIE. No!

c.c. Then what are we doing here, Margie?

MARGIE. Look! We won't be here long, O.K.? Just a visit, a quick visit.

c.c. A visit?

MARGIE. Yeah, and when you meet my mom . . . be careful, I mean she thinks I'm still working in a drugstore.

c.c. A drugstore. Oh that's rich. *(Laughs.)* You told her you worked in a drugstore?

MARGIE. I did work in a drugstore . . . that's where I met the Major.

c.c. Yeah, I believe it . . . I'd believe anything of him.

MARGIE. I didn't believe you'd been a Las Vegas showgirl!

c.c. Oh yeah, just look at this body. *(Laughing a little too loud.)* Oh shit, Margie . . . you're too goddamn serious about life, you know that?

MARGIE. Why did the Major leave for Houston so suddenly?

c.c. Nobody is supposed to know anything about it. Not until the deal is final.

MARGIE. What deal?

c.c. Well, supposedly we're to go out for four days on this yacht . . . real hotsy-totsy crowd. Some big political boss is arranging it all. Seems he needs a few girls to entertain the male guests.

MARGIE. Who are these guys?

c.c. Don't ask. As far as you are concerned, these men don't have names.

MARGIE. Anybody famous?

c.c. Maybe . . . I doubt too famous. Anyway, you better bring along your tiniest bikini and you could stand to lose a few pounds.

MARGIE. You sound just like the Major. I'm always on a diet.

c.c. Listen, honey, you lose your looks and you're out. It's as simple as that.

MARGIE. Everything's so cut-and-dried with you.

c.c. Oh not really, sweetie. I've just been playing the game longer.

MARGIE. The Major tells you everything.

c.c. Only if it pertains to the business.

MARGIE. Ginger's so dumb; he never tells her anything.

c.c. She might say the wrong thing to the wrong person . . . besides, she doesn't want to know. Not like you?

MARGIE. So what if I do? I've got a right to know what's going on.

c.c. Grow up, Miss Margie. When you signed on with this outfit, you lost all your rights. Out of the frying pan and into the fire, you've heard that before.

MARGIE. Oh shut up.

C.C. Oh now come on . . . don't you start acting like Ginger. I am sick of all this high school behavior. Besides I came down to this little ole town of yours to have a good time.

MARGIE. You are. Put your hand in this.

C.C. *(Faking a new voice.)* Why Madge, am I soaking in dishwashing liquid?

MARGIE. Come on, C.C.

C.C. Oh God you're depressing . . . you know that? Get that bottle of Chivas out of my purse . . . you got any glasses around here? It's so ungenteel to drink out of the bottle.

MARGIE. I think there are some paper cups in the back. *(She heads for the back room.)*

GINGER. *(Enters drying her hair.)* These towels are too damn small. You can't wrap your head up.

C.C. Quit complaining. You want a drink?

GINGER. Sure. I found the neatest-smelling shampoo. Smell my hair. *(MARGIE enters with some cups and GINGER bends down so C.C. can smell her hair.)* What's it smell like to you?

C.C. Contraceptive foam.

GINGER. It does not. It smells like strawberries. God, you are so crude, C.C.

C.C. Crude, rude, and unrefined, but I'm not stupid.

GINGER. Who are you calling stupid?

C.C. Oh Miss Ginger honey, please don't hit me. *(She laughs.)*

GINGER. Why you . . .

MARGIE. Shut up. Both of you.

GINGER. Have we got time for me to do my roots?

C.C. and MARGIE. No.

GINGER. O.K. Where are the rollers?

MARGIE. On that tray there.

GINGER. Oh, I see them.

C.C. How long your little grandmother owned this shop?

MARGIE. Long as I can remember. She had this place built after her first husband died.

C.C. So, what's a girl like you not doing in a nice place like this?

MARGIE. The same thing you are.

C.C. You're learning, aren't you, honey? Not like little Miss Dumb-Dumb.

GINGER. *(Angry.)* Look . . . I don't have to take this crap from you.

MARGIE. Would you two cut it out.

C.C. Have a drink, little Margie.

MARGIE. When'd you start bleaching your hair, Ginger?

GINGER. I don't know. I was still living in Germany. The Major talked me into it. Took me to this fancy salon in Munich.

MARGIE. God, I'd like to go to Europe someday.

C.C. You stay with us and you may get the chance.

GINGER. Last summer we went to some adorable little island. What did they call it, C.C.?

C.C. Martinique.

GINGER. It was so beautiful. I got the greatest tan . . . all over. The Major bought us all new clothes for the trip. Made us wear white the whole time.

MARGIE. What was the Major like . . . I mean when he was still in the army?

GINGER. No different. I met him in an officer's club. I was sitting with my parents and he came right over to our table and introduced himself . . . then he asked my father's permission to dance with me. *(Giggles.)* He was so sexy. My mom thought he was very charming.

MARGIE. He is, very charming.

C.C. Well I doubt he would be very charmed to hear that we had taken a night off and skipped down to Polly, Texas. Not while San Antonio is still filled with members of the Medical and Surgical Supply Association.

GINGER. He's gone to Houston. How's he gonna find out?

C.C. He'll find out. I think he knows every bartender and hotel clerk in the state.

MARGIE. So what if he finds out?

C.C. Then it'll cost you.

GINGER. You know, one of those Medical and Surgical dudes wanted to pay me off in a huge supply of hand soap. *(Giggles.)* Just like the surgeons use . . . big deal. *(*C.C. *and* GINGER *laugh.)*

MARGIE. Ssssh. Keep it down, would you?

C.C. What's got you so uptight? Afraid Grandma's gonna come in and make you stay? *(Pause.)* Bet your husband would like to know you're here.

MARGIE. Shut up.

GINGER. What's your husband like? Was he mean to you?

MARGIE. Mean? Jimmy? No—he's just a little crazy—anyway he was driving me crazy.

GINGER. Well, I told the Major just as soon as I find me a real nice guy with lots of money I'm getting married, settling down, and raisin' some kids.

C.C. *(She laughs.)* Ginger, you kill me . . . you know it? What are you going to tell your kids you used to do for a living?

GINGER. I'll just tell 'em . . . I traveled around a lot.

C.C. *(Still laughing.)* And what about at your first PTA meeting and you meet the principal of your little daughter's elementary school who happens to remember you from a School Administrators Convention.

GINGER. Oh, shut up. I'll move to California or someplace . . . I don't have to stay in Texas.

C.C. It doesn't matter where you go. Someone will know you. Some old, balding, nearsighted fart will remember you. You know we're a lot like the whores that would follow the armies around during the wars. Only we follow the Homebuilders, the Million Dollar Round Tablers, the AMAers, the MaBellers . . .

GINGER. Look you . . . just stop calling us whores. We are not whores. The Major said so.

c.c. Oh he did?

GINGER. We don't live like whores, Miss Know-It-All. I've got my own Corvette and a real fur coat and that's not what I call whorin' around.

c.c. I beg your pardon, Miss Sweetness and Light, but you didn't buy that car with the money made from your donut sale. And I bet that coat's not even paid for.

GINGER. Oh stop it, I am so sick of you always putting me down.

MARGIE. Goddamn it, would you two please shut up?

GINGER. I don't like the word *whore*, all right? I'm a . . . businesswoman.

c.c. Oh Ginger, come on . . . you're being a bit pretentious, aren't you?

GINGER. You stop calling me names.

MARGIE. Jesus Christ, you act like you want to wake my grandmother.

c.c. Now Miss Margie, we're sorry to cause you any concern.

GINGER. You whore.

c.c. Hey, I thought you didn't like that word?

GINGER. For you it fits.

c.c. Well I like that. You two are businesswomen, career girls, and I'm a whore . . . shit.

MARGIE. *(Changing the subject.)* Pick your polish color.

c.c. Pick your polish color. Sounds like a new game show.

GINGER. I like game shows.

c.c. I bet you do. "Frosted Passion" . . . now that's a contradiction of terms.

MARGIE. Mrs. Corey wears that color.

c.c. She does? Well slap it on, honey. This may be the only thing Mrs. Corey and I have in common.

MARGIE. *(Smiles.)* You got that right. Daizel Corey is married, has six children, teaches Sunday School at the Baptist Church . . .

c.c. And only puts out once a week.

GINGER. And she's probably a very nice person.

c.c. And I'm not?

GINGER. Bitch. O.K., how does this dryer work?

MARGIE. Here, sit down . . . now sit back. If it gets too hot just holler.

GINGER. *(Loudly.)* What? *(MARGIE turns off the dryer.)*

MARGIE. If it gets too hot let me know. *(MARGIE turns it back on.)*

c.c. God, it's gonna get a hell of a lot hotter with that thing on. Shit, it makes more noise than the air conditioner would. *(Next door, JACK wakes up. He thinks he hears something, but he is still very drowsy.)*

MARGIE. Oh all right. *(She goes over to adjust the air conditioner.)*

GINGER. Hey, Margie . . . hand me my radio and one of those movie magazines. *(JACK is now certain that the noise is coming from the shop. He gets up and goes to the back of the house, returning with a gun. He sneaks out to the front porch and sees the three women in the shop through the big glass window. He enters the shop, slamming open the door.)*

JACK. O.K., everybody just stay where you are.

c.c. *(Spilling her Scotch down her front.)* Jesus Christ!

GINGER. Oh my God.

JACK. What in the hell is going on in here? *(Finally realizes one of the women is* MARGIE LYNN.*)* Margie Lynn . . . just where in the hell have you been?

MARGIE. Uncle Jack, put that gun down before you hurt somebody . . . *(She makes a move toward him.)*

JACK. Not so fast, young lady. I asked you a question.

MARGIE. But you're scaring my friends.

C.C. Not to mention ruining my favorite T-shirt.

JACK. *(To* C.C.*)* Who the hell are you?

GINGER. *(Still under the dryer—shouting.)* Is he talking to me?

MARGIE. Turn that thing off. Now Jack, we didn't harm nothing. Just happened to be near Polly and thought I'd drop by for a minute. In fact, just as soon as Ginger here gets those rollers out of her hair we're leaving. *(*MARGIE *motions to* GINGER *to start unrolling her hair.* C.C. *catches her meaning and starts to do it for* GINGER.*)*

GINGER. Hey, my hair's not dry yet.

C.C. Oh yes it is.

JACK. Margie Lynn Kayro, you run off six months ago. Your husband Jimmy hasn't heard a word from you and your daddy's got the law looking for you . . . now damn it, you're not going nowhere till I get some answers.

C.C. Oh shit.

MARGIE. Come on, Uncle Jack. Now you should understand, especially you. I had to get out of this little town.

JACK. But why did you run off?

MARGIE. Well, I just had to.

JACK. Why?

MARGIE. Because if I had told anyone . . . then I couldn't have left. Daddy would have nailed one of my hands to the kitchen sink. I mean, don't you see, Uncle Jack, I couldn't tell anyone.

C.C. Yeah, come on, Uncle Jack . . .

JACK. You, shut up.

C.C. Margie, honey, I've really had such a nice time but we must be going. Come on, Ginger, you can fool with your hair later.

JACK. *(Covering the door.)* Hold on just a goddamn minute. You three aren't going anywhere.

C.C. Oh come off it. You're acting like some stupid cop on a bad TV series.

JACK. Now shut up, bitch. I've had just about . . .

C.C. *(Looking down at her T-shirt.)* Well mercy God, he can read!

JACK. *(Making a move toward her.)* Goddamn you woman!

MARGIE. Jack, stop it.

JACK. You better tell your friend I don't take crap like that off anyone, especially a woman.

MARGIE. Uncle Jack, now just calm down, O.K.? How about a drink?

JACK. A drink?

MARGIE. Sure . . . real expensive stuff. *(She pours him a cup.)* Now put that gun down.

JACK. Well, ain't you something now. Scotch? Real expensive Scotch. Where you livin' now, Margie Lynn?

MARGIE. I've been travelin' around.

JACK. Oh yeah, doing what?

MARGIE. Different jobs, you know.

JACK. No, I don't know. Maybe you better explain them to your Uncle Jack.

C.C. My goodness, just look what time it is. We really have got to be going. *(C.C. makes a move for the door.)*

JACK. *(Making a move toward C.C.)* Sit down . . . O.K.? *(To MARGIE.)* I want to talk to my little niece . . . you're looking good Margie Lynn, real good. I like what you've done to yourself.

MARGIE. Uncle Jack, it's awfully late. We really have to get on the road.

JACK. Now why are you in such an all-fire hurry to get out of here? I'm beginning to think you don't like my company.

C.C. How perceptive of you.

JACK. I told you to shut it, you hear me?

MARGIE. Lay off, C.C.

JACK. Yeah, or you're gonna wish you had, C.C. Now just what in the hell does that stand for?

C.C. Why, I would have thought a man of your superior intelligence could figure that one out yourself.

JACK. Oh boy, you are really asking for it.

C.C. Not me darlin' . . . I never have to. *(GINGER laughs.)*

MARGIE. *(To C.C.)* Shut up.

JACK. Who are these friends of yours, Margie? Just what kind of business are you girls in? *(Pause.)* I asked you a question, Margie.

MARGIE. *(Getting nervous.)* We . . . we're . . . C.C. and I used to work in a drug-store together and Ginger . . .

JACK. *(Laughing.)* Oh yeah. You lie real pretty, Margie.

C.C. *(Moving slowly toward JACK.)* Look, Jack, honey, you're not as dumb as I thought you were and I apologize for all those nasty things I said to you. *(Very close to him.)* Now, honey, we really do have to get out of here. So what do you suppose it would take to persuade you to let us leave . . . just real quiet like. *(Taking a hundred-dollar bill from her purse.)* I wouldn't want you to think bad things about us. I'm sure this will more than cover what little damage we did in the shop.

JACK. *(Taking the bill.)* A one-hundred-dollar bill . . . you ain't no small-town hooker, are you, baby?

C.C. *(Completely ignoring his new interest.)* Come on, campers, the bus is leaving. *(They all three make for the door.)*

JACK. Hold it. Who said anything about leaving? I'm just getting interested. I have to know all the details now. Want to get this story straight before passing it on to your daddy, Margie Lynn.

MARGIE. *(Panicky.)* Uncle Jack, you wouldn't do that.

c.c. What story, Jack? You haven't got any story . . . 'cept the one you've made up in your head.

JACK. Yeah, well Darrell Kayro's gonna find it real interesting, let me tell you.

c.c. All right, Jack, you just go ahead and tell the whole story—don't leave anything out.

JACK. If you want me to keep my mouth shut it's gonna cost you some more money.

c.c. Oh no, we wouldn't want to shut you up. You keep right on talking, Uncle Jack. 'Cause the more you say the more people are going to know how really stupid you are.

JACK. *(Runs toward* C.C. *as if to hit her.)* Oooohwee . . . ain't you tough. *(*JACK *grabs* C.C. *and they fall to the floor.* MARGIE *then tries to pull* JACK *off* C.C.*)*

MARGIE. Jack, stop it . . . stop it.

c.c. *(To* JACK.*)* Get the fuck off of me!

MARGIE. *(Still struggling.)* Ginger, get the keys out of my purse and go get the car.

GINGER. But what am I supposed to . . . ?

MARGIE. Just get out of here . . . go on back and tell the Major what happened . . . now go on.

GINGER. O.K. O.K., I'm going . . .

JACK. Oh no you don't . . . *(*GINGER *screams as* JACK *tries to grab her and she runs out leaving the door open. As* JACK *tries to grab* GINGER, MARGIE *throws a cup of Scotch in* JACK*'s face.)* What the hell . . .

MARGIE. *(Screaming.)* Stop it, Uncle Jack.

JACK. You fucking little whore . . . *(He makes a move toward* MARGIE *as* C.C. *breaks a bottle and shoves it into* JACK*'s face.)*

c.c. Not so fast, Uncle dear.

MARGIE. C.C., what are you doing?

c.c. Shit, it always worked in the movies . . . now come on, let's catch Ginger before she leaves us here . . .

> *(The door suddenly opens wide and* MAMA ALICE *appears with a huge kitchen knife. She is in her robe and nightgown, and her hair is wrapped in toilet paper and covered with a hairnet.)*

MAMA ALICE. What in God's name? *(*MAMA ALICE *takes the bottle from* C.C.*)* Give me that thing . . . My Lord what is going on in here? *(Realizing that one of the women is* MARGIE.*)* Margie Lynn?

JACK. Mama, Mama, I found them in here. One of them got away and this one . . .

MAMA ALICE. Shut up, Jack. Margie Lynn, what is going on in here?

MARGIE. Mama Alice, now don't get mad. If Jack hadn't jumped on C.C. . . . .

JACK. Don't listen to her, Mama. I found them in here, boozin' it up . . . now one of them . . .

MAMA ALICE. Shut up, Jack. Margie, how long have you been here?

MARGIE. Not long, Mama Alice. We were just leaving.

MAMA ALICE. Leaving? Not hardly. *(She shuts the front door to the shop.)* Does Jimmy know you're here?

JACK. Mama, there were three of them, I'm trying to tell you . . .

MAMA ALICE. Shut up, Jack. Margie Lynn, have you told Jimmy you are home?

MARGIE. No . . . Mama Alice, I didn't want to see anybody . . . I just . . .

MAMA ALICE. Jack, call Jimmy and tell him to come over here.

JACK. What's the number?

MARGIE. No, damn it . . . Mama Alice, you don't have to call him.

MAMA ALICE. It's in that address book on the desk.

MARGIE. *(Almost in hysterics.)* Please, Mama Alice, don't call him . . . just let me leave, O.K.? Please . . .

C.C. Hey, sweetheart, calm down. So you see your ole man, so what?

MAMA ALICE. Who are you?

C.C. Me? I'm a social worker.

JACK. Hello Jimmy. This is Jack Kayro . . . you get yourself over here, over to The Lovely Lady right this minute . . . because Margie Lynn's over here . . yeah, that's what I said. *(He hangs up the phone.)* He's coming right over.

MARGIE. Why did you have to bring him into this?

JACK. He's your husband, Margie. He's got a right to know you're here and what you've been up to all these months.

MAMA ALICE. Now Margie Lynn, get a hold of yourself. Are you in some kind of trouble? *(TISH appears at the door.)* Tish! What are you doing here?

TISH. Margie, Margie honey, I thought something might be wrong so I decided to . . .

MARGIE. Oh Mama . . . *(She runs to TISH and really begins to cry.)* Oh Mama, I'm sorry . . . I'm sorry . . .

TISH. *(Holding her.)* Hush now . . . Everything's gonna be just fine, you'll see. Just fine. Don't cry, Margie Lynn . . . you're home now. Everything is gonna be fine . . .

*(During her speech the lights fade out on the scene.)*

*Curtain*

# ★ ACT II

## SCENE I

MAMA ALICE'S *living room. The time is just a few minutes after the end of Act I.* MAMA ALICE *has just ushered everyone into her living room.*

MAMA ALICE. I swear, Margie Lynn, you picked a hell of a time to finally come home.

JACK. What time is it?

MAMA ALICE. Nearly 5:00 A.M.

JACK. Oh shit. If I don't get some sleep I'm gonna have one hell of a hangover.

MAMA ALICE. It's your own damn fault, Jack Kayro.

JACK. Now Mama Alice, don't start in on me about my drinking, my head is already . . .

MAMA ALICE. Would you hush, Jack. Well I guess we could all use some coffee. *(She starts for the kitchen.)*

JACK. Are you staying up?

MAMA ALICE. I'm up—plan to stay that way.

JACK. Well I'm going back to bed.

MAMA ALICE. Yeah, well you do that.

JACK. *(Looking at* MARGIE.*)* Hey Margie. *(She looks at him.)* I'm real glad you're home. We can have a nice long talk later, O.K.?

MARGIE. Sure, Uncle Jack.

(JACK leaves, casting one last glance at C.C.)

TISH. Margie honey, you want something to eat?

MARGIE. No Mama.

TISH. You sure have lost the weight.

MARGIE. Just a few pounds.

TISH. *(Taking a long look at* MARGIE'S *new clothes.)* That must be a new outfit.

MARGIE. Yeah.

TISH. It sure is . . . different.

MARGIE. *(Laughs.)* I didn't think you'd like it.

TISH. Oh Margie, I'm so glad you decided to come home . . . I got so anxious after you called . . . I thought somethin' might be wrong so . . .

MARGIE. Nothing's wrong, Mama.

TISH. Well, I should have brought little David with me. He was sound asleep when I took him over to Mrs. Ramos. Why don't I go get him right now . . . ?

MARGIE. No Mama, not right now. Let him sleep. I can see him later, O.K.?

TISH. Sure honey. I just thought you might . . .

MARGIE. Oh Mama, please . . .

C.C. Hey, I bet your grandmother could sure use some help with that coffee . . . Now where are my manners? I don't believe we've been properly introduced, my name is C.C.

MARGIE. Oh, I'm sorry. Mama, this is my friend . . .

C.C. Just call me C.C.

TISH. I'm very pleased to meet you, C.C.

C.C. Margie and I work in the same drugstore together.

TISH. Oh, back in Dallas.

C.C. Yeah, Dallas. A Dallas drugstore . . . well, if you two will excuse me, I'll mosey on back to the kitchen.

TISH. She's a real cute girl, Margie. Very polite.

MARGIE. C.C.? Yeah, she's one of a kind.

TISH. She drive you down from Dallas? I didn't see any car out front.

MARGIE. There were three of us came down, Mama, but when the fight started, Ginger took the car and . . .

TISH. When the fight started?

MARGIE. Yeah, Uncle Jack jumped on C.C. She said something that pissed him off. Then I grabbed Jack and tried to pull him off . . . oh it was a mess.

TISH. That Jack Kayro . . . every time you turn around he's in some kind of trouble. Your daddy would just as soon you didn't have anything to do with him, Margie . . . even if he is your uncle.

MARGIE. Whatever you say, Mama. I'll be a good little girl and do just what I'm told.

TISH. Oh honey, that's not what I meant. It's just . . . *(On the verge of tears.)* Well, I've worried so much about you. I wondered if you were taking care of yourself and eatin' right . . . you know, every time you would call I wanted to say—Now Margie Lynn, you come home right now—but I knew it was important for you to get away for awhile; get your head straight, you said.

MARGIE. Yep, that's what I said.

TISH. Oh, but honey, it's been six months. Don't you think that's long enough?

MARGIE. Six months? Yeah, Mama, I guess that's more than long enough.

TISH. Little David will be a year old on Sunday.

MARGIE. I know. One year ago I was so pregnant I could hardly walk. God I was big . . . big and ugly.

TISH. You weren't ugly, honey.

MARGIE. It all seems like such a long time ago. How is he, Mama? Does he miss me?

TISH. Oh Margie—he's gettin' so cute. I think he's gonna be big like your daddy . . .

MARGIE. Why should he miss me? You've been a better mother to him than me.

TISH. Margie, don't say that.

MARGIE. It's true. I was scared to death of that little baby. I still am. Every time he would cry I'd rush over to your house.

TISH. Well, it's not uncommon for mothers to be a little nervous, especially with their first child.

MARGIE. A little nervous. Is that what you call it, Mama? Is that how you explain my getting so drunk last December I don't even remember my baby's first Christmas morning? I couldn't talk to anybody, not even Mama Alice.

TISH. Oh baby, why didn't you come to me? We used to be able to . . .

MARGIE. But you don't understand, Mama . . . How can you . . . you stuck it out, you stayed in there and suffered all those years. Mama, why didn't you get out, divorce Daddy? Why did you stay married to him?

TISH. Divorce? I could never leave your father, Margie. We do love each other, in our own way, and he's been good to me. He has always worked real hard so that we could have a home and enough money to buy some nice things—you've never really wanted for anything—he bought you that car your senior year and he wanted you to go to college—saved enough money so you could . . .

MARGIE. Mama, please . . . don't say any more.

TISH. I guess it's my fault . . . because of his temper I shut him away from us, kept things from him . . . even lied to him. But I was just trying to do the right thing, honey, please believe me . . . please Margie, don't hate your father.

MARGIE. You never stop. You give and give and give and you think everything will be just fine. When Daddy would hit me you'd sneak me out of the house and bring me over to the shop—Mama Alice would fix my hair and you'd give me a manicure and we'd all sit around and eat peanuts and drink Cokes and pretty soon everything would be just fine.

TISH. And Mama Alice would get the hiccups.

(MAMA ALICE *enters from the kitchen.*)

MAMA ALICE. Well, those carbonated drinks would give anyone the hiccups.

MARGIE. You've been listening.

MAMA ALICE. Uh-huh. Now, how about some coffee?

C.C. This is the best cup of coffee I've ever had.

TISH. *(Takes a cup.)* Thanks, Mama Alice.

MAMA ALICE. Margie?

MARGIE. No.

TISH. You want some juice . . . How about a glass of milk, honey?

MARGIE. Please Mama . . . I don't want anything, I'm just fine.

MAMA ALICE. Well, you don't sound fine. You better have some of this coffee, it might help you to be a little nicer to people. Now here, take this cup . . . I put lots of milk in it, just like you like it. (MAMA ALICE *hands her the cup as* JIMMY *knocks at the door.*) Mornin' Jimmy.

JIMMY. Mornin' Mama Alice. *(Sees* MARGIE *and takes a long pause before he speaks.)* Hello Margie.

MARGIE. Hello Jimmy.

MAMA ALICE. Come on in, Jimmy, you want some coffee?

TISH. Won't you sit down?

JIMMY. Where's the baby?

TISH. He's with Mrs. Ramos . . . He's fine . . . Can't I get you some coffee?

JIMMY. Yes, thank you.

MAMA ALICE. I think I'd better go with you, Tish . . . show you where the cups are.

(MAMA ALICE *and* TISH *go to the kitchen.*)

C.C. *(Sensing the tension.)* So . . . you're Jimmy Bunton? *(No reply.)* My name is San Antonio Rose. *(Pause.)* Oh brother. *(Looking at her nails.)* Oh my heavens, just look at my nails . . . they're just dying for another coat of "Frosted Passion," if you two will excuse me.

MARGIE. C.C., don't go . . .

C.C. I'm just going next door, hon.

MARGIE. Please . . .

C.C. Listen, you two need a chance to talk. Besides I got to make a phone call. *(To* JIMMY.*)* See ya later, sweetcakes.

*(C.C. goes into the shop, finds the phone book, and calls the bus station.)*

JIMMY. Margie . . .

MARGIE. *(She gets a cigarette off the table.)* I don't suppose Grandmama would mind if I bummed one of her cigarettes.

JIMMY. You don't smoke.

MARGIE. I just started. *(Pause.)* Well Jimmy . . . aren't you gonna say anything?

JIMMY. Why?

MARGIE. Why what?

JIMMY. Why'd you run off?

MARGIE. Oh Jesus . . . Look, what difference does it make now? *(Pause.)* I had to get out when I did. *(He stares at her.)* Oh come on. You're acting like our marriage was in great shape when I took off last winter.

JIMMY. You don't make it easy for me, do you?

MARGIE. Easy for you . . . boy, that's a new approach.

JIMMY. What's happened to you?

MARGIE. *(Laughs.)* A lot more than you'd ever want to know.

JIMMY. You cut your hair.

MARGIE. I'm surprised you noticed.

JIMMY. Why'd you run off like that, Margie Lynn?

MARGIE. God, you're dumb. Can't you figure it out . . . do I have to spell it out for you?

JIMMY. I . . .

*(Utterly frustrated,* JIMMY *goes outside.)*

MARGIE. Jimmy, where are you going?

JIMMY. *(Emotional.)* What do you care, Margie Lynn? You don't give a damn about me or David Edward and now . . . seven months you've been gone . . . nobody knew where you were . . . if you were alive or dead, but you could care . . .

MARGIE. Mama knew I was all right.

JIMMY. What?

MARGIE. As soon as I got to Dallas I called Mama and told her I . . . I had to get away and would she look after David Edward for me.

JIMMY. Tish knew . . . she knew where you were?

MARGIE. No. She didn't know exactly where I was . . . just that I was in Dallas and that I was O.K.

JIMMY. But she never said . . .

MARGIE. I made her promise not to tell anybody . . . not you, not Daddy . . . I was afraid Daddy would find me and make me come back here.

JIMMY. This is your home.

MARGIE *(As* JIMMY *stares at her.)* Don't stare at me like that . . . it gives me the creeps. Look, it took a lot of guts for me to finally pack myself out of here . . . it wasn't easy, Jimmy. I was gonna tell you, but every time I tried . . . I couldn't, I was afraid you wouldn't let me go . . . you'd keep me here, make me stay . . . oh I don't know.

JIMMY. You're not making sense. You're talking but you're not making any sense.

MARGIE. Oh yes I am. You're not listening to me, Jimmy. You close yourself off, put some kind of a wall up and it doesn't matter what I say, you only hear what you want to . . . open up, Jimmy.

JIMMY. What for? Let some more hurt in . . . let people feel real sorry for me. Take pity on me. I don't need anyone's pity.

MARGIE. I'm sorry, Jimmy, I really didn't mean to hurt you. I thought our getting married was a good idea . . . I mean . . . I really did think I loved you.

JIMMY. Oh you did.

MARGIE. I don't know . . . I don't know anymore.

JIMMY. Well, just what do you know, Margie Lynn?

MARGIE. I've seen a lawyer in Dallas.

JIMMY. *(Not paying attention to what she is saying.)* It's a good thing you came home, Margie.

MARGIE. No it's not. Not this way . . . it wasn't gonna be like this.

JIMMY. We'll go over and get the baby and then I'll drive you both home.

MARGIE. Jimmy, stop it. Look, our marriage was a mistake. *(As he just stares at her.)* Can't you understand anything I'm saying? . . . I want a divorce.

JIMMY. *(Pause.)* No.

MARGIE. No?

JIMMY. We're a family, the three of us, and that's how it's gonna stay.

MARGIE. You're crazy.

JIMMY. *(Very serious.)* Don't you ever run off from me again.

MARGIE. You're not going to treat me like some stupid little girl.

JIMMY. Then quit acting like one.

MARGIE. Jimmy, Jimmy, listen to me. We can't go back to the way it was, can't you see that? I've changed . . . I . . . ran away from this town . . . I found . . .

JIMMY. You shouldn't have done that, Margie . . . but you're back now.

MARGIE. I'm sorry, Jimmy. I'm really sorry.

JIMMY. Quit saying you're sorry . . . now, are those all the clothes you got?

MARGIE. Talking to you is impossible, you just don't hear anything you don't want to.

JIMMY. Where are your suitcases?

MARGIE. You know who you sound like? My daddy, Darrell Kayro. Telling me what to do, what not to do . . . yes sir, no sir, I'm sorry sir . . please don't hit me, sir.

JIMMY. Get your things together and we'll go get David Edward.

MARGIE. I don't want to go get David Edward.

JIMMY. Do like I say, Margie Lynn.

MARGIE. Oh stop it . . . stop it, Jimmy.

JIMMY. You don't want to see your own baby?

MARGIE. No, I don't . . . not now. I want to see you, Jimmy. *(Pause as she looks at him.)* You don't understand, you just don't understand, do you?

TISH. *(Coming out on the porch.)* Here's your coffee, Jimmy.

MARGIE. Mama, Jimmy has something to tell you . . . Go on, Jimmy. (JIMMY *just stares at her.)* Well, I guess I'll tell you. We're gonna get a divorce.

TISH. A divorce?

JIMMY. I'm going to the garage now . . . but I'll be home for lunch, Margie. I'll see you at the house . . . you pick up the baby, O.K., and I'll be home for lunch. *(He starts to leave.)*

MARGIE. *(Desperate.)* Jimmy, don't leave . . . please . . . you've got to . . .

TISH. Come on back in the house, honey . . .

JIMMY. You do like your mama says now . . . I'll see ya later. Bye.

TISH. Bye Jimmy.

> *(He leaves.)*

MAMA ALICE. *(Standing in the doorway.)* All right, what's going on out here?

C.C. *(Coming out of The Lovely Lady.)* Hello, ladies. Which one of you knows where the bus station is in this town?

MAMA ALICE. It's downtown, right off the main square.

C.C. How far?

MAMA ALICE. A mile, maybe. You thinking on leaving?

MARGIE. C.C., you can't leave.

MAMA ALICE. You all come on inside . . . we're letting all the cool air out.

MARGIE. Mama, you go on inside . . . I want to talk to C.C. for a minute.

MAMA ALICE. *(Sensing* TISH'*s apprehension.)* It's all right, Tish . . . she's not gonna run away. Are you, Margie Lynn?

MARGIE. I'll be in in just a few minutes.

> (TISH *and* MAMA ALICE *go inside the house and back into the kitchen.)*

C.C. God, it's hot out here.

MARGIE. You're taking a bus back to San Antonio?

C.C. My word, you catch on fast.

MARGIE. But the Major will come for us.

C.C. Are you kidding? Let's go into the shop and get out of this heat.

> *(They go into the shop and as* C.C. *turns on the window unit* MARGIE *sits in one of the chairs.)*

MARGIE. I guess the Major's not back from Houston yet.

C.C. Why in the hell you sent Ginger back to San Antonio with the car I'll never figure out.

MARGIE. *(Fixing her hair.)* Are you mad at me?

C.C. It's a little late for that.

MARGIE. The Major will come and get us, you'll see. He'll probably drive down tonight.

C.C. Is that what you want? Prince Charming to come down here to your little ole town and rescue you from the clutches of your tacky husband, what's his name?

MARGIE. His name is Jimmy.

C.C. Well aren't you playing this a little dumb?

MARGIE. He'll come. He's not gonna just leave us here.

C.C. *(Laughs.)* Would you grow up? The Major's not going to set foot in this very ordinary little town . . . he's not about to risk getting involved in some soap opera scandal . . . "Ex-Prom Queen Now Call Girl" . . . I can just see the headlines.

MARGIE. Would you shut up. Nobody knows that. Nobody knows anything.

C.C. Oh come on, your Uncle Jack is going to wake up sometime today and he's just busting to spread some dirt about this whole fucking thing.

MARGIE. Look, I don't know what you're so worried about. The Major isn't going to forget about us. He'll take care of everything.

C.C. Are you in love with him? *(Pause.)* Answer me . . . are you in love with that bastard?

MARGIE. Why do you care? Besides, it's none of your business.

C.C. Jesus Christ! The Major doesn't love you.

MARGIE. How would you know? How would you know anything about love?

C.C. Would you please get your head out of your . . . that man is incapable of loving anyone. Women are just merchandise to him, items for sale. Can't you see that? Oh, I'll admit he's a real charmer, but all that's just a pitch. He's just a damn good pimp . . . everything's done with a lot of class, nothing cheap . . . the clothes, the parties, the contacts. Yeah, he knows where the big bucks are, sweetie . . . and who's gonna pay top dollar for the Major's whores.

MARGIE. You're boring me.

C.C. I'm boring you . . . listen, I couldn't believe it when the Major brought you into the business. Some dizzy little housewife who'd run away from home. You'd never even been a hooker before, right?

MARGIE. Of course not.

C.C. But then that's part of the packaging . . . some sort of country freshness for the customers, a real down-home appeal. Sweet sixteen and never been screwed.

MARGIE. So what does that make you . . . the Ice Queen?

C.C. And I'll survive this, you watch me, while you burn yourself out in a big hurry. *(Pause.)* That bus leaves for San Antonio in an hour.

MARGIE. I hear you.

C.C. I plan to be on it.

MARGIE. I'll take you to the station.

C.C. You're not coming with me?

MARGIE. No, I've got to stay.

C.C. All right. But don't count on you-know-who showing up. *(MARGIE doesn't say anything.)* And don't be stupid, Margie . . . no names, no places, no info on any of it.

MARGIE. I'll keep my mouth shut.

C.C. Good girl, and stay clear of that shit for brains uncle of yours. He doesn't know anything, right?

MARGIE. O.K., O.K.

C.C. You're sure stubborn, aren't you, Miss Margie?

*(The phone in* MAMA ALICE's *living room and in The Lovely Lady rings.* MAMA ALICE *hurries out of the kitchen to answer it. The lights are up in both The Lovely Lady and the living room.)*

MAMA ALICE. Hello . . . yes, just a minute . . . *(She goes out to the front porch and calls out to* MARGIE.*)* Margie Lynn . . . *(*MARGIE *starts for next door.)* The phone's for you. *(*MARGIE *comes out of the shop and quickly goes next door.)*

MARGIE. I'm coming.

MAMA ALICE. Sounds like long distance.

MARGIE. *(Hoping it's the Major.)* Hello . . . *(Disappointed.)* Oh, hello Ginger . . . no, we're fine . . . yeah, everything's O.K. *(*C.C. *has picked up the phone in the shop and is listening to the conversation.)* Did you tell the Major? . . .

C.C. Ginger, this is C.C., yeah . . . now listen to me . . . no, just listen. I'm taking a 6:45 bus out of here . . . Greyhound. Arrives in San Antonio at 8:55 . . . yes, you be at the station to pick me up . . . yeah right . . . now you be there, O.K.?

MARGIE. What . . . no, I'm not coming back with C.C. . . . I don't know . . a few days maybe, yeah.

C.C. Ginger, repeat to me the instructions I just gave you . . . Right . . . See you in a few hours . . . O.K. Bye. *(She hangs up and then goes over to the living room.)*

MARGIE. Ginger, you tell the Major the whole story, tell him where I am, O.K., no matter what C.C. says . . . Yeah, O.K. . . . I've got to hang up. Bye.

MAMA ALICE. Who was that?

MARGIE. Just a friend.

MAMA ALICE. Who's this Major person?

MARGIE. Nobody you'd know, Mama Alice.

MAMA ALICE. This whole business sounds awfully strange to me, young lady. Your mama is pretty upset, you know . . . and I think it's high time you started explaining this whole mess. You've got a lot of questions to answer, you hear me?

MARGIE. I hear you, Mama Alice.

C.C. Mama Alice, would you mind too terribly if I took a shower before my bus leaves?

MAMA ALICE. A shower? No, I suppose that's all right. The bathroom's at the end of the hall. When's your bus leave?

C.C. Pretty soon. Margie is going to take me to the station.

MAMA ALICE. *(Afraid* MARGIE *may leave also.)* You let Jack take her.

MARGIE. I'll take her . . . it's not that far.

MAMA ALICE. You get back on in there and talk to your mama . . . Jack can take your friend here to the station.

C.C. But Jack's asleep. We wouldn't want to disturb him.

MAMA ALICE. I'll go wake him up. You're not going to that bus station, Margie Lynn.

*(She exits down the hall toward the bedroom.)*

MARGIE. And you think I'm stubborn.

C.C. Oh well, Jack's kind I can handle. Besides, it'll give me a chance to throw him off the track.

MARGIE. *(Suspicious.)* What are you going to tell him?

C.C. I don't know . . . but you keep your mouth shut or you could find yourself in a lot of trouble.

MARGIE. You tell the Major what happened . . . you tell him the whole story, O.K.?

C.C. Yeah, sure, I'll tell him. *(As the lights are fading, we hear* MAMA ALICE *offstage.)*

MAMA ALICE. Goddamn it, Jack, I'm not going to tell you again . . . Now get your ass out of this bed.

JACK. Oh Mama . . .

*Curtain*

SCENE II

*The same day, early afternoon.* MAMA ALICE *and* TISH *are cleaning up the shop.* MAMA ALICE *is sweeping up hair and smoking a cigarette.* TISH *is at the reception desk, going over the appointment book.*

MAMA ALICE. Oh Lord, I'm tired . . . how many haircuts have we given today?

TISH. So far . . . six.

MAMA ALICE. Do you think the word is out that Margie Lynn is back, or is business really picking up?

TISH. It's the heat probably. Everybody wants to get their hair off their neck.

MAMA ALICE. Maybe so, maybe not.

TISH. Oh Mama Alice, you just look for trouble . . . none of those ladies said anything about Margie Lynn.

MAMA ALICE. They didn't have to. I could see what they were thinking. Was all I could do to keep Sarah Tinks from going next door. Had to tell her Jack was asleep on the couch and if she woke him up I wasn't gonna protect her. Ooohwee, it's warm in here. *(She goes over to adjust the air conditioner and looks out the window.)* Oh my God!

TISH. What's the matter?

MAMA ALICE. Here comes Eula Simmons and I bet it's not for a haircut.

TISH. Oh Mama Alice . . do you think Jimmy told her?

MAMA ALICE. That's a big 10-4.

TISH. Now Mama Alice, be nice.

*(EULA enters the shop, out of breath and hot.)*

MAMA ALICE. Well hello Eula, back so soon. Why you've perspired your set right out . . .

EULA. I am not here to have my hair done.

MAMA ALICE. Pity.

EULA. Tish, I need to talk to you.

MAMA ALICE. Eula, you'd best sit down, cool off a bit. Now how about a Coke, you sure look thirsty.

EULA. Well, if it wouldn't be too much . . .

MAMA ALICE. No trouble at all, compliments of The Lovely Lady. *(To* TISH.*)* While I'm getting her Coke, honey, why don't you see if you can't fix Eula's set. Looks like you've been swimming without your cap on, Eula.

EULA. *(Sitting in the styling chair.)* In this heat, it's impossible to keep a set for . . .

MAMA ALICE. *(From the back room as she enters.)* Oh I know, ain't this heat just awful. *(To* TISH.*)* That already looks so much better, Tish. I swear, you are a talented beautician. *(To* EULA.*)* Hot, ain't it? *(She goes over to adjust the air conditioner.)* Goddamn this thing . . . feels like it's just barely putting out.

EULA. Mama Alice, do not take the Lord's name in vain.

MAMA ALICE. Oh, excuse me, Eula, sometimes those "Goddamns" just slip out.

EULA. Tish, I have got to talk to you. It is most urgent. *(Pause.)* I just talked to Jimmy.

TISH. You did?

EULA. I did . . . and he told me that Margie Lynn was back in Polly. *(*TISH *does not answer.)* And he said she wanted a divorce. *(*TISH *still does not answer.)* Well Tish, I know my Jimmy wouldn't lie to me.

MAMA ALICE. Yeah Eula, Margie Lynn's back. She's been here maybe a full ten hours . . . give or take thirty minutes.

EULA. Well, she certainly hasn't gone back home to her husband and her baby.

MAMA ALICE. Aren't you just a wealth of knowledge this afternoon.

EULA. Would one of you please tell me what is going on . . . where has Margie been all these months?

MAMA ALICE. Did Jimmy tell you where she was?

EULA. No, he didn't.

MAMA ALICE. Do you suppose he knows where she is . . . I mean right this minute?

EULA. I'm sure he knows where she is.

MAMA ALICE. Then what are you so upset about? Here, let me finish up for you, Tish. *(*MAMA ALICE *takes the spray net and sprays* EULA*'s hair, managing to get a lot on her face.)* Now it's important to spray you real good so your set will stay.

EULA. I've never known Jimmy to be so upset, not since his mother died . . . *(Coughs.)* Tish, I want to see that daughter of yours . . .

MAMA ALICE. Don't talk while I'm spraying, Eula . . . close your mouth. *(*MAMA ALICE *finishes spraying and hands* EULA *a mirror, then twirls the chair around too fast and then back again.)* There, now, doesn't that look 100 percent better? *(*MAMA ALICE *takes* EULA*'s hand.)* Oh my goodness . . . if you've got the time, let's give you a manicure, Eula.

EULA. *(Pulling hand away.)* Would you please leave me alone . . . I did not come in here for a . . . a . . . beauty treatment.

MAMA ALICE. Praise the Lord!

EULA. Tish, I want to know what is going on. You can't keep this a secret, not in this town. Margie Lynn's behavior has been absolutely shameful, if you ask me.

MAMA ALICE. Who asked you?

EULA. I beg your pardon?

MAMA ALICE. Now Eula, when can I schedule your next appointment?

EULA. *(Indignant.)* I don't think I want another appointment, thank you.

MAMA ALICE. Well, all right . . . But your hair is sure gonna need it.

TISH. We're not keeping any secrets, Eula . . . but don't you think it's best to let Margie and Jimmy work this out themselves?

EULA. Don't you think Jimmy has suffered enough? I told him not to get involved with your daughter. I just knew something like this was going to happen.

MAMA ALICE. Now, Eula, what makes you say a thing like that?

EULA. No offense to you, Tish . . . but I warned Jimmy about marrying a Kayro. *(To* MAMA ALICE.*)* Your family has never been respected in this town . . . that son of yours, Jack, always drunk and been married a dozen times. In fact, I understand he was seen this morning saying good-bye to some strange woman at the bus station. A woman who gave him several one-hundred-dollar bills.

MAMA ALICE. Who told you that?

EULA. Sarah Tinks . . . and then Margie Lynn just running off, not telling anyone where she was . . .

(MARGIE *enters the room, dressed in an old housecoat of* MAMA ALICE*'s. She carries a beer with her which* TISH *immediately takes from her and tries to hide from* EULA.*)*

MARGIE. Hello Mama . . .

MAMA ALICE. Hello darlin'.

MARGIE. *(Pause.)* Well . . . would you look who's here . . . How the hell are you, Aunt Eula?

EULA. Well, I suppose you are just real proud of yourself?

MARGIE. How's the farm?

EULA. How could you do such a horrible thing? How could you do this to Jimmy, not to mention the humiliation . . .

MARGIE. Oh Aunt Eula, calm down, it's too hot for all this emotion.

MAMA ALICE. Too goddamn hot.

EULA. Just where have you been for the . . . ?

MARGIE. None of your business.

EULA. Who do you think you are? Treating Jimmy like . . . like . . . you have no respect for your own marriage.

MARGIE. Respect? What's that got to do with anything?

MAMA ALICE. Evidently, according to Eula here, we wouldn't know what respect was . . . something the Kayro family never had it seems . . .

EULA. Mama Alice, would you please stay out of this?

MAMA ALICE. Stay out, my foot.

TISH. Mama Alice, don't—don't say any more. Eula, I think it's best you leave now.

EULA. Not until I get some answers out of Margie Lynn.

TISH. Aunt Eula, I'm not going to tell you again—now please leave.

EULA. Well, I have never been so insulted . . . *(She starts to leave.)* And I hope to God Jimmy and Margie do get a divorce, it couldn't happen soon enough. *(*MAMA ALICE *makes a move toward her.)* I shall never come to this shop again.

MAMA ALICE. You better not, Eula, there's just no telling what I might do to your hair. *(*EULA *is gone.)* Goodbye Eula . . . *(To herself.)* You old bitch.

MARGIE. Who let her in?

TISH. I swear that woman . . .

MAMA ALICE. Now Tish, calm down. She's gone and we've you to thank for running her off.

TISH. It won't be ten minutes and she'll be on the phone spreading rumors . . .

MARGIE. Oh come on, Mama. What would a town like Polly do without gossip?

TISH. Did you get some sleep, honey?

MARGIE. Yeah, a little. Till Jack started snoring. He must take after you, Mama Alice, you snore something fierce.

MAMA ALICE. I do not.

TISH. Well, now that you're up—why don't I go get David Edward from Mrs. Ramos?

MARGIE. No . . . Mama. Not just yet, O.K.?

MAMA ALICE. You can't put this off any longer, Margie . . . you've got to see that baby.

MARGIE. I know, I know . . . I'm going to.

MAMA ALICE. And I suggest you call Jimmy while he's still at work and tell him to come over here.

MARGIE. Please Mama Alice . . . Why is it the minute I set foot in this town everyone starts telling me what to do?

MAMA ALICE. Well, if you weren't so all-fired stubborn we might not have to.

TISH. Are you sure you really want a divorce, honey?

MARGIE. Yeah, Mama, I just don't see any other way out.

MAMA ALICE. Well then, don't you think you'd best get Jimmy over here and talk about it?

MARGIE. What's the point? Talking to him is like talking to a brick wall. Besides, he doesn't want a divorce.

TISH. I do think Jimmy loves you, Margie.

MARGIE. O.K. That's enough . . . I'm sick of this whole conversation. Anybody want a beer?

MAMA ALICE. Lord no. I've still got work to do. (MARGIE *starts back to* MAMA ALICE'*s living room.*)

TISH. Margie, wait . . .

MAMA ALICE. Leave her be, Tish . . . come on into the back and help me with the wash—we've got nothing but dirty towels . . . come on.

　　(MARGIE *starts back to the kitchen. The lights go out in the beauty shop and come up on the living room, where* JACK *is asleep on the couch.*)

JACK. (*Kicking the blanket off him.*) goddamn it's hot in here. (*He throws the blanket off and goes over to adjust the air conditioner. Yelling.*) Who turned this damn thing off?

MARGIE. (*Entering.*) Do you always have to shout?

JACK. What's the matter, Margie Lynn? Drink too much last night?

MARGIE. You're a fine one to talk about drinking.

JACK. Oh, poor thing . . . your head hurt?

MARGIE. Shut up.

JACK. Too bad you ain't got any of that expensive Scotch left, but it won't hurt you to drink a little beer, bring you back down to where you belong.

MARGIE. Please Uncle Jack . . . would you just shut up?

JACK. Now you listen to me . . . I've kept my mouth shut, and you better start being a whole lot nicer to me . . do you hear me? (*She doesn't reply.*) Margie Lynn, I'm talking to you.

MARGIE. You don't scare me, Jack.

JACK. No, but your big ole daddy does. *(Laughs.)* You know, I just think I'd better call him and let him know what's going on around here.

MARGIE. Since when were you so all-fired concerned about ole Darrell? I thought you hated his guts.

JACK. My own brother. *(Smiles.)* Hey, why don't you go and get me one of those beers?

MARGIE. I'm not your goddamn servant. You've got two legs, go and get it yourself.

JACK. You know, you're real cute when you're mad. Makes those pretty eyes of yours shine.

MARGIE. You're sick.

JACK. I've always thought you was real pretty, Margie Lynn . . . real sweet . . . now you treat your Uncle Jack with some respect. *(He comes over very close to her.)* I'm not so dumb, honey . . . I know what you've been up to up there in Dallas. But that doesn't bother me, not so long as we understand each other. *(She tries to free herself.)*

MARGIE. Let me go.

JACK. What's the matter . . . I'm not good enough for you? Not so fast, young lady. You want me to keep this little secret, don't you? Don't want me blabbing it all over?

MARGIE. Jack, please, you're hurting me.

JACK. You play ball my way and nobody's gonna get hurt. I'll take care of you, Margie, honey . . . it'll be our little secret. *(He kisses her, she tries to struggle free.)*

MARGIE. You fucking piece of trash. You're disgusting.

JACK. What's the matter, little Margie? Nobody ever get rough with you before? Or do I have to pay extra for that? Huh? You're not answering any of my questions, honey . . . 'fraid your nice mama might hear us?

MARGIE. Shut up . . . do you hear me, shut up.

JACK. Now, wouldn't she love to know that her precious little daughter is just a goddamn whore. *(He tries to kiss her again and she spits in his face.)* When this town knows the truth about you, you'll be the piece of trash, honey. Your poor mama and grandmama ain't gonna be able to hold their heads up around here . . . and poor little David Edward . . .

MARGIE. You leave them out of this, Jack Kayro, or I swear . . .

JACK. You'll do what? Aw come on, Margie . . . you ain't gonna do nothing to me . . . 'Cause we're right down here together, sweetie . . . right on the goddamn bottom.

MARGIE. *(Screaming.)* Get out of here. Get out. Get out. *(JACK goes to the back of the house. MARGIE is trembling as she grabs the receiver and starts to dial the Major. She stops and then hangs up.)* Oh God . . .

   *(TISH and MAMA ALICE enter.)*

TISH. What's the matter, honey? Are you all right?

MARGIE. *(Really upset.)* I'm fine, just fine.

MAMA ALICE. Who were you talking to?

MARGIE. Nobody, Mama Alice . . . no one at all.

MAMA ALICE. Well who in the hell were you screaming at?

MARGIE. Was I screaming?

MAMA ALICE. Where's Jack?

MARGIE. He went back there.
> *(MAMA ALICE exits.)*

TISH. Margie . . . Margie, honey, look at me. *(MARGIE looks at TISH.)* What happened? *(No reply.)* Oh honey, please tell me what's wrong.

MARGIE. I'll be all right, Mama, really.

TISH. I wish I could do something to make you feel better.

MARGIE. *(Distantly.)* Yeah . . . well, don't worry about it.

TISH. I know it's all very difficult for you right now, but maybe if you would give Jimmy another chance . . . you could see one of those marriage counselors.

MARGIE. Who's gonna give me one?

TISH. What?

MARGIE. Who's gonna give me another chance, Mama?

TISH. I don't understand, Margie.

MARGIE. No, you don't understand . . . you want everything to be just like it was . . . me and Jimmy and the baby all living happily in our little garage apartment . . . me working at the Lovely Lady . . . it'd be so damn easy; I'd never have to make another decision, just let Jimmy and Daddy and Mama Alice tell me exactly how to live my life. God . . . wouldn't that be great, if they screw it up it ain't my fault . . . I'm not responsible. *(She pauses, staring at her mother.)* Oh Mama . . . you see, I was just gonna come down here and see you . . . and talk to you about divorcing Jimmy—that's all. I just needed to see you . . . 'cause I knew you'd help me out . . . you've always been the one . . . *(She breaks down into tears.)* You see . . . *(TISH goes over to comfort MARGIE.)* No, don't, don't touch me. *(She pulls away.)*

TISH. Margie, please . . .

MARGIE. You'll get your hands dirty, Mama.

TISH. *(Goes to her and holds her.)* Margie Lynn Kayro, now you listen to me. I don't care about anything in this world more than you—and nothing you've said or done is going to change that. I know you're in some kind of trouble, honey . . . but we'll work it out, you'll see. Now, you tell me what's wrong, Margie . . .

MARGIE. Oh Mama . . .

TISH. Honey, please talk to me.

MARGIE. *(Pause.)* I met this man.

TISH. A man?

MARGIE. And . . . we started seeing a lot of each other. He's not like any man I've ever known, Mama.

TISH. Where'd you meet this man, Margie?

MARGIE. In a drugstore.

TISH. Where you and C.C. work?

MARGIE. She doesn't work in a drugstore . . . she never did.

TISH. But she told me . . .

MARGIE. She was lying, Mama. Covering for me, just like you. Everybody covers for little Margie.

JACK. *(Enters, he is now dressed.)* Well hello Tish.

TISH. *(Coldly.)* Hello Jack.

JACK. Well, Miss Margie, I thought I'd go over to Winder's garage and see about getting my car tuned up . . . thought Jimmy could help me.

MARGIE. I bet.

JACK. Course, might be better to take it on in to San Antonio, let someone up there look at it. How'd you like to take a little trip with me to San Antone? We could see a movie, have dinner . . . maybe even stay a few days . . . now wouldn't that be fun?

TISH. Jack, I don't think Margie Lynn . . .

MARGIE. Mama, I can handle this.

JACK. That's right, Tish, this is between Margie Lynn and me. She's a big girl now.

MARGIE. Oh Uncle Jack, you are such a sweetie to include me in your plans, but I really don't think I can leave right this minute . . . I've got some things to straighten out and all . . . you understand.

JACK. Well we wouldn't have to go right this minute . . . why don't you think about it? *(He starts to leave.)* I'll be back later and you can let me know what you want to do.

*(He exits.)*

MAMA ALICE. *(She has gone out on the front porch to water the plants. She sees* JACK *as he is leaving.)* Where are you going, Jack?

JACK. Over to Shorty's for a few beers. I'll be back.

MAMA ALICE. You're gonna become a goddamn alcoholic . . . Jack, do you hear me?

TISH. Margie Lynn, what's going on between you and your uncle?

MARGIE. Nothing. Yet.

MAMA ALICE. *(She enters the living room from the porch.)* It's not even five o'clock yet and that damn Jack is already heading for Shorty's. God, it is hot out there . . . I bet it's a hundred and five degrees . . . Oooohwee . . . *(She settles herself in a chair.)* All right, Margie Lynn . . . I think we've waited long enough.

MARGIE. What are you waitin' for?

MAMA ALICE. For some explainin', that's what for.

TISH. Mama Alice, I don't think that . . .

MAMA ALICE. Now Tish, you know I love you like my own daughter, but I'll be damned, you are not going to treat this child with kid gloves any longer.

MARGIE. I am not a child, Mama Alice . . .

TISH. Margie Lynn . . .

MAMA ALICE. Let her finish, Tish.

MARGIE. Oh God help me if I ever had to make any decision for myself. I am not . . .

MAMA ALICE. You got married too young, I guess. But nobody forced you into marrying Jimmy Bunton . . . oh no, but you just had to get married.

MARGIE. Nobody forced me? Why the only real happiness for a woman is marriage and having babies . . .

MAMA ALICE. Now don't you start getting sarcastic with me, you forgot who you was talkin' to.

MARGIE. Oh yeah . . . fat chance.

TISH. Margie, all your grandmother is trying to say . . .

MAMA ALICE. Hush Tish . . . this is a discussion between Margie Lynn and me. Just what are you plannin' on doing now?

MARGIE. Doing? Hell if I know, Mama Alice.

MAMA ALICE. And what about that baby of yours? You're David Edward's mother, not Tish, not Mrs. Ramos . . . Little David didn't decide he wanted to be a part of this family; it wasn't his idea . . .

MARGIE. Well it wasn't mine either. *(Pause.)* I didn't want that baby . . . but do you think anyone in my family could understand that? Do you think if I had even mentioned the word *abortion* anyone would have been on my side? . . . God . . . Daddy was so excited and Mama, you were so happy, telling all your customers you were going to be a grandmother. Everybody was so goddamn happy I thought there must be something wrong with me.

TISH. Oh Margie, why didn't you say something?

MARGIE. Oh sure . . . and who was gonna agree with me? I had to have that baby . . .

MAMA ALICE. Because you wanted to . . . oh yes, you wanted that baby; don't you deny it, 'cause I know the truth and I am telling you, honey, that baby is your responsibility . . . to hell with Jimmy, you want to divorce him, go right ahead but . . .

MARGIE. Mama Alice please . . . I love David Edward, I do, but I had to leave . . . I knew Mama would take care of him . . . I knew he'd get all the love and attention he needed . . . I couldn't have left if I thought . . .

MAMA ALICE. Then why'd you come home, Margie?

MARGIE. Because I had to try and straighten things out, damn it.

MAMA ALICE. Oh really, and in one little brief visit you were gonna put all your ducks in a row.

MARGIE. Maybe . . . I was gonna talk to Mama and to Jimmy . . .

MAMA ALICE. And what about David Edward? Were you gonna talk to him?

MARGIE. Would you get off my back about that baby? Jesus, doesn't anybody care about me?

MAMA ALICE. Well, of course we care about you. If I didn't love you so much I wouldn't give a damn why you left. Hell, I wouldn't be arguing with you now. Margie, honey, open your eyes and quit runnin'.

TISH. Margie, please . . . let your grandmother and me help . . . we used to be able to.

MARGIE. Oh Mama . . . I never meant to hurt anybody. When I ran off I didn't think much farther than where I was going . . . I didn't want to think about Jimmy or David Edward.

MAMA ALICE. Well, you better start thinkin' about them.

MARGIE. I have, Mama Alice, but there aren't any answers to make it any easier.

MAMA ALICE. Easier? Do you think it has been easy for your mama or me? Running off like that . . . not telling anyone where you were.

MARGIE. I had to leave, don't you understand . . . I had to do what was best for me.

MAMA ALICE. Best for you . . . Margie Lynn, you don't know what you want, that's your problem. You thought you wanted to be married to Jimmy Bunton . . .

MARGIE. Yes I did. But I was wrong. I made a mistake, O.K.?

MAMA ALICE. And don't you think your running off was a mistake too?

MARGIE. What do you want from me?

MAMA ALICE. I want you to grow up, honey, and face the responsibilities you've created.

MARGIE. Oh Mama Alice, I don't think you know what you're saying.

MAMA ALICE. Now, first off, you send for your things, then, if you are still dead set on a divorce, well, you and the baby can move in with Tish . . . she's got plenty of room.

MARGIE. Oh Mama . . .

TISH. It's O.K. honey.

MAMA ALICE. And if you need some money, well, I can help you out, I've got a little stashed away for my old age . . . probably be better spent on you anyway, at least till all this gets cleared up . . .

JACK. *(He enters the living room.)* Hello ladies.

MAMA ALICE. Well that was a quick trip.

JACK. Yeah, well . . . I figured Margie Lynn here might be getting real anxious to leave . . . thought her little visit back home might be about over, right sweetie? *(No one answers him.)* What you women been talking about? Been telling 'em about your fancy life back there in Dallas, Margie?

MARGIE. Yeah Jack . . . sure.

JACK. Sure you have . . . come on, Margie, kiss your sweet mama good-bye and . . .

MARGIE. No.

JACK. What d'you mean no?

MARGIE. I'm not leaving, Jack. Not with you . . . I wouldn't be caught dead with the likes of you.

JACK. Why you stupid little bitch . . .

MAMA ALICE. Jack Kayro, you apologize for that.

JACK. Are you kidding? She's the one who'll be saying I'm sorry . . . not me.

MAMA ALICE. Now I am not going to have . . .

JACK. Just what kind of lies you been telling them, Margie?

MARGIE. Jack . . . please . . .

JACK. Well, guess I'll go on over and see Jimmy about my car.

MAMA ALICE. What's wrong with your car?

MARGIE. There's nothin' wrong with his car, Mama Alice.

MAMA ALICE. Jack Kayro . . . what are you up to?

JACK. I'm gonna make damn sure the true story about sweet little Margie gets told . . . thought I'd start with her husband and then I thought I'd call her daddy.

TISH. Jack Kayro, you leave Margie Lynn alone.

JACK. Oh no, she's not going to get away with this one, not this time.

MAMA ALICE. Margie, what is he talking about?

MARGIE. *(Pause.)* Oh let him go, Mama Alice . . . he's just got to be a big man . . . the only way he knows how.

JACK. Just remember, Margie Lynn, it was your decision . . . God, this is gonna set this town flat on its ass.

   *(JACK leaves.)*

MAMA ALICE. Jack, Jack Kayro, you come back here . . . what are you going to do?

TISH. Margie, does all of this have to do with that man you met in Dallas?

MAMA ALICE. The Major. *(A car honks outside.)* What in the hell . . . well, I don't know anybody that drives a white Lincoln.

MARGIE. I do. *(She runs out to the front porch as* C.C. *comes up to the house, soon followed by* GINGER.*)* C.C., what are you doing here?

C.C. Hello Margie . . . uh-oh, looks like you've been crying. Your face is a mess.

MARGIE. How did you know?

C.C. I've always had a talent for perfect timing.

MARGIE. Did the Major . . .

GINGER. Hi Margie.

C.C. I thought I told you to stay in the car.

GINGER. It's too hot to stay in the car. *(To* MAMA ALICE *and* TISH.*)* Hi.

MAMA ALICE. Who are you?

GINGER. I'm Ginger, pleased to meet you.

MARGIE. Oh . . . Ginger, this is my grandmother, Mama Alice Kayro, and my mom, Patricia Kayro.

GINGER. Pleased to meet you.

C.C. Well, I didn't come down here for my health, are you coming or not?

MARGIE. He sent you for me, didn't he . . . why didn't he come?

C.C. The Major is still in Houston, honey . . .

MAMA ALICE. Who the hell is the Major?

C.C. I talked with him this morning.

GINGER. We're going out on a huge yacht . . .

C.C. Shut up, Ginger . . .

MARGIE. Does he want me back?

C.C. Look honey . . . *(Pause.)* It's a long drive to Houston . . . are you coming or not?

MARGIE. What do you think, C.C.?

C.C. Oh Christ, who cares what I think . . . it's your decision, sweetie.

MARGIE. You're a real Ice Queen.

C.C. Yeah, and I'm melting in this heat. So, if you're coming, Miss Margie, come on.

MARGIE. *(Pause, then looks at her mother.)* Mama . . . I've got to go. I can't stay, not now.

TISH. I know.

MAMA ALICE. Tish.

TISH. Let me help you get your things together.

MARGIE. I'll be right back, C.C.

GINGER. Wow, look at all these plants . . . you know, the last time I was here it was real dark and . . .

C.C. Can it, Ginger.

MAMA ALICE. Well, why don't we all go into the living room . . . no use standing around in this heat. *(They all move into the living room.)* You all just go on in and have a seat. Can I get you something . . . maybe a Coke or some ice tea?

GINGER. Hey, I would love a . . .

C.C. No thank you, Mrs. Kayro. We're fine, just fine.

MAMA ALICE. Just call me Mama Alice.

GINGER. O.K. Mama Alice.

MAMA ALICE. Uh . . . Miss C.C., you all work together . . . you and Margie and Ginger?

C.C. Well Mama Alice, let's say we all run around together.

MAMA ALICE. Who's the Major?

GINGER. He's our . . .

C.C. Hush, Ginger. He's a businessman, Mrs. Kayro . . . a very good businessman.

MARGIE. *(She comes running out, followed by TISH.)* O.K. I guess I'm ready.

TISH. Now Margie, honey . . . you be careful . . .

MARGIE. Oh Mama, please don't cry, O.K.? And don't believe all you hear about me . . . only a little of it's true. *(They cling to each other.)* Now come on . . . it's gonna be all right, you'll see . . . I promise. I've got to talk to the Major. And here . . . I want you to have this . . . *(She gives TISH some money.)* It's for you and David Edward . . .

TISH. Oh Margie . . . this is so much . . .

MARGIE. Mama, please . . . just take it, O.K.? *(On the verge of tears.)* Kiss little David for me . . . tell him . . .

C.C. Oh Christ, would you come on before I start crying?

MARGIE. Good-bye Mama Alice, I know you don't approve of my running again, but . . .

MAMA ALICE. No I don't approve, Margie Lynn. I don't approve at all.

TISH. Mama Alice . . .

MAMA ALICE. Did you come home for some sort of approval . . . was that the ticket, Margie?

C.C. I believe I hear our exit music . . . come on, Margie. *(MARGIE, her eyes fixed on MAMA ALICE, does not move.)*

TISH. *(Tearfully.)* Good-bye honey.

**ʀGIE.** *(Tearfully.)* Bye Mama . . . I promise I'll let you know where I am.

**ȿH.** I know you will, Margie.

**MARGIE.** *(She goes to* MAMA ALICE.*)* Good-bye Mama Alice . . . I'm sorry . . . I just . . .

**MAMA ALICE.** *(Breaking into tears herself, she takes* MARGIE *in her arms.)* Oh Lord, Margie . . . I'm sorry too. Oh honey, what are we gonna do with you?

**MARGIE.** I don't know, Mama Alice.

**MAMA ALICE.** *(Trying to see the woman in the child.)* Oh Margie . . . I guess you do what you have to do . . . God knows you're not gonna do anything else. Now get on out of here before Jack and Jimmy show up.

**MARGIE.** O.K., Mama Alice.

**GINGER.** *(Caught up in all the emotion.)* Well, so long everybody, it was real nice to meet you.

**MARGIE.** *(As she and* GINGER *are leaving.)* Bye Mama . . .

**TISH.** Bye Margie.

**C.C.** Good-bye ladies. It was indeed a pleasure to have met you both and don't worry, I imagine we'll be seeing each other again some time.

**MAMA ALICE.** Yeah, good-bye Miss C.C.

   *(*C.C. *exits.)*

**TISH.** Oh Mama Alice, I'm not sure I want to know, but just what is Jack gonna tell Darrell and Jimmy?

**MAMA ALICE.** Well, I think I got an idea . . . yeah, and it's gonna be a long night.

**TISH.** I better make some coffee.

**MAMA ALICE.** No, first thing you're gonna do is call Darrell.

**TISH.** What am I going to say to him?

**MAMA ALICE.** I don't know yet, but I'll think of something . . . aw hell come on back into the shop, honey . . . Mrs. Corey is sending her two daughters over this afternoon for permanents.

   *(The lights begin to fade as the two women go back into the beauty shop.)*

**TISH.** You know . . . Margie sure could have used a permanent.

**MAMA ALICE.** Yeah, well she just didn't have enough time, she'll be back . . . maybe you can give her one next time.

   *(Lights out.)*

*Curtain*

# James McLure

★ ★ ★ ★ ★ ★ ★ ★ ★ ★ ★ ★ ★ ★ ★ ★ ★ ★

## ★ THE PERSON

James T. McLure was born in Alexandria, Louisiana, in 1950 and lived for a time in Oklahoma before his family settled in Shreveport, where he attended Jesuit High School. Many are surprised that he is not a native Texan because he captures the West Texas idiom and atmosphere so well in his best-known plays. The knowledge that makes this possible, though, is acquired. When he lived in Dallas during his university years, McLure became fascinated by the denizens of rural Texas honky-tonks, who appeared as exotic to him as they would have to remote midwesterners, and he observed them with care.

When he entered Southern Methodist University in 1968, the year Jack Heifner graduated, McLure already had a commitment to a theater career and a degree of exposure to dramatic practice that was rare for a freshman in the Southwest. Both were due in large part to the efforts of an exceptional high school teacher, Father Kammer, who had put on annual Shakespeare productions at Jesuit High. Like Heifner, McLure benefited from attending SMU at a time when the enthusiasm of faculty and students in the new professional theater program was at a peak. Among his many talented classmates were the actor Powers Boothe and the Pulitzer Prize–winning playwright Beth Henley. He says today that he considers SMU's theater school to have been the best in the country during those years.

From the time McLure graduated in 1973 and joined the Pacific Conservatory for the Performing Arts in Santa Maria, California, to the present, he has had fortunate professional associations with acquaintances from his student days and with fellow professionals. When an actor playing Sir Toby Belch in a West Coast production of *Twelfth Night* broke his leg on opening night, a cast member immediately persuaded the director to hire McLure for the role and to fly him out from Dallas. When McLure was in New York preparing *Pvt. Wars* as a vehicle for actor friends, a girlfriend suggested that he send the manuscript of *Lone Star* to the Actors' Theater of Louisville, where the director, Jon Jory, not only accepted it but commissioned other plays and suggested ideas for development. During the New York run of *Lone Star,* one of the city's most successful publicists volunteered his efforts to get recognition for the play, its actors, and its author.

Although McLure had been writing since his college days, acting, first on one coast and then on the other, dominated his career until the success of *Lone Star* in 1979. After that came a heady but frustrating period of writing and rewriting film scripts, only one of which got to the screen. This time was epitomized by the failure of a unified *Lone Star/Laundry and Bourbon* film to be completed, despite four years of effort and the employment of two directors and several cast members. Sigourney Weaver has publicly expressed her disappointment at being unable to play Elizabeth, the strong female lead.

Today McLure views his nontheatrical writings as deviations from his true métier. He feels that his poetry and fiction are primarily personal and that his television writing is seriously limited by the medium and its management.

McLure's dramatic subject matter has ranged widely, as have his settings, but his plays characteristically are complex in their sympathies, and his lines are lyric, as well as, in many cases, bawdy. McLure's plays are imbued with a practical performer's sense of what will work on stage, and they require audiences to face some of the darker aspects of American experience. Not for nothing did a reviewer call James McLure a cross between Neil Simon and Sam Shepherd!

★ THE PLAYS

*Lone Star* is the best of the Texas good-ol'-boy, bawdy roadhouse romps. In Roy, the main character, McLure has created a larger-than-life version of the macho West Texas "real thing," that free and energetic model of uncompromising masculinity admired and feared by the workaday, practical men of Maynard, Texas, and adored by its women. The play is appealing to audiences on this level and can be enjoyed as what Mel Gussow of the *New York Times* called "a shaggy cartoon about adults as adolescents," but it has much more to offer. McLure shows us the tawdriness of Roy's role by emphasizing the childish taste of his chosen properties—the 1959 pink Thunderbird convertible, the Lone Star beer, and the sack of popcorn and candy bars. He lets us see that the location Roy is most comfortable in, the one Roy dreamed about returning to during his army years, is not even Angel's Bar but its scruffy rear, a derelict area featuring a garbage-can rack and discarded tires. As the stage directions note, it is "a place where old worn-out things end up."

Roy appeals to us partly because he is a romantic icon, a strong figure at the end of his trail. All that is left for him is to repeat his self-destructive behavior, howl at the moon like a coyote, wish on a star like a child, and lash out at those who accommodate themselves to modern life. In its quiet moments, and sometimes indirectly, the play shows us just how unsatisfactory the mystic westerner is as a model for living. In real life, the first Marlboro man died of lung cancer. On stage, Roy ends up cuckolded by his brother and bereft of his beloved pink Thunderbird.

The remaining two characters in *Lone Star,* Ray and Cletis, play distinctly secondary roles. They serve as foils, second bananas, and as chorus. Although they express admiration and fear of Roy, they also demonstrate a practicality and adaptability that he lacks. Ray begins as very much the dim-witted, adulatory younger brother, but it is he who "survives" in the war games behind Angel's Bar, and when pressed by Roy about the extent of his dumbness, he lashes back with, "Not so dumb I didn't go to Nam and get myself shot."

This last sally calls attention to another of *Lone Star*'s subjects. It is a play about the Vietnam veteran. In Roy it shows us the veteran who was brutalized and traumatized by his experience and rendered incapable of fitting into a normal, productive social role on his return to civilian life. Probably the most telling exchange in the play comes after Roy explains to Ray, for far from the first time, that he promised himself in Vietnam that if he ever got back to Maynard safely, he would get drunk in back of Angel's and now he is doing it. Ray answers, after a meaningful pause, "You been back two years now, Roy."

Just as an audience can get carried away by Roy's swashbuckling appeal, it can also overdo its condemnation of Roy's drunken irresponsibility. All of us who were not in Vietnam, we Cletises and Rays of America, need to listen and be touched when Roy reiterates, "I served *my* time." McLure began writing this play while he was a draft-deferred college student familiar with veterans, no older than he, who had returned from Vietnam unable to cope with the demands of day-to-day life. He encourages producers of *Lone Star* to make clear to audiences that the action takes place no later than 1975, that its reality is rooted within a particular time frame.

Although *Lone Star* was originally paired with an earlier work, *Pvt. Wars*, its proper companion play is *Laundry and Bourbon*. McLure now insists that *Lone Star* be played either alone or on a bill with *Laundry and Bourbon*, the companion piece that deals with the women related to the men of *Lone Star*. The women's afternoon of drink and talk parallels the evening of Roy, Ray, and Cletis, and the audience's awareness of Roy's long-suffering and dignified wife, Elizabeth, puts his behavior into a social context. The women's play shows us the price Elizabeth has to pay for her loyal love of Roy, "the last wild thing left around here" as her friend Hattie calls him. In this play the women are occupied, if comically, with household drudgery and children, while in *Lone Star*, the men carouse with abandon. The difference is made clear by Hattie when she tells Elizabeth: "You can't leave the important things in life like marriage and children up to the menfolk. If they had their way they'd just stick to their football and their fishing and their Thunderbirds and just be boys forever."

Although *Laundry and Bourbon* has moments of effective comedy, and although Hattie and Elizabeth are believable, high-spirited partners for Roy and his high school buddy Wayne, now a convict, the targets of the play's wit are predictable. *Laundry and Bourbon* is much more effective when presented as an introduction to the stronger work, *Lone Star*, than it would be if performed alone.

When McLure's SMU classmate Chris Nichols directed the Southwest premiere of *Lone Star/Laundry and Bourbon* at Dallas's New Arts Theatre, the play was credited with drawing people who seldom, if ever, attended theater. Its run, from July 25 to September 27, 1980, was exceptionally long for the city and gave a great boost to the new company.

## ★  THE WORKS

James McLure has written a widely diversified group of plays. Like Oliver Hailey and distinctly unlike Horton Foote, who is rooted in a particular subject matter, McLure is a conscious theater artist, a wordsmith and technician who enjoys the challenges of different forms and chooses subject matter sometimes because of a familiarity based on personal experience and sometimes simply for intrinsically interesting qualities. At least twice, he has utilized ideas suggested by others.

In addition to the short plays *Lone Star* and *Laundry and Bourbon*, which together make up *1959 Pink Thunderbird*, McLure has written two more plays set in Texas: *The Very Last Lover of the River Cane* and *Loss in Least*. The first of these is of near epic proportions; set in a honky-tonk near Muleshoe, Texas, it features an annual ritual battle between Bonney McMasters and relatives of River Cane's lover, whom Bonney killed fifteen years before. Although the play includes such staples of western storytelling as large-scale barroom violence and cracker-barrel or cow-lot humor, it is dominated by its enigmatic heroine, River Cane, who seizes the initiative after the male brawling runs its course. McLure has said that one of the attractions of Texans as stage characters is that they "can be big and overtly dramatic and still true to life." In this play he successfully exploits that larger-than-life quality of his subject, but unfortunately the massive destruction of the set that the action requires will necessarily limit the number of productions.

*Loss in Least* is constructed on a much smaller scale and concerns itself with conflicts of gender and family in a small-town Texas household of declining possibilities. Once again, the plot depicts a reversal of expectations. Two sisters who have been taken advantage of in the most traditional of ways by their male lodger successfully plan to convert the double seducer into an object of mutual convenience.

*Pvt. Wars*, which now exists in a full-length version as well as in the original one-act form, is a collection of brief scenes, divided by blackouts, that all concern three wounded veterans. The play's very limited action takes place on the terrace of a veteran's hospital. *Pvt. Wars* has often been compared with *Lone Star* because the two appeared on the same bill several times before *Laundry and Bourbon* was written. One similarity is the subject—Vietnam veterans cut off from conventional society by their physical or psychic wounds. Another is the pedagogical origins of the two plays. *Lone Star* began as a class exercise in characterization at SMU, and *Pvt. Wars* was initially an exercise for McLure's fellow actors in New York. Two characters, the cocky, streetwise Italian-American Silvio and the slow, childlike Gately, reappear in McLure's *The Day They Shot John Lennon*.

This later play was created out of the author's personal experience of the crowd that congregated outside the Dakota apartment house in New York following Lennon's murder. He saw the event as one that shattered the fabric of ordinary life for vast numbers of people; and he used the play to comment on the various ways the public was touched by the event and to depict people's different responses. Interestingly, there is an additional overlap of characters between this play and a later one. In *Fran and Brian*, which premiered in Dallas in 1987, McLure takes a couple who met on the street in *The Day They Shot John Lennon* and follows them through courtship, relationship, and disillusionment. It is a stylish modern romance in which the author demonstrates his keen ear for urban dialogue and his awareness of current mores.

*Max and Maxie* and *Napoleon Nightdreams* can both be loosely described as experimental plays. They draw heavily on theatrical and avant-garde philosophical sources. Although *Max and Maxie*, based on incidents in the career of Bert Lahr, depends largely on brittle, ironic dialogue and vaudevillian associations for its effects, and although *Napoleon Nightdreams* can be called a performance piece because of its heavy reliance on dance, music, and visual effects, neither play treats time or experience one-dimensionally or refers consistently to objective reality or to the commonly accepted conventions that stand in its place.

*Wild Oats* is not an original play but is an adaptation done in Los Angeles during the 1984 Olympic Arts Festival. It is a madcap western version of John O'Keefe's eighteenth-century Irish play that was made fashionable first by a Royal Shakespeare Company production in London in 1976 and later by a New York production as well. Along with a busy plot of confused identity, lost children, and miscellaneous skulduggery, the McLure-O'Keefe work features a dazzling display of theatrical allusion and works a mad mixture of Shakespearean lines into surprising contexts.

James McLure is either a playwright still searching for his personal style and for ultimately satisfying subject matter as he moves restlessly and often brilliantly from one form to another, or he is a consummate eclectic whose works will always be most identifiable by their diversity. Regardless of the definitive judgment, it is clear from his extant works that McLure is a dynamic, original playwright whose works not only have immediate audience impact but also stimulate thoughtful analysis and reconsideration.

## LIST OF WORKS

### PLAYS

*Lone Star,* 1979
*Pvt. Wars,* 1979
*Laundry and Bourbon,* 1980
*The Day They Shot John Lennon,* 1982
*Fran and Brian,* 1983
*Thanksgiving,* 1983
*Max and Maxie,* 1984
*Wild Oats* (adaptation of eighteenth-century play by John O'Keefe), 1984
*The Very Last Lover of the River Cane,* 1985
*Napoleon Nightdreams,* 1987
*Loss in Least,* 1988

### RECOMMENDED READING

Corathers, Don. "A Conversation with James McLure." *Dramatics* 59 (January 1988): 16–19, 43–48.

# Lone Star

★ ★ ★ ★ ★ ★ ★ ★ ★ ★ ★ ★ ★ ★ ★ ★ ★

# CAST OF CHARACTERS

ROY: Lean, tough, beginnings of a beer gut. Dressed in jeans and jean jacket, beat-up cowboy hat, roach-killer boots. Uneducated, belligerent, his army service has nearly given him a sense of irony. Nearly. He voted for Nixon, likes John Wayne movies, and thinks Raquel Welch is a great actress.

RAY: His younger brother. He is larger than Roy. Slope-shouldered, sloth-like, slowww. He has no idea what irony is. Wears a John Deere hat. Probably sleeps in it.

CLETIS: A friend of Ray's. A wide-eyed asshole. His life should have been terminated in high school. He married the first girl he dated that didn't spit on him. She married him because of his father's appliance store. He works there. Gets lost in the stock room. Has a plastic pocket pencil holder. Sleeps with it.

# SETTING

*Place: Maynard, Texas. Behind Angel's Bar.*

*Time: One A.M. Summer night.*

*The rear of Angel's Bar—a roadhouse saloon in West Texas—faces the audience. It is a weatherworn, wooden building. The walls are parched and peeling. "Decorated" perhaps with a few old license plates and some beer advertisements.*

*The back of the bar has the feeling of a junkyard. A place where old worn-out things end up. Garbage cans stand against the upstage left wall containing refuse and two-by-fours. A discarded front car seat is downstage left.*

*Upstage right against the side of the bar is a two-leveled garbage-can rack holding old tires. Downstage right is a large wooden garbage-can rack about four to five feet long, two feet wide, two feet high. In the play it is used as a bench. Underneath the bench is where Roy stores his beer and his sack of "dodads."*

*As the lights come up we hear the sound of music and laughter coming from Angel's. ROY comes through the door with a bang, grinning and singing a snatch of a country song. He crosses down to the bench, gets himself a beer, sits, sips, and stares at the stars like a man who has got a grudge against them, and continues his reverie . . .*

ROY.

Starlight, starbright
Twenty-fifth star I seen tonight
I wished I may I wished I might
Have the wish I . . .
*(He sips the beer.)*
Starlight, starbright
Twenty-sixth star I seen tonight
I wished I may I wished I might
Have the wish I . . .
*(He sips the beer. Howls like a coyote. He points his finger like a gun. Holds it to his head. Fires. He falls over.)* "You all right, doc?" *(Pause. Gasping.)* "It's all right, Wyatt. It's just a flesh wound."

> *(From offstage we hear* RAY *calling for his brother. He's been running from the parking lot through Angel's; he arrives slightly out of breath.)*

RAY. Roy? You out here? Roy? Roy? *(*RAY *enters. Sees* ROY *lying down.)* Is that you, Roy?

ROY. *(Still lying.)* No. It's Dale Evans. Queen of the Goddamned West.

RAY. Have you passed out?

ROY. No. I was just killing myself. *(*ROY *sits up.)*

RAY. Are you drunk, Roy?

ROY. Is it Friday night, Ray?

RAY. It's Friday night, Roy.

ROY. Then I'm drunk, Ray. *(Pause.)* Did you take my wife home for me?

RAY. I did.

ROY. Good. *(Pause.)* How's my 1959 pink Thunderbird convertible?

RAY. It's good.

ROY. That's good. How's it runnin'?

RAY. Rough.

ROY. (Concerned.) What?

RAY. Probably need your points seein' to.

ROY. O.K.

RAY. And your plugs.

ROY. New plugs?

RAY. Maybe a new radiator cap.

ROY. Uh-huh.

RAY. And your tires are low.

ROY. Uh-huh.

RAY. *(Pause.)* Actually could use a whole new block.

ROY. Drop my block?

RAY. Uh-huh.

ROY. Still. She's a helluva automobile.

RAY. You want me to drive you home?

ROY. Little while.

RAY. You drunk ain't you, Roy?

ROY. Not much. Sorta.

RAY. I been into Angel's.

ROY. I figured.

RAY. You wanna go back in there.

ROY. What for.

RAY. Bright lights. Good music. Conversation.

ROY. Who do I want to talk to in there?

RAY. James is in there. Cletis is in there. We could talk to Cletis Fullernoy.

ROY. I'd rather talk to dirt.

RAY. You're gettin' unfriendly, Roy.

ROY. I'm a mean son of a bitch, Ray.

RAY. I know it.

ROY. War made me mean.

RAY. You were always mean.

ROY. *(Intensely.)* That goddamn Skeeter Fullernoy. I hate that little bastard.

RAY. Why?

ROY. He wears them little stupid-ass high-school loafers. I hate 'em. And he has that thing to hold pencils in his pockets. I'd like to kill him.

RAY. He runs his daddy's appliance store now.

ROY. Does that mean I can't kill him?

RAY. He's on the Junior Chamber of Commerce. *(Pause.)* Nice night.

ROY. It is.

RAY. That's for damn sure.

ROY. Look at them stars, Ray.

RAY. Any one in particular?

ROY. No. Just the whole thing. Each star is a sun, Ray. Most of 'em as big as our sun.

RAY. Some even bigger. *(Pause.)* If we went in we could listen to the jukebox. Got all your favorites, Roy. You could play A-5, "Your Cheatin' Heart." Or B-6, "Return to Sender," or C-8, "Get Offa My Cloud." *(Ray begins to sing "Get Offa My Cloud" loudly.)*

ROY. Sit down here and have a Star little brother and shutup! *(RAY takes a Lone Star beer. Sits on the bench with his brother.)*

RAY. Cold.

ROY. Uh-huh. *(Pause.)*

RAY. It's nice in there.

ROY. What do I want to go in there for. It's just a juke joint with a lot a sluts and rednecks who want to break your nose for you.

RAY. But that's your kinda place, Roy.

ROY. Normally, yeah. But not tonight.

RAY. There's some blondes in there.

ROY. Look. I'm a married man. I don't need strange all the time. Just once in a while. *(Pause. They sip.)* I like it out here.

RAY. I know you do.

ROY. We done a lot a growin' up around here. *(Pause.)* When I was in Vit Nam, I used to say to myself: "Roy."

RAY. *(Giggling.)* You called yourself Roy?

ROY. What the hell you want me to call myself?

RAY. I mean you talked to yourself out loud?

ROY. Sometimes. War is a terrible thing, Ray. Anyway I'd say, "Roy, if you ever get back to Maynard, Texas, you go out back to Angel's like you and Wayne Wilder used to do." Member Wayne?

RAY. *(Grimly.)* How could I forget.

ROY. "And you get yourself a case of Lone Star beer, some peanuts, some popcorn, some Fritos, a box of Cracker Jacks, maybe, some Baby Ruths, a couple of Mars Bars, and all the beef jerky and Slim Jims you can lay your hands on."

RAY. You got Mars Bars out here?

ROY. "And you just stretch out and look at the land and listen to the cars go by on the highway." You don't know how many times I thought about that. I promised myself that was the first damn thing I'd do, was get drunk in back of Angel's. And now I'm doin' it.

RAY. *(Pause.)* You been back two years now, Roy.

ROY. So what? *(With emphasis.)* I served *my* time.

RAY. Well, you do this every night.

ROY. But you see, when you're trying to come back to a place in your mind you want it to be how you remember it. Not how it is. This place is still the same cause the stars never change. *(Pause.)* 'Sides I got my Lone Star, and all my little dodads spread out here in front of me. I'm doin' exactly what I said I'd do.

RAY. You've always been a man of your word, Roy.

ROY. *(Pointing his finger in* RAY'*s chest for emphasis.)* And don't forget: I served my time.

RAY. *(Ashamed.)* They wouldn't take me. You know I had football knee.

ROY. What you had is football brain. And when you're too stupid to get into the army, you're too dumb to breathe. Now that's what I call dumb.

RAY. Not so dumb I didn't go to Nam and get myself shot.

ROY. What did you just call it?

RAY. Nam. That's what you call it.

ROY. Don't try to be cool. You can't say Nam. You weren't there. It's Vit Nam to you.

RAY. Vit Nam then. I didn't get my ass shot off in Vit Nam. That's for damn sure.

ROY. All I know is: *(Pointing finger.)* I served *my* time.

RAY. You been out to the house lately?

ROY. What for? Mom's gone senile and the old man's a damn fool anyway.

RAY. Why you say our father's a fool?

ROY. Named us Roy and Ray didn't he. *(*RAY *begins to rummage in the paper sacks.)* What you lookin' for?

RAY. They Mars Bar.

ROY. When are you gonna learn to talk?

RAY. I talk fine.

ROY. You talk for shit. It ain't "they Mars Bar." It's "this Mars Bar" or "that Mars Bar" or "his Mars Bars" or "her Mars Bars."

RAY. What if she only has one.

ROY. Then it's Mar Bar. She has one Mar Bar. He has one Mar Bar. They have one Mar Bar. *(Pause.)*

RAY. You got a Baby Ruth? *(ROY pulls one from his jean jacket pocket. RAY unwraps it. Takes a bite, has a sip of beer.)* Have you ever noticed how a Baby Ruth looks a lot like a turd? I mean, it's about the size of a turd. More or less. It's got little bumps on it. Worse of all it's brown. *(He takes a bite.)* Sure are good though. *(He takes a sip of beer.)*

ROY. That's not the right way to do that.

RAY. What?

ROY. Eat a Baby Ruth and drink a beer.

RAY. I been eatin' Baby Ruths all my life.

ROY. Listen to me.

RAY. Baby Ruths is one thing I know everything about.

ROY. Look, there's a right way and wrong way to do everything. That's one thing the army teaches you.

RAY. The army teaches you how to eat a Baby Ruth?

ROY. The two tastes don't mix.

RAY. I don't understand.

ROY. Look. *(Holding up his beer.)* Beer sour. *(Holding up Baby Ruth.)* Baby Ruth sweet. Now you get it?

RAY. No.

ROY. Christ. You need *(Holding up popcorn.)* popcorn.

RAY. Popcorn?

ROY. Popcorn salty.

RAY. Show.

ROY. First you eat the Baby Ruth. *(He takes a bite.)* Mm. Nutty and delicious. *(He takes popcorn.)* Then you eat the popcorn. Hm. Salty and crunchy. *(Takes beer.)* Then you drink the beer. Hm. Cold and sour. Now you try. *(RAY takes a bite of the Baby Ruth, then the popcorn, then sips the beer.)* Well?

RAY. I like it better my way.

ROY. You'd have never made it in the army.

RAY. Then I'm glad I didn't go.

ROY. You couldn't get in.

RAY. *(Mouth full.)* Football knee.

ROY. You couldn't've took it for five minutes.

RAY. Maybe I could.

ROY. You get squeamish when you see a dead armadillo out on the highway.

RAY. I don't like it when their shells are cracked open.

ROY. Shit. I saw people without heads.

RAY. Were they dead?

ROY. Think about it, Ray.

RAY. I guess so.

ROY. I saw a guy stick an M-16 up a Gook's cunt and fire it.

RAY. Ooooh.

ROY. I saw guys burn babies.

RAY. I'm glad I flunked that test.

ROY. Damn right. Here, I'm gonna show you what it was like.

RAY. Don't want to.

ROY. Now you sit there.

RAY. Who am I?

ROY. You're a Gook.

RAY. I knew it.

ROY. Now I'm gonna sneak up on you. *(RAY sits eating the popcorn.* ROY *picks up a two-by-four.* ROY *removes himself a ways and flattens himself on the ground and begins crawling.)*

RAY. Well, I'd just shoot you.

ROY. You wouldn't see me.

RAY. Hell I wouldn't.

ROY. I'm bein' too stealthy.

RAY. But I see you.

ROY. No, you're talkin' to someone.

RAY. *(Pause.)* Who am I talkin' to?

ROY. Anybody.

RAY. Can it be J.R.?

ROY. Yes!

RAY. *(Pause.)* "Well look-a there J.R. You see what I see." "I sure do, Ray. Looks like a goddamn American soldier." "Reckon we better shoot the son-bitch."

ROY. No! No! Cut! Look. You're talkin' to your friend Gung-ho. And you don't see me. Got it?

RAY. O.K. *(ROY resumes crawling.)* Well, howdy, Gung. Damn long time no see. How the wife and kids? What's that you say? No. I don't understand Chinese.

ROY. That's it. Now you see I'm sneakin' up all the time. An' you don't see me.

RAY. What's that Gung? You say you see goddamn American soldier. Reckon we better shoot the son of a bitch. *(RAY stands with a pistol in his finger. Shoots* ROY.*)* You're dead.

ROY. No I'm not.

RAY. I just killed you.

ROY. You couldn't see me!

RAY. Gung saw you.

ROY. No he didn't. Gung is blind.

RAY. Shit, I didn't know that.

ROY. You're blind too. O.K. We're gonna do it again. *(ROY resumes crawling.* RAY *closes his eyes simulating blindness. He feels the air for his friend "Gung-ho.")*

RAY. Well, Gung, how you doin' boy? You still blind? Me too. Guess we're just sitting ducks if some goddamn American soldier tries to sneak up on us. *(RAY throws a handful of popcorn into his "blind" face.)* Good thing we surrounded ourselves with land mines. *(ROY buries his face in the dirt.)*

ROY. Shit. What's the use? *(ROY gets up.)*

RAY. I don't like to play Vit Nam, Roy. *(Silence. They drink.)*

ROY. *(Suddenly.)* Where the hell *is* everybody!?

RAY. Well, Cletis and James are inside . . .

ROY. I'm not talkin' about them. I'm talkin' about people I knew. My friends from before. Guys I used to go up to Dallas with and pick up girls. Damn we had ourselves some times.

RAY. Most a your crowd done gone, Roy.

ROY. *(Nostalgically.)* There was old Palmer Jenkins.

RAY. He moved to Oklahoma.

ROY. Don't talk to me about Oklahoma.

RAY. Well, that's where he moved to. Hugo, Oklahoma.

ROY. Goddammit. I asked you. Why would anybody in their right mind move from Maynard, Texas, to Hugo, Oklahoma?

RAY. I couldn't say. But he sells used Buicks there.

ROY. *(Deathly serious.)* That's the goddamned end of the line, you know that? Sellin' used Buicks in Hugo, Oklahoma.

RAY. I wouldn't do it for money.

ROY. Goddamn. You move to Oklahoma, you know what that makes you don't it?

RAY. What?

ROY. A goddamn *Okie!* The lowest form of life that lives! *(This gives ROY an idea.)* Say Ray, what was the best time you ever had?

RAY. *(Slightest pause.)* R.O.T.C.

ROY. You liked that?

RAY. I liked them uniforms.

ROY. Well, this year we're gonna go to Texas-O.U. weekend.

RAY. Yeah?

ROY. We're gonna sit in the Cotton Bowl.

RAY. Yeah?

ROY. We're gonna watch the Longhorns beat the shit out of Oklahoma and yell hook 'em horns, just like all the other assholes.

RAY. Hook 'em horns!

ROY. Then you know what?

RAY. What?

ROY. We're gonna get a room on the tenth floor of a hotel in downtown Dallas . . .

RAY. Yeah . . .

ROY. And throw all the furniture out the window.

RAY. *(Awed.)* Man.

ROY. How does that sound?

RAY. We'll have ourselves a time!

ROY. Damn straight.

RAY. Yeoow!

ROY. Then we'll get ourselves a forty-dollar whore.

RAY. Huh?

ROY. And go to hell in a wheelbarrow!

RAY. You mean a prostitute?

ROY. Don't you like the idea?

RAY. Well, sure . . .

ROY. Say so if you don't.

RAY. Well, I just . . .

ROY. You haven't had that much experience with women is what you're tryin' to say.

RAY. *(Pause.)* I know more than Cletis knows.

ROY. What does Cletis know?

RAY. Hardly nothing at all.

ROY. I'm not surprised.

RAY. But he's been married two years.

ROY. Some girl married Skeeter Fullernoy?

RAY. *(Confidentially.)* He'd never seen a fully grown naked woman before.

ROY. He's been married two years and he's still never seen a naked woman?

RAY. Not before he got married. He'd never seen a naked woman before he got married. But he had seen a book.

ROY. A book?

RAY. Yes. It showed the female reproductive organs.

ROY. Well, that should have given him an idea.

RAY. No. It just showed a *side* view.

ROY. Uh-huh.

RAY. So I told him what I knew.

ROY. About what?

RAY. About naked women.

ROY. *(Chuckling.)* Uh-huh.

RAY. I've had some experience, Roy. I have. *(Pause.)*

ROY. Where the hell is everybody? Where the hell is Dell Henry?

RAY. He got married, moved to Snyder.

ROY. I know, I'm just talkin' out loud.

RAY. *(Darkly.)* Then there's Old Wayne.

ROY. *(With great fondness.)* Old Wayne. We won't see his like again. Biggest hell raiser this town ever saw. *(Pause.)* Guess he's still down to Huntsville.

RAY. Be out two years. Good behavior.

ROY. Now, Wayne was always smart. Remember, he got out of the army by shootin' off his toe.

RAY. Blew off half his foot.

ROY. Old Wayne. *(Pause.)* Shit. Everyone I knew is either married, moved to Oklahoma, or shot their foot off, and I can't decide which is worse. *(Pause.)*

RAY. *(Darkly.)* Wayne was a mean bastard.

ROY. *(Appalled.)* What makes you say a thing like that?

RAY. He hit me on the head with a hoe.

ROY. *(Pause.)* He was probably trying to teach you something. Probably had a moral to it.

RAY. What kind of moral can there be when somebody hits you on the head with a hoe?

ROY. Did I ever tell you about the time Ol' Wayne and me went to Bossier City, Louisiana?

RAY. About a hundred times.

ROY. *(Shouting as if in an echo canyon.)* Bossier City! Bossier City! Kinda got a sound to it, don't it? Bossier City! Babylon on the Red River! Sin. Hot women. Sticky summer nights. The biggest strip of nightclubs 'tween Vegas and Miami Beach! Bossier City! One-armed bandits! Teenage prostitutes! Drunken driving! All the things that make life worth living. One summer morning in 1967 Wayne said to me, "Roy, we can either get drunk here in Maynard or we can get drunk in Bossier City!" So we drove to Louisiana! And I mean, Ray, as soon as we got there, wham! Just like that things started to happen!

RAY. What happened?

ROY. We saw a car wreck.

RAY. Wow!

ROY. That was nothin'. We saw three before we left town. We were in two of them. *(Pause.)* Wayne was a helluva driver. I tell you we started at one end of that Bossier Strip and worked our way to the other. Club Flamingo, the Log Cabin Club, Kim's Lounge, and the immortal Merle Kimberly's Whiskey A-Go-Go. Ray, it had three dance floors that lit up!

RAY. Did you dance?

ROY. You know I don't dance. Wayne danced.

RAY. Did you get in any fights?

ROY. We got kicked out of The Ace's Lounge and Mr. Torch for fighting.

RAY. You couldn't get out of these fights.

ROY. Hell no. We started them. Then! At the Swamp Club, Wayne tried to pick up these two Italian girls. Well, their boyfriends didn't like that one little bit. And let me tell you something, Ray. If you're ever in that part of the world, don't ever get involved with no Louisiana Dagos. There ain't nothin' worse than the Southern Mafia!

RAY. Are they the ones that pull the knife on you?

ROY. Yeah, they're the ones who—hey, you've heard this story before.

RAY. Yeah.

ROY. *(Drunken pause.)* You broke into my story. Where was I?

RAY. *(With great enthusiasm.)* You were right at the part where the Italians pull out their knives, and you and Wayne run back to the truck to get your shotgun. But then the Italian guys pull out their guns and start shootin' at you! But you make it back to the truck, and while Wayne backs the truck out of the parking lot you fire out the window at the Italians. Wayne backs up into one car, hits a fence, and then as he's leaving the parking lot he sideswipes an oncoming Cadillac.

ROY. *(Annoyed.)* It was a Lincoln Continental.

RAY. Or a Lincoln Continental, depending on how drunk you are when you're telling the story.

ROY. *(Indignant.)* That story don't change! It happened. We had ourselves a time.

RAY. Well, sometimes you say a stray bullet kills an old woman.

ROY. Well, sometimes I forget that part.

RAY. How can you forget gunning down an old woman?

ROY. It wasn't an old woman exactly. What it was . . . was a bowling alley. There was a bowling alley next to the parking lot.

RAY. How could you mistake an old woman from a bowling alley?

ROY. It was dark.

RAY. Oh.

ROY. Anyway, me and Wayne ended up in Kim's Lounge. And Wayne begins to sweet-talk this girl down at the end of the bar. And pretty soon he's taking this girl out to the pickup truck. He told me it wouldn't take long. So I ordered another drink. Then, in about five minutes Old Wayne comes back in as white as a sheet and says: "Roy, let's get the hell out of Bossier City." So we did. But after only six hours on the Bossier Strip we had ourselves two fights, two car wrecks, had a gun battle with the Southern Mafia, and Wayne Wilder had french-kissed a man in a dress! *(Pause. Lifting beer.)* So Wayne, down in Huntsville—here's to you boy.

> *(They both drink.* CLETIS FULLERNOY *enters, dressed in J. C. Penney's slacks, shirt with a plastic pocket pencil holder, and a pair of loafers.)*

CLETIS. Hey Ray. Hey Roy.

RAY. Hey Cletis.

CLETIS. What you boys doin' out here?

ROY. *(Ominously.)* We were just shooting it out with the Italian Mafia.

CLETIS. Shoot. There ain't no Italians out here. *(Pause. He looks around.)* Are there?

ROY. You know any Italians, Cletis?

CLETIS. Can't say as I do.

ROY. That's just as well. I have a feeling Italians would hate you on sight. Even little baby Italians without ever being told just how hideous you are would hate you.

CLETIS. *(Pause.)* Uh . . . yes. *(Pause.)*

RAY. How are you, Cletis?

CLETIS. Fine. Perfectly fine.

RAY. That's good.

CLETIS. How are you, Ray?

RAY. I'm fine. *(Pause.)*

ROY. You know, I'm part Italian myself. That's right. My real mother was an Italian my father met during the war. *(Pause.)*

CLETIS. *(Nervously.)* I see. So, what are you boys doing out here?

RAY. Nothing.

CLETIS. Nothing?

RAY. Nothing.

CLETIS. How can you do nothing?

RAY. I can't do nothing for very long. But Roy can do nothing nigh on to forever.

ROY. What you need out here, Skeeter Fullernoy?

CLETIS. Don't call me that.

ROY. That's what I've always called you, Skeeter.

CLETIS. Yes, but I run an appliance store now.

ROY. What's your full name, Skeeter?

CLETIS. *(Reluctantly.)* Cletis T. Fullernoy.

ROY. Cletis T. Fullernoy. What does the "T" stand for?

CLETIS. Nothing. Don't stand for nothing.

ROY. It's gotta stand for somethin'.

CLETIS. No it don't. My Daddy wanted me to have a middle initial. He'd never had one himself and he said it had killed his ambition.

ROY. Are you ambitious?

CLETIS. Someday I hope to go into politics.

ROY. You do and I'll shoot you.

CLETIS. *(Smiling weakly.)* You're a caution, Roy. You really are.

ROY. Why don't you go away, Cletis? *(Pause.)* Tell you what. I'm going to close my eyes and think of pleasant thoughts like Christmas and reindeer and when I open them you'll be gone. Like a bad dream. *(ROY closes his eyes and begins humming "Rudolf the Red-Nosed Reindeer." He opens his eyes.)* You ain't gone, Cletis.

CLETIS. I know. I got something to talk to Ray about.

ROY. What?

CLETIS. It's private.

ROY. Haven't you figured out what to do in bed yet?

CLETIS. *(Flustered.)* What do you mean?!

ROY. I hear you can't find the vagina, Skeeter.

CLETIS. Who told you that? Did you tell him that?!

RAY. Now, Cletis . . .

CLETIS. You did! You did tell him that! I can't believe you told him that!

RAY. It just slipped out.

CLETIS. That's my private sex life! Things like that just don't slip out!

ROY. Is that your problem, Skeeter? Have things been slipping out lately?

CLETIS. No! And don't call me Skeeter!

ROY. What should I call you then, Skeeter?

CLETIS. I'm not talking to you.

RAY. Cletis . . .

CLETIS. I'm not talking to you either.

RAY. Cletis, if you're not talking to Roy and you're not talking to me—

ROY. Who the hell are you talking to, Skeeter?

CLETIS. Nobody and nothing. *(Silence.)* Sure are a lot of stars out tonight. Sure are. There's the Big Dipper, and the Little Dipper and there's Orion. *(Pause.)* I haven't seen stars like this since my honeymoon. Amy Lee and me, we camped out near Lake Cherokee up near Tulsa. I mean to tell you, that Oklahoma—that's God's country. *(Pause.)*

ROY. *(To RAY.)* I'm going in for a drink. When I come back, you make sure this asshole's gone.

    *(ROY exits.)*

CLETIS. I don't think Roy likes me.

RAY. He hates you, Cletis. (CLETIS *takes out a pack of cigarettes, begins to smoke.)* When did you start smokin', Cletis?

CLETIS. What time is it?

RAY. About one.

CLETIS. I started about forty-five minutes ago. *(Miserably.)* I think I'm hooked.

RAY. How do you like it so far?

CLETIS. It's all right. *(Pause.)* Tastes like shit though. Makes me dizzy too. *(Pause.)* And it makes your breath stink. Even your fingers stink.

RAY. Think you'll stick with it?

CLETIS. I don't think so. I think I'll give it up. *(Pause.)* I don't want to get lung cancer. *(Pause.)* In fact, I think I'll give it up right now. *(He drops the cigarette and steps on it.)* Whew. I feel better already. Now I can start clearing out my lungs. Tomorrow I'm going to start running track.

RAY. What made you take it up?

CLETIS. Severe depression. It was either cigarettes or alcohol. And you know what alcohol does to me. I could be a damn alcoholic if I didn't watch it.

RAY. What's your problem, Cletis?

CLETIS. Well . . .

RAY. Is it about your wife?

CLETIS. No dammit! It's not about my wife! And by the way I resent the fact that you told Roy about my private sex life.

RAY. I apologize.

CLETIS. I had a few questions, that's all! Just a few questions.

RAY. I apologize.

CLETIS. That damn book. Shit. It showed a little squiggly line with an arrow that said *vagina.* How was I to know? A vagina don't look nothin' like a squiggly line.

RAY. No. But what does it look like?

CLETIS. You know, I shouldn't be talkin' about this. I'm a Baptist and we just don't sit around talkin' about our wives' sacred reproductive organs.

RAY. O.K.

CLETIS. That's all right. I forgive you. *(Pause. Lost.)* Ray, why does Roy hate me?

RAY. He doesn't like your shoes.

CLETIS. Why?

RAY. He just doesn't like 'em.

CLETIS. *(Thoughtfully.)* I've always looked up to Roy.

RAY. So have I.

CLETIS. I don't know. He was always like an idol to me, I suppose. He was real good in sports, and he was real popular with girls. And he had that 1959 pink Thunderbird convertible.

RAY. Still does.

CLETIS. Yeah. Then too, he was the only boy from Maynard to go off to Vit Nam.

RAY. I had football knee.

CLETIS. I had to run the appliance store.

RAY. What you drivin' at, Cletis?

CLETIS. See, it's just that I always wanted to be just like Roy. See, I combed my hair like Roy. I bought cowboy shirts like Roy. I saw *Hud* six times. Nothin' worked. Girls still didn't like me. It ain't easy when you got a name like Skeeter.

RAY. I know, Cletis.

CLETIS. How do you know? How can you possibly know what it's like to go through life as Skeeter? What did they call you growin' up?

RAY. Ray.

CLETIS. Well with me it was either Skeeter or Cletis. Either way it was humiliation.

RAY. Get to the point.

CLETIS. I just always wanted to be like Roy. I had the hair combed right like him, had the shirts like him. Nothin' worked. But deep down, deep deep down, I know what was the difference beween me and Roy.

RAY. What was that?

CLETIS. *(With mystic awe.)* A 1959 pink Thunderbird convertible.

RAY. Ah, I see.

CLETIS. If I just had that car, life may have turned out different for me. I could see myself with Sandra Dee flyin' along about ninety mph, the top down, Sandra's long blonde hair wavin' in the wind, telephone posts humming by—whew, there goes one! Whew, there goes one! It would have been a beautiful thing to behold. Life would have been complete. *(Pause.)* Well, Ray, tonight I had a chance to make my life complete. You can understand that, can't you, Ray?

RAY. I don't know what the hell you're talkin' about Cletis. (CLETIS *takes out a set of car keys from his pocket.)*

CLETIS. Here.

RAY. *(Pause.)* These are the keys to Roy's car.

CLETIS. Yes they are.

RAY. Where did you get these keys?

CLETIS. You left 'em in on Angel's bar when you came back here lookin' for Roy.

RAY. Roy loves that car, Cletis.

CLETIS. It *was* a beautiful thing to behold.

RAY. Was? Was a beautiful thing to behold, Cletis? *(Pause. Whisper.)* What in the name of God have you done, Cletis?

CLETIS. I took it.

RAY. You took Roy's 1959 pink Thunderbird convertible?

CLETIS. I did.

RAY. What did you do then?

CLETIS. I broke it.

RAY. You what?

CLETIS. I was into Angel's Bar, I saw you lay the keys on the counter. You forgot you left 'em when you came out here.

RAY. And you took 'em.

CLETIS. I just wanted to take a spin. I swear, just a spin.

RAY. What happened, Cletis?

CLETIS. I run it off the road.

RAY. Where, Cletis?

CLETIS. Down past Ol' Man Purkey's place at that curve, in the road. I couldn't hold it.

RAY. Well that's flat land there. There's nothing to run into out there.

CLETIS. *(Sadly.)* Think about it, Ray.

RAY. *(Pause.)* There's one tree.

CLETIS. One gigantic, ancient, unmovable cottonwood tree.

RAY. You run the Thunderbird up against the cottonwood, didn't you, Cletis?

CLETIS. I run the Thunderbird THROUGH the cottonwood, Ray.

RAY. Is it in one piece?

CLETIS. The cottonwood is.

RAY. And the Thunderbird?

CLETIS. It hit that tree and fell apart like an old thing made of rust. There's pieces of that car spread from here to yonder. The biggest piece burst into a great wad of fire. *(Pause.)* It was pretty.

RAY. Where were you?

CLETIS. I was thrown from the car, by a miracle. By all rights I should be dead.

RAY. Don't worry. You will be.

CLETIS. He's really gonna be mad, ain't he?

RAY. Mad? Hell, Cletis, he'll kill you.

CLETIS. That's what I got to talk to you about.

RAY. I can't do nothing to help you.

CLETIS. Help me? Help US! You're my accomplice!

RAY. What d'you mean?

CLETIS. You left the keys on the counter, didn't you? It's half your fault.

RAY. *(Pause.)* That's the way Roy'll figure it too.

CLETIS. Will he? Good! Well, that's what I want to talk to you about.

RAY. What?

CLETIS. Why don't you say you wrecked the car? You're his brother! He won't kill you! Now me, he hates me to begin with! But you—what's the worst he could do?

RAY. Break my arms.

CLETIS. That's not so bad.

RAY. And my legs too.

CLETIS. Naw, his bark's worse 'n his bite.

RAY. His bark is pretty awful too.

CLETIS. Don't tell him I did it! Please don't tell him I did it. It'd be like throwing Christians to the lions. It'd be like the early Christian martyrs.

RAY. Cletis, the early Christian martyrs didn't go around wrecking people's cars!

CLETIS. *(Almost in tears.)* Please, Ray, please!

RAY. Shut up, will you, I gotta think.

CLETIS. Think about what?

RAY. Shut up!

CLETIS. What'll I do while you're thinkin'?

RAY. Look at the stars.

CLETIS. I can't look up at 'em, all I see is a dead Thunderbird.

RAY. Take up smokin' again. *(CLETIS takes out his cigarettes. Pause. He lights, shakes.)*

CLETIS. *(Talking to himself.)* He can't kill me. I'm a married man. That ought to count for something. *(Pause.)* Maybe if I move to Mexico. He might not follow me there. Or Central America! It'd be like Butch Cassidy and the Sundance Kid! I could go out in a blaze of glory shootin' it out with the Federales! *(Pause.)* I wonder if you can take a U-Haul to Central America? *(He smokes.)*

RAY. Cletis. I been thinkin'.

CLETIS. What you come up with?

RAY. Nothin'. There ain't nothin' to come up with.

CLETIS. Come on, Ray. Get in the car. We can be in San Antone by dawn!

RAY. Forget it. You just get the hell out of here. I'll take all the blame.

CLETIS. What? You mean it? *(Pumping his hand.)* Goddamn that's Christian of you goddamn. Now look, Ray, if you ever need anything from me anything at all. You just know where to find me. You come into my daddy's store an' I'll get you a goddamn 10 percent—no 15 percent discount! I don't care what Daddy says! You hear me?

RAY. I hear you, Cletis. Now get gone.

CLETIS. I just want you to know how much I . . .

    *(ROY enters . . . bandage wrapped around right hand, singing much drunker.)*

ROY.

"They say Ruby you're like a dream
Not really what you seem . . .
*(ROY walks up to CLETIS, begins dancing.)*
. . . And though I should beware
Still I just don't care.
Right from the start.
Who stole my heart.
Ruby—it's you."
*(They pull away.)*

CLETIS. Thank you. You dance really fine, Roy.

ROY. What the hell you still doin' here, Skeeter?

CLETIS. I just wanted to say . . . *(CLETIS begins pumping ROY's hand.)* . . . that you're one of the finest most respectful persons it's ever been my privilege—

ROY. Goddamnit, quit shakin' my hand.

CLETIS. I just want to say that deep down, deep down, I know you got a Christian respect for life, liberty, and love of family and friends.

ROY. C'mere Skeeter. *(Holding* CLETIS *by the lapels.)* Let's get one thing clear. I wouldn't piss in your mouth if your guts was on fire. *(Releasing* CLETIS.*)*

CLETIS. I know you wouldn't. Thank you. Thank you. Well I'll just be goin' now.

ROY. Why don't you do that little thing.

CLETIS. I'll just be goin' now—

ROY. Don't just say it . . . do it.

> *(*CLETIS *exits slowly.)*

ROY. Look a here Ray. Tore my goddamn shirt pocket.

> *(*CLETIS *reenters having heard this.)*

CLETIS. I got a whole drawer full of shirts just like that one at home. You're welcome to 'em. All of 'em.

ROY. *(Roar.)* GIT!

> *(*CLETIS *exits.)*

RAY. How'd you tear your shirt . . .

ROY. I was on my way out to the parkin' lot. I wanted to see my car.

RAY. Did you see it?

ROY. Nah. I didn't get to the parkin' lot.

RAY. Good.

ROY. No, I got in a fight with Ricky Wright.

RAY. I'm surprised he'd fight with you.

ROY. It took some doin'.

RAY. Why'd you fight him?

ROY. He was drinkin' Pearl Beer. It made me mad. Why would anybody drink that horsepiss Pearl when you could be drinkin' Lone Star?

RAY. I wouldn't drink it for money.

ROY. Want another?

RAY. Could do one.

ROY. I wished I could hear a coyote sometimes.

RAY. Me too. Ain't none no more.

ROY. I know.

RAY. We poisoned 'em all off.

ROY. *(Pause.)* I'd sell my soul to hear a coyote. *(*ROY *does a coyote howl.* RAY *does a half-hearted coyote howl.)* I wouldn't even mind a few drunken Indians now and then.

RAY. We got rid a them fore we got even rid a they coyotes.

ROY. Goddamn Texas. You ain't got coyotes; you ain't got Indians. What the hell have you got Texas?

RAY. We got International Harvester. We got plenty a them. *(Pause.)*

ROY. Sometimes you wonder what this country musta been like in the early days. Goddamn when all this country was open and breathin' free.

RAY. There were Indians then.

ROY. Yeah.

RAY. Buffalo.

ROY. Yeah.

RAY. Buffalo chips.

ROY. Yeah.

RAY. And there were . . . deer.

ROY. Uh-huh.

RAY. And antelope.

ROY. And before that . . .

RAY. Dinosaurs.

ROY. Yeah.

RAY. And dinosaur chips.

ROY. All sorts of ancient things. Hair of the dog?

RAY. No thank you.

ROY. *(Drinks.)* Damn this stuff'll kill you.

RAY. That's for damn sure. *(Silence.)*

ROY. You know what I love. I love my wife. I love my country. An I love my car. Whoooo! I tell you. I've had myself some times in that car.

RAY. I'm glad you've got your memories, Roy.

ROY. I do. I got my memories. That car's been some kind a pussy wagon. That there car's my youth.

RAY. Well we all have to grow up sometimes Roy.

ROY. In the spring of nineteen hundred and sixty-one I took Edith Ellen Hyde out in that car a mine. Took her parkin' out to Thompson's road. That was the night I looked up her dress. Up until then I had no idea what life was all about. *(Pause.)* We kissed and kissed till we got halfway good at it. Then she took off her shirt. *(Pause.)* That was the first nipple I'd had in my mouth since Mom's. But nipples are like bicycles: once you learn you never forget how. Finally we got the windows all steamed up, and I couldn't wait. Got the car to smell like the smell of a woman and I just had to see it. Edith Ellen didn't want me to see it. Said it was bad enough me touchin' it without wantin' to look at it. She even tried to scare me. Said it looked God-awful. But she couldn't talk me out of it. I was a man with a mission. So I scooted over and scrunched down under the steerin' column like this and she lifted up her skirt and I lit a match like that. And I looked at the damn thing. *(Pause.)* And y'know, y'wonder what the first explorer felt. The first explorer that climbed over that hill and saw—stretched out before him, in all its God glory—the Grand Canyon. Well that's what I felt like when Edith Ellen Hyde lifted her skirt and said, "Here it is," I looked, and it was AWE-INSPIRING. I felt like Adam. I felt like the man who discovered the Grand Canyon.

RAY. That was like a sermon.

ROY. Yes. *(Pause.)* You know, I been thinkin' about that car lately, Ray.

RAY. Me too.

ROY. Do you realize that I've had more tail in that car than anybody else in this whole town?

RAY. Well, sure. You wouldn't let no one else drive it but you.

ROY. I had myself the pleasures of my life in that backseat.

RAY. You used to let me smell the seats after you come home from a date. You used to say, "That's the smell of a woman." I appreciated it.

ROY. It was nothin'. That car's gonna be a museum piece in time. I'd like to pass on to my children and their children, somehow, a piece of that car.

RAY. You can give them each a piece, Roy. *(Pause.)* Roy, I got somethin' to tell you.

ROY. All right.

RAY. It's bad.

ROY. All right.

RAY. It's terrible.

ROY. Uh-huh.

RAY. It's like an open wound. *(Pause.)* When you were in Vit Nam.

ROY. Yes.

RAY. Me and Elizabeth . . .

ROY. You and Elizabeth what?

RAY. Me and Elizabeth . . .

ROY. Yes . . .

RAY. Well, me and Elizabeth . . .

ROY. I've heard this part, Ray. *(Pause.)* Stop playin' with that tractor gasket. *(Pause. Slowly.)* Ray—

RAY. Made love.

ROY. You and Elizabeth.

RAY. Elizabeth and me.

ROY. It's the same thing.

RAY. Yes.

ROY. While I was in Vit Nam?

RAY. Yes. *(Pause.* ROY *looks at* RAY. RAY *looks at the ground.)*

ROY. Damn. Shit damn. *(Pause.)* What have you got to say for yourself?

RAY. I'm sorry.

ROY. Is that all?

RAY. I'm real sorry.

ROY. *(Standing, pacing.)* Well, shit. I just can't believe it.

RAY. Roy—

ROY. Shut your mouth. *(Pause.)* My own little brother. I can't believe it! I taught you your life! I taught you how to swim, how to drive a car, how to pass a football, I taught you how to jack off! The most important things in life, I gave to you. And this is my reward?

RAY. What can I say?

ROY. Not a damn thing. I can't believe this is happening to me! My own goddamn little brother and my own goddamn wife! You know that's against the Ten Commandments, don't you? You've just broken one of God's biggest laws, that's all! You have coveted your own brother's wife.

RAY. What does *coveted* mean?

ROY. IT MEANS FUCK, YA DAMN FOOL! You have fucked your own brother's wife! You know what that's called?

RAY. No what?

ROY. Sodomy.

RAY. *(With terror.)* No!

ROY. That's right, Ray. Sodomy. Boy, I'd hate to be in your shoes. It says it right there in the Bible: "Thou had better not commit adultry, nor fuck thy brother's wife, nor covet thou his sheep, nor covet thou his ox . . ."

RAY. I wouldn't fuck my brother's ox.

ROY. *(Groaning.)* NO . . .

RAY. I wouldn't even fuck my own ox.

ROY. That's not what it means!

RAY. You said *covet* meant fuck.

ROY. Sometimes it does, sometimes it doesn't. See what I mean, Ray? See what I'm drivin' at?

RAY. No.

ROY. I'm talkin' about the Bible, Boy! I'm talkin' about the goddamn Garden of Eden!

RAY. You are?

ROY. Of course. In the Garden of Eden, God made Adam. And He made animals. And He looked down and He saw that it was good. Then He looked down and saw Adam was alone and He saw that that was perverted.

RAY. Why was it?

ROY. Because Adam was alone. He had nothing to occupy his mind. He was walking around perverting the Garden of Eden.

RAY. What was he doing?

ROY. Figure it out, Ray. The guy was alone and he was horny.

RAY. Oh. Then what?

ROY. Then God made Eve, and the bitch screwed the goose and they all got kicked out on their ass. Get my point?

RAY. No.

ROY. God punished them. They broke some of His major laws just like you, and He punished them. *(Pause.)* When did you and Elizabeth fornicate on me?

RAY. Uh . . . about two years ago . . .

ROY. When two years ago?

RAY. Winter . . . no, the air conditioner was on the first time—

ROY. The first time! Was there more than once?

RAY. Huh?

ROY. More than once? How many times? Did you do it a lot?

RAY. No, not a lot.

ROY. You better tell me the truth. How many times?

RAY. I'm not good at countin'. *(A horrible silence.)*

ROY. Where?

RAY. In your bed.

ROY. My weddin' bed! Is that all?

RAY. Once on the floor.

ROY. The floor!

RAY. Once in the bathroom.

ROY. What!

RAY. Once on the kitchen table.

ROY. The kitchen table. I'll never eat off it again. You goddamn degenerate. I swear. This is the most perverted thing that ever happened to me. My whole house defiled. Guess I'll just have to pitch a tent in the backyard.

RAY. Once in the backyard. *(RAY is still seated. ROY stalks around with contained rage.)*

ROY. I wonder what I'm going to do with you, Ray?

RAY. I don't know.

ROY. I think what I ought to do . . . *(ROY picks up a two-by-four near the shed.)* . . . is take this here two-by-four upside your skull.

RAY. Don't do that, Roy.

ROY. Why the hell not?

RAY. It might kill me.

ROY. You ought to be killed.

RAY. Don't say that to me. I'm your little brother.

ROY. I oughta smash your skull in.

RAY. War has made you bloodthirsty, Roy.

ROY. That's what it's supposed to do, you damn fool!

RAY. But if you killed me . . .

ROY. What?

RAY. I'll die.

ROY. So?

RAY. If I die . . . I won't know what to do.

> *(ROY throws away the lumber. RAY braces for the blow he feels sure is coming. ROY walks to RAY slowly. Stands over him. ROY snatches RAY's cap and beats RAY furiously with it. His anger subsiding, ROY walks over to the side of the bar, leans against it, groaning like an animal in pain.)*

ROY. The thing is . . . nothing has been the same since I come back. Things I see . . . people I see . . . it's like they never was. The thing is . . . I can't seem to get nothin' started no more . . . cause . . . cause . . . see, me and Elizabeth, we had it good once. And I never thought she would do me like . . . I mean I know I'm a hard man to live with . . . but . . . she's a wonderful woman . . . a wonderful woman . . . see, the thing is . . . goddamnit all to hell. *(ROY comes back to where RAY is sitting. Gives him his hat.)*

RAY. Are you gonna hit me now, Roy?

ROY. No.

RAY. Please. It'll make you feel better.

ROY. No.

RAY. Wish you would. You'll feel better. I promise.

ROY. No.

RAY. All right. *(ROY walks in front of where RAY is sitting. Without breaking stride he suddenly turns and belts RAY in the mouth. RAY flies off the car seat he is sitting on. ROY goes back to the side of the bar.)* You said you weren't going to hit me.

ROY. Changed my mind.

RAY. Do you feel any better?

ROY. No. *(Pause.)* You see, me and Elizabeth we were real close once. It's like, she trusted me . . . she knew I had my faults when she married me . . . but deep down we always loved each other. And I'll always love her, no matter what.

RAY. That's good, Roy.

ROY. No matter what comes between us, I'll always love her. *(Quietly.)* See. We were together. And we'll always be together. *(ROY crosses to the bench, sits.)* But *now* I got this hurt that I'm carrying around with me.

RAY. I understand.

ROY. No you don't. How could you understand? Ain't nobody can understand my hurt. It's deep down. No one understands. Who could possibly understand my hurt?

RAY. *(Pause.)* Hank Williams.

ROY. Shut up.

> *(RAY crosses to the bench. Sits. ROY begins drinking from a pint bottle of whiskey. He shares some with his brother. They sit in silence. From Angel's Bar drifts the sound of a song like "Your Cheating Heart." RAY begins to sing along softly. ROY joins in. They finish the first verse and together bow their heads. There is a short pause, then in unison, with extra punch, they begin singing the second verse—and finish the song with gusto. They then fall silent.)*

RAY. You still mad at me?

ROY. Yeah.

RAY. You gonna hit on me anymore?

ROY. No. You're my brother. *(Pause.)* Besides. You can't help it if you got brain damage.

RAY. I ain't got brain damage.

ROY. We been keeping it from you. Mom and me.

RAY. You made that up. I ain't got no brain damage. *(Pause.)*

ROY. I wonder why in hell she picked you?

RAY. 'Cause I was your brother. I've wanted to tell you for a long time. But everything has just fucked up tonight. I wanted to get it all over with at once. *(Pause.)*

ROY. Lotta things happen.

RAY. Yeah.

ROY. You know what we're gonna do about all this?

RAY. What?

ROY. Nothing. We're not gonna tell her you told me.

RAY. O.K.

ROY. Lotta things change. But things are gonna stay the same around here.

RAY. O.K. *(They spit in their palms and shake on it. As an afterthought* RAY *wipes his hands. Pause.)* Roy?

ROY. Huh?

RAY. I don't got brain damage like you said. Do I?

ROY. 'Course not. You're my brother ain't you?

RAY. Yeah. *(Pause. They look at each other, hug, then break away embarrassed.)*

ROY. Well, enough of this shit. Let's go home.

RAY. We can't.

ROY. Why not?

RAY. Your car ain't here.

ROY. You said it was.

RAY. I thought it was.

ROY. *(Pause.)* Where is it?

RAY. Sit down, Roy.

ROY. *(Sits.)* Where is it?

RAY. Down past Old Man Purkey's out in a field.

ROY. What's it doin' out there?

RAY. It's wrecked. *(*ROY *takes a long sip of whiskey.)*

ROY. My pink 1959 Thunderbird convertible?

RAY. She's gone, Roy.

ROY. How did it happen?

RAY. Run off the road into a tree.

ROY. That old cottonwood tree?

RAY. Yeah.

ROY. Can you fix her?

RAY. No.

ROY. Was it quick?

RAY. She burnt all up. 'Cept for the parts that don't burn. *(Pause.)* You all right, Roy?

ROY. Sure. Don't worry about it. I can handle it. No big deal. Worse things have happened in the history of man. I can't think of what . . . *(Nearly sobbing.)* My car, my car . . . why'd you do it, Ray, was it out of spite? Wasn't Elizabeth enough for you, you pig!

RAY. It wasn't me.

ROY. Who then? *(Pause.)* You were here with me all night. You took Elizabeth home, we played Vit Nam, we did the Bossier City story, then . . . then . . . then CLETIS!!

RAY. Roy!

ROY. I'm gonna kill him. I may get the chair, but I'm gonna kill him. I'm gonna torture him first and then I'm gonna kill him. *(Pause.)* I'm gonna castrate him first and then I'm gonna—I know! I'll strap him to the rear bumper and drag the sonofabitch . . . wait a minute . . . I don't even *have* a rear bumper no more. Can I borrow your pickup?

RAY. I'm using it tomorrow.

ROY. Never mind. Forget it. There's something I've gotta do first.

RAY. Before you kill Cletis?

ROY. Before I do anything.

RAY. What you gotta do?

ROY. I gotta puke.

> (ROY *runs, staggers off.*)

RAY.

Starlight, starbright

First star I seen tonight

I wished I may, I wished I might

Have the wish I wished tonight.

> (*We hear* ROY *vomit offstage. Pause.* ROY *returns, pale and shaken.*)

RAY. You O.K.?

ROY. Yeah.

RAY. You puke?

ROY. Yeah.

RAY. You want anything?

ROY. Gimme a Star. (RAY *hands him a Lone Star beer.*)

RAY. It all came up?

ROY. Yep. It all came up. The beer, Cletis, Elizabeth, Vit Nam, my car, you, me.

RAY. Breathe some of this night air, you'll feel better. *(Pause.)*

ROY. I guess my car's scattered all over the field.

RAY. Cletis said it exploded on impact.

ROY. I bet it was a beautiful sight to behold.

RAY. I bet it was too. *(Silence.)*

ROY. Guess I'll have to walk home.

RAY. I'll walk you home, Roy.

ROY. O.K.

RAY. We can follow the crick bed yonder.

ROY. O.K.

RAY. We got plenty of moon and stars. 'Member what the old man used to say about stars? "The light we seen tonight left those stars millions and millions of years ago. Some of those stars could be dead by now. They all could be dead. We might be all alone but we're still seein' 'em shine." *(Pause.* RAY *hands* ROY *his car keys.)* You can get a new car.

ROY. Won't be the same.

RAY. No.

ROY. Things is never the same. *(The brothers look at each other.)*

RAY. No. *(Pause.)* I'm going down to Minden tomorrow. Want to come?

ROY. No.

RAY. *(Pause.)* You got to look out for the silver lining, Roy.

ROY. Ain't none.

RAY. Always is, Mom says.

ROY. Mom's senile.

RAY. There's always something to be thankful for.

ROY. Well . . . *(Defiantly.)* . . . at least I ain't in *Oklahoma!* (ROY *throws his arm around* RAY, *gives a yell, and they exit.)*

*Curtain*

# Laundry and Bourbon

★ ★ ★ ★ ★ ★ ★ ★ ★ ★ ★ ★ ★ ★ ★ ★ ★ ★

# CAST OF CHARACTERS

ELIZABETH CAULDER: Strong, sensuous woman. Intelligent but under-developed. Would be capable of handling most men other than Roy, her husband. Therein lies the attraction. A woman devoid of self-pity. A forthright person who would call your bluff.

HATTIE DEALING: A woman whose bluff needs calling. Blowsy, brassy, used to getting her own way. Mother, wife, talker. Has an adage for every occasion. Anything that has gone wrong in her life is Vernon's fault. Vernon is her husband.

AMY LEE FULLERNOY: Bright, sassy, spoiled. Baptist to the teeth. Given to gossip. Life revolves around the country club. An old enemy of Hattie's.

# SETTING

*The Caulder Home. Facing the audience is the rear porch of a single-story, white, wooden frame house. There is a back door to the kitchen, flanked by two windows. Stage right is a bedroom window, stage left a kitchen window.*

*It is a large deep back porch with a western exposure. From it one sees wide-open pasture land, a hill, and the state highway beyond it. The road to the house from the highway is visible from the back porch although the road leads initially around to the front of the house.*

*The porch has railings on the side and a ceiling fan. There are two rocking chairs stage right, a low table in front of them. There is a pile of laundry waiting to be folded. Discarded magazines and papers lie around; it is obvious the porch hasn't been cleaned in days.*

*There is a sideboard stage left under the kitchen window. A black telephone is on the sideboard coming from the kitchen. Also on the sideboard is an old portable record player. Also stage left are a small kitchen table and one chair. A television set sits on a wooden crate either downstage left or downstage right.*

*At rise:* ELIZABETH *is smoking a cigarette, leaning against the porch post with a book in her arms. Music is playing on the phonograph. The doorbell rings. She doesn't move. Sound of* HATTIE *kicking front door.*

HATTIE. *(Off.)* Elizabeth! Elizabeth. You in there. *(Voice getting closer.)* Where *are* you?

ELIZABETH. *(Resigned.)* I'm back here, Hattie. *(*HATTIE *enters from around the side of the house, wearing a loud floral print dress.)*

HATTIE. Here you are. Is there something wrong with your doorbell?

ELIZABETH. I don't know.

HATTIE. I been ringing and ringing. Didn't you hear me *ring?*

ELIZABETH. Guess not.

HATTIE. Must be something wrong with your buzzer. Mmm?

ELIZABETH. I guess.

HATTIE. Your buzzer just don't buzz.

ELIZABETH. I'll have it checked. Come on in and sit a spell. *(*HATTIE *steps onto the porch.)*

HATTIE. A person could die out there in the heat. Just buzzing themselves to death. Buzz, buzz, buzz.

ELIZABETH. I'll have it checked.

HATTIE. Lord, it's like an oven out there. *(Pause.)* It's like an oven under here. Why don't we go inside where it's cool.

ELIZABETH. Can't—the air conditioner's busted. Called Fullernoy's. They're gonna send somebody out.

HATTIE. Lord. First your buzzer don't buzz, now your AC is on the blink. Looks like all your modern conveniences are just turning on you, girl. *(*HATTIE *sits, fanning herself with a magazine.)*

ELIZABETH. Can I get you something?

HATTIE. No. I'm fine.

ELIZABETH. Coffee.

HATTIE. Nuh-uh. I'm fine.

ELIZABETH. Ice tea.

HATTIE. Really. I'm fine.

ELIZABETH. Would you like some bourbon?

HATTIE. On the rocks with a splash of water. *(*ELIZABETH *exits to the kitchen.)*

ELIZABETH. You look beat.

HATTIE. I'm not beat, I'm in a frenzy.

ELIZABETH. What's the matter?

HATTIE. I'll wait'll you get back. I'm catching my breath.

ELIZABETH. Why you out of breath?

HATTIE. Mainly from buzzing your buzzer.

ELIZABETH. *(Irritated.)* I'll get it fixed. *(*ELIZABETH *returns with the drink.)* Here.

HATTIE. Thanks.

ELIZABETH. Nice dress, Hattie.

HATTIE. Thanks, but it looked better on the mannequin than it does on me . . . Say where's that worthless husband of yours?

ELIZABETH. Roy?

HATTIE. No. Burt Reynolds. I noticed that his almighty Thunderbird wasn't out front.

ELIZABETH. Oh . . . he's in town about something.

HATTIE. Don't tell me he's actually gonna get a job.

ELIZABETH. Hattie. Don't start.

HATTIE. Okay. Okay. *(Pause.)* Say, you feel all right?

ELIZABETH. Yeah. Why?

HATTIE. I don't know, you look kinda flushed.

ELIZABETH. Oh, it must be the heat.

HATTIE. Yeah. Just must be the heat. *(Pause.* ELIZABETH *takes a breath preparing for the performance she knows is coming. She enjoys playing straight man to* HATTIE.*)*

ELIZABETH. So what're you in a frenzy about?

HATTIE. Oh yeah! Today I went through living hell.

ELIZABETH. What did you do?

HATTIE. *(Grimly.)* I went shopping with my children.

ELIZABETH. Bad, huh?

HATTIE. Disastrous. When my kids hit a department store they go berserk. I think it activates something in their glands. We hadn't been in J. C. Penney's five minutes before they scattered in all directions. Now you take my little Cheryl.

ELIZABETH. Uh-huh.

HATTIE. Now she's a sweet little thing but bless her heart she's a thief.

ELIZABETH. A thief.

HATTIE. It's time I faced facts, 'Lizabeth. My daughter is a kleptomaniac. As soon as we got into that store she started stuffing her pockets. Stuffing her clothing. She ran away from me and ten minutes later I saw her. I barely recognized my only daughter. She looked like a beach ball with legs.

ELIZABETH. Did you make her put it back?

HATTIE. Yes, but it does no good. Thieving is in her blood.

ELIZABETH. Where do you suppose she gets it?

HATTIE. From Vernon Jr.

ELIZABETH. Where was Vernon Jr. all this time?

HATTIE. He was in the hardware department.

ELIZABETH. Doing what?

HATTIE. Chasing his brother with a hammer.

ELIZABETH. Chasing little Roger?

HATTIE. Yes.

ELIZABETH. What was little Roger doing?

HATTIE. Screaming.

ELIZABETH. Oh Lord.

HATTIE. Oh Lord is right. And somehow Vernon Jr. broke a solid-steel J. C. Penney hammer.

ELIZABETH. *(Laughing.)* How can you break a solid-steel hammer?

HATTIE. Don't ask me. When it comes to destruction Vernon Jr. is a genius. But I tell you it's the last time I go shopping with those kids.

ELIZABETH. Where are the kids now?

HATTIE. I took the little darlings over to Vern's mother's place. She has a nice big house. *(Pause.)* They ought to have it leveled in about an hour or so. *(She sips.* ELIZABETH *gets up, brings the laundry over.)* What you doing?

ELIZABETH. Nothing. Just sit back and enjoy your drink. I've been putting this off all afternoon.

HATTIE. Here, I'll give you a hand.

ELIZABETH. Don't be silly.

HATTIE. Hush. I don't even have to think about it. I just put it on automatic pilot and fold. *(Pause. They fold in silence.)*

ELIZABETH. You don't have to be so particular with those T-shirts. Roy's got a jillion of them.

HATTIE. So does Vernon.

ELIZABETH. Why do men wear so many T-shirts?

HATTIE. I don't know.

ELIZABETH. I don't know either. *(Pause.* ELIZABETH *stares blankly out at the land.)*

HATTIE. What you looking at?

ELIZABETH. Nothing.

HATTIE. *(Pause.)* You got a TV out here. *(*HATTIE *gets up, moves to the TV.)*

ELIZABETH. Yeah. It's an old one. I watch it out here some.

HATTIE. *(Checking watch.)* Ooooo. *(She turns on the set.)*

ELIZABETH. What's on?

HATTIE. "Let's Make a Deal." *(*HATTIE *returns to her chair and resumes folding without ever taking her eyes off the TV set.)*

ELIZABETH. Okay, but keep the volume down. I can't stand to hear them women scream.

HATTIE. I know what you mean. *(Pause.)* All that yelling. *(*ELIZABETH *goes back to work folding socks.* HATTIE, *screaming.)* Oh! Would you look at that woman!

ELIZABETH. *(Startled.)* Where?

HATTIE. There! Would you do that!

ELIZABETH. Do what?

HATTIE. Dress up like a chicken!

ELIZABETH. Is that what that's supposed to be?

HATTIE. Of course it is. It's a chicken suit. The woman has dressed herself up like a chicken to be on national television.

ELIZABETH. That's stupid.

HATTIE. Of course it's stupid. *(Folds.)* Besides, doesn't even look like a chicken. *(Folds.)* Chickens don't have bangs. *(Folds.)* Chickens don't have bangs. *(Folds.)* And I know. I've been around chickens all my life. *(They fold in silence.* HATTIE, *screaming.)* Oh God!

ELIZABETH. What?

HATTIE. Look there, it's her husband.

ELIZABETH. So.

HATTIE. So! She's got him dressed like a rooster. Bad enough her dressed like a chicken, but to get a grown man dressed like a rooster!

ELIZABETH. *(Contemptuously.)* Huh! I could never get Roy to do that.

HATTIE. I should hope not. A man loses his masculinity when he's dressed up in a rooster suit. *(Pause. Transfixed, glued to the screen.)* Look. She can't make up her mind . . . what would you take? The curtain or the box?

ELIZABETH. The box.

HATTIE. Why?

ELIZABETH. "Good things come in small packages."

HATTIE. Wrong. Small things come in small packages.

ELIZABETH. Well, wedding rings come in small packages.

HATTIE. Yeah. But once you got one of them, honey, go for the big stuff.

ELIZABETH. She chose the curtain.

HATTIE. And it is? A dream vacation to British Honduras! Just think of it! British Honduras! *(Pause.)* Say, where is British Honduras?

ELIZABETH. South America, I think.

HATTIE. Why would any person want to go there?

ELIZABETH. Well, she sure does. Look at her jump up and down. Looks like she's gonna wet her britches.

HATTIE. Well, she can relax. 'Cause she ain't going.

ELIZABETH. She just won it.

HATTIE. Well, she's gonna un-win it after this commercial.

ELIZABETH. You've seen this one before?

HATTIE. I've seen 'em all before.

ELIZABETH. How does she lose it?

HATTIE. The bitch gets greedy and goes for the grand prize.

ELIZABETH. Does she win?

HATTIE. No. She gets a year's supply of frozen meat pies.

ELIZABETH. *(Sadly.)* From British Honduras to frozen meat pies.

HATTIE. Yeah. Ain't fate weird. *(Pause. She folds.)*

ELIZABETH. Commercial's on. Want another drink? *(ELIZABETH exits to fix the drink.)*

HATTIE. Course I do. The main reason I come over here is to get away from the kids and get bombed. Lord you just don't know what it's like having a house full of kids.

ELIZABETH. No, I don't.

HATTIE. They're all the time underfoot. It's like living with midgets. *(ELIZABETH enters with the drinks.)*

ELIZABETH. You know I'll take them. Anytime you need a rest.

HATTIE. Honey, couldn't do it. It'd give me a guilty conscience. *(Pause. They begin to fold a sheet together.)* How's everything? How's Roy?

ELIZABETH. Oh . . . you know Roy.

HATTIE. *(Grinning.)* Yeah, I know Roy.

ELIZABETH. *(Stopping her, good-naturedly.)* Quit grinning. You don't know him that well.

HATTIE. I've known Roy all my life.

ELIZABETH. Yeah. But you didn't really get to know him till high school when you dated Wayne Wilder. We'd all go double-dating in Roy's Thunderbird.

HATTIE. Don't remind me.

ELIZABETH. *(Fondly.)* Why not? They were the most eligible boys in Maynard.

HATTIE. Nobody in Maynard is eligible.

ELIZABETH. Remember, we were all going to get married right after high school. Me and Roy. Wayne and you.

HATTIE. Yeah . . . but I ended up with Vernon Dealing.

ELIZABETH. Yeah. Isn't life funny?

HATTIE. Hilarious. *(Pause.* ELIZABETH *crosses to the TV.)* What're you doing?

ELIZABETH. I'm going to turn off the TV.

HATTIE. *(Restraining* ELIZABETH.*)* No!! We haven't seen the grand prize!

ELIZABETH. But you already know what it is.

HATTIE. Yeah, but you don't.

ELIZABETH. But I don't want to know.

HATTIE. Sure you do! Quick, sit down. They're about to start. First they'll open curtain #2. Wait . . . wait. Aha. Frozen meat pies! And look there on old greedy's face. Yeah, she's trying not to act disappointed. Who you kidding, honey! You coulda been in British Honduras, missy. Not that it's very nice probably. Just one big jungle. But it sure beats hell outta frozen meat pies! *Now* . . . curtain #1. An entire new kitchen and utility room ensemble. Big deal. Just look at that woman! Disappointment is carved on that face! If there's one thing no woman wants it's a new stove! Look! Look! Now she's crying and she wants us to think those are tears of joy! Baloney! You ain't gonna win no academy award with that performance.

ELIZABETH. Why do you watch this?

HATTIE. Elizabeth, TV game shows have everything. The thrill of victory, the agony of defeat! *(Slight pause.)* Mainly the agony of defeat.

ELIZABETH. Well, I think it's stupid.

HATTIE. What're you doing!

ELIZABETH. Turning it off.

HATTIE. Don't you want to know what the grand prize was?

ELIZABETH. No.

HATTIE. A brand new Lincoln Continental.

ELIZABETH. Who cares?

HATTIE. Well, you should. It's better than what you drive.

ELIZABETH. Roy's never gonna get rid of that Thunderbird.

HATTIE. He's had that car since high school.

ELIZABETH. He loves that car, Hattie.

HATTIE. What's so great about a 1959 pink Thunderbird convertible?

ELIZABETH. Roy says it's a classic.

HATTIE. It's a piece of junk.

ELIZABETH. *(Staring off.)* . . . Sometimes I think he loves that car more than me.

HATTIE. It's only a car.

ELIZABETH. Yeah, but he says it can take him where he wants to go.

HATTIE. That's stupid. *(Suspicious.)* Where does he want to go?

ELIZABETH. *(Almost to herself.)* I don't think he has any idea.

HATTIE. *(Puzzled.)* Well, good. Good. *(Pause.)* Well, we better get back to the laundry or we'll never get it done.

ELIZABETH. Oh, right. God I hate laundry.

HATTIE. Try doing it for three kids.

ELIZABETH. Week in. Week out. It's the same old clothes.

HATTIE. You can only look at so many pairs of Fruit of the Loom before you want to puke.

ELIZABETH. I'd like to burn everything in this basket and start all over. Everything except this shirt.

HATTIE. Why that shirt's all frayed.

ELIZABETH. It is now, but I remember the first time Roy wore this shirt.

HATTIE. When was that?

ELIZABETH. On our first date. He drove up in that pink Thunderbird in this shirt with all the pearl buttons. He looked just like Paul Newman in *Hud.* *(HATTIE holds up a pair of boxer shorts.)*

HATTIE. God, these shorts are big.

ELIZABETH. What?

HATTIE. These jockey shorts—they're so big. They're not that wide. They're for a narrow body, but they're so long . . .

ELIZABETH. I suppose.

HATTIE. Why're they so long?

ELIZABETH. Roy likes them big. Says he needs a lot of room. *(Pause.)*

HATTIE. Whew, it's hot out here. *(Pause.)* Lordy, how's a body supposed to keep cool?

ELIZABETH. Nothing to do but fix a bourbon and coke and just sit and sweat.

HATTIE. I can't do that.

ELIZABETH. You can't sweat?

HATTIE. No. Fix a drink in the afternoon in front of the kids.

ELIZABETH. Why not?

HATTIE. Children learn by example.

ELIZABETH. So?

HATTIE. Well, all I need is to come home to a house full of kids sitting around drinking margaritas. You don't know what it's like raising a family.

ELIZABETH. No, I don't.

HATTIE. And lemme tell you, summertime is the worst.

ELIZABETH. What do you do?

HATTIE. I send them outside.

ELIZABETH. In this heat.

HATTIE. I give 'em a salt pill and say, play outside.

ELIZABETH. Don't they collapse from heat prostration?

HATTIE. Anything to slow them down.

ELIZABETH. I wish you'd let me take them sometimes.

HATTIE. Elizabeth, you're not used to kids. The strain would kill you. *(*ELIZA-BETH *moves downstage. She leans against a porch post looking out over the land. Pause.)* Elizabeth, what are you staring out at that road for?

ELIZABETH. No reason. There's nothing to see.

HATTIE. That's the truth. Nothing green to look at. God, it's depressing living on the edge of a desert.

ELIZABETH. But just think, millions of years ago all this land was under water.

HATTIE. Well . . . at least it would have been cool.

ELIZABETH. I like this land, but sometimes it gets too hot and burnt for people. It's still too wild and hard for anything to grow. *(Pause.)* Oh, look Hattie!

HATTIE. What is it?

ELIZABETH. Look at that cloud.

HATTIE. It's just a cloud.

ELIZABETH. Yeah, but look how it's throwing a shadow across the land. God, doesn't that shadow look peaceful gliding over the land. Doesn't it look cool? It reminds me of a cool dark hand stroking a hot surface. *(Pause.)* Lately I've felt so hot and hollow inside I've wanted something to come along and touch me like that.

HATTIE. Elizabeth, what's the matter with you?

ELIZABETH. Nothing, Hattie, nothing.

HATTIE. *(Pause.)* You're doing it again, staring out at that hill. There ain't nothing out there but the highway and the road up to the house. Now, what're you expecting to see?

ELIZABETH. I was hoping to see a 1959 pink Thunderbird convertible come over that hill.

HATTIE. You've got tears in your eyes! Don't you tell me nothing's the matter! What is it? *(Pause.)*

ELIZABETH. Roy's been gone two days. *(Silence.)*

HATTIE. Why, that son of a bitch! No wonder you've been so weird. Here, you sit yourself down here. I'm gonna fix you a drink and you're gonna tell me all about it.

ELIZABETH. I don't want another drink.

HATTIE. Hush up. Hattie's taking care of you now. The doctor is *in.* *(*ELIZABETH *sits.* HATTIE *exits to the kitchen, talking.)* I knew there was something wrong the minute I laid eyes on you. First you didn't answer the doorbell, and as soon as I saw you I could tell something was the matter. That son of a bitch. *(*HATTIE *returns, having mixed drinks in record time.)* Well, what brought it on this time?

ELIZABETH. I don't know. Things haven't been the same since he came back.

HATTIE. From Vietnam?

ELIZABETH. Yeah.

HATTIE. I know. I seen the change. But believe me you've been perfect about it.

ELIZABETH. I haven't been anything. I haven't done anything. He was the one that went off for two years. He was the one got shot up. He's the one that has nightmares.

HATTIE. Nightmares.

ELIZABETH. Yeah, almost every night. *(Pause.)* Anyway, now he's back and he can't seem to get nothing started. He made me quit the job at the pharmacy. He worked some out at his dad's place. He's done some roughnecking out in the oil fields. But then he always gets in fights and gets himself fired.

HATTIE. Well . . . what's he got to say for himself?

ELIZABETH. He says he's looking for something.

HATTIE. Hmnnn. What?

ELIZABETH. He doesn't know what. He says everything has changed here in Maynard.

HATTIE. Nothing's changed in Maynard since the Civil War.

ELIZABETH. I want him back the way it used to be.

HATTIE. Elizabeth, he's always been wild and unmanageable.

ELIZABETH. *(Flaring.)* I don't want to manage him. I don't want to break his spirit. That's why I married him, his spirit. Roy Caulder wasn't going to take no crap from anyone or anything. He and Wayne Wilder were gonna shake up the world.

HATTIE. Need I remind you that Wayne Wilder is currently serving five-to-ten for car theft?

ELIZABETH. *(Quietly.)* Roy's different than Wayne.

HATTIE. I wouldn't be too sure.

ELIZABETH. I just wisht I knew he was safe. He could be hurt.

HATTIE. Or he could be with another woman.

ELIZABETH. I hope that's all it is.

HATTIE. Elizabeth, how can you say that?

ELIZABETH. Any man worthwhile is gonna look at other women. That's natural. And sometimes they wander a bit.

HATTIE. A bit? That man's done more wandering than Lewis and Clark.

ELIZABETH. You're exaggerating.

HATTIE. Last year? Last year! He took off for five days.

ELIZABETH. *(In spite of herself, smiling.)* Yeah. He had himself quite a time.

HATTIE. You mean he told you what he did?

ELIZABETH. Oh, sure.

HATTIE. Well, you never told me.

ELIZABETH. No.

HATTIE. But I'm your best friend. You're supposed to tell me everything.

ELIZABETH. It was different then. We'd had a fight and he left in a huff. Drove off to El Paso. Picked up a girl hitchhiking.

HATTIE. What was her name?

ELIZABETH. Hattie, how should I know? She was a hitchhiker.

HATTIE. A little tramp probably! A little hippie road-slut! What'd she look like?

ELIZABETH. Blonde.

HATTIE. A little blonde hippie bitch that never washed or nothing I'll bet!

ELIZABETH. Oh yeah, and there was one other thing . . .

HATTIE. What?

ELIZABETH. She had a tattoo.

HATTIE. A *tattoo* on her arm?

ELIZABETH. Not exactly on her arm.

HATTIE. God . . . where?

ELIZABETH. On her behind.

HATTIE. No! On her behind! How disgusting! . . . What did it say?

ELIZABETH. "Born to be wild."

HATTIE. Oh Lord! Lord!

ELIZABETH. Then Roy went down to El Paso, got in a four-day poker game, won a hundred bucks, and come on home.

HATTIE. Weren't you mad?!

ELIZABETH. Yes.

HATTIE. Didn't you want to shoot him?!

ELIZABETH. Yeah.

HATTIE. I would've.

ELIZABETH. I thought it was what he needed to get something out of his system. For a while it seemed to work. *(Pause.)*

HATTIE. Y'know half his trouble is that damn car of his.

ELIZABETH. What do you mean?

HATTIE. He gets behind the wheel of that car and he thinks he's the cock of the walk, the best-looking thing in these parts.

ELIZABETH. *(Proudly.)* He still is.

HATTIE. *(Grudgingly.)* Yeah.

ELIZABETH. Even the girls in high school today. I see them in town looking at him the way we did.

HATTIE. I never looked at him that way.

ELIZABETH. Hattie, you still do.

HATTIE. I tell you it's that damn car. When he gets in it he thinks he's young and free again. *(Pause.)* Somebody ought to take that car away from him.

ELIZABETH. *(Warming to the memory.)* I remember the first day he drove into town in that car.

HATTIE. So do I.

ELIZABETH. He'd worked three years, summers and winters, for the down payment.

HATTIE. Only slightly used.

ELIZABETH. Roy and Wayne drove right through the center of town.

HATTIE. They looked like a couple of sultans.

ELIZABETH. It was bright pink.

HATTIE. It glistened like sin.

ELIZABETH. I remember I was coming out of the drugstore with an ice-cream cone.

HATTIE. What flavor?

ELIZABETH. Vanilla. And the sun off the hood was blinding. Couldn't even see the car. Then it passed into one shadow and I saw it. For the first time. It was beautiful, and Roy hardly knew me then but he waved at me, and I dropped my vanilla cone right there on the pavement. And I knew . . . he was the one.

HATTIE. Yeah. All through high school we double-dated.

ELIZABETH. Remember drive-ins, Hattie?

HATTIE. I sure do. More like wrestling matches.

ELIZABETH. One couple would get the car one night.

HATTIE. The other the next.

ELIZABETH. We'd drive around and drive around and then go make out.

HATTIE. Wayne and me didn't even drive around.

ELIZABETH. *(Rising.)* God, I want them back. I wisht tonight was ten years ago. And Roy was coming to pick me up in that pink Thunderbird. I wisht I could buy back some of the nights of summer I had in that car. When everything was cool and free and driving along the highway away from this stupid town. With the wind coming at you and the stars all the way to the horizon, like diamonds that went all the way to dawn. *(Pause.)* Then driving off the road somewhere. By a lake maybe. Anywhere. Being off from town with the boy you loved better than anything ever in your whole life. I remember us making love for the first time. Really slow and gentle. God. He was gentle then. He taught me my body. I'd never really felt with my body before Roy. Suddenly it was like every pore of my skin was being opened like in a rainstorm, feeling and holding everything you possibly wanted right there in your arms. What I wouldn't give to have those nights again. Just one night when the backseat of that Thunderbird was sweeter than all the beds in the world. *(Slight pause.)*

HATTIE. They took a lot of girls out in that car.

ELIZABETH. We were different.

HATTIE. Were we? *(They stare at each other.)* Look how he's treating you now. *(Pause.)* Elizabeth, you're getting all sentimental and romantic. That happened to me once. I let a man run all over me.

ELIZABETH. What'd you do?

HATTIE. I wrote a poem.

ELIZABETH. You?

HATTIE. Yep. Worst afternoon of my life. Never do it again. That's what happens when you get all sentimental and miserable. You write poems. Just like old Emily Dickens.

ELIZABETH. Emily Dickinson.

HATTIE. That's the one. Poor gal was a miserable godforsaken old maid all her life and when she died all that was left was just a drawerful of poems.

ELIZABETH. What was your poem about, Hattie?

HATTIE. I wrote a poem about Wayne Wilder. He was a mean person and it was a mean poem. It was right after high school graduation. Wayne told me he was jilting me. You and Roy was getting married and Wayne Wilder was jilting me.

Hit me like a ton of bricks. I went out back of the girls' gym, cried, and wrote a poem. I still remember it.

"Oh Wayne you don't know, I love you so well

But you son of a bitch

I hope you roast in hell."

*(Pause.)* Not much of a poem, I guess. But then I decided to get practical like Hattie's always had to be. I went back to where everybody was in their caps and gowns and I saw Vernon Dealing standing there. He'd just been fiddlin' under some car hood. Even in his cap and gown his hands were dirty. But he was a good man and I knew he liked me. I got him to take me out. I got him to propose. Within a month we were married. Poor Vern. Never knew what hit him. *(Pause.)*

ELIZABETH. What are you telling me this for?

HATTIE. Roy's just like Wayne. He ain't never gonna change.

ELIZABETH. Maybe not.

HATTIE. I've known you all my life. I know you need a marriage and you want a family. Am I right?

ELIZABETH. Yes.

HATTIE. Then wake up. You can't leave the important things in life like marriage and children up to the menfolk. If they had their way they'd just stick to their football and their fishing and their Thunderbirds and just be boys forever. *(Pause.)* Now, if Roy straightens up, that's one thing. If not . . . well, you got to make a decision.

ELIZABETH. *(Privately.)* Maybe it's already been made for me.

HATTIE. What do you mean?

ELIZABETH. Nothing, Hattie. Forget I said that.

HATTIE. Don't tell me it's nothing . . . you're pregnant aren't you? *(Silence.)*

ELIZABETH. Yeah.

HATTIE. I knew it! I knew it the minute I walked in here today. Oh Elizabeth! That's wonderful!

ELIZABETH. What's wonderful about it? It comes at the worst possible time.

HATTIE. Wrong. It comes at the best possible time. Well, don't you see? This might be just the thing to make Roy straighten up and fly right.

ELIZABETH. And if it doesn't?

HATTIE. Then . . . to hell with him.

ELIZABETH. *(With difficulty.)* I guess . . . you're right.

HATTIE. Oh, honey! Let me give you a hug. That's the smartest thing you ever did.

ELIZABETH. *(Pulling away.)* What do you mean?

HATTIE. Getting pregnant, of course.

ELIZABETH. Hattie, I didn't get myself pregnant on purpose. I didn't plan it this way. *(Pause.)*

HATTIE. Are you sure?

ELIZABETH. *(Slightest hesitation.)* Yes! Yes, I'm sure. I don't know if Roy can take this right now. He doesn't know what he's doing himself.

HATTIE. Well, that's not your problem.

ELIZABETH. *(Angry.)* It's every bit my problem. It couldn't be any more my problem.

HATTIE. *(Pause.)* I didn't mean to get you all upset. I just meant . . .

ELIZABETH. *(Calmer.)* I know, Hattie, I know. I just don't want to talk about it anymore. *(Awkward pause.)*

HATTIE. Oh, well sure. Sure. Uh, say, mind if I use your phone?

ELIZABETH. *(Smiling.)* Of course.

HATTIE. Figure I better check on the kids. No telling what devilment they've gotten up to. *(Dialing.)* Everything's gonna turn out fine, you'll see. *(On the phone.)* Hello? Cheryl? Cheryl dear, this is Mommy . . . Mommy . . *your mother. (Aside.)* Child needs a hearing aid. What's that dear? Vernon Jr. threw a rock at you? Well, throw one back at him, honey. Show him who's boss. Cheryl, sweetheart, put Grandma on the phone . . . Cheryl, this week! *(Pause.)* Sounds like they're running her ragged. Hello? Little Roger. Is that you? I don't want to talk to you right now punkin, I want to talk to Grandma . . . 'cause I want to talk to Grandma . . . yes, Grandma does have baggy elbows. Now lemme talk to her . . . what's that? Honey, of course Mommy loves you . . . I love you all the same . . . Do I love you more than who? Fred Flintstone. Yes. More than Paul Newman, no, but Fred Flintstone, yes . . . It's a grown-up joke, honey. Now put Grandma on . . . She's what? Tied up! You untie her, you hear me? You want a switchin'? . . . Then you untie her, right now . . . Marion? That you? . . . Oh, you were playin' . . . Oh good, I thought they had you tied up for real . . . How they doing? . . . Yes . . . yes . . . yes, I agree there is too much violence on TV . . . yes, I'll pick them up at five . . . No, I won't be late . . . You have my solemn word . . . Good-bye. What's that? Little Roger? . . . Yes, it's nice to hear your voice again too . . . You're playing what? Sniper? Vernon Jr. has climbed a tree in the backyard and he has a brick? Well, little Roger, listen and listen carefully, under no circumstances go under that tree . . . He's gonna drop the brick on your head, sweetheart . . . So don't go under the tree. That's just what he wants . . . Okay . . . Okay . . . "Yabba dabba doo" to you too. *(She hangs up.)* He'll walk right under that tree. The child has no more sense than God gave a screwdriver.

ELIZABETH. What's abba dabba doo?

HATTIE. Yabba dabba doo. That's what Fred Flintstone says when he's happy. *(We hear the sound of* ELIZABETH *setting her drink down on the counter and gasping.)* Elizabeth, what's the matter?

ELIZABETH. There. There's a car coming up the road.

HATTIE. Is it Roy?

ELIZABETH. I can't tell . . . no. No.

HATTIE. Who could it be? You expecting someone?

ELIZABETH. No.

HATTIE. Isn't that just the way? Here you are all pregnant and depressed and people are dropping in unannounced.

ELIZABETH. Wait. I did call up Fullernoy's about the air conditioning.

HATTIE. Oh my God!

ELIZABETH. What?

HATTIE. That's who it is! Amy Lee Fullernoy!

ELIZABETH. Well, I asked them to send somebody out, but I didn't think they'd send Amy Lee. *(A flurry of activity begins.* ELIZABETH *begins straightening up the porch. All the carefully folded clothes get thrown helter-skelter into the laundry basket. Magazines, newspapers are collected. As* ELIZABETH *straightens up, she neglects the "long" pair of* ROY's *underwear on the table.* HATTIE *busies herself with fixing her makeup.)*

HATTIE. Of course not. What does Amy Lee Fullernoy know about fixing air conditioners?

ELIZABETH. I don't know.

HATTIE. Not a damn thing. I wonder what she wants? *(Pause.)* Are you friends with her all of a sudden?

ELIZABETH. Of course not.

HATTIE. Good, 'cause you know our bridge club isn't speaking to her bridge club.

ELIZABETH. I know, and I think it's ridiculous.

HATTIE. Of course it is, but they started it. Theirs is practically the only other game in town. If we combined groups we'd have better games. We could have teams, tournaments. We could have round robins, goddamnit! But no, they won't play with us.

ELIZABETH. *(Weary.)* That's not true. Amy Lee and her group belong to the country club. That's where they play their games. We can't play there on a regular basis 'cause we don't belong. Those are the rules.

HATTIE. Well, they're dumb rules.

ELIZABETH. But it's like Amy Lee says, "What's the point of a country club if you can't keep people out?"

HATTIE. Well, I agree with her. Keep *some* people out. But why does it have to be me?

ELIZABETH. Well, join the damn thing then if it means that much to you.

HATTIE. You better believe I am! As soon as I get Vernon off his ass and making some more money. Lord, that man's hard to motivate. It's like pulling a mule through mud. *(The doorbell rings.* ELIZABETH *moves to answer.* HATTIE *stops her, pouting.)* Don't answer it.

ELIZABETH. Why?

HATTIE. Because it's Amy Lee Fullernoy.

ELIZABETH. That's no excuse.

HATTIE. She'll ruin our afternoon. *(The doorbell rings.)*

ELIZABETH. Let go of my arm, Hattie.

HATTIE. Amy Lee is so tacky. She thinks she's cute, but she's tacky.

ELIZABETH. Quit being silly and let me go.

HATTIE. I wonder who picks out her wardrobe? Ray Charles. *(*HATTIE *laughs with a snort.)* Ray Charles! Get it?

ELIZABETH. I got it. *(Exiting.)* Hold on Amy Lee, I'm coming. *(*ELIZABETH *exits.* HATTIE *is still enjoying herself.)*

HATTIE. Ray Charles. That was a good one! *(Heard in the front room: "Elizabeth, how are you?" "Amy Lee, c'mon in" . . . etc.)* God, I hate Amy Lee. *(AMY LEE enters with* ELIZABETH, *carrying a large box, unmarked, and wearing a dress exactly the same as* HATTIE'*s.* HATTIE *turns to greet* AMY LEE.*)* Amy Lee!

AMY LEE. Hattie!

HATTIE and AMY LEE. Girl, how are youuuuuuuuuu! *(Silence.)*

HATTIE. I can't believe it.

AMY LEE. Oh no. *(*ELIZABETH *steps in between* HATTIE *and* AMY LEE.*)*

ELIZABETH. Why, Hattie, your new dress looks a lot like Amy Lee's, doesn't it?

HATTIE. That's 'cause it's the exact same dress.

ELIZABETH. You two must have the same designer. Who is it, Hattie? Mr. Charles wasn't it?

HATTIE. Yes, Mr. Charles.

AMY LEE. Mr. Charles? Who's he?

HATTIE. Frenchman. Lives in Dallas. *(Pause.)* Anyway . . . it looks real nice on you, Amy Lee.

AMY LEE. Oh, yours does too.

HATTIE. *(Pause.)* God, I feel like a bookend.

ELIZABETH. Can I get you anything?

AMY LEE. I can only stay a minute. I've something in the oven that'll burn if I don't get back.

ELIZABETH. You sure?

HATTIE. Oh stay.

AMY LEE. Well . . . what were you two having?

HATTIE. Oh, just a little highball.

AMY LEE. A highball?

HATTIE. It's a drink.

ELIZABETH. Hattie, Amy Lee's a Baptist.

HATTIE. Sorry.

AMY LEE. Oh now, I take a drink every now and then. I'm just a back-porch Baptist.

ELIZABETH. Would you like a bourbon and coke?

AMY LEE. Just a wee one.

HATTIE. Thatta girl. *(*ELIZABETH *exits.* HATTIE *stares at the box.)* My, what a big box. Have you been shopping?

AMY LEE. *(Smiling.)* Oh no. *(Pause.)*

HATTIE. *(Smiling.)* Still it's an awfully *big* package.

AMY LEE. Yes, it is.

HATTIE. Yes sir. *(Pause.)* Sure is a big box.

ELIZABETH. *(In background.)* What have you been up to, Amy Lee?

AMY LEE. Been busy as a bee. I'm on the entertainment committee for the country club, and the recreation committee for First Baptist.

HATTIE. That sounds tough.

AMY LEE. It is. Because there's very few fun things a Baptist can do without risking damnation.

HATTIE. And the country club committee too?

AMY LEE. I *am* the entertainment committee.

HATTIE. No one to help you?

AMY LEE. Clara Simms.

HATTIE. I see what you mean.

AMY LEE. One can't expect many clever ideas from a woman that's had two strokes in one year.

HATTIE. No.

AMY LEE. No. *(Pause.)* I love the way you're wearing your hair, Hattie.

HATTIE. Yes?

AMY LEE. Yeah. It's just as cute as a bug.

HATTIE. Cute as a *bug?*

AMY LEE. I mean *button.* Cute as a button. *(Pause.)* Elizabeth, how's Roy?

ELIZABETH. Roy? Roy's fine, Amy Lee.

AMY LEE. Oh I'm so glad to hear it!

ELIZABETH. How's Cletis?

AMY LEE. Oh, he's doing *so* well. So well at the store. Cletis is so funny. I have to keep a short rein on him though or he'd just overstock everything.

HATTIE. Well, we wouldn't want that to happen.

AMY LEE. No indeed.

HATTIE. Lord, this is a big box, Amy Lee. *(Pause.)*

AMY LEE. *(Laughing.)* Honey, quit worrying about that box. *(Pause.)* Well, Hattie, what have you been doing with yourself?

HATTIE. Honey, keeping up with three kids is a full-time job.

AMY LEE. Cletis and I, of course, want children . . .

HATTIE. Uh-huh.

AMY LEE. I'm just *dead* for some, but I don't want to be tied down just yet. Children can be such a lot of trouble.

HATTIE. *(Expertly.)* Well, of course they can be if they do not receive proper disciplinary guidance. Children must be taught.

AMY LEE. I'm sure you are aware of the problems, since your children are so . . . high-spirited themselves.

HATTIE. Yes, but well-behaved. Now you take my little Cheryl. A perfect angel.

AMY LEE. What about Vernon Jr.?

HATTIE. And little Roger is adorable! He's so quiet. For the first month we thought he was deaf.

AMY LEE. And Vernon Jr.?

HATTIE. *(Darkly.)* What about him?

AMY LEE. My neighbors, the Burnses, had some trouble with Vernon.

HATTIE. You friends with the Burnses?

AMY LEE. I'm neighborly with them. But never friendly. I don't want them to get the wrong impression.

HATTIE. So one of their kids played with Vernon?

AMY LEE. Yes, he's just now getting out of the cast.

HATTIE. What's his name?

AMY LEE. Chester Burns.

HATTIE. I know the Burns boy. A born liar. *(The phone rings.* ELIZABETH answers.)

ELIZABETH. Hattie, it's for you.

HATTIE. *(Rising.)* His father was a liar too! Bobby Burns. 'Member? We went to grade school with him. "Lie-a-minute Burns" we used to call him. Excuse me.

AMY LEE. Of course. (ELIZABETH *and* HATTIE *are in the doorway,* ELIZABETH *with the phone. The phone sits on the kitchen counter inside the doorway.)*

ELIZABETH. It's Marion.

HATTIE. Are the kids acting up?

ELIZABETH. Something about a bonfire.

HATTIE. *(Gaily.)* Hello. Marion? What's the matter, honey? Why're you coughing? Do you have a cold? . . . Oh. That much smoke, huh . . . Well turn on the fan . . . How're the kids? . . . They did what? . . . Oh, no, they wouldn't do that to Poochie . . . They love that dog . . . At least they wouldn't do it on purpose . . . Yes . . . yes . . . Well, you know Poochie's a Pekingese and they have long hair . . . They catch on fire easily . . . Well . . . Yes . . . Well . . . Marion, look, it coulda been worse . . . It was just the tail . . . *(The phone goes dead. Obviously Marion has hung up.* ELIZABETH *enters with a tray of drinks, crackers, cheese, etc.)*

ELIZABETH. What was all that about?

HATTIE. Oh, Marion's dog. Poochie's tail caught on fire. She's trying to frame my children. *(To* AMY LEE.*)* She's overprotective about that animal.

AMY LEE. Well, would you just look at all this?

ELIZABETH. It's nothing.

HATTIE. It looks real nice, Elizabeth.

ELIZABETH. It's only crackers and dip. What brings you out this way, Amy Lee?

AMY LEE. Just to visit.

ELIZABETH. Uh-huh . . .

AMY LEE. And to do some business.

HATTIE. Uh-huh.

AMY LEE. *(Cheerfully.)* Girls! It's that time of year again at First Baptist!

ELIZABETH. Not . . . pancake supper?

AMY LEE. You guessed!

HATTIE. How much are the tickets?

AMY LEE. Five dollars.

HATTIE. That's a lot to pay for a stack of flapjacks.

AMY LEE. All the proceeds go to charity.

HATTIE. Last year they were leathery. Made me sick.

AMY LEE. Our mission in Paraguay has worked wonders.

HATTIE. Paraguay? Where's that?

AMY LEE. South America. It's a very backward country.

HATTIE. No wonder it's backward. Only people there are people from game shows and Baptists.

AMY LEE. What?

ELIZABETH. Never mind.

AMY LEE. Anyway. There are souls need saving there. The people are starving to death. We bring them Jesus.

ELIZABETH. If they're starving, why don't you bring them a hot meal?

AMY LEE. Oh, we do. All sorts of good things.

ELIZABETH. Like what?

AMY LEE. Powdered milk. Instant eggs.

HATTIE. Um. Yummy.

AMY LEE. The underdeveloped countries need the Blood of the Lamb.

HATTIE. Blood of the Lamb?

AMY LEE. Yes. The forgiveness of God. The compassion of Christ. Christian charity. And we gotta hurry, 'cause the Catholics got a head start on us.

ELIZABETH. Frankly, I say let them have it.

AMY LEE. Elizabeth! Communism flourishes in Catholic countries! You were raised Methodist. That's practically Baptist. You ought to know that!

ELIZABETH. Well, I don't.

AMY LEE. Hattie, how were you raised?

HATTIE. With a stick.

AMY LEE. Oh, that's right.

HATTIE. Spare the rod and spoil the child.

AMY LEE. I forgot your people are from Mississippi.

HATTIE. Yes. They were in agriculture.

AMY LEE. Anyway. In many Catholic countries, Protestant missions are the only thing standing between us and the Red threat!

ELIZABETH. Lord, Amy Lee. It sounds like you've joined the John Birch Society.

AMY LEE. Honey, I can't. I'm involved in too much club work as it is. *(ELIZA-BETH goes to get her purse.* HATTIE *digs a checkbook out of her purse.* AMY LEE *produces a roll of tickets.)*

ELIZABETH. Here's my five.

AMY LEE. Think of this as a contribution to the Kingdom of Heaven.

HATTIE. Will the Kingdom of Heaven take a check?

AMY LEE. *(Continuing.)* Uh-huh. A contribution to a better world. And isn't that what we all want for our children? As mothers. And mothers-to-be?

HATTIE. Don't worry, Amy Lee. You're a real mother already. *(HATTIE rips out a check.* AMY LEE *rips off a ticket. They exchange. Pause.)* Excuse me. I've got to go to the little girl's room. *(Pause as she exits.)*

ELIZABETH. Hattie's had a few.

AMY LEE. I never listen to Hattie when she's talking like a sharecropper's daughter. *(Smiles.)* Which she is.

ELIZABETH. What's in the box?

AMY LEE. What box?

ELIZABETH. That box.

AMY LEE. Oh! I'd forget my head if it wasn't screwed on. It's the air filter.

ELIZABETH. What air filter?

AMY LEE. For your air conditioner.

ELIZABETH. Don't need one.

AMY LEE. What? Cletis told me you did.

ELIZABETH. My filter's fine. It's the motor. Damn thing won't turn on.

AMY LEE. Oh.

ELIZABETH. Yes.

AMY LEE. Well, Cletis told me y'all talked and he said it might be your air filter, so I decided to run one out.

ELIZABETH. No. *(Pause.)* Didn't talk to Cletis.

AMY LEE. Oh?

ELIZABETH. No. Talked to James.

AMY LEE. *(Recovering.)* Oh that's right! Cletis told me James had taken the order and said it sounded like it might be your filter. So I decided to run one out.

ELIZABETH. Oh. Well bless your heart. *(Her smile vanishing.)* What do you need here, Amy Lee? *(Silence.* HATTIE *returns. Immediately notices the box has been moved.)*

HATTIE. Where's the box?

AMY LEE. There.

HATTIE. Oh. Thank God. *(Smiling.)* Didn't want you to lose it. *(*HATTIE *sits. She immediately notices the hostility in the air.)*

AMY LEE. *(Nervously.)* Soooo . . .

HATTIE. Yeah? Soooo . . .

AMY LEE. How have you been, Hattie?

HATTIE. *(Wary.)* Fine.

AMY LEE. *(Overly sincere.)* I'm *so* glad. How's Vernon?

HATTIE. *(Begins to answer, then—)* Well he's—you never ask about Vernon! What the hell's going on here? What have you two been talking about? Have you two been talking about me? God! I leave the room and people talk about me! I'm an object of gossip!

ELIZABETH. No. We haven't been talking about you, Hattie.

HATTIE. Well good. Good.

ELIZABETH. No. But I think Amy Lee was about to tell me something.

AMY LEE. *(Embarrassed.)* Well, Elizabeth . . .

ELIZABETH. Go on, Amy Lee.

HATTIE. Yeah. What is it?

AMY LEE. Well . . . not in front of Hattie.

HATTIE. What do you mean "not in front of Hattie"?! Anything you can say to her you can say to me.

ELIZABETH. Go on, Amy Lee.

AMY LEE. *(Pause.)* Well . . . it's about Roy.

ELIZABETH. What about Roy?

AMY LEE. It pains me to say this . . .

HATTIE. I bet.

AMY LEE. I saw Roy yesterday . . .

ELIZABETH. *(Covering.)* Really? Where?

AMY LEE. Here in Maynard.

ELIZABETH. And . . .

AMY LEE. Well, he wasn't alone.

ELIZABETH. Who was he with?

AMY LEE. It pains me to say this . . .

ELIZABETH. Force yourself.

AMY LEE. Margaret Crowell.

HATTIE. *(Quietly.)* Margaret Crowell?

AMY LEE. Yes. (HATTIE *takes a long sip of her drink.)*

ELIZABETH. Thank you, Amy Lee.

AMY LEE. I thought you should know.

ELIZABETH. Thank you.

AMY LEE. I thought you should hear it from someone who cares. *(Pause.)* I'm sorry.

ELIZABETH. Why?

AMY LEE. *(Confused.)* Well, because . . .

ELIZABETH. Nothing to be sorry about. I knew Roy was with Margaret Crowell.

AMY LEE. You did?

HATTIE. You did?

ELIZABETH. Yeah. He called yesterday. He was late for supper. He called and said he'd given Margaret Crowell a lift.

AMY LEE. Oh Elizabeth . . .

HATTIE. You see there!

AMY LEE. I feel terrible!

HATTIE. You ought to!

AMY LEE. I feel horrible!

HATTIE. People like you start rumors!

ELIZABETH. It's okay, Amy Lee.

HATTIE. Vicious tongues!

AMY LEE. *(Standing.)* You want me to go. I know you do.

ELIZABETH. Sit down.

AMY LEE. How can you stand to look at me?

HATTIE. It's not easy.

ELIZABETH. Sit down, I'll fix you a drink.

HATTIE. *(Sweetly.)* Let me fix it.

AMY LEE. Elizabeth, can you forgive me?

ELIZABETH. I forgive you, Amy Lee.

AMY LEE. Oh, you're a Christian soul. Isn't she a Christian soul?

HATTIE. *(Pouring a huge drink at the sideboard.)* Hell, we're all Christian souls. (HATTIE *pours* AMY LEE *an enormously potent drink.)*

AMY LEE. Elizabeth, I feel so bad.

ELIZABETH. Forget it.

AMY LEE. So many bad marriages lately in Maynard has made me unnaturally suspicious.

HATTIE. What do you mean? (HATTIE *returns with the drink.)*

AMY LEE. The American family's just falling apart!

HATTIE. Cheers!

AMY LEE. Cheers!

ELIZABETH. Cheers. *(They all drink.)*

AMY LEE. Whew, that's strong.

HATTIE. The second sip is always smoother.

AMY LEE. *(Sipping, then smiling brightly.)* You're right.

HATTIE. Now, what's all this about bad marriages?

AMY LEE. Well, Maynard, Texas, has just become another Peyton Place, that's all.

HATTIE. Well, tell.

AMY LEE. Well, people are just running around on each other.

HATTIE. Well, who?

AMY LEE. Laurette Weems.

HATTIE. Who would run around with Laurette Weems?

AMY LEE. No. Her husband's been running around on her.

HATTIE. I don't blame him.

AMY LEE. This is her third marriage.

HATTIE. It sure is.

AMY LEE. Yes, there's something seriously wrong in Laurette's approach to modern marriage.

HATTIE. Who else?

AMY LEE. Dorthea Hicks is expecting.

HATTIE. What do you expect? She's Catholic.

AMY LEE. But six children.

HATTIE. She doesn't have children. She drops litters. *(*AMY LEE *shares a dirty laugh with* HATTIE.*)* Who else?

AMY LEE. Jenny Jo Gilcrease.

HATTIE. Divorced?

AMY LEE. Pregnant.

HATTIE. No! They can't afford that child.

AMY LEE. Of course not.

HATTIE. What does her husband do?

AMY LEE. Works at the amusement park over in Snyder. Runs the go-cart ride.

HATTIE. *Oh brother.*

AMY LEE. But you want to hear the best part?

HATTIE. What?

AMY LEE. He doesn't want the child!

HATTIE. Oh no!

AMY LEE. Yes! She told me that he told her that if she got pregnant that was her tough luck. She could just raise it herself.

HATTIE. That man has no sense of responsibility.

AMY LEE. But listen to this.

HATTIE. There's more?

AMY LEE. Do you know what Jenny Jo is contemplating?

HATTIE. What?

AMY LEE. Abortion.

HATTIE. Abortion?

AMY LEE. Yes ma'am.

HATTIE. Nooooo . . .

AMY LEE. Where she'd get it I don't know. She can't get one in Maynard. She'd have to go to someplace that didn't have any morality. Like Dallas or Houston.

ELIZABETH. But can you imagine her position?

HATTIE. She shouldn't have gotten herself pregnant by a man who raced go-carts.

AMY LEE. *(Virtuous.)* Hattie, you're being heartless.

HATTIE. Hattie's just telling it like it is. *(Right at* AMY LEE.*)* I know plenty of people who've married for money.

ELIZABETH. *(Angry.)* I wisht you could hear yourselves.

AMY LEE. Why?

HATTIE. What's up?

ELIZABETH. So Jenny Jo has gone and gotten herself pregnant. What business is it of yours? So her husband doesn't want it? What business is it of yours? She probably told you all that 'cause she had nobody else to listen. Somebody she could open up to. God, don't you know she feels like the loneliest person in the world?

HATTIE. *(Pause.)* Elizabeth, you're right. I'm sorry.

AMY LEE. Yeah. We shouldn't have picked on that poor pregnant Catholic girl like that.

ELIZABETH. *(Embarrassed.)* Uhmmm . . . Sorry. I don't know what got into me there. I didn't mean to spoil the party. Here, have some dip.

AMY LEE. This is good dip.

ELIZABETH. Fresh avocadoes. I grow 'em myself out in the garden. *(Pause.* AMY LEE *mistakes the "long" pair of Roy's underwear, which* ELIZABETH *neglected to remove from the coffee table, for a table napkin. She demurely wipes her mouth with the underwear. They all realize what it is at the same time and break up. As the laughter subsides,* ELIZABETH *gamely tries to get the conversation back to a polite level.)* Well, Amy Lee, so how's your bridge game, girl?

AMY LEE. *(With elaborate boredom.)* Oh that. It's fine.

HATTIE. Don't tell me you've given up bridge?

AMY LEE. Well, no.

HATTIE. Thank heavens. It took me forever to learn bridge.

AMY LEE. But in just a few months I doubt whether anyone will be playing bridge at all.

HATTIE. *(Panic.)* What!?

AMY LEE. You mean you haven't heard the news?

HATTIE. News? What news?

AMY LEE. Haven't you heard?

HATTIE. No. What news?

AMY LEE. Elizabeth, surely you know.

HATTIE. No she doesn't.

AMY LEE. Oh, you must.

HATTIE. I tell you she doesn't!

AMY LEE. How do you know?

HATTIE. Because if she knew, she'd tell me, and then I'd know. But she didn't, so I don't, what news? *(Dramatic pause.)*

AMY LEE. Bridge is on the way out.

HATTIE. *(Crushed.)* Oh God!

AMY LEE. There is a new game.

HATTIE. Is it hard?

AMY LEE. It is an Oriental parlor game.

HATTIE. Is it harder than bridge?

ELIZABETH. What's the name of it?

AMY LEE. I'm sure it's going to be the new rage.

ELIZABETH. What's its name?

HATTIE. But, I just got through learning bridge!!

ELIZABETH. Hattie, hush up, what's its name, Amy?

AMY LEE. *(Pause.)* Mah-jongg.

HATTIE. Mah-jongg.

ELIZABETH. Mah-jongg. *(Pause.)* I've heard of that game.

HATTIE. *(Scared.)* Well, I haven't.

AMY LEE. Trudy Stevens just came back from Dallas and she bought a Mah-jongg set at Neiman-Marcus.

ELIZABETH. That sounds like Trudy . . .

HATTIE. *(To ELIZABETH.)* Don't you just know it's gonna be hard.

ELIZABETH. Calm down, we don't know anything about this game except it's Oriental. It might not be bad.

HATTIE. I'm real good at Chinese checkers.

ELIZABETH. See there.

AMY LEE. This is nothing like Chinese checkers. Mah-jongg is a cultured parlor game that has been around for thousands of years.

HATTIE. See? They've had all that time to make it even harder!

ELIZABETH. Settle down! You don't know if it's going to be hard.

AMY LEE. It is *very* hard.

HATTIE. I knew it!

AMY LEE. Even Trudy Stevens can't figure it out. And she does comparative shopping!

ELIZABETH. Hattie, you're getting worked up over nothing.

AMY LEE. You mustn't let it upset you so.

HATTIE. I'm not upset! How do you play this game?

AMY LEE. It's played with tiles.

HATTIE. Tiles? Bathroom tiles?

AMY LEE. No, silly, with ivory tiles. Like dominoes. Only instead of little dots each tile represents a different style of tile. Like one tile will be four bamboos or three winds, or five dragons. Then you pass to your left, then you pass to your right, then, of course, there's your courtesy pass, a whirlwind of excitement! Then you want to build your wall.

HATTIE. *(Rising panic.)* Stop! I ain't building nothing. Bamboos, winds, dragons. It's no good. It took me a year to learn bridge. I concentrated my entire being on bridge. I neglected my housework. My children nearly starved, all for bridge which I finally learned. But I can't do it again. I can't go through that hell again. It'd kill me.

AMY LEE. Well, of course, if you don't want to learn the game, you won't be able to play.

HATTIE. Shut up! I'll play if I want to.

AMY LEE. You won't play if you don't know the rules.

HATTIE. I'll know the rules 'cause we're still gonna play bridge. We're not changing games in midstream.

ELIZABETH. Hattie . . .

AMY LEE. What are you talking about?

HATTIE. I know what you're doing. You're trying to pull a fast one. You and Trudy Stevens are the only two that know the rules. You're trying to get us all to play this stupid game so you two can clean up!

AMY LEE. We are not!

HATTIE. You just want to be a couple of Mah-jongg hustlers. I know for a fact you and her cheat at bridge.

AMY LEE. We what!?

HATTIE. What'd you come over here for?

AMY LEE. To give Elizabeth this. (AMY LEE *picks up the box.* HATTIE *snatches the box.)*

HATTIE. Yes, and what is this! I've been wanting to know all afternoon . . . *(Gasps.)* Is this Mah-jongg!? *(Gasps.)* Are these the *tiles!* God, they're big!!

AMY LEE. Those aren't the tiles.

HATTIE. Well, what's in here?

ELIZABETH. An air filter!

HATTIE. What's all this got to do with an Oriental parlor game?

AMY LEE. Nothing! Absolutely nothing! God, you're stupid! You're an idiot! You're as stupid as that husband of yours and he's a moron.

HATTIE. Are you calling me a moron?

AMY LEE. No, you're just an idiot. He's the moron.

ELIZABETH. Shut up, Amy Lee!

HATTIE. Watch what you say about Vernon Dealing. He's twice the man Skeeter Fullernoy is.

AMY LEE. They don't call him Skeeter no more.

HATTIE. Everybody calls him Skeeter.

AMY LEE. He may have been Skeeter once. But he's married to me now and he ain't never gonna be Skeeter again.

HATTIE. How come?

AMY LEE. Because of the appliance store, the chamber of commerce, and the country club, that's how come!

HATTIE. Oh yeah? Well I'm breaking into that country club next year!

AMY LEE. Huh! You and what army?

HATTIE. You can't keep me out!

AMY LEE. What makes you think I can't?

HATTIE. Why you little bitch!

ELIZABETH. Calm down both of you!

HATTIE. She can't talk to me that way! We grew up together, Amy Lee Braddley! Your folks were just as poor as mine!

AMY LEE. Yes, but at least my daddy wasn't a sharecropper.

HATTIE. Yeah, well at least I didn't marry for money.

AMY LEE. *(All cards on the table.)* Yes. I married Skeeter Fullernoy! And I've done all right for myself. I'm in the country club, aren't I? There's nobody eligible in this stupid town, we all know that. Wayne Wilder was the best thing that ever happened to you. And he was a car thief!

ELIZABETH. Amy Lee!

AMY LEE. Wayne Wilder jilted you, you married Vernon, and then you had a kid right off the bat. That always seemed funny to me!

HATTIE. *(Pause.)* Take that back.

AMY LEE. I don't have to.

HATTIE. You do if you want to stay healthy. (HATTIE *advances on* AMY LEE. HATTIE *begins to chase* AMY LEE *about the stage, first around the table grouping right stage, then around the table left, knocking chairs, props, etc., over as they go.* ELIZABETH *follows them trying to intercede,* HATTIE *and* AMY LEE *screaming all the while.)*

AMY LEE. Hattie! Hattie!

HATTIE. You little bitch.

AMY LEE. Oh Lord! Lord! *(Finally,* ELIZABETH *manages to restrain* HATTIE, *at which point* AMY LEE *begrudgingly speaks.)* Okay. I'm sorry. *(Hiccups.)* I apologize. *(Hiccups.)* Oh God.

ELIZABETH. What is it?

AMY LEE. I got the hiccups. *(Hiccups.)*

ELIZABETH. You sure?

AMY LEE. *(Hiccups.)* Yes. *(Hiccups.)*

ELIZABETH. C'mon in the kitchen. (ELIZABETH *takes her inside.* HATTIE *follows, pauses in the doorway.)*

HATTIE. *(Calling after them.)* They say best way to cure the hiccups is to scare someone. (HATTIE *follows* AMY LEE *and* ELIZABETH *into the kitchen. We hear a tremendous scream from* HATTIE *followed by much commotion.)*

AMY LEE. Oooooh.

ELIZABETH. Look what you've done. *(*AMY LEE *and* ELIZABETH *come back onstage to retrieve* AMY LEE'S *purse.)*

AMY LEE. Oh my God!

ELIZABETH. It's okay, Amy. It's okay.

AMY LEE. I want to go home.

ELIZABETH. Sure you don't want to—

AMY LEE. No, home. *(Sweetly.)* I want to thank you for a real nice day.

ELIZABETH. You're sure you're okay?

AMY LEE. I'm fine. Perfectly fine. *(She sways a bit.)* Well, bye-bye.

ELIZABETH. Bye-bye, Amy Lee. *(ELIZABETH exits with AMY LEE to see her to her car. HATTIE comes onstage holding one of her shoes. She sits on the table.)*

AMY LEE. *(Off.)* Thank you for buying tickets to the pancake supper.

ELIZABETH. *(Off.)* Thank you, Amy. *(ELIZABETH enters, sits in the chair left stage).*

HATTIE. Well. It's been a great day. My daughter was nearly arrested for shoplifting. My eldest son set fire to my mother-in-law's Pekingese—and now a Baptist has barfed on my shoe. *(Pause. The two women chuckle together.)* Damn, that's a pretty sunset.

ELIZABETH. Yeah, it's my favorite time.

HATTIE. That's one thing Texas is good for—sunsets.

ELIZABETH. It's the only time things get soft. *(Pause.)* Look, Hattie. The evening star. *(Pause.)*

HATTIE. That was quick thinking about Margaret Crowell.

ELIZABETH. Hattie.

HATTIE. Huh?

ELIZABETH. I'm sorry it never worked out for you and Wayne.

HATTIE. What's that supposed to mean?

ELIZABETH. I think that's what we've been talking about all afternoon. Roy and I. Wayne and you.

HATTIE. Hell no. That's all over with years ago. I'm better off with old Vernon. He isn't worth kicking off the porch . . . but we're, well, comfortable together . . . Now, Wayne was . . . he was too . . . hell, Wayne was Wayne . . . Sure, I loved him. You bet. *(Pause.)*

ELIZABETH. Well I love Roy, Hattie, and he needs me right now. He doesn't know it. But he does. *(Pause.)* And I'm going to be here. *(Pause.)*

HATTIE. *(Standing.)* Well, I gotta go get the kids.

ELIZABETH. Okay.

HATTIE. Never did finish folding your laundry.

ELIZABETH. I'll get to it. *(Pause. The women stand facing each other. HATTIE unconsciously touches ELIZABETH's stomach. They smile, then pull away.)*

HATTIE. You hang on to Roy.

ELIZABETH. I intend to.

HATTIE. He's the last wild thing left around here. *(Pause.)* Talk to you tomorrow?

ELIZABETH. Yeah. Call me. *(HATTIE exits. ELIZABETH turns on the phonograph again. As the lights fade to black, ELIZABETH takes a deep breath. Blackout.)*

*Curtain*

# SOURCES

*A Cloud of Witnesses*, by Ramsey Yelvington.
   Reprinted from *The Drama of the Alamo: A Cloud of Witnesses* (Austin:
   University of Texas Press, 1959).

*The Trip to Bountiful*, by Horton Foote.
   Reprinted from *The Trip to Bountiful*. New York: Dramatists Play Service, 1954.

*Who's Happy Now?* by Oliver Hailey.
   Reprinted from *Who's Happy Now?* New York: Dramatists Play Service, 1970.

*Patio/Porch*, by Jack Heifner.
   Reprinted from *Patio/Porch*. New York: Dramatists Play Service, 1978.

*The Regions of Noon*, by R. G. Vliet.
   Reprinted from manuscript final draft, October 1982.

*El Jardín*, by Carlos Morton.
   Reprinted, with revisions made in 1989 by the author, from *The Many Deaths of
   Danny Rosales and Other Plays*. Houston: Arte Público Press, 1983.

*Lu Ann Hampton Laverty Oberlander*, by Preston Jones.
   Reprinted from *A Texas Trilogy*. New York: Hill and Wang, 1976.

*Ladybug, Ladybug, Fly Away Home*, by Mary Rohde.
   Reprinted from manuscript acting script, 1980.

*Lone Star*, by James McLure.
   Reprinted from *Lone Star*. New York: Dramatists Play Service, 1980.

*Laundry and Bourbon*, by James McLure.
   Reprinted from *Laundry and Bourbon*. New York: Dramatists Play Service, 1981.